The Stick of Joseph
In the Hand of Ephraim

עץ יוסף
אשר ביד אפרים

Originally Translated by Yosef ben Yosef
First Edition Published 5590/1830 CE

Translation Updated and Restored 5780/2019 CE

© 2019 Restoration Scriptures Foundation. All rights reserved.
Restoration Scriptures Foundation is a trademark of Restoration Archive LLC.

First Edition
ISBN 978-1-951168-60-5
TEXT V1.006 - 2020.10.6
www.StickofJoseph.info

CONTENTS

Dedication	v
Introduction	vii
1 Nefi	1
2 Nefi	59
Ya'akov	135
Enosh	156
Yahram	159
Ameni	161
Words of M'raman	165
Moshiyah	168
Alma	242
Cheleman	442
3 Nefi	490
4 Nefi	561
M'raman	566
'Eter	588
M'roni	625
Glossary	643
Appendices	652

Dedication

First, and above all else, this book is dedicated to Mashiach—the anointed one—who will bring Shalom. Those who labored both anciently and recently to make these words available did so, and continue to do so, as an act of dedication to him.

Second, this book is dedicated, as Ezekiel prophesied, to "all the House of Israel," both scattered remnants and gathered branches, as evidence that YHWH has not forgotten His covenants with Abraham, Isaac, and Jacob. His breath of life now breathes upon all the remnants of Israel, to restore life and gather scattered Israel home.

And finally, this book is dedicated specifically to the Y'hudim, or the Jewish People:

> *And because my words shall hiss forth, many of the Goyim shall say, A bible, a bible, we have got a bible, and there cannot be any more bible. But thus says Adonai YHWH: Oh fools, they shall have a bible and it shall proceed forth from the Y'hudim, my ancient covenant people. And what thank they the Y'hudim for the bible which they receive from them? Yes, what do the Goyim mean? Do they remember the travails, and the labors, and the pains of the Y'hudim? And their diligence unto me in bringing forth salvation unto the Goyim? Oh you Goyim, have you remembered the Y'hudim, my ancient covenant people?* (2 Nefi 12:8-9)

We remember, and we thank those ancient covenant people, the Jews, who have suffered and sacrificed so much to preserve light and truth for the world.

Introduction

The ancient House of Israel consisted of twelve families, or tribes, named for the twelve sons of Jacob (Israel). Ten of those tribes were conquered, driven from their homelands, and scattered throughout the world. Although their bloodlines continue, they have lost their identity with the House of Israel. The remaining two tribes have retained their identity, and are now known as the Jewish people, named for the tribe of Judah.

Over two thousand five hundred years ago, the prophet Ezekiel foretold a future day when the spirit of YHWH would stir the scattered remnants of Israel and restore them to life (Ezek. 37:11–14). He also prophesied of a second scriptural record that would come forth from the tribe of Joseph to Judah, in the hand of Joseph's son, Ephraim. This record would be used by YHWH to gather all of scattered Israel home to their lands, into one people and one family that He would again call His own (Ezek. 37:15–23; see also Appendix E).

This is that prophesied record.

The Stick of Joseph in the Hand of Ephraim is a sacred, first-temple-period, Israelite text, written by a prophetic family from the tribe of Joseph who fled Jerusalem in 601 BCE, prior to the Babylonian destruction. YHWH led them for years in the wilderness and finally brought them "over the wall" to the American continent, in fulfillment of Jacob's final blessing to Joseph (Gen. 49:22).

For a thousand years, these ancient Israelites built their civilization, fought wars, served the God of Israel, and kept sacred records. When their civilization ended in destruction (420 CE), their final prophet, M'roni, hid this record in the ground, to come forth at a future time and begin the prophesied restoration of scattered Israel to its former glory.

This is the only Hebrew Messianic/ascension document in existence that has not been influenced by entanglements with Babylon, Greece, or Rome, because those who kept the record left Jerusalem and the Eastern Hemisphere prior to the Babylonian captivity. It is the most sublime and direct Jewish ascension text in existence.

Initial Discovery and Publication of the Text

In 1820 CE, the God of Israel called a prophet to begin the long-prophesied work of restoration. When He appeared to that prophet, Yosef ben Yosef (Joseph Smith, Jr.), He declared the corruption of all Christian religions and His intent to restore His covenant people. On Rosh Hashanah 5588 (1827 CE), Yosef received this ancient record from an angel at the place where it had been buried for over 1400 years. Yosef received divine power and means to translate the ancient text and publish it to the world.

Yosef ben Yosef first published the text for a Gentile audience, in antiquated English, under a different title. As happened with the Bible, Gentile churches and institutions attempted to claim the book as their own, make profit from it, and use it to gain converts—all while utterly failing to appreciate its authors, purpose, message, or destiny (see 2 Nefi 12:8). For more information about the first published text, see the Appendices at the back of this book.

Although the text itself acknowledges it will convince some few Gentiles to believe in Israel's God, the text's main focus is directed to the scattered remnants of the House of Israel, with the stated purpose of restoring the knowledge of YHWH's covenants and gathering YHWH's people, in preparation for the time of Mashiach.

Current Translation

Nearly 190 years after the first English translation of the text, YHWH set His hand again the second time to gather His people (Isaiah 11:11) and called servants to prepare and publish the text in its current form, without the encumbrance of Gentile language and concepts. Part of this effort involved removing antiquated English words and expressions, as well as restoring Hebraic terms that would have been used by the original writers. This Hebraic-roots English translation reveals the ancient Hebraic nature of this record and provides a clear understanding of Israel's God, His work now underway, and the coming age of Mashiach.

The original, intended title of the work has also been restored, as stated by Yosef ben Yosef, who called it *The Stick of Joseph in the Hand of Ephraim* on multiple, recorded occasions.[1]

---

1 Letter to Stephen Post, 17 September 1838, p. 2; Joseph Smith History, Part 19 (April–May 1830) paragraph 7.

Numerous footnotes have been added to explain Hebraic concepts, reference language and ideas also found in the Tanakh, and provide deeper understanding and explanations. Many footnotes also provide cross references to other areas of the text to enhance the reader's understanding. However, the reader should know that the footnotes are not part of the original text and should not be regarded as anything more than the opinions of those preparing this current version for publication. Likewise, because the text is so thoroughly Hebraic in nature, the number of footnotes regarding Hebraisms has been intentionally limited to a few representative cases. A thorough treatment of the Hebraic nature of the text would fill multiple volumes.

Many ideas presented in this ancient work persisted in Jewish thought for thousands of years and appeared again in later Jewish sources. Such sources have been referenced when applicable; see *Abbreviations and References* in Appendix A for further information. Text found within *The Stick of Joseph* that also appears in the Tanakh is featured in **bold**.

A *Glossary* is provided at the end of the volume, with explanations of Hebraic names and terms.

YHWH, who keeps His covenants, has now decreed the restoration of His people Israel, by sending *The Stick of Joseph* to Judah in the hand of Ephraim. The glory of this accomplishment belongs to YHWH alone. This is His work and His text, though it came through the hands of imperfect mortals. If there are errors, they are the fault of those who have labored to recover this text.

Purpose and Intent of this Translation

This effort is a direct response to the promise of YHWH that He would restore the House of Israel. Because true worship always requires sacrifice, thousands of dollars and thousands of hours have been freely given to this project on a volunteer basis, without compensation. Those who have contributed their time and means have done so to offer a gift to the world, with no intent other than to obey YHWH and see His covenants fulfilled. Therefore, this book is sold at publisher's cost, with the specific intent of eliminating any profit. The text is also available at no cost online at www.StickOfJoseph.info.

First published in this form at Rosh Hashanah 5780 (2019 CE), *The Stick of Joseph* is YHWH's call to all the House of Israel. He has not forgotten His people, and He invites all to return to Him, remember His covenants with their fathers, obey His commandments, and prepare for the glorious day of Mashiach.

Within this sacred text, YHWH issues a specific warning against those who would attempt to profit financially, elevate themselves above others, or attempt to gain control over others in any way by using this book or its teachings:

> *He commands that there shall be no priestcrafts; for behold, priestcrafts are that men preach and set themselves up for a light unto the world, that they may get gain and praise of the world, but they seek not the welfare of Tziyon...But the laborer in Tziyon shall labor for Tziyon, for if they labor for money, they shall perish.* (2 Nefi 11:17)

This record was originally published separately from any church, assembly, or organization. Therefore, accepting *The Stick of Joseph* does not require one to be institutionally loyal to any organization, group, or man. It was written unto all nations (see Dedication in Appendix F). Those who believe these words are invited to repent, obey the Mitzvot of YHWH, and be immersed as a sign of acceptance. More information is available at www.StickOfJoseph.info.

The House of Israel, the Jewish People, and *The Stick of Joseph*

Three major world religions claim Abraham as patriarch. Jews and Christians also acknowledge Abraham's son, Isaac, and grandson, Jacob, as Abraham's successors in YHWH's covenant. Jacob was renamed Israel and given twelve sons who became the "twelve tribes" or "house" of Israel. The texts of every Abrahamic religion record the story of the second youngest son, Joseph, who was sold into Egyptian slavery by his brothers and who subsequently saved Israel's entire family from a decimating famine.

The family of Israel eventually became scattered throughout the world. Most lost their identity and connection to Israel, with the exception of the tribe of Judah, for whom the Jews are named. The tribe of Judah's tenacity and sacrifice over thousands of years preserved sacred texts, traditions, and teachings going all the way back to the patriarchs. Although the Jews are but one of the twelve tribes, their very name has become synonymous with Israel.

The remaining "lost" tribes do not know their identity, though they carry the blood of Abraham, Isaac, and Jacob. Prophecy foretells their future return to the family, and promised lands, of Israel. Malachi prophesied that Elijah would come to turn the hearts of the children back to their fathers (Mal. 3:23–24 [4:5–6]). This text is sent in the spirit of Elijah, as part of that mission. Its purpose is to turn the hearts of all the family of Israel, not only to the covenants of Abraham, Isaac, and Jacob, but also to Mashiach, who will come.

Both supporters and detractors of the modern state of Israel recognize its founding and growth as a phenomenon without parallel in world history. The book you are now reading boldly predicts a future for Israel beyond what any without the spirit of prophecy could foretell. Those scattered remnants who yet carry the blood of Israel will resonate in a singular way with its message.

Isaiah holds special significance in this text and is quoted extensively by the first prophet-writer, Nefi. This is due to Isaiah's singular position as a seer who saw and prophesied of our present day. You are encouraged to consider the Isaiah materials in light of the explanations given within this text.

Other first-temple-period prophets are also referenced or quoted by the writers of *The Stick of Joseph*. Likewise the Torah is quoted, with comments and explanations by the ancient prophet-writers of this work.

A Note of Warning About this Book

The Stick of Joseph in the Hand of Ephraim is not just another book. Rather it is all of the following unique and extraordinary things:

- The sounding of the shofar to the scattered tribes of Israel as YHWH's final attempt to gather His people;
- A dire warning to the United States of America and a cry of repentance to the modern state of Israel. Any nation that does not honor the Elohim of Israel will not survive;
- An independent witness of the prophets, Mashiach, and the covenants given by YHWH to Israel;

- A record of the means whereby all mankind can, as Moses, ascend to stand in the presence of YHWH;
- An invitation to believe and receive the promises that YHWH extends to those who will be His people.

As is always the case with Elohim's work, there will be opposition to this effort. Those who fight against it or say, "This is just..." or "That is not..." in an attempt to re-cast this text as something other than what it says it is are dangerously ignorant, wicked, or both. They do not know or honor the God of Abraham who vouches for these words; in fact, they fight against Him. They are trifling with your soul, and if you pay them heed, you will receive only disappointment.

It is true that various forms of this book have been in continuous publication since 1830 CE, and millions of people from dozens of sects have embraced it as holy scripture, but effectively none have comprehended its underlying message, and consequently all have failed to fulfill its purpose or offer it to its intended audience. This translation is unique and fundamentally different than any version that has come before because it is focused entirely on God's covenant people, to whom He promised this record would be sent.

We, who have prepared this current translation, testify that the God of Israel is the God of all the earth and He has scattered Israel among all people. Yosef ben Yosef was called by the God of Israel to fulfill part of the promises and prophecies made by Him. This book is a record of a branch of Israel and testifies that there are other branches led away by God to places known to God, and these scattered branches, including the keepers of this record, were visited and taught by Mashiach.

A Promise to the Reader

The only way to know the truth of this record is to examine it for yourself. You are invited to study the contents of *The Stick of Joseph* and to experiment upon M'roni's petition, found in the final chapter:

> *Behold, I would exhort you that when you shall read these things, if it be wisdom in Elohim that you should read them, that you would remember how merciful YHWH has been unto the children of men, from the creation of Adam even down until the time that you shall receive these things, and ponder it in your hearts. And when you shall receive*

> *these things, I would exhort you that you would ask Elohim the Eternal Father, in the name of Mashiach, if these things are not true. And if you shall ask with a sincere heart, with real intent, having faith in Mashiach, and he will manifest the truth of it unto you by the power of the Ruach HaKodesh. And by the power of the Ruach HaKodesh, you may know the truth of all things.* (M'roni 10:2)

Elohim, who cannot lie, will keep His word.

ספר נפי הראאשון שלטונו ומשרדו
1 NEFI
THE FIRST BOOK OF NEFI
HIS REIGN AND MINISTRY

An account of Lechi, and his wife Saryah, and his four sons being called, beginning at the eldest, Laman, L'mu'el, Sam, and Nefi. YHWH warns Lechi to depart out of the land of Yerushalayim because he prophesies unto the people concerning their iniquity and they seek to destroy his life. He takes three days journey into the wilderness with his family. Nefi takes his brothers and returns to the land of Yerushalayim after the record of the Y'hudim. The account of their sufferings. They take the daughters of Yishma'el to wife. They take their families and depart into the wilderness. Their sufferings and afflictions in the wilderness. The course of their travels. They come to the large waters. Nefi's brothers rebel against him. He confounds them and builds a ship. They call the name of the place Bountiful. They cross the large waters into the promised land, and so forth. This is according to the account of Nefi, or in other words, I, Nefi, wrote this record.

I NEFI,[1] having been born of goodly parents, therefore I was taught somewhat in all the learning of my father. And having seen many afflictions in the course of my days, nevertheless, having been highly favored of YHWH in all my days, yes, having had a great knowledge of the goodness and the mysteries of Elohim, therefore I make a record of my proceedings in my days. Yes, I make a record in the language[2] of my father, which consists of the learning of the Y'hudim and the language of the Egyptians. And I know that the record which I make is true; and I make it with my own hand, and I make it according to my knowledge.

2 For it came to pass in the commencement of the first year[3] of the reign of Tzidkiyahu,[4] king of Y'hudah — my father Lechi having dwelt at Yerushalayim[5] in all his days — and in that same year there came many prophets, prophesying unto the people[6] that they must repent or the great city Yerushalayim must be destroyed.

---

1 See *Nefi* in Glossary   2 Moshiyah 1:1; M'raman 4:11   3 ~ 601 BCE   4 Ameni 1:7
5 2 Nefi 1:1; Cheleman 3:9   6 2 Chron. 36:15–16; Jer. 7:13, 25; 25:3

³ Wherefore, it came to pass that my father Lechi, as he went forth, prayed unto YHWH, yes, even with all his heart in behalf of his people. And it came to pass as he prayed unto YHWH, there came a **pillar of fire**⁷ and dwelt⁸ upon a rock before him, and he saw and heard much. And because of the things which he saw and heard, he did quake and tremble exceedingly.

The Ma'aseh Merkavah (account of the divine throne-chariot) of Lechi

And it came to pass that he returned to his own house at Yerushalayim. And he cast himself upon his bed, being overcome with the spirit and the things which he had seen. And being thus overcome with the spirit, he was carried away in a vision, even that he saw the Heavens open and he thought he saw Elohim sitting upon his throne, surrounded with numberless concourses of angels in the attitude of singing and praising their Elohim. And it came to pass that he saw one descending out of the midst of Heaven, and he beheld that his luster was above that of the sun at noonday. And he also saw twelve others following him, and their brightness did exceed that of the stars in the firmament. And they came down and went forth upon the face of the earth. And the first came and stood before my father and gave unto him a book and directed him that he should read. And it came to pass that as he read he was filled with the spirit of YHWH. And he read, saying, Woe, woe unto Yerushalayim,⁹ for I have seen your abominations. Yes, and many things did my father read concerning Yerushalayim: that it should be destroyed and the inhabitants thereof; many should perish by the sword and many should be carried away captive into Babylon.¹⁰ And it came to pass that when my father had read and saw many great and marvelous things, he did exclaim many things unto YHWH, such as, Great and marvelous are your works, O Adonai YHWH Tzva'ot! Your throne is high in the Heavens, and your power, and goodness, and mercy are over all the inhabitants of the earth; and because you are merciful, you will not allow those who come¹¹ unto you that they shall perish! And after this manner was the

---

7 Ex. 14:24 8 The underlying Hebrew word is most likely *yashav* ישׁב (Strong's 3427), meaning "to sit or to dwell." The noun form is *yeshiva*. It is interesting to note that this same word correlates with the Uto-Aztecan word *yesipa*, which has exactly the same range of meaning. 9 2 Nefi 11:4 10 2 Chron. 36:17-21 11 2 Nefi 11:16; Alma 3:5; 3 Nefi 4:7

language of my father in the praising of his Elohim, for his soul did rejoice[12] and his whole heart was filled because of the things which he had seen, yes, which YHWH had shown unto him.

4 And now I, Nefi, do not make a full account of the things which my father had written, for he has written many things which he saw in visions and in dreams.[13] And he also has written many things which he prophesied and spoke unto his children, of which I shall not make a full account. But I shall make an account of my proceedings in my days. Behold, I make an abridgment of the record of my father upon plates which I have made with my own hands. Wherefore, after that I have abridged the record of my father, then will I make an account of my own life.

5 Therefore, I would that you should know that after YHWH had shown so many marvelous things unto my father Lechi, yes, concerning the destruction of Yerushalayim, behold, he went forth among the people and began to prophesy and to declare unto them concerning the things which he had both seen and heard. And it came to pass that the Judeans did mock him because of the things which he testified of them, for he truly testified of their wickedness and their abominations. And he testified that the things which he saw and heard, and also the things which he read in the book, manifested plainly of the coming of a Mashiach and also the redemption of the world. And when the Judeans heard these things they were angry with him, yes, even as with the prophets of old, whom they had cast out and stoned and slain; and they also sought his life that they might take it away. But behold, I, Nefi, will show unto you that the tender mercies of YHWH are over all those whom he has chosen because of their faith to make them mighty, even unto the power of deliverance.

6 For behold, it came to pass that YHWH spoke unto my father, yes, even in a dream, and said unto him, Blessed are you Lechi because of the things which you have done. And because you have been faithful and declared unto this people the things which I commanded you, behold, they seek to take away your life. And it came to pass that YHWH commanded my father, even in a dream, that he should take his family and depart into the wilderness. And it came to pass that

---

12 The Hebrew word behind "rejoice" here may have been *giyl* גיל (Strong's 1523), which can mean "rejoice" but can also mean "tremble."   13 1 Nefi 2:7-13

he was obedient unto the word of YHWH; wherefore, he did as YHWH commanded him.

7 And it came to pass that he departed into the wilderness. And he left his house, and the land of his inheritance, and his gold, and his silver, and his precious things, and took nothing with him except it were his family, and provisions, and tents, and he departed into the wilderness. And he came down by the borders near the shore of the Red Sea, and he traveled in the wilderness in the borders which were nearer the Red Sea. And he did travel in the wilderness with his family, which consisted of my mother, Saryah, and my elder brothers, who were Laman, L'mu'el, and Sam. And it came to pass that when he had traveled three days in the wilderness, he pitched his tent in a valley by the side of a river of water.

8 And it came to pass that he built an **altar of stones**,[14] and he made an offering unto YHWH, and gave thanks unto YHWH our Elohim. And it came to pass that he called the name of the river Laman, and it emptied into the Red Sea; and the valley was in the borders near the mouth thereof. And when my father saw that the waters of the river emptied into the fountain of the Red Sea, he spoke unto Laman, saying, Oh that you might be like unto this river, continually running into the fountain of all righteousness. And he also spoke unto L'mu'el, saying, Oh that you might be like unto this valley, firm, and steadfast, and immovable in keeping the mitzvot of YHWH. Now this he spoke because of the stiffneckedness of Laman and L'mu'el;[15] for behold, they did murmur in many things against their father because that he was a visionary man and that he had led them out of the land of Yerushalayim, to leave the land of their inheritance, and their gold, and their silver, and their precious things, and to perish in the wilderness. And this they said that he had done because of the foolish imaginations of his heart. And thus Laman and L'mu'el, being the eldest, did murmur against their father. And they did murmur because they knew not the dealings of that Elohim who had created them. Neither did they believe that Yerushalayim, that great city, could be destroyed according to the words of the prophets. And they

---

14 Deut. 27:5   **15** L'mu'el (Lemuel) is an appropriate name for a rebellious son. As we read in Midrash Rabbah 10:4, "Why was Solomon called Lemuel?... Lemuel is because he cast off the yoke of the Kingdom of Heaven from his shoulders; as if to say: *Lammah lo El* (What [use] is God to him?)."

were like unto the Judeans who were at Yerushalayim, who sought to take away the life of my father. And it came to pass that my father did speak unto them in the valley of L'mu'el with power, being filled with the spirit, until their frames did shake before him. And he did confound them that they dared not utter against him; wherefore, they did do as he commanded them. And my father dwelt in a tent.

9 And it came to pass that I, Nefi, being exceedingly young, nevertheless, being large in stature, and also having great desires to know of the mysteries of Elohim, wherefore I cried unto YHWH. And behold, he did visit me and did soften my heart that I did believe all the words which had been spoken by my father; wherefore, I did not rebel against him like unto my brothers. And I spoke unto Sam, making known unto him the things which YHWH had manifested unto me by his Holy Spirit. And it came to pass that he believed in my words. But behold, Laman and L'mu'el would not hearken unto my words. And being grieved because of the hardness of their hearts, I cried unto YHWH for them. And it came to pass that YHWH spoke unto me, saying, Blessed are you, Nefi, because of your faith, for you have sought me diligently with humility of heart. And inasmuch as you shall keep my mitzvot, you shall prosper and shall be led to a land of promise, yes, even a land which I have prepared for you, a land which is choice above all other lands.[16] And inasmuch as your brothers shall rebel against you, they shall be cut off[17] from the presence of YHWH. And inasmuch as you shall keep my mitzvot, you shall be made a ruler and a teacher over your brothers. For behold, in that day that they shall rebel against me, I will curse them even with a sore curse, and they shall have no power over your seed except they shall rebel against me also. And if it so be that they rebel against me, they shall be a scourge unto your seed to stir them up in the ways of remembrance.

10 And it came to pass that I, Nefi, returned from speaking with YHWH, to the tent of my father. And it came to pass that he spoke unto me, saying, Behold, I have dreamed a dream[18] in the which YHWH has commanded me that you and your brothers shall return to Yerushalayim. For behold, Lavan has the record of the Y'hudim

---

[16] Deut. 33:13-17   [17] 2 Nefi 4:4; Alma 7:3; Alma 18:1   [18] This is an example of the Hebraism known as the Cognate Accusative, where a noun pairs with the verb which is the noun's root.

and also a genealogy[19] of your forefathers, and they are engraved upon plates of brass. Wherefore, YHWH has commanded me that you and your brothers should go unto the house of Lavan and seek the records and bring them down here into the wilderness. And now behold, your brothers murmur, saying it is a hard thing which I have required of them; but behold, I have not required it of them, but it is a mitzvah of YHWH. Therefore go, my son, and you shall be favored of YHWH because you have not murmured. And it came to pass that I, Nefi, said unto my father, I will go and do the things which YHWH has commanded, for I know that YHWH gives no mitzvot unto the children of men except he shall prepare a way for them that they may accomplish the thing which he commands them. And it came to pass that when my father had heard these words he was exceedingly glad, for he knew that I had been blessed of YHWH.

[11] And I, Nefi, and my brothers took our journey in the wilderness with our tents to go up[20] to the land of Yerushalayim. And it came to pass that when we had gone up to the land of Yerushalayim, I and my brothers did consult one with another. And we cast lots — who of us should go in unto the house of Lavan. And it came to pass that the lot fell upon Laman. And Laman went in unto the house of Lavan, and he talked with him as he sat in his house.[21] And he desired of Lavan the records which were engraved upon the plates of brass, which contained the genealogy of my father. And behold, it came to pass that Lavan was angry and thrust him out from his presence, and he would not that he should have the records. Wherefore, he said unto him, Behold, you are a robber and I will slay you. But Laman fled out of his presence and told the things which Lavan had done unto us.

---

19 1 Nefi 1:22   **20** The likely underlying Hebrew was *alah* (עלה Strong's 5927), which means "go up, ascend, climb." This expression is commonly used to denote travel to Jerusalem (e.g. Isa. 2:3; 7:1; Ps. 24:3) because, regardless of elevation, one "ascends" to the Holy City, and more specifically to the Temple, which makes the city holy. In modern usage, the term "making Aliyah" still specifically denotes emigration to Israel. The ancient authors of this text associated this language not only with travel to Jerusalem (1 Nefi 1:15; 2:2), but also with travel to the cities on the American continent where Nefite Temples were located (Moshiyah 5:2; 6:1; 12:2; Alma 12:1), and with travel to the Temple itself (Moshiyah 1:4-5). Likewise, they used "go down" in reference to leaving Jerusalem (1 Nefi 1:12).   **21** The Hebrew may have read וּדבר אתו בשבת ביתו which could also mean "And he spoke with him on the Sabbath in his house." If this event occurred on the Sabbath, it would have been especially egregious for Lavan to violate the peace of the Sabbath with an outburst of anger, and to drive a guest out of his home on the Sabbath— a time at which there was strict travel limit (see Ex. 16:29; Acts 1:12).

And we began to be exceedingly sorrowful, and my brothers were about to return unto my father in the wilderness.

12 But behold, I said unto them that as YHWH lives and as we live, we will not go down[22] unto our father in the wilderness until we have accomplished the thing which YHWH has commanded us. Wherefore, let us be faithful in keeping the mitzvot of YHWH. Therefore, let us go down to the land of our father's inheritance, for behold, he left gold and silver and all manner of riches. And all this he has done because of the mitzvot of YHWH. For he knew that Yerushalayim must be destroyed because of the wickedness of the people. For behold, they have rejected the words of the prophets. Wherefore, if my father should dwell in the land after he has been commanded to flee out of the land, behold, he would also perish; wherefore, it must necessarily be that he flee out of the land. And behold, it is wisdom in Elohim that we should obtain these records that we may preserve unto our children the language of our fathers, and also that we may preserve unto them the words which have been spoken by the mouth of all the holy prophets, which have been delivered unto them by the spirit and power of Elohim since the world began, even down unto this present time. And it came to pass that after this manner of language did I persuade my brothers that they might be faithful in keeping the mitzvot of Elohim.

13 And it came to pass that we went down to the land of our inheritance, and we did gather together our gold, and our silver, and our precious things. And after we had gathered these things together we went up again unto the house of Lavan. And it came to pass that we went in unto Lavan and desired him that he would give unto us the records which were engraved upon the plates of brass, for which we would give unto him our gold, and our silver, and all our precious things. And it came to pass that when Lavan saw our property, that it was exceedingly great, he did lust after it, insomuch that he thrust us out and sent his servants to slay us that he might obtain our property. And it came to pass that we did flee before the

---

22 The likely underlying Hebrew was *yarad* (ירד Strong's 3381), which means "to go down, descend." This expression denotes leaving Jerusalem because the Holy City is, spiritually speaking, the highest place. Leaving Jerusalem is a descent, regardless of elevation. See footnote 20 and 1 Nefi 1:20.

servants of Lavan, and we were obliged to leave behind our property, and it fell into the hands of Lavan.

14 And it came to pass that we fled into the wilderness, and the servants of Lavan did not overtake us, and we hid ourselves in the cavity of a rock. And it came to pass that Laman was angry with me and also with my father — and also was L'mu'el, for he hearkened unto the words of Laman — wherefore, Laman and L'mu'el did speak many hard words unto us, their younger brothers, and they did strike us even with a rod. And it came to pass as they did strike us with a rod, behold, an angel of YHWH came and stood before them, and he spoke unto them, saying, Why do you strike your younger brother with a rod? Do you not know that YHWH has chosen him to be a ruler over you, and this because of your iniquities? Behold, you shall go up to Yerushalayim again, and YHWH will deliver Lavan into your hands. And after the angel had spoken unto us, he departed. And after the angel had departed, Laman and L'mu'el again began to murmur, saying, How is it possible that YHWH will deliver Lavan into our hands? Behold, he is a mighty man and he can command fifty, yes, even he can slay fifty, then why not us?[23]

15 And it came to pass that I spoke unto my brothers, saying, Let us go up again unto Yerushalayim, and let us be faithful in keeping the mitzvot of YHWH. For behold, he is mightier than all the earth, then why not mightier than Lavan and his fifty? Yes, or even than his tens of thousands?[24] Therefore, let us go up. Let us be strong like unto Moshe, for he truly spoke unto the **waters** of the Red Sea and they **divided** hither and thither and our fathers came through out of captivity on **dry ground**,[25] and the armies of Pharaoh did follow and were drowned in the waters of the Red Sea. Now behold, you know that this is true; and you also know that an angel has spoken unto you. Wherefore, can you doubt? Let us go up. YHWH is able to deliver us, even as our fathers, and to destroy Lavan, even as the Egyptians.

16 Now when I had spoken these words, they were yet angry and did still continue to murmur; nevertheless, they did follow me up until we came without the walls of Yerushalayim. And it was by night,

---

23 This is an example of the Kal va-homer thought form, which serves as the first of the Seven Rules of Hillel. This classic Jewish thought form expresses that that which applies in a less important case will certainly apply in a more important case.   **24** Another example of the Kal va-homer thought form.   **25** Ex. 14:21

and I caused that they should hide themselves without the walls. And after they had hidden themselves, I, Nefi, crept into the city and went forth towards the house of Lavan. And I was led by the spirit, not knowing beforehand the things which I should do. Nevertheless, I went forth. And as I came near unto the house of Lavan I beheld a man, and he had fallen to the earth before me, for he was drunken with wine. And when I came to him, I found that it was Lavan, and beheld his sword, and I drew it forth from the sheath thereof. And the hilt thereof was of pure gold, and the workmanship thereof was exceedingly fine, and I saw that the blade thereof was of the most precious steel.

17 And it came to pass that I was constrained by the spirit that I should kill Lavan, but I said in my heart, Never at any time have I shed the blood of man. And I shrunk and would that I might not slay him. And the spirit said unto me again, Behold, YHWH has delivered him into your hands. Yes, and I also knew that he had sought to take away my own life. Yes, and he would not hearken unto the mitzvot of YHWH; and he also had taken away our property. And it came to pass that the spirit said unto me again, Slay him, for YHWH has delivered him into your hands. Behold, YHWH slays the wicked[26] to bring forth his righteous purposes. It is better that one man should perish than that a nation should dwindle and perish in unbelief. And now when I, Nefi, had heard these words, I remembered the words of YHWH which he spoke unto me in the wilderness, saying that inasmuch as your seed shall keep my mitzvot, they shall prosper in the land of promise. Yes, and I also thought that they could not keep the mitzvot of YHWH according to the Torah of Moshe except they should have the Torah. And I also knew that the Torah was engraved upon the plates of brass. And again, I knew that YHWH had delivered Lavan into my hands for this cause, that I might obtain the records according to his mitzvot. Therefore, I did obey the voice of the spirit and took Lavan by the hair of the head, and I smote off his head with his own sword.

18 And after I had struck off his head with his own sword, I took the garments of Lavan and put them upon my own body, yes, even every whit; and I did gird on his armor about my loins. And after I had done this, I went forth unto the genizah[27] of Lavan. And as I

---

26 1 Nefi 5:19-20   27 "Treasury." The Hebrew was likely *genizah* גניזה, which can mean

went forth towards the genizah of Lavan, behold, I saw the servant of Lavan who had the keys of the genizah. And I commanded him in the voice of Lavan that he should go with me into the genizah. And he supposing me to be his master Lavan, for he beheld the garments and also the sword girded about my loins, and he spoke unto me concerning the elders of the Y'hudim, he knowing that his master Lavan had been out by night among them. And I spoke unto him as if it had been Lavan. And I also spoke unto him that I should carry the engravings which were upon the plates of brass to my elder brothers, who were without the walls. And I also directed him that he should follow me. And he supposing that I spoke of the brothers of the assembly[28] and that I was truly that Lavan whom I had slain, wherefore he did follow me. And he spoke unto me many times concerning the elders of the Y'hudim as I went forth unto my brothers, who were without the walls.

19 And it came to pass that when Laman saw me, he was exceedingly frightened, and also L'mu'el and Sam. And they fled from before my presence, for they supposed it was Lavan and that he had slain me and had sought to take away their lives also. And it came to pass that I called after them and they did hear me; wherefore, they did cease to flee from my presence. And it came to pass that when the servant of Lavan beheld my brothers, he began to tremble and was about to flee from before me and return to the city of Yerushalayim. And now I, Nefi, being a man large in stature, and also having received much strength of YHWH, therefore I did seize upon the servant of Lavan and held him that he should not flee.

20 And it came to pass that I spoke with him, that if he would hearken unto my words, as YHWH lives and as I live, even so that

---

"treasury" but can also refer to a storage room for sacred texts.   **28** The 1830 text uses the word "church" instead of "assembly," reflecting standard KJV language. This may not refer to the Assembly of Israel, but rather to the Assembly of Elders, aligned with the usage of the word "church" in KJV Matt. 18:16-17. This Matthew passage draws on Deut. 19:15 where the "assembly" that hears these witnesses is "the priests and judges which shall be in those days" (Deut. 19:17). This council of Elders was known in the Second Temple Era as the "Great Assembly." It appears this term may have been in use even earlier, in the First Temple Era. When Nefi spoke of "my elder brothers, who were without the walls" the servant of Lavan may have thought he was speaking of the brothers of the Great Assembly. The Hebrew phrase for "older brothers" is actually "achim gadolim" (אחים גדולים) literally, "great [big] brothers." The word "Great" in "Great Assembly" is gadol (גדול). The servant of Lavan wrongly thought that when Nefi referred to "achim gadolim," he was referring to the brothers of the Great Assembly, or the council of Elders.

if he would hearken unto our words, we would spare his life. And I spoke unto him, even with an oath, that he need not fear, that he should be a free man like unto us if he would go down in the wilderness with us. And I also spoke unto him, saying, Surely YHWH has commanded us to do this thing. And shall we not be diligent in keeping the mitzvah of YHWH? Therefore, if you will go down in the wilderness to my father, you shall have place with us. And it came to pass that Tzuram did take courage at the words which I spoke. Now Tzuram[29] was the name of the servant, and he promised that he would go down into the wilderness unto our father; yes, and he also made an oath unto us that he would remain with us from that time forth. Now we were desirous that he should remain with us for this cause: that the Y'hudim might not know concerning our flight into the wilderness, for fear that they should pursue us and destroy us. And it came to pass that when Tzuram had made an oath unto us, our fears did cease concerning him. And it came to pass that we took the plates of brass and the servant of Lavan and departed into the wilderness and journeyed unto the tent of our father.

21 And it came to pass that after we had come down into the wilderness unto our father, behold, he was filled with joy. And also my mother Saryah[30] was exceedingly glad, for she truly had mourned because of us, for she had supposed that we had perished in the wilderness. And she also had complained against my father, telling him that he was a visionary man, saying, Behold, you have led us forth from the land of our inheritance, and my sons are no more, and we perish in the wilderness. And after this manner of language had my mother complained against my father. And it had came to pass that my father spoke unto her, saying, I know that I am a visionary man, for if I had not seen the things of Elohim in a vision, I should not have known the goodness of Elohim, but had remained at Yerushalayim and had perished with my brothers. But behold, I have obtained a land of promise,[31] in the which things I do rejoice. Yes, and I know that YHWH will deliver my sons out of the hands of

---

29 Possibly meaning "Rock of the Nation." Tzur was used as a metaphor for Elohim as Mighty One or protector of Israel (Deut. 32:37; Isa. 30:29; Ps. 18:3 (2), 32 (31), 47 (46)). See also 2 Nefi 3:8. **30** "My prince is Yah." **31** This is an example of the Hebraism known as the Prophetic Perfect, in which a prophet speaks of a future event in the perfect form (completed action), as if it had already occurred.

Lavan and bring them down again unto us in the wilderness. And after this manner of language did my father Lechi comfort my mother Saryah concerning us while we journeyed in the wilderness up to the land of Yerushalayim to obtain the record of the Y'hudim. And when we had returned to the tent of my father, behold, their joy was full, and my mother was comforted. And she spoke, saying, Now I know of a surety that YHWH has commanded my husband to flee into the wilderness; yes, and I also know of a surety that YHWH has protected my sons and delivered them out of the hands of Lavan and given them power by which they could accomplish the thing which YHWH has commanded them. And after this manner of language did she speak.

22 And it came to pass that they did rejoice exceedingly and did offer sacrifice and burnt offerings unto YHWH, and they gave thanks unto the Elohim of Isra'el. And after they had given thanks unto the Elohim of Isra'el, my father Lechi took the records which were engraved upon the plates of brass and he did search them from the beginning. And he beheld that they did contain the five books of Moshe, which gave an account of the creation of the world and also of Adam and Havah who were our first parents, and also a record of the Y'hudim from the beginning, even down to the commencement of the reign of Tzidkiyahu, king of Y'hudah, and also the prophecies of the holy prophets from the beginning, even down to the commencement of the reign of Tzidkiyahu, and also many prophecies which have been spoken by the mouth of Yirmeyahu.[32] And it came to pass that my father Lechi also found upon the plates of brass a genealogy of his fathers; wherefore, he knew that he was a descendant of Yosef, yes, even that Yosef who was the son of Ya'akov, who was sold into Egypt and who was preserved by the hand of YHWH that he might preserve his father Ya'akov and all his household from perishing with famine. And they were also led out of captivity and out of the land of Egypt by that same Elohim who had preserved them. And thus my father Lechi did discover the genealogy of his fathers. And Lavan also was a descendant of Yosef; wherefore, he and his fathers had kept the records. And now when my father saw all these things, he was filled with the spirit and began to prophesy concerning his

---

32 The threefold division of the Tanakh: the *Torah* (Law), "the five books of Moshe"; the *Nevi'im* (Prophets), "the prophecies of the holy prophets"; and the *Ketuvim* (Writings), "a record of the Jews." The first letter of each spells TNK (Tanakh).

seed — that these plates of brass should go forth unto all nations, kindreds, and tongues, and people, who were of his seed. Wherefore, he said that these plates of brass should never perish; neither should they be dimmed anymore by time. And he prophesied many things concerning his seed.

23 And it came to pass that thus far I and my father had kept the mitzvot with which YHWH had commanded us. And we had obtained the record which YHWH had commanded us and searched them and found that they were desirable, yes, even of great worth unto us, insomuch that we could preserve the mitzvot of YHWH unto our children. Wherefore, it was wisdom in YHWH that we should carry them with us as we journeyed in the wilderness toward the land of promise.

2 And now I, Nefi, do not give the genealogy of my fathers in this part[33] of my record, neither at any time shall I give it after upon these plates which I am writing, for it is given in the record which has been kept by my father; wherefore, I do not write it in this work, for it suffices me to say that we are a descendant of Yosef. And it matters not to me that I am particular to give a full account of all the things of my father, for they cannot be written upon these plates, for I desire the room that I may write of the things of Elohim. For the fulness of my intent is that I may persuade[34] men to come unto the Elohim of Avraham, and the Elohim of Yitz'chak, and the Elohim of Ya'akov and be saved. Wherefore, the things which are pleasing unto the world I do not write, but the things which are pleasing unto Elohim and unto those who are not of the world. Wherefore, I shall give commandment unto my seed that they shall not occupy these plates with things which are not of worth unto the children of men.

2 And now I would that you might know that after my father Lechi had made an end of prophesying concerning his seed, it came to pass that YHWH spoke unto him again, that it was not suitable for him, Lechi, that he should take his family into the wilderness alone, but that his sons should take daughters to wife, that they might raise up seed unto YHWH in the land of promise. And it came to pass that YHWH commanded him that I, Nefi, and my brothers should again

---

33 2 Nefi 3:6   34 2 Nefi 11:8; 2 Nefi 15:2

return into the land of Yerushalayim and bring down Yishma'el and his family into the wilderness. And it came to pass that I, Nefi, did again with my brothers go forth into the wilderness to go up to Yerushalayim. And it came to pass that we went up unto the house of Yishma'el, and we did gain favor in the sight of Yishma'el, insomuch that we did speak unto him the words of YHWH. And it came to pass that YHWH did soften the heart of Yishma'el and also his whole household, insomuch that they took their journey with us down into the wilderness to the tent of our father.

3 And it came to pass that as we journeyed in the wilderness, behold, Laman, and L'mu'el, and two of the daughters of Yishma'el, and the two sons of Yishma'el, and their families did rebel against us; yes, against I, Nefi, and Sam, and their father Yishma'el, and his wife, and his three other daughters. And it came to pass that in the which rebellion they were desirous to return unto the land of Yerushalayim. And now I, Nefi, being grieved for the hardness of their hearts, therefore I spoke unto them, saying—yes, even unto Laman and unto L'mu'el—Behold, you are my elder brothers, and how is it that you are so hard in your hearts and so blind in your minds that you have need that I, your younger brother, should speak unto you? Yes, and set an example for you? How is it that you have not hearkened unto the word of YHWH? How is it that you have forgotten that you have seen an angel of YHWH? Yes, and how is it that you have forgotten what great things YHWH has done for us in delivering us out of the hands of Lavan? And also that we should obtain the record? Yes, and how is it that you have forgotten that YHWH is able to do all things according to his will for the children of men, if it so be that they exercise faith in him? Wherefore, let us be faithful to him.[35] And if it so be that we are faithful to him, we shall obtain the land of promise.[36] And you shall know at some future period that the word of YHWH shall be fulfilled concerning the destruction of Yerushalayim,[37] for all things which YHWH has spoken concerning the destruction of Yerushalayim must be fulfilled. For behold, the spirit of YHWH ceases soon to strive with them; for behold, they have rejected the prophets, and Yirmeyahu have they cast into prison,[38] and they have

---

35 Another example of the Kal va-homer thought form. See footnote 23.   36 1 Nefi 5:32
37 2 Nefi 5:4; 2 Nefi 11:4   38 Jer. 37:15

sought to take away the life of my father, insomuch that they have driven him out of the land. Now behold, I say unto you that if you will return unto Yerushalayim, you shall also perish with them. And now if you have choice, go up to the land and remember the words which I speak unto you, that if you go, you will also perish. For thus the spirit of YHWH constrains me that I should speak.

4 And it came to pass that when I, Nefi, had spoken these words unto my brothers, they were angry with me. And it came to pass that they did lay their hands upon me, for behold, they were exceedingly angry; and they did bind me with cords, for they sought to take away my life, that they might leave me in the wilderness to be devoured by wild beasts. But it came to pass that I prayed unto YHWH, saying, O YHWH, according to my faith which is in you, will you deliver me from the hands of my brothers? Yes, even give me strength that I may burst these bands with which I am bound? And it came to pass that when I had said these words, behold, the bands[39] were loosed from off my hands and feet, and I stood before my brothers and I spoke unto them again. And it came to pass that they were angry with me again and sought to lay hands upon me. But behold, one of the daughters of Yishma'el, yes, and also her mother, and one of the sons of Yishma'el, did plead with my brothers, insomuch that they did soften their hearts and they did cease striving to take away my life. And it came to pass that they were sorrowful because of their wickedness, insomuch that they did bow down before me and did plead with me that I would forgive them of the thing that they had done against me. And it came to pass that I did frankly forgive them all that they had done, and I did exhort them that they would pray unto YHWH their Elohim for forgiveness. And it came to pass that they did so. And after they had done praying unto YHWH, we did again travel on our journey towards the tent of our father.

5 And it came to pass that we did come down unto the tent of our father. And after I and my brothers and all the house of Yishma'el had come down unto the tent of my father, they did give thanks unto YHWH their Elohim, and they did offer sacrifice and burnt offerings unto him.

---

39 Alma 10:10

⁶And it came to pass that we had gathered together all manner of seeds of every kind, both of grain of every kind and also of the seeds of fruits of every kind.

⁷And it came to pass that while my father remained in the wilderness, he spoke unto us, saying, Behold, I have dreamed a dream, or in other words, I have seen a vision. And behold, because of the thing which I have seen, I have reason to rejoice in YHWH because of Nefi and also of Sam; for I have reason to suppose that they and also many of their seed will be saved. But behold, Laman and L'mu'el, I fear exceedingly because of you. For behold, it seemed to me I saw in my dream a dark and dreary wilderness. And it came to pass that I saw a man and he was dressed in a white robe; and he came and stood before me. And it came to pass that he spoke unto me and invited me to follow him. And it came to pass that as I followed him, I beheld myself that I was in a dark and dreary waste. And after I had traveled for the space of many hours in darkness, I began to pray unto YHWH that he would have mercy on me according to the multitude of his tender mercies.

⁸And it came to pass, after I had prayed unto YHWH, I beheld a large and spacious field. And it came to pass that I beheld a tree[40] whose fruit was desirable to make one happy. And it came to pass that I did go forth and partake of the fruit thereof, and beheld that it was most sweet, above all that I ever before tasted. Yes, and I beheld that the fruit thereof was white to exceed all the whiteness that I had ever seen.

⁹And as I partook of the fruit thereof, it filled my soul with exceedingly great joy; wherefore, I began to be desirous[41] that my family should partake of it also, for I knew that it was desirable above all other fruit. And as I cast my eyes around about, that perhaps I might discover my family also, and I beheld a river[42] of water and it ran along, and it was near the tree of which I was partaking the fruit. And I looked to behold from where it came, and I saw the head thereof a little way off. And at the head thereof I beheld your mother Saryah, and Sam, and Nefi, and they stood as if they knew not where they should go. And it came to pass that I beckoned unto them; and I also did say unto them with a loud voice that they should come unto me and partake of the fruit, which was desirable above all other fruit.

---

40 1 Nefi 3:7–10   41 Enosh 1:2; Alma 17:5   42 1 Nefi 3:17;   1 Nefi 4:5

And it came to pass that they did come unto me and partake of the fruit also. And it came to pass that I was desirous that Laman and L'mu'el should come and partake of the fruit also; wherefore, I cast my eyes towards the head of the river that perhaps I might see them. And it came to pass that I saw them, but they would not come unto me and partake of the fruit.

10 And I beheld a rod[43] of iron, and it extended along the bank of the river and led to the tree by which I stood. And I also beheld a straight[44] and narrow path which came along by the rod of iron, even to the tree by which I stood; and it also led by the head of the fountain unto a large and spacious field, as if it had been a world. And I saw numberless concourses of people, many of whom were pressing forward that they might obtain the path which led unto the tree by which I stood. And it came to pass that they did come forth and commenced in the path which led to the tree. And it came to pass that there arose a mist[45] of darkness, yes, even an exceedingly great mist of darkness, insomuch that they who had commenced in the path did lose their way, that they wandered off and were lost. And it came to pass that I beheld others pressing forward, and they came forth and caught hold of the end of the rod of iron; and they did press forward through the mists of darkness, clinging to the rod of iron, even until they did come forth and partook of the fruit of the tree. And after they had partaken of the fruit of the tree, they did cast their eyes about as if they were ashamed.

11 And I also cast my eyes around about and beheld, on the other side of the river of water, a great and spacious[46] building. And it stood as it were in the air, high above the earth. And it was filled with people, both old and young, both male and female, and their manner of dress was exceedingly fine; and they were in the attitude of mocking and pointing their fingers towards those who had come up and were partaking of the fruit. And after they had tasted of the fruit, they were ashamed because of those that were a scoffing at them; and they fell away into forbidden paths and were lost.

12 And now I, Nefi, do not speak all the words of my father. But to be short in writing, behold, he saw other multitudes pressing forward; and they came and caught hold of the end of the rod of iron.

---

43 1 Nefi 4:5   **44** 2 Nefi 13:3-4   **45** 1 Nefi 3:17   **46** 1 Nefi 3:14, 17

And they did press their way forward, continually holding fast to the rod of iron, until they came forth and fell down and partook of the fruit of the tree. And he also saw other multitudes pressing their way towards that great and spacious building. And it came to pass that many were drowned in the depths of the fountain, and many were lost from his view, wandering in strange roads. And great was the multitude that did enter into that strange building. And after they did enter into that building, they did point the finger of scorn at me and those that were partaking of the fruit also. But we heeded them not — thus are the words of my father — for as many as heeded them had fallen away. And Laman and L'mu'el partook not of the fruit, said my father.

13 And it came to pass after my father had spoken all the words of his dream or vision, which were many, he said unto us, because of these things which he saw in a vision, he exceedingly feared for Laman and L'mu'el; yes, he feared that they should be cast off from the presence of YHWH. And he did exhort them then with all the feeling of a tender parent that they would hearken to his words, in that perhaps YHWH would be merciful to them and not cast them off; yes, my father did preach unto them. And after he had preached unto them, and also prophesied unto them of many things, he exhorted them to keep the mitzvot of YHWH; and he did cease speaking unto them. And all these things did my father see, and hear, and speak as he dwelt in a tent in the valley of L'mu'el, and also a great many more things which cannot be written upon these plates.

14 And now as I have spoken concerning these plates, behold, they are not the plates upon which I make a full account of the history of my people; for the plates upon which I make a full account of my people I have given the name of Nefi; wherefore, they are called the plates of Nefi, after my own name. And these plates also are called the plates of Nefi. Nevertheless, I have received a mitzvah of YHWH that I should make these plates for the special purpose that there should be an account engraved of the ministry of my people. And upon the other plates should be engraved an account of the reigns of the kings, and the wars and contentions of my people. Wherefore, these plates are for the more part of the ministry, and the other plates are for the more part of the reigns of the kings, and the wars and contentions of my people. Wherefore, YHWH has commanded me to

make these plates for a wise purpose in him, which purpose I know not. But YHWH knows all things from the beginning; wherefore, he prepares a way to accomplish all his works among the children of men. For behold, he has all power unto the fulfilling of all his words. And thus it is. Amen.

3

And now I, Nefi, proceed to give an account upon these plates of my proceedings and my reign and ministry; wherefore, to proceed with my account, I must speak somewhat of the things of my father and also of my brothers.

2 For behold, it came to pass after my father had made an end of speaking the words of his dream,[47] and also of exhorting them to all diligence, he spoke unto them concerning the Y'hudim, that after they should be destroyed — even that great city Yerushalayim[48] — and many be carried away captive into Babylon, according to the own due time of YHWH, they should return again, yes, even should be brought back out of captivity. And after that they should be brought back out of captivity, they should possess again their land of inheritance. Yes, even six hundred years from the time that my father left Yerushalayim, a prophet[49] would Adonai YHWH raise up among the Y'hudim, even a Mashiach,[50] or in other words, a savior of the world. And he also spoke concerning the prophets, how great a number had testified[51] of these things concerning this Mashiach of whom he had spoken, or this Redeemer of the world. Wherefore, all mankind were in a lost and in a fallen state, and always would be except they should rely on this Redeemer.

3 And he spoke also concerning a prophet[52] who should come before the Mashiach to prepare the way of YHWH. Yes, even he should go forth and **cry in the wilderness, Prepare you the way of YHWH and make his paths straight!**[53] For there stands one among you whom you know not; and he is mightier than I, whose shoe's latchet I am not worthy to unloose. And much spoke my father concerning this thing. And my father said he should immerse in Beit Avarah beyond Yarden; and he also said he should wash by immersion with water, even that he should immerse[54] the Mashiach with water. And after

---

47 1 Nefi 2:7-13 48 2 Nefi 5:4; 11:4 49 1 Nefi 7:5 50 1 Nefi 5:36-37 51 Moshiyah 8:2
52 1 Nefi 3:11 53 Isa. 40:3 54 2 Nefi 13:1-3

1 NEFI 3:4

he had immersed the Mashiach with water, he should behold and bear record that he had washed the Lamb of Elohim, who should take away the sins of the world.

4 And it came to pass, after my father had spoken these words, he spoke unto my brothers concerning the besorah[55] which should be preached among the Y'hudim, and also concerning the dwindling of the Y'hudim in unbelief.[56] And after they had slain the Mashiach who should come, and after he had been slain, he should rise from the dead and should make himself manifest[57] by the Ruach HaKodesh unto the Goyim. Yes, even my father spoke much concerning the Goyim, and also concerning the house of Isra'el, that they should be compared like unto an olive tree whose branches should be broken off and should be scattered upon all the face of the earth. Wherefore, he said it must necessarily be that we should be led with one accord into the land of promise, unto the fulfilling of the word of YHWH that we should be **scattered**[58] **upon all the face of the earth**. And after the house of Isra'el should be **scattered, they should be gathered together again**,[59] or in short, after the Goyim had received the fulness of the besorah, the natural branches of the olive tree — or the remnants of the house of Isra'el — should be grafted in,[60] or come[61] to the knowledge of the true Mashiach, their Adonai and their Redeemer. And after this manner of language did my father prophesy and speak unto my brothers, and also many more things which I do not write in this book; for I have written as many of them as were expedient for me in my other[62] book. And all these things of which I have spoken were done as my father dwelt in a tent in the valley of L'mu'el.

5 And it came to pass after I, Nefi, having heard all the words of my father concerning the things which he saw in a vision, and also the things which he spoke by the power of the Ruach HaKodesh, which power he received by faith on the Son of Elohim — and the Son of Elohim was the Mashiach who should come — I, Nefi, was desirous also that I might see, and hear, and know of these things by the power of the Ruach HaKodesh, which is the gift of Elohim unto all those who diligently seek him, as well in times of old as in

---

55 *Besorah* בשורה (Strong's 1309) means "good tidings, good news." Answers to the English word "gospel." **56** Ya'akov 3:5-6 **57** 3 Nefi 7:3 **58** 1 Nefi 7:1-3 **59** Deut. 30:3-4; Isa. 11:12 **60** The Zohar also uses the imagery of being "grafted in" to describe a proselyte being "grafted in" to Y'hudah (Zohar 1:26). **61** 1 Nefi 3:24; 3 Nefi 9:7-9 **62** 2 Nefi 3:6

the time that he should manifest himself unto the children of men, for he is the same[63] yesterday, and today, and for ever. And the way is prepared for all men from the foundation of the world, if it so be that they repent and come unto him. For he that diligently seeks shall find, and the mysteries of Elohim shall be unfolded to them[64] by the power of the Ruach HaKodesh, as well in this time as in times of old, and as well in times of old as in times to come; wherefore, the course of YHWH is one eternal round. Therefore remember, O man, for all your doings you shall be brought into judgment. Wherefore, if you have sought to do wickedly in the days of your probation, then you are found unclean before the judgment seat of Elohim, and no unclean thing can dwell with Elohim; wherefore, you must be cast off for ever. And the Ruach HaKodesh gives authority that I should speak these things and deny them not.

6 For it came to pass, after I had desired to know the things that my father had seen, and believing that YHWH was able to make them known unto me, as I sat pondering in my heart, I was caught away in the spirit of YHWH, yes, into an exceedingly high mountain,[65] a mountain which I never had before seen and upon which I never had before set my foot. And the spirit said unto me, Behold, what do you desire? And I said, I desire to behold the things which my father saw. And the spirit said unto me, Do you believe that your father saw the tree[66] of which he has spoken? And I said, Yes, you know that I believe all the words of my father. And when I had spoken these words, the spirit cried with a loud voice, saying, Hoshianna to YHWH, the El Elyon, for he is Elohim over all the earth, yes, even above all! And blessed are you, Nefi, because you believe in the Son of the El Elyon; wherefore, you shall behold the things which you have desired. And behold, this thing shall be given unto you for a sign, that after you have beheld the tree which bears the fruit of which your father tasted, you shall also behold a man descending out of Heaven, and him shall you witness. And after you shall have witnessed him, you shall bear record that it is the Son of Elohim.

---

63 M'raman 4:7   **64** Compare with the Gospel according to the Hebrews as quoted by Clement of Alexandria: "Even (or also, in the Gospel according to the Hebrews) is written the saying, 'he that wondereth shall reign, and he that reigneth shall rest'" (Stromateis ii. 9. 45). "For those words have the same force as these: 'He shall not cease from seeking until he find, and having found, he will be amazed, and having been amazed will reign, and having reigned will rest.'"(Stromateis v. 14. 96).   **65** 2 Nefi 3:7   **66** 1 Nefi 2:8-9

7 And it came to pass that the spirit said unto me, Look. And I looked and beheld a tree, and it was like unto the tree which my father had seen; and the beauty thereof was far beyond, yes, exceeding of all beauty, and the whiteness thereof did exceed the whiteness of the driven snow. And it came to pass after I had seen the tree, I said unto the spirit, I behold you have shown unto me the tree which is most precious above all. And he said unto me, What do you desire? And I said unto him, To know the interpretation thereof — for I spoke unto him as a man speaks, for I beheld that he was in the form of a man. Yet nevertheless, I knew that it was the spirit of YHWH; and he spoke unto me as a man speaks with another.

8 And it came to pass that he said unto me, Look. And I looked as if to look upon him and I saw him not, for he had gone from before my presence. And it came to pass that I looked and beheld the great city Yerushalayim, and also other cities. And I beheld the city of Natzrat, and in the city of Natzrat I beheld a virgin,[67] and she was exceedingly fair and white. And it came to pass that I saw the Heavens open, and an angel came down and stood before me; and he said unto me, Nefi, what do you behold? And I said unto him, A virgin most beautiful and fair above all other virgins. And he said unto me, Do you know the condescension of Elohim? And I said unto him, I know that he loves his children; nevertheless, I do not know the meaning of all things. And he said unto me, Behold, the virgin whom you see is the Mother[68] of the Son of Elohim, after the manner of the flesh. And it came to pass that I beheld that she was carried away in the spirit.

9 And after she had been carried away in the spirit for the space of a time, the angel spoke unto me, saying, Look. And I looked and beheld the virgin again bearing a child in her arms. And the angel said unto me, Behold the Lamb of Elohim, yes, even the Son of the Eternal Father. Do you know the meaning of the tree which your father saw? And I answered him, saying, Yes, it is the love of Elohim, which sheds itself abroad in the hearts of the children of men; wherefore, it is the most desirable above all things. And he spoke unto me, saying, Yes, and the most joyous to the soul.

10 And after he had said these words, he said unto me, Look. And I looked, and I beheld the Son of Elohim going forth among the

---

67 Alma 5:3 **68** Moshiyah 1:14; Alma 12:20

children of men; and I saw many fall down at his feet and worship him. And it came to pass that I beheld that the **rod of iron**⁶⁹ which my father had seen was the word of Elohim, which led to the **fountain of living waters**,⁷⁰ or to the **tree of life**,⁷¹ which waters are a representation of the love of Elohim. And I also beheld that the tree of life was a representation of the love of Elohim.

¹¹ And the angel said unto me again, Look and behold the condescension of Elohim. And I looked and beheld the Redeemer of the world, of whom my father had spoken; and I also beheld the prophet who should **prepare the way before him**.⁷² And the Lamb of Elohim went forth and was immersed of him; and after he was washed by immersion, I beheld the Heavens open, and the **Ruach HaKodesh** came down out of Heaven and **abode upon him**⁷³ in the form of a dove. And I beheld that he went forth ministering unto the people in power and great glory, and the multitudes were gathered together to hear him; and I beheld that they cast him out from among them. And I also beheld twelve others following him. And it came to pass that they were carried away in the spirit from before my face, that I saw them not.

¹² And it came to pass that the angel spoke unto me, saying, Look. And I looked, and I beheld the Heavens open again, and I saw angels descending upon the children of men, and they did minister unto them.

¹³ And he spoke unto me again, saying, Look. And I looked and I beheld the Lamb of Elohim going forth⁷⁴ among the children of men. And I beheld multitudes of people who were sick and who were afflicted with all manner of diseases, and with demons and unclean spirits; and the angel spoke and showed all these things unto me. And they were healed by the power of the Lamb of Elohim, and the demons and the unclean spirits were cast out.

¹⁴ And it came to pass that the angel spoke unto me again, saying, Look. And I looked and beheld the Lamb of Elohim, that he was taken by the people, yes, the Son of the El Olam was judged of the world; and I saw and bear record. And I, Nefi, saw that he was lifted up⁷⁵ upon the Tz'lav⁷⁶ and slain⁷⁷ for the sins of the world. And after he

---

69 Ps. 2:9   **70** Jer. 2:13; 17:13   **71** Gen. 2:9; 3:22–24; Prov. 3:18; 11:30; 13:12; 15:4   **72** Isa. 40:3   **73** Isa. 11:2; 42:1; 61:1   **74** Moshiyah 1:14   **75** 3 Nefi 12:5   **76** צלב A wooden instrument of execution by hanging or crucifixion. "Cross."   **77** 2 Nefi 7:1

was slain, I saw the multitudes of the earth, that they were gathered together to fight against the emissaries of the Lamb, for thus were the twelve called by the angel of YHWH. And the multitude of the earth was gathered together, and I beheld that they were in a large and spacious building, like unto the building which my father saw. And the angel of YHWH spoke unto me again, saying, Behold, the world and the wisdom thereof; yes, behold, the house of Isra'el has gathered together to fight against the twelve emissaries of the Lamb. And it came to pass that I saw and bear record that the great and spacious building was the pride of the world; and the fall thereof was exceedingly great. And the angel of YHWH spoke unto me, saying, Thus shall be the destruction of all nations, kindreds, tongues, and people, that shall fight against the twelve emissaries of the Lamb.

15 And it came to pass that the angel said unto me, Look and behold your seed, and also the seed of your brothers. And I looked and beheld the land of promise; and I beheld multitudes of people, yes, even as it were in number as many as the sand of the sea. And it came to pass that I beheld multitudes gathered together to battle one against the other. And I beheld wars and rumors of wars and great slaughters with the sword among my people. And it came to pass that I beheld many generations pass away after the manner of wars and contentions in the land. And I beheld many cities, yes, even that I did not number them. And it came to pass that I saw a mist of darkness on the face of the land of promise. And I saw lightnings,[78] and I heard thunderings, and earthquakes, and all manner of tumultuous noises. And I saw the earth and the rocks, that they split, and I saw mountains tumbling into pieces, and I saw the plains of the earth, that they were broken up. And I saw many cities, that they were sunk, and I saw many that they were burnt with fire, and I saw many that did tumble to the earth because of the quaking thereof. And it came to pass after I saw these things, I saw the vapor[79] of darkness, that it passed from off the face of the earth. And behold, I saw the multitudes who had not fallen because of the great and terrible judgments of YHWH. And I saw the Heavens open and the Lamb of Elohim descending out of Heaven, and he came down and he showed himself[80] unto them.

---

78 3 Nefi 4:2-3   79 3 Nefi 4:4   80 2 Nefi 11:10; 3 Nefi 5:2-6

16 And I also saw and bear record that the Ruach HaKodesh fell upon twelve[81] others, and they were ordained of Elohim and chosen. And the angel spoke unto me, saying, Behold the twelve talmidim of the Lamb, who were chosen to minister unto your seed. And he said unto me, You remember the twelve emissaries[82] of the Lamb. Behold, they are they who shall judge the twelve tribes of Isra'el. Wherefore, the twelve servants of your seed shall be judged of them, for you are of the house of Isra'el; and these twelve servants whom you behold shall judge your seed. And behold, they are righteous for ever, for because of their faith in the Lamb of Elohim, their garments are made white in his blood.

17 And the angel said unto me, Look. And I looked and beheld three[83] generations pass away in righteousness, and their garments were white, even like unto the Lamb of Elohim. And the angel said unto me, These are made white in the blood of the Lamb because of their faith in him. And I, Nefi, also saw many of the fourth generation[84] who passed away in righteousness. And it came to pass that I saw the multitudes of the earth gathered together. And the angel said unto me, Behold your seed and also the seed of your brothers. And it came to pass that I looked and beheld the people of my seed gathered together in multitudes against the seed of my brothers, and they were gathered together to battle. And the angel spoke unto me, saying, Behold the fountain of filthy water which your father saw, yes, even the river of which he spoke; and the depths thereof are the depths of She'ol. And the mists of darkness are the temptations of HaSatan which blind the eyes and harden the hearts of the children of men and lead them away into broad roads, that they perish and are lost. And the large and spacious building which your father saw is vain imaginations and the pride of the children of men. And a great and a terrible gulf[85] divides them, yes, even the sword of the justice of the Elohe Kedem and Mashiach who is the Lamb of Elohim, of whom the Ruach HaKodesh bears record from the beginning of the world until this time, and from this time henceforth and for ever.

18 And while the angel spoke these words, I beheld and saw that the seed of my brothers did contend against my seed, according to

---

81 3 Nefi 5:10 82 1 Nefi 3:11 83 2 Nefi 11:11; 3 Nefi 13:1 84 4 Nefi 1:4 85 1 Nefi 4:5

the word of the angel. And because of the pride of my seed and the temptations of HaSatan, I beheld that the seed of my brothers did overpower the people of my seed. And it came to pass that I beheld and saw the people of the seed of my brothers, that they had overcome my seed, and they went forth in multitudes upon the face of the land. And I saw them gathered together in multitudes; and I saw wars and rumors of wars among them, and in wars and rumors of wars I saw many generations pass away. And the angel said unto me, Behold, these shall dwindle in unbelief. And it came to pass that I beheld, after they had dwindled in unbelief, they became a dark, and loathsome, and a filthy people, full of idleness and all manner of abominations.

19 And it came to pass that the angel spoke unto me, saying, Look. And I looked and beheld many nations and kingdoms. And the angel said unto me, What do you behold? And I said, I behold many nations and kingdoms. And he said unto me, These are the nations and kingdoms of the Goyim. And it came to pass that I saw among the nations of the Goyim the formation of a great church.[86] And the angel said unto me, Behold the formation of a church which is most abominable above all other churches, which slays the k'doshim of Elohim, yes, and tortures them, and binds them down, and yokes them with a yoke of iron, and brings them down into captivity. And it came to pass that I beheld this great and abominable church, and I saw HaSatan that he was the foundation of it. And I also saw gold,[87] and silver, and silks, and scarlets, and fine twined linen, and all manner of precious clothing; and I saw many harlots. And the angel spoke unto me, saying, Behold, the gold, and the silver, and the silks, and the scarlets, and the fine twined linen, and the precious clothing, and the harlots are the desires of this great and abominable church. And also for the praise of the world do they destroy the k'doshim of Elohim and bring them down into captivity.

20 And it came to pass that I looked and beheld many waters, and they divided the Goyim from the seed of my brothers. And it came to pass that the angel said unto me, Behold, the wrath of Elohim is upon the seed of your brothers. And I looked and beheld a man among the Goyim, who was separated from the seed of my brothers by the many waters; and I beheld the Ruach Elohim, that it came down and

---

86 1 Nefi 7:4   87 M'raman 4:5

worked upon the man, and he went forth upon the many waters, even unto the seed of my brothers who were in the promised land. And it came to pass that I beheld the Ruach Elohim, that it worked upon other Goyim, and they went forth out of captivity upon the many waters. And it came to pass that I beheld many multitudes of the Goyim upon the land of promise; and I beheld the wrath of Elohim, that it was upon the seed of my brothers; and they were scattered[88] before the Goyim and were smitten. And I beheld the spirit of YHWH, that it was upon the Goyim, that they did prosper and obtain the land for their inheritance. And I beheld that they were white, and exceedingly fair and beautiful, like unto my people before they were slain. And it came to pass that I, Nefi, beheld that the Goyim who had gone forth out of captivity did humble themselves before YHWH, and the power of YHWH was with them. And I beheld that their mother Goyim were gathered together upon the waters, and upon the land also, to battle against them. And I beheld that the power of Elohim was with them, and also that the wrath of Elohim was upon all those that were gathered together against them to battle. And I, Nefi, beheld that the Goyim that had gone out of captivity were delivered by the power of Elohim[89] out of the hands of all other nations. And it came to pass that I, Nefi, beheld that they did prosper in the land.

21 And I beheld a book, and it was carried forth among them. And the angel said unto me, Do you know the meaning of the book? And I said, I know not. And he said, Behold, it proceeds out of the mouth of a Y'hudi[90] — and I, Nefi, beheld it. And he said unto me, The book that you behold is a record of the Y'hudim, which contains the covenants of YHWH which he has made unto the house of Isra'el; and it also contains many of the prophecies of the holy prophets. And it is a record like unto the engravings which are upon the plates of brass,[91] except there are not so many. Nevertheless, they contain the covenants of YHWH which he has made unto the house of Isra'el; wherefore, they are of great worth unto the Goyim. And the angel of YHWH said unto me, You have beheld that the book proceeded forth from the mouth of a Y'hudi. And when it proceeded forth from the mouth of a Y'hudi, it contained the fulness of the besorah of the Lamb, of whom the twelve emissaries bore record; and they bore record according to

---

88 1 Nefi 7:2 89 3 Nefi 9:11; 'Eter 1:7 90 2 Nefi 12:8 91 1 Nefi 1:22-23

the truth which is in the Lamb of Elohim. Wherefore, these things go forth from the Y'hudim in purity unto the Goyim, according to the truth which is in Elohim. And after they go forth by the hand of the twelve emissaries of the Lamb from the Y'hudim unto the Goyim, you see the formation of that great and abominable church, which is the most abominable of all other churches. For behold, they have taken away[92] from the besorah of the Lamb many parts which are plain and most precious; and also many covenants of YHWH have they taken away. And all this have they done that they might pervert the right ways of YHWH, that they might blind the eyes and harden the hearts of the children of men. Wherefore, you see that after the book has gone forth through the hands of the great and abominable church, that there are many plain and most precious things taken away from the book, which is the book of the Lamb of Elohim. And after these plain and precious things were taken away, it goes forth unto all the nations of the Goyim.

22 And after it goes forth unto all the nations of the Goyim, yes, even across the many waters (which you have seen) with the Goyim which have gone forth out of captivity, you see, because of the many plain and precious things which have been taken out of the book — which were plain unto the understanding of the children of men, according to the plainness which is in the Lamb of Elohim — that because of these things which are taken away out of the besorah of the Lamb, an exceedingly great many do stumble,[93] yes, insomuch that HaSatan has great power over them. Nevertheless, you behold that the Goyim who have gone forth out of captivity and have been lifted up by the power of Elohim above all other nations upon the face of the land — which is choice above all other lands, which is the land Adonai YHWH has covenanted with your father that his seed should have for the land of their inheritance — will not utterly destroy the mixture of your seed who are among your brothers. Neither will he allow that the Goyim shall destroy the seed of your brothers; neither will Adonai YHWH allow that the Goyim shall for ever remain in that awful state of blindness, which you behold they are in because of the plain and most precious parts of the besorah of the Lamb which have been kept back by that abominable church, whose formation you have

---

92 1 Nefi 3:21   93 2 Nefi 11:15

seen. Wherefore, says the Lamb of Elohim, I will be merciful unto the Goyim, unto the visiting of the remnant of the house of Isra'el in great judgment.

23 And it came to pass that the angel of YHWH spoke unto me, saying, Behold, says the Lamb of Elohim, after I have visited the remnant of the house of Isra'el (and this remnant of whom I speak is the seed of your father), wherefore, after I have visited them in judgment and smitten them by the hand of the Goyim, and after that the Goyim do stumble exceedingly because of the most plain and precious parts of the besorah of the Lamb which has been kept back by that abominable church, which is the mother of harlots, says the Lamb, I will be merciful unto the Goyim in that day, insomuch that I will bring forth unto them in my own power much of my besorah which shall be plain and precious, says the Lamb. For behold, says the Lamb, I will manifest myself unto your seed,[94] that they shall write many things which I shall minister unto them, which shall be plain and precious. And after your seed shall be destroyed and dwindle in unbelief, and also the seed of your brothers, behold, these things shall be hid up to come forth[95] unto the Goyim by the gift and power of the Lamb. And in them shall be written my besorah, says the Lamb, and my rock and my salvation. And blessed are they who shall seek to bring forth my Tziyon at that day, for they shall have the gift and the power of the Ruach HaKodesh. And if they endure unto the end, they shall be lifted up at the last day and shall be saved in the everlasting kingdom of the Lamb. Yes, **whoever shall publish shalom,**[96] **yes, tidings of great joy, how beautiful upon the mountains shall they be!**[97]

24 And it came to pass that I beheld the remnant of the seed of my brothers and also the book of the Lamb of Elohim which had proceeded forth from the mouth of the Y'hudi, that it came forth from the Goyim unto the remnant of the seed of my brothers. And after it had come forth unto them, I beheld other books which came forth by the power of the Lamb from the Goyim unto them, unto the convincing of the Goyim, and the remnant of the seed of my brothers, and also the Y'hudim who were scattered upon all the face of the earth, that the records of the prophets and of the twelve emissaries

---

[94] 3 Nefi 4:11; 3 Nefi 5:3-4 [95] 1 Nefi 7:3; 2 Nefi 11:19 [96] 3 Nefi 9:10 [97] Isa. 52:7

of the Lamb are true. And the angel spoke unto me, saying, These last records which you have seen among the Goyim shall establish the truth of the first, which are of the twelve emissaries of the Lamb, and shall make known the plain and precious things which have been taken away from them, and shall make known to all kindreds, tongues, and people that the Lamb of Elohim is the Son of the Eternal Father and the Savior of the world, and that all men must come unto him or they cannot be saved. And they must come according to the words which shall be established by the mouth of the Lamb; and the words of the Lamb shall be made known in the records of your seed, as well as in the records of the twelve emissaries of the Lamb. Wherefore, they both shall be established in one,[98] for there is one Elohim and one Shepherd over all the earth. And the time comes that he shall manifest himself unto all nations, both unto the Y'hudim and also unto the Goyim. And after he has manifested himself unto the Y'hudim and also unto the Goyim, then he shall manifest himself unto the Goyim and also unto the Y'hudim; and the last shall be first, and the first[99] shall be last.

25 And it shall come to pass that if the Goyim shall hearken[100] unto the Lamb of Elohim in that day that he shall manifest himself unto them in word and also in power, in very deed, unto the taking away of their stumbling blocks, and harden not their hearts against the Lamb of Elohim, they shall be numbered among the seed of your father. Yes, they shall be numbered among the house of Isra'el; and they shall be a blessed people upon the promised land for ever. They shall be no more brought down into captivity, and the house of Isra'el shall no more be confounded. And that great pit which has been dug for them by that great and abominable church — which was founded by HaSatan and his children, that he might lead away the souls of men down to Gehinnom — yes, that great pit which has been dug for the destruction of men shall be filled by those who dug it, unto their utter destruction, says the Lamb of Elohim, not the destruction of the soul, except it be the casting of it into that Gehinnom which has no end. For behold, this is according to the captivity of HaSatan, and also according to the justice of Elohim, upon all those who will work wickedness and abomination before him.

---

98 Ezek. 37:16-17   99 1 Nefi 3:4; 'Eter 6:3   100 3 Nefi 10:1

26 And it came to pass that the angel spoke unto me, Nefi, saying, You have beheld that if the Goyim repent, it shall be well with them; and you also know concerning the covenants of YHWH unto the house of Isra'el. And you also have heard that whoever repents not must perish. Therefore, woe be unto the Goyim[101] if it so be that they harden their hearts against the Lamb of Elohim. For the time comes, says the Lamb of Elohim, that I will work a **great and a marvelous**[102] **work**[103] among the children of men, a work which shall be everlasting, either on the one hand or on the other, either to the convincing of them unto shalom and life Eternal, or unto the deliverance of them to the hardness of their hearts and the blindness of their minds, unto their being brought down into captivity and also unto destruction, both temporally and spiritually, according to the captivity of HaSatan of which I have spoken.

27 And it came to pass that when the angel had spoken these words, he said unto me, Do you remember the covenants of the Father unto the house of Isra'el? I said unto him, Yes. And it came to pass that he said unto me, Look and behold that great and abominable church, which is the mother of abominations, whose foundation is HaSatan. And he said unto me, Behold, there are only two assemblies: the one is the assembly of the Lamb of Elohim, and the other is the assembly of HaSatan.[104] Wherefore, whoever belongs not to the assembly of the Lamb of Elohim belongs to that great assembly which is the mother of abominations, and she is the whore of all the earth.

28 And it came to pass that I looked and beheld the whore of all the earth, and she sat upon many waters, and she had dominion over all the earth, among all nations, kindreds, tongues, and people. And it came to pass that I beheld the assembly of the Lamb of Elohim, and its numbers were few because of the wickedness and abominations of the whore who sat upon many waters. Nevertheless, I beheld that the assembly of the Lamb, who were the k'doshim of Elohim, were also upon all the face of the earth; and their dominions upon the face of the earth were small because of the wickedness of the great whore whom I saw. And it came to pass that I beheld that the great mother of abominations did gather together in multitudes upon the face of

---

101 3 Nefi 7:4-5; 9:7-8   102 3 Nefi 9:10-11; 10:1   103 Another example of the Cognate Accusative Hebraic construction. See footnote 18.   104 1 Nefi 7:5

all the earth, among all the nations of the Goyim, to fight against the Lamb of Elohim. And it came to pass that I, Nefi, beheld the power of the Lamb of Elohim, that it descended upon the k'doshim of the assembly of the Lamb and upon the covenant people of YHWH, who were scattered upon all the face of the earth. And they were armed with righteousness and with the power of Elohim in great glory.

²⁹ And it came to pass that I beheld that the wrath of Elohim was poured out upon that great and abominable church, insomuch that there were wars[105] and rumors of wars among all the nations and kindreds of the earth. And as there began to be wars and rumors of wars among all the nations which belonged to the mother of abominations, the angel spoke unto me, saying, Behold, the wrath of Elohim is upon the mother of harlots, and behold, you see all these things. And when the day comes that the wrath of Elohim is poured out upon the mother of harlots — which is the great and abominable church of all the earth, whose foundation is HaSatan — then at that day the work of the Father shall commence in preparing the way for the fulfilling of his covenants which he has made to his people who are of the house of Isra'el.

³⁰ And it came to pass that the angel spoke unto me, saying, Look. And I looked and beheld a man, and he was dressed in a white robe; and the angel said unto me, Behold one of the twelve emissaries of the Lamb. Behold, he shall see and write the remainder of these things, yes, and also many things which have been; and he shall also write concerning the end of the world. Wherefore, the things which he shall write are just and true; and behold, they are written in the book which you beheld proceeding out of the mouth of the Y'hudi. And at the time they proceeded out of the mouth of the Y'hudi, or at the time the book proceeded out of the mouth of the Y'hudi, the things which were written were plain, and pure, and most precious, and easy to the understanding of all men. And behold, the things which this emissary of the Lamb shall write are many things which you have seen; and behold, the remainder shall you see. But the things which you shall see hereafter you shall not write, for Adonai YHWH has ordained the emissary of the Lamb of Elohim that he should write them. And also others who have been, to them has he

---

[105] 1 Nefi 7:4

shown all things, and they have written them. And they **are sealed up to come forth**[106] in their purity, according to the truth which is in the Lamb, in the own due time of YHWH, unto the house of Isra'el.

31 And I, Nefi, heard and bear record that the name of the emissary of the Lamb was Yochanan, according to the word of the angel. And behold, I, Nefi, am forbidden that I should write the remainder of the things which I saw. Wherefore, the things which I have written suffice me, and I have not written but a small part of the things which I saw. And I bear record that I saw the things which my father saw, and the angel of YHWH did make them known unto me. And now I make an end of speaking concerning the things which I saw while I was carried away in the spirit; and if all the things which I saw are not written, the things which I have written are true. And thus it is. Amen.

4 And it came to pass that after I, Nefi, had been carried away in the spirit and seen all these things, I returned to the tent of my father. And it came to pass that I beheld my brothers, and they were disputing one with another concerning the things which my father had spoken unto them; for he truly spoke many great things unto them which were hard to be understood except a man should inquire of YHWH. And they being hard in their hearts, therefore they did not look unto YHWH as they ought. And now I, Nefi, was grieved because of the hardness of their hearts, and also because of the things which I had seen, and knew they must unavoidably come to pass because of the great wickedness of the children of men. And it came to pass that I was overcome because of my afflictions, for I considered that my afflictions were great above all because of the destructions[107] of my people, for I had beheld their fall.

2 And it came to pass that after I had received strength, I spoke unto my brothers, desiring to know of them the cause of their disputations. And they said, Behold, we cannot understand the words which our father has spoken concerning the natural branches of the olive tree,[108] and also concerning the Goyim. And I said unto them, Have you inquired of YHWH? And they said unto me, We have not, for YHWH makes no such thing known unto us. Behold, I said unto them, How is it that you do not keep the mitzvot of YHWH? How is it that you will

---

106 Dan. 12:9 **107** M'raman 4:1 **108** 1 Nefi 3:2-4

1 NEFI 4:3

perish because of the hardness of your hearts? Do you not remember the thing which YHWH has said, If you will not harden your hearts, and ask[109] me in faith, believing that you shall receive, with diligence in keeping my mitzvot, surely these things shall be made known unto you?

3 Behold, I say unto you that the house of Isra'el was compared unto an olive tree by the spirit of YHWH which was in our father. And behold, are we not broken off from the house of Isra'el? And are we not a branch of the house of Isra'el? And now the thing which our father means concerning the grafting in of the natural branches through the Milo HaGoyim[110] is that in the latter days, when our seed shall have dwindled in unbelief—yes, for the space of many years and many generations after the Mashiach shall be manifested in body unto the children of men—then[111] shall the fulness of the besorah of the Mashiach come unto the Goyim, and from the Goyim unto the remnant of our seed. And at that day shall the remnant of our seed know that they are of the house of Isra'el and that they are the covenant people of YHWH. And then shall they know and come to the knowledge of their forefathers, and also to the knowledge of the besorah of their Redeemer, which was taught unto their fathers by him. Wherefore, they shall come to the knowledge of their Redeemer and the very points of his doctrine, that they may know how to come unto him and be saved. And then at that day, will they not rejoice and give praise unto their El Olam, their rock, and their salvation? Yes, at that day, will they not receive strength and nourishment from the true vine? Yes, will they not come unto the true fold of Elohim? Behold, I say unto you, yes, they shall be numbered again among the house of Isra'el; they shall be grafted in, being a natural branch of the olive tree, into the true olive tree; and this is what our father means. And he means that it will not come to pass until after they are scattered[112] by the Goyim. And he means that it shall come by way of

---

109 Enosh 1:4; 3 Nefi 6:7; M'roni 7:5   110 "Fulness of the Gentiles." See Gen. 48:19; Rom. 11:25; 3 Nefi 7:4. This phrase (מלא הגוים) appears in Rom. 11:25 where the KJV has "fulness of the Gentiles" as part of the explanation of the Olive Tree parable. It also appears in Gen. 48:19, where the KJV translates it as "a multitude of nations" as part of Jacob's blessing on Ephraim. Jacob plainly states that Ephraim's descendants will become the fulness of the Gentiles. Hence this work began among the Gentiles and goes to all of scattered Israel in the hand of Ephraim. See also Ezek. 37:19.   111 3 Nefi 9:10
112 1 Nefi 7:2-3

the Goyim, that YHWH may show his power unto the Goyim for the very cause that he shall be rejected of the Y'hudim, or of the house of Isra'el. Wherefore, our father has not spoken of our seed alone, but also of all the house of Isra'el, pointing to the covenant which should be fulfilled in the latter days, which covenant YHWH made to our father Avraham, saying, In your seed shall all the kindreds of the earth be blessed.

⁴And it came to pass that I, Nefi, spoke much unto them concerning these things; yes, I spoke unto them concerning the restoration of the Y'hudim[113] in the latter days. And I did rehearse unto them the words of Yesha'yahu, who spoke concerning the restoration of the Y'hudim, or of the house of Isra'el; and after they were restored, they should no more be confounded, neither should they be scattered again. And it came to pass that I did speak so many words unto my brothers that they were pacified and did humble themselves before YHWH.

⁵And it came to pass that they did speak unto me again, saying, What is the meaning of this thing which our father saw in a dream? What is the meaning of the tree which he saw? And I said unto them, It was a representation of the tree of life.[114] And they said unto me, What is the meaning of the rod of iron which our father saw that led to the tree? And I said unto them that it was the word of Elohim, and that whoever would hearken unto the word of Elohim and would hold fast unto it, they would never perish, neither could the temptations and the fiery darts of the adversary overpower them unto blindness, to lead them away to destruction. Wherefore, I, Nefi, did exhort them to give heed unto the word of YHWH; yes, I did exhort them with all the energies of my soul, and with all the faculty which I possessed, that they would give heed to the word of Elohim and remember to keep his mitzvot always, in all things. And they said unto me, What is the meaning of the river of water which our father saw? And I said unto them that the water which my father saw was tum'ah;[115] and so much was his mind swallowed up in other things that he beheld not the uncleanness of the water. And I said unto them that it was an awful gulf which separates the wicked from the tree of life, and also from the k'doshim of Elohim. And I said unto them that it

---

113 2 Nefi 6:1; 7:2; 12:10; 3 Nefi 10:1   114 Gen. 2:9; 3:22-24; Prov. 3:18; 11:30; 13:12; 15:4
115 טומאה Ritual uncleanness

was a representation of that awful Gehinnom which the angel said unto me was prepared for the wicked. And I said unto them that our father also saw that the justice of Elohim did also divide the wicked from the righteous, and the brightness thereof was like unto the brightness of a flaming fire which ascends up unto Elohim for ever and ever and has no end.

⁶And they said unto me, Does this thing mean the torment of the body in the days of probation? Or does it mean the final state of the soul after the death of the temporal body? Or does it speak of the things which are temporal? And it came to pass that I said unto them that it was a representation of things both temporal and spiritual; for the day should come that they must be judged of their works, yes, even the works which were done by the temporal body in their days of probation. Wherefore, if they should die in their wickedness, they must be cast off also as to the things which are spiritual, which are pertaining unto righteousness. Wherefore, they must be brought to stand before Elohim to be judged of their works. And if their works have been tum'ah, they must necessarily be unclean; and if they be unclean, it must necessarily be that they cannot dwell in the kingdom of Elohim — if so, the kingdom of Elohim must be unclean also. But behold, I say unto you that the kingdom of Elohim is not unclean, that there cannot any tamé[116] thing enter into the kingdom of Elohim; wherefore, there must necessarily be a place of tum'ah prepared for that which is unclean. And there is a place prepared, yes, even that awful Gehinnom of which I have spoken, and HaSatan is the foundation of it. Wherefore, the final state of the souls of man is to dwell in the kingdom of Elohim or to be cast out because of that justice of which I have spoken. Wherefore, the wicked are separated from the righteous, and also from that tree of life whose fruit is most precious and most desirable of all other fruits; yes, and it is the greatest of all the gifts of Elohim. And thus I spoke unto my brothers. Amen.

5 And now it came to pass that after I, Nefi, had made an end of speaking to my brothers, behold, they said unto me, You have declared unto us hard things, more than which we are able to bear.

---

116 טמא Ritually impure

And it came to pass that I said unto them that I knew that I had spoken hard things against the wicked according to the truth, and the righteous have I justified and testified that they should be lifted up at the last day. Wherefore, the guilty take the truth to be hard, for it cuts them to the very center. And now my brothers, if you were righteous and were willing to hearken to the truth and give heed unto it, that you might walk uprightly before Elohim, then you would not murmur because of the truth and say, You speak hard things against us. And it came to pass that I, Nefi, did exhort my brothers with all diligence to keep the mitzvot of YHWH. And it came to pass that they did humble themselves before YHWH, insomuch that I had joy and great hopes of them, that they would walk in the paths of righteousness. Now all these things were said and done as my father dwelt in a tent in the valley which he called L'mu'el.

2 And it came to pass that I, Nefi, took one of the daughters of Yishma'el to wife, and also my brothers took of the daughters of Yishma'el to wife, and also Tzuram took the eldest daughter of Yishma'el to wife. And thus my father had fulfilled all the mitzvot of YHWH which had been given unto him. And also I, Nefi, had been blessed of YHWH exceedingly.

3 And it came to pass that the voice of YHWH spoke unto my father by night and commanded him that the next day he should take his journey into the wilderness. And it came to pass that as my father arose in the morning and went forth to the tent door, and to his great astonishment, he beheld upon the ground a round ball[117] of elegant workmanship, and it was of fine brass. And within the ball were two spindles, and the one pointed the way where we should go into the wilderness.

4 And it came to pass that we did gather together whatsoever things we should carry into the wilderness, and all the remainder of our provisions which YHWH had given unto us. And we did take seed of every kind that we might carry into the wilderness.

5 And it came to pass that we did take our tents and departed into the wilderness across the river Laman. And it came to pass that we traveled for the space of four days, nearly a south-southeast direction,

---

117 Alma 17:15-17

and we did pitch our tents again; and we did call the name of the place Shazar.[118]

6 And it came to pass that we did take our bows and our arrows and go forth into the wilderness to slay food for our families; and after we had slain food for our families, we did return again to our families in the wilderness, to the place of Shazer. And we did go forth again in the wilderness, following the same direction, keeping in the most fertile parts of the wilderness which were in the borders near the Red Sea. And it came to pass that we did travel for the space of many days, slaying food by the way with our bows, and our arrows, and our stones, and our slings; and we did follow the directions of the ball, which led us in the more fertile parts of the wilderness. And after we had traveled for the space of many days, we did pitch our tents for the space of a time, that we might again rest ourselves and obtain food for our families.

7 And it came to pass that as I, Nefi, went forth to slay food, behold, I did break my bow which was made of fine steel; and after I did break my bow, behold, my brothers were angry with me because of the loss of my bow, for we did obtain no food. And it came to pass that we did return without food to our families. And being much fatigued because of their journeying, they did suffer much for the want of food. And it came to pass that Laman, and L'mu'el, and the sons of Yishma'el did begin to murmur exceedingly because of their sufferings and afflictions in the wilderness; and also my father began to murmur against YHWH his Elohim; yes, and they were all exceedingly sorrowful, even that they did murmur against YHWH. Now it came to pass that I, Nefi, having been afflicted with my brothers because of the loss of my bow, and their bows having lost their springs, it began to be exceedingly difficult, yes, insomuch that we could obtain no food. And it came to pass that I, Nefi, did speak much unto my brothers because they had hardened their hearts again, even unto complaining against YHWH their Elohim. And it came to pass that I, Nefi, did make out of wood a bow, and out of a straight stick an arrow; wherefore, I did arm myself with a bow and an arrow, with a sling and with stones. And I said unto my father, Where shall I go to obtain food? And it came to pass that he did inquire of YHWH,

---

118 *Shazar* שזר (Strong's 7806), to be twisted

for they had humbled themselves because of my words; for I did say many things unto them in the energy of my soul. And it came to pass that the voice of YHWH came unto my father, and he was truly chastened because of his murmurings against YHWH, insomuch that he was brought down into the depths of sorrow.

8 And it came to pass that the voice of YHWH said unto him, Look upon the ball and behold the things which are written. And it came to pass that when my father beheld the things which were written upon the ball, he did fear and tremble exceedingly, and also my brothers, and the sons of Yishma'el, and our wives. And it came to pass that I, Nefi, beheld the pointers which were in the ball, that they did work according to the faith, and diligence, and heed, which we did give unto them. And there was also written upon them a new writing which was plain to be read, which did give us understanding concerning the ways of YHWH; and it was written and changed from time to time according to the faith and diligence which we gave unto it. And thus we see that by small[119] means YHWH can bring about great things. And it came to pass that I, Nefi, did go forth up into the top of the mountain, according to the directions which were given upon the ball. And it came to pass that I did slay wild beasts, insomuch that I did obtain food for our families. And it came to pass that I did return to our tents bearing the beasts which I had slain; and now when they beheld that I had obtained food, how great was their joy! And it came to pass that they did humble themselves before YHWH and did give thanks unto him.

9 And it came to pass that we did again take our journey, traveling nearly the same course as in the beginning; and after we had traveled for the space of many days, we did pitch our tents again, that we might remain for the space of a time.

10 And it came to pass that Yishma'el died and was buried in the place which was called Nahom.[120] And it came to pass that the daughters of Yishma'el did mourn exceedingly because of the loss of their father and because of their afflictions in the wilderness. And they did murmur[121] against my father because he had brought them out of the land of Yerushalayim, saying, Our father is dead. Yes, and

---

119 Alma 17:8 120 *Nacham* נחם (Strong's 5162), to grieve 121 They were "sitting shiva," at which time such murmuring would have been excused.

we have wandered much in the wilderness, and we have suffered much afflictions, hunger, thirst, and fatigue; and after all these sufferings we must perish in the wilderness with hunger. And thus they did murmur against my father and also against me; and they were desirous to return again to Yerushalayim. And Laman said unto L'mu'el, and also unto the sons of Yishma'el, Behold, let us slay our father, and also our brother Nefi who has taken it upon him to be our ruler and our teacher, who are his elder brothers. Now he says that YHWH has talked with him, and also that angels have ministered unto him. But behold, we know that he lies unto us; and he tells us these things, and he works many things by his cunning arts, that he may deceive our eyes, thinking perhaps that he may lead us away into some strange wilderness. And after he has led us away, he has thought to make himself a king and a ruler over us, that he may do with us according to his will and pleasure. And after this manner did my brother Laman stir up their hearts to anger. And it came to pass that YHWH was with us, yes, even the voice of YHWH came and did speak many words unto them and did chasten them exceedingly. And after they were chastened by the voice of YHWH, they did turn away their anger and did repent of their sins, insomuch that YHWH did bless us again with food, that we did not perish.

11 And it came to pass that we did again take our journey in the wilderness; and we did travel nearly eastward from that time forth. And we did travel and wade through much affliction in the wilderness, and our women bore children in the wilderness. And so great were the blessings of YHWH upon us that while we did live upon raw meat in the wilderness, our women did give plenty of milk for their children and were strong, yes, even like unto the men; and they began to bear their journeyings without murmurings.

12 And thus we see that the mitzvot of Elohim must be fulfilled. And if it so be that the children of men keep the mitzvot of Elohim, he does nourish them, and strengthen them, and provide[122] ways and means by which they can accomplish the thing which he has commanded them. Wherefore, he did provide ways and means for us while we did sojourn in the wilderness.

---

[122] 1 Nefi 1:10

13 And we did sojourn for the space of many years, yes, even eight years[123] in the wilderness. And we did come to the land which we called Bountiful, because of its much fruit[124] and also wild honey; and all these things were prepared of YHWH that we might not perish. And we beheld the sea, which we called Irreantum, which (being interpreted) is many waters.

14 And it came to pass that we did pitch our tents by the seashore. And even though we had suffered many afflictions and much difficulty, yes, even so much that we cannot write them all, we rejoiced exceedingly when we came to the seashore; and we called the place Bountiful because of its much fruit.

15 And it came to pass that after I, Nefi, had been in the land Bountiful for the space of many days, the voice of YHWH came unto me, saying, Arise and get you into the mountain. And it came to pass that I arose and went up into the mountain and cried unto YHWH. And it came to pass that YHWH spoke unto me, saying, You shall construct a ship after the manner which I shall show you, that I may carry your people across these waters. And I said, YHWH, where shall I go that I may find ore to molten that I may make tools to construct the ship after the manner which you have shown unto me? And it came to pass that YHWH told me where I should go to find ore, that I might make tools.

16 And it came to pass that I, Nefi, did make bellows, with which to blow the fire, of the skins of beasts. And after I had made bellows, that I might have the means to blow the fire, I did strike two stones together that I might make fire. For YHWH had not thus far allowed that we should make much fire as we journeyed in the wilderness, for he said, I will make your food become sweet, that you cook it not. And I will also be your light in the wilderness; and I will prepare the way before you, if it so be that you shall keep my mitzvot. Wherefore, inasmuch as you shall keep my mitzvot, you shall be led towards the promised land; and you shall know that it is by me that you are led. Yes, and YHWH said also that after you have arrived to the promised land, you shall know that I, YHWH, am Elohim, and that I, YHWH, did deliver you from destruction, yes, that I did bring you out of

---

123 ~593 BCE **124** The beauty of this phrase is clearer as we see it in the Hebrew: "And we did come to the land which we called Bountiful (רב), because of its much fruit (הרבים פרותיה)...." "Bountiful" (רב) is obviously derived from "much" (רבים).

the land of Yerushalayim. Wherefore, I, Nefi, did strive to keep the mitzvot of YHWH, and I did exhort my brothers to faithfulness and diligence. And it came to pass that I did make tools of the ore which I did molten out of the rock. And when my brothers saw that I was about to build a ship, they began to murmur against me, saying, Our brother is a fool, for he thinks that he can build a ship; yes, and he also thinks that he can cross these great waters. And thus my brothers did complain against me and were desirous that they might not labor, for they did not believe that I could build a ship, neither would they believe that I was instructed of YHWH.

17 And now it came to pass that I, Nefi, was exceedingly sorrowful because of the hardness of their hearts. And now when they saw that I began to be sorrowful, they were glad in their hearts, insomuch that they did rejoice over me, saying, We knew that you could not construct a ship, for we knew that you were lacking in judgment; wherefore, you cannot accomplish so great a work. And you are like unto our father, led away by the foolish imaginations of his heart. Yes, he has led us out of the land of Yerushalayim, and we have wandered in the wilderness for these many years.[125] And our women have labored, being big with child; and they have borne children in the wilderness and suffered all things except it were death. And it would have been better that they had died before they came out of Yerushalayim than to have suffered these afflictions. Behold, these many years we have suffered in the wilderness, which time we might have enjoyed our possessions and the land of our inheritance; yes, and we might have been happy. And we know that the people who were in the land of Yerushalayim were a righteous people, for they keep the statutes and the judgments of YHWH, and all his mitzvot according to the Torah of Moshe; wherefore, we know that they are a righteous people. And our father has judged them and has led us away because we would hearken unto his word; yes, and our brother is like unto him. And after this manner of language did my brothers murmur and complain against us.

18 And it came to pass that I, Nefi, spoke unto them, saying, Do you believe that our fathers, who were the children of Isra'el, would have been led away out of the hands of the Egyptians if they had not

---

[125] 1 Nefi 5:13

hearkened unto the words of YHWH? Yes, do you suppose that they would have been led out of bondage if YHWH had not commanded Moshe that he should lead them out of bondage? Now you know that the children of Isra'el were in bondage, and you know that they were laden with tasks which were grievous to be borne. Wherefore, you know that it must necessarily be a good thing for them that they should be brought out of bondage. Now you know that Moshe was commanded of YHWH to do that great work, and you know that by his word the waters of the Red Sea were **divided** hither and thither, and they passed through **on dry ground.**[126] But you know that the Egyptians were drowned in the Red Sea, who were the armies of Pharaoh.[127] And you also know that they were fed with **manna** in the wilderness.[128] Yes, and you also know that Moshe, by his word, according to the power of Elohim which was in him, **smote the rock and there came forth water,** that the children of Isra'el might quench their thirst.[129] And despite their being led — YHWH their Elohim, their Redeemer, **going before them,** leading them **by day, and giving light unto them by night,**[130] and doing all things for them which were expedient for man to receive — they hardened their hearts and blinded their minds, and reviled against Moshe and against the true and living Elohim. And it came to pass that according to his word he did destroy them, and according to his word he did lead them, and according to his word he did do all things for them; and there was not anything done except it were by his word. And after they had crossed the river Yarden, he did make them mighty unto the driving out the children of the land, yes, unto the scattering them to destruction.[131]

19 And now, do you suppose that the children of this land, who were in the land of promise, who were driven out by our fathers, do you suppose that they were righteous? Behold, I say unto you, no. Do you suppose that our fathers would have been more choice than they if they had been righteous? I say unto you, no. Behold, YHWH esteems[132] all flesh in one; he that is righteous is favored of Elohim. But behold, this people had rejected every word of Elohim, and they were ripe in iniquity, and the fulness of the wrath of Elohim was upon

---

126 Ex. 14:16   **127** Ex. 14:23-31   **128** Ex. 16:15   **129** Ex. 17:6   **130** Ex. 13:21   **131** Ex. 34:11   **132** 2 Nefi 11:16-17

them. And YHWH did curse the land against them and bless it unto our fathers; yes, he did curse it against them unto their destruction, and he did bless it unto our fathers, unto their obtaining power over it.

20 Behold, YHWH has **created the earth**[133] that it should be inhabited, and he has created his children that they should possess it. And he raises up a righteous nation and destroys the nations of the wicked. And he leads away the righteous into precious lands, and the wicked he destroys, and curses the land unto them for their sakes. He rules high in **the Heavens, for it is his throne, and this earth is his footstool.**[134] And he loves them who will have him to be their Elohim. Behold, he loved our fathers; and he covenanted with them, yes, even Avraham, and Yitz'chak, and Ya'akov, and he remembered the covenants which he had made; wherefore, he did bring them out of the land of Egypt. And he did distress them in the wilderness with his rod, for they hardened their hearts, even as you have; and YHWH distressed them because of their iniquity. **He sent flying fiery serpents**[135] **among them;**[136] and after they were bitten, he prepared a way that they might be healed; and the labor which they had to perform was to look. And because of the simpleness of the way, or the easiness of it, there were many who perished. And they did harden their hearts from time to time, and they did revile against Moshe and also against Elohim. Nevertheless, you know that they were led forth by his matchless power into the land of promise.

21 And now after all these things, the time has come that they have become wicked, yes, nearly unto ripeness. And I know not but they are at this day about to be destroyed, for I know that the day must surely come that they must be destroyed, except a few only, who shall be led away into captivity; wherefore, YHWH commanded[137] my father that he should depart into the wilderness. And the Judeans also sought to take away his life; yes, and you also have sought to take away his life. Wherefore, you are murderers in your hearts and you are like unto them. You are swift to do iniquity but slow to remember YHWH your Elohim. You have seen an angel and he spoke unto you. Yes, you have heard his voice from time to time, and he has spoken unto you in a still, small voice, but you were past feeling, that you could not feel his words. Wherefore, he has spoken unto you like unto the

---

133 Gen. 1:1 **134** Isa. 66:1 **135** Alma 16:32 **136** Num. 21:6 **137** 1 Nefi 1:6

voice of thunder, which did cause the earth to shake as if it were to divide asunder. And you also know that by the power of his almighty word he can cause the earth that it shall pass away; yes, and you know that by his word he can cause that rough places to be made smooth, and smooth places shall be broken up. Oh then, why is it that you can be so hard in your hearts? Behold, my soul is torn with anguish because of you, and my heart is pained. I fear that you shall be cast off for ever. Behold, I am full of the Ruach Elohim, insomuch that my frame has no strength.

22 And now it came to pass that when I had spoken these words, they were angry with me and were desirous to throw me into the depths of the sea. And as they came forth to lay their hands upon me, I spoke unto them, saying, In the name of El Shaddai I command you that you touch me not, for I am filled with the power of Elohim, even unto the consuming of my flesh. And whoever shall lay their hands upon me shall wither even as a dried weed, and he shall be as nothing before the power of Elohim, for Elohim shall smite him. And it came to pass that I, Nefi, said unto them that they should murmur no more against their father, neither should they withhold their labor from me, for Elohim had commanded me that I should build a ship. And I said unto them, If Elohim had commanded me to do all things, I could do them. If he should command me that I should say unto this water, Be you earth — and it shall be earth. And if I should say it, it would be done. And now, if YHWH has such great power and has worked so many miracles among the children of men, how is it that he cannot instruct me that I should build a ship?[138] And it came to pass that I, Nefi, said many things unto my brothers, insomuch that they were confounded and could not contend against me; neither dared they lay their hands upon me nor touch me with their fingers, even for the space of many days. Now they dared not do this for fear that they should wither before me, so powerful was the Ruach Elohim; and thus it had worked upon them.

23 And it came to pass that YHWH said unto me, Stretch forth your hand again unto your brothers and they shall not wither before you, but I will shake them, says YHWH, and this will I do that they may know that I am YHWH their Elohim. And it came to pass that I

---

138 Another example of the Kal va-homer thought form. See footnote 23.

stretched forth my hand unto my brothers, and they did not wither before me, but YHWH did shake them, even according to the word which he had spoken. And now they said, We know of a surety that YHWH is with you, for we know that it is the power of YHWH that has shaken us. And they fell down before me and were about to worship me, but I would not allow them, saying, I am your brother, yes, even your younger brother. Wherefore, worship YHWH your Elohim, and **honor your father and your mother, that your days may be long in the land which YHWH your Elohim shall give you.**[139]

24 And it came to pass that they did worship YHWH and did go forth with me, and we did work timbers of exact workmanship. And YHWH did show me from time to time after what manner I should work the timbers of the ship. Now I, Nefi, did not work the timbers after the manner which was learned by men, neither did I build the ship after the manner of man, but I did build it after the manner which YHWH had shown unto me; wherefore, it was not after the manner of men.

25 And I, Nefi, did go into the mount often, and I did pray often unto YHWH; wherefore, YHWH showed unto me great things.

26 And it came to pass that after I had finished the ship according to the word of YHWH, my brothers beheld that it was good and that the workmanship thereof was exceedingly fine; wherefore, they did humble themselves again before YHWH.

27 And it came to pass that the voice of YHWH came unto my father that we should arise and go down into the ship. And it came to pass that the next day, after we had prepared all things, much fruits and meat from the wilderness, and honey in abundance, and provisions, according to that which YHWH had commanded us, we did go down into the ship with all our loading, and our seeds, and whatsoever things we had brought with us, every one according to his age. Wherefore, we did all go down into the ship with our wives and our children. And now my father had fathered two sons in the wilderness; the elder was called Ya'akov, and the younger, Yosef.

28 And it came to pass, after we had all gone down into the ship, and had taken with us our provisions and things which had been commanded us, we did put forth into the sea and were driven forth before the wind towards the promised land.

---

139 Ex. 20:12; Deut. 5:16

29 And after we had been driven forth before the wind for the space of many days, behold, my brothers, and the sons of Yishma'el, and also their wives, began to make themselves merry, insomuch that they began to dance and to sing and to speak with much rudeness, yes, even that they did forget by what power they had been brought to that point; yes, they were lifted up unto exceeding rudeness. And I, Nefi, began to fear exceedingly that YHWH should be angry with us and smite us because of our iniquity, that we should be swallowed up in the depths of the sea. Wherefore, I, Nefi, began to speak to them with much soberness, but behold, they were angry with me, saying, We will not that our younger brother shall be a ruler over us.

30 And it came to pass that Laman and L'mu'el did take me and bind me with cords, and they did treat me with much harshness. Nevertheless, YHWH allowed[140] it, that he might show forth his power unto the fulfilling of his word which he had spoken concerning the wicked. And it came to pass that after they had bound me, insomuch that I could not move, the compass[141] which had been prepared of YHWH did cease to work. Wherefore, they knew not where they should steer the ship, insomuch that there arose a great storm — yes, a great and terrible tempest — and we were driven back upon the waters for the space of three days. And they began to be exceedingly frightened that they should be drowned in the sea; nevertheless, they did not loose me. And on the fourth day which we had been driven back, the tempest began to be exceedingly sore. And it came to pass that we were about to be swallowed up in the depths of the sea. And after we had been driven back upon the waters for the space of four days, my brothers began to see that the judgments of Elohim were upon them, and that they must perish except that they should repent of their iniquities. Wherefore, they came unto me and loosed the bands which were upon my wrists, and behold, they had swollen exceedingly; and also my ankles were much swollen, and great was the soreness thereof. Nevertheless, I did look unto my Elohim, and I did praise him all the day long, and I did not murmur against YHWH because of my afflictions.

31 Now my father Lechi had said many things unto them, and also unto the sons of Yishma'el, but behold, they did breathe out

---

140 Alma 10:7   141 1 Nefi 5:3

much threatenings against anyone that should speak for me. And my parents, being stricken in years and having suffered much grief because of their children, they were brought down, yes, even upon their sickbeds. Because of their grief, and much sorrow, and the iniquity of my brothers, they were brought near even to be carried out of this time to meet their Elohim. Yes, their gray hairs were about to be brought down to lie low in the dust, yes, even they were near to be cast with sorrow into a watery grave. And Ya'akov and Yosef also being young, having need of much nourishment, were grieved because of the afflictions of their mother. And also my wife with her tears and prayers, and also my children, did not soften the hearts of my brothers that they would loose me. And there was nothing, except it were the power of Elohim which threatened them with destruction, could soften their hearts. Wherefore, when they saw that they were about to be swallowed up in the depths of the sea, they repented of the thing which they had done, insomuch that they loosed me.

32 And it came to pass after they had loosed me, behold, I took the compass, and it did work[142] where I desired it. And it came to pass that I prayed unto YHWH; and after I had prayed, the winds did cease, and the storm did cease, and there was a great calm. And it came to pass that I, Nefi, did guide the ship that we sailed again towards the promised land. And it came to pass that after we had sailed for the space of many days, we did arrive to the promised land. And we went forth upon the land and did pitch our tents, and we did call it the promised land.

33 And it came to pass that we did begin to till the earth, and we began to plant seeds; yes, we did put all our seeds into the earth which we had brought from the land of Yerushalayim. And it came to pass that they did grow exceedingly; wherefore, we were blessed in abundance. And it came to pass that we did find upon the land of promise, as we journeyed in the wilderness, that there were beasts in the forests of every kind, both the cow, and the ox, and the ass, and the horse, and the goat, and the wild goat, and all manner of wild animals, which were for the use of man. And we did find all manner of ore, both of gold, and of silver, and of copper.

---

142 Alma 17:15-17

34 And it came to pass that YHWH commanded me; wherefore, I did make plates of ore, that I might engrave upon them the record of my people. And upon the plates which I made, I did engrave the record of my father, and also our journeyings in the wilderness, and the prophecies of my father; and also many of my own prophecies have I engraved upon them. And I knew not at the time when I made them that I should be commanded of YHWH to make these plates. Wherefore, the record of my father, and the genealogy of his forefathers, and the more part of all our proceedings in the wilderness, are engraved upon those first plates of which I have spoken; wherefore, the things which transpired before I made these plates are of a truth more particularly made mention upon the first plates.

35 And after I made these plates by way of mitzvah, I, Nefi, received a mitzvah that the ministry and the prophecies — the more plain and precious parts of them — should be written upon these plates, and that the things which were written should be kept for the instruction of my people, who should possess the land, and also for other wise purposes, which purposes are known unto YHWH. Wherefore, I, Nefi, did make a record upon the other plates, which gives an account — or which gives a greater account — of the wars, and contentions, and destructions of my people. And now this have I done, and commanded my people that they should do after I was gone, and that these plates should be handed down from one generation to another, or from one prophet to another, until further mitzvot of YHWH. And an account of my making these plates shall be given hereafter; and then behold, I proceed according to that which I have spoken. And this I do that the more sacred things may be kept for the knowledge of my people. Nevertheless, I do not write anything upon plates except it be that I think it be sacred. And now if I do err, even did they err of old; not that I would excuse myself because of other men, but because of the weakness which is in me according to the flesh, I would excuse myself.

36 For the things which some men esteem to be of great worth, both to the body and soul, others set at no value[143] and trample under their feet, yes, even the very Elohim of Isra'el do men trample under their feet. I say trample under their feet, but I would speak in other words: They set him at no value and hearken not to the voice of his

---

143 2 Nefi 15:1

counsels. And behold, he comes, according to the words of the angel, in six hundred[144] years from the time my father left Yerushalayim. And the world, because of their iniquity, shall judge him to be a thing of no value. Wherefore, they scourge him and he allows it; and they smite him and he allows it; yes, they spit upon him and he allows it, because of his lovingkindness and his long-suffering towards the children of men. And the Elohim of our fathers who were led out of Egypt, out of bondage, and also were preserved in the wilderness by him — yes, the Elohim of Avraham, and of Yitz'chak, and the Elohim of Ya'akov — yields himself, according to the words of the angel, as a man into the hands of wicked men, to be lifted up according to the words of Zenoch, and to be crucified according to the words of Ne'um, and to be buried in a sepulcher according to the words of Zenos, which he spoke concerning the three days[145] of darkness which should be a sign given of his death unto those who should inhabit the isles of the sea — more especially given unto those who are of the house of Isra'el.

37 For thus spoke the prophet: The Adonai YHWH surely shall visit all the house of Isra'el at that day, some with his voice because of their righteousness, unto their great joy and salvation, and others with the thunderings and the lightnings of his power — by tempest, by fire, and by smoke and vapor of darkness, and by the opening of the earth, and by mountains which shall be carried up. And all these things must surely come, says the prophet Zenos. And the rocks of the earth must split. And because of the groanings of the earth, many of the kings of the isles of the sea shall be worked upon by the Ruach Elohim to exclaim, The Elohim of nature suffers![146] And as for they who are at Yerushalayim, says the prophet, they shall be afflicted by all people because they crucified the Elohim of Isra'el and turn their hearts aside, rejecting signs, and wonders, and power, and glory of the Elohim of Isra'el. And because they turn their hearts aside, says the prophet, and have despised HaKodesh of Isra'el,[147] they shall wander in the flesh, and perish, and become a hiss and a byword, and be hated among all nations. Nevertheless, when that day comes, says the prophet, that they no more turn aside their hearts against HaKodesh of Isra'el, then will he remember the covenants which

---

144 Mic. 5:2-3; 1 Nefi 3:2-4   145 Cheleman 5:13; 3 Nefi 4:4-5. See also Ex. 10:21-23
146 3 Nefi 4:3-5   147 Moshiyah 8:2-3

he made to their fathers.¹⁴⁸ Yes, then will he remember the isles of the sea, yes, and all the people who are of the house of Isra'el will I **gather** in, says YHWH, according to the words of the prophet Zenos, **from the four quarters of the earth.**¹⁴⁹ Yes, and all the earth shall see the salvation of YHWH, says the prophet: every nation, kindred, tongue, and people shall be blessed.

38 And I, Nefi, have written these things unto my people, that perhaps I might persuade them that they would remember YHWH their Redeemer. Wherefore, I speak unto all the house of Isra'el, if it so be that they should obtain these things. For behold, I have workings in the spirit which do weary me, even that all my joints are weak, for those who are at Yerushalayim. For had not YHWH been merciful to show unto me concerning them, even as he had prophets of old, I should have perished also. He surely did show unto prophets of old all things concerning them, and also he did show unto many concerning us. Wherefore, it must necessarily be that we know concerning them, for they are written upon the plates of brass.

6 Now it came to pass that I, Nefi, did teach my brothers these things. And it came to pass that I did read many things to them which were engraved upon the plates of brass, that they might know concerning the doings of YHWH in other lands among people of old. And I did read many things unto them which were written in the books of Moshe. But that I might more fully persuade them to believe in YHWH their Redeemer, I did read unto them that which was written by the prophet Yesha'yahu; for I did apply all scriptures unto us, that it might be for our profit and learning. Wherefore, I spoke unto them, saying, Hear you the words of the prophet, you who are a remnant of the house of Isra'el, a branch who have been broken off. Hear you the words of the prophet which were written unto all the house of Isra'el and apply them unto yourselves, that you may have hope as well as your brothers from whom you have been broken off.

Yesha'yahu 48 from the Plates of Brass

2 For after this manner has the prophet written: **Hearken and hear this, O house of Ya'akov, who are called by the name of Isra'el**

---
148 Compare Deut. 30:1-5   149 Isa. 11:12

and are come forth out of the waters of Y'hudah (or out of the waters of immersion), who swear by the name of YHWH and make mention of the Elohim of Isra'el; yet they swear not in truth nor in righteousness. Nevertheless, they call themselves of the holy city, but they do not stay themselves upon the Elohim of Isra'el, who is YHWH Tzva'ot; yes, YHWH Tzva'ot is his name. Behold, I have declared the former things from the beginning; and they went forth out of my mouth, and I showed them. I did show them suddenly. And I did it because I knew that you are obstinate, and your neck was an iron sinew, and your brow brass. And I have, even from the beginning, declared to you; before it came to pass, I showed them you. And I showed them for fear that you should say, My idol has done them, and my graven image and my molten image have commanded them. You have heard and seen all this,[150] and will you not declare them? And that I have showed you new things from this time, even hidden things, and you did not know them? They are created now, and not from the beginning; even before the day when you heard them not, they were declared unto you, for fear that you should say, Behold, I knew them. Yes, and you heard not, yes, you knew not; yes, from that time your ear was not opened. For I knew that you would deal very treacherously and were called a transgressor from the womb. Nevertheless, for my name's sake will I defer my anger, and for my praise will I refrain from you, that I cut you not off. For behold, I have refined you; I have chosen you in the furnace of affliction. For my own sake — yes, for my own sake — will I do this; for I will not allow my name to be polluted.[151] And I will not give my glory unto another.

3 Hearken unto me, O Ya'akov, and Isra'el my called, for I am he: I am the First, and I am also the Last. My hand has also laid the foundation of the earth, and my right hand has spanned

---

150 In this verse of Isaiah (Isa. 48:6), the *Plates of Brass* reading "You have heard and seen" agrees with both the Septuagint and the Aramaic Peshitta text against the Masoretic text, which has "You have heard, see...." This agreement demonstrates that the *Plates of Brass* are an authentic source for the ancient textual tradition of Isaiah.   151 In this verse of Isaiah (Isa. 48:11) the *Plates of Brass* agree with the reading of the Peshitta Aramaic text of Isaiah "that [my name] be not polluted" (דלא אתטושי) against the Hebrew Masoretic Text, which has "for how should [my name] be polluted" (כי איך יחל). This agreement demonstrates that the *Plates of Brass* are an authentic source for the ancient textual tradition of Isaiah.

the heavens; and I call unto them and they stand up together. All of you, assemble yourselves and hear: Who among them has declared these things unto them? YHWH has loved him; yes, and he will fulfill his word which he has declared by them.[152] And he will do his pleasure on Babylon, and his arm shall come upon the Chaldeans also, says YHWH. I, YHWH, yes, I have spoken; yes, I have called him to declare; I have brought him, and he shall make his way prosperous.

4 Come you near unto me. I have not spoken in secret from the beginning; from the time that it was declared have I spoken; and Adonai YHWH and his spirit have sent me. And thus says YHWH your Redeemer, HaKodesh of Isra'el: I have sent him. YHWH your Elohim who teaches you to profit, who leads you by the way you should go, has done it. Oh that you had hearkened to my mitzvot; then had your shalom been as a river[153] and your righteousness as the waves of the sea. Your seed also had been as the sand, the offspring of your bowels like the gravel thereof. His name should not have been cut off nor destroyed from before me.

5 Go forth out of Babylon, flee you from the Chaldeans; with a voice of singing declare you, tell this, utter to the end of the earth, say you, YHWH has redeemed his servant Ya'akov and they thirsted not; he led them through the deserts, he caused the waters to flow out of the rock for them; he split the rock also and the waters gushed out. And though he has done all this, and greater also, there is no shalom, says YHWH, unto the wicked.

Yesha'yahu 49 from the Plates of Brass

6 And again, Hearken, O you house of Isra'el, all you that are broken[154] off and are driven out because of the wickedness of the shepherds of my people, yes, all you that are broken off, that are scattered abroad, who are of my people, O house of Isra'el. Listen, O isles, unto me, and hearken you people from

---

152 In this verse of Isaiah (Isa. 48:14), the *Plates of Brass* reading "has declared these things unto them" agrees with the Septuagint reading of "has told them these things." The Masoretic Text omits the word "them." The word "fulfill" agrees with the reading of the Septuagint but is also omitted from the Masoretic Text. These readings help demonstrate that the *Plates of Brass* are an authentic source for the ancient textual tradition of Isaiah.   153 1 Nefi 1:8   154 1 Nefi 7:2; 2 Nefi 7:5

far. YHWH has called me from the womb; from the bowels of my mother has he made mention of my name. And he has made my mouth like a sharp sword; in the shadow of his hand has he hid me and made me a polished shaft; in his quiver has he hid me and said unto me, You are my servant, O Isra'el, in whom I will be glorified. Then I said, I have labored in vain, I have spent my strength for nothing and in vain; surely my judgment is with YHWH, and my work with my Elohim.

⁷ And now says YHWH, that formed me from the womb, that I should be his servant to bring Ya'akov again to him. Though Isra'el be not gathered, yet shall I be glorious in the eyes of YHWH, and my Elohim shall be my strength. And he said, It is a light thing that you should be my servant to raise up the tribes of Ya'akov and to restore the preserved of Isra'el. I will also give you for a light to the Goyim, that you may be my salvation unto the end of the earth. Thus says YHWH, the Redeemer of Isra'el, his Kadosh, to him whom man despises, to him whom the nation abhors, to a servant of rulers: Kings shall see and arise, princes also shall worship, because of YHWH that is faithful. Thus says YHWH: In an acceptable time have I heard you, O isles of the sea, and in a day of salvation have I helped you. And I will preserve you and give you my servant for a covenant of the people, to strengthen the earth, to cause to inherit the desolate heritages, that you may say to the prisoners, Go forth — to them that sit in darkness, Show yourselves. They shall feed in the ways, and their pastures shall be in all high places. They shall not hunger nor thirst, neither shall the heat nor the sun afflict them; for he that has mercy on them shall lead them, even by the springs of water shall he guide them. And I will make all my mountains a way, and my highways shall be exalted. And then, O house of Isra'el, behold, these shall come from far, and lo, these from the north, and from the west, and these from the land of Sinim.

⁸ Sing, O heavens, and be joyful, O earth, for the feet of those who are in the east shall be established; and break forth into singing, O mountains, for they shall be smitten no more. For YHWH has comforted his people and will have mercy upon his afflicted. But behold, Tziyon has said, YHWH has abandoned

me, and my YHWH[155] has forgotten me — but he will show that he has not. For can a woman forget her sucking child, that she should not have compassion on the son of her womb? Yes, they may forget, yet will I not forget you, O house of Isra'el. Behold, I have graven you upon the palms[156] of my hands; your walls are continually before me. Your children shall make haste against your destroyers, and they that made you waste shall go forth of you.

9 Lift up your eyes round about and behold, all these gather themselves together, and they shall come to you. And as I live, says YHWH, you shall surely clothe you with them all, as with an ornament, and bind them on, even as a bride. For your waste and your desolate places, and the land of your destruction shall even now be too narrow by reason of the inhabitants. And they that swallowed you up shall be far away. The children whom you shall have, after you have lost the first, shall again in your ears say, The place is too narrow for me, give place to me that I may dwell. Then shall you say in your heart, Who has begotten me these, seeing I have lost my children and am desolate, a captive, and removing to and fro? And who has brought up these? Behold, I was left alone; these, where have they been?

10 Thus says Adonai YHWH: Behold, I will lift up my hand to the Goyim and set up my standard to the people. And they shall bring your sons in their arms,[157] and your daughters shall be carried upon their shoulders. And kings shall be your nursing fathers, and their queens your nursing mothers. They shall bow down to you with their face towards the earth and lick up the dust of your feet; and you shall know that I am YHWH, for they shall not be ashamed that wait for me. For shall the prey be taken from the mighty, or the lawful captive delivered? But thus says YHWH: Even the captive of the mighty shall be taken away and the prey of the terrible shall be delivered, for I will contend with him that contends with you and I will save your children. And I will feed them that oppress you with their own flesh; they shall be drunken with their own blood as with sweet

---

155 Original reading was "YHWH", but was altered by scribes to read "Adonai" in the Masoretic Text. See footnote to 2 Nefi 8:8.   156 3 Nefi 5:5-6   157 1 Nefi 7:3; 2 Nefi 7:2

wine. And all flesh shall know that I YHWH am your Savior and your Redeemer, the Mighty One of Ya'akov.

7 And now it came to pass that after I, Nefi, had read these things which were engraved upon the plates of brass, my brothers came unto me and said unto me, What is the meaning of these things which you have read? Behold, are they to be understood according to things which are spiritual, which shall come to pass according to the spirit and not the flesh? And I, Nefi, said unto them, Behold, they were made manifest unto the prophets by the voice of the spirit, for by the spirit are all things made known unto the prophets which shall come upon the children of men according to the flesh. Wherefore, the things of which I have read are things pertaining to things both temporal and spiritual.

2 For it appears that the house of Isra'el, sooner or later, will be **scattered** upon all the face of the earth, and also among all nations; and behold, there are many who are already lost from the knowledge of those who are at Yerushalayim. Yes, the more part of all the tribes have been led away, and they are **scattered** to and fro upon the isles of the sea; and where they are, none of us knows, except that we know that they have been led away. And since they have been led away, these things have been prophesied concerning them, and also concerning all those who shall hereafter be **scattered** and be confounded because of HaKodesh of Isra'el, for against him will they harden their hearts. Wherefore, they shall be **scattered**[158] among all nations and shall be hated by all men.

3 Nevertheless, after they have been **nursed** by the Goyim, and YHWH has lifted up his hand upon the Goyim, and set them up for a standard, **and their children have been carried in their arms, and their daughters have been carried upon their shoulders**[159] — behold, these things of which are spoken are temporal, for thus are the covenants of YHWH with our fathers. And it means us in the days to come, and also all our brothers who are of the house of Isra'el. And it means that the time comes that after all the house of Isra'el have been scattered and confounded, that Adonai YHWH will

---

158 Isa. 49:1 (*Plates of Brass* version); see 1 Nefi 6:6; "Plates of Brass" in *Appendix B: Source Documents* and *Groups*. **159** Isa. 49:23

raise up a mighty nation among the Goyim, yes, even upon the face of this land, and by them shall our seed be **scattered**. And after our seed is **scattered**, Adonai YHWH **will proceed to do a marvelous work**[160] among the Goyim which shall be of great worth unto our seed. Wherefore, it is compared unto them being nursed by the Goyim **and being carried in their arms and upon their shoulders.**[161] And it shall also be of worth unto the Goyim, and not only unto the Goyim but unto all the house of Isra'el, unto the making known of the covenants of the Father of Heaven unto Avraham, saying, **In your seed shall all the kindreds of the earth be blessed.**[162] And I would, my brothers, that you should know that **all the kindreds of the earth cannot be blessed** unless he shall **make bare his arm in the eyes of the nations.**[163] Wherefore, Adonai YHWH will proceed to **make bare his arm in the eyes of all the nations,** in bringing about his covenants and his besorah unto those who are of the house of Isra'el. Wherefore, he will bring them again out of captivity, and they shall be **gathered together**[164] to the lands of their first inheritance, and they shall be brought out of obscurity and out of darkness, and they shall know that YHWH is their Savior and their Redeemer, the Mighty One of Isra'el.

4 And the blood of that great and abominable church, which is the whore of all the earth, shall turn upon their own heads, for they shall war among themselves, and the sword of their own hands shall fall upon their own heads, **and they shall be drunken with their own blood.**[165] And every nation which shall war against you, O house of Isra'el, shall be turned one against another, and they shall fall into the pit which they dug to ensnare the people of YHWH. And all they that fight against Tziyon shall be destroyed. And that great whore who has perverted the right ways of YHWH — yes, that great and abominable church — shall tumble to the dust, and great shall be the fall of it. For behold, says the prophet, the time comes speedily that HaSatan shall have no more power over the hearts of the children of men. **For the day soon comes that all the proud and they who do wickedly shall be as stubble; and the day comes that they must be burned.**[166] For the time soon comes that the fulness of the wrath

---

160 Isa. 29:14 161 Isa. 49:23 162 Gen. 12:2 163 Isa. 52:10 164 Isa. 11:12 165 Isa. 49:26 166 Mal. 3:19 (4:1)

of Elohim shall be poured out upon all the children of men, for he will not allow that the wicked shall destroy the righteous. Wherefore, he will preserve the righteous by his power, even if it so be that the fulness of his wrath must come and the righteous be preserved, even unto the destruction of their enemies by fire. Wherefore, the righteous need not fear, for thus says the prophet: They shall be saved, even if it so be as by fire. Behold, my brothers, I say unto you that these things must shortly come; yes, even blood, and fire, and vapor of smoke must come. And it must necessarily be upon the face of this earth; and it comes unto men according to the flesh, if it so be that they will harden their hearts against HaKodesh of Isra'el. For behold, the righteous shall not perish, for the time surely must come that all they who fight against Tziyon shall be cut off.

5 And YHWH will surely prepare a way for his people, unto the fulfilling of the words of Moshe, which he spoke, saying, **A prophet shall YHWH your Elohim raise up unto you, like unto me. Him shall you hear in all things whatsoever he shall say unto you. And it shall come to pass that all those who will not hear that prophet shall be cut off from among the people.**[167] And now I, Nefi, declare unto you that this prophet of whom Moshe spoke was HaKodesh of Isra'el; wherefore, he shall execute judgment in righteousness. And the righteous need not fear, for they are those who shall not be confounded, but it is the kingdom of HaSatan, which shall be built up among the children of men, which kingdom is established among them which are in the flesh. For the time speedily shall come that all churches which are built up to get gain, and all those who are built up to get power over the flesh, and those who are built up to become popular in the eyes of the world, and those who seek the lusts of the flesh and the things of the world and to do all manner of iniquity — yes, in short, all those who belong to the kingdom of HaSatan — are they who need fear, and tremble, and quake. They are those who must be brought low in the dust, they are those who must be consumed as **stubble;**[168] and this is according

---

[167] Deut. 18:15, 18-19. Nefi says he "shall be cut off from among the people" while Deut. 18:19 says, "I will require it of him." The Targum Onkelos states, "My Word shall take vengeance upon him"; and similarly, the Greek Septuagint translation renders the phrase, "I shall take vengeance upon him." The Mishnah explains the phrase "I will require it of him" to mean "death at the hands of heaven" (m.Sanhedrin 11:5; b.Sanhedrin 89a).
[168] Mal. 3:19 (4:1)

to the words of the prophet. And the time comes speedily that the righteous must be led up as calves of the stall, and HaKodesh of Isra'el must reign in dominion, and might, and power, and great glory. And he **gathers** his children **from the four quarters of the earth**,[169] and he numbers his sheep, and they know him. And there shall be one fold and one shepherd, and he shall feed his sheep, and in him they shall find pasture. And because of the righteousness of his people, HaSatan has no power. Wherefore, he cannot be loosed for the space of many years, for he has no power over the hearts of the people, for they dwell in righteousness, and HaKodesh of Isra'el reigns. And now behold, I, Nefi, say unto you that all these things must come according to the flesh. But behold, all nations, kindreds, tongues, and people shall dwell safely in HaKodesh of Isra'el if it so be that they will repent.

6 And now I, Nefi, make an end, for I dare not speak further as yet concerning these things. Wherefore, my brothers, I would that you should consider that the things which have been written upon the plates of brass are true, and they testify that a man must be obedient to the mitzvot of Elohim. Wherefore, you need not suppose that I and my father are the only ones that have testified and also taught them. Wherefore, if you shall be obedient to the mitzvot and endure to the end, you shall be saved at the last day. And thus it is. Amen.

ספר נפי השני
2 NEFI
THE SECOND BOOK OF NEFI

An account of the death of Lechi. Nefi's brothers rebel against him. YHWH *warns Nefi to depart into the wilderness. His journeyings in the wilderness, and so forth.*

AND now it came to pass after I, Nefi, had made an end of teaching my brothers, our father Lechi also spoke many things unto them and rehearsed unto them how great things YHWH had done for them

---

169 Isa. 11:12

2 NEFI 1:2

in bringing them out of the land of Yerushalayim.¹ And he spoke unto them concerning their rebellions² upon the waters, and the mercies of Elohim in sparing their lives, that they were not swallowed up in the sea. And he also spoke unto them concerning the land of promise which they had obtained, how merciful YHWH had been in warning us that we should flee out of the land of Yerushalayim. For behold, said he, I have seen a vision in the which I know that Yerushalayim is destroyed; and had we remained in Yerushalayim, we should also have perished. But, said he, despite our afflictions, we have obtained a land of promise, a land which is choice above all other lands, a land which Adonai YHWH has covenanted with me should be a land for the inheritance of my seed. Yes, YHWH has consecrated this land unto me and to my children for ever, and also all they who should be led out of other countries by the hand of YHWH. Wherefore, I, Lechi, prophesy according to the workings of the spirit which is in me, that there shall none come into this land except they shall be brought by the hand of YHWH. Wherefore, this land is consecrated³ unto him whom he shall bring. And if it so be that they shall serve him according to the mitzvot which he has given, it shall be a land of liberty unto them. Wherefore, they shall never be brought down into captivity; if so, it shall be because of iniquity. For if iniquity shall abound, cursed shall be the land for their sakes, but unto the righteous it shall be blessed for ever. And behold, it is wisdom that this land should be kept as yet from the knowledge of other nations; for behold, many nations would overrun this land, that there would be no place for an inheritance.

²Wherefore, I, Lechi, have obtained a promise that inasmuch as those whom Adonai YHWH shall bring out of the land of Yerushalayim shall keep his mitzvot, they shall prosper upon the face of this land; and they shall be kept from all other nations,⁴ that they may possess this land unto themselves. And if it so be that they shall keep his mitzvot, they shall be blessed upon the face of this land, and there shall be none to molest them nor to take away the land

---

1 This phrase "land of Yerushalayim" (land of Jerusalem) does not appear in the Tanakh. However, it has turned up in the Amarna Letters, dated to the early 14th Century BCE. These letters were written in Akkadian on 350 clay tablets discovered in 1887 and in the Dead Sea Scrolls (4Q385b), which mentions "Jeremiah the Prophet" as one of those who "were taken captive from the land of Jerusalem." 2 1 Nefi 5:29-31 3 'Eter 1:7 4 1 Nefi 3:20; M'raman 2:6

of their inheritance, and they shall dwell safely for ever. But behold, when the time comes that they shall dwindle in unbelief, after they have received so great blessings from the hand of YHWH, having a knowledge of the creation of the earth and all men, knowing the great and marvelous works of YHWH from the creation of the world, having power given them to do all things by faith, having all the mitzvot from the beginning, and having been brought by his infinite goodness into this precious land of promise, behold, I say, if the day shall come that they will reject HaKodesh of Isra'el, the true Mashiach, their Redeemer and their Elohim, behold, the judgments of him that is just shall rest upon them. Yes, he will bring other nations unto them, and he will give unto them power, and he will take away from them the lands of their possessions, and he will cause them to be scattered and slain. Yes, as one generation passes to another, there shall be bloodsheds and great visitations among them.

3 Wherefore, my sons, I would that you would remember; yes, I would that you would hearken unto my words. Oh that you would awake, awake from a deep sleep, yes, even from the sleep of She'ol, and shake off the awful chains[5] by which you are bound, which are the chains which bind the children of men, that they are carried away captive down to the eternal gulf of misery and woe. Awake and arise from the dust, and hear the words of a trembling parent, whose limbs you must soon lay down in the cold and silent grave, from which no traveler can return; a few more days and I go the way of all the earth. But behold, YHWH has redeemed[6] my soul from She'ol — I have beheld his glory,[7] and I am encircled about eternally in the arms of his love. And I desire that you should remember to observe the statutes and the judgments of YHWH; behold, this has been the anxiety of my soul from the beginning. My heart has been weighed down with sorrow from time to time, for I have feared, that because of the hardness of your hearts, YHWH your Elohim should come out in the fulness of his wrath upon you, that you be cut off and destroyed for ever, or that a cursing should come upon you[8] for the space of many generations, and you are visited by **sword**[9] and by famine,[10] and are hated, and are led according to the will and captivity of HaSatan. O my sons,

---

5 Alma 9:3   6 Moshiyah 11:28; 'Eter 1:13   7 1 Nefi 1:3, 8-9   8 Lev. 26:14-39; Deut. 28:15-68   9 Lev. 26:25, 33; Deut. 28:22   10 Lev. 26:16, 20, 26; Deut. 28:18, 38, 51

that these things might not come upon you, but that you might be a choice and a favored people of YHWH.

4 But behold, his will be done, for his ways are righteousness for ever. And he has said that inasmuch as you shall keep my mitzvot, you shall prosper in the land;[11] but inasmuch as you will not keep my mitzvot, you shall be cut off from my presence.[12] And now, that my soul might have joy in you, and that my heart might leave this world with gladness because of you, that I might not be brought down with grief and sorrow to the grave — arise from the dust my sons, and be men. And be determined in one mind and in one heart, united in all things, that you may not come down into captivity, that you may not be cursed with a sore cursing,[13] and also that you may not incur the displeasure of a just Elohim upon you unto the destruction — yes, the Eternal destruction — of both soul and body. Awake my sons, **put on the armor of righteousness,**[14] shake off the chains with which you are bound, and come forth out of obscurity, and arise from the dust. Rebel no more against your brother, whose views have been glorious, and who has kept the mitzvot from the time we left Yerushalayim, and who has been an instrument in the hands of Elohim in bringing us forth into the land of promise; for were it not for him, we must have perished with hunger[15] in the wilderness. Nevertheless, you sought to take away his life; yes, and he has suffered much sorrow because of you. And I exceedingly fear and tremble because of you, for fear that he shall suffer again. For behold, you have accused him that he sought power and authority over you, but I know that he has not sought for power nor authority over you, but he has sought the glory of Elohim and your own eternal welfare. And you have murmured because he has been plain unto you. You say that he has used sharpness, you say that he has been angry with you. But behold, his sharpness was the sharpness of the power of the word of Elohim which was in him, and that which you call anger was the truth according to that which is in Elohim, which he could not restrain, manifesting boldly concerning your iniquities. And it must necessarily be that the power of Elohim must be with him, even unto his commanding you that you must obey. But behold, it was not him,

---

11 Lev. 26:1-13; Deut. 28:1-14   12 Lev. 26:14-39; Deut. 28:15-68   13 This is an example of the Hebraism known as the Cognate Accusative, where a noun pairs with the verb which is the noun's root.   14 Isa. 59:17; Ps. 91:4   15 1 Nefi 5:7-8

but it was the spirit of YHWH which was in him which opened his mouth to utterance, that he could not shut it.

5 And now my son Laman, and also L'mu'el, and Sam, and also my sons who are the sons of Yishma'el, behold, if you will hearken unto the voice of Nefi, you shall not perish. And if you will hearken unto him, I leave unto you a blessing, yes, even my first blessing. But if you will not hearken unto him, I take away my first blessing — yes, even my blessing — and it shall rest upon him. And now Tzuram,[16] I speak unto you: Behold, you are the servant of Lavan; nevertheless, you have been brought out of the land of Yerushalayim, and I know that you are a true friend unto my son Nefi for ever. Wherefore, because you have been faithful, your seed shall be blessed with his seed, that they dwell in prosperity long upon the face of this land. And nothing, except it shall be iniquity among them, shall harm or disturb their prosperity upon the face of this land for ever. Wherefore, if you shall keep the mitzvot of YHWH, YHWH has consecrated this land for the security of your seed with the seed of my son.

6 And now Ya'akov, I speak unto you: You are my first born in the days of my tribulation in the wilderness. And behold, in your childhood you have suffered afflictions and much sorrow because of the rudeness of your brothers. Nevertheless, Ya'akov, my first born in the wilderness, you know the greatness of Elohim; and he shall consecrate your afflictions for your gain. Wherefore, your soul shall be blessed, and you shall dwell safely with your brother Nefi, and your days shall be spent in the service of your Elohim. Wherefore, I know that you are redeemed because of the righteousness of your Redeemer, for you have beheld that in the fulness of time he comes to bring salvation unto men. And you have beheld[17] in your youth his glory; wherefore, you are blessed, even as they unto whom he shall minister in the flesh; for the spirit is the same yesterday, today, and for ever, and the way is prepared from the Fall of man, and salvation is free. And men are instructed sufficiently that they know good from evil. And the Torah is given unto men; and by the Torah no flesh is justified, or by the Torah men are cut off. Yes, by the temporal Torah[18]

---

16 1 Nefi 1:18, 20   17 2 Nefi 8:2   18 The temporal Torah is the Torah as it exists in this temporal world. The spiritual Torah is the Torah as it exists in the upper worlds. According to the Midrash Rabbah, the Torah was one of six things that pre-existed the creation of this world (Midrash Genesis Rabbah 1:4) where the Zohar says it was written with black

they were cut off, and also by the spiritual Torah they perish from that which is good and become miserable for ever. Wherefore, redemption comes in and through the Holy Mashiach, for he is full of grace and truth. Behold, he offers himself a sacrifice for sin,[19] to answer the ends of the Torah unto all those who have a broken heart and **a contrite spirit**,[20] and unto none else can the ends[21] of the Torah be answered. Wherefore, how great the importance to make these things known unto the inhabitants of the earth that they may know that there is no flesh that can dwell in the presence of Elohim, except it be through the merits, and mercy, and grace of the Holy Mashiach, who lays down his life according to the flesh and takes it again by the power of the spirit, that he may bring to pass the resurrection of the dead, being the first that should rise. Wherefore, he is the firstfruits[22] unto Elohim, inasmuch as he shall make intercession[23] for all the children of men, and they that believe in him shall be saved. And because of the intercession for all, all men come unto Elohim. Wherefore, they stand in the presence of him, to be judged of him according to the truth and holiness which is in him.

7 Wherefore, the ends of the Torah which HaKodesh has given, unto the inflicting[24] of the punishment which is affixed, which punishment that is affixed is in opposition to that of the happiness which is affixed, to answer the ends of the atonement—for it must necessarily be that there is an opposition in all things. If not so, my first born in the wilderness, righteousness could not be brought

---

fire written on white fire (Zohar 2:84a). And we read in the Midrash Rabbah: "R. Hezekiah said in the name of R. Simon b. Zabdi: 'All the Torah which you learn in this world is "vanity" in comparison with Torah in the World to Come; because in this world a man learns Torah and forgets it, but with reference to the World to Come what is written there? I will put My Torah in their inward parts (Jer. 31:32 (33))'" (Midrash Rabbah Eccl. II:1). **19** In the Hebrew reading, Mashiach offers "his soul" (*nefesh*) for sin. See Isa. 53:7, 10. **20** Isa. 57:15; 66:22; Ps. 34:19 (18); 51:3-19 (1-17); 'Eter 1:19; M'roni 6:1   **21** The Hebrew word for "ends" may have been *tak'lit* תכלית (Strong's 8503), which can mean "ends" but can also mean "purpose, aim, intention, or goal." "[F]or this end has the Torah been given" (2 Nefi 8:2). This passage runs parallel to Rom. 10:4 where the word translated "end" (in the KJV) is *telos* in the Greek and *saka* סכא in the Aramaic Peshitta text. In the *Jewish New Testament*, David Stern renders the Greek word *telos* as "goal." James Murdock's 1893 translation of the Peshitta renders the word *saka* as "aim," while a note in the margin shows that the Aramaic word is *saka* and can be understood as "end, scope, summary." See also 2 Nefi 8:2 and 3 Nefi 7:2.   **22** Mashiach fulfills the typology of the Firstfruits offering (Lev. 23:9-14), being the firstfruits of the resurrection. See also 1 Cor. 15:20; Rev. 14:4.   **23** Isa. 53:12; M'roni 7:5   **24** There is a wordplay here in the original Hebrew between the words יפגיע (yap'gia) "intercession" (in 2 Nefi 1:6) and פגע (p'ga) "inflicting," pointing to the Hebrew origin of *The Stick of Joseph*.

to pass, neither wickedness, neither holiness nor misery, neither good nor bad; wherefore, all things must necessarily be a compound in one. Wherefore, if it should be one body, it must necessarily remain as dead, having no life neither death, nor corruption nor incorruption, happiness nor misery, neither sense nor insensibility. Wherefore, it must necessarily have been created for a thing of nothing; wherefore, there would have been no purpose in the end of its creation. Wherefore, this thing must necessarily destroy the wisdom of Elohim and his eternal purposes, and also the power, and the mercy, and the justice of Elohim.[25] And if you shall say there is no Torah, you shall also say there is no sin.[26] And if you shall say there is no sin, you shall also say there is no righteousness. And if there be no righteousness, there be no happiness. And if there be no righteousness nor happiness, there be no punishment nor misery. And if these things are not, there is no Elohim. And if there is no Elohim, we are not, neither the earth; for there could have been no creation of things, neither to act nor to be acted upon; wherefore, all things must have vanished away.

8 And now my sons, I speak unto you these things for your profit and learning; for there is an Elohim and he has created all things, both the heavens and the earth, and all things that in them are, both things to act and things to be acted upon.[27] And to bring about his eternal purposes in the end of man — after he had created our first parents, and the **beasts of the field, and the fowls of the air,**[28] and in short, all things which are created — it must necessarily be that there was an

---

25 Wisdom [*chochma*], eternal [*natzach*], power [*gevurah*], mercy [*chesed*], justice [*din*]: In Kabbalah, these are four of the ten *Sefirot* of the Tree of Life (power and justice being alternate names for the same *Sefira*). **26** Alma 19:15 **27** The first century Jewish writer, Philo of Alexandria writes: "But Moses, who had early reached the very summits of philosophy, and who had learnt from the oracles of God the most numerous and important of the principles of nature, was well aware that it is indispensable that in all existing things there must be an active cause, and a passive subject; and that the active cause is the intellect of the universe, thoroughly unadulterated and thoroughly unmixed, superior to virtue and superior to science, superior even to abstract good or abstract beauty; while the passive subject is something inanimate and incapable of motion by any intrinsic power of its own, but having been set in motion, and fashioned, and endowed with life by the intellect, became transformed into that most perfect work, this world" (Philo; On Creation 8-9). And Maimonides says "He is the Knowledge and the Knower...and this is not within the power of any man to comprehend clearly" (Code, Hilchot Yesodei ha-Torah 2:10). And as we read in the Tanya "He is wise—but not through a knowable wisdom, because He and His wisdom are one" (Tanya; Likutei Amarim Chapter 2). **28** Gen. 2:19-20

opposition, even the forbidden[29] **fruit**[30] in opposition to **the tree of life,**[31] the one being sweet and the other bitter.[32] Wherefore, Adonai YHWH gave unto man that he should act for himself; wherefore, man could not act for himself except it should be that he were enticed by the one or the other.

9 And I, Lechi, according to the things which I have read, must necessarily suppose that an angel of Elohim, according to that which is written, had **fallen from Heaven.**[33] Wherefore, he became a demon, having sought that which was evil before Elohim. And because he had fallen from Heaven and had become miserable for ever, he sought also the misery of all mankind. Wherefore, he said unto Havah— yes, even that old serpent which is HaSatan, which is the father of all lies — wherefore, he said, Partake of the forbidden fruit and **you shall not die, but you shall be as Elohim, knowing good and evil.**[34] And after Adam and Havah had partaken of the forbidden fruit, **they were driven out from the Garden of Eden to till the earth.**[35] And they have brought forth children, yes, even the family of all the earth. And the days of the children of men were prolonged according to the will of Elohim, that they might repent while in the flesh. Wherefore, their state became a state of probation,[36] and their time was lengthened, according to the mitzvot which Adonai YHWH gave unto the children of men. For he gave mitzvah that all men must repent, for he showed unto all men that they were lost because of the transgression of their parents.

10 And now behold, if Adam had not transgressed, he would not have fallen, but he would have remained in the Garden of Eden. And all things which were created must have remained in the same state which they were after they were created; and they must have remained for ever and had no end. And they would have had no children. Wherefore, they would have remained in a state of innocence, having no joy for they knew no misery, doing no good for they knew no sin. But behold, all things have been done in the wisdom of him who knows all things. Adam fell that men might be, and men are that

---

29 The phrase "forbidden fruit" never appears in the Tanakh, but is found in the Zohar (Zohar 2:144a).   **30** Gen. 3:3   **31** Gen. 2:9; 3:22-24   **32** We read similarly in the Zohar: "The tree of good and evil: This tree was not in the middle. It is called by this name because it draws sustenance from two opposite sides, which it distinguishes as clearly as one distinguishes sweet and bitter, and therefore it is called 'good and evil'" (Zohar 1:35a).   **33** Isa. 14:12   **34** Gen. 3:5   **35** Gen. 3:23-24   **36** Alma 9:6-9

they might have joy.³⁷ And the Mashiach comes in the fulness of time, that he may redeem the children of men from the Fall.³⁸ And because that they are redeemed from the Fall, they have become free for ever —knowing good from evil — to act for themselves and not to be acted upon, except it be by the punishment of the Torah at the great and last day, according to the mitzvot which Elohim has given. Wherefore, men are free according to the flesh, and all things are given them which are expedient unto man. And they are free to choose liberty and Eternal life through the great Mediator of all men, or to choose captivity and death according to the captivity and power of HaSatan, for he seeks that all men might be miserable like unto himself.

11 And now my sons, I would that you should look to the great Mediator, and hearken unto his great mitzvot, and be faithful unto his words, and choose Eternal life according to the will of his Holy Spirit, and not choose Eternal death according to the will of the flesh and the evil which is therein, which gives the spirit of HaSatan power to captivate, to bring you down to Gehinnom, that he may reign over you in his own kingdom. I have spoken these few words unto you all, my sons, in the last days of my probation; and I have chosen the good part according to the words of the prophet. And I have no other object except it be the everlasting welfare of your souls. Amen.

---

37 Compare with the Zohar: "For indeed, if Adam had brought offspring with him out of the Garden of Eden, these would never have been destroyed ... and all would have lived for ever; and not even the angels would have equalled them in illumination and wisdom, as we read, 'In the image of God he created him' (Gen. 1:27). But since, through his sin, he left the Garden by himself and bore offspring outside it, these did not endure in the world, and this ideal was, therefore, not realised. Said R. Hizkiah: 'How could they have begotten children there, seeing that, had the evil inclination (*yetzer ra*) not enticed him to sin, Adam would have dwelt for ever in the world by himself and would not have begotten children?'" (Zohar 1:60a-61a). And with the Midrash Rabbah, "Nachman said, In the name of Rabbi Shmu'el: 'and behold it was very good' (Gen. 1:31) refers to the *yetzer ra* [evil inclination]. But can the *yetzer ra* be 'very good?' Amazingly enough, yes—were it not for the *yetzer ra* no man would build a house, take a wife and father children, or engage in business; as Solomon said, 'I considered all labor and excellence in work and concluded that it comes from a man's rivalry with his neighbor' (Eccles. 4:4)" (Gen. Rabbah 9:7).   38 "But in the days of the Messiah, the choice of their [genuine] good will be natural; the heart will not desire the improper and it will have no craving whatever for it. This is the 'circumcision' mentioned here, for lust and desire are the 'foreskin' of the heart, and circumcision of the heart means that it will not covet or desire evil. Man will return at that time to what he was before the sin of Adam, when by his nature he did what should properly be done, and there were no conflicting desires in his will" (Ramban on Deut. 29:6).

2 And now I speak unto you, Yosef, my last born. You were born in the wilderness of my afflictions, yes, in the days of my greatest sorrow did your mother bear you. And may YHWH consecrate also unto you this land, which is a most precious land, for your inheritance and the inheritance of your seed with your brothers, for your security for ever, if it so be that you shall keep the mitzvot of HaKodesh of Isra'el.

2 And now Yosef, my last born whom I have brought out of the wilderness of my afflictions, may YHWH bless you for ever, for your seed shall not utterly be destroyed. For behold, you are the fruit of my loins, and I am a descendant of Yosef[39] who was carried captive into Egypt.[40] And great were the covenants of YHWH which he made unto Yosef. Wherefore, Yosef truly saw our day. And he obtained a promise of YHWH that, out of the fruit of his loins, Adonai YHWH would raise up a righteous branch unto the house of Isra'el, not the Mashiach, but a branch which was to be broken off, nevertheless to be remembered in the covenants of YHWH, that the Mashiach should be made manifest unto them in the latter days in the spirit of power unto the bringing of them out of darkness unto light, yes, out of hidden darkness and out of captivity unto freedom.

3 For Yosef truly testified, saying, A seer shall YHWH my Elohim raise up, who shall be a choice seer unto the fruit of my loins. Yes, Yosef truly said, Thus says YHWH unto me: A choice seer will I raise up out of the fruit of your loins, and he shall be esteemed highly among the fruit of your loins. And unto him will I give mitzvah that he shall do a work for the fruit of your loins, his brothers, which shall be of great worth unto them, even to the bringing of them to the knowledge of the covenants which I have made with your fathers. And I will give unto him a mitzvah that he shall do no other work except the work which I shall command him. And I will make him great in my eyes, for he shall do my work. And he shall be great like unto Moshe, whom I have said I would raise up unto you to deliver my people, O house of Isra'el.[41] And Moshe will I raise up to deliver

---

39 1 Nefi 1:22 **40** Gen. 37:36 **41** We read in Targum Neofiti concerning Joseph's interpretation of the butler's dream "The three branches are the three fathers of the world, namely: Abraham, Isaac and Jacob, the sons of whose sons are to be enslaved in the slavery of the land of Egypt and are to be delivered by the hands of three faithful leaders: Moses, Aaron, and Miriam, who are to be likened to the cluster of grapes." (Targum Neofiti to Gen. 40:12). The Talmud says concerning this same dream: "It was taught: R.

your people out of the land of Egypt. But a seer will I raise up out of the fruit of your loins, and unto him will I give power to bring forth my word unto the seed of your loins; and not to the bringing forth my word only, says YHWH, but to the convincing them of my word which shall have already gone forth among them.

4 Wherefore, the fruit of your loins **shall write**, and the fruit of the loins of **Y'hudah**[42] shall write. And that which shall be written by the fruit of your loins, and also that which shall be written by the fruit of the loins of Y'hudah, shall grow **together**[43] unto the confounding of false doctrines, and laying down of contentions, and establishing shalom among the fruit of your loins, and bringing them to the knowledge of their fathers[44] in the latter days, and also to the knowledge of my covenants, says YHWH. And out of weakness he shall be made strong, in that day when my work shall commence among all my people, unto the restoring you, O house of Isra'el, says YHWH.

5 And thus prophesied Yosef, saying, Behold, that seer will YHWH bless; and they that seek to destroy him shall be confounded, for this promise of which I have obtained of YHWH, of the fruit of your loins, shall be fulfilled. Behold, I am sure of the fulfilling of this promise. And his name shall be called after me, and it shall be after the name of his father. And he shall be like unto me, for the thing which YHWH

Eliezer says: 'The "vine" is the world, the "three branches" are [the patriarchs] Abraham, Isaac and Jacob; "and as it was budding its blossoms shot forth", these are the matriarchs; "and the clusters thereof brought forth ripe grapes", these are the tribes.' Thereupon R. Joshua said to him: 'Is a man shown [in a dream] what has happened? Surely he is only shown what is to happen! Therefore, I say: The "vine" is the Torah, the "three branches" are Moses, Aaron and Miriam…'" (b.Hullin 92a). Moreover, in Targum Pseudo-Jonathan to Gen. 50:24 Joseph says "Behold you will be enslaved in Egypt, but do not make plans to go out of Egypt until the time that the two deliverers come and say to you, 'The Lord remembers you.'" **42** 1 Nefi 3:21-22; 2 Nefi 12:10. See *Appendix E: Ezekiel's Prophecy of this Work.* **43** Ezek. 37:16-19 "Moreover, you son of man, take you one stick, and write upon it, For Y'hudah, and for the children of Yisra'el his companions: then take another stick, and write upon it, For Yosef, the stick of Efrayim, and for all the house of Yisra'el his companions: And join them one to another into one stick; and they shall become one in your hand. And when the children of your people shall speak unto you, saying, Will you not show us what you mean by these? Say unto them, Thus says the YHWH Adonai; Behold, I will take the stick of Yosef, which is in the hand of Efrayim, and the tribes of Yisra'el his fellows, and will put them with him, even with the stick of Y'hudah, and make them one stick, and they shall be one in my hand." Targum Jonathan to these verses interprets "stick" (Hebrew *etz* עץ) with the Aramaic word *lucha* לוחא meaning "plate" or "writing tablet" so that two "plates" become "one." This prophecy is fulfilled not only by the union of the two houses of Israel (Ezek. 37:21-22) but by the growing together of two written records; the "Plate of Y'hudah" (*Plates of Brass*/the Bible) and the "Plate of Yosef" (*The Stick of Joseph*—this record). **44** 1 Nefi 4:3; 2 Nefi 12:12

shall bring forth by his hand, by the power of YHWH, shall bring my people unto salvation. Yes, thus prophesied Yosef: I am sure of this thing, even as I am sure of the promise of Moshe; for YHWH has said unto me, I will preserve your seed for ever. And YHWH has said, I will raise up a Moshe,[45] and I will give power unto him in a **rod**;[46] and I will give judgment unto him in writing. Yet I will not loose his **tongue**[47] that he shall speak much, for I will not make him mighty in speaking. But I will **write unto him my Torah by the finger of my own hand**,[48] and I will make one a **spokesman** for him.[49]

6 And YHWH said unto me also, I will raise up unto the fruit of your loins, and I will make for him a spokesman. And I, behold, I will give unto him that he shall write the writing of the fruit of your loins unto the fruit of your loins; and the spokesman of your loins shall declare it. And the words which he shall write shall be the words which are expedient in my wisdom should go forth unto the fruit of your loins. And it shall be as if the fruit of your loins had cried unto them **from the dust**, for I know their faith. And they shall cry **from the dust**,[50] yes, even repentance unto their brothers, even that after many generations have gone by them. And it shall come to pass that their cry shall go, even according to the simpleness of their words, because of their faith. Their words shall proceed forth out of my mouth unto their brothers who are the fruit of your loins; and the weakness of their words will I make strong in their faith unto the remembering of my covenant which I made unto your fathers.

7 And now behold, my son Yosef, after this manner did my father of old prophesy. Wherefore, because of this covenant, you are blessed; for your seed shall not be destroyed, for they shall hearken unto the words of the book. And there shall raise up one mighty among them who shall do much good, both in word and in deed, being an instrument in the hands of Elohim with exceeding faith to work mighty wonders and do that thing which is great in the sight of Elohim, unto the bringing to pass much restoration unto the house of Isra'el and unto the seed of your brothers. And now blessed are you, Yosef. Behold, you are little; wherefore, hearken unto the words of your brother Nefi, and it shall be done unto you even according to

---

45 Ex. 3:1-22 **46** Ex. 4:2, 17 **47** Ex. 4:10 **48** Ex. 31:18 **49** Ex. 4:14-16 **50** Isa. 29:4

the words which I have spoken. Remember the words of your dying father. Amen.

3 And now I, Nefi, speak concerning the prophecies of which my father has spoken concerning Yosef, who was carried into Egypt. For behold, he truly prophesied concerning all his seed. And the prophecies which he wrote, there are not many greater. And he prophesied concerning us and our future generations, and they are written upon the plates of brass.

2 Wherefore, after my father had made an end of speaking concerning the prophecies of Yosef, he called the children of Laman, his sons and his daughters, and said unto them, Behold, my sons and my daughters who are the sons and the daughters of my first born, I would that you should give ear unto my words. For Adonai YHWH has said that inasmuch as you shall keep my mitzvot, you shall prosper in the land,[51] and inasmuch as you will not keep my mitzvot, you shall be cut off from my presence.[52] But behold, my sons and my daughters, I cannot go down to my grave except I should leave a blessing upon you. For behold, I know that if you are **brought up in the way you should go, you will not depart from it.**[53] Wherefore, if you are cursed, behold, I leave my blessing upon you that the cursing may be taken from you and be answered upon the heads of your parents. Wherefore, because of my blessing, Adonai YHWH will not allow that you shall perish. Wherefore, he will be merciful unto you and unto your seed for ever.

3 And it came to pass that after my father had made an end of speaking to the sons and daughters of Laman, he caused the sons and daughters of L'mu'el to be brought before him. And he spoke unto them, saying, Behold, my sons and my daughters who are the sons and the daughters of my second son, behold, I leave unto you the same blessing which I left unto the sons and daughters of Laman. Wherefore, you shall not utterly be destroyed, but in the end, your seed shall be blessed.

4 And it came to pass that when my father had made an end of speaking unto them, behold, he spoke unto the sons of Yishma'el, yes, and even all his household. And after he had made an end of

---

51 Lev. 26:1-13; Deut. 28:1-14 52 Lev. 26:14-39; Deut. 28:15-68 53 Prov. 22:6

speaking unto them, he spoke unto Sam, saying, Blessed are you and your seed, for you shall inherit the land like unto your brother Nefi. And your seed shall be numbered with his seed; and you shall be even like unto your brother, and your seed like unto his seed; and you shall be blessed in all your days.

5 And it came to pass that after my father Lechi had spoken unto all his household, according to the feelings of his heart and the spirit of YHWH which was in him, he grew old. And it came to pass that he died and was buried.

6 And it came to pass that not many days after his death, Laman and L'mu'el and the sons of Yishma'el were angry with me because of the admonitions of YHWH; for I, Nefi, was constrained to speak unto them according to his word. For I had spoke many things unto them, and also my father before his death, many of which sayings are written upon my other plates, for a more historical part is written upon my other plates. And upon these I write the things of my soul and many of the scriptures which are engraved upon the plates of brass.

The Psalm of Nefi

For my soul delights in the scriptures,
and my heart ponders them and writes them
    for the learning and the profit of my children.
Behold, my soul delights in the things of YHWH,
and my heart ponders continually upon the things
    which I have seen and heard.
7 Nevertheless, despite the great goodness of YHWH
in showing me his great and marvelous works,

My heart exclaims, O wretched man that I am!
Yes, my heart sorrows because of my flesh,
my soul grieves because of my iniquities.

I am encompassed about because of the temptations
and the sins which do so easily entangle me,
and when I desire to rejoice, my heart groans because of my sins.
Nevertheless, I know in whom I have trusted.[54]

---

[54] This reads identically to a phrase in 2 Tim. 1:12 except for one word: "nevertheless...I

My Elohim has been my support.
He has led me through my afflictions in the wilderness
and he has preserved me upon the waters of the great deep.
He has filled me with his love,
>even unto the consuming of my flesh.
He has confounded my enemies,
>unto the causing of them to quake before me.
Behold, he has heard my cry by day,
and he has given me knowledge by visions in the night time.

And by day have I grown bold in mighty prayer before him;
yes, my voice have I sent up on high,
and angels came down and ministered unto me.
And upon the wings of his spirit has my body been carried away
>up on exceedingly high mountains.
And my eyes have beheld great things —
>yes, even too great for man —
therefore I was bidden[55] that I should not write them.

8 Oh then, if I have seen so great things,
if YHWH, in his condescension unto the children of men,
>has visited me in so much mercy,
why should my heart weep
and my soul linger in the valley of sorrow,
and my flesh waste away
and my strength slacken because of my afflictions?

And why should I yield to sin because of my flesh?
Yes, why should I give way to temptations,
that the Evil One have place in my heart
to destroy my shalom and afflict my soul?
Why am I angry because of my enemy?

>Awake my soul! No longer droop in sin.
>Rejoice, O my heart, and give place no more

---

know in whom I believed." The underlying Hebrew word behind both must have been *aman* אמן (Strong's 539), which can mean "to trust, to have faith, or to believe." This points to a Hebrew original behind 2 Nefi 3:7. **55** 1 Nefi 3:31

for the enemy of my soul.
Do not anger again because of my enemies.
Do not slacken my strength because of my afflictions.
Rejoice, O my heart, and cry unto YHWH
and say, O YHWH, I will praise you for ever.
Yes, my soul will rejoice in you,
my Elohim and the Rock of my salvation.[56]

O YHWH, will you redeem my soul?
Will you deliver me out of the hands of my enemies?
Will you make me that I may shake at the appearance of sin?

May the gates of She'ol be shut continually before me
because that my heart is broken
and my spirit is contrite?
O YHWH, will you not shut the gates of your righteousness
    before me,
that I may walk in the path of the low valley,
that I may be strict in the plain road?

O YHWH, will you encircle me around in the robe
    of your righteousness?
O YHWH, will you make a way for my escape
    before my enemies?
Will you make my path straight before me?
Will you not place a stumbling block in my way,
but that you would clear my way before me
and hedge not up my way, but the ways of my enemy?

O YHWH, I have trusted in you
and I will trust in you for ever.
I will not put my trust in the arm of flesh,
for I know that **cursed is he that puts his trust**
    in the arm of flesh.
Yes, **cursed is he that puts his trust in man**
    or makes flesh his arm.[57]

---

56 Deut. 32:15; 2 Sam. 22:47; Ps. 89:27 (26); 95:1 **57** Jer. 17:5

Yes, I know that Elohim will give liberally to him that asks.
Yes, my Elohim will give me if I ask not amiss;
therefore I will lift up my voice unto you.
Yes, I will cry unto you, my Elohim,
    the Rock of my righteousness.
Behold, my voice shall for ever ascend up unto you,
    my Rock and my El Olam.
Amen.

4 Behold, it came to pass that I, Nefi, did cry much unto YHWH my Elohim because of the anger of my brothers. But behold, their anger did increase against me, insomuch that they did seek to take away my life. Yes, they did murmur against me, saying, Our younger brother thinks to rule over us, and we have had much trial because of him; wherefore, now let us slay him, that we may not be afflicted more because of his words. For behold, we will not have him to be our ruler, for it belongs unto us, who are the elder brothers, to rule over this people. Now I do not write upon these plates all the words which they murmured against me, but it suffices me to say that they did seek to take away my life.

2 And it came to pass that YHWH did warn me that I, Nefi, should depart from them and flee into the wilderness, and all those who would go with me. Wherefore, it came to pass that I, Nefi, did take my family, and also Tzuram and his family, and Sam, my elder brother, and his family, and Ya'akov and Yosef, my younger brothers, and also my sisters, and all those who would go with me. And all those who would go with me were those who believed in the warnings and the revelations of Elohim; wherefore, they did hearken unto my words. And we did take our tents and whatsoever things were possible for us, and did journey in the wilderness for the space of many days. And after we had journeyed for the space of many days, we did pitch our tents. And my people would that we should call the name of the place Nefi; wherefore, we did call it Nefi. And all those who were with me did take upon them to call themselves the people of Nefi. And we did observe to keep the judgments, and the statutes,[58] and the mitzvot

---

[58] "Judgments" (*mishpatim*) are moral and ethical laws. "Statutes" (*chokim*) are commandments with no apparent rationale, except that Elohim has decreed them.

of YHWH in all things according to the Torah of Moshe.[59] And YHWH was with us and we did prosper exceedingly, for we did sow seed and we did reap again in abundance. And we began to raise flocks, and herds, and animals of every kind. And I, Nefi, had also brought the records which were engraved upon the plates of brass, and also the ball,[60] or the compass, which was prepared for my father by the hand of YHWH according to that which is written.

3 And it came to pass that we began to prosper exceedingly and to multiply in the land. And I, Nefi, did take the sword of Lavan, and after the manner of it did make many swords, for fear that by any means the people who were now called Lamanites should come upon us and destroy us. For I knew their hatred towards me, and my children, and those who were called my people. And I did teach my people to build buildings and to work in all manner of wood, and of iron, and of copper, and of brass, and of steel, and of gold, and of silver, and of precious ores, which were in great abundance. And I, Nefi, did build a Temple;[61] and I did construct it after the manner of the Temple of Solomon, except it were not built of so many precious things, for they were not to be found upon the land. Wherefore, it could not be built like unto Solomon's Temple. But the manner of the construction was like unto the Temple of Solomon, and the workmanship thereof was exceedingly fine.[62]

4 And it came to pass that I, Nefi, did cause my people to be industrious and to labor with their hands. And it came to pass that they would that I should be their king, but I, Nefi, was desirous that they should have no king; nevertheless, I did for them according to that which was in my power. And behold, the words of YHWH had

---

59 2 Nefi 11:8; Ya'akov 3:2   60 1 Nefi 5:3, 8   61 Ya'akov 1:4; Moshiyah 1:4; 5:7
62 According to both the first century Jewish historian Josephus and the Talmud, there was also a Jewish Temple for YHWH at Leontopolis in Egypt, built by Onias, which was "like indeed to that in Jerusalem" (Josephus, *Antiquities of the Jews*. xiii, 3, 3) when he fled to Egypt (Josephus, *Antiquities of the Jews*. xiii, 3, 1-4; *The Wars of the Jews*. vii, 10, 2-4). This Temple is also mentioned in the Babylonian Talmud which says, "the Temple of Onias was not an idolatrous shrine" and was seen as a fulfillment of the prophecy of Yesha'yahu 19:19 "that there would be "an altar of YHWH in the midst of the land of Egypt" (b.Menahot 109b), which appears to justify the existence of a Temple outside of Jerusalem. Archaeological evidence has established that certain other ancient Jewish communities also built Temples outside of Jerusalem (for example, at Arad—near Beer Sheba; see: Aharoni, Herzog, and Rainey. [March/April 1987] Arad—An Ancient Isra'elite Fortress with a Temple to Yahweh. Biblical Archaeology Review 13:2; see also Lemaire. [July/August 2004] Elephantine, Egypt (Another Temple to the Isra'elite God; Aramaic Hoard Documents Life in Fourth Century B.C.). Biblical Archaeology Review 30:4).

been fulfilled unto my brothers, which he spoke concerning them, that I should be their ruler and their teacher; wherefore, I had been their ruler and their teacher according to the mitzvot of YHWH until the time they sought to take away my life. Wherefore, the word of YHWH was fulfilled which he spoke unto me, saying that inasmuch as they will not hearken unto your words, they shall be cut off from the presence of YHWH. And behold, they were cut off from his presence. And he had caused the cursing to come upon them, yes, even a sore cursing because of their iniquity. For behold, they had hardened their hearts against him, that they had become like unto a flint. Wherefore, as they were white and exceedingly fair and delightful, that they might not be enticing unto my people, Adonai YHWH did cause a skin of blackness to come upon them.[63] And thus says Adonai YHWH: I will cause that they shall be loathsome unto your people, except they shall repent of their iniquities. And cursed shall be the seed of him that mixes with their seed,[64] for they shall be cursed even with the same cursing. And YHWH spoke it, and it was done. And because of their cursing which was upon them, they did become an idle people, full of mischief and subtlety, and did seek in the wilderness for beasts of prey.[65] And Adonai YHWH said unto me, They shall be a scourge unto your seed to stir them up in remembrance of me; and inasmuch as they will not remember me and hearken unto my words, they shall scourge them even unto destruction.

5 And it came to pass that I, Nefi, did consecrate Ya'akov and Yosef that they should be kohanim and teachers over the land of my people.[66] And it came to pass that we lived after the manner of

---

63 Similarly, we read of Ham in the Talmud: "Our Rabbis taught: Three copulated in the ark, and they were all punished; the dog, the raven, and Ham. The dog was doomed to be tied, the raven expectorates [his seed into his mate's mouth] and Ham was smitten in his skin" (b.Sanhedrin 108b). A similar account appears in the Midrash Rabbah but says "Ham came forth black-skinned" (Gen. Rabbah XXXVI:7). 64 Compare Deut. 7:3-4 and Neh. 10:30; 13:23-31. 65 "[B]easts of prey" are unkosher; Lev. 11:2-8. 66 Ya'akov and Yosef were both sons of Lechi (1 Nefi 5:27), and Lechi was a Yosefite (1 Nefi 1:22). Thus Ya'akov and Yosef were both from the Tribe of Yosef and *not* from the Tribe of Levi. Rabbi Abraham ben Meir Ibn Ezra (one of the most distinguished Jewish biblical commentators and philosophers of the Middle Ages and one of the classic commentators included in the Miqrat Gedolot) writes in his commentary on Ex. 19:6: "A Kingdom of Priests. In my opinion, 'priest' in the Bible means 'one who serves,' just as the verbal form is taken in 28:41 to mean 'serve me as priests.' Jethro is the 'priest of Midian' (18:1) because he served God, as did Melchizedek of Salem, the 'priest of God Most High' (Gen. 14:18). The same is true when David's sons are called 'priests' in 2 Sam. 8:18. There would be no point in telling us that they were 'princes,' for we know that a king's sons possess

happiness. And thirty⁶⁷ years had passed away from the time we left Yerushalayim. And I, Nefi, had kept the records, upon my plates which I had made, of my people thus far.

⁶And it came to pass that Adonai YHWH said unto me, Make other plates; and you shall engrave many things upon them which are good in my sight for the profit of your people. Wherefore, I, Nefi, to be obedient to the mitzvot of YHWH, went and made these plates upon which I have engraved these things. And I engraved that which is pleasing unto Elohim. And if my people are pleased with the things of Elohim, they will be pleased with my engravings which are upon these plates. And if my people desire to know the more particular part of the history of my people, they must search my other plates. And it suffices me to say that forty years⁶⁸ had passed away, and we had already had wars and contentions with our brothers.

5 The words of Ya'akov, the brother of Nefi, which he spoke unto the people of Nefi: Behold, my beloved brothers, I, Ya'akov, having been called of Elohim and ordained after the manner of his Holy Order, and having been consecrated by my brother Nefi, unto whom you look as a king or a protector and on whom you depend for safety, behold, you know that I have spoken unto you exceedingly many things. Nevertheless, I speak unto you again, for I am desirous for the welfare of your souls. Yes, my anxiety is great for you; and you yourselves know that it always has been, for I have exhorted you with all diligence. And I have taught you the words of my father, and I have spoken unto you concerning all things which are written from the creation of the world.

²And now behold, I would speak unto you concerning things which are and which are to come; wherefore, I will read you the words of Yesha'yahu. And they are the words which my brother has desired that I should speak unto you. And I speak them unto you for your sakes, that you may learn and glorify the name of your Elohim. And now the words which I shall read are they which Yesha'yahu spoke

---

high rank; this verse informs us that they served God. So telling Israel that they will be 'a kingdom of priests' means, 'By means of you, My kingdom shall appear, when you are serving Me.' But others understand it to mean 'There is no kingship other than serving Me.'" As cited by Rabbi Abraham ben Meir Ibn Ezra above, the actual Hebrew of 2 Sam. 8:18 identifies David's sons as kohanim (priests), where the KJV translates it as "chief rulers." **67** ~ 571 BCE; 1 Nefi 1:7 **68** ~ 561 BCE

concerning all the house of Isra'el; wherefore, they may be applied unto you, for you are of the house of Isra'el. And there are many things which have been spoken by Yesha'yahu which may be applied unto you because you are of the house of Isra'el.

3 And now these are the words: **Thus says Adonai YHWH: Behold,[69] I will lift up my hand to the Goyim and set up my standard to the people; and they shall bring your sons in their arms, and your daughters shall be carried upon their shoulders. And kings shall be your nursing fathers and their queens your nursing mothers. They shall bow down to you with their faces towards the earth and lick up the dust of your feet. And you shall know that I am YHWH, for they shall not be ashamed that wait for me.**[70]

4 And now I, Ya'akov, would speak somewhat concerning these words. For behold, YHWH has shown me that those who were at Yerushalayim, from where we came, have been slain and carried away captive; nevertheless, YHWH has shown unto me that they should return[71] again. And he also has shown unto me that Adonai YHWH, HaKodesh of Isra'el, should manifest himself unto them in the flesh. And after he should manifest himself, they should scourge him and crucify[72] him, according to the words of the angel who spoke it unto me. And after they have hardened their hearts and stiffened their necks against HaKodesh of Isra'el, behold, the judgments of HaKodesh of Isra'el shall come upon them. And the day comes that they shall be smitten and afflicted. Wherefore, after they are driven to and fro, for thus says the angel, many shall be afflicted in the flesh, and shall not be allowed to perish because of the prayers of the faithful. They shall be scattered, and smitten, and hated; nevertheless, YHWH will be merciful unto them, that when they shall come to the knowledge of their Redeemer, they shall be gathered[73] together again to the lands of their inheritance.

5 And blessed are the **Goyim**,[74] they of whom the prophet has written. For behold, if it so be that they shall repent, and fight not against Tziyon, and do not unite themselves to that great and abominable church, they shall be saved. For Adonai YHWH will fulfill

---

69 1 Nefi 6:10   **70** Isa. 49:22-23; see also 1 Nefi 6:10   **71** 1 Nefi 3:2   **72** Moshiyah 1:14   **73** 2 Nefi 6:1   **74** Isa. 49:22; 1 Nefi 3:25-26

his covenants which he has made unto his children; and for this cause the prophet has written these things. Wherefore, they that fight against Tziyon and the covenant people of YHWH shall **lick up the dust of** their feet; and the people of YHWH shall not be ashamed. For the people of YHWH are they who wait for him; for they still wait for the coming of the Mashiach. And behold, according to the words of the prophet, the Mashiach **will set himself again the second time to recover them.**[75] Wherefore, he will manifest himself unto them in power and great glory, unto the destruction of their enemies, when that day comes when they shall believe in him; and none will he destroy that believes in him. And they that believe not in him shall be destroyed,[76] both by fire, and by tempest, and by earthquakes, and by bloodsheds, and by pestilence, and by famine. And they shall know that YHWH is Elohim, HaKodesh of Isra'el. **For shall the prey be taken from the mighty? Or the lawful captive delivered? But thus says YHWH: Even the captives of the mighty shall be taken away, and the prey of the terrible shall be delivered, for the mighty Elohim shall deliver his covenant people. For thus says YHWH: I will contend with them that contend with you; and I will feed them that oppress you with their own flesh, and they shall be drunken with their own blood as with sweet wine. And all flesh shall know that I, YHWH, am your Savior and your Redeemer, the Mighty One of Ya'akov.**[77]

Yesha'yahu 50 from the Plates of Brass

⁶Yes, for thus says YHWH: **Have I put you away? Or have I cast you off for ever? For thus says YHWH: Where is the bill of your Mother's divorcement? To whom have I put you away? Or to which of my creditors have I sold you? Yes, to whom have I sold you? Behold, for your iniquities have you sold yourselves, and for your transgressions is your Mother put away. Wherefore,**

---

75 Isa. 11:11; see also 2 Nefi 11:6   76 The Torah warns concerning Mashiach: "I will raise them up a prophet from among their brothers, like unto you, and I will put My words in his mouth, and he shall speak unto them all that I shall command him. And it shall come to pass, that whosoever will not hearken unto My words which he shall speak in My Name, I will require it of him" (Deut. 18:18-19). Targum Onkelos paraphrases "I will require it of them" with "My Word shall take vengeance upon him," and the Mishnah explains the phrase "I will require it of him" to mean "death at the hands of heaven" (m.Sanhedrin 11:5; b.Sanhedrin 89a).   77 Isa. 49:24-26

when I came, there was no man; when I called, yes, there was none to answer. O house of Isra'el, is my hand shortened at all that it cannot redeem? Or have I no power to deliver? Behold, at my rebuke I dry up the sea. I make the rivers a wilderness and their fish to stink because the waters are dried up,[78] and they die because of thirst. I clothe the heavens with blackness and I make sackcloth their covering.

7 Adonai YHWH has given me the tongue of the learned, that I should know how to speak a word in season unto you, O house of Isra'el, when you are weary. He wakes morning by morning; he wakes my ear to hear as the learned. Adonai YHWH has opened my ear, and I was not rebellious, neither turned away back. I gave my back to the smiter and my cheeks to them that plucked off the hair. I hid not my face from shame and spitting. For Adonai YHWH will help me, therefore shall I not be confounded. Therefore have I set my face like a flint, and I know that I shall not be ashamed. And YHWH is near, and he justifies me. Who will contend with me? Let us stand together. Who is my adversary? Let him come near me and I will smite him with the strength of my mouth. For Adonai YHWH will help me. And all they who shall condemn me, behold, all they shall become old as a garment, and the moth shall eat them up. Who is among you that fears YHWH, that obeys the voice of his servant, that walks in darkness and has no light? Behold, all you that kindle fire, that compass yourselves about with sparks, walk in the light of your fire and in the sparks which you have kindled. This shall you have of my hand: You shall lie down in sorrow.

Yesha'yahu 51:1 – 52:2 from the Plates of Brass

8 Hearken to me, you that follow after righteousness. Look unto the rock from which you are cut, and to the hole of the pit from which you are dug. Look unto Avraham, your father, and unto Sarah, she that bore you; for I called him alone and blessed him. For YHWH shall comfort Tziyon; he will comfort all

---

[78] In this verse of Isaiah (Isa. 50:2), the *Plates of Brass* has the reading "their fish to stink because the waters are dried up." The Masoretic Text omits "dried up" and has only "their fish stink because there is no water." The Septuagint has "their fish shall be dried up because there is no water."

her waste places, and he will make her wilderness like Eden and her desert like the garden of YHWH. Joy and gladness shall be found therein, thanksgiving and the voice of melody. Hearken unto me, my people, and give ear unto me, O my nation, for a torah shall proceed from me and I will make my judgment to rest for a light for the people. My Righteousness is near, my Salvation is gone forth, and my Arm shall judge the people. The isles shall wait upon me, and on my Arm shall they trust. Lift up your eyes to the heavens and look upon the earth beneath, for the heavens shall vanish away like smoke, and the earth shall become old like a garment, and they that dwell therein shall die in like manner. But my Salvation shall be for ever, and my Righteousness shall not be abolished. Hearken unto me, you that know righteousness, the people in whose heart I have written my torah. Fear you not the reproach of men, neither be you afraid of their revilings. For the moth shall eat them up like a garment and the worm shall eat them like wool. But my Righteousness shall be for ever, and my Salvation from generation to generation.

9 Awake, awake, put on strength, O arm of YHWH. Awake as in the ancient days. Are you not he who has cut Rahav and wounded the dragon? Are you not he who has dried the sea, the waters of the great deep, that has made the depths of the sea a way for the ransomed to pass over? Therefore, the redeemed of YHWH shall return and come with singing unto Tziyon, and everlasting joy and holiness[79] shall be upon their heads. And they shall obtain gladness and joy; sorrow and mourning shall flee away. I am he, yes, I am he that comforts you.

10 Behold,[80] who are you, that you should be afraid of man who shall die and of the son of man who shall be made like unto grass, and forget YHWH your maker that has stretched forth the heavens and laid the foundations of the earth, and has feared continually every day because of the fury of the oppressor, as if he were ready to destroy? And where is the fury of the oppressor?

---

[79] In this verse of Isaiah (Isa. 51:11), the Masoretic Text omits "holiness," while the Septuagint has "praise" (αινεσις) in place of "holiness." [80] In this verse of Isaiah (Isa. 51:12), "Behold" is omitted in the Masoretic Text, while the Septuagint has "know" (γνωθι) in place of "Behold."

The captive exile hastens that he may be loosed and that he should not die in the pit, nor that his bread should fail. But I am YHWH your Elohim, whose waves roared; YHWH Tzva'ot is my name. And I have put my words in your mouth and have covered you in the shadow of my hand, that I may plant the heavens and lay the foundations of the earth, and say unto Tziyon, Behold, you are my people.

¹¹ Awake, awake, stand up, O Yerushalayim, which has drunk at the hand of YHWH the cup of his fury; you have drunken the dregs of the cup of trembling wrung out — and none to guide her, among all the sons she has brought forth, neither that takes her by the hand, of all the sons she has brought up. These two sons are come unto you. Who shall be sorry for you — your desolation and destruction, and the famine and the sword? And by whom shall I comfort you? Your sons have fainted, except these two; they lie at the head of all the streets, as a wild bull in a net. They are full of the fury of YHWH, the rebuke of your Elohim.

¹² Therefore, hear now this, you afflicted, and drunken and not with wine. Thus says your Adon — YHWH and your Elohim pleads the cause of his people: Behold, I have taken out of your hand the cup of trembling, the dregs of the cup of my fury; you shall no more drink it again. But I will put it into the hand of them that afflict you, who have said to your soul, Bow down that we may go over — and you have laid your body as the ground and as the street to them that went over.

¹³ Awake, awake, put on your strength, O Tziyon. Put on your beautiful garments, O Yerushalayim, the holy city. For henceforth there shall no more come into you the uncircumcised and the unclean. Shake yourself from the dust. Arise, sit down, O Yerushalayim. Loose yourself from the bands of your neck, O captive daughter of Tziyon.

6 And now my beloved brothers, I have read these things that you might know concerning the covenants of YHWH, that he has covenanted with all the house of Isra'el, that he has spoken unto the Y'hudim by the mouth of his holy prophets, even from the beginning, down from generation to generation, until the time comes that they shall be restored to the true assembly and fold of Elohim, when they

shall be gathered[81] home to the lands of their inheritance and shall be established in all their lands of promise.

2 Behold, my beloved brothers, I speak unto you these things that you may rejoice and lift up your heads for ever because of the blessings which Adonai YHWH shall bestow upon your children. For I know that you have searched much, many of you, to know of things to come; wherefore, I know that you know that our flesh must waste away and die; nevertheless, in our bodies we shall see Elohim. Yes, and I know that you know that in the body he shall show[82] himself unto those at Yerushalayim, from where we came, for it is expedient that it should be among them. For it is necessary that the great Creator allow himself to become subject unto man in the flesh and die[83] for all men, that all men might become subject unto him. For as death has passed upon all men to fulfill the merciful plan of the great Creator, there must necessarily be a power of resurrection. And the resurrection must necessarily come unto man by reason of the Fall, and the Fall came by reason of transgression. And because man became fallen, they were cut off from the presence of YHWH. Wherefore, it must necessarily be an infinite atonement; except it should be an infinite atonement,[84] this corruption could not put on incorruption. Wherefore, the first judgment which came upon man must necessarily have remained to an endless duration. And if so, this flesh must have laid down to rot and to crumble to its mother earth, to rise no more.

3 Oh the wisdom of Elohim, his mercy and grace. For behold, if the flesh should rise no more, our spirits must become subject to that angel who fell[85] from before the presence of the Elohe Kedem and became HaSatan, to rise no more. And our spirits must have become like unto him and we become demons, angels to a demon, to be shut out from the presence of our Elohim, and to remain with the father of lies, in misery like unto himself; yes, to that being who beguiled our first parents,[86] who transforms himself nearly unto an angel of light, and stirs up the children of men unto secret conspiracies of murder and all manner of secret works of darkness.

4 Oh how great the goodness of our Elohim, who prepares a way for our escape from the grasp of this awful monster, yes, that monster death and She'ol, which I call the death of the body and also the death

---

81 2 Nefi 5:4; 7:2 82 1 Nefi 3:8-13 83 2 Nefi 11:16; 3 Nefi 12:5 84 Alma 16:34 85 2 Nefi 1:9 86 'Eter 3:19

of the spirit! And because of the way of deliverance of our Elohim, HaKodesh of Isra'el, this death of which I have spoken, which is the temporal, shall deliver up its dead, which death is the grave. And this death of which I have spoken, which is the spiritual death, shall deliver up its dead, which spiritual death is She'ol. Wherefore, death and She'ol must deliver up its dead. And She'ol must deliver up its captive spirits, and the grave must deliver up its captive bodies, and the bodies and the spirits of men will be restored one to the other; and it is by the power of the resurrection[87] of HaKodesh of Isra'el.[88]

5 Oh how great the plan of our Elohim! For on the other hand, the pardes of Elohim must deliver up the spirits of the righteous, and the grave deliver up the body of the righteous. And the spirit and the body is restored to itself again, and all men become incorruptible and immortal; and they are living souls, having a perfect knowledge like unto us in the flesh, except it be that our knowledge shall be perfect. Wherefore, we shall have a perfect knowledge of all our guilt, and our uncleanness, and our nakedness; and the righteous shall have a perfect knowledge of their enjoyment and their righteousness, being clothed with purity, yes, even with the robe of righteousness.

6 And it shall come to pass that when all men shall have passed from this first death unto life, insomuch as they have become immortal, they must appear before the judgment seat of HaKodesh of Isra'el. And then comes the judgment, and then must they be judged according to the holy judgment of Elohim. And assuredly as YHWH lives — for Adonai YHWH has spoken it and it is his Eternal word, which cannot pass away — that they who are righteous shall be righteous still, and they who are unclean shall be unclean still. Wherefore, they who are unclean are HaSatan and his angels, and they shall go away into everlasting fire prepared for them. And their torment is as a lake of fire and brimstone, whose flames ascend up for ever and ever and has no end.[89]

7 Oh the greatness and the justice of our Elohim. For he executes all his words, and they have gone forth out of his mouth, and his Torah must be fulfilled. But behold, the righteous — the k'doshim of

---

[87] Alma 8:16-17; 19:8-9 [88] "And in those days shall the earth also give back that which has been entrusted to it, and She'ol will also give back that which it received. And hell shall give back that which it owes" (1 Enoch 51:1; see also Rev. 20:13). [89] See *Gehinnom* in Glossary.

HaKodesh of Isra'el, they who have believed in HaKodesh of Isra'el, they who have endured the Tz'livot of the world and despised the shame of it — they shall inherit the kingdom of Elohim which was prepared for them from the foundation of the world; and their joy shall be full for ever. Oh the greatness of the mercy of our Elohim, HaKodesh of Isra'el. For he delivers his k'doshim from that awful monster, HaSatan, and death, and She'ol, and that lake of fire and brimstone, which is Endless[90] torment. Oh how great the holiness of our Elohim! For he knows all things, and there is not anything except he knows it. And he comes into the world that he may save all men, if they will hearken unto his voice. For behold, he suffers the pains of all men, yes, the pains of every living creature, both men, women, and children, who belong to the family of Adam. And he suffers this that the resurrection might pass upon all men, that all might stand before him at the great and judgment day. And he commands all men that they must repent and be washed by immersion in his name, having perfect faith in HaKodesh of Isra'el, or they cannot be saved in the kingdom of Elohim. And if they will not repent, and believe in his name, and be immersed in his name, and endure to the end, they must be damned, for Adonai YHWH, HaKodesh of Isra'el, has spoken it. Wherefore, he has given a Torah; and where there is no Torah given there is no punishment; and where there is no punishment there is no condemnation; and where there is no condemnation the mercies of HaKodesh of Isra'el have claim upon them because of the atonement, for they are delivered by the power of him. For the atonement satisfies the demands of his justice upon all those who have not the Torah given to them, that they are delivered from that awful monster, death, and She'ol, and HaSatan, and the lake of fire and brimstone, which is Endless torment. And they are restored to that Elohim who gave them breath, which is HaKodesh of Isra'el.

8 But woe unto him that has the Torah given, yes, that has all the mitzvot of Elohim like unto us, and that transgresses them and that wastes the days of his probation,[91] for awful is his state.

9 Oh that cunning plan of the Evil One. Oh the vainness, and the frailties, and the foolishness of men! When they are learned they think

---

90 "Endless" is used as a title of deity, as well as an adjective describing torment.
91 Alma 9:6

they are wise, and they hearken not unto the counsel of Elohim, for they set it aside, supposing they know of themselves. Wherefore, their wisdom is foolishness[92] and it profits them not; and they shall perish. But to be learned is good if they hearken unto the counsels of Elohim.

10 But woe unto the rich who are rich as to the things of the world, for because they are rich, they despise the poor, and they persecute the meek, and their hearts are upon their treasures; wherefore, their treasure is their god. And behold, their treasure shall perish with them also. And woe unto the deaf that will not hear, for they shall perish. Woe unto the blind that will not see, for they shall perish also. Woe unto **the uncircumcised of heart**,[93] for a knowledge of their iniquities shall smite them at the last day. Woe unto the liar, for he shall be thrust down to Gehinnom. Woe unto the murderer who deliberately kills, for he shall die. Woe unto them who commit whoredoms, for they shall be thrust down to Gehinnom. Yes, woe unto those that worship idols, for the demon of all demons delights in them. And in short, woe unto all those who die in their sins, for they shall return to Elohim, and behold his face, and remain in their sins.

11 O my beloved brothers, remember the awfulness in transgressing against that holy Elohim, and also the awfulness of yielding to the enticings of that cunning one. Remember, to be carnally minded is death and to be spiritually minded is life Eternal. O my beloved brothers, give ear to my words. Remember the greatness of HaKodesh of Isra'el. Do not say that I have spoken hard things against you, for if you do, you will revile against the truth; for I have spoken the words of your Maker. I know that the words of truth are hard against all uncleanness, but the righteous fear them not, for they love the truth and are not shaken. O then, my beloved brothers, come unto YHWH, HaKodesh. Remember that his paths are righteousness. Behold, the way for man is narrow, but it lies in a straight course before him, and the keeper of the gate is HaKodesh of Isra'el, and he employs no servant there. And there is no other way except it be by the gate, for he cannot be deceived, for Adonai YHWH is his name. And whoever knocks, to him will he open. And the wise, and the learned, and they that are rich — who are puffed up because of their learning, and their wisdom, and their riches — yes, they are they whom he despises. And

---

[92] Isa. 29:14   [93] Lev. 26:40-42; Deut. 10:16; Jer. 4:4; 9:24-26; Ezek. 44:9

except they shall cast these things away, and consider themselves fools before Elohim, and come down in the depths of humility, he will not open unto them; but the things of the wise and the prudent shall be hid from them for ever, yes, that happiness which is prepared for the k'doshim.

12 O my beloved brothers, remember my words. Behold, I take off my garments and I shake them before you. I pray the Elohim of my salvation that he view me with his all-searching eye. Wherefore, you shall know at the last day, when all men shall be judged of their works, that the Elohim of Isra'el did witness that I shook your iniquities from my soul, and that I stand with brightness before him and am rid of your blood.[94] O my beloved brothers, turn away from your sins. Shake off the chains of him that would bind you fast. Come unto that **Elohim** who is **the Rock of** your **salvation**.[95] Prepare your souls for that glorious day when justice shall be administered unto the righteous, even the day of judgment, that you may not shrink with awful fear, that you may not remember your awful guilt in perfectness and be constrained to exclaim, Holy, holy are your judgments, O Adonai YHWH Tzva'ot, but I know my guilt. I transgressed your Torah and my transgressions are mine; and HaSatan has obtained me, that I am a prey to his awful misery. But behold, my brothers, is it expedient that I should awake you to an awful reality of these things? Would I torment your souls if your minds were pure? Would I be plain unto you, according to the plainness of the truth, if you were freed from sin? Behold, if you were holy, I would speak unto you of holiness; but as you are not holy, and you look upon me as a teacher, it must necessarily be expedient that I teach you the consequences of sin.

13 Behold, my soul abhors sin and my heart delights in righteousness; and I will praise the holy name of my Elohim. Come, my brothers, **everyone that thirsts, come you to the waters; and he that has no money, come buy and eat, yes, come buy wine and milk without money and without price. Wherefore, do not spend money for that which is of no worth, nor your labor for that which cannot satisfy. Hearken diligently unto me**, and remember the words which I have spoken, and come unto HaKodesh of Isra'el, and feast upon that which perishes not, neither can be corrupted,

---

94 Acts 18:6 **95** Deut. 32:15; 2 Sam. 22:47; Ps. 89:27 (26); 95:1

and let your soul delight in fatness.⁹⁶ Behold, my beloved brothers, remember the words of your Elohim. Pray unto him continually by day, and give thanks unto his holy name by night. Let your hearts rejoice. And behold, how great the covenants of YHWH, and how great his condescensions unto the children of men. And because of his greatness, and his grace, and mercy, he has promised unto us that our seed shall not utterly be destroyed according to the flesh, but that he would preserve them. And in future generations they shall become a righteous branch unto the house of Isra'el.

¹⁴ And now my brothers, I would speak unto you more, but tomorrow I will declare unto you the remainder of my words. Amen.

7 And now I, Ya'akov, speak unto you again, my beloved brothers, concerning this righteous branch of which I have spoken. For behold, the promises which we have obtained are promises unto us according to the flesh. Wherefore, as it has been shown unto me that many of our children shall perish in the flesh because of unbelief, nevertheless, Elohim will be merciful unto many; and our children shall be restored, that they may come to that which will give them the true knowledge of their Redeemer. Wherefore, as I said unto you, it must necessarily be expedient that Mashiach (for, in the last night, the angel spoke unto me that this should be his name), that he should come among the Judeans, among those who are the more wicked part of the world. And they shall crucify him – for it is required by our Elohim – and there is no other nation on earth that would crucify their Elohim. For should the mighty miracles be worked among other nations, they would repent and know that he is their Elohim. But because of priestcrafts⁹⁷ and iniquities, they at Yerushalayim will stiffen their necks against him, that he be crucified. Wherefore, because of their iniquities, destructions, famines, pestilences, and bloodsheds shall come upon them; and they who shall not be destroyed shall be scattered among all nations.

² But behold, thus says Adonai YHWH: When the day comes that they shall believe in me, that I am Mashiach, then have I covenanted with their fathers that they shall be restored in the flesh upon the earth unto the lands of their inheritance.⁹⁸ And it shall come to pass

---

96 Isa. 44:3; 55:1–2 **97** 2 Nefi 11:17 **98** 3 Nefi 9:9

that they shall be gathered in from their long dispersion, from **the isles of the sea.**[99] and **from the four parts of the earth.**[100] And the nations of the Goyim shall be great in the eyes of me, says Elohim, in carrying them forth to the lands of their inheritance. **Yes, the kings of the Goyim shall be nursing fathers unto them, and their queens shall become nursing mothers.**[101] Wherefore, the promises of YHWH are great unto the Goyim, for he has spoken it, and who can dispute? But behold, this land, says Elohim, shall be a land of your inheritance, and the Goyim shall be blessed upon the land. And this land shall be a land of liberty unto the Goyim, and there shall be no kings upon the land who shall raise up unto the Goyim, and I will fortify this land against all other nations. And he that fights against Tziyon shall perish, says Elohim, for he that raises up a king against me shall perish. For I YHWH, the King of Heaven, will be their king, and I will be a light unto them for ever that hear my words.

3 Wherefore, for this cause, that my covenants may be fulfilled which I have made unto the children of men, that I will do unto them while they are in the flesh, I must necessarily destroy the secret works of darkness, and of murders, and of abominations. Wherefore, he that fights against Tziyon, both Y'hudi and Goy, both bond and free, both male and female, shall perish; for they are they who are the whore of all the earth. For they who are not for me are against me, says our Elohim. For I will fulfill my promises which I have made unto the children of men that I will do unto them while they are in the flesh.

4 Wherefore, my beloved brothers, thus says our Elohim: I will afflict your seed by the hand of the Goyim; nevertheless, I will soften the hearts of the Goyim, that they shall be like unto a father to them. Wherefore, the Goyim shall be blessed and numbered among the house of Isra'el. Wherefore, I will consecrate this land unto your seed, and they who shall be numbered among your seed, for ever, for the land of their inheritance; for it is a choice land, says Elohim unto me, above all other lands.[102] Wherefore, I will have all men that dwell thereon that they shall worship me, says Elohim.

5 And now my beloved brothers, seeing that our merciful Elohim has given us so great knowledge concerning these things, let us

---

99 Isa. 42:10 100 Deut. 30:4; Isa. 11:12; Zech. 2:6 101 Isa. 49:22-23; see also 1 Nefi 6:10 and 1 Nefi 7:3 102 Deut. 33:13-16

remember him, and lay aside our sins, and not hang down our heads; for we are not cast off. Nevertheless, we have been driven out of the land of our inheritance, but we have been led to a better land, for YHWH has made the sea our path, and we are upon **an isle of the sea.** But great are the promises of YHWH unto those who are upon **the isles of the sea.**[103] Wherefore, as it says isles, there must necessarily be more than this, and they are inhabited also by our brothers. For behold, Adonai YHWH has led away from time to time from the house of Isra'el, according to his will and pleasure. And now behold, YHWH remembers all these who have been broken off; wherefore, he remembers us also. Therefore, cheer up your hearts and remember that you are free to act for yourselves, to choose the way of everlasting death or the way of Eternal life. Wherefore, my beloved brothers, reconcile yourselves to the will of Elohim, and not to the will of HaSatan and the flesh. And remember after you are reconciled unto Elohim that it is only in and through the grace of Elohim that you are saved. Wherefore, may Elohim raise you from death by the power of the resurrection, and also from everlasting death by the power of the atonement, that you may be received into the Eternal kingdom of Elohim, that you may praise him through grace divine. Amen.

8 And now Ya'akov spoke many more things to my people at that time. Nevertheless, only these things have I caused to be written, for the things which I have written suffice me.

2 And now I, Nefi, write more of the words of Yesha'yahu, for my soul delights in his words. For I will apply his words unto my people, and I will send them forth unto all my children; for he truly saw my Redeemer, even as I have seen him. And my brother Ya'akov also has seen him as I have seen him. Wherefore, I will send their words forth unto my children to prove unto them that my words are true. Wherefore, by the words of three, Elohim has said, I will confirm my word. Nevertheless, Elohim sends more witnesses and he proves all his words. Behold, my soul delights in proving unto my people the truth of the coming of Mashiach, for, for this end has the Torah of Moshe[104] been given.[105] And all things which have been given of

---

103 Isa. 11:11-12; 42:4; 51:5   **104** 2 Nefi 11:8; Ya'akov 3:2   **105** See footnote to "ends of the Torah" in 2 Nefi 1:6. See also 3 Nefi 7:2.

Elohim from the beginning of the world unto man are the typifying of him. And also my soul delights in the covenants of YHWH which he has made to our fathers; yes, my soul delights in his grace, and his justice, and power, and mercy, in the great and eternal plan of deliverance from death.[106] And my soul delights in proving unto my people that, except Mashiach should come, all men must perish. For if there be no Mashiach, there be no Elohim; and if there be no Elohim, we are not, for there could have been no creation. But there is an Elohim, and he is Mashiach, and he comes[107] in the fulness of his own time.

3 And now I write some of the words of Yesha'yahu, that whoever of my people shall see these words may lift up their hearts and rejoice for all men. Now these are the words, and you may compare them unto you and unto all men.

Yesha'yahu 2 from the Plates of Brass

The word that Yesha'yahu the son of Amotz, saw concerning Y'hudah and Yerushalayim.

4 And it shall come to pass in the last days, when the mountain of YHWH's house shall be established in the top of the mountains, and shall be exalted above the hills, and all the Goyim shall flow unto it. And many people shall go and say, Come you, and let us go up to the mountain of YHWH, to the house of the Elohim of Ya'akov, and he will teach us of his ways and we will walk in his paths. For out of Tziyon shall go forth the Torah, and the word of YHWH from Yerushalayim. And he shall judge among the nations and shall rebuke many people. And they shall beat their swords into plowshares and their spears into pruning hooks; nation shall not lift up sword against nation, neither shall they learn war anymore.

5 O house of Ya'akov, come you and let us walk in the light of YHWH, yes, come, for you have all gone astray, everyone to his wicked ways. Therefore, O YHWH, you have abandoned your people, the house of Ya'akov, because they be replenished from

---

106 Justice [*din*], power [*gevurah*], mercy [*chesed*]: In Kabbalah, these are two of the ten *Sefirot* of the Tree of Life (power and justice being alternate names for the same *Sefira*).
107 Moshiyah 8:2, 6

the east, and hearken unto soothsayers like the P'lishtim, and they please themselves in the children of strangers. Their land also is full of silver and gold, neither is there any end of their treasures. Their land is also full of horses, neither is there any end of their chariots. Their land also is full of idols; they worship the work of their own hands, that which their own fingers have made. And the mean man bows not down, and the great man humbles himself not; therefore, forgive him not.

⁶ O you wicked ones, enter into the rock and hide you in the dust, for the fear of YHWH and the glory of his majesty shall smite you. And it shall come to pass that the lofty looks of man shall be humbled, and the arrogance of men shall be bowed down, and YHWH alone shall be exalted in that day. For the day of YHWH Tzva'ot soon comes upon all nations, yes, upon everyone; yes, upon the proud and lofty, and upon everyone who is lifted up; and he shall be brought low. Yes, and the day of YHWH shall come upon all the cedars of L'vanon, for they are high and lifted up, and upon all the oaks of Bashan, and upon all the high mountains, and upon all the hills, and upon all the nations which are lifted up, and upon every people, and upon every high tower, and upon every fenced wall, and upon all the ships of the sea, and upon all the ships of Tarshish, and upon all the pleasant pictures.[108] And the loftiness of man shall be bowed down, and the arrogance of men shall be made low, and YHWH alone shall be exalted in that day. And the idols he shall utterly abolish. And they shall go into the holes of the rocks and into the caves of the earth, for the fear of YHWH shall come upon them and the glory of his majesty shall smite them when

---

108 In this verse of Isaiah (Isa. 2:16) there is a variant reading between the reading of the Masoretic Text, which has "ships of Tarshish" and the Hebrew text underlying the Greek Septuagint, which reads "ships of the sea." The *Plates of Brass* version contains both readings. This may be an example of what is called in textual criticism "conflation." Conflation occurred when a scribe had two or more manuscripts in front of him that contained conflicting readings, and so he included both of them in his copy. Alternatively, the *Plates of Brass* might express the original reading, and the readings of the Masoretic Text and the Septuagint could represent two separate instances of the scribal error known in textual criticism as "haplography," in which a scribe's eye skips from a word or phrase to a similar or identical word or phrase, inadvertently omitting the text in between. (This is less likely because it would require two scribal errors instead of just one.) In either case, this reading demonstrates that the *Plates of Brass* are an authentic source for the ancient textual tradition of Isaiah.

he arises to shake terribly the earth.¹⁰⁹ In that day, a man shall cast his idols of silver and his idols of gold, which he has made for himself to worship, to the moles and to the bats, to go into the clefts of the rocks and into the tops of the ragged rocks; for the fear of YHWH shall come upon them and the majesty of his glory shall smite them when he arises to shake terribly the earth. Cease you from man, whose breath is in his nostrils, for how is he to be accounted of?

Yesha'yahu 3 from the Plates of Brass

⁷ For behold, the Adon YHWH Tzva'ot does take away from Yerushalayim and from Y'hudah the stay and the staff, the whole staff of bread and the whole stay of water, the mighty man, and the man of war, the judge, and the prophet, and the prudent, and the ancient, the captain of fifty, and the honorable man, and the counselor, and the skillful artificer, and the eloquent orator. And I will give children unto them to be their princes, and babes shall rule over them. And the people shall be oppressed, everyone by another and everyone by his neighbor. The child shall behave himself proudly against the ancient, and the base against the honorable. When a man shall take hold of his brother of the house of his father, and shall say, You have clothing, be you our ruler and let not this ruin come under your hand — in that day shall he swear, saying, I will not be a healer, for in my house there is neither bread nor clothing; make me not a ruler of the people. For Yerushalayim is ruined and Y'hudah is fallen because their tongues and their doings have been against YHWH, to provoke the eyes of his glory. The show of their countenance does witness against them, and does declare their sin to be even as Sodom, and they cannot hide it. Woe unto their souls, for they have rewarded evil unto themselves. Say unto the righteous that it is well with them, for they shall eat the fruit of their doings.

---

109 In this verse of Isaiah (Isa. 2:21), the *Plates of Brass* has "and the majesty of his glory shall smite them, when he arises to shake terribly the earth." The Masoretic Text omits "shall smite them." The Septuagint has "...glory of his might, when he shall arise to smite (θραυσαι) the earth." The Aramaic Peshitta has "...glory of his majesty, when he arises to subdue (למכבש) the earth."

Woe unto the wicked, for they shall perish, for the reward of their hands shall be upon them.

⁸And my people, children are their oppressors and women rule over them. O my people, they who lead you cause you to err and destroy the way of your paths. YHWH stands up to plead, and stands to judge the people. YHWH will enter into judgment with the ancients of his people and the princes thereof; for you have eaten up the vineyard and the spoil of the poor in your houses. What mean you? You beat my people to pieces and grind the faces of the poor, says Adonai YHWH Tzva'ot. Moreover, YHWH says, Because the daughters of Tziyon are haughty, and walk with stretched forth necks and wanton eyes, walking and mincing as they go, and making a tinkling with their feet, therefore YHWH[110] will smite with a scab the crown of the head of the daughters of Tziyon, and YHWH will uncover their secret parts. In that day, YHWH[111] will take away the bravery of tinkling ornaments, and cauls, and round tires like the moon, the chains, and the bracelets, and the mufflers, the bonnets, and the ornaments of their legs, and the headbands, and the tablets, and the earrings, the rings, and nose jewels, the changeable suits of apparel, and the mantles, and the wimples, and the crisping pins, the glasses, and the fine linen, and hoods, and the veils. And it shall all come to pass, instead of sweet smell there shall be stink; and instead of a girdle, a tear; and instead of well-set hair, baldness; and instead of a stomacher, a girding of sackcloth; burning instead of beauty. Your men shall fall by the sword, and your mighty in the war. And her gates shall lament and mourn, and she shall be desolate and shall sit upon the ground.

Yesha'yahu 4 from the Plates of Brass

⁹And in that day, seven women shall take hold of one man, saying, We will eat our own bread and wear our own apparel, only let us be called by your name to take away our reproach.

---

[110] This is one of 134 places where the Massorah (notes transmited by the Masorites in the margins of the Masoretic Text) states that the original reading was "YHWH", but was altered by the scribes to read "Adonai" in the Masoretic Text. [111] Original reading was "YHWH", but was altered by scribes to read "Adonai" in the Masoretic Text. See footnote 110.

¹⁰ In that day shall the Branch of YHWH be beautiful and glorious, the fruit of the earth excellent and becoming to them that are escaped of Isra'el. And it shall come to pass, them that are left in Tziyon and remain in Yerushalayim shall be called holy, everyone that is written among the living in Yerushalayim when YHWH¹¹² shall have washed away the filth of the daughters of Tziyon, and shall have purged the blood of Yerushalayim from the midst thereof by the spirit of judgment and by the spirit of burning. And YHWH will create upon every dwelling place of Mount Tziyon, and upon her assemblies, a cloud and smoke by day, and the shining of a flaming fire by night; for upon all, the glory of Tziyon shall be a defense. And there shall be a sukkah for a shadow in the daytime from the heat, and for a place of refuge, and a covert from storm and from rain.

Yesha'yahu 5 from the Plates of Brass

¹¹ And then will I sing to my well-beloved a song of my beloved, touching his vineyard: My well-beloved has a vineyard in a very fruitful hill. And he fenced it, and gathered out the stones thereof, and planted it with the choicest vine, and built a tower in the midst of it, and also made a winepress therein. And he looked that it should bring forth grapes, and it brought forth wild grapes. And now O inhabitants of Yerushalayim and men of Y'hudah, judge, I pray you, between me and my vineyard. What could have been done more to my vineyard that I have not done in it? Wherefore, when I looked that it should bring forth grapes, it brought forth wild grapes. And now go to, I will tell you what I will do to my vineyard: I will take away the hedge thereof, and it shall be eaten up; and I will break down the wall thereof, and it shall be trampled down; and I will lay it waste. It shall not be pruned nor dug, but there shall come up briers and thorns. I will also command the clouds that they rain no rain upon it. For the vineyard of YHWH Tzva'ot is the house of Isra'el, and the men of Y'hudah his pleasant plant. And he looked for judgment, and behold, oppression; for righteousness, but behold, a cry.

---

112 Original reading was "YHWH", but was altered by scribes to read "Adonai" in the Masoretic Text. See footnote 110.

12 Woe unto them that join house to house till there can be no place that they may be placed alone in the midst of the earth. In my ears says YHWH Tzva'ot, Of a truth many houses shall be desolate, and great and fair cities without inhabitant. Yes, ten acres of vineyard shall yield one bath, and the seed of a homer shall yield an ephah.

13 Woe unto them that rise up early in the morning that they may follow strong drink, that continue until night, and wine inflame them. And the harp and the viol, the tabret and pipe, and wine are in their feasts, but they regard not the work of YHWH, neither consider the operation of his hands. Therefore, my people are gone into captivity because they have no knowledge, and their honorable men are famished, and their multitude dried up with thirst. Therefore, She'ol has enlarged herself, and opened her mouth without measure; and their glory, and their multitude, and their pomp, and he that rejoices shall descend into it. And the mean man shall be brought down, and the mighty man shall be humbled, and the eyes of the lofty shall be humbled; but YHWH Tzva'ot shall be exalted in judgment, and the El HaKodesh shall be sanctified in righteousness. Then shall the lambs feed after their manner, and the waste places of the fat ones shall strangers eat.

14 Woe unto them that draw iniquity with cords of vanity and sin as it were with a cart rope, that say, Let him make speed; hasten his work, that we may see it; and let the counsel of HaKodesh of Isra'el draw near and come, that we may know it.

15 Woe unto them that call evil good and good evil, that put darkness for light and light for darkness, that put bitter for sweet and sweet for bitter.

16 Woe unto the wise[113] in their own eyes and prudent in their own sight.

17 Woe unto the mighty to drink wine, and men of strength to mingle strong drink, which justify the wicked for reward, and take away the righteousness of the righteous from him. Therefore, as the fire devours the stubble and the flame consumes the chaff, their root shall be rottenness and their

---

113 Isa. 5:21; Prov. 3:7; 2 Nefi 8:16

blossom shall go up as dust, because they have cast away the Torah of YHWH Tzva'ot, and despised the word of HaKodesh of Isra'el. Therefore is the anger of YHWH kindled against his people, and he has stretched forth his hand against them and has smitten them. And the hills did tremble, and their carcasses were torn in the midst of the streets. For all this his anger is not turned away, but his hand stretched out still.

18 And he will lift up an ensign to the nations from far, and will hiss unto them from the end of the earth. And behold, they shall come with speed, swiftly; none shall be weary nor stumble among them; none shall slumber nor sleep; neither shall the girdle of their loins be loosed, nor the latchet of their shoes be broken; whose arrows shall be sharp, and all their bows bent, and their horses' hoofs shall be counted like flint, and their wheels like a whirlwind, their roaring like a lion. They shall roar like young lions; yes, they shall roar, and lay hold of the prey, and shall carry away safe, and none shall deliver. And in that day, they shall roar against them like the roaring of the sea; and if they look unto the land, behold, darkness and sorrow, and the light is darkened in the heavens thereof.

Yesha'yahu 6 from the Plates of Brass

9 In the year that king 'Uziyahu died, I saw also YHWH[114] sitting upon a throne, high and lifted up, and his train filled the Temple. Above it stood the s'rafim. Each one had six wings: with two he covered his face, and with two he covered his feet, and with two he did fly. And one cried unto another, and said, Holy, holy, holy is YHWH Tzva'ot! The whole earth is full of his glory! And the posts of the door moved at the voice of him that cried, and the house was filled with smoke.

2 Then said I, Woe is unto me, for I am undone because I am a man of unclean lips, and I dwell in the midst of a people of unclean lips; for my eyes have seen the King, YHWH Tzva'ot. Then flew one of the s'rafim unto me, having a live coal in his hand, which he had taken with the tongs from off the altar. And he

---

114 Original reading was "YHWH", but was altered by scribes to read "Adonai" in the Masoretic Text. See footnote 110.

laid upon my mouth and said, Lo, this has touched your lips, and your iniquity is taken away, and your sin purged. Also, I heard the voice of YHWH,[115] saying, Whom shall I send? And who will go for us? Then I said, Here am I; send me. And he said, Go and tell this people, Hear you indeed — but they understand not; and, See you indeed — but they perceived not. Make the heart of this people fat, and make their ears heavy, and shut their eyes, lest they see with their eyes, and hear with their ears, and understand with their heart, and be converted, and be healed. Then said I, YHWH,[116] how long? And he said, Until the cities be wasted without inhabitant, and the houses without man, and the land be utterly desolate, and YHWH have removed men far away; for there shall be a great forsaking in the midst of the land. But yet in it there shall be a tenth, and they shall return and shall be eaten as a teil tree and as an oak, whose substance is in them when they cast their leaves, so the holy seed shall be the substance thereof.

Yesha'yahu 7 from the Plates of Brass

3 And it came to pass in the days of Achaz the son of Yotam, the son of 'Uziyahu king of Y'hudah, that Retzin king of Syria, and Pekach the son of Remalyah king of Isra'el, went up towards Yerushalayim to war against it, but could not prevail against it. And it was told the house of David, saying, Syria is allied with Efrayim. And his heart was moved, and the heart of his people, as the trees of the wood are moved with the wind.

4 Then said YHWH unto Yesha'yahu, Go forth now to meet Achaz — thou, and Shear-jashub your son — at the end of the conduit of the upper pool in the highway of the fuller's field. And say unto him, Take heed and be quiet; fear not, neither be faint-hearted for the two tails of these smoking firebrands, for the fierce anger of Retzin with Syria, and of the son of Remalyah, because Syria, Efrayim, and the son of Remalyah have taken evil counsel against you, saying, Let us go up against Y'hudah and vex it, and let us make a breach therein for us, and set a king in

---

115 Original reading was "YHWH", but was altered by scribes to read "Adonai" in the Masoretic Text. See footnote 110.   116 Original reading was "YHWH", but was altered by scribes to read "Adonai" in the Masoretic Text. See footnote 110.

the midst of it, yes, the son of Tav'el. Thus says Adonai YHWH: It shall not stand, neither shall it come to pass. For the head of Syria is Damascus, and the head of Damascus, Retzin. And within threescore and five years shall Efrayim be broken, that it be not a people. And the head of Efrayim is Samaria, and the head of Samaria is Remalyah's son. If you will not believe, surely you shall not be strengthened.

5 Moreover, YHWH spoke again unto Achaz, saying, Ask you a sign of YHWH your Elohim; ask either in the depths or in the heights above. But Achaz said, I will not ask, neither will I tempt YHWH. And he said, Hear you now, O house of David: Is it a small thing for you to weary men, but will you weary my Elohim also? Therefore, YHWH[117] himself shall give you a sign: behold, a virgin[118] shall conceive, and shall bear a son, and shall call his name Immanuel. Butter and honey shall he eat, that he may know to refuse the evil and to choose the good. For before the child shall know to refuse the evil and choose the good, the land that you abhor shall be abandoned of both her kings. YHWH shall bring upon you, and upon your people, and upon your father's house — days that have not come from the day that Efrayim departed from Y'hudah — the king of Assyria. And it shall come to pass in that day that YHWH shall hiss for the fly that is in the uttermost part of Egypt, and for the bee that is in the land of Assyria. And they shall come and shall rest all of them in the desolate valleys, and in the holes of the rocks, and upon all thorns, and upon all bushes. In the same day shall YHWH[119] shave with a razor that is hired — by them beyond the river, by the king of Assyria — the head, and the hair of the feet; and it shall also consume the beard.

6 And it shall come to pass that in that day, a man shall nourish a young cow and two sheep. And it shall come to pass, for the abundance of milk they shall give, he shall eat butter; for butter and honey shall everyone eat that is left in the land. And it shall come to pass in that day, every place shall be, where there were

---

117 Original reading was "YHWH", but was altered by scribes to read "Adonai" in the Masoretic Text. See footnote 110.   118 1 Nefi 3:8-9; Alma 5:3   119 Original reading was "YHWH", but was altered by scribes to read "Adonai" in the Masoretic Text. See footnote 110.

a thousand vines at a thousand silverlings, which shall be for briers and thorns. With arrows and with bows shall men come there because all the land shall become briers and thorns. And all hills that shall be dug with the mattock, there shall not come there the fear of briers and thorns, but it shall be for the sending forth of oxen, and the treading of lesser cattle.

Yesha'yahu 8 from the Plates of Brass

7 Moreover, the word of YHWH said unto me, Take you a great roll and write in it with a man's pen concerning Maher-shalal-hash-baz. And I took unto me faithful witnesses to record — Uriyah the kohen and Z'kharyahu the son of Y'verekhyahu. And I went unto the prophetess, and she conceived and bore a son. Then said YHWH to me, Call his name Maher-shalal-hash-baz. For behold, the child shall not have knowledge to cry, My father and my mother — before the riches of Damascus and the spoil of Samaria shall be taken away before the king of Assyria.

8 YHWH spoke also unto me again, saying, Forasmuch as this people refuse the waters of Shilo'ach that go softly, and rejoice in Retzin and Remalyah's son, now therefore behold, YHWH[120] brings up upon them the waters of the river, strong and many, even the king of Assyria and all his glory. And he shall come up over all his channels, and go over all his banks, and he shall pass through Y'hudah. He shall overflow and go over, he shall reach even to the neck. And the stretching out of his wings shall fill the breadth of your land, O Immanuel. Associate yourselves, O you people, and you shall be broken in pieces. And give ear, all you of far countries: Gird yourselves, and you shall be broken in pieces; gird yourselves, and you shall be broken in pieces. Take counsel together, and it shall come to nothing; speak the word, and it shall not stand; for El is with us.

9 For YHWH spoke thus to me with a strong hand, and instructed me that I should not walk in the way of this people, saying, Say you not, A confederacy — to all to whom this people

---

120 Original reading was "YHWH", but was altered by scribes to read "Adonai" in the Masoretic Text. See footnote 110.

shall say, A confederacy; neither fear you their fear nor be afraid. Sanctify YHWH Tzva'ot himself, and let him be your fear, and let him be your dread, and he shall be for a sanctuary; but for a stone of stumbling and for a rock of offense to both the houses of Isra'el, for a gin and a snare to the inhabitants of Yerushalayim. And many among them shall stumble and fall, and be broken, and be snared, and be taken.

10 Bind up the testimony, seal the Torah among my students. And I will wait upon YHWH that hides his face from the house of Ya'akov, and I will look for him. Behold, I and the children whom YHWH has given me are for signs and for wonders in Isra'el from YHWH Tzva'ot which dwells in Mount Tziyon. And when they shall say unto you, Seek unto them that have familiar spirits, and unto wizards that peep and mutter — should not a people seek unto their Elohim? For the living to hear from the dead — to the Torah and to the testimony? And if they speak not according to this word, it is because there is no light in them. And they shall pass through it hardly distressed and hungry; and it shall come to pass that when they shall be hungry, they shall fret themselves, and curse their king and their Elohim, and look upward. And they shall look unto the earth and behold trouble and darkness, dimness of anguish, and shall be driven to darkness.

Yesha'yahu 9 from the Plates of Brass

11 Nevertheless, the dimness shall not be such as was in her vexation, when at the first he lightly afflicted the land of Z'vulun, and the land of Naftali, and afterward did more grievously afflict by the way of the Red Sea beyond Yarden, in Galil of the Goyim. The people that walked in darkness have seen a great light; they that dwell in the land of the shadow of death, upon them has the light shined. You have multiplied the nation and increased the joy; they joy before you according to the joy in harvest, and as men rejoice when they divide the spoil. For you have broken the yoke of his burden, and the staff of his shoulder, the rod of his oppressor, for every battle of the warrior with confused noise and garments rolled in blood; but this shall be

with burning and fuel of fire. For unto us a child is born, unto us a son is given, and the government shall be upon his shoulder. And his name shall be called Wonderful Counselor, the Mighty El, the Everlasting Father, the Prince of Shalom. Of the increase of government and shalom there is no end, upon the throne of David and upon his kingdom, to order it and to strengthen it with judgment and with justice from henceforth even for ever. The zeal of YHWH Tzva'ot will perform this.

12 YHWH[121] sent his word unto Ya'akov, and it has lighted upon Isra'el. And all the people shall know, even Efrayim and the inhabitants of Samaria, that say in the pride and the stoutness of heart, The bricks are fallen down, but we will build with cut stones; the sycamores are cut down, but we will change them into cedars. Therefore, YHWH shall set up the adversaries of Retzin against him and join his enemies together — the Syrians before and the P'lishtim behind — and they shall devour Isra'el with open mouth. For all this his anger is not turned away, but his hand stretched out still.

13 For the people turn not unto him that smites them, neither do they seek YHWH Tzva'ot. Therefore will YHWH cut off from Isra'el head and tail, branch and rush, in one day. The ancient, he is the head; and the prophet that teaches lies, he is the tail. For the leaders of this people cause them to err,[122] and they that are led of them are destroyed. Therefore, YHWH[123] shall have no joy in their young men, neither shall have mercy on their fatherless and widows; for every one of them is a hypocrite and an evildoer, and every mouth speaks folly. For all this his anger is not turned away, but his hand stretched out still.

14 For wickedness burns as the fire; it shall devour the briers and thorns, and shall kindle in the thickets of the forests, and they shall mount up like the lifting up of smoke. Through the wrath of YHWH Tzva'ot is the land darkened, and the people shall be as the fuel of the fire; no man shall spare his brother. And he shall snatch on the right hand and be hungry, and he shall eat on the left hand and they shall not be satisfied. They shall eat, every

---

121 Original reading was "YHWH", but was altered by scribes to read "Adonai" in the Masoretic Text. See footnote 110.   122 2 Nefi 12:2   123 Original reading was "YHWH", but was altered by scribes to read "Adonai" in the Masoretic Text. See footnote 110.

man, the flesh of his own arm: M'nasheh, Efrayim; and Efrayim, M'nasheh; they together shall be against Y'hudah. For all this his anger is not turned away, but his hand stretched out still.

Yesha'yahu 10 from the Plates of Brass

15 Woe unto them that decree unrighteous decrees and that write grievousness which they have prescribed, to turn aside the needy from judgment and to take away the right from the poor of my people, that widows may be their prey and that they may rob the fatherless. And what will you do in the day of visitation, and in the desolation which shall come from far? To whom will you flee for help? And where will you leave your glory? Without me they shall bow down under the prisoners, and they shall fall under the slain. For all this his anger is not turned away, but his hand stretched out still.

16 O Assyrian, the rod of my anger, and the staff in their hand is their indignation. I will send him against a hypocritical nation, and against the people of my wrath will I give him a charge to take the spoil, and to take the prey, and to tread them down like the mire of the streets. Howbeit he means not so, neither does his heart think so, but in his heart it is to destroy and cut off nations not a few. For he says, Are not my princes altogether kings? Is not Kalno as Kark'mish? Is not Hamat as Arpad? Is not Samaria as Damascus? As my hand has founded the kingdoms of the idols, and whose graven images did excel them of Yerushalayim and of Samaria, shall I not, as I have done unto Samaria and her idols, so do to Yerushalayim and to her idols?

17 Wherefore, it shall come to pass that when YHWH[124] has performed his whole work upon Mount Tziyon and upon Yerushalayim, I will punish the fruit of the stout heart of the king of Assyria, and the glory of his high looks. For he says, By the strength of my hand and by my wisdom I have done these things, for I am prudent. And I have removed the borders of the people, and have robbed their treasures, and I have put down the inhabitants like a valiant man. And my hand has found as

---

[124] Original reading was "YHWH", but was altered by scribes to read "Adonai" in the Masoretic Text. See footnote 110.

a nest the riches of the people, and as one gathers eggs that are left have I gathered all the earth; and there was none that moved the wing, or opened the mouth, or peeped. Shall the ax boast itself against him that cuts therewith? Shall the saw magnify itself against him that shakes it? As if the rod should shake itself against them that lift it up, or as if the staff should lift up itself as if it were no wood. Therefore shall the Adon YHWH Tzva'ot, send among his fat ones leanness; and under his glory he shall kindle a burning like the burning of a fire. And the Light of Isra'el shall be for a fire, and his Holy One for a flame, and shall burn and shall devour his thorns and his briers in one day, and shall consume the glory of his forest and of his fruitful field, both soul and body. And they shall be as when a standard-bearer faints. And the rest of the trees of his forest shall be few, that a child may write them.

18 And it shall come to pass in that day that the remnant of Isra'el, and such as are escaped of the house of Ya'akov, shall no more again stay upon him that smote them, but shall stay upon YHWH, HaKodesh of Isra'el, in truth. The remnant shall return, yes, even the remnant of Ya'akov, unto the mighty El. For though your people Isra'el be as the sand of the sea, yet a remnant of them shall return. The consumption decreed shall overflow with righteousness; for Adonai YHWH Tzva'ot shall make a consumption, even determined, in all the land.

19 Therefore, thus says Adonai YHWH Tzva'ot: O my people that dwell in Tziyon, be not afraid of the Assyrian (he shall strike you with a rod, and shall lift up his staff against you, after the manner of Egypt), for yet a very little while, and the indignation shall cease and my anger in their destruction. And YHWH Tzva'ot shall stir up a scourge for him, according to the slaughter of Midian at the rock of 'Orev; and as his rod was upon the sea, so shall he lift it up after the manner of Egypt. And it shall come to pass in that day, that his burden shall be taken away from off your shoulder, and his yoke from off your neck, and the yoke shall be destroyed because of the anointing.

20 He is come to Aiath, he is passed to Migron; at Michmash, he has laid up his carriages. They are gone over the passage, they have taken up their lodging at Geba. Ramath is afraid,

Giv'at-Sh'ul is fled. Lift up the voice, O daughter of Gallim; cause it to be heard unto Laish, O poor Anathoth. Madmenah is removed, the inhabitants of Gebim gather themselves to flee. As yet shall he remain at Nob that day; he shall shake his hand against the mount of the daughter of Tziyon, the hill of Yerushalayim. Behold, the Adon YHWH Tzva'ot shall lop the bough with terror, and the high ones of stature shall be cut down, and the haughty shall be humbled. And he shall cut down the thickets of the forests with iron, and L'vanon shall fall by a mighty one.

Yesha'yahu 11 from the Plates of Brass

21 And there shall come forth a rod out of the stem of Yishai, and a branch shall grow out of his roots. And the spirit of YHWH shall rest upon him — the spirit of wisdom and understanding, the spirit of counsel and might, the spirit of knowledge and of the fear of YHWH — and shall make him of quick understanding in the fear of YHWH. And he shall not judge after the sight of his eyes, neither reprove after the hearing of his ears, but with righteousness shall he judge the poor, and reprove with equity for the meek of the earth. And he shall smite the earth with the rod of his mouth, and with the breath of his lips shall he slay the wicked. And righteousness shall be the girdle of his loins, and faithfulness the girdle of his reins. The wolf also shall dwell with the lamb, and the leopard shall lie down with the kid; and the calf, and the young lion, and the fatling together, and a little child shall lead them. And the cow and the bear shall feed, their young ones shall lie down together, and the lion shall eat straw like the ox. And the sucking child shall play on the hole of the asp, and the weaned child shall put his hand on the cockatrice's den. They shall not hurt nor destroy in all my holy mountain, for the earth shall be full of the knowledge of YHWH as the waters cover the sea.

22 And in that day, there shall be a root of Yishai which shall stand for an ensign of the people; to it shall the Goyim seek,

---

125 Original reading was "YHWH", but was altered by scribes to read "Adonai" in the Masoretic Text. See footnote 110.

and his rest shall be glorious. And it shall come to pass in that day that YHWH[125] shall set his hand again the second time[126] to recover the remnant of his people which shall be left from Assyria, and from Egypt, and from Patros, and from Cush, and from Elam, and from Shin'ar, and from Hamat, and from the islands of the sea. And he shall set up an ensign for the nations, and shall assemble the outcasts of Isra'el, and gather together[127] the dispersed of Y'hudah, from the four corners of the earth. The envy of Efrayim also shall depart, and the adversaries of Y'hudah shall be cut off. Efrayim shall not envy Y'hudah and Y'hudah shall not vex Efrayim. But they shall fly upon the shoulders of the P'lishtim toward the west, they shall spoil them of the east together, they shall lay their hand upon Edom and Moab, and the children of Ammon shall obey them. And YHWH shall utterly destroy the tongue of the Egyptian sea, and with his mighty wind he shall shake his hand over the river, and shall strike it in the seven streams, and make men go over dry-shod. And there shall be a highway for the remnant of his people which shall be left from Assyria, like as it was to Isra'el in the day that he came up out of the land of Egypt.

Yesha'yahu 12 from the Plates of Brass

23 And in that day, you shall say, O YHWH, I will praise you; though you were angry with me, your anger is turned away and you comforted me. Behold, El is my salvation. I will trust and not be afraid, for Yah YHWH is my strength and my song; he also is become my salvation. Therefore, with joy shall you draw water out of the wells of salvation. And in that day shall you say, Praise YHWH, call upon his name, declare his doings among the people, make mention that his name is exalted. Sing unto YHWH, for he has done excellent things; this is known in all the earth. Cry out and shout, you inhabitant of Tziyon, for great is HaKodesh of Isra'el in the midst of you.

Yesha'yahu 13 from the Plates of Brass

The burden of Babylon, which Yesha'yahu the son of Amotz did see.

---

126 2 Nefi 11:6   **127** 1 Nefi 7:3

10 Lift you up a banner upon the high mountain, exalt the voice unto them, shake the hand, that they may go into the gates of the nobles. I have commanded my sanctified ones, I have also called my mighty ones, for my anger is not upon them that rejoice in my highness.[128] The noise of the multitude in the mountains, like as of a great people, a tumultuous noise of the kingdoms of nations gathered together; YHWH Tzva'ot musters the host of the battle. They come from a far country, from the end of heaven — yes, YHWH and the weapons of his indignation — to destroy the whole land.

2 Howl you, for the day of YHWH is at hand; it shall come as a destruction from Shaddai. Therefore shall all hands be faint, every man's heart shall melt, and they shall be afraid. Pangs and sorrows shall take hold of them, they shall be amazed one at another, their faces shall be as flames. Behold, the day of YHWH comes, cruel both with wrath and fierce anger, to lay the land desolate; and he shall destroy the sinners thereof out of it. For the stars of heaven and the constellations thereof shall not give their light; the sun shall be darkened in his going forth, and the moon shall not cause her light to shine. And I will punish the world for evil, and the wicked for their iniquity. I will cause the arrogance of the proud to cease, and will lay down the arrogance of the terrible. I will make a man more precious than fine gold, even a man than the golden wedge of Ofir. Therefore, I will shake the heavens, and the earth shall remove out of her place, in the wrath of YHWH Tzva'ot and in the day of his fierce anger. And it shall be as the chased roe, and as a sheep that no man takes up; they shall every man turn to his own people and flee everyone into his own land. Everyone that is proud shall be thrust through, yes, and everyone that is joined to the wicked shall fall by the sword. Their children also shall be dashed to pieces before their eyes, their houses shall be spoiled, and their wives ravished. Behold, I will stir up the Medes against them, which shall not regard silver and gold, nor they shall not delight

---

128 The *Plates of Brass* reading of "my anger is not upon them that rejoice in my highness" must have read לא אפי על עליזי גאותי. The Masoretic Text appears to reflect a scribal error with the similar-appearing text "mine anger, [even] them that rejoice in my highness" לאפי עליזי גאותי.

in it. Their bows shall also dash the young men to pieces, and they shall have no pity on the fruit of the womb; their eyes shall not spare children.

³And Babylon, the glory of kingdoms, the beauty of the Chaldees' excellency, shall be as when Elohim overthrew Sodom and Gomorrah. It shall never be inhabited, neither shall it be dwelt in from generation to generation, neither shall the Arabian pitch tent there, neither shall the shepherds make their fold there. But wild beasts of the desert shall lie there, and their houses shall be full of doleful creatures, and owls shall dwell there, and satyrs shall dance there. And the wild beasts of the islands shall cry in their desolate houses, and dragons in their pleasant palaces. And her time is near to come, and her day shall not be prolonged, for I will destroy her speedily; yes, for I will be merciful unto my people, but the wicked shall perish.

Yesha'yahu 14 from the Plates of Brass

⁴For YHWH will have mercy on Ya'akov, and will yet choose Isra'el, and set them in their own land, and the strangers shall be joined with them, and they shall cling to the house of Ya'akov. And the people shall take them and bring them to their place, yes, from far unto the ends of the earth, and they shall return to their lands of promise. And the house of Isra'el shall possess them, and the land of YHWH shall be for servants and handmaids; and they shall take them captives unto whom they were captives, and they shall rule over their oppressors. And it shall come to pass in that day that YHWH shall give you rest from your sorrow, and from your fear, and from the hard bondage in which you were made to serve.

⁵And it shall come to pass in that day, that you shall take up this proverb against the king of Babylon, and say, How has the oppressor ceased, the golden city ceased! YHWH has broken the staff of the wicked, the scepters of the rulers. He who smote the people in wrath with a continual stroke, he that ruled the nations in anger, is persecuted, and none hinders. The whole earth is at rest and is quiet; they break forth into singing. Yes, the fir trees rejoice at you, and also the cedars of L'vanon, saying,

Since you are laid down, no feller is come up against us. She'ol from beneath is moved for you to meet you at your coming. It stirs up the dead for you, even all the chief ones of the earth; it has raised up from their thrones all the kings of the nations. All they shall speak and say unto you, Are you also become weak as we? Are you become like unto us? Your pomp is brought down to the grave, the noise of your viols is not heard,[129] the worm is spread under you, and the worms cover you.

6 How are you fallen[130] from Heaven, O Hellel, son of the morning! Are you cut down to the ground, which did weaken the nations? For you have said in your heart, I will ascend into Heaven; I will exalt my throne above the stars of El; I will sit also upon the mount of the congregation, in the sides of the north; I will ascend above the heights of the clouds; I will be like HaElyon. Yet you shall be brought down to She'ol, to the sides of the pit. They that see you shall narrowly look upon you, and shall consider you, and shall say, Is this the man that made the earth to tremble, that did shake kingdoms, and made the world as a wilderness, and destroyed the cities thereof, and opened not the house of his prisoners?

7 All the kings of the nations, yes, all of them lie in glory, every one of them in his own house. But you are cast out of your grave like an abominable branch, and the remnant of those that are slain, thrust through with a sword, that go down to the stones of the pit, as a carcass trampled under feet. You shall not be joined with them in burial because you have destroyed your land and slain your people; the seed of evildoers shall never be renowned. Prepare slaughter for his children for the iniquities of their fathers, that they do not rise, nor possess the land, nor fill the face of the world with cities. For I will rise up against them, says YHWH Tzva'ot, and cut off from Babylon the name, and remnant, and son, and nephew, says YHWH. I will also make it a possession for the bittern and pools of water; and I will sweep it with the besom of destruction, says YHWH Tzva'ot.

---

129 The *Plates of Brass* have "the noise of your viols is not heard" whereas the Masoretic Text omits "is not heard". The Aramaic Peshitta text agrees closely with the Brass Plates with the reading "[the noise of] your viols is dead" (ומית כנרך).   130 2 Nefi 1:9

⁸YHWH Tzva'ot has sworn, saying, Surely as I have thought, so shall it come to pass; and as I have purposed, so shall it stand, that I will break the Assyrian in my land, and upon my mountains tread him underfoot. Then shall his yoke depart from off them, and his burden depart from off their shoulders. This is the purpose that is purposed upon the whole earth, and this is the hand that is stretched out upon all nations. For YHWH Tzva'ot has purposed, and who shall disannul? And his hand stretched out, and who shall turn it back?

In the year that king Achaz died was this burden.

⁹ Rejoice not you, whole P'leshet, because the rod of him that smote you is broken; for out of the serpent's root shall come forth a cockatrice, and his fruit shall be a fiery flying serpent. And the first born of the poor shall feed, and the needy shall lie down in safety. And I will kill your root with famine, and he shall slay your remnant. Howl, O gate; cry, O city; you whole P'leshet are dissolved, for there shall come from the north a smoke, and none shall be alone in his appointed times. What shall then answer the messengers of the nations? That YHWH has founded Tziyon, and the poor of his people shall trust in it.

11

Now I, Nefi, do speak somewhat concerning the words which I have written, which have been spoken by the mouth of Yesha'yahu. For behold, Yesha'yahu spoke many things which were hard for many of my people to understand, for they know not concerning the manner of prophesying among the Y'hudim; for I, Nefi, have not taught them many things concerning the manner of the Y'hudim, for their works were works of darkness, and their doings were doings of abominations.[131] Wherefore I write unto my people, unto all those that shall receive hereafter these things which I write, that they may know the judgments of Elohim, that they come upon all nations according to the word which he has spoken.

---

[131] At the time in question, Nefi's people "know not concerning the manner of prophesying among the Y'hudim." This is why Nefi says "I, Nefi, have not taught my children after the manner of the Y'hudim" (2 Nefi 11:2). By contrast, Nefi says, "[T]he Y'hudim do understand the things of the prophets. And there is no other people that understand the things which were spoken unto the Y'hudim like unto them, except it be that they are taught after the manner of the things of the Y'hudim" (2 Nefi 11:1-2).

Wherefore hearken, O my people which are of the house of Isra'el, and give ear unto my words, for because the words of Yesha'yahu are not plain unto you, nevertheless, they are plain unto all those that are filled with the spirit of prophecy. But I give unto you a prophecy according to the spirit which is in me. Wherefore, I shall prophesy according to the plainness which has been with me from the time that I came out from Yerushalayim with my father. For behold, my soul delights in plainness unto my people, that they may learn; yes, and my soul delights in the words of Yesha'yahu.

2 For I came out from Yerushalayim, and my eyes have beheld the things of the Y'hudim, and I know that the Y'hudim do understand the things of the prophets. And there is no other people that understand the things which were spoken unto the Y'hudim like unto them, except it be that they are taught after the manner of the things of the Y'hudim. But behold, I, Nefi, have not taught my children after the manner of the Y'hudim. But behold, I, of myself, have dwelt at Yerushalayim; wherefore, I know concerning the regions round about. And I have made mention unto my children concerning the judgments of Elohim which have come to pass among the Y'hudim, unto my children, according to all that which Yesha'yahu has spoken, and I do not write them.

3 But behold, I proceed with my own prophecy according to my plainness, in the which I know that no man can err. Nevertheless, in the days that the prophecies of Yesha'yahu shall be fulfilled, men shall know of a surety at the times when they shall come to pass; wherefore, they are of worth unto the children of men. And he that supposes that they are not, unto them will I speak particularly and confine the words unto my own people. For I know that they shall be of great worth unto them in the last days, for in that day shall they understand them; wherefore, for their good have I written them.

4 And as one generation has been destroyed among the Y'hudim because of iniquity, even so have they been destroyed from generation to generation according to their iniquities. And never have any of them been destroyed except it were foretold them by the prophets of YHWH. Wherefore, it has been told[132] them concerning the destruction which should come upon them immediately after my

---

132 Jer. 26:17-18; 1 Nefi 1:5

father left Yerushalayim; nevertheless, they hardened their hearts. And according to my prophecy they have been destroyed, except it be those which are carried away captive into Babylon. And now this I speak because of the spirit which is in me. And even though they have been carried away, they shall return again and possess the land of Yerushalayim; wherefore, they shall be restored again to the lands of their inheritance. But behold, they shall have wars and rumors of wars.

5 And when the day comes that the Only Begotten of the Father — yes, even the Father of Heaven and of earth — shall manifest[133] himself unto them in the flesh, behold, they will reject him because of their iniquities, and the hardness of their hearts, and the stiffness of their necks. Behold, they will crucify him. And after he is laid in a sepulcher for the space of three days, he shall rise from the dead with **healing in his wings**,[134] and all those who shall believe on his name shall be saved in the kingdom of Elohim. Wherefore, my soul delights to prophesy concerning him, for I have seen his day and my heart does magnify his holy name. And behold, it shall come to pass that after the Mashiach has risen from the dead, and has manifested himself unto his people, unto as many as will believe on his name, behold, Yerushalayim shall be destroyed again; for woe unto them that fight against Elohim and the people of his assembly. Wherefore, the Y'hudim shall be scattered among all nations, yes, and also Babylon shall be destroyed; wherefore, the Y'hudim **shall be scattered by other nations.**[135]

6 And after they have been scattered, and Adonai YHWH has scourged them by other nations for the space of many generations, yes, even down from generation to generation until they shall be persuaded to believe in Mashiach, the Son of Elohim, and the atonement which is infinite for all mankind, and when that day shall come that they shall believe in Mashiach, and worship the Father in

---

133 Moshiyah 8:5-6   **134** Mal. 3:19-20 (4:1-2 KJV) is never cited as a Mashiach prophecy in the New Testament. However, it is used as a Mashiach prophecy in the Midrash Rabbah: "Moses asked: 'Shall they remain in pledge for ever?' God replied: 'No, only until the sun appears' that is, till the coming of the Messiah; for it says, But unto you that fear My name shall the sun of righteousness arise with healing in its wings (Mal. 3:20)" (Midrash Rabbah on Ex. 31:10). The Hebrew word for "wing" in this verse of Malachi is *kanaf*, a word which means "wing" or "corner." This is the Hebrew word for "corner" in Num. 15:37-41, where we are told to put the *tzitzit* on the "corners" of our garments. In Matt. 9:20-22; 14:36; Mark 3:10; Luke 6:19, persons were healed after touching Yeshua's *tzitzit* because there was healing in his "wings." It appears the same thing would happen with the resurrected Messiah among the Nefites. See also 2 Nefi 11:10-11 and 3 Nefi 11:5.   **135** Neh. 1:8

his name, with pure hearts and clean hands, and look not forward anymore for another mashiach — and then, at that time, the day will come that it must be necessary that they should believe these things — YHWH[136] **will set his hand again the second time**[137] to restore his people from their lost and fallen state. **Wherefore, he will proceed to do a marvelous work and a wonder among**[138] the children of men. Wherefore, he shall bring forth his words unto them, which words shall judge them at the last day. For they shall be given them for the purpose of convincing them of the true Mashiach, who was rejected by them, and unto the convincing of them that they need not look forward anymore for a Mashiach to come; for there should not any come, except it should be a false mashiach which should deceive the people, for there is only one Mashiach spoken of by the prophets, and that Mashiach is he which **should be rejected**[139] of the Y'hudim. For according to the words of the prophets, the Mashiach comes in six hundred years from the time that my father left Yerushalayim.[140] And according to the words of the prophets, and also the word of the angel of Elohim, his name shall be Yeshua HaMashiach, the Son of Elohim.

7 And now my brothers, I have spoken plainly that you cannot err. And as Adonai YHWH lives that brought Isra'el up out of the land of Egypt, and gave unto Moshe power that he should heal the nations after they had been bitten by the poisonous serpents, if they would cast their eyes unto the serpent which he did raise up before them, and also gave him power that he should strike the rock and the water should come forth, yes, behold, I say unto you that as these things are true, and as Adonai YHWH lives, there is no other name given under Heaven, except it be this Yeshua HaMashiach of which I have spoken, by which man can be saved. Wherefore, for this cause has Adonai YHWH promised unto me that these things which I write shall be kept, and preserved, and handed down unto my seed from generation to generation — that the promise may be fulfilled unto Yosef that his seed should never perish as long as the earth should stand. Wherefore, these things shall go from generation to generation as long as the earth shall stand, and they shall go according to the will

---

136 Original reading was "YHWH", but was altered by scribes to read "Adonai" in the Masoretic Text. See footnote 110.   **137** Isa. 11:11-12   **138** Isa. 29:14   **139** Isa. 53:3   **140** 3 Nefi 1:9

and pleasure of Elohim. And the nations which shall possess them shall be judged of them according to the words which are written.

8 For we labor diligently to write, to persuade our children and also our brothers to believe in Mashiach, and to be reconciled to Elohim, for we know that it is by grace that we are saved after all that we can do. And even though we believe in Mashiach, we keep the Torah of Moshe, and look forward with steadfastness unto Mashiach until the Torah shall be fulfilled;[141] for, for this end was the Torah given. Wherefore, the Torah has become dead unto us, and we are made alive in Mashiach because of our faith; yet we keep the Torah because of the mitzvot. And we talk of Mashiach, we rejoice in Mashiach, we preach of Mashiach, we prophesy of Mashiach, and we write according to our prophecies, that our children may know to what source they may look for a remission of their sins. Wherefore, we speak concerning the Torah, that our children may know the deadness of the Torah;[142] and they, by knowing the deadness of the Torah, may look forward unto that life which is in Mashiach, and know for what end the Torah was given; and after the Torah is fulfilled in Mashiach, that they need not harden their hearts against him when the Torah ought to be done away.[143]

9 And now behold, my people, you are a stiffnecked people; wherefore, I have spoken plainly unto you, that you cannot misunderstand. And the words which I have spoken shall stand as a

---

141 What does it mean to fulfill the Torah? David Bivin and Roy Blizzard wrote: "'Destroy' and 'fulfill' are technical terms used in rabbinic argumentation. When a rabbi felt that his colleague had misinterpreted a passage of Scripture, he would say, 'You are destroying the Law!' Needless to say, in most cases his colleague strongly disagreed. What was 'destroying the Law' for one rabbi, was 'fulfilling the Law' (correctly interpreting Scripture) for another" (Bivin, D. and Blizzard, R. (1983) *Understanding the Difficult Words of Jesus*. Arcadia, CA: Makor Publishing, p. 154). Yosef ben Yosef understood "fulfilled the law" to mean that Mashiach "magnified" the Torah and made it "honorable" and not that he destroyed it. He said that Mashiach himself "fulfil[l]ed all righteousness in becoming obedient to the the (sic) Law which himself had given to Moses on the mount and thereby magnified it and made it honorable instead of destroying it" (Cook, L.W. & Ehat, A.F. (Eds.) (1980) *The Words of Joseph Smith*. Salt Lake City, UT: Bookcraft, pgs. 162-3)." **142** We read in the Torah, "Cursed be he that confirms not all the words of this Torah to do them" (Deut. 27:26). This deadness is not from Torah observance, but from Torah violations. Yet Torah is life (Deut. 30:10-20; 32:46-47), and the Mashiach is the Torah (3 Nefi 7:2). **143** The underlying Hebrew may have been *chalaf* חלף (Strong's 2498), which can mean "done away" but can also mean "changed, renewed, or revived." This same word (that is translated in the KJV as "renewed") is found in Isa. 40:31 and 41:1. Yeshua later testifies to the Nefites (in 3 Nefi 5:31) in parallel thought that "things which were of old time… [were] all fulfilled. Old things are done away and all things have become new" (see note to 3 Nefi 5:31; M'roni 8:2).

testimony against you, for they are sufficient to teach any man the right way. For the right way is to believe in Mashiach and deny him not, for by denying him you also deny the prophets and the Torah. And now behold, I say unto you that the right way is to believe in Mashiach and deny him not, and Mashiach is HaKodesh of Isra'el. Wherefore, you must bow down before him and worship him **with all your might, mind, and strength, and your whole soul;**[144] and if you do this, you shall in no way be cast out. And inasmuch as it shall be expedient, you must keep the performances and ordinances of Elohim until[145] the Torah shall be fulfilled[146] which was given unto Moshe.

10 And after Mashiach shall have risen from the dead, he shall show himself unto you, my children and my beloved brothers, and the words which he shall speak unto you shall be the Torah which you shall do. For behold, I say unto you that I have beheld that many generations shall pass away, and there shall be great wars and contentions among my people. And after the Mashiach shall come, there shall be signs given unto my people of his birth, and also of his death and resurrection. And great and terrible shall that day be unto the wicked, for they shall perish. And they perish because they cast out the prophets and the k'doshim, and stone them, and slay them. Wherefore, the cry of the blood of the k'doshim shall ascend up to Elohim from the ground against them. **Wherefore, all those who are proud, and that do wickedly, the day that comes shall burn them up, says YHWH Tzva'ot, for they shall be as stubble.**[147] And they that kill the prophets and the k'doshim, the depths of the earth shall swallow them up, says YHWH Tzva'ot, and mountains shall cover them, and whirlwinds shall carry them away, and buildings shall fall upon them, and crush them to pieces, and grind them to powder. And they shall be visited with thunderings, and lightnings,

---

144 Deut. 6:4-5 **145** Underlying Hebrew for "until" would likely be *ad* עד (Strong's 5704), meaning "as far (or long or much) as, whether in space (even unto) or time (during, while, until) or degree (equally with)." Thus, this passage could be understood to mean that they kept the Torah to the degree that the performances and ordinances were fulfilled. Torah observance reveals Mashiach to us, because the Mashiach is the Torah (3 Nefi 7:2); it is a tutor that brings us each, as individuals, to a knowledge of Mashiach (Gal. 3:23-29). Passover was a type that Mashiach fulfilled; hence, Paul says, "Therefore let us keep the feast" (1 Cor. 5:7-8). So the fact that an outward observance of the Torah is a type of Mashiach may be considered a reason to continue the outward observance. **146** See footnote for "Torah shall be fulfilled" in paragraph 8. **147** Mal. 3:19 (4:1)

and earthquakes, and all manner of destructions; for the fire of the anger of YHWH shall be kindled against them, **and they shall be as stubble, and the day that comes shall consume them, says YHWH Tzva'ot.**[148]

11 Oh the pain and the anguish of my soul for the loss of the slain of my people. For I, Nefi, have seen it, and it very nearly consumes me before the presence of YHWH. But I must cry unto my Elohim, Your ways are just! But behold, the righteous that hearken unto the words of the prophets and destroy them not, but look forward unto Mashiach with steadfastness for the signs which are given, despite all persecutions, behold, they are they which shall not perish. But the **Son of Righteousness**[149] shall appear unto them and **he shall heal them,**[150] and they shall have shalom with him until three generations shall have passed away and many of the fourth generation shall have passed away in righteousness. And when these things shall have passed away, a speedy destruction[151] comes unto my people. For despite the pains of my soul, I have seen it; wherefore, I know that it shall come to pass. And they sell themselves for no value, for, for the reward of their pride and their foolishness they shall reap destruction. For because they yield unto HaSatan and choose works of darkness rather than light, therefore they must go down to She'ol. For the **spirit of YHWH will not always strive with man,**[152] and when the spirit ceases to strive with man, then comes speedy destruction. And this grieves my soul.

12 And as I spoke concerning the convincing of the Y'hudim that Yeshua is the very Mashiach, it must necessarily be that the Goyim be convinced also that Yeshua is the Mashiach, the Elohe Kedem, and that he manifests himself unto all those who believe in him by the power of the Ruach HaKodesh, yes, unto every nation, kindred, tongue, and people, working mighty miracles, signs, and wonders among the children of men according to their faith.

13 But behold, I prophesy unto you concerning the last days, concerning the days when Adonai YHWH shall bring these things forth unto the children of men. After my seed and the seed of my brothers shall have dwindled in unbelief, and shall have been slain

---

148 Mal. 3:19 (4:1)   **149** Mal. 3:20 (4:2); 3 Nefi 5:3-5   **150** 3 Nefi 8:2-3   **151** Alma 21:2; M'raman 3:1-4   **152** Gen. 6:3

by the Goyim, yes, after Adonai YHWH shall have **camped against them round about, and shall have laid siege against them**[153] with a mount, and raised forts against them, and after they shall have been brought down **low in the dust**,[154] even that they are not, yet the words of the righteous shall be written, and the prayers of the faithful shall be heard, and all those who have dwindled in unbelief shall not be forgotten. **For those who shall be destroyed shall speak unto them out of the ground, and their speech shall be low out of the dust, and their voice shall be as one that has a familiar spirit, for Adonai YHWH will give unto him power that he may whisper concerning them, even as it were out of the ground, and their speech shall whisper out of the dust.**[155]

14 For thus says Adonai YHWH: They shall write the things which shall be done among them, and they shall be written and **sealed up in a book**,[156] and those who have dwindled in unbelief shall not have them, for they seek to destroy the things of Elohim. Wherefore, as those who have been destroyed have been destroyed speedily, and the multitude of **their terrible ones**[157] shall be as chaff that passes away, yes, thus says Adonai YHWH: It shall be at an instant, suddenly.

15 And it shall come to pass that those who have dwindled in unbelief shall be slain by the hand of the Goyim. And the Goyim are lifted up in the pride of their eyes, and have stumbled because of the greatness of their stumbling block, that they have built up many churches; nevertheless, they put down the power and the miracles of Elohim, and preach up unto themselves their own wisdom and their own learning, that they may get gain and **grind upon the face of the poor**.[158] And there are many churches built up which cause envyings, and strifes, and malice; and there are also secret conspiracies, even as in times of old, according to the conspiracies of HaSatan. For he is the foundation of all these things, yes, the foundation of murder and works of darkness; yes, and he leads them by the neck with a flaxen cord until he binds them with his strong cords for ever.

16 For behold, my beloved brothers, I say unto you that Adonai YHWH works not in darkness. He does not do anything except it be for the benefit of the world, for he loves the world, even that he lays down his own life, that he may draw all men unto him. Wherefore, he

---

153 Isa. 29:3 154 Isa. 29:4 155 Isa. 29:4 156 Isa. 29:11 157 Isa. 29:20 158 Isa. 3:15

commands none that they shall not partake of his salvation. Behold, does he cry unto any, saying, Depart from me? Behold, I say unto you, no; but he says, Come unto me all you ends of the earth, **buy milk** and honey **without money and without price**.¹⁵⁹ Behold, has he commanded any that they should depart out of the synagogues or out of the houses of worship? Behold, I say unto you, no. Has he commanded any that they should not partake of his salvation? Behold, I say unto you, no, but he has given it free for all men; and he has commanded his people that they should persuade all men unto repentance. Behold, has YHWH commanded any that they should not partake of his goodness? Behold, I say unto you, no, but all men are privileged, the one like unto the other, and none are forbidden.

¹⁷ He commands that there shall be no priestcrafts; for behold, priestcrafts are that men preach and set themselves up for a light unto the world, that they may get gain¹⁶⁰ and praise of the world, but they seek not the welfare of Tziyon. Behold, YHWH has forbidden this thing; wherefore, Adonai YHWH has given a mitzvah that all men should have charity, which charity is love. And except they should have charity, they were nothing; wherefore, if they should have charity, they would not allow the laborer in Tziyon to perish. But the laborer in Tziyon shall labor for Tziyon, for if they labor for money, they shall perish. And again, Adonai YHWH has commanded that men **should not murder**,¹⁶¹ that they **should not lie**, that they **should not steal**,

---

159 Isa. 55:1   **160** "He [the Tanna] informs us this: that even where a fee is taken, it may be accepted only for Scripture, but not for Midrash. Now, why does Midrash differ, that remuneration is forbidden? Because it is written, And the Lord commanded me at that time to teach you (Deut. 4:14); and it is also written, Behold I have taught you statutes and judgments, even as the Lord my God commanded me (Deut. 4:5) just as I [taught you] gratuitously, so you must teach gratuitously? Then should not Scripture too be unremunerated? — Rab said: The fee is for guarding [the children]. R. Johanan maintained: The fee is for the teaching of accentuation" (b.Nedarim 37a). "Rab Judah reported in the name of Rab: Scripture says: Behold I have taught you, etc. (Deut. 4:14) Just as I teach gratuitously, so you should teach gratuitously. It has also been taught to the same effect Scripture says: Even as the Lord my God commanded me (Deut. 4:5), [intimating], just as I teach gratuitously, so you should teach gratuitously. And whence do we derive that if he cannot find someone to teach him gratuitously, he must pay for learning? The text states: Buy the truth. And whence do we infer that one should not say 'as I learnt the Torah by paying, so I shall teach it for payment'? The text states: And sell it not" (b. Bekhorot 29a).   **161** The Hebrew word for "murder" here must be *ratsach* רָצַח (Strong's 7523), which appears in the Ten Commandments (*Aseret HaDibrot*) (Ex. 20:13; Deut. 5:17). When Yosef ben Yosef translated direct quotes of this mitzvah (Moshiyah 7:21; 3 Nefi 5:24), he used the KJV "thou shalt not kill," but when he only alluded to the mitzvah, he translated the word more correctly as "murder" (2 Nefi 11:17; Alma 16:2).

that they **should not take the name of YHWH their Elohim in vain, that they should not envy,**[162] that they should not have malice, that they should not contend one with another, that they should not commit whoredoms, and that they should do none of these things.[163] For whoever does them shall perish, for none of these iniquities come of YHWH. For he does that which is good among the children of men, and he does nothing except it be plain unto the children of men. And he invites them all to come unto him and partake of his goodness, and he denies none that come unto him, black and white, bond and free, male and female; and he remembers the heathen, and all are alike unto Elohim, both Y'hudi and Goy.

An Aggadic Midrash on Yesha'yahu 29

18 But behold, in the last days, or in the days of the Goyim, yes, behold, all the nations of the Goyim, and also the Y'hudim, both those who shall come upon this land and those who shall be upon other lands, yes, even upon all the lands of the earth, behold, they will be drunken with iniquity and all manner of abominations. And when that day shall come, they shall be visited of YHWH Tzva'ot with thunder, and with earthquake, and with a great noise, and with storm and tempest, and with the flame of devouring fire. **And all the nations that fight against Tziyon and that distress her shall be as a dream of a night vision. Yes, it shall be unto them even as unto a hungry man which dreams, and behold, he eats, but he awakes and his soul is empty. Or like unto a thirsty man which dreams, and behold, he drinks, but he awakes and behold, he is faint and his soul has appetite. Yes, even so shall the multitude of all the nations be that fight against Mount Tziyon.**[164] For behold, all you that do iniquity, **stay yourselves and wonder, for you shall cry out and cry. Yes, you shall be drunken, but not with wine; you shall stagger, but not with strong drink.**[165] For behold, **YHWH has poured out upon you the spirit of deep sleep**, for behold, **you have closed your eyes, and** you have rejected **the prophets, and your rulers and the seers has he covered**[166] because of your iniquity.

19 And it shall come to pass that Adonai YHWH shall bring forth unto you **the words of a book,**[167] and they shall be the words of them

---
162 Deut. 5:17–21; Isa. 20:13–17 163 Ex. 20:7–17; Deut. 5:11–21 164 Isa. 29:7–8 165 Isa. 29:9 166 Isa. 29:10 167 Isa. 29:11

which have slumbered. And behold, the **book shall be sealed**, and in the book shall be a revelation from Elohim, from the beginning of the world to the ending thereof. Wherefore, because of the **things which are sealed up**, the things which are sealed shall not **be delivered**[168] in the day of the wickedness and abominations of the people; wherefore, the book shall be kept from them. But the book shall be delivered unto a man, and he shall deliver the words of the book, which are the words of those who have slumbered in the dust, and he shall deliver these words unto another. But the words which are **sealed** he shall not **deliver**, neither shall he **deliver the book**, for the book shall be sealed by the power of Elohim, and the revelation which was sealed shall be kept in the book until the own due time of YHWH, that they may come forth; for behold, they reveal all things from the foundation of the world unto the end thereof. And the day comes that the **words of the book which were sealed** shall be read upon the housetops, and they shall be read by the power of Mashiach. And all things shall be revealed unto the children of men which ever have been among the children of men, and which ever will be, even unto the end of the earth. Wherefore, at that day when the book shall be delivered unto the man of whom I have spoken, the book shall be hid from the eyes of the world, that the eyes of none shall behold it, except it be that three witnesses[169] shall behold it by the power of Elohim, besides him to whom the book shall be delivered; and they shall testify to the truth of the book and the things therein. And there is no other which shall view it, except it be a few according to the will of Elohim, to bear testimony of his word unto the children of men. For Adonai YHWH has said that the words of the faithful should speak as if it were from the dead. Wherefore, Adonai YHWH will proceed to bring forth **the words of the book**; and in the mouth of as many witnesses as seems him good will he confirm his word; and woe be unto him that rejects the word of Elohim.

20 But behold, it shall come to pass that Adonai YHWH shall say unto him to whom he **shall deliver the book,** Take these words which are not **sealed and deliver them to** another, that he may show them unto the **learned, saying, Read this, I ask you.** And the **learned shall say**, Bring here the book and I will read it. And now because

---

168 Isa. 29:12 169 See *Testimony of Three Witnesses* in Appendix F.

of the glory of the world and to get gain will they say this, and not for the glory of Elohim. And the man shall say, **I cannot bring the book, for it is sealed.**[170] Then shall the learned say, I cannot read it. Wherefore, it shall come to pass that Adonai YHWH **will deliver again the book and the words thereof to him that is not learned; and the man that is not learned shall say, I am not learned.**[171] Then shall Adonai YHWH say unto him, The learned shall not read them, for they have rejected them, and I am able to do my own work; wherefore, you shall read the words which I shall give unto you. Touch not the things which are sealed, for I will bring them forth in my own due time, for I will show unto the children of men that I am able to do my own work. Wherefore, when you have read the words which I have commanded you, and obtained the witnesses which I have promised unto you, then shall you seal up the book again and hide it up unto me, that I may preserve the words which you have not read, until I shall see fit in my own wisdom to reveal all things unto the children of men. For behold, I am Elohim, and I am an Elohim of miracles, and I will show unto the world that I am the same yesterday, today, and for ever, and I work not among the children of men except it be according to their faith.

21 And again it shall come to pass that YHWH shall say unto him that shall read the words that shall be delivered him, **Forasmuch as this people draw near unto me with their mouth, and with their lips do honor me, but have removed their heart far from me, and their fear towards me is taught by the precept of men, therefore, I will proceed to do a marvelous work among this people, yes, a marvelous work and a wonder; for the wisdom of their wise and learned shall perish, and the understanding of their prudent shall be hid. And woe unto them that seek deep to hide their counsel from YHWH, and their works are in the dark, and they say, Who sees us? And who knows us? And they also say, Surely your turning of things upside down shall be esteemed as the potter's clay. But behold, I will show unto them, says YHWH Tzva'ot, that I know all their works. For shall the work say of him that made it, He made me not? Or shall the thing framed say of him that framed it, He had no understanding?** But behold, says

---

170 Isa. 29:11 171 Isa. 29:12

YHWH Tzva'ot, I will show unto the children of men that **it is not yet a very little while and L'vanon shall be turned into a fruitful field, and the fruitful field shall be esteemed as a forest. And in that day shall the deaf hear the words of the book, and the eyes of the blind shall see out of obscurity and out of darkness. And the meek also shall increase, and their joy shall be in** YHWH, **and the poor among men shall rejoice in HaKodesh of Isra'el.** For assuredly as YHWH lives, they shall see **that the terrible one is brought to nothing, and the scorner is consumed; and all that watch for iniquity are cut off, and they that make a man an offender for a word, and lay a snare for him that reproves in the gate, and turn aside the just for a thing of no value. Therefore, thus says** YHWH, **who redeemed Avraham, concerning the house of Ya'akov: Ya'akov shall not now be ashamed, neither shall his face now grow pale. But when he sees his children, the work of my hands, in the midst of him, they shall sanctify my name, and sanctify HaKodesh of Ya'akov, and shall fear the Elohim of Isra'el. They also that erred in spirit shall come to understanding, and they that murmured shall learn doctrine.**[172]

12 And now behold, my brothers, I have spoken unto you according as the spirit has constrained me; wherefore, I know that they must surely come to pass. And the things which shall be written out of the book shall be of great worth unto the children of men, and especially unto our seed, which is a remnant of the house of Isra'el. For it shall come to pass in that day that the churches[173] which are built up, and not unto YHWH, when the one shall say unto the other, Behold, I, I am YHWH's — and the other shall say, I, I am YHWH's — and thus shall everyone say that has built up churches and not unto YHWH. And they shall contend one with another, and their kohanim shall contend one with another, and they shall teach with their learning,[174] and deny the Ruach HaKodesh which gives utterance. And they deny the power of Elohim, HaKodesh of Isra'el. And they say unto the people, Hearken unto us and hear you our precept, for behold, there is no Elohim today, for YHWH and the Redeemer has done his work, and he has given his power unto

---

[172] Isa. 29:13-24 [173] 1 Nefi 7:5 [174] 2 Nefi 6:9; 11:15

men. Behold, hearken you unto my precept. If they shall say there is a miracle worked by the hand of YHWH, believe it not; for this day he is not an Elohim of miracles; he has done his work. Yes, and there shall be many which shall say, **Eat, drink, and be merry, for tomorrow we die**[175] and it shall be well with us. And there shall also be many which shall say, **Eat, drink, and be merry**; nevertheless, fear Elohim, he will justify in committing a little sin. Yes, lie a little, take the advantage of one because of his words, dig a pit for your neighbor, there is no harm in this. And do all these things, **for tomorrow we die**. And if it so be that we are guilty, Elohim will beat us with a few stripes and at last we shall be saved in the kingdom of Elohim. Yes, and there shall be many which shall teach after this manner false, and vain, and foolish doctrines, and shall be puffed up in their hearts, and shall seek deep to hide their counsels from YHWH. And their works shall be in the dark, and the blood of the k'doshim shall cry from the ground against them.

2 Yes, they have all gone out of the way, they have become corrupted; because of pride, and because of false teachers, and false doctrine, their churches have become corrupted,[176] and their churches are lifted up; because of pride, they are puffed up. They rob the poor because of their fine sanctuaries; they rob the poor because of their fine clothing, and they persecute the meek and the poor in heart because in their pride they are puffed up. They wear stiff necks and high heads, yes, and because of pride, and wickedness, and abominations, and whoredoms, they have all gone astray, except it be a few who are the humble followers of Mashiach. Nevertheless, they are led, that in many instances they do err because they are taught by the precepts of men.

3 O the wise, and the learned, and the rich, that are puffed up in the pride of their hearts, and all those who preach false doctrines, and all those who commit whoredoms and pervert the right way of YHWH, Woe, woe, woe be unto them, says Adonai YHWH Tzva'ot, for they shall be thrust down to Gehinnom.

4 Woe unto them that turn aside the just for a thing of no value, and revile against that which is good and say that it is of no worth, for the day shall come that Adonai YHWH will speedily visit the inhabitants

---

175 Isa. 22:13   176 M'raman 4:4-5

of the earth. And in that day that they are fully ripe in iniquity, they shall perish. But behold, if the inhabitants of the earth shall repent of their wickedness and abominations, they shall not be destroyed, says YHWH Tzva'ot. But behold, that great and abominable church, the whore of all the earth, must tumble to the earth, and great must be the fall thereof. For the kingdom of HaSatan must shake, and they which belong to it must necessarily be stirred up unto repentance, or HaSatan will grasp them with his everlasting chains and they be stirred up to anger and perish. For behold, at that day shall he rage in the hearts of the children of men and stir them up to anger against that which is good. And others will he pacify, and lull them away into carnal security, that they will say, All is well in Tziyon, yes, Tziyon prospers, all is well. And thus HaSatan cheats their souls and leads them away carefully down to Gehinnom. And behold, others he soothes away and tells them there is no Gehinnom. And he says unto them, I am no adversary, for there is none. And thus he whispers in their ears until he grasps them with his awful chains, from which there is no deliverance. Yes, they are grasped with death and She'ol; and death, and She'ol, and HaSatan, and all that have been seized therewith must stand before the throne of Elohim and be judged according to their works, from where they must go into the place prepared for them, even a lake of fire and brimstone, which is Endless torment. Therefore, woe be unto him that is at ease in Tziyon.

5 Woe be unto him that cries, All is well. Yes, woe be unto him that hearkens unto the precepts of men, and denies the power of Elohim and the gift of the Ruach HaKodesh. Yes, woe be unto him that says, We have received and we need no more. And in short, woe unto all those who tremble and are angry because of the truth of Elohim. For behold, he that is built upon the rock receives it with gladness, and he that is built upon a sandy foundation trembles, for fear that he shall fall.

6 Woe be unto him that shall say, We have received the word of Elohim, and we need no more of the word of Elohim, for we have enough. For behold, thus says Adonai YHWH, I will give unto the children of **men line upon line, precept upon precept, here a little and there a little.**[177] And blessed are those who hearken unto

---

177 Isa. 28:10, 13

my precepts and lend an ear unto my counsel, for they shall learn wisdom. For unto him that receives[178] I will give more; and from them that shall say, We have enough — shall be taken away even that which they have. **Cursed is he that puts his trust in man, or makes flesh his arm,**[179] or shall hearken unto the precepts of men, except their precepts shall be given by the power of the Ruach HaKodesh.

7 Woe be unto the Goyim, says Adonai YHWH Tzva'ot, for even though I shall **lengthen out my arm** unto them **from day to day,** they will deny me. Nevertheless, I will be merciful unto them, says Adonai YHWH, if they will repent and come unto me, **for my** arm is **lengthened out all the day long,**[180] says Adonai YHWH Tzva'ot.

8 But behold, there shall be many at that day when **I shall proceed to do a marvelous work among**[181] them, that I may remember my covenants[182] which I have made unto the children of men, that **I may set my hand again the second time to recover my people**[183] which are of the house of Isra'el, and also that I may remember the promises which I have made unto you, Nefi, and also unto your father, that I would remember your seed, and that the words of your seed should proceed forth out of my mouth unto your seed. And my words **shall hiss forth unto the ends of the earth for a standard unto my people**[184] which are of the house of Isra'el. And because my words **shall hiss forth,** many of the Goyim shall say, A bible, a bible, we have got a bible, and there cannot be any more bible. But thus says Adonai YHWH: O fools, they shall have a bible and it shall proceed forth from the Y'hudim, my ancient covenant people.[185] And what thank they the Y'hudim for the bible which they receive from them? Yes, what do the Goyim mean? Do they remember the travails, and the labors, and the pains of the Y'hudim? And their diligence unto me in bringing forth salvation unto the Goyim?[186]

9 O you Goyim, have you remembered the Y'hudim, my ancient covenant people? No, but you have cursed them, and have hated them, and have not sought to recover them. But behold, I will return all these things upon your own heads, for I YHWH have not forgotten my people. You fool that shall say, A bible, we have got a bible and we

---

178 Alma 9:3   **179** Jer. 17:5   **180** Isa. 65:2   **181** Isa. 29:14   **182** Deut. 28:69 (29:1); 30:1–5. More broadly, see Deut. 28:69–30:20.   **183** Isa. 11:11   **184** Isa. 5:26   **185** "Unto them [the Y'hudim] were committed the oracles of Elohim" (Rom. 3:2).   **186** "[S]alvation is of the Y'hudim" (John 4:22).

need no more bible. Have you obtained a bible, except it were by the Y'hudim? Do you not know that there are more nations than one? Do you not know that I, YHWH your Elohim, have created all men, and that I remember those who are upon the isles of the sea? And that I rule in the heavens above and in the earth beneath, and I bring forth my word unto the children of men, yes, even upon all the nations of the earth? Why do you murmur because you shall receive more of my word? Do you not know that the testimony of **two nations**[187] is a witness unto you that I am Elohim? That I remember one nation like unto another? Wherefore, I speak the same words unto one nation like unto another. And when the **two nations shall run together**, the testimony of the **two nations shall run together also.**[188] And I do this that I may prove unto many that I am the same yesterday, today, and for ever, and that I speak forth my words according to my own pleasure.

10 And because that I have spoken one word, you need not suppose that I cannot speak another, for my work is not yet finished, neither shall it be until the end of man, neither from that time henceforth and for ever. Wherefore, because that you have a bible, you need not suppose that it contains all my words, neither need you suppose that I have not caused more to be written. For I command all men, both in the east, and in the west, and in the north, and in the south, and in the islands of the sea, that they shall write the words which I speak unto them. For out of the books which shall be written I will judge the world, every man according to their works, according to that which is written. For behold, I shall speak unto the Y'hudim and they shall write it, and I shall also speak unto the Nefites and they shall write it. And I shall also speak unto the other tribes of the house of Isra'el which I have led away and they shall write it, and I shall also speak unto all the nations of the earth and they shall write it. And it shall come to pass that the Y'hudim shall have the words of the Nefites, and the Nefites shall have the words of the Y'hudim, and the Nefites and the Y'hudim shall have the words of the lost tribes of Isra'el, and the lost tribes of Isra'el shall have the words of the Nefites and the Y'hudim. And it shall come to pass that my people which are of the house of Isra'el shall be gathered home unto the lands of

---

187 Ezek. 35:10; 37:15–22   **188** Ezek. 37:22

their possessions, and my word also shall be gathered in one. And I will show unto them that fight against my word, and against my people who are of the house of Isra'el, that I am Elohim, and that I covenanted with Avraham that I would remember his seed for ever.

11 And now behold, my beloved brothers, I would speak unto you, for I, Nefi, would not allow that you should suppose that you are more righteous than the Goyim shall be. For behold, except you shall keep the mitzvot of Elohim, you shall all likewise perish. And because of the words which have been spoken, you need not suppose that the Goyim are utterly destroyed. For behold, I say unto you, as many of the Goyim as will repent are the covenant people of YHWH, and as many of the Y'hudim as will not repent shall be cast off. For YHWH covenants with none except it be with them that repent and believe in his Son, who is HaKodesh of Isra'el.

12 And now I would prophesy somewhat more concerning the Y'hudim and the Goyim. For after the book of which I have spoken shall come forth, and be written unto the Goyim, and sealed up again unto YHWH, there shall be many which shall believe the words which are written, and they shall carry them forth unto the remnant of our seed. And then shall the remnant of our seed know concerning us, how that we came out from Yerushalayim, and that they are descendants of the Y'hudim. And the besorah of Yeshua HaMashiach shall be declared among them; wherefore, they shall be restored unto the knowledge of their fathers, and also to the knowledge of Yeshua HaMashiach which was had among their fathers. And then shall they rejoice, for they shall know that it is a blessing unto them from the hand of Elohim. And their scales of darkness shall begin to fall from their eyes, and many generations shall not pass away among them except they shall be a pure and a delightful people. And it shall come to pass that the Y'hudim which are scattered also shall begin to believe in Mashiach, and they shall begin to gather in upon the face of the land. And as many as shall believe in Mashiach shall also become a delightful people.

13 And it shall come to pass that Adonai YHWH shall commence his work among all nations, kindreds, tongues, and people, to bring about the restoration of his people upon the earth.[189] **And with**

---

189 The Hebrew word here was likely *eretz* ארץ, which could mean "earth" or "land."

righteousness shall Adonai YHWH judge the poor and reprove with equity for the meek of the earth. And he shall smite the earth with the rod of his mouth, and with the breath of his lips shall he slay the wicked.[190] For the time speedily comes that Adonai YHWH shall cause a great division among the people, and the wicked will he destroy. And he will spare his people, yes, even if it so be that he must destroy the wicked by fire. **And righteousness shall be the girdle of his loins and faithfulness the girdle of his reins. And then shall the wolf dwell with the lamb, and the leopard shall lie down with the kid, and the calf, and the young lion, and the fatling together, and a little child shall lead them. And the cow and the bear shall feed, their young ones shall lie down together, and the lion shall eat straw like the ox. And the sucking child shall play on the hole of the asp, and the weaned child shall put his hand on the cockatrice's den. They shall not hurt nor destroy in all my holy mountain, for the earth shall be full of the knowledge of YHWH as the waters cover the sea.**[191] Wherefore, the things of all nations shall be made known, yes, all things shall be made known unto the children of men. There is nothing which is secret except it shall be revealed, there is no work of darkness except it shall be made manifest in the light, and there is nothing which is sealed upon earth except it shall be loosed. Wherefore, all things which have been revealed unto the children of men shall at that day be revealed, and HaSatan shall have power over the hearts of the children of men no more for a long time. And now my beloved brothers, I make an end of my sayings.

13 And now I, Nefi, make an end of my prophesying unto you, my beloved brothers. And I cannot write but a few things which I know must surely come to pass, neither can I write but a few of the words of my brother Ya'akov. Wherefore, the things which I have written suffice me, except it be a few words which I must speak concerning the doctrine of Mashiach. Wherefore, I shall speak unto you plainly, according to the plainness of my prophesying. For my soul delights in plainness, for after this manner does Adonai

---

Based on the phrase "gather in upon the face of the land" (2 Nefi 12:12), the meaning here may also have been "land." **190** Isa. 11:4 **191** Isa. 11:5-9

YHWH work among the children of men. For Adonai YHWH gives light unto the understanding, for he speaks unto men according to their language, unto their understanding. Wherefore, I would that you should remember that I have spoken unto you concerning that prophet[192] which YHWH showed unto me that should immerse the Lamb of Elohim, which should take away the sin of the world.

2 And now, if the Lamb of Elohim, he being holy, should have need to be washed by immersion in water to fulfill all righteousness, oh, then, how much more need have we, being unholy, to be washed by immersion, yes, even by water?[193] And now I would ask of you, my beloved brothers, how did the Lamb of Elohim fulfill[194] all righteousness in being washed by water?[195] Do you not know that he was holy? But despite he being holy, he shows unto the children of men that according to the flesh he humbles himself before the Father, and witnesses unto the Father that he would be obedient unto him in keeping his mitzvot. Wherefore, after he was immersed with water, **the Ruach HaKodesh descended upon him**[196] in the form of a dove.[197] And again, it shows unto the children of men the straitness of the path and the narrowness of the gate by which they should enter, he having set the example before them. And he said unto the children of men, Follow me. Wherefore, my beloved brothers, can we follow Yeshua except we shall be willing to keep the mitzvot of the Father?[198] And the Father said, Repent, repent, and be immersed in the name of my Beloved Son. And also the voice of the Son came unto me, saying, He that is washed by immersion in my name, to him

---

192 1 Nefi 3:3   193 This is an example of the Kal va-homer thought form, which serves as the first of the Seven Rules of Hillel. This classic Jewish thought form expresses that that which applies in a less important case will certainly apply in a more important case. 194 This is one of the "mitzvot" that Mashiach "fulfilled," but that did not mean the practice of immersion was abolished.   195 The fourth century "Church Father" Jerome writes: "In the Gospel according to the Hebrews, which is written in the Chaldee and Syrian language, but in Hebrew letters, and is used by the Nazarenes to this day (I mean the Gospel according to the Apostles, or, as is generally maintained, the Gospel according to Matthew), a copy of which is in the library at Caesarea, we find: 'Behold, the mother of our Lord and His brothers said to him, John the Baptist baptizes for the remission of sins; let us go and be baptized by him. But He said to them, what sin have I committed that I should go and be baptized by him? Unless perchance, the very words which I have said are [a sin of] ignorance'" (Jerome; Against Pelagius 3:2).   196 Isa. 42:1; 61:1. The Talmud says "The Messiah—as it is written, And the spirit of the Lord shall rest upon him..." (b.Sanhedrin 93); 1 Nefi 3:11.   197 This is an example of the Hebraism known as the Prophetic Perfect, in which a prophet speaks of a future event in the perfect form (completed action), as if it had already occurred.   198 Immersion being a practice of the Mosaic Torah.

will the Father give the Ruach HaKodesh like unto me. Wherefore, follow me and do the things which you have seen me do. Wherefore, my beloved brothers, I know that if you shall follow the Son with full purpose of heart, acting no hypocrisy and no deception before Elohim, but with real intent, repenting of your sins, witnessing unto the Father that you are willing to take upon you the name of Mashiach by immersion — yes, by following your Adonai and Savior down into the water according to his word — behold, then shall you receive the Ruach HaKodesh. Yes, then comes the immersion of fire and of the Ruach HaKodesh, and then can you speak with the tongue of angels and shout praises unto HaKodesh of Isra'el.

3 But behold, my beloved brothers, thus came the voice of the Son unto me, saying, After you have repented of your sins, and witnessed unto the Father that you are willing to keep my mitzvot by the immersion of water, and have received the immersion of fire and of the Ruach HaKodesh, and can speak with a new tongue — yes, even with the tongue of angels — and after this should deny me, it would have been better for you that you had not known me. And I heard a voice from the Father saying, Yes, the words of my beloved are true and faithful. He that endures to the end, the same shall be saved. And now my beloved brothers, I know by this that unless a man shall endure to the end in following the example of the Son of the living Elohim, he cannot be saved. Wherefore, do the things which I have told you I have seen that your Adonai and your Redeemer should do; for, for this cause have they been shown unto me: that you might know the gate by which you should enter. For the gate by which you should enter is repentance and washing by immersion in water,[199] and then comes a remission of your sins by fire and by the Ruach HaKodesh. And then are you in this strait and narrow path which leads to Eternal life. Yes, you have entered in by the gate, you have done according to the mitzvot of the Father and the Son, and you have received the Ruach HaKodesh, which witnesses of the Father

---

[199] We read in the Talmud: "A Ger (proselyte/stranger) who is circumcised and not immersed; Rabbi Eliezer said: Behold this is a Ger. Thus we find of the fathers, they were circumcised and not immersed, immersed and not circumcised: Rabbi Joshua said: Behold this is a Ger; thus we find of the mothers, they were immersed and not circumcised. And the sages say: Immersed and not circumcised, circumcised and not immersed, He is not a Ger until he is circumcised and immersed" (b.Yevamot 46a). *Ger* is short for *Ger HaShar* (The Ger at the Gate) (Deut. 14:21; 24:14).

and the Son unto the fulfilling of the promise which he has made, that if you entered in by the way, you should receive.

4 And now my beloved brothers, after you have gotten into this strait and narrow path, I would ask if all is done. Behold, I say unto you, no, for you have not come thus far except it were by the word of Mashiach, with unshaken faith in him, relying wholly upon the merits of him who is mighty to save. Wherefore, you must press forward with a steadfastness in Mashiach, having a perfect brightness of hope, and a love of Elohim and of all men. Wherefore, if you shall press forward, feasting upon the word of Mashiach, and endure to the end, behold, thus says the Father: You shall have Eternal life.

5 And now behold, my beloved brothers, this is the way; and there is no other way nor name given under Heaven by which man can be saved in the kingdom of Elohim. And now behold, this is the doctrine of Mashiach, and the only and true doctrine of the Father, and of the Son, and of the Ruach HaKodesh, which is one Elohim without end. Amen.

14

And now behold, my beloved brothers, I suppose that you ponder somewhat in your hearts concerning that which you should do after you have entered in by the way. But behold, why do you ponder these things in your hearts? Do you not remember that I said unto you that after you had received the Ruach HaKodesh, you could speak with the tongue of angels? And now, how could you speak with the tongue of angels except it were by the Ruach HaKodesh? Angels speak by the power of the Ruach HaKodesh; wherefore, they speak the words of Mashiach. Wherefore, I said unto you, Feast upon the words of Mashiach; for behold, the words of Mashiach will tell you all things what you should do. Wherefore, now after I have spoken these words, if you cannot understand them, it will be because you ask not, neither do you knock. Wherefore, you are not brought into the light, but must perish in the dark. For behold, again I say unto you that if you will enter in by the way and receive the Ruach HaKodesh, it will show unto you all things what you should do.[200] Behold, this is the doctrine of Mashiach, and

---

200 "And I will give them one heart, and *I will put a new spirit within you*; and I will take the stony heart out of their flesh, and will give them a heart of flesh: *That they may walk*

there will be no more doctrine given until after he shall manifest himself unto you in the flesh. And when he shall manifest himself unto you in the flesh, the things which he shall say unto you shall you observe to do.

2 And now I, Nefi, cannot say more. The spirit stops my utterance and I am left to mourn because of the unbelief, and the wickedness, and the ignorance, and the stiffneckedness of men. For they will not search knowledge nor understand great knowledge when it is given unto them in plainness, even as plain as word can be.

3 And now my beloved brothers, I perceive that you ponder still in your hearts, and it grieves me that I must speak concerning this thing. For if you would hearken unto the spirit which teaches a man to pray, you would know that you must pray; for the evil spirit teaches not a man to pray, but teaches him that he must not pray. But behold, I say unto you that you must pray always and not faint, that you must not perform anything unto YHWH except in the first place you shall pray unto the Father in the name of Mashiach that he will consecrate your performance unto you, that your performance may be for the welfare of your soul.[201]

15

And now I, Nefi, cannot write all the things which were taught among my people, neither am I mighty in writing, like unto speaking; for when a man speaks by the power of the Ruach HaKodesh, the power of the Ruach HaKodesh carries it unto the hearts of the children of men. But behold, there are many that harden their hearts against the Holy Spirit, that it has no place in them. Wherefore, they cast many things away which are written and esteem them as things of no value. But I, Nefi, have written what I have written, and I esteem it as of great worth, and especially unto my people. For I pray continually for them by day, and my eyes water

---

in my statutes, and keep my ordinances, and do them: and they shall be my people, and I will be their Elohim" (Ezek. 11:19–20 emphasis added; see also Ezek. 18:29–32; 36:25–27). **201** As stated in *The Complete Book of Jewish Observance*: "Before we perform a Mitzvah, we put ourselves 'in tune' by speaking: *Barukh attah Adonai Elohenu Melekh ha-Olam asher kid-shanu be-mitzvotav vetzivanu* ... Blessed are You, Lord our God, Ruler of the universe, You are He, who has sanctified us by His commandments, and commanded us ... This is followed by the Mitzvah we are about to perform, for instance, on putting on the Tallit: *lehitatef ba-Tzitzit* to wrap ourselves in Tzitzit" Trepp, L. (1980) *The Complete Book of Jewish Observance*. New York, NY: Behrman House, Inc. and Summit Books, p. 45.

my pillow by night because of them. And I cry unto my Elohim in faith, and I know that he will hear my cry, and I know that Adonai YHWH will consecrate my prayers for the gain of my people. And the word which I have written in weakness will he make strong unto them, for it persuades men to do good. It makes known unto them of their fathers, and it speaks of Yeshua and persuades men to believe in him and to endure to the end, which is life Eternal. And it speaks harshly against sin according to the plainness of the truth; wherefore, no man will be angry at the words which I have written, except he shall be of the spirit of the adversary. I glory in plainness; I glory in truth; I glory in my Yeshua, for he has redeemed my soul from She'ol. I have charity for my people and great faith in Mashiach that I shall meet many souls spotless at his judgment seat. I have charity for the Y'hudi – I say Y'hudi because I mean them from where I came. I also have charity for the Goyim. But behold, for none of these can I hope except they shall be reconciled unto Mashiach, and enter into the narrow gate, and walk in the straight path which leads to life, and continue in the path until the end of the day of probation.

2 And now my beloved brothers, and also Y'hudi, and all you ends of the earth, hearken unto these words and believe in Mashiach; and if you believe not in these words, believe in Mashiach. And if you shall believe in Mashiach, you will believe in these words, for they are the words of Mashiach; and he has given them unto me, and they teach all men that they should do good. And if they are not the words of Mashiach, judge you, for Mashiach will show unto you with power and great glory that they are his words at the last day. And you and I shall stand face to face before his bar, and you shall know that I have been commanded of him to write these things, despite my weakness. And I pray the Father in the name of Mashiach that many of us, if not all, may be saved in his kingdom at that great and last day.

3 And now my beloved brothers, all those who are of the house of Isra'el, and all you ends of the earth, I speak unto you as the voice of one crying **from the dust**.[202] Shalom until that great day shall come. And you that will not partake of the goodness of Elohim, and respect the words of the Y'hudim, and also my words, and the words which

---

202 Isa. 29:4

shall proceed forth out of the mouth of the Lamb of Elohim, behold, I bid you an everlasting shalom, for these words shall condemn you at the last day. For what I seal on earth shall be brought against you at the judgment bar, for thus has YHWH commanded me and I must obey. Amen.

ספר יעקב אח נפי
YA'AKOV
THE BOOK OF YA'AKOV
THE BROTHER OF NEFI

The words of his preaching unto his people. He confounds a man who seeks to overthrow the doctrine of Mashiach. A few words concerning the history of the people of Nefi.

For behold, it came to pass that fifty and five years[1] had passed away from the time that Lechi left Yerushalayim. Wherefore, Nefi gave me, Ya'akov, a commandment[2] concerning these small plates upon which these things are engraved. And he gave me, Ya'akov, a commandment that I should write upon these plates a few of the things which I considered to be most precious;[3] that I should not touch, except it were lightly, concerning the history of this people which are called the people of Nefi. For he said that the history of his people should be engraved upon his other plates, and that I should preserve these plates and hand them down unto my seed, from generation to generation. And if there were preaching which was sacred, or revelation which was great, or prophesying, that I should engrave the chief points of them upon these plates and touch upon them as much as it were possible, for Mashiach's sake, and for the sake of our people. For because of faith and great anxiety, it truly had been made manifest unto us concerning our people, what things should happen unto them. And we also had many revelations and the spirit of much prophecy. Wherefore, we knew[4] of Mashiach and his kingdom which should come. Wherefore, we labored diligently among our people that we might persuade them to come[5] unto Mashiach and

---

1 ~545 BCE; 1 Nefi 1:7 **2** 1 Nefi 2:14; 5:35 **3** 1 Nefi 2:1 **4** Ya'akov 3:1–2 **5** 2 Nefi 6:11;

partake of the goodness of Elohim, **that they might enter into his rest**,⁶ for fear that by any means he **should swear in** his **wrath they should not enter in**,⁷ as in the provocation in the days of temptation **while the children of Isra'el were in the wilderness**.⁸ Wherefore, we would to Elohim that we could persuade all men not to rebel against Elohim, **to provoke him to anger**,⁹ but that all men would believe in Mashiach,¹⁰ and view his death,¹¹ and suffer his Tz'lav, and bear the shame of the world. Wherefore, I, Ya'akov, take it upon me to fulfill the commandment of my brother Nefi.

2 Now Nefi began to be old, and he saw that he must soon die; wherefore, he anointed a man to be a king and a ruler over his people. Now, according to the reigns of the kings, the people having loved Nefi exceedingly, he having been a great protector for them, having wielded the sword of Lavan in their defense, and having labored in all his days for their welfare; wherefore, the people were desirous to retain in remembrance his name. And whoever should reign in his place were called by the people, Second Nefi, and Third Nefi, and so forth, according to the reigns of the kings; and thus they were called by the people, let them be of whatsoever name they would.

3 And it came to pass that Nefi died. Now the people which were not Lamanites were Nefites; nevertheless, they were called Nefites, Ya'akovites, Yosefites, Tzuramites, Lamanites, L'mu'elites, and Yishma'elites. But I, Ya'akov, shall not hereafter distinguish them by these names, but I shall call them Lamanites that seek to destroy the people of Nefi; and they who are friendly to Nefi I shall call Nefites, or the people of Nefi, according to the reigns of the kings.

4 And now it came to pass that the people of Nefi, under the reign of the second king, began to grow hard in their hearts and indulge themselves somewhat in wicked practices, such as like unto David of old, desiring many wives and concubines, and also Solomon, his son.¹² Yes, and they also began to search much gold and silver, and began to be lifted up somewhat in pride.¹³ Wherefore, I, Ya'akov, gave unto them these words as I taught them in the Temple, having firstly obtained my errand from YHWH. For I, Ya'akov, and my brother Yosef,

---

Ameni 1:10; Moshiyah 8:14 **6** Alma 9:8-9; Alma 19:6 **7** Ps. 95:11 **8** Ex. 20:18-21; Deut. 9:23 **9** Deut. 4:25 **10** Moshiyah 2:3; M'roni 10:6 **11** Zech. 13:6; Ps. 22. **12** Deut. 17:17; 1 Sam. 25:42-43; 2 Sam. 5:13; 20:3; 1 Kings 11:1-8; see also Ya'akov 2:6-7. **13** 3 3 Nefi 3:2-3

had been consecrated kohanim and teachers of this people by the hand of Nefi.[14] And we did magnify our office unto YHWH, taking upon us the responsibility, answering the sins of the people upon our own heads if we did not teach them the word of Elohim with all diligence. Wherefore, by laboring with our might,[15] their blood might not come upon our garments; otherwise, their blood would come upon our garments and we would not be found spotless at the last day.

2 The words which Ya'akov, the brother of Nefi, spoke unto the people of Nefi, after the death of Nefi: Now, my beloved brothers, I, Ya'akov, according to the responsibility which I am under to Elohim to magnify my office with soberness, and that I might rid my garments of your sins, I come up into the Temple this day that I might declare unto you the word of Elohim. And you yourselves know that I have thus far been diligent in the office of my calling, but I this day am weighed down with much more desire and anxiety for the welfare of your souls than I have previously been. For behold, as yet you have been obedient unto the word of YHWH which I have given unto you. But behold, hearken unto me and know that by the help of the all-powerful Creator of Heaven and earth, I can tell you concerning your thoughts,[16] how that you are beginning to labor in sin, which sin appears very abominable unto me, yes, and abominable unto Elohim. Yes, and it grieves my soul, and causes me to shrink with shame before the presence of my Maker, that I must testify unto you concerning the wickedness of your hearts. And also it grieves me that I must use so much boldness of speech concerning you before your wives and your children, many of whose feelings are exceedingly tender, and chaste, and delicate before Elohim, which thing is pleasing unto Elohim. And I suppose that they have come up here to hear the pleasing word of Elohim, yes, the word which heals the wounded soul.

2 Wherefore, it burdens my soul that I should be constrained, because of the strict mitzvah which I have received from Elohim, to admonish you according to your crimes, to enlarge the wounds of those who are already wounded, instead of consoling and healing

---

14 See footnote to 2 Nefi 4:5 regarding kohanim and teachers. **15** 2 Nefi 11:8-9; Yahram 1:5; Moshiyah 1:8-9 **16** Moshiyah 2:6

their wounds. And those who have not been wounded, instead of feasting upon the pleasing word of Elohim, have daggers placed to pierce their souls and wound their delicate minds. But despite the greatness of the task, I must do according to the strict commands of Elohim and tell you concerning your wickedness and abominations in the presence of the pure in heart,[17] and the broken heart, and under the glance of the piercing eye of El Shaddai.

3 Wherefore, I must tell you the truth according to the plainness[18] of the word of Elohim. For behold, as I inquired of YHWH, thus came the word unto me, saying, Ya'akov, get you up into the Temple tomorrow and declare the word which I shall give you unto this people.

4 And now behold, my brothers, this is the word which I declare unto you: that many of you have begun to search for gold, and for silver, and all manner of precious ores, in the which this land, which is a land of promise unto you and to your seed, abounds most plentifully. And the hand of Providence has smiled upon you most pleasingly, that you have obtained many riches. And because some of you have obtained more abundantly than that of your brothers, you are lifted up in the pride of your hearts,[19] and wear stiff necks and high heads because of the costliness of your apparel, and persecute your brothers because you suppose that you are better than they.

5 And now my brothers, do you suppose that Elohim justifies you in this thing? Behold, I say unto you, no, but he condemns you; and if you persist in these things, his judgments must speedily come unto you. Oh that he would show you that he can pierce you, and with one glance of his eye he can smite you to the dust. Oh that he would rid you from this iniquity and abomination. And, oh that you would listen unto the word of his commands, and let not this pride of your hearts destroy your souls. Think of your brothers like unto yourselves,[20] and be familiar with all and free with your substance, that they may be rich like unto you. But before you seek for riches, seek you for the kingdom of Elohim. And after you have obtained a hope in Mashiach, you shall obtain riches if you seek them. And you will seek them for the intent to do good: to clothe the naked, and to feed the hungry, and to liberate the captive, and administer relief to the sick and the afflicted.[21]

---

17 3 Nefi 5:17 **18** 2 Nefi 11:1, 3, 7 **19** M'raman 4:4-5 **20** Matt. 7:12; Alma 2:4-5
21 Moshiyah 2:4-6

6 And now my brothers, I have spoken unto you concerning pride. And those of you which have afflicted your neighbor and persecuted him because you were proud in your hearts of the things which Elohim has given you, what say you of it? Do you not suppose that such things are abominable unto him who created all flesh? And the one being is as precious in his sight as the other.[22] And all flesh is of the dust. And for the very same end has he created them, that they should keep his mitzvot[23] and glorify him for ever. And now I make an end of speaking unto you concerning this pride. And were it not that I must speak unto you concerning a more shameful crime, my heart would rejoice exceedingly because of you. But the word of Elohim burdens me because of your more shameful crimes. For behold, thus says YHWH: This people begins to grow[24] in iniquity; they understand not the scriptures,[25] for they seek to excuse themselves in committing whoredoms because of the things which are written concerning David, and Solomon his son. Behold, David and Solomon truly had many wives and concubines,[26] which thing was abominable before me, says YHWH.[27]

7 Wherefore, thus says YHWH: I have led this people forth out of the land of Yerushalayim by the power of my arm, that I might raise up unto me a righteous branch from the fruit of the loins of Yosef. Wherefore, I, Adonai YHWH, will not allow that this people shall do like unto them of old.[28] Wherefore, my brothers, hear me and hearken to the word of YHWH: For there shall not any man among you have except it be one wife, and concubines he shall have none;[29] for I, Adonai YHWH, delight in the chastity of women. And whoredoms are an abomination before me; thus says YHWH Tzva'ot. Wherefore, this people shall keep my mitzvot, says YHWH Tzva'ot, or cursed be the land for their sakes.

8 For if I will, says YHWH Tzva'ot, raise up seed unto me, I will command my people. Otherwise, they shall hearken unto these

---

22 Moshiyah 13:9 23 Alma 14:15 24 1 Nefi 5:21 25 1 Nefi 4:2; Ya'akov 5:2 26 1 Sam 25:42-43; 2 Sam. 5:13; 20:3; 1 Kings 11:1-8 27 Deut. 17:17 28 Ya'akov 2:11; Alma 21:3 29 In the Dead Sea Scrolls, we read this strong rebuke of polygamy: "They are caught in fornication, by taking two wives in their lifetime although the principle of creation is 'male and female He Created them' (Gen. 1:27) and those who entered the ark 'went into the ark two by two' (Gen. 7:9). Concerning the Leaders it is written 'he shall not multiply wives to himself' (Deut. 17:17)" (Damascus Document 4.20-5.2). Compare Matt. 19:3-9 and 1 Tim. 3:2.

things: for behold, I, YHWH, have seen[30] the sorrow and heard the mourning of the daughters of my people in the land of Yerushalayim, yes, and in all the lands of my people, because of the wickedness and abominations of their husbands. And I will not allow, says YHWH Tzva'ot, that the cries of the fair daughters of this people, which I have led out of the land of Yerushalayim, shall come up unto me against the men of my people, says YHWH Tzva'ot. For they shall not lead away captive the daughters of my people because of their tenderness, except I shall visit them with a sore curse, even unto destruction. For they shall not commit whoredoms like unto them of old, says YHWH Tzva'ot.

9 And now behold, my brothers, you know that these mitzvot were given to our father, Lechi.[31] Wherefore, you have known them before, and you have come unto great condemnation, **for you have done these things which you ought not to have done.**[32] Behold, you have done greater iniquity than the Lamanites, our brothers. You have broken the hearts of your tender wives and lost the confidence of your children because of your bad examples before them, and the sobbings of their hearts ascend up to Elohim against you. And because of the strictness of the word of Elohim which comes down against you, many hearts died, pierced with deep wounds.

10 But behold, I, Ya'akov, would speak unto you that are pure in heart. Look unto Elohim with firmness of mind, and pray unto him with exceeding faith, and he will console you in your afflictions, and he will plead your cause and send down justice upon those who seek your destruction.

11 O all you that are pure in heart,[33] lift up your heads, and receive the pleasing word of Elohim, and feast upon his love, for you may, if your minds are firm for ever. But woe, woe unto you that are not pure in heart, that are unclean this day before Elohim; for except you shall repent, the land is cursed for your sakes.[34] And the Lamanites, who are not unclean like unto you — nevertheless, they are cursed with a sore cursing[35] — shall scourge you even unto destruction. And the time speedily comes that except you repent, they shall possess the land

---

30 Alma 2:3-4; M'raman 1:6   31 1 Nefi 1:6-7; 5:18-21   32 Gen. 20:9   33 2 Nefi 11:5-6
34 Alma 21:3; 'Eter 1:7   35 This is an example of the Hebraism known as the Cognate Accusative, where a noun pairs with the verb which is the noun's root (cursed with a... cursing).

of your inheritance, and Adonai YHWH will lead away the righteous out from among you. Behold, the Lamanites, your brothers whom you hate because of their uncleanness and the cursings which have come upon their skins, **are more righteous than you;**[36] for they have not forgotten the mitzvah of YHWH which was given unto our father, that they should have except it were one wife, and concubines they should have none, and there should not be whoredoms committed among them. And now this mitzvah they observe to keep. Wherefore, because of this observance in keeping this mitzvah, Adonai YHWH will not destroy them, but will be merciful unto them, and one day they shall become a blessed people. Behold, their husbands love their wives, and their wives love their husbands, and their husbands and their wives love their children; and their unbelief and their hatred towards you is because of **the iniquity of their fathers.**[37] Wherefore, how much better are you than they in the sight of your great Creator?

12 O my brothers, I fear that unless you shall repent of your sins, that their skins will be whiter than yours when you shall be brought with them before the throne of Elohim. Wherefore, a mitzvah I give unto you, which is the word of Elohim, that you revile no more against them because of the darkness of their skin, neither shall you revile against them because of their uncleanness, but you shall remember your own uncleanness, and remember that their uncleanness came because of their fathers. Wherefore, you shall remember your children, how that you have grieved their hearts because of the example that you have set before them, and also remember that you may, because of your uncleanness, bring your children unto destruction, and their sins be heaped upon your heads at the last day.

13 O my brothers, hearken unto my words; arouse the faculties of your souls. Shake yourselves, that you may awake from the slumber of death, and loose yourselves from the pains of She'ol, that you may not become angels to HaSatan, to be cast into that lake of fire and brimstone which is the second death.[38] And now I, Ya'akov, spoke many more things unto the people of Nefi, warning them against fornication, and lustfulness, and every kind of sin, telling them the awful consequences of them. And a hundredth part of the proceedings of this people, which now began to be numerous, cannot

---

36 Ezek. 16:52 **37** Lev. 26:40 **38** 2 Nefi 1:10-11; Moshiyah 1:18

be written upon these plates; but many of their proceedings are written upon the larger plates, and their wars, and their contentions, and the reigns of their kings. These plates are called the Plates of Ya'akov, and they were made by the hand of Nefi. And I make an end of speaking these words.

3 Now behold, it came to pass that I, Ya'akov, having ministered much unto my people in word, and I cannot write but a few of my words because of the difficulty of engraving our words upon plates; and we know that the things which we write upon plates must endure, but whatsoever things we write upon anything except it be upon plates must perish and vanish away; but we can write a few words upon plates which will give our children, and also our beloved brothers, a small degree of knowledge concerning us, or concerning their fathers. Now in this thing we do rejoice, and we labor diligently to engrave these words upon plates, hoping that our beloved brothers and our children will receive them with thankful hearts and look upon them, that they may learn with joy, and not with sorrow, neither with contempt, concerning their first parents. For, for this intent have we written these things: that they may know that we knew of Mashiach,[39] and we had a hope of his glory many hundred years before his coming. And not only we ourselves had a hope of his glory, but also all the holy prophets which were before us.

2 Behold, they **believed** in Mashiach[40] and worshipped the Father in his name, and also we worship the Father in his name. And for this intent we keep the Torah of Moshe,[41] it pointing our souls to him. And for this cause it is sanctified unto us **for righteousness**, even as it was **accounted unto Avraham**[42] in the wilderness to be obedient unto the commands of Elohim in offering up his son Yitz'chak,[43] which was a similitude of Elohim and his only begotten Son. Wherefore, we search the prophets, and we have many revelations and the spirit of prophecy. And having all these witnesses, we obtain a hope and our faith[44] becomes unshaken, insomuch that we truly can command in the name of Yeshua and the very trees obey us, or the mountains,

---

[39] 1 Nefi 3:2-5; Ya'akov 1:1 [40] 2 Nefi 11:7-8 [41] Alma 16:34 [42] Gen. 15:6. The Targum Onkelos reads: "And Abraham trusted in the Word [*Memra*] of YHWH, and He counted it to him for righteousness" (Targum Onkelos Gen. 15:6). [43] Gen. 22:1-18 [44] Alma 16:27-30; 'Eter 5:2-3

or the waves of the sea. Nevertheless, Adonai YHWH shows us our weakness,[45] that we may know that it is by his grace and his great condescensions unto the children of men that we have power to do these things.

3 Behold, great and marvelous are the works[46] of YHWH; how unsearchable are the depths of the mysteries of him. And it is impossible that man should find out all his ways. And no man knows of his ways except it be revealed unto him; wherefore, brothers, despise not the revelations of Elohim. For behold, by the power of his word, man came upon the face of the earth, which earth was created by the power of his word. Wherefore, if Elohim being able to speak and the world was, and to speak and man was created, oh then why not able to command the earth or the workmanship of his hands upon the face of it according to his will and pleasure? Wherefore, brothers, seek not to counsel YHWH, but to take counsel from his hand; for behold, you yourselves know that he counsels in wisdom, and in justice, and in great mercy, over all his works. Wherefore, beloved, be reconciled unto him through the atonement of Mashiach, his only begotten Son, that you may obtain a resurrection according to the power of the resurrection which is in Mashiach, and be presented as the firstfruits of Mashiach unto Elohim, having faith and obtained a good hope of glory in him before he manifests himself in the flesh.

4 And now beloved, marvel not that I tell you these things; for why not speak of the atonement of Mashiach and attain to a perfect knowledge[47] of him, as to attain to the knowledge of a resurrection and the world to come? Behold, my brothers, he that prophesies, let him prophesy to the understanding of men. For the spirit speaks the truth, and lies not; wherefore, it speaks of things as they really are, and of things as they really will be. Wherefore, these things are manifested unto us plainly for the salvation of our souls. But behold, we are not witnesses alone in these things, for Elohim also spoke them unto prophets of old.

5 But behold, the Judeans were a stiffnecked people, and they despised the words of plainness, and killed the prophets, and sought for things that they could not understand.[48] Wherefore, because of their blindness, which blindness came by looking beyond the mark,

---

45 'Eter 5:5 **46** 1 Nefi 1:3; M'raman 4:4–5 **47** 2 Nefi 6:5 **48** As we read in the Talmud,

they must necessarily fall; for Elohim has taken away his plainness from them, and delivered unto them many things **which they cannot understand**[49] because they desired it. And because they desired it, Elohim has done it that they may stumble.

6 And now I, Ya'akov, am led on by the spirit unto prophesying, for I perceive by the workings of the spirit which is in me that by the stumbling of the Y'hudim, they will reject the stone upon which they might build and have safe foundation. But behold, according to the scriptures, this stone shall become the great, and the last, and the only **sure foundation**[50] upon which the Y'hudim can build.[51] And now my beloved, how is it possible that these, after having rejected the sure foundation, can ever build upon it that it may become the **head of their corner**?[52] Behold, my beloved brothers, I will unfold this mystery unto you, if I do not by any means get shaken from my firmness in the spirit and stumble because of my overanxiety for you.

7 Behold, my brothers, do you not remember to have read the words of the prophet Zenos which he spoke unto the house of Isra'el, saying, Hearken, O you house of Isra'el, and hear the words of me,[53] a prophet of YHWH? For behold, thus says YHWH: I will compare you, O house of Isra'el, like unto a tame olive tree[54] which a man took and nourished in his vineyard.[55] And it grew, and became old, and began to decay. And it came to pass that the master of the vineyard went forth, and he saw that his olive tree began to decay. And he said, I will prune it, and dig about it, and nourish it, that perhaps it may shoot forth young and tender branches and it perish not. And it came to pass that he pruned it, and dug about it, and nourished it, according to his word. And it came to pass that after many days

---

"...it is written in the Book of Ben Sira 'Seek not things that are too hard for you' (Ben Sira 3:21-22), and search not things that are hidden from you. The things that have permitted you, think thereupon; you have no business with the things that are secret..." (b.Chagigah 13a). This is said in regards to the statement in the Mishnah (concerning Kabbalah), "Do not expound upon…the account of Creation before two, or the account of the divine throne chariot before one, unless he was a sage and understands of his own knowledge" (m.Chagigah 2:1). **49** Isa. 44:18 **50** Isa. 28:16 **51** Cheleman 2:17 **52** Ps. 118:22 **53** This unusual order of words ("words of me") would be normal in Hebrew where the pronominal suffix would have been used. **54** 1 Nefi 3:4 **55** While the Torah prohibits sowing diverse seeds in a vineyard (Deut. 22:9), the Mishnah does not consider the presence of olive trees in a vineyard as violating this commandment (m.Kilayim 6:3-5). Since ancient times, olive trees have traditionally been cultivated alongside grapes due to their mutual affinity for the same soil and climate, their staggered harvest seasons, and the protection the trees afford the grapes from certain weather phenomena. This practice continues today.

it began to put forth somewhat a little, young and tender branches; but behold, the main top thereof began to perish. And it came to pass that the master of the vineyard saw it, and he said unto his servant, It grieves me that I should lose this tree. Wherefore, go and pluck the branches from a wild olive tree and bring them here unto me; and we will pluck off those main branches which are beginning to wither away, and we will cast them into the fire that they may be burned. And behold, said the Adon of the vineyard, I take away many of these young and tender branches, and I will graft them wherever I will, and it matters not that if it so be that the root of this tree will perish, I may preserve the fruit thereof unto myself. Wherefore, I will take these young and tender branches, and I will graft them wherever I will; you take the branches of the wild olive tree and graft them in,[56] in the place thereof. And these which I have plucked off, I will cast into the fire and burn them,[57] that they may not encumber the ground of my vineyard.

8 And it came to pass that the servant of the Adon of the vineyard did according to the word of the Adon of the vineyard, and grafted in the branches of the wild olive tree. And the Adon of the vineyard caused that it should be dug about, and pruned, and nourished, saying unto his servant, It grieves me that I should lose this tree. Wherefore, that perhaps I might preserve the roots thereof, that they perish not, that I might preserve them unto myself, I have done this thing. Wherefore, go your way, watch the tree, and nourish it according to my words. And these will I place in the lowest part of my vineyard, wherever I will; it is not your concern. And I do it that I may preserve unto myself the natural branches of the tree, and also that I may lay up fruit thereof against the season unto myself; for it grieves me that I should lose this tree and the fruit thereof.

9 And it came to pass that the Adon of the vineyard went his way and hid the natural branches of the tame olive tree in the lowest parts of the vineyard, some in one and some in another,[58] according to his will and pleasure. And it came to pass that a long time passed away, and the Adon of the vineyard said unto his servant, Come, let us go down into the vineyard, that we may labor in the vineyard.

---

56 The Zohar also uses the allegory of being "grafted in" to describe proselytes becoming part of Israel (Zohar 1:26).   57 Jer. 11:16   58 Isa. 27:6; 37:31

¹⁰ And it came to pass that the Adon of the vineyard, and also the servant, went down into the vineyard to labor. And it came to pass that the servant said unto his master, Behold, look here; behold the tree. And it came to pass that the Adon of the vineyard looked and beheld the tree in the which the wild olive branches had been grafted, and it had sprung forth and began to bear fruit. And he beheld that it was good, and the fruit thereof was like unto the natural fruit. And he said unto the servant, Behold, the branches of the wild tree have taken hold of the moisture of the root thereof, that the root thereof has brought forth much strength. And because of the much strength of the root thereof, the wild branches have brought forth tame fruit. Now, if we had not grafted in these branches, the tree thereof would have perished. And now behold, I shall lay up much fruit which the tree thereof has brought forth; and the fruit thereof I shall lay up against the season unto my own self.

¹¹ And it came to pass that the Adon of the vineyard said unto the servant, Come, let us go to the lowest parts of the vineyard and see if the natural branches of the tree have not brought forth much fruit also, that I may lay up of the fruit thereof against the season unto my own self. And it came to pass that they went forth, where the master of the vineyard had hidden the natural branches of the tree, and he said unto the servant, Behold these. And he beheld the first, that it had brought forth much fruit, and he beheld also that it was good. And he said unto the servant, Take of the fruit thereof and lay it up against the season, that I may preserve it unto my own self. For behold, said he, this long time have I nourished it and it has brought forth much fruit.

¹² And it came to pass that the servant said unto his master, Why did you come here to plant this tree, or this branch of the tree? For behold, it was the poorest spot in all the land of your vineyard. And the Adon of the vineyard said unto him, Counsel me not. I knew that it was a poor spot of ground; wherefore, I said unto you I have nourished it this long time, and you can see that it has brought forth much fruit.

¹³ And it came to pass that the Adon of the vineyard said unto his servant, Look here. Behold, I have planted another branch of the tree also, and you know that this spot of ground was poorer than the first, but behold the tree. I have nourished it this long time and it has

brought forth much fruit. Therefore, gather it and lay it up against the season, that I may preserve it unto my own self.

14 And it came to pass that the Adon of the vineyard said again unto his servant, Look here and behold another branch also which I have planted. Behold that I have nourished it also, and it has brought forth fruit. And he said unto the servant, Look here and behold the last. Behold, this have I planted in a good spot of ground, and I have nourished it this long time, and only a part of the tree has brought forth tame fruit; and the other part of the tree has brought forth wild fruit. Behold, I have nourished this tree like unto the others.

15 And it came to pass that the Adon of the vineyard said unto the servant, Pluck off the branches that have not brought forth good fruit and cast them into the fire. But behold, the servant said unto him, Let us prune it, and dig about it, and nourish it a little longer, that perhaps it may bring forth good fruit unto you, that you can lay it up against the season. And it came to pass that the Adon of the vineyard, and the servant of the Adon of the vineyard, did nourish all the fruit of the vineyard.

16 And it came to pass that a long time had passed away, and the Adon of the vineyard said unto his servant, Come, let us go down in the vineyard, that we may labor again in the vineyard. For behold, the time draws near and the end soon comes. Wherefore, I must lay up fruit against the season unto my own self. And it came to pass that the Adon of the vineyard and the servant went down into the vineyard, and they came to the tree whose natural branches had been broken off and the wild branches had been grafted in; and behold, all sorts of fruit did encumber the tree.

17 And it came to pass that the Adon of the vineyard did taste of the fruit, every sort according to its number. And the Adon of the vineyard said, Behold, this long time have we nourished this tree, and I have laid up unto myself against the season much fruit. But behold, this time it has brought forth much fruit, and there is none of it which is good. And behold, there are all kinds of bad fruit, and it profits me nothing, despite all our labor; and now it grieves me that I should lose this tree. And the Adon of the vineyard said unto the servant, What shall we do unto the tree that I may preserve again good fruit thereof unto my own self? And the servant said unto his master, Behold, because you did graft in the branches of the wild olive

tree, they have nourished the roots, that they are alive and they have not perished; wherefore, you can see that they are yet good.

18 And it came to pass that the Adon of the vineyard said unto his servant, The tree profits me nothing and the roots thereof profit me nothing, so long as it shall bring forth evil fruit. Nevertheless, I know that the roots are good, and for my own purpose I have preserved them. And because of their much strength, they have previously brought forth from the wild branches good fruit. But behold, the wild branches have grown and have overrun the roots thereof. And because that the wild branches have overcome the roots thereof, it has brought forth much evil fruit. And because that it has brought forth so much evil fruit, you can see that it begins to perish; and it will soon become ripened, that it may be cast into the fire, except we should do something for it to preserve it.

19 And it came to pass that the Adon of the vineyard said unto his servant, Let us go down into the lowest parts of the vineyard and see if the natural branches have also brought forth evil fruit. And it came to pass that they went down into the lowest parts of the vineyard. And it came to pass that they beheld that the fruit of the natural branches had become corrupt also, yes, the first, and the second, and also the last; and they had all become corrupt. And the wild fruit of the last had overcome that part of the tree which brought forth good fruit, even that the branch had withered away and died.

20 And it came to pass that the Adon of the vineyard wept and said unto the servant, **What could I have done more for my vineyard?**[59] Behold, I knew that all the fruit of the vineyard, except it were these, had become corrupted. And now these, which have once brought forth good fruit, have also become corrupted. And now all the trees of my vineyard are good for nothing, except it be to be cut down and cast into the fire. And behold, this last, whose branch has withered away, I did plant in a good spot of ground, yes, even that which was choice unto me, above all other parts of the land of my vineyard.

21 And you can see that I also cut down that which encumbered this spot of ground, that I might plant this tree in the place thereof. And you can see that a part thereof brought forth good fruit, and a part thereof brought forth wild fruit. And because I plucked not

---

59 Isa. 5:4

the branches thereof and cast them into the fire, behold, they have overcome the good branch, that it has withered away. And now behold, despite all the care which we have taken of my vineyard, the trees thereof have become corrupted, that they bring forth no good fruit. And these I had hoped to preserve, to have laid up fruit thereof against the season unto my own self. But behold, they have become like unto the wild olive tree, and they are of no worth but to be cut down and cast into the fire; and it grieves me that I should lose them. But what could I have done more in my vineyard? Have I slackened my hand, that I have not nourished it? No, I have nourished it, and I have dug about it, and I have pruned it, and I have dunged it, **and I have stretched forth my hand almost all the day long,**[60] and the end draws near. And it grieves me that I should cut down all the trees of my vineyard and cast them into the fire that they should be burned. Who is it that has corrupted my vineyard?

22 And it came to pass that the servant said unto his master, Is it not the loftiness of your vineyard? Have not the branches thereof overcome the roots which are good? And because the branches have overcome the roots thereof — behold, they grew faster than the strength of the roots, taking strength unto themselves — behold, I say, is not this the cause that the trees of your vineyard have become corrupted?

23 And it came to pass that the Adon of the vineyard said unto the servant, Let us go to, and cut down the trees of the vineyard, and cast them into the fire, that they shall not encumber the ground of my vineyard, for I have done all. What could I have done more for my vineyard? But behold, the servant said unto the Adon of the vineyard, Spare it a little longer.[61] And the Adon said, Yes, I will spare it a little longer, for it grieves me that I should lose the trees of my vineyard. Wherefore, let us take of the branches of these which I have planted in the lowest parts of my vineyard, and let us graft them into the tree from which they came. And let us pluck from the tree those branches whose fruit is most bitter, and graft in the natural branches of the tree in the place thereof. And this will I do that the tree may not perish, that perhaps I may preserve unto myself the roots thereof for my own purpose. And behold, the roots of the natural branches of the tree

---

60 Isa. 65:2 **61** 1 Nefi 4:2-4

which I planted wherever I would are yet alive. Wherefore, that I may preserve them also for my own purpose, I will take of the branches of this tree, and I will graft them in unto them. Yes, I will graft in unto them the branches of their mother tree, that I may preserve the roots also unto my own self, that when they shall be sufficiently strong, perhaps they may bring forth good fruit unto me, and I may yet have glory in the fruit of my vineyard.

24 And it came to pass that they took from the natural tree which had become wild, and grafted in unto the natural trees which also had become wild. And they also took of the natural trees which had become wild and grafted into their mother tree. And the Adon of the vineyard said unto the servant, Pluck not the wild branches from the trees, except it be those which are most bitter; and in them, you shall graft according to that which I have said. And we will nourish again the trees of the vineyard, and we will trim up the branches thereof, and we will pluck from the trees those branches which are ripened that must perish and cast them into the fire. And this I do that perhaps the roots thereof may take strength because of their goodness, and because of the change of the branches, that the good may overcome the evil. And because that I have preserved the natural branches and the roots thereof, and that I have grafted in the natural branches again into their mother tree, and have preserved the roots of their mother tree — that perhaps the trees of my vineyard may bring forth again good fruit, and that I may have joy again in the fruit of my vineyard, and perhaps that I may rejoice exceedingly that I have preserved the roots and the branches of the first fruit — wherefore, go to, and call servants, that we may labor diligently with our might in the vineyard, that we may prepare the way, that I may bring forth again the natural fruit, which natural fruit is good, and the most precious above all other fruit.

25 Wherefore, let us go to and labor with our might this last time; for behold, the end draws near, and this is the last time that I shall prune my vineyard. Graft in the branches. Begin at the last, that they may be first and that the first may be last;[62] and dig about the trees, both old and young, the first and the last, and the last and the first, that all may be nourished once again for the last time. Wherefore,

---

62 1 Nefi 3:24; 'Eter 6:2-3

dig about them, and prune them, and dung them once more for the last time, for the end draws near. And if it so be that these last grafts shall grow and bring forth the natural fruit, then shall you prepare the way for them that they may grow. And as they begin to grow, you shall clear away the branches which bring forth bitter fruit, according to the strength of the good and the size thereof. And you shall not clear away the bad thereof all at once, lest the roots thereof should be too strong for the graft and the graft thereof shall perish, and I lose the trees of my vineyard; for it grieves me that I should lose the trees of my vineyard. Wherefore, you shall clear away the bad according as the good shall grow, that the root and the top may be equal in strength, until the good shall overcome the bad and the bad be cut down and cast into the fire, that they encumber not the ground of my vineyard. And thus will I sweep away the bad out of my vineyard. And the branches of the natural tree will I graft in again into the natural tree, and the branches of the natural tree will I graft into the natural branches of the tree, and thus will I bring them together again, that they shall bring forth the natural fruit, and they shall be one. And the bad shall be cast away, yes, even out of all the land of my vineyard; for behold, only this once will I prune my vineyard.

26 And it came to pass that the Adon of the vineyard sent his servant, and the servant went and did as the Adon had commanded him and brought other servants, and they were few. And the Adon of the vineyard said unto them, Go to and labor in the vineyard with your might, for behold, this is the last time that I shall nourish my vineyard, for the end is near at hand and the season speedily comes. And if you labor with your might with me, you shall have joy in the fruit which I shall lay up unto myself against the time which will soon come.

27 And it came to pass that the servants did go and labor with their might, and the Adon of the vineyard labored also with them. And they did obey the commandments of the Adon of the vineyard in all things. And there began to be the natural fruit again in the vineyard. And the natural branches began to grow and thrive exceedingly, and the wild branches began to be plucked off and to be cast away; and they did keep the root and the top thereof equal, according to the strength thereof. And thus they labored with all diligence, according to the commandments of the Adon of the vineyard, even until the bad had been cast away out of the vineyard and the Adon had preserved

unto himself, that the trees had become again the natural fruit. And they became like unto one body, and the fruits were equal. And the Adon of the vineyard had preserved unto himself the natural fruit, which was most precious unto him from the beginning.

28 And it came to pass that when the Adon of the vineyard saw that his fruit was good and that his vineyard was no more corrupt, he called up his servants and said unto them, Behold, for this last time have we nourished my vineyard.[63] And you can see that I have done according to my will, and I have preserved the natural fruit, that it is good, even as if it were in the beginning. And blessed are you, for because you have been diligent in laboring with me in my vineyard, and have kept my commandments, and have brought unto me again the natural fruit, that my vineyard is no more corrupted and the bad is cast away, behold, you shall have joy with me because of the fruit of my vineyard. For behold, for a long time will I lay up of the fruit of my vineyard unto my own self against the season which speedily comes. And for the last time have I nourished my vineyard, and pruned it, and dug about it, and dunged it. Wherefore, I will lay up unto my own self of the fruit for a long time, according to that which I have spoken. And when the time comes that evil fruit shall again come into my vineyard, then will I cause the good and the bad to be gathered. And the good will I preserve unto myself, and the bad will I cast away into its own place. And then comes the season and the end, and my vineyard will I cause to be burned with fire.

4 And now behold, my brothers, as I said unto you that I would prophesy, behold, this is my prophecy, that the things which this prophet Zenos spoke concerning the house of Isra'el, in the which he compared them unto a tame olive tree, must surely come to pass.[64] And in the day that he **shall set his hand again the second time to recover his people**,[65] is the day, yes, even the last time, that the servants of YHWH shall go forth in his power to nourish and prune his vineyard. And after that, the end soon comes. And how blessed are they who have labored diligently in his vineyard, and how cursed

---

63 As we read in the Talmud concerning Israel: "The Lord called your name a leafy olive-tree, fair with goodly fruit (Jer. 11:16): as the olive-tree produces its best only at the very end, so Israel will flourish at the end of time" (b.Menachot 53b).   **64** Words of M'raman 1:2-3   **65** Isa. 11:11; 2 Nefi 5:5; 9:18; 11:6; 12:8

are they who shall be cast out into their own place. And the world shall be burned with fire. And how merciful is our Elohim unto us, for he remembers the house of Isra'el, both roots and branches; and he stretches forth his hands unto them all the day long. And they are a stiffnecked and an argumentative people, but as many as will not harden their hearts shall be saved in the kingdom of Elohim.

2 Wherefore, my beloved brothers, I implore you in words of soberness that you would repent, and come with full purpose of heart,[66] and cling unto Elohim as he clings unto you. And while his arm of mercy is extended towards you in the light of the day, harden not your hearts. Yes, today, if you will hear his voice, harden not your hearts; for why will you die? For behold, after you have been nourished by the good word of Elohim all the day long, will you bring forth evil fruit that you must be cut down and cast into the fire? Behold, will you reject these words? Will you reject the words of the prophets? And will you reject all the words which have been spoken concerning Mashiach after so many have spoken concerning him? And deny the good word of Mashiach, and the power of Elohim, and the gift of the Ruach HaKodesh, and quench the Holy Spirit? And make a mockery of the great plan of redemption which has been laid for you? Do you not know that if you will do these things, that the power of the redemption and the resurrection which is in Mashiach will bring you to stand with shame and awful guilt before the bar of Elohim? And according to the power of justice — for justice cannot be denied — you must go away into that lake of fire and brimstone, whose flames are unquenchable, and whose smoke ascends up for ever and ever, which lake of fire and brimstone is Endless torment. O then, my beloved brothers, repent, and enter in at the strait gate,[67] and continue in the way which is narrow until you shall obtain Eternal life. Oh be wise. What can I say more? Finally, I bid you shalom, until I shall meet you before the pleasing bar of Elohim, which bar strikes the wicked with awful dread and fear. Amen.

5 And now it came to pass, after some years had passed away, and there came a man among the people of Nefi whose name was Sherem. And it came to pass that he began to preach among the

---

66 2 Nefi 13:2-3   67 2 Nefi 6:11

people and to declare unto them that there should be no Mashiach. And he preached many things which were flattering[68] unto the people, and this he did that he might overthrow the doctrine of Mashiach. And he labored diligently that he might lead away the hearts of the people, insomuch that he did lead away many hearts. And he knowing that I, Ya'akov, had faith in Mashiach, who should come, he sought much opportunity that he might come unto me. And he was learned, that he had a perfect knowledge of the language of the people; wherefore, he could use much flattery and much power of speech, according to the power of HaSatan. And he had hope to shake me from the faith, despite the many revelations and the many things which I had seen concerning these things; for I truly had seen angels[69] and they had ministered unto me. And also I had heard the voice of YHWH speaking unto me in very word from time to time; wherefore, I could not be shaken.

2 And it came to pass that he came unto me, and in this manner did he speak unto me, saying, Brother Ya'akov, I have sought much opportunity that I might speak unto you, for I have heard and also know that you go about much, preaching that which you call the besorah or the doctrine of Mashiach. And you have led away much of this people, that they pervert the right way of Elohim, and keep not the Torah of Moshe, which is the right way, and convert the Torah of Moshe into the worship of a being who you say shall come many hundred years hence. And now behold, I, Sherem, declare unto you that this is blasphemy; for no man knows of such things, for he cannot tell of things to come. And after this manner did Sherem contend against me. But behold, Adonai YHWH poured his spirit into my soul, insomuch that I did confound him in all his words. And I said unto him, Do you deny the Mashiach who shall come? And he said, If there should be a Mashiach, I would not deny him; but I know that there is no Mashiach, neither has been, nor ever will be. And I said unto him, Do you believe the scriptures? And he said, Yes. And I said unto him, Then you do not understand them, for they truly testify of Mashiach.[70] Behold, I say unto you that none of the prophets have written nor prophesied, except they have spoken concerning this

---

68 Moshiyah 11:18   **69** M'roni 7:4-7   **70** Alma 16:32; Cheleman 3:9; 3 Nefi 3:4; 4:11; 5:4; 7:2

Mashiach. And this is not all. It has been made manifest unto me, for I have heard and seen, and it also has been made manifest unto me by the power of the Ruach HaKodesh; wherefore, I know if there should be no atonement made, all mankind must be lost.

3 And it came to pass that he said unto me, Show me a sign by this power of the Ruach HaKodesh in the which you know so much.

4 And I said unto him, What am I that I should tempt Elohim to show unto you a sign in the thing which you know to be true? Yet you will deny it because you are of HaSatan. Nevertheless, not my will be done, but if Elohim shall smite you, let that be a sign unto you that he has power, both in Heaven and in earth, and also that Mashiach shall come. And your will, O YHWH, be done, and not mine.

5 And it came to pass that when I, Ya'akov, had spoken these words, the power of YHWH came upon him, insomuch that he fell to the earth. And it came to pass that he was nourished for the space of many days. And it came to pass that he said unto the people, Gather together tomorrow, for I shall die; wherefore, I desire to speak unto the people before I shall die.

6 And it came to pass that the next day the multitude were gathered together. And he spoke plainly unto them, and denied the things which he had taught them, and confessed the Mashiach, and the power of the Ruach HaKodesh, and the ministering of angels. And he spoke plainly unto them that he had been deceived by the power of HaSatan. And he spoke of Gehinnom, and of eternity, and of Eternal punishment. And he said, I fear that I have committed the unpardonable sin, for I have lied unto Elohim; for I denied the Mashiach and said that I believed the scriptures, and they truly testify of him. And because I have thus lied unto Elohim, I greatly fear that my case shall be awful but I confess unto Elohim.

7 And it came to pass that when he had said these words, he could say no more, and he gave up the ghost. And when the multitude had witnessed that he spoke these things as he was about to give up the ghost, they were astonished exceedingly, insomuch that the power of Elohim came down upon them and they were overcome, that they fell to the earth. Now, this thing was pleasing unto me, Ya'akov, for I had requested it of my Father who was in Heaven, for he had heard my cry and answered my prayer.

⁸And it came to pass that shalom and the love of Elohim was restored again among the people, and they searched the scriptures[71] and hearkened no more to the words of this wicked man. And it came to pass that many means were devised to reclaim and restore the Lamanites to the knowledge of the truth, but it all was vain; for they delighted in wars and bloodsheds, and they had an eternal hatred against us, their brothers. And they sought by the power of their arms to destroy us continually; wherefore, the people of Nefi did fortify themselves against them with their arms and with all their might, trusting in the Elohim and **the Rock of their salvation.**[72] Wherefore, they became as yet conquerors of their enemies.

⁹And it came to pass that I, Ya'akov, began to be old. And the record of this people being kept on the other plates of Nefi, wherefore, I conclude this record, declaring that I have written according to the best of my knowledge by saying that the time passed away with us, and also our lives passed away as if it were unto us a dream, we being a lonesome and a solemn people, wanderers cast out from Yerushalayim, born in tribulation in a wild wilderness, and hated of our brothers, which caused wars and contentions. Wherefore, we did mourn out our days.

¹⁰And I, Ya'akov, saw that I must soon go down to my grave; wherefore, I said unto my son Enosh, Take these plates. And I told him the things which my brother Nefi had commanded me, and he promised obedience unto the commands. And I make an end of my writing upon these plates, which writing has been small. And to the reader I bid shalom, hoping that many of my brothers may read my words. Brothers, Shalom.

ספר אנוש
ENOSH
THE BOOK OF ENOSH

BEHOLD, it came to pass that I, Enosh, knowing my father, that he was a just man, for he taught me in his language, and also in the nurture and admonition of YHWH; and blessed be the name

---

71 Alma 10:5   72 Deut. 32:15; 2 Sam. 22:47; Ps. 89:27 (26); 95:1

of my Elohim for it. And I will tell you of the wrestle which I had before Elohim before I received a remission[1] of my sins. Behold, I went to hunt beasts[2] in the forest, and the words which I had often heard my father speak concerning Eternal life[3] and the joy of the k'doshim sunk deep into my heart; and my soul hungered,[4] and I kneeled down before my Maker, and I cried[5] unto him in mighty prayer and supplication for my own soul. And all the day long did I cry unto him; yes, and when the night came, I did still raise my voice high, that it reached the heavens. And there came a voice unto me, saying, Enosh, your sins are forgiven you[6] and you shall be Blessed. And I, Enosh, knew that Elohim could not lie; wherefore, my guilt[7] was swept away. And I said, YHWH, how is it done? And he said unto me, Because of your faith in Mashiach,[8] whom you have never before heard nor seen. And many years pass away before he shall manifest himself in the flesh. Wherefore, go to, your faith has made you whole.

2 Now it came to pass that when I had heard these words, I began to feel a desire for the welfare[9] of my brothers the Nefites; therefore, I did pour out my whole soul unto Elohim for them. And while I was thus struggling in the spirit, behold, the voice of YHWH came into my mind again, saying, I will visit your brothers according to their diligence in keeping my mitzvot.[10] I have given unto them this land, and it is a holy land; and I curse it not, except[11] it be for the cause of iniquity. Wherefore, I will visit your brothers according as I have said, and their transgressions will I bring down with sorrow upon their own heads.[12] And after I, Enosh, had heard these words, my faith began to be unshaken[13] in YHWH. And I prayed unto him with many long struggles for my brothers the Lamanites.

3 And it came to pass that after I had prayed and labored with all diligence, YHWH said unto me, I will grant unto you according to your desires because of your faith. And now behold, this was the desire which I desired of him:[14] that if it should so be that my people

---

1 Moshiyah 2:3; Alma 18:3; Cheleman 5:11; 3 Nefi 3:12   2 Eating of hunted meat is permitted by Torah: "And whatever man...hunts and catches any beast or fowl that may be eaten; he shall even pour out the blood thereof, and cover it with dust..." (Lev. 17:13). 3 2 Nefi 1:10-11   4 2 Nefi 6:13   5 1 Nefi 1:9; 'Eter 1:3   6 Moshiyah 2:1-2   7 Alma 14:7 8 M'roni 7:5; 'Eter 5:2-3   9 1 Nefi 4:5   10 2 Nefi 1:4   11 1 Nefi 1:9; 2 Nefi 1:1   12 Lev. 26:15-46; Deut. 28:15-68   13 2 Nefi 13:4; Ya'akov 3:2   14 This is an example of the Hebraism known as the Cognate Accusative, where a noun pairs with the verb which is the noun's root (desire which I desired of him).

the Nefites should fall into transgression, and by any means be destroyed, and the Lamanites should not be destroyed, that Adonai YHWH would preserve a record of my people the Nefites, even if it so be by the power of his holy arm, that it might be brought forth[15] some future day unto the Lamanites, that perhaps they might be brought unto salvation. For at the present, our struggles were vain in restoring them to the true faith. And they swore in their wrath that if it were possible, they would destroy our records, and us, and also all the traditions of our fathers.[16]

4 Wherefore, I knowing that Adonai YHWH was able to preserve our records, I cried unto him continually, for he had said unto me, Whatsoever thing you shall ask[17] in faith, believing that you shall receive, in the name of Mashiach, you shall receive it. And I had faith, and I did cry unto Elohim that he would preserve the records. And he covenanted with me that he would bring them forth unto the Lamanites in his own due time. And I, Enosh, knew that it would be according to the covenant which he had made; wherefore, my soul did rest. And YHWH said unto me, Your fathers have also required of me this thing, and it shall be done unto them according to their faith,[18] for their faith was like unto yours.

5 And now it came to pass that I, Enosh, went about among the people of Nefi, prophesying of things to come and testifying of the things which I had heard and seen. And I bear record that the people of Nefi did seek diligently to restore[19] the Lamanites unto the true faith in Elohim, but our labors were vain. Their hatred was fixed, and they were led by their evil nature, that they became wild and ferocious, and a bloodthirsty[20] people, full of idolatry and tum'ah,[21] feeding upon beasts of prey, dwelling in tents, and wandering about in the wilderness with a short skin girded about their loins and their heads shaven.[22] And their skill was in the bow, and the cimeter, and

---

15 2 Nefi 2:7; 11:19; Alma 17:9-11   16 "...the Pharisees have delivered to the people a great many observances by succession from their fathers, which are not written in the law of Moses; for that reason it is that the Sadducees reject them, and say that we are to esteem those observances to be obligatory which are in the written word, but are not to observe what are delivered from the tradition of our forefathers..." (Josephus; Ant. 13:11:6). See also Ps. 78:1-4.   17 M'raman 4:1; M'roni 7:5   18 2 Nefi 2:6-7; Ya'akov 3:1
19 Ya'akov 5:8   20 Literally, as we read in Yahram 1:3, they would "drink the blood of beasts" in violation of Torah (Gen. 9:4; Lev. 17:11-12).   21 טומאה (Ritual uncleanness).
22 "You shall not round the corners of your heads, neither shall you mar the corners of your beard" (Lev. 19:27).

the ax; and many of them did eat nothing except it was raw meat. And they were continually seeking to destroy us.

⁶And it came to pass that the people of Nefi did till the land and raise all manner of grain, and of fruit, and flocks, and herds of all manner of cattle of every kind, and goats, and wild goats, and also many horses. And there were exceedingly many prophets among us; and the people were a stiffnecked people, hard to understand. And there was nothing except it was exceeding harshness, preaching and prophesying of wars and contentions and destructions, and continually reminding them of death and of the duration of eternity and the judgments and the power of Elohim — and all these things stirring them up continually to keep them in the fear of YHWH — I say there was nothing short of these things and exceedingly great plainness of speech that would keep them from going down speedily to destruction. And after this manner do I write concerning them. And I saw wars between the Nefites and the Lamanites in the course of my days.

⁷And it came to pass that I began to be old. And a hundred and seventy and nine years had passed away from the time that our father Lechi left Yerushalayim.[23] And as I saw that I must soon go down to my grave, having been worked upon by the power of Mashiach that I must preach and prophesy unto this people and declare the word according to the truth which is in Mashiach — and I have declared it in all my days and have rejoiced in it above that of the world. And I soon go to the place of my rest, which is with my Redeemer; for I know that in him I shall rest. And I rejoice in the day when my mortal shall put on immortality and shall stand before him. Then shall I see his face with pleasure, and he will say unto me, Come unto me, you Blessed; there is a place prepared for you in the mansions of my Father. Amen.

ספר יהרם
YAHRAM
THE BOOK OF YAHRAM

Now behold, I, Yahram, write a few words according to the commandment of my father Enosh, that our genealogy[1] may be

---

23 1 Nefi 1:7 **1** 1 Nefi 1:22

kept. And as these plates are small, and as these things are written for the intent of the benefit[2] of our brothers, the Lamanites; wherefore, it must necessarily be that I write a little; but I shall not write the things of my prophesying, nor of my revelations. For what could I write more than my fathers have written? For have not they revealed the plan of salvation?[3] I say unto you, yes, and this suffices me.

2 Behold, it is expedient that much should be done among this people because of the hardness of their hearts, and the deafness of their ears, and the blindness of their minds, and the stiffness of their necks. Nevertheless, Elohim is exceedingly merciful[4] unto them, and has not, as yet, swept them off from the face of the land. And there are many among us who have many revelations, for they are not all stiffnecked. And as many as are not stiffnecked, and have faith, have communion with the Holy Spirit, which makes manifest unto the children of men according to their faith.

3 And now behold, two hundred years had passed away and the people of Nefi had grown strong in the land. They observed to keep the Torah of Moshe,[5] and the Shabbat holy unto YHWH, and they profaned not, neither did they blaspheme. And the laws of the land were exceedingly strict. And they were scattered upon much of the face of the land, and the Lamanites also. And they were exceedingly more numerous than were they of the Nefites, and they loved murder and would drink the blood of beasts.[6]

4 And it came to pass that they came many times against us, the Nefites, to battle. But our kings and our leaders were mighty men in the faith of YHWH, and they taught the people the ways of YHWH. Wherefore, we withstood the Lamanites and swept them away out of our lands, and began to fortify our cities, or whatsoever place of our inheritance. And we multiplied exceedingly, and spread upon the face of the land, and became exceedingly rich in gold, and in silver, and in precious things, and in fine workmanship of wood, in buildings, and in machinery, and also in iron, and copper, and brass, and steel, making all manner of tools of every kind to till the ground, and weapons of war — yes, the sharp pointed arrow, and the quiver, and the dart, and the javelin, and all preparations for war. And thus

---

2 Enosh 1:3 **3** Ya'akov 4:2; Alma 9:7 **4** 2 Nefi 6:13 **5** 2 Nefi 8:2 **6** In violation of Torah (Gen. 9:4; Lev. 17:11–12).

being prepared to meet the Lamanites, they did not prosper against us. But the word of YHWH was verified which he spoke unto our fathers, saying that inasmuch as you will keep my mitzvot, you shall prosper in the land.[7]

5 And it came to pass that the prophets of YHWH did threaten the people of Nefi, according to the word of Elohim, that if they did not keep the mitzvot, but should fall into transgression, they should be destroyed from off the face of the land. Therefore, the prophets, and the kohanim, and the teachers did labor diligently, exhorting with all long-suffering the people to diligence, teaching the Torah of Moshe and the intent for which it was given, persuading them to look forward unto the Mashiach[8] and believe in him to come, as though he already was.[9] And after this manner did they teach them. And it came to pass that by so doing, they kept them from being destroyed upon the face of the land; for they did prick their hearts with the word, continually stirring[10] them up unto repentance.

6 And it came to pass that two hundred and thirty and eight years[11] had passed away, after the manner of wars, and contentions, and dissensions, for the space of much of the time. And I, Yahram, do not write more, for the plates are small. But behold, my brothers, you can go to the other plates of Nefi; for behold, upon them the record of our wars are engraved according to the writings of the kings, or that which they cause to be written. And I deliver these plates into the hands of my son Ameni, that they may be kept according to the commandments of my fathers.

ספר אמני
AMENI
THE BOOK OF AMENI

BEHOLD, it came to pass that I, Ameni, being commanded by my father Yahram[1] that I should write somewhat upon these plates

---

7 Lev. 26:1-14; Deut. 28:1-14; 1 Nefi 1:9; 2 Nefi 1:4; Alma 17:1   8 2 Nefi 11:8   9 This is an example of the Hebraism known as the Prophetic Perfect, in which a prophet speaks of a future event in the perfect form (completed action), as if it had already occurred.
10 Alma 2:5   11 ~362 BCE   1 Yahram 1:6

to preserve our genealogy; wherefore, in my days, I would that you should know that I fought much with the sword to preserve my people, the Nefites, from falling into the hands of their enemies, the Lamanites. But behold, I, of myself, am a wicked man,[2] and I have not kept the statutes and the mitzvot[3] of YHWH as I ought to have done.

2 And it came to pass that two hundred and seventy and six years had passed away; and we had many seasons of shalom, and we had many seasons of serious war and bloodshed. Yes, and in short, two hundred and eighty and two years had passed away; and I had kept these plates according to the commandments of my fathers, and I conferred them upon my son Amaron. And I make an end.

3 And now I, Amaron, write the things whatsoever I write, which are few, in the book of my father. Behold, it came to pass that three hundred and twenty years had passed away; and the more wicked part of the Nefites were destroyed. For YHWH would not allow, after he had led them out of the land of Yerushalayim, and kept and preserved them from falling into the hands of their enemies, yes, he would not allow that the words should not be verified[4] which he spoke unto our fathers, saying that inasmuch as you will not keep[5] my mitzvot, you shall not prosper in the land. Wherefore, YHWH did visit them in great judgment; nevertheless, he did spare the righteous, that they should not perish, but did deliver them out of the hands of their enemies. And it came to pass that I did deliver the plates unto my brother Chamesh.

4 Now I, Chamesh,[6] write what few things I write in the same book with my brother. For behold, I saw the last which he wrote, that he wrote it with his own hand; and he wrote it in the day that he delivered them unto me. And after this manner we keep the record, for it is according to the commandments of our fathers. And I make an end.

5 Behold, I, Avinodam, am the son of Chamesh. Behold, it came to pass that I saw much war and contention between my people, the

---

2 The Talmud records a Jewish tradition that states that at the time a soul is sent into the world, an oath is administered to the soul by Elohim, as follows: "Be righteous and be not wicked; and even if the whole world tells you that you are righteous, regard yourself as if you were wicked" (b.Niddah 30b). **3** Alma 16:17 **4** Alma 22:4 **5** 1 Nefi 1:16–18; Alma 7:3 **6** The 1830 text has "Chemish"; the underlying Hebrew appears to be *Chamesh* חמש, meaning "five." The masculine form is Chamishah. He was the fifth generation after the departure from Jerusalem.

Nefites, and the Lamanites; and I, with my own sword, have taken the lives of many of the Lamanites in the defense of my brothers. And behold, the record of this people is engraved upon plates which is had by the kings, according to the generations. And I know of no revelation,[7] except that which has been written, neither prophecy. Wherefore, that which is sufficient is written. And I make an end.

6 Behold, I am Amaleki, the son of Avinodam. Behold, I will speak unto you somewhat concerning Moshiyah, who was made king over the land of Zerach'mla.[8] For behold, he was warned of YHWH that he should flee out of the land of Nefi—and as many as would hearken unto the voice of YHWH should also depart out of the land with him into the wilderness—and it came to pass that he did according as YHWH had commanded him. And they departed out of the land into the wilderness, as many as would hearken unto the voice of YHWH. And they were led by many preachings and prophesyings, and they were admonished continually by the word of Elohim. And they were led by the power of his arm through the wilderness until they came down into the land which is called the land of Zerach'mla. And they discovered a people who were called the people of Zerach'mla. Now, there was great rejoicing among the people of Zerach'mla, and also, Zerach'mla did rejoice exceedingly because YHWH had sent the people of Moshiyah with the plates of brass, which contained the record of the Y'hudim.

7 Behold, it came to pass that Moshiyah discovered that the people of Zerach'mla came out from Yerushalayim at the time[9] that Tzidkiyahu king of Y'hudah was carried away captive into Babylon. And they journeyed in the wilderness and were brought by the hand of YHWH across the great waters, into the land where Moshiyah discovered them; and they had dwelt there from that time forth. And at the time that Moshiyah discovered them, they had become exceedingly numerous. Nevertheless, they had had many wars and serious contentions, and had fallen by the sword from time to time. And their language had become corrupted; and they had brought no records with them; and they denied the being of their Creator. And neither Moshiyah, nor the people of Moshiyah, could understand

---

7 Ya'akov 1:1   8 Aramaic: זרעחמלא *Zera* (seed/dispersed) and *Ch'mla* (gathered in). Suggests the group who came with Muloch and founded Zerach'mla may have spoken Aramaic.   9 ~ 591 BCE; 2 Kings 25:1-7

them.¹⁰ But it came to pass that Moshiyah caused that they should be taught in his language.¹¹ And it came to pass that after they were taught in the language of Moshiyah, Zerach'mla gave a genealogy of his fathers, according to his memory. And they are written, but not in these plates.

8 And it came to pass that the people of Zerach'mla and of Moshiyah did unite together, and Moshiyah was appointed to be their king. And it came to pass in the days of Moshiyah, there was a large stone brought unto him with engravings on it, and he did interpret the engravings by the gift and power of Elohim. And they gave an account of one Coriantumr and the slain of his people. And Coriantumr was discovered by the people of Zerach'mla, and he dwelt with them for the space of nine moons. It also spoke a few words concerning his fathers. And his first parents who came out from the tower at the time YHWH confounded the language of the people; and the severity of YHWH fell upon them according to his judgments, which are just. And their bones lay scattered in the land northward.

9 Behold, I, Amaleki, was born in the days of Moshiyah, and I have lived to see his death; and Binyamin, his son, reigns in his place. And behold, I have seen in the days of king Binyamin a serious war, and much bloodshed, between the Nefites and the Lamanites. But behold, the Nefites did obtain much advantage over them; yes, insomuch that king Binyamin did drive them out of the land of Zerach'mla.

10 And it came to pass that I began to be old; and having no seed, and knowing king Binyamin¹² to be a just man before YHWH; wherefore, I shall deliver up these plates unto him, exhorting all men to come unto Elohim, HaKodesh of Isra'el,¹³ and believe in prophesying, and in revelations, and in the ministering of angels, and in the gift of speaking with tongues, and in the gift of interpreting

---

10 The people of Zerach'mla (commonly called Mulochites) and the Nefites had each only been in the land of Promise about 400 years—not long enough for language corruption alone to make their language unintelligible to one another. *The Stick of Joseph* tells us very little about the Mulochites, only that they were descendants of Muloch, the son of king Tzidkiyahu, and those who came with Muloch into the wilderness and across the sea (Ameni 1:6-7; Moshiyah 11:13; Cheleman 2:29; 3:9). We are never told who smuggled a son of Tzidkiyahu, heir to David's throne, out of Jerusalem. Could they have been Babylonian dissidents? Whereas the Nefites spoke Hebrew (M'raman 4:11), there is internal evidence that the Mulochites may have been Aramaic speakers. Zerach'mla is Aramaic, and after the merger of the Nefites and Mulochites, Aramaic names like "Alma" (the Aramaic form of the Hebrew name "Elam") begin to appear.   **11** Moshiyah 1:1   **12** Moshiyah 1:1   **13** 1 Nefi 7:5

languages, and in all things which are good. For there is nothing which is good, except it comes from YHWH, and that which is evil comes from HaSatan. And now my beloved brothers, I would that you should come[14] unto Mashiach, who is HaKodesh of Isra'el, and partake of his salvation and the power of his redemption. Yes, come unto him, and offer your whole souls as an offering unto him, and continue in fasting and praying, and endure to the end, and as YHWH lives, you will be saved.

11 And now I would speak somewhat concerning a certain number who went up into the wilderness to return to the land of Nefi, for there was a large number who were desirous to possess the land of their inheritance; wherefore, they went up into the wilderness. And their leader, being a strong and a mighty man, and a stiffnecked man; wherefore, he caused a contention among them. And they were all slain, except fifty, in the wilderness; and they returned again to the land of Zerach'mla. And it came to pass that they also took others, to a considerable number, and took their journey again into the wilderness. And I, Amaleki, had a brother who also went with them; and I have not since known concerning them. And I am about to lie down in my grave; and these plates are full. And I make an end of my speaking.

דברי מרמן
WORDS OF M'RAMAN
THE WORDS OF M'RAMAN

And now I, M'raman, being about to deliver up the record which I have been making into the hands of my son M'roni, behold, I have witnessed almost all the destruction of my people,[1] the Nefites. And it is many hundred years after the coming of Mashiach that I deliver these records into the hands of my son. And I suppose that he will witness the entire destruction of my people. But may Elohim grant that he may survive them, that he may write somewhat concerning them, and somewhat concerning Mashiach, that perhaps some day it may profit them.[2]

---

14 M'roni 10:6 **1** M'raman 3:4 **2** 2 Nefi 11:6

2 And now I speak somewhat concerning that which I have written. For after I had made an abridgment from the plates of Nefi, down to the reign of this king Binyamin, of whom Amaleki spoke, I searched among the records which had been delivered into my hands, and I found these plates,[3] which contained this small account of the prophets, from Ya'akov down to the reign of this king Binyamin, and also many of the words of Nefi. And the things which are upon these plates pleasing me because of the prophecies of the coming of Mashiach,[4] and my fathers knowing that many of them have been fulfilled — yes, and I also know that as many things as have been prophesied concerning us down to this day have been fulfilled, and as many as go beyond this day must surely come to pass[5] — wherefore, I chose these things, to finish my record upon them, which remainder of my record I shall take from the plates of Nefi. And I cannot write a hundredth part of the things of my people.

3 But behold, I shall take these plates, which contain these prophesyings and revelations, and put them with the remainder of my record, for they are choice unto me; and I know they will be choice unto my brothers. And I do this for a wise purpose, for thus it is whispered to me, according to the workings of the spirit of YHWH which is in me. And now I do not know all things, but YHWH knows all things which are to come; wherefore, he works in me to do according to his will. And my prayer to Elohim is concerning my brothers, that they may once again come to the knowledge of Elohim — yes, the redemption[6] of Mashiach — that they may once again be a delightful people.

4 And now I, M'raman, proceed to finish out my record, which I take from the plates of Nefi; and I make it according to the knowledge and the understanding which Elohim has given me. Wherefore, it came to pass that after Amaleki had delivered up these plates into the hands of king Binyamin, he took them and put them with the other plates, which contained records which had been handed down by the kings, from generation to generation, until the days of king Binyamin. And they were handed down from king Binyamin, from generation to generation, until they have fallen into my hands. And

---

3 1 Nefi 2:14 **4** 2 Nefi 8:2 **5** 3 Nefi 5:2–6 **6** Moshiyah 8:9, 14; M'raman 4:7

I, M'raman, pray to Elohim that they may be preserved[7] from this time henceforth. And I know that they will be preserved, for there are great things written upon them, out of which my people and their brothers shall be judged[8] at the great and last day, according to the word of Elohim which is written.

⁵And now concerning this king Binyamin, he had a number of contentions among his own people. And it came to pass also that the armies of the Lamanites came down out of the land of Nefi to battle against his people. But behold, king Binyamin gathered together his armies, and he did stand against them. And he did fight with the strength of his own arm, with the sword of Lavan; and in the strength of YHWH they did contend against their enemies until they had slain many thousands of the Lamanites. And it came to pass that they did contend against the Lamanites until they had driven them out of all the lands of their inheritance.

⁶And it came to pass that after there had been false mashiachs — and their mouths had been shut, and they punished according to their crimes — and after there had been false prophets, and false preachers and teachers among the people — and all these having been punished according to their crimes — and after there had been many contentions and many defections away unto the Lamanites, behold, it came to pass that king Binyamin, with the assistance of the holy prophets who were among his people — for behold, king Binyamin was a holy man, and he did reign over his people in righteousness; and there were many holy men in the land, and they did speak the word of Elohim with power and with authority, and they did use much sharpness because of the stiffneckedness of the people — wherefore, with the help of these, king Binyamin, by laboring with all the might of his body and the faculty of his whole soul, and also the prophets, did once more establish shalom in the land.

---

7 Enosh 1:4 8 M'raman 1:12

ספר מושעיה
MOSHIYAH
THE BOOK OF MOSHIYAH

AND now there was no more contention in all the land of Zerach'mla, among all the people who belonged to king Binyamin, so that king Binyamin had continual shalom all the remainder of his days. And it came to pass that he had three sons, and he called their names Moshiyah, and Helorum, and Cheleman. And he caused that they should be taught in all the language of his fathers,[1] that thereby they might become men of understanding, and that they might know concerning the prophecies[2] which had been spoken by the mouths of their fathers, which were delivered to them by the hand of YHWH. And he also taught them concerning the records which were engraved upon the plates of brass,[3] saying, My sons, I would that you should remember that were it not for these plates which contain these records and these mitzvot, we must have suffered in ignorance, even at this present time, not knowing the mysteries of Elohim. For it was not possible that our father Lechi could have remembered all these things, to have taught them to his children, except it were for the help of these plates. For he had been taught in the language of the Egyptians, therefore he could read these engravings and teach them to his children, that thereby they could teach them to their children, and so fulfilling the mitzvot of Elohim even down to this present time. I say unto you my sons, were it not for these things which have been kept and preserved by the hand of Elohim, that we might read and understand of his mysteries[4] and have his mitzvot always before our eyes, that even our fathers would have dwindled in unbelief. And we should have been like unto our brothers the Lamanites, who know nothing concerning these things, or even do not believe them when they are taught them, because of the traditions of their fathers[5] which are not correct. O my sons, I would that you should remember that these sayings are true, and also that these records are true. And behold also the plates of Nefi, which contain the records and the sayings of our fathers from the

---

[1] 1 Nefi 1:1; M'raman 4:11 [2] 2 Nefi 3:1 [3] 1 Nefi 1:10, 22–23 [4] 1 Nefi 3:5; Alma 9:3 [5] Moshiyah 6:12

time they left Yerushalayim[6] until now; that they are true. And we can know of their surety because we have them before our eyes. And now my sons, I would that you should remember to search them diligently, that you may profit thereby. And I would that you **should keep the mitzvot of Elohim, that you may prosper** in the land according to the promises which YHWH made unto our fathers.[7] And many more things did king Binyamin teach his sons, which are not written in this book.

2 And it came to pass that after king Binyamin had made an end of teaching his sons, that he became old and he saw that he must very soon go the way of all the earth. Therefore, he thought it expedient that he should confer the kingdom upon one of his sons; therefore, he had Moshiyah brought before him. And these are the words which he spoke unto him, saying, My son, I would that you should make a proclamation throughout all this land, among all this people, or the people of Zerach'mla[8] and the people of Moshiyah who dwell in this land, that thereby they may be gathered together;[9] for tomorrow I shall proclaim unto this my people out of my own mouth that you are a king and a ruler over this people **whom YHWH our Elohim has given us**.[10] And moreover, I shall give this people a name that thereby they may be distinguished above all the people which Adonai YHWH has brought out of the land of Yerushalayim. And this I do because they have been a diligent people in keeping the mitzvot of YHWH. And I give unto them a name that never shall be blotted out, except it be through transgression. Yes, and moreover I say unto you that if this highly favored people of YHWH should fall into transgression, and become a wicked and an adulterous people, that YHWH will deliver them up, that thereby they become weak like unto their brothers. And he will no more preserve them by his matchless and marvelous power as he has previously preserved our fathers.[11] For I say unto you that if he had not extended his arm in the preservation of our fathers, they must have fallen into the hands of the Lamanites and become victims to their hatred.

---

6 1 Nefi 1:1, 7   **7** Deut. 29:8 (9); Lev. 26:1-13; Deut. 28:1-14; 2 Nefi 1:1-2   **8** Aramaic: זרעחמלא Zera (seed/dispersed) and *Ch'mla* (gathered in). Suggests the group who came with Muloch and founded Zerach'mla may have spoken Aramaic.   **9** Compare with the proclamation to come to Jerusalem for Passover (2 Chron. 30:5).   **10** Deut. 17:14-15   **11** Ameni 1:3; Alma 7:2

3 And it came to pass that after king Binyamin had made an end of these sayings to his son, that he gave him charge concerning all the affairs of the kingdom. And moreover, he also gave him charge concerning the records which were engraved upon the plates of brass, and also the plates of Nefi,[12] and also the sword of Lavan,[13] and the ball or director[14] which led our fathers through the wilderness, which was prepared by the hand of YHWH that thereby they might be led, every one, according to the heed and diligence which they gave unto him. Therefore, as they were unfaithful, they did not prosper nor progress in their journey, but were driven back, and incurred the displeasure of Elohim upon them. And therefore, they were smitten with famine and sore afflictions to stir them up in remembrance of their duty.

4 And now it came to pass that Moshiyah went and did as his father had commanded him, and proclaimed unto all the people who were in the land of Zerach'mla, that thereby they might gather themselves together to go up[15] to the Temple[16] to hear the words which his father should speak unto them.[17]

5 And it came to pass that after Moshiyah had done as his father had commanded him and had made a proclamation throughout all the land, that the people gathered themselves together throughout all the land, that they might go up to the Temple to hear the words which king Binyamin should speak unto them. And there were a great number, even so many that they did not number them, for they had multiplied exceedingly and grown great in the land. And they also **took of the firstlings of their flocks,**[18] that they might offer sacrifice and burnt offerings according to the Torah of Moshe,[19] and also that they might give thanks to **YHWH their Elohim, who had brought them out of** the land of Yerushalayim, **and who had delivered them out of the hands of their enemies,**[20] and had appointed just men to be their teachers, and also a just man to be their king, who had

---

12 1 Nefi 2:14; 5:34-35 **13** 1 Nefi 1:16-17 **14** 1 Nefi 5:3 **15** See footnote for "go up" in 1 Nefi 1:11 **16** 2 Nefi 4:3; Ya'akov 2:3; 3 Nefi 5:1 **17** Moshiyah 1:2. The people were gathered together to the Temple. Sukkot is one of the three pilgrimage feasts requiring the people to gather to "the place which he shall choose", i.e. the Temple (Deut. 16:16). **18** Gen. 4:4; Ex. 13:12; 34:19; Lev. 27:26; Num. 3:41; 18:15-18; Deut. 12:6, 17; 14:23; Neh. 10:36. Neh. 10:36 is just two days after Sukkot (Neh. 8:2 and 9:1). Sukkot coincides with lambing season, so firstlings would have been available. Moreover, the Talmud indicates a firstling could be offered up even more than a year after birth (b.Rosh Hashanah 5b). **19** At Sukkot, "fourteen lambs of the first year" served as a burnt offering (Num. 29:13). **20** Judg. 2:12; 8:34

established shalom in the land of Zerach'mla, and who had taught them to keep the mitzvot of Elohim, that thereby they might rejoice[21] and be filled with love towards Elohim and all men.

6 And it came to pass that when they came up to the Temple, they pitched their sukkah booths[22] round about, every man according to his family, consisting of his wife, and his sons, and his daughters, and their sons, and their daughters, from the eldest down to the youngest, every family being separate one from another. And they pitched their sukkah booths round about the Temple, every man having his sukkah booth with the door thereof towards the Temple, that thereby they might remain in their sukkah booths and hear the words which king Binyamin should speak unto them. For the multitude was so great that king Binyamin could not teach them all within the walls of the Temple, therefore he caused a tower to be erected, that thereby his people might hear the words which he should speak unto them.

7 And it came to pass that he began to speak to his people from the tower, and they could not all hear his words because of the greatness of the multitude. Therefore, he caused that the words which he spoke should be written and sent forth among those that were not under the sound of his voice, that they might also receive his words. And these are the words which he spoke and caused to be written, saying, My brothers, all you that have assembled yourselves together, you that can hear my words which I shall speak unto you this day, for I have not commanded you to come up here to trifle with the words which I shall speak, but that you should hearken unto me, and open your ears that you may hear, and your hearts that you may understand, and your minds that the mysteries of Elohim may be unfolded to your view. I have not commanded you to come up here that you should fear me, or that you should think that I of myself am more than a mortal man. But I am like as yourselves, subject to all manner of infirmities in body and mind. Yet as I have been chosen by this people, and was consecrated by my father, and was sustained by the hand of YHWH that I should be a ruler and a king over this people, and have been

---

21 As we are commanded, "You shall rejoice before YHWH your Elohim seven days" (Lev. 23:40) at Sukkot. 22 Throughout this paragraph, the 1830 English text has "tent(s)" rather than "sukkah booth(s)"; however, the context of this event appears to be Sukkot, and one translation of the Hebrew word *sukkah* is "tent." Therefore, *sukkah* appears to be the likely underlying Hebrew.

MOSHIYAH 1:8

kept and preserved by his matchless power to serve you with all the might, mind, and strength which YHWH has granted unto me, I say unto you that as I have been allowed to spend my days in your service, even up to this time, and have not sought gold, nor silver, nor any manner of riches of you, neither have I allowed that you should be confined in dungeons, nor that you should make slaves one of another, or that you should murder, or plunder, or steal, or commit adultery, or even I have not allowed that you should commit any manner of wickedness, and have taught you that you should keep the mitzvot of YHWH in all things which he has commanded you. And even I myself have labored with my own hands that I might serve you, and that you should not be laden with taxes, and that there should nothing come upon you which was grievous to be borne. And of all these things which I have spoken, you yourselves are witnesses this day. Yet my brothers, I have not done these things that I might boast, neither do I tell these things that thereby I might accuse you; but I tell you these things that you may know that I can answer a clear conscience before Elohim[23] this day. Behold, I say unto you that because I said unto you that I had spent my days in your service, I do not desire to boast,[24] for I have only been in the service of Elohim.

8 And behold, I tell you these things that you may learn wisdom, that you may learn that when you are in the service of your fellow beings, you are only in the service of your Elohim. Behold, you have called me your king. And if I, whom you call your king, do labor to serve you, then had not you ought to labor to serve one another? And behold also, if I, whom you call your king, who has spent his days in your service and yet has been in the service of Elohim, do merit any thanks from you, oh how had you ought to thank your Heavenly King! I say unto you, my brothers, that if you should render all the thanks and praise which your whole souls have power to possess, to that Elohim who has created you, and has kept and preserved you, and has caused that you should rejoice, and has granted that you

---

[23] This is almost identical to 1 Kefa (1 Pet.) 3:21, "the answer of a good conscience toward Elohim," pointing to an underlying Hebrew word *pashat* פשט (Strong's 6584), which is affected by the meaning of the Aramaic cognate *peshitta* פשיטא. This word could be translated "clear," as in the Jerusalem Talmud, "things doubtful to the Rabbis are clear to you; those clear to the Rabbis are doubtful to you" (y.Betzah I, 60b) or "good" as in Matt. 6:22 in the Aramaic Peshitta, "If your eye therefore is good" (see footnote to 3 Nefi 5:37 concerning meaning of "good eye" in Matt. 6:22).   [24] Deut. 17:20

should live in shalom one with another[25] — I say unto you that if you should serve him who has created you from the beginning, and is preserving you from day to day by lending you breath that you may live, and move, and do according to your own will, and even supporting you from one moment to another — I say, if you should serve him with all your whole soul, yet you would be unprofitable servants. And behold, all that he requires of you is to keep his mitzvot. And he has promised you that if you would keep his mitzvot, you should prosper in the land. And he never does vary from that which he has said. Therefore, if you do keep his mitzvot, he does bless you and prosper you.

9 And now in the first place he has created you, and granted unto you your lives, for which you are indebted unto him. And secondly, he does require that you should do as he has commanded you, for which, if you do, he does immediately bless you, and therefore he has paid you. And you are still indebted unto him, and are and will be for ever and ever. Therefore, of what have you to boast? And now I ask, can you say anything of yourselves? I answer you, no. You cannot say that you are even as much as the dust of the earth, yet you were created of the dust of the earth; but behold, it belongs to him who created you. And I, even I whom you call your king, am no better than you yourselves are, for I am also of the dust. And you can see that I am old and am about to yield up this mortal frame to its mother earth. Therefore, as I said unto you that I had served you, walking with a clear conscience before Elohim, even so I, at this time, have caused that you should assemble yourselves together, that I might be found blameless, and that your blood should not come upon me when I shall stand to be judged of Elohim of the things whereof he has commanded me concerning you. I say unto you that I have caused that you should assemble yourselves together that I might rid my garments of your blood at this period of time when I am about to go down to my grave, that I might go down in peace, and my immortal spirit may join the choirs above in singing the praises of a just Elohim. And moreover, I say unto you that I have caused that you should assemble yourselves

---

[25] This closely parallels the Jewish prayer known as the *Shehecheyanu*: "Praised are you...YHWH our God, King of the universe, who has kept us, and has preserved us, and enabled us to reach this season," which is said at special occasions and feasts, such as Sukkot.

together that I might declare unto you that I can no longer be your teacher nor your king; for even at this time my whole frame does tremble exceedingly while attempting to speak unto you. But Adonai YHWH does support me, and has sustained me that I should speak unto you, and has commanded me that I should declare unto you this day that my son Moshiyah is a king and a ruler over you.

10 And now my brothers, I would that you should do as you have previously done. As you have kept my commandments, and also the commandments of my father, and have prospered, and have been kept from falling into the hands of your enemies, even so, if you shall keep the commandments of my son, or the mitzvot of Elohim which shall be delivered unto you by him, you shall prosper in the land and your enemies shall have no power over you. But O my people, beware lest there shall arise contentions among you, and you hearken to obey the evil spirit which was spoken of by my father, Moshiyah. For behold, there is a woe pronounced upon him who hearkens to obey that spirit; for if he hearkens to obey him, and remains and dies in his sins, the same drinks damnation[26] to his own soul,[27] for he receives for his wages an Everlasting punishment, having transgressed the Torah of Elohim, contrary to his own knowledge. I say unto you that there are not any among you, except it be your little children, that have not been taught concerning these things but that knows that you are eternally indebted to your Heavenly Father, to render to him all that you have and are, and also have been taught concerning the records which contain the prophecies which have been spoken by the holy prophets, even down to the time our father Lechi left Yerushalayim, and also all that has been spoken by our fathers until now. And behold also, they spoke that which was commanded them of YHWH; therefore, they are just and true.

11 And now I say unto you, my brothers, that after you have known and have been taught all these things, if you should transgress and go contrary to that which has been spoken, that you do withdraw yourselves from the spirit of YHWH, that it may have no place in you to guide you in Wisdom's[28] paths that you may be blessed, prospered, and preserved, I say unto you that the man that does this, the same

---

[26] Cheleman 4:11; Moshiyah 8:11 [27] This is almost identical to 1 Cor. 11:29, "drinks damnation to himself" pointing to an underlying Hebrew word *nefesh* נפש (Strong's 5315), meaning "soul, life, or self" (see 3 Nefi 8:9). [28] 2 Nefi 12:6

comes out in open rebellion against Elohim. Therefore, he hearkens to obey the evil spirit and becomes an enemy to all righteousness. Therefore, YHWH has no place in him, for he dwells not in unholy temples.[29] Therefore, if that man repents not, and remains and dies an enemy to Elohim, the demands of divine justice do awaken his immortal soul to a lively sense of his own guilt, which does cause him to shrink from the presence of YHWH, and does fill his breast with guilt, and pain, and anguish, which is like an unquenchable fire whose flames ascend up for ever and ever. And now I say unto you that mercy has no claim on that man; therefore, his final doom is to endure a never-ending torment.

12 O all you old men, and also you young men, and you little children who can understand my words — for I have spoken plainly unto you that you might understand — I pray that you should awaken to a remembrance of the awful situation of those that have fallen into transgression. And moreover, I would desire that you should consider on the blessed and happy state of those that keep the mitzvot[30] of Elohim; for behold, they are blessed in all things, both temporal and spiritual. And if they hold out faithful to the end, they are received into Heaven, that thereby they may dwell with Elohim in a state of never-ending happiness. Oh remember, remember that these things are true, for Adonai YHWH has spoken it.

13 And again my brothers, I would call for your attention, for I have somewhat more to speak unto you. For behold, I have things to tell you concerning that which is to come. And the things which I shall tell you are made known unto me by an angel[31] from Elohim. And he said unto me, Awake. And I awoke. And behold, he stood before me. And he said unto me, Awake and hear the words which I shall tell you; for behold, I am come to declare unto you glad tidings of great joy.[32] For YHWH has heard your prayers, and has judged of your righteousness, and has sent me to declare unto you that you may rejoice, and that you may declare unto your people that they may also be filled with joy.

---

29 This keeps with the Sukkot theme of Binyamin's speech. Each of the biblical Temples was dedicated at Sukkot (1 Kings 8:2, 65; Neh. 8:13-18; 2 Macc. 10:5-8). See also Alma 16:37. **30** 3 Nefi 5:23 **31** M'roni 7:6 **32** These words, which parallel the Sukkot liturgy, are in harmony with the words of the angels in Luke 2:10-11 relating to Mashiach's birth, which may have also occurred at Sukkot.

14 For behold, the time comes and is not far distant that with power YHWH Omnipotent who reigns, who was and is from all eternity to all eternity, shall come down from Heaven among the children of men, and shall dwell in a tabernacle of clay,[33] and shall go forth among men, working mighty miracles such as healing the sick, raising the dead, causing the lame to walk, the blind to receive their sight, and the deaf to hear, and curing all manner of diseases. And he shall cast out demons, or the evil spirits which dwell in the hearts of the children of men.[34] And lo, he shall suffer temptations and pain of body, hunger, thirst, and fatigue, even more than man can suffer except it be unto death. For behold, blood comes from every pore, so great shall be his anguish for the wickedness and the abominations of his people.[35] And he shall be called Yeshua HaMashiach, the Son of Elohim the Father of Heaven and of earth, the Creator of all things from the beginning; and his Mother shall be called Miryam. And lo, he comes unto his own, that salvation might come unto the children of men, even through faith on his name. And even after all this, they shall consider him as a man and say that he has a demon,[36] and shall scourge him, and shall crucify him. And he shall rise the third day from the dead.

15 And behold, he stands to judge the world. And behold, all these things are done that a righteous judgment might come upon the children of men. For behold, and also his blood atones for the sins of those who have fallen by the transgression of Adam, who have died not knowing the will of Elohim concerning them, or who have ignorantly sinned. But woe, woe unto him who knows that he rebels against Elohim; for salvation comes to none such except it be through repentance and faith on Adonai Yeshua HaMashiach. And Adonai YHWH has sent his holy prophets among all the children of men to declare these things to every kindred, nation, and tongue, that thereby whosoever should believe that Mashiach should come, the same might receive remission of their sins and rejoice with exceedingly great joy, even as though he had already come among them.[37]

---

33 Alluding to the future birth of Mashiach with a Sukkot theme (1 Nefi 3:8-14; Alma 5:3). **34** Following the Sukkot theme of man as a tabernacle. **35** See Luke 22:44. This verse (Luke 22:44) appears in the KJV but does not appear in some other Bible versions. It is found in the Aramaic of the Old Syriac Curetonian and the Aramaic Peshitta but does not appear in the Old Syriac Siniatic. **36** This prophecy was fulfilled in John 8:48; it was also a Sukkot event (John 7:2). **37** This is an example of the Hebraism known as the

16 Yet Adonai YHWH saw that his people were a stiffnecked people, and he appointed unto them a Torah, even the Torah of Moshe. And many signs, and wonders, and types, and shadows[38] showed he unto them concerning his coming; and also holy prophets spoke unto them concerning his coming. And yet they hardened their hearts and understood not that the Torah of Moshe avails nothing except it were through the atonement of his blood. And even if it were possible that little children[39] could sin, they could not be saved. But I say unto you, they are blessed; for behold, as in Adam or by nature they fall, even so the blood of Mashiach atones for their sins. And moreover, I say unto you that there shall be no other name given, nor any other way nor means by which salvation can come unto the children of men, only in and through the name of Mashiach YHWH Omnipotent. For behold, he judges, and his judgment is just. And the infant perishes not that dies in his infancy, but men drink damnation to their own souls except they humble themselves, and become as little children,[40] and believe that salvation was, and is, and is to come, in and through the atoning blood of Mashiach, YHWH Omnipotent. For the natural man is an enemy to Elohim, and has been from the fall of Adam, and will be for ever and ever unless he yields to the enticings of the Holy Spirit, and puts off the natural man, and becomes a kadosh through the atonement of Mashiach YHWH, and becomes as a child: submissive, meek, humble, patient, full of love, willing to submit to all things which YHWH sees fit to inflict upon him, even as a child does submit to his father.

17 And moreover, I say unto you that the time shall come when the knowledge of a savior shall spread throughout every nation, kindred, tongue, and people. And behold, when that time comes, none shall be found blameless before Elohim, except it be little children, only through repentance and faith on the name of YHWH Elohim Omnipotent. And even at this time, when you shall have taught your people the things which YHWH your Elohim has commanded you,

---

Prophetic Perfect, in which a prophet speaks of a future event in the perfect form (completed action), as if it had already occurred. **38** The biblical feasts are a "shadow of things to come" (Col. 2:17). Binyamin has been presenting Sukkot as such a type and shadow. For example, the Passover was a shadow which Mashiach fulfilled; hence Paul says, "Therefore let us keep the feast" (1Cor. 5:7-8). **39** M'roni 8:3; 3 Nefi 4:7 **40** 3 Nefi 5:9

even then are they found no more blameless in the sight of Elohim, only according to the words which I have spoken unto you.

18 And now I have spoken the words which Adonai YHWH has commanded me. And thus says YHWH: They shall stand as a bright testimony against this people at the judgment day, whereof they shall be judged, every man according to his works, whether they be good or whether they be evil. And if they be evil, they are consigned to an awful view of their own guilt and abominations, which does cause them to shrink from the presence of YHWH into a state of misery and Endless torment, from which they can no more return. Therefore, they have drunk damnation to their own souls. Therefore, they have drunk out of the cup of the wrath of Elohim, which justice could no more deny unto them than it could deny that Adam should fall because of his partaking of the forbidden fruit.[41] Therefore, mercy could have claim on them no more for ever, and their torment is as a lake of fire and brimstone whose flames are unquenchable and whose smoke ascends up for ever and ever. Thus has YHWH commanded me. Amen.

2 And now it came to pass that when king Binyamin had made an end of speaking the words which had been delivered unto him by the angel of YHWH, that he cast his eyes round about on the multitude, and behold, they had fallen to the earth, for the fear of YHWH had come upon them; and they had viewed themselves in their own carnal state, even less than the dust of the earth. And they all cried aloud with one voice, saying, Oh have mercy and apply the atoning blood of Mashiach, that we may receive forgiveness of our sins and our hearts may be purified! For we believe in Yeshua HaMashiach, the Son of Elohim who created Heaven and earth and all things, who shall come down among the children of men.

2 And it came to pass that after they had spoken these words, the spirit of YHWH came upon them and they were filled with joy, having received a remission of their sins and having shalom of conscience because of the exceeding faith which they had in Yeshua HaMashiach, who should come, according to the words which king Binyamin had spoken unto them. And king Binyamin again opened his mouth and

---

41 The phrase "forbidden fruit" never appears in the Tanakh, but is found in the Zohar (Zohar 2:144a).

began to speak unto them, saying, My friends and my brothers, my kindred and my people, I would again call for your attention, that you may hear and understand the remainder of my words which I shall speak unto you. For behold, if the knowledge of the goodness of Elohim at this time has awakened you to a sense of your nothingness, and your worthless and fallen state, I say unto you, if you have come to a knowledge of the goodness of Elohim, and his matchless power, and his wisdom, and his patience, and his long-suffering towards the children of men, and also the atonement which has been prepared from the foundation of the world,[42] that thereby salvation might come to him that should put his trust in YHWH, and should be diligent in keeping his mitzvot, and continue in the faith, even unto the end of his life (I mean the life of the mortal body), I say that this is the man that receives salvation through the atonement which was prepared from the foundation of the world for all mankind who ever were, ever since the fall of Adam, or who are, or who ever shall be, even unto the end of the world. And this is the means by which salvation comes. And there is no other salvation except this which has been spoken of; neither are there any conditions by which man can be saved except the conditions which I have told you.

3 Believe in Elohim. Believe that he is, and that he created all things both in Heaven and in earth; believe that he has all wisdom and all power both in Heaven and in earth; believe that man does not comprehend all the things which YHWH can comprehend. And again, believe that you must repent of your sins, and abandon them, and humble yourselves before Elohim, and ask in sincerity of heart that he would forgive you. And now if you believe[43] all these things, see that you do them. And again I say unto you as I have said before, that as you have come to the knowledge of the glory of Elohim, or if you have known of his goodness, and have tasted of his love, and have received a remission[44] of your sins, which causes such exceedingly great joy in your souls, even so I would that you should remember and always retain in remembrance the greatness of Elohim and your own nothingness, and his goodness and long-suffering towards you unworthy creatures, and humble yourselves even in the depths of humility, calling on the name of YHWH daily, and standing steadfastly

---

42 'Eter 1:13 **43** Alma 16:27-28 **44** 3 Nefi 5:11

in the faith of that which is to come, which was spoken by the mouth of the angel. And behold, I say unto you that if you do this, you shall always rejoice, and be filled with the love of Elohim, and always retain a remission of your sins. And you shall grow in the knowledge[45] of the glory of him that created you, or in the knowledge of that which is just and true. And you will not have a mind to injure one another, but to live peaceably, and to render to every man according to that which is his due. And you will not allow your children that they go hungry or naked, neither will you allow that they transgress the laws of Elohim, and fight and quarrel one with another, and serve HaSatan, who is the master of sin, or who is the evil spirit which has been spoken of by our fathers, he being an enemy to all righteousness. But you will teach them to walk in the ways of truth and soberness; you will teach them to love one another and to serve one another.

4 And also, you yourselves will relieve those that stand in need of your relief. You will administer of your substance unto him that stands in need, and you will not allow that the beggar puts up his petition to you in vain, and turn him out to perish. Perhaps you shall say, The man has brought upon himself his misery; therefore I will stay my hand and will not give unto him of my food, nor impart unto him of my substance that he may not suffer, for his punishments are just. But I say unto you, O man, whosoever does this, the same has great cause to repent; and except he repents of that which he has done, he perishes[46] for ever and has no interest in the kingdom of Elohim.[47] For behold, are we not all beggars? Do we not all depend upon the same being, even Elohim, for all the substance which we have,[48] for both food and raiment, and for gold, and for silver, and for all the riches which we have of every kind? And behold, even at this time you have been calling on his name and begging for a remission of your sins. And has he allowed that you have begged in vain? No, he has poured out his spirit[49] upon you and has caused that your hearts

---

45 Alma 16:29-30 46 Alma 16:36 47 One of the prophetic meanings of Sukkot is that of the millennial Kingdom and the Mashiach tabernacling with us (see Zech. 14:16). The Kingdom and Kingdom-living are important themes in king Binyamin's message (see Moshiyah 2:3-4). 48 Sukkot teaches us our dependence on Elohim and reminds us of the forty years in the wilderness in which we were totally dependent. 49 A reference to the water libation ceremony performed at Sukkot, in which the priests poured out water and wine, mixing them together over the altar (m.Sukkah 4:9 [b.Sukkah 48a-b]). In John 7:37-38 (which was also at Sukkot, see also John 7:2), Yeshua referred to this

should be filled with joy and has caused that your mouths should be stopped, that you could not find utterance, so exceedingly great was your joy.

⁵And now if Elohim, who has created you, on whom you are dependent for your lives, and for all that you have and are, does grant unto you whatsoever you ask that is right, in faith, believing that you shall receive, oh then how had you ought to impart of the substance that you have one to another! And if you judge the man who puts up his petition to you for your substance that he perish not, and condemn him, how much more just will be your condemnation for withholding your substance, which does not belong to you, but to Elohim, to whom also your life belongs.⁵⁰ And yet you put up no petition, nor repent of the thing which you have done.⁵¹ I say unto you, woe be unto that man, for his substance shall perish with him. And now I say these things unto those who are rich as pertaining to the things of this world. And again I say unto the poor, you who have not, and yet have sufficient that you remain from day to day (I mean all you who deny the beggar because you have not), I would that you say in your hearts that I give not because I have not, but if I had, I would give. And now if you say this in your hearts, you remain guiltless; otherwise, you are condemned, and your condemnation is just, for you covet that which you have not received.

⁶And now, for the sake of these things which I have spoken unto you — that is, for the sake of retaining a remission of your sins from day to day, that you may walk guiltless before Elohim — I would that you should impart of your substance to the poor, every man according to that which he has, such as feeding the hungry, clothing the naked, visiting the sick and administering to their relief, both spiritually and temporally, according to their wants. And see that all these things are done in wisdom and order, for it is not requisite that a man should run faster than he has strength. And again, it is

---

ceremony as well, saying, "If anyone thirsts, let him come to me and drink. Whoever believes in me, as the Scriptures have said, rivers of water of life will flow from his belly." **50** This is an example of the Kal va-homer thought form, which serves as the first of the Seven Rules of Hillel. This classic Jewish thought form expresses that that which applies in a less important case will certainly apply in a more important case. **51** Parallel to Yeshua's Sukkot teaching, "Judge not according to the appearance, but judge with a righteous judgment" (John 7:2, 24). As we read in the Mishnah, Hillel taught, "And do not judge your fellow until you are in his place" (m.Avot 2:4).

expedient that he should be diligent, that thereby he might win the prize. Therefore, all things must be done in order. And I would that you should remember that whosoever among you that borrows of his neighbor should return the thing that he borrows, according as he does agree, or else you shall commit sin, and perhaps you shall cause your neighbor to commit sin also. And finally, I cannot tell you all the things by which you may commit sin; for there are diverse ways and means, even so many that I cannot number them. But this much I can tell you, that if you do not watch yourselves, and your thoughts, and your words, and your deeds,[52] and observe to keep the mitzvot of Elohim, and continue in the faith of what you have heard concerning the coming of our Adonai, even unto the end of your lives, you must perish. And now, O man, remember and perish not.

3 And now it came to pass that when king Binyamin had thus spoken to his people, he sent among them, desiring to know of his people if they believed the words which he had spoken unto them. And they all cried with one voice, saying, Yes, we believe all the words which you have spoken unto us! And also, we know of their surety and truth because of the spirit of YHWH Omnipotent, which has worked a mighty change in us, or in our hearts, that we have no more disposition to do evil, but to do good continually. And we, ourselves, also through the infinite goodness of Elohim and the manifestations of his spirit, have great views of that which is to come; and were it expedient, we could prophesy of all things. And it is the faith which we have had on the things which our king has spoken unto us that has brought us to this great knowledge, by which we do rejoice with such exceedingly great joy. And we are willing to enter into a covenant[53] with our Elohim[54] to do his will, and to be obedient to his mitzvot in all things that he shall command us,[55] all the remainder of our days, that we may not bring upon ourselves a never-ending torment as has been spoken by the angel, that we may not drink out of **the cup of the wrath**[56] of Elohim.

2And now these are the words which king Binyamin desired of them, and therefore, he said unto them, You have spoken the

---

52 The repetition of the possessive pronoun here is normative in Hebrew, where a pronominal suffix is normally attached to each object of possession. 53 Moshiyah 9:7; Alma 5:4 54 Deut. 29:12 55 Deut. 31:12-13 56 Isa. 51:17

words that I desired, and the covenant which you have made is a righteous covenant. And now, because of the covenant which you have made, you shall be called the children of Mashiach, his sons and his daughters; for behold, this day he has spiritually begotten you. For you say that your hearts are changed through faith on his name, therefore you are born of him and have become his sons and his daughters. And under this head you are made free, and there is no other head by which you can be made free; there is no other name given by which salvation comes. Therefore I would that you should take upon you the name of Mashiach, all you that have entered into the covenant with Elohim that you should be obedient unto the end of your lives. And it shall come to pass that whosoever does this shall be found at the right hand of Elohim, for he shall know the name by which he is called; for he shall be called by the name of Mashiach.

³And now it shall come to pass that whosoever shall not take upon them the name of Mashiach must be called by some other name; therefore he finds himself on the left hand of Elohim.[57] And I would that you should remember also that this is the name that I said I should give unto you that never should be blotted out, except it be through transgression; therefore, take heed that you do not transgress, that the name be not blotted out of your hearts. I say unto you, I would that you should remember to retain the name written always in your hearts, that you are not found on the left hand of Elohim, but that you hear and know the voice by which you shall be called, and also the name by which he shall call you. For how knows a man the master whom he has not served, and who is a stranger unto him, and is far from the thoughts and intents of his heart? And again, does a man take an ass which belongs to his neighbor and keep him? I say unto you, no. He will not even allow that he shall feed among his flocks, but will drive him away and cast him out. I say unto you that even so shall it be among you if you know not the name by which you are called. Therefore I would that you should be steadfast and immovable, always abounding in good works, that Mashiach, YHWH Elohim Omnipotent, may seal you his,[58] that you

---

[57] A word play: "Binyamin" means "a son of the right hand." [58] Binyamin is speaking at Sukkot and reflecting on the themes of the other recent fall holy days. As we read in the Talmud: "For it has been taught: 'All are judged on Rosh Hashanah and their doom is sealed on Yom Kippur' (b.Rosh Hashanah 16a), and it has been taught: 'Beth Shammai says: There will be three groups at the Day of Judgment: one of thoroughly righteous,

may be brought to Heaven, that you may have everlasting salvation and Eternal life through the wisdom, and power, and justice, and mercy of him who created all things in Heaven and in earth, who is Elohim above all. Amen.

4 And now king Binyamin thought it was expedient, after having finished speaking to the people, that he should take the names of all those who had entered into a covenant with Elohim to keep his mitzvot. And it came to pass that there was not one soul, except it were little children, but that had entered into the covenant and had taken upon them the name of Mashiach. And again, it came to pass that when king Binyamin had made an end of all these things, and had consecrated his son Moshiyah to be a ruler and a king over his people, and had given him all the charges concerning the kingdom, and also had appointed kohanim to teach the people, that thereby they might hear and know the mitzvot of Elohim, and to stir them up in remembrance of the oath which they had made, he dismissed the multitude and they returned, everyone according to their families, to their own houses.

2 And Moshiyah began to reign in his father's place, and he began to reign in the thirtieth year of his age, making in the whole about four hundred and seventy-six years[59] from the time that Lechi left Yerushalayim. And king Binyamin lived three years, and he died.[60] And it came to pass that king Moshiyah did walk in the ways of YHWH, and did observe his judgments and his statutes, and did keep his mitzvot in all things whatsoever he commanded him.

3 And king Moshiyah did cause his people that they should till the earth, and he also himself did till the earth, that thereby he might not become burdensome to his people, that he might do according to that which his father had done in all things. And there was no contention among all his people for the space of three years.

5 And now it came to pass that after king Moshiyah had had continual shalom for the space of three years, he was desirous

---

one of thoroughly wicked, and one of intermediate. The thoroughly righteous will forthwith be inscribed definitively as entitled to everlasting life; the thoroughly wicked will forthwith be inscribed definitively as doomed to Gehinnom'" (b.Rosh Hashanah 16b).
59 ~ 126 BCE; 1 Nefi 1:7   60 ~ 123 BCE

to know concerning the people who went up to dwell in the land of Lechi-Nefi, or in the city of Lechi-Nefi; for his people had heard nothing from them from the time they left the land of Zerach'mla; therefore, they wearied him with their teasings.

2 And it came to pass that king Moshiyah granted that sixteen of their strong men might go up to the land of Lechi-Nefi to inquire concerning their brothers. And it came to pass that the next day they started to go up, having with them one Ammon, he being a strong and mighty man, and a descendant of Zerach'mla, and he was also their leader. And now they knew not the course they should travel in the wilderness to go up to the land of Lechi-Nefi; therefore they wandered many days in the wilderness, even forty days did they wander. And when they had wandered forty days, they came to a hill which is north of the land of Shilom, and there they pitched their tents. And Ammon took three of his brothers — and their names were Amaleki, Helem, and Hem — and they went down into the land of Nefi. And behold, they met the king of the people who was in the land of Nefi and in the land of Shilom, and they were surrounded by the king's guard, and were taken, and were bound, and were committed to prison.

3 And it came to pass, when they had been in prison two days, they were again brought before the king and their bands were loosed. And they stood before the king and were permitted, or rather commanded, that they should answer the questions which he should ask them. And he said unto them, Behold, I am Limhi, the son of Noah, who was the son of Zeniff, who came up out of the land of Zerach'mla to inherit this land which was the land of their fathers, who was made a king by the **voice of the people.** And now I desire to know the cause by which you were so bold as to come near the walls of the city when I myself was with my guards without the gate. And now for this cause have I allowed that you should be preserved, that I might inquire of you, or else I should have caused that my guards should have put you to death. You are permitted to speak.

4 And now when Ammon saw that he was permitted to speak, he went forth and bowed himself before the king. And rising again, he said, O king, I am very thankful before Elohim this day that I am yet alive and am permitted to speak. And I will endeavor to speak with boldness; for I am assured that if you had known me, you would not

have allowed that I should have worn these bands. For I am Ammon, and am a descendant of Zerach'mla, and have come up out of the land of Zerach'mla to inquire concerning our brothers whom Zeniff brought up out of that land.

5 And now it came to pass that after Limhi had heard the words of Ammon, he was exceedingly glad and said, Now I know of a surety that my brothers who were in the land of Zerach'mla are yet alive. And now I will rejoice, and tomorrow I will cause that my people shall rejoice also. For behold, we are in bondage to the Lamanites and are taxed with a tax[61] which is grievous to be borne. And now behold, our brothers will deliver us out of our bondage, or out of the hands of the Lamanites, and we will be their slaves; for it is better that we be slaves to the Nefites than to pay tribute to the king of the Lamanites.

6 And now king Limhi commanded his guards that they should no more bind Ammon nor his brothers, but caused that they should go to the hill which was north of Shilom and bring their brothers into the city, that thereby they might eat, and drink, and rest themselves from the labors of their journey, for they had suffered many things; they had suffered hunger, thirst, and fatigue.

7 And now it came to pass on the next day, that king Limhi sent a proclamation among all his people, that thereby they might gather themselves together to the Temple to hear the words which he should speak unto them. And it came to pass that when they had gathered themselves together, that he spoke unto them in this way, saying, O my people, lift up your heads and be comforted. For behold, the time is at hand, or is not far distant, when we shall no longer be in subjection to our enemies; despite our many struggles which have been in vain, yet I trust there remains an effective struggle to be made. Therefore, lift up your heads and rejoice, and put your trust in Elohim, in that Elohim who was the Elohim of Avraham, and Yitz'chak, and Ya'akov, and also that **Elohim who brought the children of Isra'el out of the land of Egypt,**[62] and caused that they should **walk through the Red Sea on dry ground,**[63] and fed them with manna that they might not perish **in the wilderness;**[64] and many more things did he do for them. And again, that same

---

[61] This is an example of the Hebraism known as the Cognate Accusative, where a noun pairs with the verb which is the noun's root. **62** Ex. 12:51 **63** Ex. 14:21 **64** Deut. 8:16; Ex. 16:15, 35

Elohim has brought our fathers out of the land of Yerushalayim, and has kept and preserved his people, even until now. And behold, it is because of our iniquities and abominations that we have been brought into bondage.

8 And you all are witnesses this day that Zeniff, who was made king over this people, he being overzealous to inherit the land of his fathers, therefore being deceived by the cunning and craftiness of king Laman, who, having entered into a treaty with king Zeniff, and having yielded up into his hands the possessions of a part of the land, or even the city of Lechi-Nefi, and the city of Shilom, and the land round about, and all this he did for the sole purpose of bringing this people into subjection or into bondage. And behold, we, at this time, do pay tribute to the king of the Lamanites, to the amount of one half of our corn, and our barley, and even all our grain of every kind, and one half of the increase of our flocks and our herds; and even one half of all we have or possess, the king of the Lamanites does exact of us — or our lives. And now, is not this grievous to be borne? And is not this our affliction great? Now behold, how great reason have we to mourn. Yes, I say unto you, great are the reasons which we have to mourn. For behold, how many of our brothers have been slain, and their blood has been spilled in vain, and all because of iniquity. For if this people had not fallen into transgression, YHWH would not have allowed that this great evil should come upon them. But behold, they would not hearken unto his words, but there arose contentions among them, even so much that they did shed blood among themselves.

9 And a prophet[65] of YHWH have they slain, yes, a chosen man of Elohim who told them of their wickedness and abominations, and prophesied of many things which are to come, yes, even the coming of Mashiach. And because he said unto them that Mashiach was the Elohim, the Father of all things, and said that he should take upon him the image of man, and it should be the image after which man was created in the beginning, or in other words, he said that man was created after the image of Elohim, and that Elohim should come down among the children of men, and take upon him flesh and blood, and go forth upon the face of the earth — and now because he said

---

65 Moshiyah 9:5

this, they did put him to death. And many more things did they do which brought down the wrath of Elohim upon them.

10 Therefore, who wonders that they are in bondage and that they are smitten with sore afflictions? For behold, YHWH has said, I will not relieve my people in the day of their transgression, but **I will hedge up their ways**,[66] that they prosper not; and their doings shall be as **a stumbling block before them**.[67] And again he said, If my people shall sow uncleanness, they **shall reap** the chaff thereof in **the whirlwind**,[68] and the effect thereof is poison. And again he said, If my people shall sow uncleanness, they shall reap the east wind, which brings immediate destruction. And now behold, the promise of YHWH is fulfilled, and you are smitten and afflicted. But if you will turn to YHWH with full purpose of heart, and put your trust in him, and serve him with all diligence of mind — if you do this, he will, according to his own will and pleasure, deliver you out of bondage.

11 And it came to pass that after king Limhi had made an end of speaking to his people — for he spoke many things unto them, and only a few of them have I written in this book — he told his people all the things concerning their brothers who were in the land of Zerach'mla. And he caused that Ammon should stand up before the multitude and rehearse unto them all that had happened unto their brothers, from the time that Zeniff went up out of the land even until the time that he himself came up out of the land. And he also rehearsed unto them the last words which king Binyamin had taught them, and explained them to the people of king Limhi so that they might understand all the words which he spoke. And it came to pass that after he had done all this, that king Limhi dismissed the multitude and caused that they should return everyone unto his own house.

12 And it came to pass that he caused that the plates, which contained the record of his people from the time that they left the land of Zerach'mla, should be brought before Ammon, that he might read them. Now as soon as Ammon had read the record, the king inquired of him to know if he could interpret languages. And Ammon told him that he could not. And the king said unto him, Being grieved for the afflictions of my people, I caused that forty and three of my

---

66 Hos. 2:6 **67** Ezek. 3:20 **68** Hos. 8:7

people should take a journey into the wilderness, that thereby they might find the land of Zerach'mla, that we might appeal unto our brothers to deliver us out of bondage. And they were lost in the wilderness for the space of many days, yet they were diligent, and found not the land of Zerach'mla but returned to this land, having traveled in a land among many waters, having discovered a land which was covered with bones of men and of beasts, and so forth, and was also covered with ruins of buildings of every kind; having discovered a land which had been peopled with a people who were as numerous as the hosts of Isra'el. And for a testimony that the things that they have said are true, they have brought twenty-four plates[69] which are filled with engravings; and they are of pure gold. And behold also, they have brought breastplates which are large, and they are of brass and of copper, and are perfectly sound. And again they have brought swords; the hilts thereof have perished, and the blades thereof were cankered with rust. And there is no one in the land that is able to interpret the language or the engravings that are on the plates. Therefore, I said unto you, can you translate? And I say unto you again, do you know of anyone that can translate? For I am desirous that these records should be translated into our language, for perhaps they will give us a knowledge of a remnant of the people who have been destroyed, from which these records came. Or perhaps they will give us a knowledge of this very people who have been destroyed. And I am desirous to know the cause of their destruction.

13 Now Ammon said unto him, I can assuredly tell you, O king, of a man that can translate the records; for he has that with which he can look and translate all records that are of ancient date, and it is a gift from Elohim. And the things are called interpreters, and no man can look in them except he be commanded, lest he should look for that he ought not and he should perish. And whosoever is commanded to look in them, the same is called seer.[70] And behold, the king of the people who are in the land of Zerach'mla is the man that is commanded to do these things, and who has this high gift from Elohim. And the king said that a seer is greater than a prophet. And Ammon said that a seer is a revelator and a prophet also. And a gift which is greater can no man have, except he should possess the

---

69 'Eter 1:1 **70** Moshiyah 12:3

power of Elohim, which no man can; yet a man may have great power given him from Elohim. But a seer can know of things which have passed, and also of things which are to come. And by them shall all things be revealed, or rather shall secret things be made manifest, and hidden things shall come to light, and things which are not known shall be made known by them, and also things shall be made known by them which otherwise could not be known.[71] Thus, Elohim has provided a means that man, through faith, might work mighty miracles.[72] Therefore he becomes a great benefit to his fellow beings.

14 And now when Ammon had made an end of speaking these words, the king rejoiced exceedingly and gave thanks to Elohim, saying, Doubtless a great mystery is contained within these plates; and these interpreters were doubtless prepared for the purpose of unfolding all such mysteries to the children of men. Oh how marvelous are the works of YHWH. And how long does he bear with his people. Yes, and how blind and impenetrable are the understandings of the children of men, for they will not seek Wisdom, neither do they desire that she should rule over them. Yes, they are as a wild flock which flees from the shepherd, and scatters, and are driven, and are devoured by the beasts of the forest.

THE RECORD OF ZENIFF

An account of his people from the time they left the land of Zerach'mla until the time that they were delivered out of the hands of the Lamanites.

6 I, Zeniff, having been taught in all the language of the Nefites, and having had a knowledge of the land of Nefi, or of the land of our fathers' first inheritance, therefore I was sent as a spy among the Lamanites, that I might spy out their forces, that our army might come upon them and destroy them. But when I saw that which was good among them, I was desirous that they should not be destroyed. Therefore I contended with my brothers in the wilderness, for I would that our ruler should make a treaty with them; but he, being

---

71 Throughout this verse, the underlying Hebrew word behind "things" would be *devarim* דברים, which can mean "things" but can also mean "words." The words "secret" and "hidden" point to the underlying Hebrew word *sod* סוד. The *sod* level of interpretation deals with hidden messages in the original Hebrew of the Scriptures.   72 'Eter 5:3; M'roni 7:7

an austere and a bloodthirsty man, commanded that I should be slain. But I was rescued by the shedding of much blood, for father fought against father and brother against brother until the greatest number of our army was destroyed in the wilderness. And we returned, those of us that were spared, to the land of Zerach'mla, to relate that tale to their wives and their children. And yet I, being overzealous to inherit the land of our fathers, collected as many as were desirous to go up[73] to possess the land, and started again on our journey into the wilderness to go up to the land. But we were smitten with famine and sore affliction, for we were slow to remember YHWH our Elohim. Nevertheless, after many days wandering in the wilderness, we pitched our tents in the place where our brothers were slain, which was near to the land of our fathers.

2 And it came to pass that I went again with four of my men into the city, in unto the king, that I might know of the disposition of the king and that I might know if I might go in with my people and possess the land in shalom. And I went in unto the king, and he covenanted with me that I might possess the land of Lechi-Nefi and the land of Shilom. And he also commanded that his people should depart out of that land, and I and my people went into the land that we might possess it. And we began to build buildings and to repair the walls of the city, yes, even the walls of the city of Lechi-Nefi and the city of Shilom. And we began to till the ground, yes, even with all manner of seeds: with seeds of corn, and of wheat, and of barley, and with neas, and with sheum, and with seeds of all manner of fruits. And we did begin to multiply and prosper in the land. Now it was the cunning and crafty purpose of king Laman to bring my people into bondage, so he yielded up the land that we might possess it.

3 Therefore it came to pass that after we had dwelt in the land for the space of twelve years, king Laman began to grow uneasy, for fear that by any means my people should grow strong in the land, and they could not overpower them and bring them into bondage. Now they were a lazy and an idolatrous people; therefore they were desirous to bring us into bondage, that they might gorge themselves with the labors of our hands, yes, that they might feast themselves upon the flocks of our fields.

---

73 See note for "go up" in 1 Nefi 1:11

⁴Therefore it came to pass that king Laman began to stir up his people that they should contend with my people; therefore there began to be wars and contentions in the land. For in the thirteenth year of my reign in the land of Nefi, away on the south of the land of Shilom, when my people were watering and feeding their flocks and tilling their lands, a numerous host of Lamanites came upon them, and began to slay them, and to take of their flocks and the corn of their fields. Yes, and it came to pass that they fled, all that were not overtaken, even into the city of Nefi, and did call upon me for protection.

⁵And it came to pass that I did arm them with bows and with arrows, with swords and with cimeters, and with clubs, and with slings, and with all manner of weapons which we could invent. And I and my people did go forth against the Lamanites to battle; yes, in the strength of YHWH did we go forth to battle against the Lamanites. For I and my people did cry mightily to YHWH that he would deliver us out of the hands of our enemies, for we were awakened to a remembrance of the deliverance⁷⁴ of our fathers. And Elohim did hear our cries and did answer our prayers, and we did go forth in his might; yes, we did go forth against the Lamanites. And in one day and a night we did slay three thousand and forty-three; we did slay them even until we had driven them out of our land. And I myself with my own hands did help bury their dead. And behold, to our great sorrow and lamentation, two hundred and seventy-nine of our brothers were slain.

⁶And it came to pass that we again began to strengthen the kingdom, and we again began to possess the land in shalom. And I caused that there should be weapons of war made of every kind, that thereby I might have weapons for my people against the time the Lamanites should come up again to war against my people. And I set guards round about the land, that the Lamanites might not come upon us again unawares and destroy us. And thus I did guard my people and my flocks, and keep them from falling into the hands of our enemies.

⁷And it came to pass that we did inherit the land of our fathers for many years, yes, for the space of twenty and two years. And I

---

74 1 Nefi 1:15; Alma 7:2

did cause that the men should till the ground and raise all manner of grain and all manner of fruit of every kind. And I did cause that the women should spin, and labor, and work, and work all manner of fine linen, yes, and cloth of every kind, that we might clothe our nakedness. And thus we did prosper in the land; thus, we did have continual peace in the land for the space of twenty and two years.

8 And it came to pass that king Laman died, and his son began to reign in his place. And he began to stir his people up in rebellion against my people. Therefore, they began to prepare for war and to come up to battle against my people, but I had sent my spies out, round about the land of Shemlon, that I might discover their preparations, that I might guard against them, that they might not come upon my people and destroy them.

9 And it came to pass that they came up upon the north of the land of Shilom with their numerous hosts, men armed with bows, and with arrows, and with swords, and with cimeters, and with stones, and with slings. And they had their heads shaved that they were naked, and they were girded with a leather girdle about their loins.

10 And it came to pass that I caused that the women and children of my people should be hidden in the wilderness. And I also caused that all my old men that could bear arms, and also all my young men that were able to bear arms, should gather themselves together to go to battle against the Lamanites; and I did place them in their ranks, every man according to his age.

11 And it came to pass that we did go up to battle against the Lamanites. And I, even I, in my old age, did go up to battle against the Lamanites. And it came to pass that we did go up in the strength of YHWH to battle.

12 Now the Lamanites knew nothing concerning YHWH nor the strength of YHWH, therefore they depended upon their own strength; yet they were a strong people as to the strength of men. They were a wild, and ferocious, and a bloodthirsty people, believing in the tradition of their fathers, which is this: believing that they were driven out of the land of Yerushalayim because of the iniquities of their fathers, and that they were wronged in the wilderness by their brothers, and they were also wronged while crossing the sea, and again, that they were wronged while in the land of their first inheritance after they had crossed the sea — and all this because

Nefi was more faithful in keeping the mitzvot of YHWH. Therefore he was favored of YHWH, for YHWH heard his prayers and answered them, and he took the lead of their journey in the wilderness. And his brothers were angry with him because they understood not the dealings of YHWH. They were also angry with him upon the waters because they hardened their hearts against YHWH. And again they were angry with him when they had arrived in the promised land, because they said that he had taken the ruling of the people out of their hands; and they sought to kill him. And again they were angry with him because he departed into the wilderness as YHWH had commanded him and took the records which were engraved upon the plates of brass, for they said that he robbed them. And thus they have taught their children that they should hate them, and that they should murder them, and that they should rob and plunder them, and do all they could to destroy them. Therefore they have an eternal hatred towards the children of Nefi. And for this very cause has king Laman — by his cunning, and lying craftiness, and his fair promises — deceived me, that I have brought this my people up into this land that they may destroy them. Yes, and we have suffered this many years in the land.

13 And now I, Zeniff, after having told all these things unto my people concerning the Lamanites, I did stimulate them to go to battle with their might, putting their trust in YHWH. Therefore we did contend with them face to face. And it came to pass that we did drive them again out of our land; and we slew them with a great slaughter, even so many that we did not number them.

14 And it came to pass that we returned again to our own land, and my people again began to tend their flocks and to till their ground. And now I, being old, did confer the kingdom upon one of my sons; therefore I say no more. And may YHWH bless my people. Amen.

7 And now it came to pass that Zeniff conferred the kingdom upon Noah, one of his sons; therefore Noah began to reign in his place. And he did not walk in the ways of his father; for behold, he did not keep the mitzvot of Elohim, but he did walk after the desires of his own heart. And he had many wives and concubines.[75] And he did

---

[75] Deut. 17:17

cause his people to commit sin and do that which was abominable in the sight of YHWH; yes, and they did commit whoredoms and all manner of wickedness. And he laid a tax of one-fifth part of all they possessed: a fifth part of their gold and of their silver, and a fifth part of their ziff, and of their copper, and of their brass, and their iron, and a fifth part of their fatlings, and also a fifth part of all their grain.[76] And all this did he take to support himself, and his wives, and his concubines, and also his kohanim, and their wives, and their concubines. Thus, he had changed the affairs of the kingdom, for he put down all the kohanim that had been consecrated by his father and consecrated new ones in their place, such as were lifted up in the pride of their hearts. Yes, and thus were they supported in their laziness, and in their idolatry, and in their whoredoms by the taxes which king Noah had put upon his people. Thus did the people labor exceedingly to support iniquity. Yes, and they also became idolatrous because they were deceived by the vain and flattering words of the king and kohanim, for they did speak flattering things unto them.

2 And it came to pass that king Noah built many elegant and spacious buildings, and he ornamented them with fine work of wood and of all manner of precious things; of gold, and of silver, and of iron, and of brass, and of ziff, and of copper. And he also built him a spacious palace and a throne in the midst thereof, all of which was of fine wood and was ornamented with gold, and silver, and with precious things. And he also caused that his workmen should work all manner of fine work[77] within the walls of the Temple, of fine wood, and of copper, and of brass. And the seats which were set apart for the Kohanim HaGadolim, which were above all the other seats, he did ornament with pure gold. And he caused a breastwork to be built before them that they might rest their bodies and their arms upon while they should speak lying and vain words to his people.

3 And it came to pass that he built a tower near the Temple, yes, a very high tower, even so high that he could stand upon the top thereof and overlook the land of Shilom, and also the land of Shemlon, which was possessed by the Lamanites; and he could even look over all the land round about.

---

76 The repetition of the possessive pronoun here is normative in Hebrew, where a pronominal suffix is normally attached to each object of possession.   77 Another example of the Cognate Accusative Hebraic construction. See footnote 61.

⁴And it came to pass that he caused many buildings to be built in the land Shilom. And he caused a great tower to be built on the hill north of the land Shilom, which had been a refuge for the children of Nefi at the time they fled out of the land. And thus he did do with the riches which he obtained by the taxation of his people.

⁵And it came to pass that he placed his heart upon his riches, and he spent his time in riotous living with his wives and his concubines; and so did also his kohanim spend their time with harlots. And it came to pass that he planted vineyards round about in the land, and he built winepresses, and made wine in abundance; and therefore he became a winebibber, and also his people.

⁶And it came to pass that the Lamanites began to come in upon his people, upon small numbers, and to slay them in their fields and while they were tending their flocks. And king Noah sent guards round about the land to keep them off, but he did not send a sufficient number, and the Lamanites came upon them, and killed them, and drove many of their flocks out of the land. Thus the Lamanites began to destroy them and to exercise their hatred upon them.

⁷And it came to pass that king Noah sent his armies against them and they were driven back, or they drove them back for a time. Therefore they returned, rejoicing in their spoil. And now because of this great victory, they were lifted up in the pride of their hearts. They did boast in their own strength, saying that their fifty could stand against thousands of the Lamanites. And thus they did boast, and did delight in blood and the shedding of the blood of their brothers — and this because of the wickedness of their king and kohanim.

⁸And it came to pass that there was a man among them whose name was Avinodi; and he went forth among them and began to prophesy, saying, Behold, thus says YHWH and thus has he commanded me, saying, Go forth and say unto this people, Thus says YHWH: Woe be unto this people, for I have seen their abominations, and their wickedness, and their whoredoms; and except they repent, I will visit them in my anger. And except they repent and turn to YHWH their Elohim, behold, I will deliver them into the hands of their enemies; yes, and they shall be brought into bondage, and they shall be afflicted by the hand of their enemies. And it shall come to pass that they shall know that I am YHWH their Elohim and am a jealous Elohim, visiting the iniquities of my people. And it shall come to pass that

except this people repent and turn unto YHWH their Elohim, they shall be brought into bondage; and none shall deliver them except it be YHWH, El Shaddai. Yes, and it shall come to pass that when they shall cry unto me, I will be slow to hear their cries. Yes, and I will allow that they be smitten by their enemies. And except they repent in sackcloth and ashes, and cry mightily to YHWH their Elohim, I will not hear their prayers, neither will I deliver them out of their afflictions. And thus says YHWH, and thus has he commanded me.

9 Now it came to pass that when Avinodi had spoken these words unto them, they were angry with him and sought to take away his life; but YHWH delivered him out of their hands. Now when king Noah had heard of the words which Avinodi had spoken unto the people, he was also angry, and he said, Who is Avinodi that I and my people should be judged of him? Or who is YHWH that shall bring upon my people such great affliction? I command you to bring Avinodi here that I may slay him, for he has said these things that he might stir up my people to anger one with another, and to raise contentions among my people; therefore I will slay him. Now the eyes of the people were blinded; therefore they hardened their hearts against the words of Avinodi, and they sought from that time forward to take him. And king Noah hardened his heart against the word of YHWH, and he did not repent of his evil doings.

10 And it came to pass that after the space of two years, that Avinodi came among them in disguise, that they knew him not, and began again to prophesy among them,[78] saying, Thus has YHWH commanded me, saying, Avinodi, go and prophesy unto this my people, for they have hardened their hearts against my words; they have repented not of their evil doings. Therefore I will visit them in my anger; yes, in my fierce anger will I visit them in their iniquities and abominations; yes, woe be unto this generation. And YHWH said unto me, Stretch forth your hand[79] and prophesy, saying, Thus says YHWH: It shall come to pass that this generation, because of their iniquities, shall be brought into bondage and shall be struck on the cheek, yes, and

---

[78] Avinodi would almost certainly have chosen an opportune time to re-enter the city. A festival would have given him a large audience (compare John 7:1–10, where Yeshua secretly returned to Jerusalem for Sukkot). It appears that this occasion was Shavuot, evidenced by Avinodi's strong use of Shavuot imagery, themes, and liturgy in his message. (See footnotes to Moshiyah 7:18, 20–21; 8:5). [79] 1 Nefi 5:23; Alma 10:3

shall be driven by men and shall be slain. And the vultures of the air, and the dogs, yes, and the wild beasts shall devour their flesh.

11 And it shall come to pass that the life of king Noah shall be valued even as a garment in a hot furnace, for he shall know that I am YHWH. And it shall come to pass that I will smite this my people with sore afflictions, yes, with famine and with pestilence. And I will cause that they shall howl all the day long. Yes, and I will cause that they shall have burdens lashed upon their backs, and they shall be driven before like a dumb ass.[80]

12 And it shall come to pass that I will send forth hail among them, and it shall smite them, and they shall also be smitten with the east wind, and insects shall pester their land also and devour their grain;[81] and they shall be smitten with a great pestilence. And all this will I do because of their iniquities and abominations.

13 And it shall come to pass that except they repent, I will utterly destroy them from off the face of the earth. Yet they shall leave a record behind them, and I will preserve them for other nations which shall possess the land. Yes, even this will I do that I may uncover the abominations of this people to other nations. And many things did Avinodi prophesy against this people.

14 And it came to pass that they were angry with him; and they took him and carried him bound before the king, and said unto the king, Behold, we have brought a man before you who has prophesied evil concerning your people, and says that Elohim will destroy them. And he also prophesies evil concerning your life, and says that your life shall be as a garment in a furnace of fire. And again he says that you shall be as a stalk, even as a dry stalk of the field, which is run over by the beasts and trampled underfoot. And again he says you shall be as the blossoms of a thistle, which, when it is fully ripe, if the wind blows, it is driven forth upon the face of the land. And he pretends YHWH has spoken it. And he says all this shall come upon you except you repent, and this because of your iniquities.

15 And now, O king, what great evil have you done? Or what great sins have your people committed that we should be condemned of Elohim or judged of this man? And now, O king, behold, we are

---

[80] Shavuot is the wrapping up of Passover after the Counting of the Omer. Avinodi begins using Exodus imagery in Moshiyah 7:10-11 (see also Moshiyah 7:8). Compare Ex. 1:11.
[81] These words were particularly relevant, as Shavuot is a harvest festival.

guiltless. And you, O king, have not sinned. Therefore this man has lied concerning you, and he has prophesied in vain. And behold, we are strong; we shall not come into bondage or be taken captive by our enemies. Yes and you have prospered in the land, and you shall also prosper. Behold, here is the man. We deliver him into your hands. You may do with him as seems good to you.

16 And it came to pass that king Noah caused that Avinodi should be cast into prison; and he commanded that the kohanim should gather themselves together, that he might hold a council with them regarding what he should do with him. And it came to pass that they said unto the king, Bring him here that we may question him. And the king commanded that he should be brought before them. And they began to question him, that they might cross him, that thereby they might have that with which to accuse him. But he answered them boldly and withstood all their questions, yes, to their astonishment; for he did withstand them in all their questions and did confound them in all their words.

17 And it came to pass that one of them said unto him, What do the words mean which are written and which have been taught by our fathers, saying, **How beautiful upon the mountains are the feet of him that brings good tidings, that publishes shalom,[82] that brings good tidings of good, that publishes salvation, that says unto Tziyon, Your Elohim reigns! Your watchmen shall lift up the voice; with the voice together shall they sing.[83] For they shall see eye to eye when YHWH shall bring again Tziyon. Break forth into joy. Sing together you waste places of Yerushalayim. For YHWH has comforted his people; he has redeemed[84] Yerushalayim. YHWH has made bare his holy arm in the eyes of all the nations, and all the ends of the earth shall see the salvation of our Elohim.[85]** And now Avinodi said unto them, Are you kohanim and pretend to teach this people and to understand the spirit of prophesying, and yet desire to know of me what these things mean? I say unto you, woe be unto you for perverting the ways

---

82 We read in the Talmud and in Midrash Rabbah: "Rabbi Jose the Galilean says: Great is peace—for at the hour the King Messiah reveals himself unto Israel, he will begin in no other way than with 'peace' as it is written: 'How beautiful upon the mountains are the feet of the messenger of good news, that announces peace' (Is. 52:7)" (Perek HaShalom in some Talmud editions and Numbers Rabbah XI, 16-20).   83 2 Nefi 5:9; 3 Nefi 7:6   84 3 Nefi 9:9   85 Isa. 52:7-10

of YHWH. For if you understand these things, you have not taught them. Therefore you have perverted the ways of YHWH. You have not applied your hearts to understanding; therefore you have not been wise. Therefore, what do you teach this people? And they said, We teach the Torah of Moshe. And again he said unto them, If you teach the Torah of Moshe, why do you not keep it? Why do you set your hearts upon riches? Why do you commit whoredoms and spend your strength with harlots? Yes, and cause this people to commit sin, that YHWH has cause to send me to prophesy against this people, yes, even a great evil against this people? Do you not know that I speak the truth? Yes, you know that I speak the truth, and you ought to tremble before Elohim.

18 And it shall come to pass that you shall be smitten for your iniquities, for you have said that you teach the Torah of Moshe. And what know you concerning the Torah of Moshe? Does salvation come by the Torah of Moshe?[86] What say you? And they answered and said that salvation did come by the Torah of Moshe. But now Avinodi said unto them, I know if you keep the mitzvot of Elohim, you shall be saved; yes, if you keep the mitzvot which YHWH delivered unto Moshe in the mount of Sinai,[87] saying, **I am YHWH your Elohim, who has brought you out of the land of Egypt, out of the house of bondage. You shall have no other Elohim before me. You shall not make unto you any graven image, or any likeness of anything in the Heaven above, or things which are in the earth beneath.**[88] Now Avinodi said unto them, Have you done all this? I say unto you, no, you have not. And have you taught this people that they should do all these things? I say unto you, no, you have not.

19 And now when the king had heard these words, he said unto his kohanim, Away with this fellow and slay him. For what have we to do with him? For he is mad. And they stood forth and attempted to lay their hands on him, but he withstood them and said unto them, Touch me not. For Elohim shall smite you if you lay your hands upon me, for I have not delivered the message which YHWH sent me to deliver, neither have I told you that which you requested that I should tell. Therefore Elohim will not allow that I shall be destroyed

---

86 Alma 14:15   **87** Shavuot is traditionally the anniversary of Moshe receiving the Torah on Mount Sinai (b.Shabbat 86b).   **88** Ex. 20:2-4

at this time. But I must fulfill the mitzvot with which Elohim has commanded me. And because I have told you the truth, you are angry with me. And again because I have spoken the word of Elohim, you have judged me that I am mad.

20 Now it came to pass after Avinodi had spoken these words that the people of king Noah dared not lay their hands on him, for the spirit of YHWH was upon him. And **his face shone** with exceeding luster, even as **Moshe's** did while in the **mount of Sinai while speaking with**[89] YHWH. And he spoke with power and authority[90] from Elohim. And he continued his words, saying, You see that you have not power to slay me; therefore I finish my message. Yes, and I perceive that it cuts you to your hearts because I tell you the truth concerning your iniquities. Yes, and my words fill you with wonder and amazement, and with anger. But I finish my message, and then it matters not where I go if it so be that I am saved. But this much I tell you, what you do with me after this shall be as a type and a shadow of things which are to come.[91] And now I read unto you the remainder of the mitzvot of Elohim, for I perceive that they are not written in your hearts. I perceive that you have studied and taught iniquity the most part of your lives.

21 And now you remember that I said unto you, **You shall not make unto you any graven image, or any likeness of things which are in Heaven above, or which are in the earth beneath, or which are in the water under the earth.** And again, **You shall not bow yourself down unto them nor serve them, for I, YHWH your Elohim, am a jealous Elohim, visiting the iniquities of the fathers upon the children unto the third and fourth generation of them that hate me,** and showing mercy unto thousands of them that love me and keep my mitzvot. **You shall not take the name of YHWH your Elohim in vain,** for YHWH will not hold him guiltless that takes his name in vain. **Remember Shabbat, to keep it holy. Six days shall you labor and do all your work; but the seventh day, the Shabbat of YHWH your Elohim, you shall not do any work, neither you, nor your son, nor your daughter, neither your manservant nor your maidservant, nor your cattle, nor**

---

89 Ex. 34:29. The Shavuot imagery continues with Avinodi's face shining as Moshe's did when he received the Torah.   90 Cheleman 2:19   91 Moshiyah 9:5, 17

the stranger that is within your gates. For in six days YHWH made Heaven, and earth, and the sea, and all that in them is; wherefore, YHWH blessed the Shabbat and hallowed it. Honor your father and your mother, that your days may be long upon the land which YHWH your Elohim gives you. You shall not kill. You shall not commit adultery. You shall not steal. You shall not bear false witness against your neighbor. You shall not covet your neighbor's house; you shall not covet your neighbor's wife, nor his manservant, nor his maidservant, nor his ox, nor his ass, nor anything that is your neighbor's.[92]

8 And it came to pass that after Avinodi had made an end of these sayings, that he said unto them, Have you taught this people that they should **observe to do all these** things and to keep **these mitzvot?**[93] I say unto you, no; for if you had, YHWH would not have caused me to come forth and to prophesy evil concerning this people. And now you have said that salvation comes by the Torah of Moshe. I say unto you that it is expedient that you should keep the Torah of Moshe as yet; but I say unto you that the time shall come when it shall no more be expedient to keep the Torah[94] of Moshe.[95] And moreover, I say unto you that salvation does not come by the Torah alone; and were it not for the atonement which Elohim himself shall make for the sins and iniquities of his people, that they must

---

92 Ex. 20:4-17. The Shavuot imagery continues with Avinodi's recitation of the mitzvot.
93 Deut. 6:6-7   94 3 Nefi 4:7   95 The underlying Hebrew might be understood as a rhetorical question rather than as a statement. Torrey states, "It sometimes happens in the O.T. Hebrew that an interrogative sentence is not provided with any interrogative word or particle. In such cases the context is supposed to leave no room for doubt, but there are some instances of resulting misunderstanding and mistranslation, more or less disturbing. The Greek translator ordinarily reproduces his original exactly, word for word, without undertaking to interpret; but in such passages as Isa. 1:18 and (more significant) Isa. 43:23a and 24a the decision between the two varieties of sentence carries much with it" (Torrey, C.C. (1936) *Our Translated Gospels*. London, England: Hodder and Stoughton, p. 55). For example, the KJV of Ex. 6:3 says, "And I appeared unto Abraham, unto Isaac, and unto Jacob, by the name of God Almighty, but by my name JEHOVAH was I not known to them" (Ex. 6:3 KJV); however, "The Scriptures" version from the Institute for Scripture Research has translated this declaration as a question, as follows: "And I appeared to Abraham, to Yitshaq, and to Ya'aqob, as El Shaddai. And by My Name, Fulness, was I not known to them?" (Ex. 6:3 ISR). Yosef ben Yosef also made use of this fact in his rendering of the same passage: "And I appeared unto Abraham, unto Isaac, and unto Jacob, I am the Lord God Almighty, the Lord Jehovah. And was not my name known unto them?" (Ex. 6:3 JST). If this is a rhetorical question, it would fit the context, as Avinodi is asking a series of rhetorical questions (see Moshiyah 8:1-2).

unavoidably perish, despite the Torah of Moshe. And now I say unto you that it was expedient that there should be a Torah given to the children of Isra'el, yes, even a very strict Torah. For they were a stiffnecked people, quick to do iniquity and slow to remember YHWH their Elohim. Therefore there was a Torah given them, yes, a Torah of performances and of ordinances, a Torah which they were to observe strictly from day to day, to keep them in remembrance of Elohim and their duty towards him. But behold, I say unto you that all these things were types of things to come.

2 And now did they understand the Torah? I say unto you, no, they did not all understand the Torah — and this because of the hardness of their hearts — for they understood not that there could not any man be saved except it were through the redemption of Elohim. For behold, did not Moshe prophesy unto them concerning the coming of the Mashiach and that Elohim should redeem his people? Yes, and even all the prophets[96] who have prophesied ever since the world began — have they not spoken more or less concerning these things? Have they not said that Elohim himself should come down among the children of men, and take upon him the form of man, and go forth in mighty power upon the face of the earth? Yes, and have they not said also that he should bring to pass the resurrection of the dead? And that he himself should be oppressed and afflicted?[97]

3 Yes, does not even Yesha'yahu say, **Who has believed our report? And to whom is the arm of YHWH revealed? For he shall grow up before him as a tender plant, and as a root out of dry ground.**[98] **He has no form nor comeliness, and when we shall see him, there is no beauty that we should desire him. He is despised and rejected of men — a man of sorrows and acquainted with grief. And we hid, as it were, our faces from him. He was despised and we esteemed him not. Surely he has borne our griefs and carried our sorrows, yet we did esteem him stricken, smitten of Elohim, and afflicted.**[99]

---

96 Cheleman 3:9   97 1 Nefi 3:8-14   98 Rambam writes, "Regarding the mission by which Messiah will present himself Isaiah states, 'He grew like a tender plant and as a root out of dry land. At him will kings shut their mouths, for what had not been told unto them shall they see, and what they never heard shall they understand'"(Rambam on Isa. 52:15-53:2).   99 We read in the Talmud: "The Rabanan says that Messiah's name is the Suffering Scholar of Rabbi's House (or the Leper Scholar) for it is written, 'Surely he has borne our grief and carried our sorrows, yet we did esteem him stricken, smitten of God and afflicted' (Isa. 53:4)" (b.Sanhedrin 98a). And: "'The Messiah—what is his name?' The

4 But he was wounded for our transgressions, he was bruised for our iniquities;[100] the chastisement of our shalom was upon him, and with his stripes we are healed.[101] All we, like sheep, have gone astray — we have turned every one to his own way; and YHWH has laid on him the iniquities of us all. He was oppressed and he was afflicted, yet he opened not his mouth; he is brought as a lamb to the slaughter; and as a sheep before her shearers is dumb, so he opened not his mouth. He was taken from prison and from judgment. And who shall declare his generation? For he was cut off out of the land of the living; for the transgressions of my people was he stricken. And he made his grave with the wicked, and with the rich in his death. Because he had done no evil,[102] neither was any deceit in his mouth; yet it pleased YHWH to bruise him; he has put him to grief.

5 When you shall make his soul an offering for sin, he shall see his seed; he shall prolong his days, and the pleasure of YHWH shall prosper in his hand.[103] He shall see[104] of the travail of his soul and shall be satisfied; by his knowledge shall my righteous

---

House of Rabbi Judah the Holy One says: 'The Sick One,' 'Surely he has borne our sicknesses' (Isa. 53:4)" (b.Sanhedrin 98b).   **100** As we read in the Talmud: "Rabbi Joshua came upon the prophet Elijah as he was standing at the entrance of Rabbi Simeon ben Yohai's cave. He asked him: 'When is the Messiah coming?' The other replied: 'Go and ask him yourself.' 'Where shall I find him?' 'Before the gates of Rome.' 'By what sign shall I know him?' 'He is sitting among the poor people and covered with wounds (see Isa. 53:5)'" (b.Sanhedrin 98a).   **101** We read in the Zohar: "In the Garden of Eden there is a hall that is called the 'hall of the afflicted.' Now it is into this hall that the Messiah goes and summons all the afflictions and pains and sufferings of Israel to come upon him. And so they all come upon him. And had he not eased the children of Israel of their sorrow, and taken their burden upon himself, there would be none who could endure the suffering of Israel in penalty of neglecting the Torah. Thus it is written: 'Surely our diseases he did bear and our pains he carried' (Isa. 53:5). As long as the children of Israel dwelt in the Holy Land, they averted all afflictions and sufferings from the world by the service of the sanctuary and by sacrifice. But now it is the Messiah who is averting them from the habitants of the world" (Zohar 2:212a).   **102** In this verse of Isaiah (Isa. 53:9), the Masoretic Text has "violence" (חמס). The *Plates of Brass* reading here of "evil" agrees with the Septuagint, which has "iniquity, lawless" (ανομιαν), and the Aramaic Peshitta text of Isaiah which has "iniquity" (עויא).   **103** "It is the will of the Lord to purify and to acquit as innocent the remnant of His people, to cleanse their souls of sin, so that they may see the Kingdom of their Messiah, have many sons and daughters, enjoy long life, and observe the Torah of the Lord, prospering according to His will" (Targum Jonathan on Isa. 53:10).   **104** The Masoretic Text has literally: "From the travail of his soul he shall see and shall be satisfied in his understanding." There appears to be a missing word here, as there is no object for the verb "see." However, two Hebrew copies found in the Dead Sea Scrolls and the Greek Septuagint text include the word "light" as the object, testifying to the resurrection. The word may also have been absent from The *Plates of Brass* version; however, Avinodi was clearly aware of it, as he comments upon it later in Moshiyah 8:14.

Servant justify many, for he shall bear their iniquities. Therefore will I divide him a portion with the great, and he shall divide the spoil with the strong — because he has poured out his soul unto death, and he was numbered with the transgressors, and he bore the sins of many, and made intercession[105] for the transgressors.[106]

6 And now Avinodi said unto them, I would that you should understand that **Elohim himself shall come down among the children of men**[107] and shall redeem his people. And because he dwells in flesh, he shall be called the Son of Elohim; and having subjected the flesh to the will of the Father, being the Father and the Son — the Father because he was conceived by the power of Elohim, and the Son because of the flesh, thus becoming the Father and Son (and they are echad, yes, the very Eternal Father of Heaven and of earth), and thus the flesh becoming subject to the spirit, or the Son to the Father, being one Elohim — suffers temptation and yields not to the temptation, but allows himself to be mocked, and scourged, and cast out, and disowned by his people.

7 And after all this, and after working many mighty miracles among the children of men, he shall be led, yes, even as Yesha'yahu said, **as a sheep before the shearer is dumb, so he opened not his mouth.**[108] Yes, even so he shall be led, crucified, and slain, the flesh becoming subject even unto death, the will of the Son being swallowed up in the will of the Father. And thus Elohim breaks the bands of death, having gained the victory over death, giving the Son power to make intercession for the children of men, having ascended into Heaven, having the bowels of mercy, being filled with compassion toward the children of men, standing between them and justice, having broken the bands of death, having taken upon himself their iniquity and their transgressions, having redeemed them and satisfied the demands of justice.

---

[105] 2 Nefi 1:6 [106] Isa. 53:1-12 [107] Ex. 19:11; Ps. 50:3. Ps. 50 is an important part of the Shavuot imagery and has many parallels with Avinodi's message. Ps. 50:13-14 emphasizes that Elohim prefers thanksgiving over sacrifices, while Avinodi calls for the mitzvot to be "written in your hearts" (Moshiyah 7:20). Ps. 50:16-21, like Avinodi, gives a strong rebuke to observe the Torah; Ps. 50:16, 22, also like Avinodi (in Moshiyah 7:8; 7:17), calls us to keep the Torah, not merely proclaim the Torah. [108] Isa. 53:7

⁸And now I say unto you, **who shall declare his generation?**¹⁰⁹ Behold, I say unto you that **when his soul has been made an offering for sin, he shall see his seed.**¹¹⁰ And now what do you say? And who shall be **his seed?** Behold, I say unto you that whosoever has heard the words of the prophets, yes, all the holy prophets who have prophesied concerning the coming of YHWH, I say unto you that all those who have hearkened unto their words, and believed that YHWH would redeem his people, and have looked forward to that day for a remission of their sins, I say unto you that these are his seed, or they are heirs of the kingdom of Elohim.¹¹¹ For these are they whose sins he has borne; these are they for whom he has died,¹¹² to redeem them from their transgressions. And now, are they not his seed? Yes, and are not the prophets, every one that has opened his mouth to prophesy that has not fallen into transgression? (I mean all the holy prophets ever since the world began.) I say unto you that they are his seed. And these are they who have **published shalom, who have brought good tidings of good, who have published salvation and said unto Tziyon, Your Elohim reigns.** And oh how beautiful upon the mountains were their feet! And again, **how beautiful upon the mountains are the feet of those that are still publishing peace.** And again, **how beautiful upon the mountains are the feet of those who** shall hereafter **publish shalom,** yes, from this time henceforth and for ever!

⁹And behold, I say unto you, this is not all; for **oh how beautiful upon the mountains are the feet of him that brings good tidings**¹¹³— that is, the Founder of shalom, yes, even YHWH, who has redeemed¹¹⁴ his people, yes, he who has granted salvation unto his people! For were it not for the redemption which he has made for his people, which was prepared from the foundation of the world, I say unto you, were it not for this, that all mankind must have perished. But behold, the bands of death shall be broken, and the Son reigns and has power over the dead; therefore he brings to pass the resurrection of the dead. And there comes a resurrection, even a first resurrection, yes, even a resurrection of those that have been, and who are, and who shall be, even until the resurrection of Mashiach — for so shall

---

109 Isa. 53:8   110 Isa. 53:10   111 2 Nefi 13:5; 3 Nefi 4:10, 5:9   112 This another example of the Prophetic Perfect Hebraic form. See footnote 37.   113 Isa. 52:7   114 'Eter 1:13

he be called.[115] And now the resurrection of all the prophets and all those that have believed in their words (or all those that have kept the mitzvot of Elohim) shall come forth in the first resurrection; therefore, they are the first resurrection. They are raised to dwell with Elohim, who has redeemed them. Thus they have Eternal life through Mashiach, who has broken the bands of death.

10 And there are those who have part in the first resurrection; and these are they that have died before Mashiach came, in their ignorance, not having salvation declared unto them. And thus YHWH brings about the restoration of these, and they have a part in the first resurrection or have Eternal life, being redeemed by YHWH. And little children also have Eternal life.

11 But behold, and fear, and tremble before Elohim — for you ought to tremble — for YHWH redeems none such that rebel against him and die in their sins, yes, even all those that have perished in their sins ever since the world began, that have willfully rebelled[116] against Elohim, that have known the mitzvot of Elohim and would not keep them. These are they that have no part in the first resurrection. Therefore, ought you not to tremble? For salvation comes to none such, for YHWH has redeemed none such. Yes, neither can YHWH redeem such, for he cannot deny himself; for he cannot deny justice when it has its claim.

12 And now I say unto you that the time shall come that the salvation of YHWH shall be declared to every nation, kindred, tongue, and people.[117] **Yes, YHWH, your watchmen shall lift up their voice; with the voice together shall they sing. For they shall see eye to eye when YHWH shall bring again Tziyon. Break forth into joy. Sing together, you waste places of Yerushalayim. For YHWH has comforted his people; he has redeemed Yerushalayim. YHWH has made bare his holy arm in the eyes of all the nations, and all the ends of the earth shall see the salvation of our Elohim.**[118]

13 And now it came to pass that after Avinodi had spoken these words, he stretched forth his hands and said, The time shall come

---

115 "Behold, My Servant the Messiah shall prosper; he shall be exalted and great and very powerful" (Targum Jonathan on Isa. 52:13). "It is the will of the Lord to purify and to acquit as innocent the remnant of His people, to cleanse their souls of sin, so that they may see the Kingdom of their Messiah, have many sons and daughters, enjoy long life, and observe the Torah of the Lord, prospering according to His will" (Targum Jonathan on Is. 53:10). **116** Alma 7:4 **117** 2 Nefi 8:4; Moshiyah 1:15; 3 Nefi 10:1 **118** Isa. 52:8-10

when all shall see the salvation of YHWH, when every nation, kindred, tongue, and people shall see eye to eye and shall confess before Elohim that his judgments are just. And then shall the wicked be cast out, and they shall have cause to howl, and weep, and wail, and gnash their teeth; and this because they would not hearken unto the voice of YHWH. Therefore YHWH redeems them not. For they are carnal and demonic; and HaSatan has power over them, yes, even that old serpent that did beguile our first parents, which was the cause of their fall, which was the cause of all mankind's becoming carnal, sensual, demonic, knowing evil from good, subjecting themselves to HaSatan. Thus, all mankind were lost. And behold, they would have been endlessly lost were it not that Elohim redeemed his people from their lost and fallen state. But remember that he that persists in his own carnal nature, and goes on in the ways of sin and rebellion against Elohim, he remains in his fallen state and HaSatan has all power over him. Therefore, he is as though there was no redemption made, being an enemy to Elohim; and also is HaSatan an enemy to Elohim.

14 And now, if Mashiach had not come into the world, speaking of things to come as though they had already come, there could have been no redemption.[119] And if Mashiach had not risen from the dead, or had not broken the bands of death, that **the grave** should have no **victory** and that **death** should have no **sting**, there could have been no resurrection. But there is a resurrection; therefore the **grave** has no **victory**, and the **sting** of **death** is **swallowed up**[120] in Mashiach. He is the light[121] and the life of the world[122] — yes, a light that is Endless,[123] that can never be darkened, yes, and also a life which is Endless, that there can be no more death. Even this mortal shall put on immortality, and this corruption shall put on incorruption, and shall be brought to stand before the bar of Elohim to be judged of him according to their works, whether they be good or whether they be evil: if they be

---

119 This another example of the Prophetic Perfect Hebraic form. See footnote 37.   120 Isa. 25:8; Hos. 13:14   121 In Isa. 53:11, the Masoretic Text says: "From the travail of his soul he shall see and shall be satisfied in his understanding." There appears to be a missing word here, as there is no object for the verb "see." However, two Hebrew copies found in the Dead Sea Scrolls and the Greek Septuagint text include the word "light" as the object, testifying to the resurrection. The word may also have been absent from the *Plates of Brass* version (see Moshiyah 8:4); however, Avinodi was clearly aware of it, as he comments upon it here. This may have been the passage of Tanakh spoken of by Paul in 1 Cor. 15:1-4, which spoke of the death, burial, and resurrection of the Mashiach.   122 3 Nefi 4:7; 5:4; 'Eter 1:19   123 Endless; literally *Eyn* (without) *Sof* (end).

good, to the resurrection of Endless life and happiness, and if they be evil, to the resurrection of Endless damnation, being delivered up to HaSatan who has subjected them, which is damnation, having gone according to their own carnal wills and desires, having never called upon YHWH while the arms of mercy were extended towards them. For the arms of mercy were extended towards them and they would not, they being warned of their iniquities, and yet they would not depart from them. And they were commanded to repent, and yet they would not repent.

15 And now ought you not to tremble and repent of your sins? And remember, only in and through Mashiach can you be saved. Therefore, if you teach the Torah of Moshe, also teach that it is a shadow of those things which are to come.[124] Teach them that redemption comes through Mashiach YHWH, who is the very Eternal Father. Amen.

9 And now it came to pass that when Avinodi had finished these sayings, that the king commanded that the kohanim should take him and cause that he should be put to death. But there was one among them whose name was Alma, he also being a descendant of Nefi, and he was a young man. And he believed the words which Avinodi had spoken, for he knew concerning the iniquity which Avinodi had testified against them. Therefore he began to plead with the king that he would not be angry with Avinodi, but allow that he might depart in shalom. But the king was more angry, and caused that Alma should be cast out from among them, and sent his servants after him that they might slay him. But he fled from before them and hid himself that they found him not. And he, being concealed for many days, did write all the words which Avinodi had spoken.

2 And it came to pass that the king caused that his guards should surround Avinodi and take him; and they bound him and cast him into prison. And after three days, having counseled with his kohanim, he caused that he should again be brought before him. And he said unto him, Avinodi, we have found an accusation against you, and you are worthy of death. For you have said that Elohim himself should come down among the children of men. And now for this cause you

---

124 For example, the Passover was a shadow which Mashiach fulfilled; therefore, Paul says, "Therefore let us keep the feast" (1 Cor. 5:7-8).

shall be put to death, unless you will recall all the words which you have spoken evil concerning me and my people.

3 Now Avinodi said unto him, I say unto you, I will not recall the words which I have spoken unto you concerning this people, for they are true. And that you may know of their surety, I have allowed myself that I have fallen into your hands, yes, and I will suffer even until death. And I will not recall my words, and they shall stand as a testimony against you. And if you slay me, you will shed innocent blood; and this shall also stand as a testimony against you at the last day.

4 And now king Noah was about to release him, for he feared his word; for he feared that the judgments of Elohim would come upon him. But the kohanim lifted up their voices against him and began to accuse him, saying, He has reviled the king. Therefore the king was stirred up in anger against him, and he delivered him up that he might be slain.

5 And it came to pass that they took him, and bound him, and scourged his skin with fagots, yes, even unto death. And now when the flames began to scorch him, he cried unto them, saying, Behold, even as you have done unto me, so shall it come to pass that your seed shall cause that many shall suffer the pains that I do suffer, even the pains of death by fire — and this because they believe in the salvation of YHWH their Elohim! And it will come to pass that you shall be afflicted with all manner of diseases because of your iniquities. Yes, and you shall be smitten on every hand, and shall be driven and scattered to and fro, even as a wild flock is driven by wild and ferocious beasts. And in that day, you shall be hunted, and you shall be taken by the hand of your enemies. And then you shall suffer as I suffer the pains of death by fire. Thus, Elohim executes vengeance upon those that destroy his people. O Elohim, receive my soul. And now when Avinodi had said these words, he fell, having suffered death by fire, yes, having been put to death because he would not deny the mitzvot of Elohim, having sealed the truth of his words by his death.

6 And now it came to pass that Alma, who had fled from the servants of king Noah, repented of his sins and iniquities, and went about privately among the people, and began to teach the words of Avinodi — yes, concerning that which was to come, and also concerning the resurrection of the dead, and the redemption

of the people, which was to be brought to pass through the power, and sufferings, and death of Mashiach, and his resurrection and ascension into Heaven. And as many as would hear his word he did teach; and he taught them privately, that it might not come to the knowledge of the king. And many did believe his words. And it came to pass that as many as did believe him did go forth to a place which was called M'raman, having received its name from the king, being in the borders of the land, having been infested by times or at seasons by wild beasts. Now there was in M'raman a fountain of pure water, and Alma took refuge in that place, there being near the water a thicket of small trees where he did hide himself in the daytime from the searches of the king. And it came to pass that as many as believed him went there to hear his words. And it came to pass after many days there were a good number gathered together to the place of M'raman to hear the words of Alma; yes, all were gathered together that believed on his word to hear him. And he did teach them and did preach unto them repentance, and redemption, and faith on YHWH.

7 And it came to pass that he said unto them, Behold, here are the waters of M'raman — for thus were they called — and now, as you are desirous to come into the fold of Elohim and to be called his people, and are willing to bear one another's burdens, that they may be light, yes, and are willing to mourn with those that mourn, yes, and comfort those that stand in need of comfort, and to stand as witnesses of Elohim at all times, and in all things, and in all places that you may be in, even until death, that you may be redeemed of Elohim and be numbered with those of the first resurrection, that you may have Eternal life, now I say unto you, if this be the desire of your hearts, what have you against being washed by immersion, in the name of YHWH, as a witness before **him that you have entered into a covenant with him that you will serve him and keep his mitzvot**,[125] that he may pour out his spirit more abundantly upon you? And now when the people had heard these words, they clapped their hands for joy and exclaimed, This is the desires of our hearts!

8 And now it came to pass that Alma took Helam, he being one of the first, and went and stood forth in the water, and cried, saying, O YHWH, pour out your spirit upon your servant, that he may do this

---

[125] Deut. 29:12; 30:10

work with holiness of heart. And when he had said these words, the spirit of YHWH was upon him, and he said, Helam, I immerse you, having s'mikhah[126] from El Shaddai, as a testimony that you have entered into a covenant to serve him until you are dead as to the mortal body; and may the spirit of YHWH be poured out upon you, and may he grant unto you Eternal life through the redemption of Mashiach, whom he has prepared from the foundation of the world. And after Alma had said these words, both Alma and Helam were buried in the water. And they arose and came forth out of the water rejoicing, being filled with the spirit. And again Alma took another, and went forth a second time into the water, and immersed him according to the first, only he did not bury himself again in the water. And after this manner, he did immerse everyone that went forth to the place of M'raman, and they were in number about two hundred and four souls; yes, and they were immersed in the waters of M'raman, and were filled with the grace of Elohim. And they were called the assembly of Elohim, or the assembly of Mashiach,[127] from that time forward. And it came to pass that whosoever was immersed by the power and s'mikhah of Elohim was added to his assembly.

9 And it came to pass that Alma, having s'mikhah from Elohim, ordained kohanim; even one kohen to every fifty of their number did he ordain, to preach unto them and to teach them concerning the things pertaining to the kingdom of Elohim. And he commanded them that they should teach nothing except it were the things which he had taught and which had been spoken by the mouth of the holy prophets. Yes, even he commanded them that they should preach nothing except it were repentance and faith on YHWH, who had redeemed his people. And he commanded them that there should be no contention one with another, but that they should look forward with one eye, having one faith and one immersion, having their hearts knit together in unity and in love one towards another. And thus he commanded them to preach. And thus they became the children of Elohim.

10 And he commanded them that they should observe **the Shabbat and keep it holy**,[128] and also every day they should give thanks to

---

[126] "Authority, ordination." From a word meaning "laying on of hands." [127] 3 Nefi 12:4 [128] Ex. 20:8

YHWH their Elohim. And he also commanded them that the kohanim whom he had ordained should labor with their own hands for their support. And there was one day in every week that was set apart that they should gather themselves together to teach the people, and to worship YHWH their Elohim, and also as often as it was in their power to assemble themselves together. And the kohanim were not to depend upon the people for their support, but for their labor they were to receive the grace of Elohim, that they might grow strong in the spirit, having the knowledge of Elohim, that they might teach with power and s'mikhah from Elohim.

11 And again Alma commanded that the people of the assembly should impart of their substance, everyone according to that which he had: if he have more abundantly, he should impart more abundantly; and he that had but little, but little should be required; and to him that had not, should be given. And thus they should impart of their substance of their own free will and good desires towards Elohim, to those kohanim that stood in need, yes, and to every needy, naked soul. And this he said unto them, having been commanded of Elohim. And they did walk uprightly before Elohim, imparting to one another both temporally and spiritually according to their needs and their wants.

12 And now it came to pass that all this was done in M'raman, yes, by the waters of M'raman, in the forest that was near the waters of M'raman — yes, the place of M'raman, the waters of M'raman, the forest of M'raman, how beautiful are they to the eyes of those who there came to the knowledge of their Redeemer! Yes, and how blessed are they, for they shall sing to his praise for ever.

13 And these things were done in the borders of the land that they might not come to the knowledge of the king. But behold, it came to pass that the king, having discovered a movement among the people, sent his servants to watch them. Therefore on the day that they were assembling themselves together to hear the word of YHWH, they were uncovered unto the king. And now the king said that Alma was stirring up the people to a rebellion against him; therefore he sent his army to destroy them. And it came to pass that Alma and the people of YHWH were apprised of the coming of the king's army; therefore they took their tents and their families and departed into the wilderness. And they were in number about four hundred and fifty souls.

¹⁴ And it came to pass that the army of the king returned, having searched in vain **for the people of YHWH**.¹²⁹ And now behold, the forces of the king were small, having been reduced. And there began to be a division among the remainder of the people. And the lesser part began to breathe out threatenings against the king, and there began to be a great contention among them. And now there was a man among them whose name was Gideon, and he being a strong man and an enemy to the king, therefore he drew his sword and swore in his wrath that he would slay the king. And it came to pass that he fought with the king. And when the king saw that he was about to overpower him, he fled, and ran, and got upon the tower which was near the Temple. And Gideon pursued after him and was about to get upon the tower to slay the king. And the king cast his eyes round about towards the land of Shemlon, and behold, the army of the Lamanites were within the borders of the land. And now the king cried out in the anguish of his soul, saying, Gideon, spare me! For the Lamanites are upon us and they will destroy them—yes, they will destroy my people. And now the king was not so concerned about his people as he was about his own life; nevertheless, Gideon did spare his life.

¹⁵ And the king commanded the people that they should flee before the Lamanites, and he himself did go before them. And they did flee into the wilderness with their women and their children. And it came to pass that the Lamanites did pursue them, and did overtake them, and began to slay them. Now it came to pass that the king commanded them that all the men should leave their wives and their children and flee before the Lamanites. Now there were many that would not leave them but had rather stay and perish with them. And the rest left their wives and their children and fled.

¹⁶ And it came to pass that those that remained with their wives and their children caused that their fair daughters should stand forth and plead with the Lamanites that they would not slay them. And it came to pass that the Lamanites had compassion on them, for they were charmed with the beauty of their women. Therefore the Lamanites did spare their lives, and took them captives, and carried them back to the land of Nefi, and granted unto them that they might

---

129 2 Sam. 1:12

possess the land under the conditions that they would deliver up the king, Noah, into the hands of the Lamanites and deliver up their property, even one half of all they possessed: one half of their gold, and their silver, and all their precious things. And thus they should pay tribute to the king of the Lamanites from year to year. And now there was one of the sons of the king among those that were taken captive, whose name was Limhi. And now Limhi was desirous that his father should not be destroyed. Nevertheless, Limhi was not ignorant of the iniquities of his father, he himself being a just man.

17 And it came to pass that Gideon sent men into the wilderness secretly to search for the king and those that were with him. And it came to pass that they met the people in the wilderness, all except the king and his kohanim. Now they had sworn in their hearts that they would return to the land of Nefi, and if their wives and their children were slain, and also those that had remained with them, that they would seek revenge and also perish with them. And the king commanded them that they should not return, and they were angry with the king and caused that he should suffer, even unto death by fire. And they were about to take the kohanim also, to put them to death, and they fled before them.

18 And it came to pass that they were about to return to the land of Nefi, and they met the men of Gideon. And the men of Gideon told them of all that had happened to their wives and their children, and that the Lamanites had granted unto them that they might possess the land by paying tribute to the Lamanites of one half of all they possessed. And the people told the men of Gideon that they had slain the king, and his kohanim had fled from them farther into the wilderness. And it came to pass that after they had ended the ceremony, that they returned to the land of Nefi, rejoicing because their wives and their children were not slain; and they told Gideon what they had done to the king.

19 And it came to pass that the king of the Lamanites made an oath unto them that his people should not slay them. And also Limhi, being the son of the king, having the kingdom conferred upon him by the people, made an oath unto the king of the Lamanites that his people should pay tribute unto him, even one half of all they possessed.

20 And it came to pass that Limhi began to strengthen the kingdom and to establish peace among his people. And the king of the Lamanites set guards round about the land that he might keep the people of Limhi in the land, that they might not depart into the wilderness. And he did support his guards out of the tribute which he did receive from the Nefites. And now king Limhi did have continual shalom in his kingdom for the space of two years, that the Lamanites did not molest them nor seek to destroy them.

21 Now there was a place in Shemlon where the daughters of the Lamanites did gather themselves together, to sing, and to dance, and to make themselves merry. And it came to pass that there was one day[130] a small number of them gathered together to sing and to dance. And now the kohanim of king Noah, being ashamed to return to the city of Nefi, yes, and also fearing that the people would slay them, therefore they dared not return to their wives and their children. And having remained in the wilderness, and having discovered the daughters of the Lamanites, they laid and watched them. And when there were but few of them gathered together to dance, they came forth out of their secret places and took them,[131] and carried them into the wilderness, yes, twenty and four of the daughters of the Lamanites they carried into the wilderness.

22 And it came to pass that when the Lamanites found that their daughters had been missing, they were angry with the people of Limhi; for they thought it was the people of Limhi. Therefore they sent their armies forth, yes, even the king himself went before his people, and they went up to the land of Nefi to destroy the people

---

130 The underlying Hebrew may have been *yom echad* יוֹם אֶחָד, which can be used idiomatically to mean "a certain day." The context here is that the "certain day" was Tu B'av (the 15th of Av), an ancient, minor Jewish festival that marks the beginning of the grape harvest. It is similar in romantic character with Valentine's Day and is traditionally celebrated with maidens dancing. This event parallels that of Judg. 21:16-23, which also occurred at a "feast of YHWH" (Judg. 21:19). According to the Talmud, this "feast of YHWH" was the 15th of Av: "Rabbi Simeon ben Gamliel said, 'There never were in Israel greater days of joy than the Fifteenth of Av and the Day of Atonement.'...what happened on the fifteenth of Av?... Rabbi Joseph said in the name of Rabbi Nahman: 'It is the day on which the Tribe of Benjamin was permitted to re-enter the congregation [of Israel], as it is said, now the men of Israel had sworn in Mizpah, saying: There shall not any of us give his daughter unto Benjamin to wife (Judg. 21:1). From what was their exposition?' Rab said: From the phrase 'any of us' which was interpreted to mean, 'but not from any of our children'" (b.Ta'anit 30b). 131 See Judg. 21:16-23, where the men of Benjamin, who could not otherwise obtain wives, were permitted to kidnap the maidens who danced at Tu B'av.

of Limhi. And now Limhi had discovered them from the tower, even all their preparations for war did he discover. Therefore he gathered his people together and laid wait for them in the fields and in the forests. And it came to pass that when the Lamanites had come up, that the people of Limhi began to fall upon them from their waiting places and began to slay them.

23 And it came to pass that the battle became exceedingly sore, for they fought like lions for their prey. And it came to pass that the people of Limhi began to drive the Lamanites before them. Yet they were not half so numerous as the Lamanites, but they fought for their lives, and for their wives, and for their children. Therefore, they exerted themselves and like dragons did they fight.

24 And it came to pass that they found the king of the Lamanites among the number of their dead, yet he was not dead, having been wounded and left upon the ground, so speedy was the flight of his people. And they took him, and bound up his wounds, and brought him before Limhi, and said, Behold, here is the king of the Lamanites; he, having received a wound, has fallen among their dead and they have left him. And behold, we have brought him before you. And now let us slay him. But Limhi said unto them, You shall not slay him, but bring him here that I may see him. And they brought him, and Limhi said unto him, What cause have you to come up to war against my people? Behold, my people have not broken the oath that I made unto you; therefore, why should you break the oath which you made unto my people? And now the king said, I have broken the oath because your people did carry away the daughters of my people. Therefore, in my anger did I cause my people to come up to war against your people. Now Limhi had heard nothing concerning this matter; therefore he said, I will search among my people, and whosoever has done this thing shall perish. Therefore he caused a search to be made among his people.

25 Now when Gideon had heard these things, he being the king's captain, he went forth and said unto the king, I implore you to show restraint, and do not search this people, and lay not this thing to their charge. For do you not remember the kohanim of your father whom this people sought to destroy? And are they not in the wilderness? And are not they the ones who have stolen the daughters of the Lamanites? And now behold, and tell the king of these things, that he may tell

his people, that they may be pacified towards us. For behold, they are already preparing to come against us. And behold also, there are but few of us; and behold, they come with their numerous hosts. And except the king does pacify them towards us, we must perish. For are not the words of Avinodi fulfilled which he prophesied against us — and all this because we would not hearken unto the word of YHWH and turn from our iniquities? And now let us pacify the king, and fulfill the oath which we have made unto him. For it is better that we should be in bondage than that we should lose our lives. Therefore, let us put a stop to the shedding of so much blood. And now Limhi told the king all the things concerning his father and the kohanim that had fled into the wilderness, and attributed the carrying away of their daughters to them.

26 And it came to pass that the king was pacified towards his people, and he said unto them, Let us go forth to meet my people without arms, and I swear unto you with an oath that my people shall not slay your people. And it came to pass that they followed the king and went forth without arms to meet the Lamanites. And it came to pass that they did meet the Lamanites, and the king of the Lamanites did bow himself down before them and did plead in behalf of the people of Limhi. And when the Lamanites saw the people of Limhi, that they were without arms, they had compassion on them, and were pacified towards them, and returned with their king in shalom to their own land.

27 And it came to pass that Limhi and his people returned to the city of Nefi and began to dwell in the land again in shalom. And it came to pass that after many days the Lamanites began again to be stirred up in anger against the Nefites, and they began to come into the borders of the land round about. Now they dared not slay them, because of the oath which their king had made unto Limhi, but they would strike them on their cheeks and exercise authority over them, and began to put heavy burdens upon their backs and drive them as they would a dumb ass. Yes, all this was done that the word of YHWH might be fulfilled. And now the afflictions of the Nefites were great. And there was no way that they could deliver themselves out of their hands, for the Lamanites had surrounded them on every side.

28 And it came to pass that the people began to murmur with the king because of their afflictions. And they began to be desirous

to go against them to battle, and they did afflict the king sorely with their complaints. Therefore he granted unto them that they should do according to their desires. And they gathered themselves together again, and put on their armor, and went forth against the Lamanites to drive them out of their land. And it came to pass that the Lamanites did beat them, and drove them back, and slew many of them. And now there was a great mourning and lamentation among the people of Limhi: the widow mourning for her husband, the son and the daughter mourning for their father, and the brothers for their brothers.

29 Now there were a great many widows in the land, and they did cry mightily from day to day, for a great fear of the Lamanites had come upon them. And it came to pass that their continual cries did stir up the remainder of the people of Limhi to anger against the Lamanites. And they went again to battle, but they were driven back again, suffering much loss. Yes, they went again, even the third time, and suffered in like manner. And those that were not slain returned again to the city of Nefi. And they did humble themselves even to the dust, subjecting themselves to the yoke of bondage, submitting themselves to be smitten, and to be driven to and fro, and burdened according to the desires of their enemies. And they did humble themselves even in the depths of humility. And they did cry mightily to Elohim, yes, even all the day long did they cry unto their Elohim **that he would deliver them out of their afflictions.**[132]

30 And now YHWH was slow to hear their cry because of their iniquities. Nevertheless, YHWH did hear their cries, and began to soften the hearts of the Lamanites, that they began to ease their burdens; yet YHWH did not see fit to deliver them out of bondage.

31 And it came to pass that they began to prosper by degrees in the land, and began to raise grain more abundantly, and flocks, and herds, that they did not suffer from hunger. Now there was a great number of women, more than there was of men. Therefore king Limhi commanded that every man should impart to the support of the widows and their children, that they might not perish with hunger. And this they did because of the greatness of their number that had been slain. Now the people of Limhi kept together in a body

---

132 Ps. 107:6

as much as it was possible, and secured their grain and their flocks. And the king himself did not trust his person without the walls of the city unless he took his guards with him, fearing that he might by some means fall into the hands of the Lamanites. And he caused that his people should watch the land round about, that by some means they might take those kohanim that fled into the wilderness, who had stolen the daughters of the Lamanites, and that had caused such a great destruction to come upon them. For they were desirous to take them that they might punish them, for they had come into the land of Nefi by night and carried off of their grain and many of their precious things. Therefore they laid wait for them.

32 And it came to pass that there was no more disturbance between the Lamanites and the people of Limhi, even until the time that Ammon and his brothers came into the land. And the king, having been without the gates of the city with his guard, he discovered Ammon and his brothers; and supposing them to be kohanim of Noah, therefore he caused that they should be taken, and bound, and cast into prison. And had they been the kohanim of Noah, he would have caused that they should be put to death. But when he found that they were not, but that they were his brothers and had come from the land of Zerach'mla, he was filled with exceedingly great joy.

33 Now king Limhi had sent, previous to the coming of Ammon, a small number of men to search for the land of Zerach'mla, but they could not find it and they were lost in the wilderness. Nevertheless, they did find a land which had been peopled, yes, a land which was covered with dry bones, yes, a land which had been peopled and which had been destroyed.[133] And they, having supposed it to be the land of Zerach'mla, returned to the land of Nefi, having arrived in the borders of the land not many days before the coming of Ammon. And they brought a record with them, even a record of the people[134] whose bones they had found; and they were engraved upon plates of ore. And now Limhi was again filled with joy on learning from the mouth of Ammon that king Binyamin had a gift from Elohim by which he could interpret such engravings; yes, and Ammon also did rejoice. Yet Ammon and his brothers were filled with sorrow

---

133 Note that the discovery of Coriantumr shortly after the final destruction of the Yeredite nation may have taken place much earlier (perhaps around ~ 550 BCE), with only the report of that discovery being made during the days of Moshiyah the 1st.   134 'Eter 1:1

because so many of their brothers had been slain, and also that king Noah and his kohanim had caused the people to commit so many sins and iniquities against Elohim. And they also did mourn for the death of Avinodi, and also for the departure of Alma and the people that went with him, who had formed an assembly of Elohim through the strength and power of Elohim and faith on the words which had been spoken by Avinodi. Yes, they did mourn for their departure, for they knew not where they had fled. Now they would have gladly joined with them, for they themselves had **entered into a covenant with Elohim to serve him and keep his mitzvot**.[135] And now since the coming of Ammon, king Limhi had also entered into a covenant with Elohim, and also many of his people, to serve him and keep his mitzvot.

34 And it came to pass that king Limhi and many of his people were desirous to be washed by immersion, but there was none in the land that had s'mikhah from Elohim. And Ammon declined doing this thing, considering himself an unworthy servant. Therefore they did not at that time form themselves into an assembly, waiting upon the spirit of YHWH. Now they were desirous to become even as Alma and his brothers, who had fled into the wilderness. They were desirous to be immersed as a witness and a testimony that they were willing to serve Elohim with all their hearts. Nevertheless, they did await their time, and an account of their immersion shall be given hereafter. And now the study of Ammon and his people, and king Limhi and his people, was to deliver themselves out of the hands of the Lamanites and from bondage.

10 And now it came to pass that Ammon and king Limhi began to consult with the people regarding how they should deliver themselves out of bondage. And even they did cause that all the people should gather themselves together; and this they did that they might have the **voice of the people** concerning the matter. And it came to pass that they could find no way to deliver themselves out of bondage except it were to take their women and children, and their flocks, and their herds and their tents, and depart into the wilderness, for the Lamanites were so numerous that it was

---

135 Deut. 29:11 (12); 30:10

impossible for the people of Limhi to contend with them, thinking to deliver themselves out of bondage by the sword.

2 Now it came to pass that Gideon went forth and stood before the king, and said unto him, Now, O king, you have previously hearkened unto my words many times when we have been contending with our brothers the Lamanites. And now, O king, if you have not found me to be an unprofitable servant, or if you have previously listened to my words in any degree, and they have been of service to you, even so I desire that you would listen to my words at this time; and I will be your servant and deliver this people out of bondage. And the king granted unto him that he might speak, and Gideon said unto him, Behold the back pass through the back wall on the back side of the city. The Lamanites, or the guards of the Lamanites, by night are drunken. Therefore let us send a proclamation among all this people that they gather together their flocks and herds, that they may drive them into the wilderness by night. And I will go according to your command and pay the last tribute of wine to the Lamanites, and they will be drunken; and we will pass through the secret pass on the left of their camp when they are drunken and asleep. Thus we will depart with our women and our children, our flocks and our herds, into the wilderness; and we will travel around the land of Shilom. And it came to pass that the king hearkened unto the words of Gideon. And king Limhi caused that his people should gather their flocks together. And he sent the tribute of wine to the Lamanites, and he also sent more wine as a present unto them, and they did drink freely of the wine which king Limhi did send unto them.

3 And it came to pass that the people of king Limhi did depart by night into the wilderness with their flocks and their herds. And they went round about the land of Shilom in the wilderness and bent their course towards the land of Zerach'mla, being led by Ammon and his brothers. And they had taken all their gold, and silver, and their precious things which they could carry, and also their provisions, with them into the wilderness; and they pursued their journey. And after being many days in the wilderness, they arrived in the land of Zerach'mla, and joined his people and became his subjects. And it came to pass that Moshiyah received them with joy, and he also received their records, and also the records which had been found by the people of Limhi. And now it came to pass, when the Lamanites

had found that the people of Limhi had departed out of the land by night, that they sent an army into the wilderness to pursue them. And after they had pursued them two days, they could no longer follow their tracks; therefore they were lost in the wilderness.

An account of Alma and the people of YHWH who were driven into the wilderness by the people of king Noah.

11 Now Alma having been warned of YHWH that the armies of king Noah would come upon them, had made it known to his people, therefore they gathered together their flocks, and took of their grain, and departed into the wilderness before the armies of king Noah. And YHWH did strengthen them, that the people of king Noah could not overtake them to destroy them. And they fled eight days' journey into the wilderness, and they came to a land, yes, even a very beautiful and pleasant land, a land of pure water. And they pitched their tents, and began to till the ground, and began to build buildings, and so forth. Yes, they were industrious and did labor exceedingly.

2 And the people were desirous that Alma should be their king, for he was beloved by his people. But he said unto them, Behold, it is not expedient that we should have a king, for thus says YHWH: You shall not esteem one flesh above another, or one man shall not think himself above another. Therefore I say unto you, it is not expedient that you should have a king; nevertheless, if it were possible that you could always have just men to be your kings, it would be well for you to have a king; but remember the iniquity of king Noah and his kohanim. And I myself was caught in a snare, and did many things which were abominable in the sight of YHWH, which caused me sore repentance. Nevertheless, after much tribulation, YHWH did hear my cries and did answer my prayers, and has made me an instrument in his hands in bringing so many of you to a knowledge of his truth. Nevertheless, in this I do not glory, for I am unworthy to glory of myself. And now I say unto you, you have been oppressed by king Noah, and have been in bondage to him and his kohanim, and have been brought into iniquity by them; therefore, you were bound with the bands of iniquity. And now as you have been delivered by the power of Elohim out of these bonds, yes, even out of the hands of king

Noah and his people, and also from the bonds of iniquity, even so I desire that you should stand fast in this liberty with which you have been made free, and that you trust no man to be a king over you; and also trusting no one to be your teacher nor your guide except he be a man of Elohim, walking in his ways and keeping his mitzvot. Thus did Alma teach his people that **every man should love his neighbor as himself,**[136] that there should be no contention among them.

3 And now Alma was their Kohen HaGadol, he being the founder of their assembly. And it came to pass that none received s'mikhah to preach or to teach except it were by him from Elohim; therefore he consecrated all their kohanim and all their teachers, and none were consecrated except they were just men. Therefore they did watch over their people and did nourish them with things pertaining to righteousness. And it came to pass that they began to prosper exceedingly in the land, and they called the land Helam. And it came to pass that they did multiply and prosper exceedingly in the land of Helam; and they built a city which they called the city of Helam. Nevertheless, YHWH sees fit to chasten his people; yes, he tries their patience and their faith. Nevertheless, whosoever puts his trust in him, the same shall be lifted up at the last day; yes, and thus it was with this people. For behold, I will show unto you that they were brought into bondage, and none could deliver them but YHWH their Elohim, yes, even the Elohim of Avraham, and of Yitz'chak, and of Ya'akov. And it came to pass that he did deliver them, and he did show forth his mighty power unto them; and great were their rejoicings.

4 For behold, it came to pass that while they were in the land of Helam, yes, in the city of Helam, while tilling the land round about, behold, an army of the Lamanites were in the borders of the land. Now it came to pass that the brothers of Alma fled from their fields and gathered themselves together into the city of Helam, and they were much frightened because of the appearance of the Lamanites. But Alma went forth and stood among them, and exhorted them that they should not be frightened, but that they should remember YHWH their Elohim and he would deliver them. Therefore they hushed their fears and began to cry unto YHWH that he would soften the hearts of the Lamanites, that they would spare them, and their

---

[136] Lev. 19:18

wives, and children. And it came to pass that YHWH did soften the hearts of the Lamanites. And Alma and his brothers went forth and delivered themselves up into their hands, and the Lamanites took possession of the land of Helam.

5 Now the armies of the Lamanites which had followed after the people of king Limhi had been lost in the wilderness for many days. And behold, they had found those kohanim of king Noah in a place which they called Amulon, and they had begun to possess the land of Amulon and had begun to till the ground. Now the name of the leader of those kohanim was Amulon. And it came to pass that Amulon did plead with the Lamanites, and he also sent forth their wives, who were the daughters of the Lamanites, to plead with their brothers that they should not destroy their husbands. And the Lamanites had compassion on Amulon and his brothers and did not destroy them, because of their wives. And Amulon and his brothers did join the Lamanites, and they were traveling in the wilderness in search of the land of Nefi when they discovered the land of Helam, which was possessed by Alma and his brothers.

6 And it came to pass that the Lamanites promised unto Alma and his brothers that if they would show them the way which led to the land of Nefi, that they would grant unto them their lives and their liberty. But after Alma had shown them the way that led to the land of Nefi, the Lamanites would not keep their promise, but they set guards round about the land of Helam over Alma and his brothers, and the remainder of them went to the land of Nefi. And a part of them returned to the land of Helam, and also brought with them the wives and the children of the guards who had been left in the land. And the king of the Lamanites had granted unto Amulon that he should be a king and a ruler over his people who were in the land of Helam; nevertheless, he should have no power to do anything contrary to the will of the king of the Lamanites.

7 And it came to pass that Amulon did gain favor in the eyes of the king of the Lamanites; therefore, the king of the Lamanites granted unto him and his brothers that they should be appointed teachers over his people, yes, even over the people who were in the land of Shemlon, and the land of Shilom, and in the land of Amulon. For the Lamanites had taken possession of all these lands; therefore, the king of the Lamanites had appointed kings over all these lands.

And now the name of the king of the Lamanites was Laman, being called after the name of his father; and therefore, he was called king Laman. And he was king over a numerous people. And he appointed teachers from among the brothers of Amulon in every land which was possessed by his people. And thus the language of Nefi began to be taught among all the people of the Lamanites. And they were a people friendly one with another. Nevertheless, they knew not Elohim; neither did the brothers of Amulon teach them anything concerning YHWH their Elohim, neither the Torah of Moshe, nor did they teach them the words of Avinodi. But they taught them that they should keep their record, and that they might write one to another. And thus the Lamanites began to increase in riches, and began to trade one with another and grow great, and began to be a cunning and a wise people as to the wisdom of the world — yes, a very cunning people, delighting in all manner of wickedness and plunder, except it were among their own brothers.

⁸And now it came to pass that Amulon began to exercise authority over Alma and his brothers, and began to persecute him, and cause that his children should persecute their children. For Amulon knew Alma, that he had been one of the king's kohanim, and that it was he that believed the words of Avinodi and was driven out before the king; and therefore he was angry with him. For he was subject to king Laman, yet he exercised authority over them, and put tasks upon them, and put taskmasters over them. And it came to pass that so great were their afflictions that they began to cry mightily to Elohim. And Amulon commanded them that they should stop their cries, and put guards over them to watch them, that whosoever should be found calling upon Elohim should be put to death. And Alma and his people did not raise their voices to YHWH their Elohim, but did pour out their hearts to him; and he did know the thoughts of their hearts.

⁹And it came to pass that the voice of YHWH came to them in their afflictions, saying, Lift up your heads and be of good comfort,[137] for I know of the covenant which you have made unto me. And I will covenant with this my people and deliver them out of bondage. And I will also ease the burdens which are put upon your shoulders, that

---

[137] 1 Nefi 6:8

even you cannot feel them upon your backs, even while you are in bondage. And this will I do that you may stand as witnesses for me hereafter, and that you may know of a surety that I, Adonai YHWH, do visit my people in their afflictions. And now it came to pass that the burdens which were laid upon Alma and his brothers were made light; yes, YHWH did strengthen them, that they could bear up their burdens with ease, and they did submit cheerfully and with patience to all the will of YHWH.

10 And it came to pass that so great was their faith and their patience that the voice of YHWH came unto them again, saying, Be of good comfort, for tomorrow I will deliver you out of bondage. And he said unto Alma, You shall go before this people, and I will go with you and deliver this people out of bondage.

11 Now it came to pass that Alma and his people in the nighttime gathered their flocks together, and also of their grain; yes, even all the nighttime were they gathering their flocks together. And in the morning, YHWH caused a deep sleep to come upon the Lamanites; yes, and all their taskmasters were in a profound sleep. And Alma and his people departed into the wilderness. And when they had traveled all day, they pitched their tents in a valley; and they called the name of the valley Alma, because he led their way in the wilderness. Yes, and in the valley of Alma they poured out their thanks to Elohim because he had been merciful unto them, and eased their burdens, and had delivered them out of bondage — for they were in bondage, and none could deliver them except it were YHWH their Elohim. And they gave thanks to Elohim — yes, all their men, and all their women, and all their children that could speak, lifted their voices in the praises of their Elohim.

12 And now YHWH said unto Alma, Hasten and get yourself and this people out of this land, for the Lamanites have awoken and do pursue you; therefore get yourself out of this land. And I will stop the Lamanites in this valley, that they come no further in pursuit of this people. And it came to pass that they departed out of the valley and took their journey into the wilderness. And after they had been in the wilderness twelve days, they arrived to the land of Zerach'mla; and king Moshiyah did also receive them with joy.

13 And now king Moshiyah caused that all the people should be gathered together. Now there were not so many of the children of

Nefi, or so many of those who were descendants of Nefi, as there were of the people of Zerach'mla, who was a descendant of Muloch and those who came with him into the wilderness. And there were not so many of the people of Nefi and of the people of Zerach'mla as there were of the Lamanites; yes, they were not half so numerous. And now all the people of Nefi were assembled together, and also all the people of Zerach'mla, and they were gathered together in two bodies.

14 And it came to pass that Moshiyah did read, and caused to be read, the records of Zeniff to his people; yes, he read the records of the people of Zeniff from the time they left the land of Zerach'mla until the time they returned again. And he also read the account of Alma and his brothers, and all their afflictions from the time they left the land of Zerach'mla until the time they returned again. And now when Moshiyah had made an end of reading the records, his people who remained in the land were struck with wonder and amazement, for they knew not what to think. For when they beheld those that had been delivered out of bondage, they were filled with exceedingly great joy. And again, when they thought of their brothers who had been slain by the Lamanites, they were filled with sorrow, and even shed many tears of sorrow. And again, when they thought of the immediate goodness of Elohim, and his power [138] in delivering Alma and his brothers out of the hands of the Lamanites and of bondage, they did raise their voices and give thanks to Elohim. And again, when they thought upon the Lamanites, who were their brothers, of their sinful and polluted state, they were filled with pain and anguish for the welfare of their souls.

15 And it came to pass that those who were the children of Amulon and his brothers, who had taken to wife the daughters of the Lamanites, were displeased with the conduct of their fathers, and they would no longer be called by the names of their fathers. Therefore, they took upon themselves the name of Nefi, that they might be called the children of Nefi and be numbered among those who were called Nefites. And now all the people of Zerach'mla were numbered with the Nefites, and this because the kingdom had been conferred upon none but those who were descendants of Nefi.

---

[138] 1 Nefi 5:18

16 And now it came to pass that when Moshiyah had made an end of speaking and reading to the people, he desired that Alma should also speak to the people. And Alma did speak unto them when they were assembled together in large bodies; and he went from one body to another, preaching unto the people repentance and faith on YHWH. And he did exhort the people of Limhi and his brothers — all those that had been delivered out of bondage — that they should remember that it was YHWH that did deliver them. And it came to pass that after Alma had taught the people many things, and had made an end of speaking to them, that king Limhi was desirous that he might be washed by immersion; and all his people were desirous that they might be immersed also. Therefore, Alma did go forth into the water and did immerse them; yes, he did immerse them after the manner he did his brothers in the waters of M'raman. Yes, and as many as he did wash by immersion did belong to the assembly of Elohim,[139] and this because of their belief on the words of Alma.

17 And it came to pass that king Moshiyah granted unto Alma that he might establish assemblies throughout all the land of Zerach'mla, and gave him power to ordain kohanim and teachers over every assembly. Now this was done because there were so many people that they could not be all governed by one teacher, neither could they all hear the word of Elohim in one assembly. Therefore, they did assemble themselves together in different bodies, being called assemblies, every assembly having their kohanim and their teachers, and every kohen preaching the word according as it was delivered to him by the mouth of Alma. And thus, even though there were many assemblies, they were all one assembly, yes, even the assembly of Elohim; for there was nothing preached in all the assemblies except it were repentance and faith in Elohim. And now there were seven assemblies in the land of Zerach'mla. And it came to pass that whosoever were desirous to take upon them the name of Mashiach, or of Elohim, they did join the assemblies of Elohim; and they were called the people of Elohim. And YHWH did pour out his spirit upon them, and they were blessed and prospered in the land.

---

139 "Although circumcision is the token of the covenant (Gen. 17:11; Ex. 12:47-48), the Talmud indicates that it is immersion that marks the point that a proselyte has entered the covenant and become part of the Assembly of Israel" (b.Yevamot 46a).

18 Now it came to pass that there were many of the rising generation that could not understand the words of king Binyamin, being little children at the time he spoke unto his people; and they did not believe the tradition of their fathers. They did not believe what had been said concerning the resurrection of the dead, neither did they believe concerning the coming of Mashiach. And now, because of their unbelief, they could not understand the word of Elohim, and their hearts were hardened. And they would not be immersed, neither would they join the assembly. And they were a separate people as to their faith, and remained so ever after, even in their carnal and sinful state, for they would not call upon YHWH their Elohim. And now in the reign of Moshiyah, they were not half so numerous as the people of Elohim; but because of the dissensions among the brothers, they became more numerous. For it came to pass that they did deceive many — with their flattering words — who were in the assembly, and did cause them to commit many sins. Therefore, it became expedient that those who committed sin, that were in the assembly, should be admonished by the assembly.

19 And it came to pass that they were brought before the kohanim and delivered up unto the kohanim by the teachers, and the kohanim brought them before Alma, who was the Kohen HaGadol. Now king Moshiyah had given Alma the authority over the assembly. And it came to pass that Alma did know concerning them, for there were many witnesses against them; yes, the people stood and testified of their iniquity in abundance. Now there had not any such thing happened before in the assembly. Therefore, Alma was troubled in his spirit, and he caused that they should be brought before the king. And he said unto the king, Behold, here are many whom we have brought before you, who are accused of their brothers. Yes, and they have been taken in diverse iniquities, and they do not repent of their iniquities. Therefore we have brought them before you, that you may judge them according to their crimes. But king Moshiyah said unto Alma, Behold, I judge them not; therefore I deliver them into your hands to be judged. And now the spirit of Alma was again troubled. And he went and inquired of YHWH what he should do concerning this matter, for he feared that he should do wrong in the sight of Elohim.

20 And it came to pass that after he had poured out his whole soul to Elohim, the voice of YHWH came to him, saying, Blessed[140] are you Alma, and blessed are they who were immersed in the waters of M'raman. You are blessed because of your exceeding faith in the words alone of my servant Avinodi. And blessed are they because of their exceeding faith in the words alone which you have spoken unto them. And blessed are you because you have established an assembly among this people. And they shall be strengthened, and they shall be my people. Yes, blessed is this people who are willing to bear my name, for in my name shall they be called, and they are mine. And because you have inquired of me concerning the transgressor, you are blessed. You are my servant, and I covenant with you that you shall have Eternal life.

21 And you shall serve me, and go forth in my name, and shall gather together my sheep. And he that will hear my voice shall be my sheep;[141] and him shall you receive into the assembly, and him will I also receive. For behold, this is my assembly. Whosoever is immersed shall be washed unto repentance, and whosoever you receive shall believe in my name, and him will I freely forgive. For it is I that take upon myself the sins of the world, for it is I that have created them. And it is I that grant unto him that believes unto the end a place at my right hand. For behold, in my name are they called; and if they know me, they shall come forth and shall have a place eternally at my right hand. And it shall come to pass that when the second shofar shall sound, then shall they that never knew me come forth and shall stand before me. And then shall they know that I am YHWH their Elohim, that I am their Redeemer, but they would not be redeemed. And then will I confess unto them that I never knew them, and they shall depart into everlasting fire prepared for HaSatan and his angels. Therefore I say unto you that he that will not hear my voice, the same shall you not receive into my assembly, for him will I not receive at the last day.

22 Therefore I say unto you, go, and whosoever transgress against me, him shall you judge according to the sins which he has committed. And if he confess his sins before you and me, and repents in the sincerity of his heart, him shall you forgive, and I will forgive him

---

140 Ya'akov 3:28; Enosh 1:1 **141** 1 Nefi 7:5; Alma 3:7; 3 Nefi 7:3

also. Yes, and as often as my people repent will I forgive them their trespasses against me. And you shall also forgive one another your trespasses. For truly I say unto you, he that forgives not his neighbor's trespasses when he says that he repents, the same has brought himself under condemnation. Now I say unto you, go, and whosoever will not repent of his sins, the same shall not be numbered among my people. And this shall be observed from this time forward.

23 And it came to pass when Alma had heard these words, he wrote them down that he might have them and that he might judge the people of that assembly according to the mitzvot of Elohim. And it came to pass that Alma went and judged those that had been taken in iniquity, according to the word of YHWH. And whosoever repented of their sins and did confess them, those he did number among the people of the assembly. And those that would not confess their sins and repent of their iniquity, the same were not numbered among the people of the assembly; and their names were blotted out. And it came to pass that Alma did regulate all the affairs of the assembly. And they began again to have peace and to prosper exceedingly in the affairs of the assembly, walking circumspectly before Elohim, receiving many and immersing many. And now all these things did Alma and his fellow laborers do who were over the assembly, walking in all diligence, teaching the word of Elohim in all things, suffering all manner of afflictions, being persecuted by all those who did not belong to the assembly of Elohim. And they did admonish their brothers, and they were also admonished, every one by the word of Elohim, according to his sins, or to the sins which he had committed, being commanded of Elohim to pray without ceasing and to give thanks in all things. And now it came to pass that the persecutions which were inflicted on the assembly by the unbelievers became so great that the assembly began to murmur and complain to their leaders concerning the matter; and they did complain to Alma. And Alma laid the case before their king, Moshiyah, and Moshiyah consulted with his kohanim.

24 And it came to pass that king Moshiyah sent a proclamation throughout the land round about that there should not any unbeliever persecute any of those who belonged to the assembly of Elohim. And there was a strict command throughout all the assemblies that there should be no persecutions among them, that

there should be an equality among all men, that they should let no pride nor arrogance disturb their shalom, that **every man should esteem his neighbor as himself**,[142] laboring with their own hands for their support. Yes, and all their kohanim and teachers should labor with their own hands for their support in all cases, except it were in sickness or in much want; and doing these things they did abound in the grace of Elohim. And there began to be much shalom again in the land. And the people began to be very numerous, and began to scatter abroad upon the face of the earth — yes, on the north and on the south, on the east and on the west, building large cities and villages in all quarters of the land. And YHWH did visit them and prosper them, and they became a large and a wealthy people.

25 Now the sons of Moshiyah were numbered among the unbelievers; and also one of the sons of Alma was numbered among them, he being called Alma after his father. Nevertheless, he became a very wicked and an idolatrous man; and he was a man of many words and did speak much flattery to the people. Therefore he led many of the people to do after the manner of his iniquities. And he became a great hinderance to the prosperity of the assembly of Elohim: stealing away the hearts of the people, causing much dissension among the people, giving a chance for the enemy of Elohim to exercise his power over them.

26 And now it came to pass that while he was going about to destroy the assembly of Elohim — for he did go about secretly with the sons of Moshiyah, seeking to destroy the assembly and to lead astray the people of YHWH contrary to the mitzvot of Elohim, or even the king — and as I said unto you, as they were going about rebelling against Elohim, behold, the angel of YHWH appeared unto them, and he descended as it were in a cloud. And he spoke as it were with a voice of thunder, which caused the earth to shake upon which they stood. And so great was their astonishment that they fell to the earth and understood not the words which he spoke unto them. Nevertheless, he cried again, saying, Alma, arise and stand forth! For why do you persecute the assembly of Elohim? For YHWH has said, This is my assembly, and I will strengthen it; and nothing shall overthrow it,

---

142 Lev. 19:18. As the Talmud records, Hillel said, "What is hateful to you, do not to your neighbour" (b.Shabbat 21a).

except it is the transgression of my people. And again the angel said, Behold, YHWH has heard the prayers of his people, and also the prayers of his servant Alma, who is your father. For he has prayed with much faith concerning you, that you might be brought to the knowledge of the truth. Therefore, for this purpose have I come, to convince you of the power and authority of Elohim, that the prayers of his servants might be answered according to their faith. And now behold, can you dispute the power of Elohim? For behold, does not my voice shake the earth? And can you not also behold me before you? And I am sent from Elohim. Now I say unto you, go, and remember the captivity of your fathers in the land of Helam, and in the land of Nefi, and remember how great things he has done for them. For they were in bondage, and he has delivered them. And now I say unto you, Alma, go your way, and seek to destroy the assembly no more, that their prayers may be answered. And this, even if you will of yourself be cast off. And now it came to pass that these were the last words which the angel spoke unto Alma, and he departed.

27 And now Alma and those that were with him fell again to the earth, for great was their astonishment; for with their own eyes they had beheld an angel of YHWH, and his voice was as thunder which shook the earth. And they knew that there was nothing except the power of Elohim that could shake the earth and cause it to tremble as though it would part asunder. And now the astonishment of Alma was so great that he became dumb, that he could not open his mouth; yes, and he became weak, even that he could not move his hands. Therefore, he was taken by those that were with him, and carried helpless, even until he was laid before his father. And they rehearsed unto his father all that had happened unto them. And his father rejoiced, for he knew that it was the power of Elohim. And he caused that a multitude should be gathered together, that they might witness what YHWH had done for his son, and also for those that were with him. And he caused that the kohanim should assemble themselves together. And they began to fast and to pray to YHWH their Elohim that he would open the mouth of Alma, that he might speak, and also that his limbs might receive their strength, that the eyes of the people might be opened to see and know of the goodness and glory of Elohim.

28 And it came to pass, after they had fasted and prayed for the space of two days and two nights, the limbs of Alma received their strength. And he stood up and began to speak unto them, bidding them to be of good comfort. For, said he, I have repented of my sins and have been redeemed of YHWH. Behold, I am born of the spirit. And YHWH said unto me, Marvel not that all mankind, yes, men and women — all nations, kindreds, tongues, and people — must be born again, yes, born of Elohim,[143] changed from their carnal and fallen state to a state of righteousness, being redeemed of Elohim, becoming his sons and daughters.[144] And thus they become new creatures; and unless they do this, they can in no way inherit the kingdom of Elohim. I say unto you, unless this be the case, they must be cast off. And this I know because I was about to be cast off. Nevertheless, after wading through much tribulation, repenting nearly unto death, YHWH in mercy has seen fit to snatch me out of an everlasting burning; and I am born of Elohim. My soul has been redeemed from the gall of bitterness and bonds of iniquity. I was in the darkest abyss, but now I behold the marvelous light of Elohim. My soul was racked with Eternal torment, but I am snatched away, and my soul is pained no more. I rejected my Redeemer and denied that which had been spoken of by our fathers. But now, that they may foresee that he will come and that he remembers every creature of his creating, he will make himself manifest unto all. Yes, every knee shall bow and every tongue confess before him. Yes, even at the last day, when all men shall stand to be judged of him, then shall they confess that he is Elohim; then shall they confess, who live without Elohim in the world, that the judgment of an everlasting punishment is just upon them. And they shall quake, and tremble, and shrink beneath the glance of his all-searching eye.

29 And now it came to pass that Alma began from this time forward to teach the people, and those who were with Alma at the time the angel appeared unto them: traveling round about through all the land, publishing to all the people the things which they had heard and seen, and preaching the word of Elohim in much tribulation, being greatly persecuted by those who were unbelievers, being smitten by many of them. But despite all this, they did impart much consolation

---

143 Alma 3:3; 17:2, 5; 3 Nefi 5:9   144 Ps. 2:7; Moshiyah 3:2; 'Eter 1:13

to the assembly, confirming their faith, and exhorting them with long-suffering and much travail to keep the mitzvot of Elohim. And four of them were the sons of Moshiyah. And their names were Ammon, and Aharon, and Omner, and Himni — these were the names of the sons of Moshiyah. And they traveled throughout all the land of Zerach'mla, and among all the people who were under the reign of king Moshiyah, zealously striving to repair all the injuries which they had done to the assembly, confessing all their sins, and publishing all the things which they had seen, and explaining the prophecies and the scriptures to all who desired to hear them. And thus they were instruments in the hands of Elohim in bringing many to the knowledge of the truth, yes, to the knowledge of their Redeemer. **And how blessed are they, for they did publish shalom; they did publish good tidings of good, and they did declare unto the people that YHWH reigns.**[145]

12 Now it came to pass that after the sons of Moshiyah had done all these things, they took a small number with them and returned to their father the king, and desired of him that he would grant unto them that they might, with those whom they had selected, go up to the land of Nefi, that they might preach the things which they had heard, and that they might make known the word of Elohim to their brothers the Lamanites, that perhaps they might bring them to the knowledge of YHWH their Elohim and convince them of the iniquity of their fathers, and that perhaps they might cure them of their hatred towards the Nefites, that they might also be brought to rejoice in YHWH their Elohim, that they might become friendly to one another, and that there should be no more contentions in all the land which YHWH their Elohim had given them. Now they were desirous that salvation should be declared to every creature, for they could not bear that any human soul should perish; yes, even the very thought that any soul should endure Endless torment did cause them to quake and tremble. And thus did the spirit of YHWH work upon them. For they were the very vilest of sinners, and YHWH saw fit in his infinite mercy to spare them. Nevertheless, they suffered much anguish of soul because

---

[145] Isa. 52:7

of their iniquities; and suffered much fear that they should be cast off for ever.

2 And it came to pass that they did plead with their father many days that they might go up to the land of Nefi. King Moshiyah went and inquired of YHWH if he should let his sons go up among the Lamanites to preach the word. And YHWH said unto Moshiyah, Let them go up, for many shall believe on their words and they shall have Eternal life. And I will deliver your sons out of the hands of the Lamanites.

3 And it came to pass that Moshiyah granted that they might go and do according to their request. And they took their journey into the wilderness to go up to preach the word among the Lamanites. And I shall give an account of their proceedings hereafter. Now king Moshiyah had no one to confer the kingdom upon, for there were not any of his sons who would accept the kingdom. Therefore, he took the records which were engraved upon the plates of brass, and also the plates of Nefi, and all the things which he had kept and preserved according to the mitzvot of Elohim, after having translated and caused to be written the records which were on the plates of gold which had been found by the people of Limhi, which were delivered to him by the hand of Limhi; and this he did because of the great anxiety of his people, for they were desirous beyond measure to know concerning those people who had been destroyed. And now he translated them by the means of those two stones which were fastened into the two rims of a bow. Now these things were prepared from the beginning, and were handed down from generation to generation, for the purpose of interpreting languages. And they have been kept and preserved by the hand of YHWH, that he should uncover to every creature who should possess the land the iniquities and abominations of his people. And whosoever has these things is called seer,[146] after the manner of old times.

4 Now after Moshiyah had finished translating these records, behold, it gave an account of the people[147] who were destroyed — from the time that they were destroyed, back to the building of the great tower, at the time YHWH confounded the language of the people and they were scattered abroad upon the face of all the earth, yes, and

---

146 Moshiyah 5:13   **147** 'Eter 1:1

even from that time until the creation of Adam. Now this account did cause the people of Moshiyah to mourn exceedingly; yes, they were filled with sorrow. Nevertheless, it gave them much knowledge, in the which they did rejoice. And this account shall be written hereafter; for behold, it is expedient that all people should know the things which are written in this account.

13 And now as I said unto you that after king Moshiyah had done these things, he took the plates of brass and all the things which he had kept, and conferred them upon Alma, who was the son of Alma — yes, all the records, and also the interpreters — and conferred them upon him, and commanded him that he should keep and preserve them, and also keep a record of the people, handing them down from one generation to another, even as they had been handed down from the time that Lechi left Yerushalayim.

2 Now when Moshiyah had done this, he sent out through all the land, among all the people, desiring to know their will concerning who should be their king. And it came to pass that the **voice of the people**[148] came, saying, We are desirous that Aharon your son should be our king and our ruler. Now Aharon had gone up to the land of Nefi; therefore, the king could not confer the kingdom upon him. Neither would Aharon take upon him the kingdom, neither was any of the sons of Moshiyah willing to take upon them the kingdom. Therefore, king Moshiyah sent again among the people — yes, even a written word sent he among the people. And these were the words that were written, saying, Behold, O you my people — or my brothers, for I esteem you as such — I desire that you should consider the cause which you are called to consider; for you are desirous to have a king. Now I declare unto you that he to whom the kingdom does rightly belong has declined and will not take upon himself the kingdom. And now, if there should be another appointed in his place, behold, I fear there would arise contentions among you. And who knows but that my son, to whom the kingdom does belong, should turn and become angry and draw away a part of this people after him, which will cause wars and contentions among you, which would be the cause of shedding much blood and perverting the way of YHWH — yes, and

---

148 1 Sam. 8:7; Alma 1:8-9

destroy the souls of many people. Now I say unto you, let us be wise and consider these things. For we have no right to destroy my son, neither should we have any right to destroy another if he should be appointed in his place. And if my son should turn again to his pride and vain things, he would recall the things which he had said and claim his right to the kingdom, which would cause him and also this people to commit much sin. And now let us be wise, and look forward to these things, and do that which will make for the peace of this people. Therefore, I will be your king the remainder of my days.

3 Nevertheless, let us appoint judges to judge this people according to our law, and we will newly arrange the affairs of this people. For we will appoint wise men to be judges that will judge this people according to the mitzvot of Elohim. Now it is better that a man should be judged of Elohim than of man; for the judgments of Elohim are always just, but the judgments of man are not always just. Therefore, if it were possible that you could have just men to be your kings, who would establish the laws of Elohim and judge this people according to his mitzvot, yes, if you could have men for your kings who would do even as my father Binyamin did for this people, I say unto you, if this could always be the case, then it would be expedient that you should always have kings to rule over you. And even I myself have labored with all the power and faculties which I have possessed to teach you the mitzvot of Elohim and to establish shalom throughout the land, that there should be no wars nor contentions, no stealing, nor plundering, nor murdering, nor any manner of iniquity. And whosoever has committed iniquity, him have I punished according to the crime which he has committed, according to the law which has been given to us by our fathers.

4 Now I say unto you that because all men are not just, it is not expedient that you should have a king or kings to rule over you. For behold, how much iniquity does one wicked king cause to be committed; yes, and what great destruction. Yes, remember king Noah, his wickedness and his abominations, and also the wickedness and abominations of his people. Behold, what great destruction did come upon them. And also because of their iniquities they were brought into bondage. And were it not for the intervention of their all-wise Creator — and this because of their sincere repentance — they must have unavoidably remained in bondage until now. But behold,

he did deliver them because they did humble themselves before him; and because they cried mightily unto him, he did deliver them out of bondage. And thus does YHWH work with his power in all cases among the children of men, extending the arm of mercy **towards them that put their trust in him.**[149]

5 And behold, now I say unto you, you cannot dethrone an iniquitous king except it be through much contention and the shedding of much blood. For behold, he has his friends in iniquity, and he keeps his guards about him, and he tears up the laws of those who have reigned in righteousness before him, and he tramples under his feet the mitzvot of Elohim. And he enacts laws and sends them forth among his people, yes, laws after the manner of his own wickedness; and whosoever does not obey his laws, he causes to be destroyed. And whosoever does rebel against him, he will send his armies against them to war; and if he can, he will destroy them. And thus an unrighteous king does pervert the ways of all righteousness. And now behold, I say unto you, it is not expedient that such abominations should come upon you.

6 Therefore, choose you by the **voice of this people,**[150] judges,[151] that you may be judged according to the laws which have been given you by our fathers, which are correct and which were given them by the hand of YHWH. Now it is not common that the voice of the people desires anything contrary to that which is right, but it is common for the lesser part of the people to desire that which is not right. Therefore, this shall you observe and make it your law: to do your business by the voice of the people.

7 And if the time comes that the **voice of the people** does choose iniquity, then is the time that the judgments of Elohim will come upon you. Yes, then is the time he will visit you with great destruction, even as he has previously visited this land. And now, if you have judges, and they do not judge you according to the law which has been given, you can cause that he may be judged of a higher judge. If your higher judges do not judge righteous judgments, you shall cause that a small number of your lower judges should be gathered together, and they shall judge your higher judges according to the

---

149 Prov. 30:5; 2 Nefi 3:8   **150** Cheleman 1:1   **151** The Torah directs us: "Judges and officers shall you make you in all your gates" (Deut. 16:18).

voice of the people. And I command you to do these things in the fear of YHWH. And I commanded you to do these things, and that you have no king, that if these people commit sins and iniquities, they shall be answered upon their own heads. For behold, I say unto you, the sins of many people have been caused by the iniquities of their kings; therefore, their iniquities are answered upon the heads of their kings.

8 And now I desire that this inequality should be no more in this land, especially among this my people. But I desire that this land be a land of liberty, and every man may enjoy his rights and privileges alike, so long as YHWH sees fit that we may live and inherit the land, yes, even as long as any of our posterity remains upon the face of the land. And many more things did king Moshiyah write unto them, unfolding unto them all the trials and troubles of a righteous king, yes, all the travails of soul for their people, and also all the murmurings of the people to their king; and he explained it all unto them. And he told them that these things ought not to be, but that the burden should come upon all the people, that every man might bear his part. And he also unfolded unto them all the disadvantages they labored under by having an unrighteous king to rule over them, yes, all his iniquities and abominations, and all the wars, and contentions, and bloodshed, and the stealing, and the plundering, and the committing of whoredoms, and all manner of iniquities which cannot be enumerated, telling them that these things ought not to be, that they were expressly repugnant to the mitzvot of Elohim.

9 And now it came to pass, after king Moshiyah had sent these things forth among the people, they were convinced of the truth of his words. Therefore, they relinquished their desires for a king and became exceedingly anxious that every man should have an equal chance throughout all the land; yes, and every man expressed a willingness to answer for his own sins. Therefore, it came to pass that they assembled themselves together in bodies throughout the land, to cast in their voices concerning who should be their judges to judge them according to the law which had been given them. And they rejoiced exceedingly because of the liberty which had been granted unto them. And they did grow strong in love towards Moshiyah; yes, they did esteem him more than any other man. For they did not

look upon him as a tyrant who was seeking for gain—yes, for that lucre which does corrupt the soul—for he had not exacted riches of them, neither had he delighted in the shedding of blood, but he had established shalom in the land. And he had granted unto his people that they should be delivered from all manner of bondage. Therefore they did esteem him, yes, exceedingly beyond measure. And it came to pass that they did appoint judges to rule over them, or to judge them according to the law; and this they did throughout all the land.

10 And it came to pass that Alma was appointed to be the chief judge, he being also the Kohen HaGadol, his father having conferred the office upon him and had given him the charge concerning all the affairs of the assembly. And now it came to pass that Alma did walk in the ways of YHWH, and he did keep his mitzvot, and he did judge righteous judgments.[152] And there was continual shalom through the land. And thus commenced the reign of the judges throughout all the land of Zerach'mla, among all the people who were called the Nefites; and Alma was the first and chief judge.

11 And now it came to pass that his father died, being eighty and two years old, having lived to fulfill the mitzvot of Elohim. And it came to pass that Moshiyah died also, in the thirty and third year of his reign, being sixty and three years, making in the whole five hundred and nine years from the time Lechi left Yerushalayim. And thus ended the reign of the kings over the people of Nefi. And thus ended the days of Alma, who was the founder of their assembly.

ספר עלמא בן עלמא
ALMA
THE BOOK OF ALMA
THE SON OF ALMA

The account of Alma, who was the son of Alma, the first and chief judge over the people of Nefi, and also the Kohen HaGadol over the assembly. An account of the reign of the judges, and the wars and contentions among the people. And also an account of a war between the Nefites and the Lamanites according to the record of Alma, the first and chief judge.

---

[152] Another example of the Cognate Accusative Hebraic construction. See footnote 61 in Moshiyah.

Now it came to pass that in the first year[1] of the reign of the judges over the people of Nefi, from this time forward, king Moshiyah having gone the way of all the earth, having warred a good warfare, walking uprightly before Elohim, leaving none to reign in his place – nevertheless, he established laws and they were acknowledged by the people; therefore, they were obliged to abide by the laws which he had made – and it came to pass that in the first year of the reign of Alma in the judgment seat, there was a man brought before him to be judged, a man who was large and was noted for his great strength. And he had gone about among the people, preaching to them that which he termed to be the word of Elohim, bearing down against the assembly, declaring unto the people that every kohen and teacher ought to become popular and they ought not to labor with their own hands, but that they ought to be supported by the people.[2] And he also testified unto the people that all mankind should be saved at the last day, and that they need not fear nor tremble, but that they might lift up their heads and rejoice, for YHWH had created all men and had also redeemed all men; and in the end, all men should have Eternal life. And it came to pass that he did teach these things so much that many did believe on his words, even so many that they began to support him and give him money. And he began to be lifted up in the pride of his heart and to wear very costly apparel, yes, and even began to establish an assembly after the manner of his preaching.

2 And it came to pass, as he was going to preach to those who believed on his word, he met a man who belonged to the assembly of Elohim, yes, even one of their teachers. And he began to contend with him sharply, that he might lead away the people of the assembly; but the man withstood him, admonishing him with the words of Elohim. Now the name of the man was Gideon, and it was he that was an instrument in the hands of Elohim in delivering the people of Limhi out of bondage. Now, because Gideon withstood him with the words of Elohim, he was angry with Gideon, and drew his sword and began to strike him. Now Gideon being stricken with many years, therefore he was not able to withstand his blows; therefore, he was slain by the sword. And the man who slew him was taken by the

---

1 ~93 BCE 2 Moshiyah 9:10

people of the assembly and was brought before Alma to be judged according to the crime which he had committed. And it came to pass that he stood before Alma and pled for himself with much boldness. But Alma said unto him, Behold, this is the first time that priestcraft has been introduced among this people. And behold, you are not only guilty of priestcraft, but have endeavored to enforce it by the sword. And were priestcraft to be enforced among this people, it would prove their entire destruction. And you have shed the blood of a righteous man, yes, a man who has done much good among this people. And were we to spare you, his blood would come upon us for vengeance. Therefore, you are condemned to die according to the law which has been given us by Moshiyah, our last king. And they have been acknowledged by this people, therefore this people must abide by the law.

3 And it came to pass that they took him (and his name was Nehor) and they carried him up on the top of the hill Manti, and there he was caused or rather did acknowledge between the heavens and the earth that what he had taught to the people was contrary to the word of Elohim. And there he suffered an ignominious death.

4 Nevertheless, this did not put an end to the spreading of priestcraft through the land, for there were many who loved the vain things of the world. And they went forth preaching false doctrines, and this they did for the sake of riches and honor. Nevertheless, they dared not lie, if it were known, for fear of the law, for liars were punished. Therefore, they pretended to preach according to their belief. And now the law could have no power on any man for his belief. And they dared not steal for fear of the law, for such were punished. Neither dared they rob nor murder, for he that murdered was punished unto death.

5 But it came to pass that whosoever did not belong to the assembly of Elohim began to persecute those that did belong to the assembly of Elohim and had taken upon them the name of Mashiach. Yes, they did persecute them and afflict them with all manner of words, and this because of their humility, because they were not proud in their own eyes, and because they did teach the word of Elohim one to another without money and without price. Now there was a strict law among the people of the assembly that there should not any man belonging to the assembly arise and persecute those that did not belong to the

assembly, and that there should be no persecution among themselves. Nevertheless, there were many among them who began to be proud and began to contend warmly with their adversaries, even unto blows; yes, they would strike one another with their fists. Now this was in the second year of the reign of Alma, and it was a cause of much affliction to the assembly; yes, it was the cause of much trial with the assembly. For the hearts of many were hardened, and **their names were blotted out,** that **they were remembered no more**[3] among the people of Elohim; and also many withdrew themselves from among them. Now this was a great trial to those that did stand fast in the faith; nevertheless, they were steadfast and immovable in keeping the mitzvot of Elohim, and they bore with patience the persecution which was heaped upon them. And when their kohanim left their labor to teach the word of Elohim unto the people, the people also left their labors to hear the word of Elohim. And when the kohen had taught unto them the word of Elohim, they all returned again diligently unto their labors, and the kohen, not esteeming himself above his hearers; for the preacher was no better than the hearer, neither was the teacher any better than the learner. And thus they were all equal; and they did all labor, every man according to his strength. And they did impart of their substance, every man according to that which he had, to the poor, and the needy, and the sick, and the afflicted. And they did not wear costly apparel, yet they were neat and becoming. And thus they did strengthen the affairs of the assembly; and thus they began to have continual shalom again, despite all their persecutions.

6 And now, because of the steadiness of the assembly, they began to be exceedingly rich, **having abundance of all things**[4] whatsoever they stood in need: abundance of flocks, and herds, and fatlings of every kind, and also abundance of grain, and of gold, and of silver, and of precious things, and abundance of silk, and fine-twined linen, and all manner of good plain cloth. And thus, in their prosperous circumstances, they did not send away any who were naked, or that were hungry, or that were thirsty, or that were sick, or that had not been nourished. And they did not set their hearts upon riches. Therefore, they were liberal to all, both old and young, both bond

---

3 Ps. 109:13   4 Deut. 28:47

and free, both male and female, whether out of the assembly or in the assembly, having no respect to persons as to those who stood in need. And thus they did prosper and become far more wealthy than those who did not belong to their assembly. For those who did not belong to their assembly did indulge themselves in sorceries, and in idolatry or idleness, and in lashon hara,[5] and in envyings, and strife, and wearing costly apparel, being lifted up in the pride of their own eyes, persecuting, lying, thieving, robbing, committing whoredoms, and murdering, and all manner of wickedness. Nevertheless, the law was put in force upon all those who did transgress it, inasmuch as it were possible.

7 And it came to pass that by thus exercising the law upon them, every man suffering according to that which he had done, they became more restrained, and dared not commit any wickedness, if it were known. Therefore, there was much shalom among the people of Nefi until the fifth year of the reign of the judges.

8 And it came to pass in the commencement of the fifth year[6] of their reign, there began to be a contention among the people. For a certain man, being called Amlici,[7] he being a very cunning man, yes, a wise man as to the wisdom of the world, he being after the order of the man that slew Gideon by the sword, who was executed according to the law — now this Amlici had, by his cunning, drawn away many people after him, even so much that they began to be very powerful; and they began to endeavor to establish Amlici to be a king over the people. Now this was alarming to the people of the assembly, and also to all those who had not been drawn away after the persuasions of Amlici, for they knew that according to their law that such things must be confirmed by the **voice of the people**.[8] Therefore, if it were possible that Amlici should gain the **voice of the people**,[9] he, being a wicked man, would deprive them of their rights and privileges of the assembly, and so forth, for it was his intent to destroy the assembly of Elohim.

9 And it came to pass that the people assembled themselves together throughout all the land, every man according to his mind, whether it was for or against Amlici, in separate bodies, having many

---

5 Talebearing, babbling, derogatory or damaging speech about a person. 6 ~ 88 BCE
7 It is likely no coincidence that his name seems built upon the Hebrew root *mlk* (מלך), meaning "to rule" or, in the noun form, "king." 8 Moshiyah 13:6-7 9 1 Sam. 8:7

disputations and awful contentions one with another. And thus they did assemble themselves together to cast in their voices concerning the matter; and it was laid before the judges. And it came to pass that the **voice of the people** came against Amlici, that he was not made king over the people. Now this did cause much joy in the hearts of those who were against him, but Amlici did stir up those who were in his favor to anger against those who were not in his favor.

10 And it came to pass that they gathered themselves together and did consecrate Amlici to be their king. Now when Amlici was made king over them, he commanded them that they should take up arms against their brothers; and this he did that he might subject them to him. Now the people of Amlici were distinguished by the name of Amlici, being called Amlicites, and the remainder were called Nefites, or the people of Elohim. Therefore, the people of the Nefites were aware of the intent of the Amlicites. And therefore, they did prepare to meet them; yes, they did arm themselves with swords, and with cimeters, and with bows, and with arrows, and with stones, and with slings, and with all manner of weapons of war of every kind. And thus they were prepared to meet the Amlicites at the time of their coming. And there were appointed captains, and higher captains, and chief captains, according to their numbers.

11 And it came to pass that Amlici did arm his men with all manner of weapons of war of every kind; and he also appointed rulers and leaders over his people to lead them to war against their brothers. And it came to pass that the Amlicites came up upon the hill of Amnihu, which was east of the river Tzidon, which ran by the land of Zerach'mla and there they began to make war with the Nefites. Now Alma, being the chief judge and the governor of the people of Nefi, therefore he went up with his people, yes, with his captains and chief captains, yes, at the head of his armies against the Amlicites to battle. And they began to slay the Amlicites upon the hill east of Tzidon and the Amlicites did contend with the Nefites with great strength, insomuch that many of the Nefites did fall before the Amlicites. Nevertheless, YHWH did strengthen the hand of the Nefites, that they slew the Amlicites with a great slaughter, that they began to flee before them. And it came to pass that the Nefites did pursue the Amlicites all that day and did slay them with much slaughter, insomuch that there was slain of the Amlicites twelve thousand five

hundred thirty and two souls; and there was slain of the Nefites six thousand five hundred sixty and two souls.

¹² And it came to pass that when Alma could pursue the Amlicites no longer, he caused that his people should pitch their tents in the valley of Gideon, the valley being called after that Gideon who was slain by the hand of Nehor with the sword. And in this valley, the Nefites did pitch their tents for the night. And Alma sent spies to follow the remnant of the Amlicites, that he might know of their plans and their plots, by which he might guard himself against them, that he might preserve his people from being destroyed. Now those whom he had sent out to watch the camp of the Amlicites were called Zeram, and Amnor, and Manti, and Limher; these were they who went out with their men to watch the camp of the Amlicites.

¹³ And it came to pass that the next day they returned into the camp of the Nefites in great haste, being greatly astonished and struck with much fear, saying, Behold, we followed the camp of the Amlicites. And to our great astonishment, in the land of Minon, above the land of Zerach'mla, in the course of the land of Nefi, we saw a numerous host of the Lamanites; and behold, the Amlicites have joined them. And they are upon our brothers in that land, and they are fleeing before them with their flocks, and their wives, and their children, towards our city. And except we make haste, they will obtain possession of our city; and our fathers, and our wives, and our children will be slain.

¹⁴ And it came to pass that the people of Nefi took their tents and departed out of the valley of Gideon towards their city, which was the city of Zerach'mla. And behold, as they were crossing the river Tzidon, the Lamanites and the Amlicites — being as numerous almost, as it were, as the sands of the sea — came upon them to destroy them. Nevertheless, the Nefites being strengthened by the hand of YHWH, having prayed mightily to him that he would deliver them out of the hands of their enemies, therefore YHWH did hear their cries and did strengthen them; and the Lamanites and the Amlicites did fall before them. And it came to pass that Alma fought with Amlici with the sword face to face, and they did contend mightily one with another.

¹⁵ And it came to pass that Alma, being a man of Elohim, being exercised with much faith, cried, saying, O YHWH, have mercy and spare my life, that I may be an instrument in your hands to save

and protect this people! Now when Alma had said these words, he contended again with Amlici; and he was strengthened insomuch that he slew Amlici with the sword. And he also contended with the king of the Lamanites, but the king of the Lamanites fled back from before Alma, and sent his guards to contend with Alma. But Alma, with his guards, contended with the guards of the king of the Lamanites until he slew and drove them back. And thus he cleared the ground, or rather the bank which was on the west of the river Tzidon, throwing the bodies of the Lamanites whom he had slain into the waters of Tzidon, that thereby his people might have room to cross and contend with the Lamanites and the Amlicites on the west side of the river Tzidon.

16 And it came to pass that when they had all crossed the river Tzidon, that the Lamanites and the Amlicites began to flee before them, even though they were so numerous that they could not be numbered. And they fled before the Nefites towards the wilderness which was west and north, away beyond the borders of the land. And the Nefites did pursue them with their might and did slay them; yes, they were met on every side, and slain, and driven, until they were scattered on the west and on the north, until they had reached the wilderness which was called Hermounts; and it was that part of the wilderness which was infested by wild and ravenous beasts. And it came to pass that many died in the wilderness of their wounds and were devoured by those beasts, and also the vultures of the air. And their bones have been found and have been heaped up on the earth.

17 And it came to pass that the Nefites who were not slain by the weapons of war, after having buried those who had been slain — now the number of the slain were not numbered because of the greatness of their number — after they had finished burying their dead, they all returned to their lands and to their houses, and their wives, and their children. Now many women and children had been slain with the sword, and also many of their flocks and their herds; and also many of their fields of grain were destroyed, for they were trampled down by the hosts of men. And now as many of the Lamanites and the Amlicites who had been slain upon the bank of the river Tzidon were cast into the waters of Tzidon. And behold, their bones are in the depths of the sea, and they are many.

18 And the Amlicites were distinguished from the Nefites, for they had marked themselves with red in their foreheads after the manner of the Lamanites; nevertheless, they had not shorn their heads like unto the Lamanites. Now the heads of the Lamanites were shorn; and they were naked except it were skin which was girded about their loins, and also their armor which was girded about them, and their bows, and their arrows, and their stones, and their slings, and so forth. And the skins of the Lamanites were dark, according to the mark which was set upon their fathers,[10] which was a curse upon them because of their transgression and their rebellion against their brothers,[11] who consisted of Nefi, Ya'akov, and Yosef, and Sam, who were just and holy men; and their brothers sought to destroy them, therefore they were cursed, and Adonai YHWH set a mark upon them — yes, upon Laman and L'mu'el, and also the sons of Yishma'el, and the Yishma'elite women. And this was done that their seed might be distinguished from the seed of their brothers, that thereby Adonai YHWH might preserve his people, that they might not mix and believe in incorrect traditions which would prove their destruction.

19 And it came to pass that whosoever did mingle his seed with that of the Lamanites did bring the same curse upon his seed. Therefore, whosoever allowed himself to be led away by the Lamanites were called under that head, and there was a mark set upon him. And it came to pass that whosoever would not believe in the tradition of the Lamanites, but believed those records which were brought out of the land of Yerushalayim, and also in the tradition of their fathers which was correct,[12] who believed in the mitzvot of Elohim and kept them, were called the Nefites or the people of Nefi from that time forth. And it is they who have kept the records, which are true, of their people, and also of the people of the Lamanites.

20 Now we will return again to the Amlicites, for they also had a mark set upon them; yes, they set the mark upon themselves, yes, even a mark of red upon their foreheads. Thus the word of Elohim is fulfilled, for these are the words which he said to Nefi: Behold, the Lamanites have I cursed, and I will set a mark upon them, that they and their seed may be separated from you and your seed from this time henceforth and for ever, except they repent of their wickedness

---

10 2 Nefi 4:4   11 1 Nefi 2:3; 2 Nefi 4:1   12 1 Nefi 1:10, 22-23

and turn to me, that I may have mercy upon them. And again, I will set a mark upon him that mingles his seed with your brothers, that they may be cursed also. And again, I will set a mark upon him that fights against you and your seed. And again, I say, he that departs from you shall no more be called your seed. And I will bless you, and so forth, and whosoever shall be called your seed, henceforth and for ever. And these were the promises of YHWH unto Nefi and to his seed. Now the Amlicites knew not that they were fulfilling the words of Elohim when they began to mark themselves in their foreheads. Nevertheless, as they had come out in open rebellion against Elohim, therefore it was expedient that the curse should fall upon them. Now I would that you should see that they brought upon themselves the curse; and even so does every man that is cursed bring upon himself his own condemnation.

21 Now it came to pass that not many days after the battle which was fought in the land of Zerach'mla by the Lamanites and the Amlicites, that there was another army of the Lamanites that came in upon the people of Nefi, in the same place where the first army met the Amlicites. And it came to pass that there was an army sent to drive them out of their land. Now Alma himself, being afflicted with a wound, did not go up to battle at this time against the Lamanites, but he sent up a numerous army against them. And they went up and slew many of the Lamanites, and drove the remainder of them out of the borders of their land. And then they returned again and began to establish shalom in the land, being troubled no more for a time with their enemies. Now all these things were done, yes, all these wars and contentions were commenced and ended in the fifth year of the reign of the judges. And in one year were thousands and tens of thousands of souls sent to the eternal world, that they might reap their rewards according to their works, whether they were good or whether they were bad — to reap eternal happiness or eternal misery, according to the spirit which they hearkened to obey, whether it be a good spirit or a bad one. For every man receives wages of him whom he hearkens to obey, and this according to the words of the spirit of prophecy; therefore, let it be according to the truth. And thus ended the fifth year of the reign of the judges.

2 Now it came to pass in the sixth year[13] of the reign of the judges over the people of Nefi, there were no contentions nor wars in the land of Zerach'mla. But the people were afflicted, yes, greatly afflicted, for the loss of their brothers, and also for the loss of their flocks and herds, and also for the loss of their fields of grain, which were trampled underfoot and destroyed by the Lamanites. And so great were their afflictions that every soul had cause to mourn. And they believed that it was the judgments of Elohim sent upon them because of their wickedness and their abominations; therefore they were awakened to a remembrance of their duty, and they began to strengthen the assembly more fully. Yes, and many were immersed in the waters of Tzidon and were joined to the assembly of Elohim; yes, they were immersed by the hand of Alma, who had been consecrated the Kohen HaGadol over the people of the assembly by the hand of his father, Alma.

2 And it came to pass in the seventh year of the reign of the judges, there were about three thousand five hundred souls that united themselves to the assembly of Elohim and were washed by immersion. And thus ended the seventh year of the reign of the judges over the people of Nefi; and there was continual shalom in all that time.

3 And it came to pass in the eighth year of the reign of the judges that the people of the assembly began to grow proud because of their exceeding riches, and their fine silks, and their fine-twined linen, and because of their many flocks and herds, and their gold, and their silver, and all manner of precious things, which they had obtained by their industry. And in all these things were they lifted up in the pride of their eyes, for they began to wear very costly apparel. Now this was the cause of much affliction to Alma, yes, and to many of the people whom Alma had consecrated to be teachers, and kohanim, and elders, over the assembly. Yes, many of them were sorely grieved for the wickedness which they saw had begun to be among their people. For they saw and beheld with great sorrow that the people of the assembly began to be lifted up in the pride of their eyes, and to set their hearts upon riches and upon the vain things of the world, that they began to be scornful one towards another. And they began to persecute those that did not believe according to their own will and pleasure. And

---

13 ~87 BCE

thus, in this eighth year of the reign of the judges, there began to be great contentions among the people of the assembly; yes, there were envyings, and strifes, and malice, and persecutions, and pride, even to exceed the pride of those who did not belong to the assembly of Elohim. And thus ended the eighth year of the reign of the judges. And the wickedness of the assembly was a great stumbling block to those who did not belong to the assembly; and thus the assembly began to fail in its progress.

4 And it came to pass in the commencement of the ninth year, Alma saw the wickedness of the assembly, and he also saw that the example of the assembly began to lead those who were unbelievers on from one piece of iniquity to another, thus bringing on the destruction of the people; yes, he saw great inequality among the people, some lifting themselves up with their pride, despising others, turning their backs upon the needy, and the naked, and those who were hungry, and those who were thirsty, and those who were sick and afflicted — now this was a great cause for lamentations among the people — while others were humbling themselves, relieving those who stood in need of their relief, such as imparting their substance to the poor and the needy, feeding the hungry, and suffering all manner of afflictions for Mashiach's sake,[14] who should come according to the spirit of prophecy, looking forward to that day, thus retaining a remission of their sins, being filled with great joy because of the resurrection of the dead, according to the will, and power, and deliverance of Yeshua HaMashiach from the bands of death.

5 And now it came to pass that Alma having seen the afflictions of the humble followers of Elohim, and the persecutions which were heaped upon them by the remainder of his people, and seeing all their inequality, began to be very sorrowful; nevertheless, the spirit of YHWH did not fail him. And he selected a wise man, who was among the elders of the assembly, and gave him power according to the **voice of the people**, that he might have power to enact laws, according to the laws which had been given, and to put them in force according to the wickedness and the crimes of the people. Now this man's name was Nefihah, and he was appointed chief judge; and he sat in the judgment seat to judge and to govern the people. Now Alma did not

---

14 Moshiyah 2:6

grant unto him the office of being Kohen HaGadol over the assembly, but he retained the office of Kohen HaGadol unto himself, but he delivered the judgment seat unto Nefihah. And this he did that he himself might go forth among his people, or among the people of Nefi, that he might preach the word of Elohim unto them, to stir them up in remembrance of their duty, and that he might pull down, by the word of Elohim, all the pride and craftiness, and all the contentions which were among his people, seeing no way that he might reclaim them except it were in bearing down in pure testimony against them. And thus, in the commencement of the ninth year of the reign of the judges over the people of Nefi, Alma delivered up the judgment seat to Nefihah, and confined himself wholly to the High Priesthood of the Holy Order of Elohim,[15] to the testimony of the word, according to the spirit of revelation and prophecy.[16]

The words which Alma, the Kohen HaGadol according to the Holy Order of Elohim, delivered to the people in their cities and villages throughout the land.

3 Now it came to pass that Alma began to declare the word of Elohim unto the people, first in the land of Zerach'mla, and from there throughout all the land. And these are the words which he spoke to the people in the assembly which were established in the city of Zerach'mla, according to his own record, saying, I, Alma, having been consecrated by my father Alma to be a Kohen HaGadol over the assembly of Elohim[17] – he having power and s'mikhah from Elohim[18] to do these things – behold, I say unto you that he began to establish an assembly[19] in the land which was in the borders of Nefi – yes, the land was called the land of M'raman – yes, and he did immerse his brothers in the waters of M'raman. And behold, I say unto you, they were delivered out of the hands of the people of king Noah by the mercy and power of Elohim. And behold, after that, they were brought into bondage by the hands of the Lamanites in the wilderness. Yes, I say unto you, they were in captivity, and again YHWH did deliver them out of bondage by the power of his word.[20] And we were brought into this land, and here we began to establish the assembly of Elohim throughout this land also.

---

15 Ordained by Adonai YHWH; see Alma 9:10. Malki-Tzedek (Melchizedek) is the prototypical example of such; see Alma 10:1-2. **16** Alma 3:8; 7:4 **17** Moshiyah 13:10; 2 Nefi 5:1 **18** 1 Nefi 3:5; Cheleman 2:19; 3 Nefi 3:9; 5:10 **19** Moshiyah 11:20-21 **20** M'raman 4:8

2 And now behold, I say unto you, my brothers, you that belong to this assembly, have you sufficiently retained in remembrance the captivity of your fathers? Yes, and have you sufficiently retained in remembrance his mercy and long-suffering towards them? And moreover, have you sufficiently retained in remembrance that he has **delivered** their **souls from She'ol**?[21] Behold, he changed their hearts; yes, he awakened them out of a deep sleep, and they awoke unto Elohim.[22] Behold, they were in the midst of darkness; nevertheless, their souls were illuminated by the light of the everlasting word. Yes, they were encircled about by the bands of death and the chains of She'ol, and an everlasting destruction did await them. And now I ask of you, my brothers, were they destroyed? Behold, I say unto you, no, they were not. And again I ask, were the bands of death broken? And the chains of She'ol which encircled them about, were they loosed? I say unto you, yes, they were loosed. And their souls did expand, and they did sing redeeming love. And I say unto you that they are saved. And now I ask of you, on what conditions are they saved? Yes, what grounds had they to hope for salvation? What is the cause of their being loosed from the bands of death, yes, and also the chains of She'ol? Behold, I can tell you. Did not my father Alma believe in the words which were delivered by the mouth of Avinodi? And was he not a holy prophet? Did he not speak the words of Elohim? And my father Alma believed them. And according to his faith, there was a mighty change worked in his heart. Behold, I say unto you that this is all true. And behold, he preached the word unto your fathers, and a mighty change was also worked in their hearts, and they humbled themselves and put their trust in the true and living Elohim. And behold, they were faithful until the end; therefore, they were saved.

3 And now behold, I ask of you, my brothers of the assembly, have you spiritually been born of Elohim? Have you received his image in your own countenances? Have you experienced this mighty change in your hearts? Do you exercise faith in the redemption of he who created you? Do you look forward with an eye of faith and view this mortal body raised in immortality, and this corruption raised in incorruption? To stand before Elohim to be judged according to the deeds which have been done in the mortal body? I say unto you, can

---

21 Ps. 86:13; Prov. 23:14   22 2 Nefi 1:3; 5:13; M'roni 10:6

you imagine to yourselves that you hear the voice of YHWH saying unto you in that day, Come unto me, you blessed, for behold, your works have been the works of righteousness upon the face of the earth — or do you imagine to yourselves that you can lie unto YHWH at that day and say, Adonai, our works have been righteous works upon the face of the earth — and that he will save you? Or otherwise, can you imagine yourselves brought before the tribunal of Elohim with your souls filled with guilt and remorse, having a remembrance of all your guilt, yes, a perfect remembrance of all your wickedness, yes, a remembrance that you have set at defiance the mitzvot of Elohim? I say unto you, can you look up to Elohim at that day with **a pure heart and clean hands?**[23] I say unto you, can you look up, having the image of Elohim engraved upon your countenances? I say unto you, can you think of being saved when you have yielded yourselves to become subjects to HaSatan? I say unto you, you will know at that day that you cannot be saved; for there can no man be saved except his garments are washed white. Yes, his garments must be purified until they are cleansed from all stain through the blood of he of whom it has been spoken by our fathers, who should come to redeem his people from their sins.

4 And now I ask of you, my brothers, how will any of you feel if you shall stand before the bar of Elohim, having your garments stained with blood and all manner of uncleanness? Behold, what will these things testify against you? Behold, will they not testify that you are murderers? Yes, and also that you are guilty of all manner of wickedness? Behold, my brothers, do you suppose that such a person can have a place to sit down in the kingdom of Elohim with Avraham, with Yitz'chak, and with Ya'akov, and also all the holy prophets whose garments are cleansed and are spotless, pure, and white?[24] I say unto you, no, except you make our Creator a liar from the beginning, or suppose that he is a liar from the beginning. You cannot suppose that such can have place in the kingdom of Heaven, but he shall be cast out, for they are the children of the kingdom of HaSatan.

5 And now behold, I say unto you, my brothers, if you have experienced a change of heart, and if you have felt to sing the song[25]

---

23 Ps. 24:3-4; Ya'akov 2:11   **24** 3 Nefi 12:5; 'Eter 6:3   **25** This is an example of the Hebraism known as the Cognate Accusative, where a noun pairs with the verb which is the noun's root.

of redeeming love, I would ask, can you feel so now? Have you walked keeping yourselves blameless before Elohim? Could you say — if you were called to die at this time — within yourselves that you have been sufficiently humble, that your garments have been cleansed and made white through the blood of Mashiach, who will come to redeem his people from their sins? Behold, are you stripped of pride? I say unto you, if you are not, you are not **prepared to meet Elohim**.[26] Behold, you must prepare quickly; for the kingdom of Heaven is soon at hand, and such a person does not have Eternal life. Behold, I say, is there one among you who is not stripped of envy? I say unto you that such a person is not prepared. And I would that he should prepare quickly, for the hour is close at hand; and he does not know when the time shall come, for such a person is not found guiltless.

6 And again I say unto you, is there one among you that mocks his brother or that heaps upon him persecutions? Woe unto such a person, for he is not prepared; and the time is at hand that he must repent, or he cannot be saved. Yes, even woe unto **all you workers of iniquity**.[27] Repent, repent, for Adonai YHWH has spoken it. Behold, he sends an invitation unto all men; for the arms of mercy are extended towards them, and he says, Repent and I will receive you. Yes, he says, Come unto me and you shall partake of the fruit of the tree of life;[28] yes, you shall eat and drink of the bread and the waters of life freely. Yes, come unto me and bring forth works of righteousness, and you shall not be cut down and cast into the fire.[29] For behold, the time is at hand that whosoever does not bring forth good fruit, or whosoever does not the works of righteousness, the same shall have cause to wail and mourn.

7 O you workers of iniquity, you that are puffed up in the vain things of the world, you that have professed to have known the ways of righteousness — nevertheless, you have gone astray as sheep having no shepherd, even though a shepherd has called after you, and is still calling after you, but you will not hearken unto his voice. Behold, I say unto you that the Good Shepherd does call you; yes, and in his own name[30] he does call you, which is the name of Mashiach. And if you will not hearken unto the voice of the good shepherd, to the name

---

[26] Amos 4:12 [27] Ps. 6:9 (8) [28] 1 Nefi 3:7-10; Alma 3:12 [29] 3 Nefi 6:10 [30] Moshiyah 3:2; 3 Nefi 12:4

by which you are called, behold, you are not the sheep of the good shepherd. And now if you are not the sheep of the good shepherd, of what fold are you? Behold, I say unto you that HaSatan is your shepherd, and you are of his fold. And now who can deny this? Behold, I say unto you, whosoever denies this is a liar and a child of HaSatan.

8 For I say unto you that whatsoever is good comes from Elohim, and whatsoever is evil comes from HaSatan. Therefore, if a man bring forth good works, he hearkens unto the voice of the good shepherd, and he does follow him. But whosoever brings forth evil works, the same becomes a child of HaSatan, for he hearkens unto his voice and does follow him. And whosoever does this must receive his wages of him. Therefore, for his wages he receives death as to things pertaining unto righteousness, being dead unto all good works. And now, my brothers, I would that you should hear me, for I speak in the energy of my soul. For behold, I have spoken unto you plainly, that you cannot err, or have spoken according to the mitzvot of Elohim. For I am called to speak after this manner, according to the Holy Order of Elohim, which is in the Mashiach, Yeshua. Yes, I am commanded to stand and testify unto this people of the things which have been spoken by our fathers concerning the things which are to come. And this is not all; do you not suppose that I know of these things myself? Behold, I testify unto you that I do know that these things whereof I have spoken are true. And how do you suppose that I know of their surety? Behold, I say unto you, they are made known unto me by the holy Ruach Elohim. Behold, I have fasted and prayed many days that I might know these things for myself. And now I do know for myself that they are true, for Adonai YHWH has made them manifest unto me by his Holy Spirit; and this is the spirit of revelation which is in me.[31] And moreover, I say unto you that as it has thus been revealed unto me that the words which have been spoken by our fathers are true, even so according to the spirit of prophecy which is in me, which is also by the manifestation of the Ruach Elohim, I say unto you that I know of myself that whatsoever I shall say unto you concerning that which is to come is true. And I say unto you that I know that Yeshua HaMashiach shall come, yes, the Son, the Only Begotten of the Father, full of grace, and mercy, and truth. And behold, it is he

---

31 1 Nefi 3:6; Alma 7:4

that comes to take away the sins of the world, yes, the sins of every man who steadfastly believes on his name.

9 And now I say unto you that this is the Order after which I am called, yes, to preach unto my beloved brothers, yes, and everyone that dwells in the land — yes, to preach unto all, both old and young, both bond and free, yes, I say unto you, the aged, and also the middle-aged, and the rising generation — yes, to cry unto them that they must repent and be born again.[32] Yes, thus says the spirit: Repent, all you ends of the earth, for the kingdom of Heaven is soon at hand. Yes, the Son of Elohim comes in his glory, in his might, majesty, power, and dominion. Yes, my beloved brothers, I say unto you that the spirit says, Behold, the glory of the **King of all the earth**[33] and also **the King of Heaven**[34] shall very soon shine forth among all the children of men. And also the spirit says unto me, yes, cries unto me with a mighty voice, saying, Go forth and say unto this people, Repent, for except you repent, you can in no way inherit the kingdom of Heaven. And again I say unto you, the spirit says, Behold, the ax is laid at the root of the tree; therefore, every tree that brings not forth good fruit shall be cut down and cast into the fire,[35] yes, a fire which cannot be consumed, even an unquenchable fire. Behold, and remember, HaKodesh has spoken it.

10 And now, my beloved brothers, I say unto you, can you withstand these sayings? Yes, can you lay aside these things and trample HaKodesh under your feet? Yes, can you be puffed up in the pride of your hearts? Yes, will you still persist in the wearing of costly apparel and **setting your hearts upon** the **vain** things of the world? Upon your **riches?**[36] Yes, will you persist in supposing that you are better one than another? Yes, will you persist in the persecutions of your brothers who humble themselves and do walk after the Holy Order of Elohim[37] with which they have been brought into this assembly, having been sanctified by the Holy Spirit? And they do bring forth works showing repentance. Yes, and will you persist in turning your backs upon the poor and the needy? And in withholding your substance from them? And finally, all you that will persist in your

---

32 3 Nefi 5:9   **33** Ps. 47:8 (7)   **34** Dan. 4:37   **35** Ya'akov 3:15; 3 Nefi 6:10   **36** Ps. 62:11 (10)   **37** Alma 10:1-2

wickedness, I say unto you that these are they who shall be cut down and cast into the fire, except they speedily repent.

11 And now I say unto you, all you that are desirous to follow the voice of the good shepherd, come out from among the wicked and be separate, and touch not their unclean things. And behold, their names shall be blotted out, that the names of the wicked shall not be numbered among the names of the righteous, that the word of Elohim may be fulfilled which says, The names of the wicked shall not be mingled with the names of my people, for the names of the righteous shall be written in the Book of Life,[38] and unto them will I grant an inheritance at my right hand. And now, my brothers, what have you to say against this? I say unto you, if you speak against it, it matters not, for the word of Elohim must be fulfilled. For what shepherd is there among you, having many sheep, does not watch over them that the wolves enter not and devour his flock? And behold, if a wolf enter his flock, does he not drive him out? Yes, and at the last, if he can, he will destroy him. And now I say unto you that the good shepherd does call after you. And if you will hearken unto his voice, he will bring you into his fold and you are his sheep. And he commands you that you allow no ravenous wolf to enter among you, that you may not be destroyed.

12 And now I, Alma, do command you in the language of he who has commanded me that you observe to do the words which I have spoken unto you. I speak by way of command unto you that belong to the assembly. And unto those who do not belong to the assembly, I speak by way of invitation, saying, Come and be immersed unto repentance, that you also may be partakers of the fruit of the tree of life.

4 And now it came to pass that after Alma had made an end of speaking unto the people of the assembly which was established in the city of Zerach'mla, he ordained kohanim and elders by laying on his hands, according to the Order of Elohim, to preside and watch over the assembly. And it came to pass that whosoever did not belong to the assembly, who repented of their sins, were washed by immersion unto repentance and were received into the assembly.

---

[38] 3 Nefi 11:4

And it also came to pass that whosoever did belong to the assembly, that did not repent of their wickedness and humble themselves before Elohim (I mean those who were lifted up in the pride of their hearts), the same were rejected and their names were blotted out, that their names were not numbered among those of the righteous. And thus they began to strengthen the order of the assembly in the city of Zerach'mla. Now I would that you should understand that the word of Elohim was liberal unto all, that none were deprived of the privilege of assembling themselves together to hear the word of Elohim. Nevertheless, the children of Elohim were commanded that they should gather themselves together often, and join in fasting and mighty prayer in behalf of the welfare of the souls of those who knew not Elohim.

2 And now it came to pass that when Alma had made these regulations, he departed from them — yes, from the assembly which was in the city of Zerach'mla — and went over upon the east of the river Tzidon into the valley of Gideon, there having been a city built which was called the city of Gideon, which was in the valley that was called Gideon, being called after the man who was slain by the hand of Nehor with the sword. And Alma went and began to declare the word of Elohim unto the assembly which was established in the valley of Gideon, according to the revelation of the truth of the word which had been spoken by his fathers, and according to the spirit of prophecy which was in him — according to the testimony of Yeshua HaMashiach, the Son of Elohim who should come to redeem his people from their sins — and the Holy Order by which he was called. And thus it is written. Amen.

The words of Alma which he delivered to the people in Gideon, according to his own record.

5 Behold, my beloved brothers, seeing that I have been permitted to come unto you, therefore I attempt to address you in my language, yes, by my own mouth, seeing that it is the first time that I have spoken unto you by the words of my mouth, I having been wholly confined to the judgment seat, having had much business, that I could not come unto you. And even I could not have come now at this time, were it not that the judgment seat has been given to another to reign in my place. And YHWH, in much mercy, has granted that I

ALMA 5:2

should come unto you; and behold, I have come, having great hopes and much desire that I should find that you had humbled yourselves before Elohim, and that you had continued in supplicating for his grace, that I should find that you were blameless before him, that I should find that you were not in the awful dilemma that our brothers were in at Zerach'mla. But blessed be the name of Elohim, that he has given unto me to know, yes, has given unto me the exceedingly great joy of knowing that they are established again in the way of his righteousness. And I trust according to the Ruach Elohim which is in me that I shall also have joy over you.

2 Nevertheless, I do not desire that my joy over you should come by the cause of so much affliction and sorrow as I have had for the brothers at Zerach'mla. For behold, my joy over them comes after wading through much affliction and sorrow. But behold, I trust that you are not in a state of so much unbelief as were your brothers. I trust that you are not lifted up in the pride of your hearts. Yes, I trust that you have not set your hearts upon riches and the vain things of the world. Yes, I trust that you do not worship idols, but that you do worship the true and the living Elohim, and that you look forward for the remission of your sins, with an everlasting faith, which is to come.

3 For behold, I say unto you, there are many things to come. And behold, there is one thing which is of more importance than they all, for behold, the time is not far distant that the Redeemer lives and comes among his people. Behold, I do not say that he will come among us at the time of his dwelling in his mortal tabernacle; for behold, the spirit has not said unto me that this should be the case. Now as to this thing I do not know; but this much I do know, that Adonai YHWH has power to do all things which are according to his word. But behold, the spirit has said this much unto me, saying, Cry unto this people, saying, Repent, repent, and prepare the way of YHWH, and walk in his paths, which are straight; for behold, the kingdom of Heaven is at hand, and the Son of Elohim comes upon the face of the earth. And behold, he shall be born of Miryam at Yerushalayim,[39] which is the land of our forefathers, she being a virgin, a precious and

---

[39] Not in the "City of Yerushalyim" but the "land of Yerushalayim" (see footnote to 2 Nefi 1:1). The Mashiach was to be born in Beit Lechem (Bethlehem), a small town just outside of the City of Yerushalayim and within the land of Yerushalayim. As we read in the Targum: "And you, O Bethlehem Ephrath, you who were too small to be numbered

chosen vessel, who shall be overshadowed and conceive by the power of the Ruach HaKodesh and bring forth a son, yes, even the Son of Elohim. And he shall go forth suffering **pains**, and **afflictions**, and temptations of every kind, and this that the word might be fulfilled which says, He will take upon him the **pains** and the **sicknesses**[40] of his people. And he will take upon him death, that he may loose the bands of death which bind his people. And he will take upon him their infirmities, that his bowels may be filled with mercy according to the flesh, that he may know according to the flesh how to deliver his people according to their infirmities. Now the spirit knows all things; nevertheless, the Son of Elohim suffers according to the flesh, that he might take upon him the sins of his people, that he might **blot out** their **transgressions**[41] according to the power of his deliverance. And now behold, this is the testimony which is in me.

4 Now I say unto you that you must repent and be born again, for the spirit says, If you are not born again, you cannot inherit the kingdom of Heaven. Therefore, come and be immersed unto repentance, that you may be washed from your sins, that you may have faith on the Lamb of Elohim, who takes away the sins of the world, who is **mighty to save**[42] and to cleanse from all unrighteousness. Yes, I say unto you, come, and fear not, and lay aside every sin which easily does entangle you, which does bind you down to destruction. Yes, come, and go forth, and show unto your Elohim that you are willing to repent of your sins, and **enter into a covenant**[43] with him to **keep his mitzvot**,[44] and witness it unto him this day by going into the waters of immersion.[45] And whosoever does this, and keeps the mitzvot of Elohim from that time forward, the same will remember that I say unto him, yes, he will remember that I have said unto him, He shall have Eternal life, according to the testimony of the Holy Spirit which testifies in me.

---

among the thousands of the house of Judah, from you shall come forth before Me the Messiah, to exercise dominion over Israel, he whose name was mentioned from before, from the days of creation" (Targum Jonathan; Micah 5:1).   **40** Isa. 53:3-4. When *The Stick of Joseph* actually quotes these verses, the standard KJV terms "sorrows" and "grief" are used for Hebrew *makov* מכאב (Strong's 4341) and Hebrew *khali* חלי (Strong's 2483); but when only alluding to the verses, *The Stick of Joseph* uses the more literal translation "pains, sicknesses, and afflictions." "Pains" and "afflictions" are used for *makov* and "sicknesses" for *khali*, pointing to a Hebrew original behind the English.   **41** Ps. 51:1   **42** Isa. 63:1   **43** Deut. 29:11 (12)   **44** Deut. 30:10   **45** Moshiyah 11:20-21

5 And now, my beloved brothers, do you believe these things? Behold, I say unto you, yes, I know that you believe them. And the way that I know that you believe them is by the manifestation of the spirit which is in me. And now because your faith is strong concerning that, yes, concerning the things which I have spoken, great is my joy. For as I said unto you from the beginning, that I had much desire that you were not in the state of dilemma like your brothers, even so I have found that my desires have been gratified. For I perceive that you are **in the paths of righteousness**.[46] I perceive that you are in the path which leads to the kingdom of Elohim. Yes, I perceive that you are making his paths straight. I perceive that it has been made known unto you by the testimony of his word that he cannot walk in crooked paths, neither does he vary from that which he has said, neither has he a shadow of turning from the right to the left, or from that which is right to that which is wrong. Therefore, his course is one eternal round.[47] And he does not dwell in unholy temples, neither can impurity or anything which is unclean be received into the kingdom of Elohim. Therefore, I say unto you, the time shall come, yes, and it shall be at the last day, that he who is unclean shall remain in his impurity.

6 And now, my beloved brothers, I have said these things unto you that I might awaken you to a sense of your duty to Elohim, that you may walk blameless before him, that you may walk after the Holy Order of Elohim after which you have been received. And now I would that you should be humble, and be submissive and gentle, easy to be entreated, full of patience and long-suffering, being temperate in all things, being diligent in keeping the mitzvot of Elohim at all times, asking for whatsoever things you stand in need, both spiritual and temporal, always returning thanks unto Elohim for whatsoever things you do receive. And see that you have faith, hope, and charity,[48] and then you will always abound in good works. And may YHWH bless you and keep your garments spotless, that you may, at last, be brought to sit down with Avraham, Yitz'chak, and Ya'akov, and the holy prophets[49] who have been ever since the world began, having your garments spotless even as their garments are spotless, in the kingdom of Heaven, to go no more out.

---

46 Ps. 23:3 **47** 1 Nefi 3:5 **48** M'roni 7:7-9; 10:4 **49** Cheleman 2:7; Alma 3:4; 15:14; 'Eter 5:7

7 And now, my beloved brothers, I have spoken these words unto you according to the spirit which testifies in me. And my soul does exceedingly rejoice because of the great diligence and heed which you have given unto my word. And now, may the shalom of Elohim rest upon you, and upon your houses and lands, and upon your flocks and herds, and all that you possess, your women and your children, according to your faith and good works, from this time forth and for ever. And thus I have spoken. Amen.

6 And now it came to pass that Alma returned from the land of Gideon, after having taught the people of Gideon many things which cannot be written, having strengthened the order of the assembly according as he had before done in the land of Zerach'mla, yes, he returned to his own house at Zerach'mla to rest himself from the labors which he had performed. And thus ended the ninth year of the reign of the judges over the people of Nefi.

2 And it came to pass in the commencement of the tenth year of the reign of the judges over the people of Nefi that Alma departed from that place and took his journey over into the land of Melek, on the west of the river Tzidon, on the west by the borders of the wilderness. And he began to teach the people in the land of Melek according to the Holy Order of Elohim by which he had been called,[50] and he began to teach the people throughout all the land of Melek.

3 And it came to pass that the people came to him throughout all the borders of the land which was by the wilderness side. And they were washed by immersion throughout all the land, so that when he had finished his work at Melek, he departed from there and traveled three days' journey on the north of the land of Melek; and he came to a city which was called Ammonihah. Now it was the custom of the people of Nefi to call their lands, and their cities, and their villages — yes, even all their small villages — after the name of him who first possessed them; and thus it was with the land of Ammonihah.

4 And it came to pass that when Alma had come to the city of Ammonihah, he began to preach the word of Elohim unto them. Now HaSatan had gotten great hold upon the hearts of the people

---

[50] Alma 9:10

of the city of Ammonihah; therefore, they would not hearken unto the words of Alma. Nevertheless, Alma labored much in the spirit, wrestling with Elohim in mighty prayer,⁵¹ that he would pour out his spirit upon the people who were in the city, that he would also grant that he might immerse them unto repentance. Nevertheless, they hardened their hearts, saying unto him, Behold, we know that you are Alma; and we know that you are Kohen HaGadol over the assembly which you have established in many parts of the land according to your tradition. And we are not of your assembly, and we do not believe in such foolish traditions. And now we know that because we are not of your assembly, we know that you have no power over us. And you have delivered up the judgment seat unto Nefihah; therefore, you are not the chief judge over us. Now when the people had said this, and had withstood all his words, and reviled him, and spit upon him, and caused that he should be cast out of their city, he departed from there and took his journey towards the city which was called Aharon.

⁵And it came to pass that while he was journeying there, being weighed down with sorrow, wading through much tribulation and anguish of soul because of the wickedness of the people who were in the city of Ammonihah, it came to pass that while Alma was thus weighed down with sorrow, behold, an angel of YHWH appeared unto him, saying, Blessed are you, Alma.⁵² Therefore, lift up your head and rejoice, for you have great cause to rejoice; for you have been faithful in keeping the mitzvot of Elohim from the time which you received your first message from him. Behold, I am he that delivered it unto you. And behold, I am sent to command you that you return to the city of Ammonihah and preach again unto the people of the city, yes, preach unto them, yes, say unto them, except they repent Adonai YHWH will destroy them. For behold, they do study at this time that they may destroy the liberty of your people — for thus says YHWH — which is contrary to the statutes and judgments and mitzvot which he has given unto his people.

⁶Now it came to pass that after Alma had received his message from the angel of YHWH, he returned speedily to the land of Ammonihah. And he entered the city by another way, yes, by the way which was

---

51 Enosh 1:1   **52** 1 Nefi 1:6; Enosh 1:1; Moshiyah 11:20

on the south of the city Ammonihah. And it came to pass that as he entered the city, he was hungry; and he said to a man, Will you give to a humble servant of Elohim something to eat? And the man said unto him, I am a Nefite, and I know that you are a holy prophet of Elohim, for you are the man whom an angel said in a vision, You shall receive. Therefore, go with me into my house, and I will impart unto you of my food. And I know that you will be a blessing unto me and my house. And it came to pass that the man received him into his house. And the man was called Amulek; and he brought forth bread and meat, and set it before Alma.

7 And it came to pass that Alma ate bread and he was filled; and he blessed Amulek and his house, and he gave thanks unto Elohim.[53] And after he had eaten and was filled, he said unto Amulek, I am Alma, and am the Kohen HaGadol over the assemblies of Elohim throughout the land. And behold, I have been called to preach the word of Elohim among all this people according to the spirit of revelation and prophecy. And I was in this land, and they would not receive me, but they cast me out. And I was about to set my back towards this land for ever. But behold, I have been commanded that I should turn again and prophesy unto this people, yes, and to testify against them concerning their iniquities. And now, Amulek, because you have fed me and took me in, you are blessed; for I was hungry, for I had fasted many days. And Alma remained many days with Amulek before he began to preach unto the people.

8 And it came to pass that the people did grow more shameful in their iniquities. And the word came to Alma, saying, Go; and also say unto my servant Amulek, Go forth and prophesy unto this people, saying, Repent, for thus says YHWH: Except you repent, I will visit this people in my anger; yes, and I will not turn my fierce anger away. And Alma went forth, and also Amulek, among the people, to declare the words of Elohim unto them. And they were filled with the Ruach HaKodesh, and they had power given unto them, insomuch that they could not be confined in dungeons, neither was it possible that any man could slay them. Nevertheless, they did not exercise their power

---

53 The giving of thanks after meals is a Jewish practice prescribed by the Talmud (b. Berakhot 47b-49a) that is also found in the Dead Sea Scrolls in the hymn "Invitation to Grace after Meals." The practice is derived from Deut. 8:10.

until they were bound in bands and cast into prison. Now this was done that YHWH might show forth his power in them.⁵⁴

⁹And it came to pass that they went forth and began to preach and to prophesy unto the people according to the spirit and power which YHWH had given them.

The words of Alma, and also the words of Amulek, which were declared unto the people who were in the land of Ammonihah. And also, they are cast into prison, and delivered by the miraculous power of Elohim which was in them, according to the record of Alma.

7 And again I, Alma, having been commanded of Elohim that I should take Amulek and go forth and preach again unto this people, or the people who were in the city of Ammonihah, it came to pass, as I began to preach unto them, that they began to contend with me, saying, Who are you? Do you suppose that we shall believe the testimony of one man although he should preach unto us that the earth should pass away? Now they understood not the words which they spoke, for they knew not that the earth should pass away.⁵⁵ And they said also, We will not believe your words if you should prophesy that this great city should be destroyed in one day. Now they knew not that Elohim could do such marvelous works, for they were a hard-hearted and a stiffnecked people. And they said, Who is Elohim that sends no more authority than one man among this people to declare unto them the truth of such great and marvelous things? And they stood forth to lay their hands on me, but behold, they did not.⁵⁶

²And I stood with boldness to declare unto them, yes, I did boldly testify unto them, saying, Behold, O you wicked and perverse generation, how have you forgotten the tradition of your fathers? Yes, how soon you have forgotten the mitzvot of Elohim! Do you not remember that our father Lechi was brought out of Yerushalayim by the hand of Elohim? Do you not remember that they were all led by him through the wilderness? And have you forgotten so soon how many times he delivered our fathers out of the hands of their enemies and preserved them from being destroyed, even by the hands of their own brothers? Yes, and if it had not been for his matchless power, and his mercy, and his long-suffering towards us, we should

---

54 Cheleman 2:20   55 3 Nefi 11:6; 'Eter 6:3   56 Moshiyah 7:19-20

unavoidably have been cut off from the face of the earth long before this period of time, and perhaps been consigned to a state of Endless misery and woe. Behold, now I say unto you that he commands you to repent. And except you repent, you can in no way inherit the kingdom of Elohim. But behold, this is not all. He has commanded you to repent, or he will utterly destroy you from off the face of the earth. Yes, he will visit you in his anger, and **in his fierce anger**[57] he will not turn away.

3 Behold, do you not remember the words which he spoke unto Lechi, saying that inasmuch as you shall keep my mitzvot, you shall prosper in the land?[58] And again it is said that inasmuch as you will not keep my mitzvot, **you shall be cut off from the presence of YHWH.**[59] Now I would that you should remember that inasmuch as the Lamanites have not kept the mitzvot of Elohim, they have been cut off from the presence of YHWH. Now we see that the word of YHWH has been verified in this thing, and the Lamanites have been cut off from his presence from the beginning of their transgressions in the land. Nevertheless, I say unto you that it shall be more tolerable for them in the day of judgment than for you if you remain in your sins, yes, and even more tolerable for them in this life than for you, except you repent. For there are many promises which are extended to the Lamanites, for it is because of the traditions of their fathers that cause them to remain in their state of ignorance. Therefore, YHWH will be merciful unto them and prolong their existence in the land. And at some period of time, they will be brought to believe in his word and to know of the incorrectness of the traditions of their fathers; and many of them will be saved, for YHWH will be merciful unto all who call on his name.

4 But behold, I say unto you that if you persist in your wickedness, **that your days shall not be prolonged in the land,**[60] for the Lamanites shall be sent upon you. And if you repent not, they shall come in a time when you know not, and you shall be visited with utter destruction. And it shall be according to the fierce anger of YHWH, for he will not allow you that you shall live in your iniquities to destroy his people. I say unto you, no, he would rather allow

---

57 Deut. 29:22 (23)   **58** Lev. 26:3–13; Deut. 28:1–14   **59** Lev. 22:3; 26:14–46; Deut 28:15–68; 1 Nefi 1:9; 2 Nefi 1:1–2   **60** Deut. 30:18

that the Lamanites might destroy all this people who are called the people of Nefi, if it were possible that they could fall into sins and transgressions after having had so much light and so much knowledge given unto them of YHWH their Elohim — yes, after having been such a highly favored people of YHWH; yes, after having been favored above every other nation, kindred, tongue, or people; after having had all things made known unto them according to their desires, and their faith, and prayers, of that which has been, and which is, and which is to come; having been visited by the Ruach Elohim, having conversed with angels, and having been spoken unto by the voice of YHWH; and having the spirit of prophecy and the spirit of revelation; and also many gifts: the gift of speaking with tongues, and the gift of preaching, and the gift of the Ruach HaKodesh, and the gift of translation; yes, and after having been delivered by Elohim out of the land of Yerushalayim by the hand of YHWH; having been saved from famine, and from sickness, and all manner of diseases of every kind; and they having been made strong in battle, that they might not be destroyed; having been brought out of bondage time after time, and having been kept and preserved until now; and they have been prospered until they are rich in all manner of things.

5 And now behold, I say unto you that if this people, who have received so many blessings from the hand of YHWH, should transgress contrary to the light and knowledge which they do have, I say unto you that if this be the case, that if they should fall into transgression, that it would be far more tolerable for the Lamanites than for them. For behold, the promises of YHWH are extended to the Lamanites, but they are not unto you if you transgress; for has not YHWH expressly promised and firmly decreed that if you will rebel against him, that you shall utterly be destroyed from off the face of the earth?[61]

6 And now for this cause — that you may not be destroyed — YHWH has sent his angel to visit many of his people, declaring unto them that they must go forth and cry mightily unto this people, saying, Repent, repent, for the kingdom of Heaven is nearly at hand. And not many days hence, the Son of Elohim shall come in his glory, and his glory shall be the glory of the Only Begotten of the Father, full of grace, equity, and truth; full of patience, mercy, and long-suffering,

---

61 Cheleman 3:5

quick to hear the cries of his people and to answer their prayers. And behold, he comes to redeem those who will be immersed unto repentance through faith on his name. Therefore, prepare you the way of YHWH, for the time is at hand that all men shall reap a reward for their works, according to that which they have been: if they have been righteous, they shall reap the salvation of their souls according to the power and deliverance of Yeshua HaMashiach; and if they have been evil, they shall reap the damnation of their souls according to the power and captivity of HaSatan; now behold, this is the voice of the angel crying unto the people. And now, my beloved brothers, for you are my brothers and you ought to be beloved, and you ought to bring forth works showing repentance, seeing that your hearts have been enormously hardened against the word of Elohim, and seeing that you are a lost and a fallen people.[62]

7 Now it came to pass that when I, Alma, had spoken these words, behold, the people were angry with me because I said unto them that they were a hard-hearted and a stiffnecked people. And also because I said unto them that they were a lost and fallen people, they were angry with me and sought to lay their hands upon me, that they might cast me into prison. But it came to pass that YHWH did not allow them that they should take me at that time and cast me into prison.

8 And it came to pass that Amulek went and stood forth, and began to preach unto them also. And now the words of Amulek are not all written; nevertheless, a part of his words are written in this book.

8 Now these are the words that Amulek preached unto the people who were in the land of Ammonihah, saying, I am Amulek. I am the son of Gidanah, who was the son of Yishma'el, who was a descendant of Aminadi; and it was that same Aminadi who interpreted the writing which was upon the wall of the Temple, which was written by the finger of Elohim. And Aminadi was a descendant of Nefi, who was the son of Lechi, who came out of the land of Yerushalayim, who was a descendant of M'nasheh, who was

---

[62] Avinodi taught that those who rebel against Elohim remain lost and fallen, despite the redemption offered through Mashiach (Moshiyah 8:13–14). Alma's characterization of those at Ammonihah was entirely accurate because they were in a state of rebellion, not ignorance, and they specifically denied Mashiach.

the son of **Yosef, who was sold into Egypt**[63] by the hands of his brothers. And behold, I am also a man of no small reputation among all those who know me; yes, and behold, I have many kindred and friends. And I have also acquired great riches by the hand of my industry. Nevertheless, after all this, I have never known much of the ways of YHWH, and his mysteries and marvelous power. I said I never had known much of these things, but behold, I misspoke, for I have seen much of his mysteries and his miraculous power, yes, even in the preservation of the lives of this people. Nevertheless, I did harden my heart, for I was called many times and I would not hear. Therefore, I knew concerning these things, yet I chose not to know. Therefore, I went on rebelling against Elohim in the wickedness of my heart, even until the fourth day of this seventh month, which is in the tenth year of the reign of our judges.

2 As I was journeying to see a very near kindred, behold, an angel of YHWH appeared unto me and said, Amulek, return to your own house, for you shall feed a prophet of YHWH, yes, a holy man who is a chosen man of Elohim; for he has fasted many days because of the sins of this people, and he is hungry. And you shall receive him into your house and feed him. And he shall bless you and your house, and the blessing of YHWH shall rest upon you and your house.[64]

3 And it came to pass that I obeyed the voice of the angel and returned towards my house. And as I was going there, I found the man whom the angel said unto me, You shall receive him into your house; and behold, it was this same man who has been speaking unto you concerning the things of Elohim. And the angel said unto me, He is a holy man. Wherefore, I know he is a holy man because it was said by an angel of Elohim. And again I know that the things whereof he has testified are true. For behold, I say unto you that as YHWH lives, even so he has sent his angel to make these things manifest unto me; and this he has done while this Alma has dwelt at my house. For

---

63 Gen. 45:4   64 When we compare Alma's account of these events (Alma 6:5-7) with Amulek's account of the same (Alma 8:1-3), an interesting picture develops that points to a Passover setting. Amulek tells us the events begin on the fourth day of the seventh month (Alma 8:1). Counting from Rosh Hashanah as the new year, this is just ten days before Passover. Amulek was traveling to visit a near kinsman, perhaps with whom to observe the Seder (Alma 8:2). An angel appears to him and directs him to return to his own home and prepare an additional place for a prophet who has been blessed. He and his house will be blessed if he does this. One cannot help but recall the tradition of setting an extra place for Elijah at the Seder.

behold, he has blessed my house; he has blessed me, and my women, and my children, and my father, and my kinsfolk — yes, even all my kindred has he blessed. And the blessing of YHWH has rested upon us according to the words which he spoke.

4 And now when Amulek had spoken these words, the people began to be astonished, seeing there was more than one witness who testified of the things whereof they were accused, and also of the things which were to come, according to the spirit of prophecy which was in them. Nevertheless, there were some among them who thought to question them, that by their cunning schemes they might catch them in their words, that they might find evidence against them, that they might deliver them to the judges, that they might be judged according to the law, and that they might be slain or cast into prison, according to the crime which they could make appear or witness against them.

5 Now those men who sought to destroy them were lawyers, who were hired or appointed by the people to administer the law at their times of trial, or at the trials of the crimes of the people before the judges — now these lawyers were learned in all the arts and cunning of the people, and this was to enable them that they might be skillful in their profession. And it came to pass that they began to question Amulek, that thereby they might make him cross his words or contradict the words which he should speak. Now they knew not that Amulek could know of their design; but it came to pass, as they began to question him, he perceived their thoughts. And he said unto them, O you wicked and perverse generation, you lawyers and hypocrites, for you are laying the foundations of HaSatan, for you are laying traps and snares to catch the holy ones of Elohim. You are laying plans to pervert the ways of the righteous and to bring down the wrath of Elohim upon your heads, even to the utter destruction of this people. Yes, well did Moshiyah say, who was our last king, when he was about to deliver up the kingdom, having no one to confer it upon, causing that this people should be governed by their own voices — yes, well did he say that if the time should come that the voice of this people should cause iniquity, that is, if the time should come that this people should fall into transgression, they would be ripe for destruction. And now I say unto you that well does YHWH judge of your iniquities; well does he cry unto this people by the voice of his angels, Repent, repent, for the kingdom of Heaven is at hand. Yes, well

does he cry by the voice of his angels that I will come down among my people with equity and justice in my hands. Yes, and I say unto you that if it were not for the prayers of the righteous who are now in the land, that you would even now be visited with utter destruction. Yet it would not be by flood, as were the people in the days of Noach, but it would be by famine, and by pestilence, and the sword. But it is by the prayers of the righteous that you are spared. Now therefore, if you will cast out the righteous from among you, then YHWH will not stay his hand, but in his fierce anger he will come out against you; then you shall be smitten by famine, and by pestilence, and by the sword.[65] And the time is soon at hand except you repent.

6 And now it came to pass that the people were more angry with Amulek, and they cried out, saying, This man does revile against our laws, which are just, and our wise lawyers whom we have selected! But Amulek stretched forth his hand and cried the mightier unto them, saying, O you wicked and perverse generation! Why has HaSatan got such great hold upon your hearts? Why will you yield yourselves unto him, that he may have power over you to blind your eyes, that you will not understand the words which are spoken according to their truth? For behold, have I testified against your law? You do not understand. You say that I have spoken against your law, but I have not; but I have spoken in favor of your law, to your condemnation. And now behold, I say unto you that the foundation of the destruction of this people is beginning to be laid by the unrighteousness of your lawyers and your judges.

7 And now it came to pass that when Amulek had spoken these words, the people cried out against him, Now we know that this man is a child of HaSatan! For he has lied unto us, for he has spoken against our law and now he says that he has not spoken against it! And again he has reviled against our lawyers and our judges and so forth. And it came to pass that the lawyers put it into their hearts that they should remember these things against him. And there was one among them whose name was Zeezrom. Now he was the foremost to accuse Amulek and Alma, he being one of the most expert among them, having much business to do among the people. Now the object

---

65 Alma 11:5. The prophecy of utter destruction is swiftly and completely fulfilled.

of these lawyers was to get gain, and they got gain according to their employment.

8 Now it was in the law of Moshiyah that every man who was a judge of the law, or those who were appointed to be judges, should receive wages according to the time which they labored to judge those who were brought before them to be judged.

9 Now if a man owed another, and he would not pay that which he did owe, he was complained of to the judge; and the judge executed authority and sent forth officers, that the man should be brought before him. And he judged the man according to the law and the evidences which were brought against him; and thus the man was compelled to pay that which he owed, or be whipped, or be cast out from among the people as a thief and a robber. And the judge received for his wages according to his time: a senine of gold for a day, or a senum of silver, which is equal to a senine of gold. And this is according to the law which was given.

10 Now these are the names of the different pieces of their gold and of their silver according to their value; and the names are given by the Nefites. For they did not reckon after the manner of the Y'hudim who were at Yerushalayim, neither did they measure after the manner of the Y'hudim; but they altered their reckoning and their measure according to the minds and the circumstances of the people, in every generation until the reign of the judges, they having been established by king Moshiyah.

11 Now the reckoning is thus: a senine of gold, a seon[66] of gold, a shum of gold, and a limnah of gold. A senum of silver, an amnor of silver, an ezrum of silver, and an onti of silver. A senum of silver was equal to a senine of gold, and either for a measure of barley, and also for a measure of every kind of grain. Now the amount of a seon of gold was twice the value of a senine. And a shum of gold was twice the value of a seon. And a limnah of gold was the value of them all. And an amnor of silver was as great as two senums. And an ezrum of silver was as great as four senums. And an onti was as great as all of them. Now this is the value of the lesser numbers of their reckoning: a shiblon is half of a senum; therefore, a shiblon for a half a measure

---

66 Compare Hebrew *s'ah* סאה (Strong's 5429), a measure of volume of grain (6.5 to 7.5 liters).

of barley. And a shilum[67] is a half of a shiblon. And a leah is the half of a shilum. Now an antion of gold is equal to three shiblons. Now this is their number according to their reckoning.

12 Now it was for the sole purpose to get gain, because they received their wages according to their employment, therefore they did stir up the people to riotings and all manner of disturbances and wickedness, that they might have more employment, that they might get money according to the suits which were brought before them; therefore, they did stir up the people against Alma and Amulek. And this Zeezrom began to question Amulek, saying, Will you answer me a few questions which I shall ask you? Now Zeezrom was a man who was expert in the schemes of HaSatan, that he might destroy that which was good; therefore, he said unto Amulek, Will you answer the questions which I shall put unto you? And Amulek said unto him, Yes, I will, if they be according to the spirit of YHWH which is in me; for I shall say nothing which is contrary to the spirit of YHWH. And Zeezrom said unto him, Behold, here are six onties of silver, and all these will I give unto you if you will deny the existence of a supreme being.

13 Now Amulek said, O you child of She'ol, why do you tempt me? Do you know that the righteous yield to no such temptations? Do you believe that there is no Elohim? I say unto you, no, you know that there is an Elohim; but you love that lucre more than him. And now you have lied before Elohim unto me; for you said unto me, Behold, these six onties, which are of great worth, I will give unto you, when you had it in your heart to retain them from me. And it was only your desire that I should deny the true and living Elohim, that you might have cause to destroy me. And now behold, for this great evil you shall have your reward.

14 And Zeezrom said unto him, You say there is a true and a living Elohim? And Amulek said, Yes, there is a true and a living Elohim. Now Zeezrom said, Is there more than **one Elohim**?[68] And he answered, No. Now Zeezrom said unto him again, How do you know these things? And he said, An angel has made them known unto me. And Zeezrom said again, Who is he that shall come? Is it

---

67 Compare Hebrew *shillum* שׁלוּם (Strong's 7966), "recompence, payment." 68 Deut. 6:4

the Son of Elohim? And he said unto him, Yes. And Zeezrom said again, Shall he save his people in their sins? And Amulek answered and said unto him, I say unto you, he shall not; for it is impossible for him to deny his word.

15 Now Zeezrom said unto the people, See that you remember these things, for he said there is but one Elohim, yet he said that the Son of Elohim shall come, but he shall not save his people, as though he had authority to command Elohim. Now Amulek said again unto him, Behold, you have lied; for you say that I speak as though I had authority to command Elohim because I said he shall not save his people in their sins. And I say unto you again that he cannot save them in their sins, for I cannot deny his word. And he has said that no unclean thing can inherit the kingdom of Heaven. Therefore, how can you be saved except you inherit the kingdom of Heaven? Therefore, you cannot be saved in your sins. Now Zeezrom said again unto him, Is the Son of Elohim the very Eternal Father? And Amulek said unto him, yes, he is the very Eternal Father of Heaven and earth and all things which in them are; he is the beginning and the end, **the first and the last**.[69] And he shall come into the world to redeem his people; and he shall take upon himself the transgressions of those who believe on his name; and these are they that shall have Eternal life, and salvation comes to none else. Therefore, the wicked remain as though there had been no redemption made, except it be the loosing of the bands of death. For behold, the day comes that all shall rise from the dead, and stand before Elohim, and be judged according to their works.

16 Now there is a death which is called temporal death, and the death of Mashiach shall loose the bands of this temporal death, that all shall be raised from this temporal death; the spirit and the body shall be reunited again in its perfect form; both limb and joint shall be restored to its proper frame, even as we now are at this time. And we shall be brought to stand before Elohim, knowing even as we know now, and have a bright recollection of all our guilt. Now this restoration shall come to all, both old and young, both bond and free, both male and female, both the wicked and the righteous. And even there shall not so much as a hair of their heads be lost; but all things

---

[69] Isa. 41:4; 44:6; 48:12

shall be restored to its perfect frame, as it is now, or in the body, and shall be brought and be arraigned before the bar of Mashiach the Son, and Elohim the Father, and the Holy Spirit, which is one Elohe Kedem, to be judged according to their works, whether they be good or whether they be evil.

17 Now behold, I have spoken unto you concerning the death of the mortal body, and also concerning the resurrection of the mortal body. I say unto you that this mortal body is raised to an immortal body, that is from death, even from the first death unto life, that they can die no more; their spirits uniting with their bodies, never to be divided, thus the whole becoming spiritual and immortal, that they can no more see corruption.

18 Now when Amulek had finished these words, the people began again to be astonished; and also Zeezrom began to tremble. And thus ended the words of Amulek, or this is all that I have written.

9 Now Alma, seeing that the words of Amulek had silenced Zeezrom – for he beheld that Amulek had caught him in his lying and deceiving to destroy him – and seeing that he began to tremble under a consciousness of his guilt, he opened his mouth and began to speak unto him, and to confirm the words of Amulek, and to explain things beyond, or to unfold the scriptures beyond that which Amulek had done. Now the words that Alma spoke unto Zeezrom were heard by the people round about, for the multitude was great, and he spoke in this manner: Now Zeezrom, seeing that you have been taken in your lyings and craftiness, for you have not lied unto men only, but you have lied unto Elohim, for behold, he knows all your thoughts, and you see that your thoughts are made known unto us by his spirit. And you see that we know that your plan was a very subtle plan, as to the subtlety of HaSatan, to lie and to deceive this people, that you might set them against us, to revile us and to cast us out. Now this was a plan of your adversary, and he has exercised his power in you. Now I would that you should remember that what I say unto you, I say unto all. And behold, I say unto you all that this was a snare of the adversary which he has laid to catch this people, that he might bring you into subjection unto him, that he might encircle you about with his chains, that he might chain you down to everlasting destruction according to the power of his captivity.

2 Now when Alma had spoken these words, Zeezrom began to tremble more exceedingly, for he was convinced more and more of the power of Elohim. And he was also convinced that Alma and Amulek had a knowledge of him, for he was convinced that they knew the thoughts and intents of his heart; for power was given unto them that they might know of these things according to the spirit of prophecy. And Zeezrom began to inquire of them diligently, that he might know more concerning the kingdom of Elohim. And he said unto Alma, What does this mean which Amulek has spoken concerning the resurrection of the dead, that all shall rise from the dead, both the just and the unjust, and are brought to stand before Elohim to be judged according to their works?

3 And now Alma began to explain these things unto him, saying, It is given unto many to know the mysteries of Elohim; nevertheless, they are laid under a strict command that they shall not make them known — only according to the portion of his word which he does grant unto the children of men, according to the heed and diligence which they give unto him. And therefore, he that will harden his heart, the same receives the lesser portion of the word. And he that will not harden his heart, to him is given the greater portion of the word, until it is given unto him to know the mysteries of Elohim, until they know them in full. And they that will harden their hearts, to them is given the lesser portion of the word until they know nothing concerning his mysteries; and then they are taken captive by HaSatan and led by his will down to destruction. Now this is what is meant by the chains of She'ol.[70]

4 And Amulek has spoken plainly concerning death, and being raised from this mortality to a state of immortality, and being brought before the bar of Elohim to be judged according to our works. Then, if our hearts have been hardened, yes, if we have hardened our hearts against the word insomuch that it has not been found in us, then will our state be awful, for then we shall be condemned. For our words will condemn us, yes, all our works will condemn us; we shall not be

---

70 Alma is alluding to the concept in Judaism of the four levels of understanding known as *Pardes* פרדס. *Pardes* is the Hebrew word for "paradise." *PaRDeS* is also an acronym for the four levels of understanding of the Scriptures: *Pashat* (literal); *Remez* (implied, hinted); *Drash* (allegorical, homiletical); and *Sod* (hidden, secret). Alma is telling us that a person who has hardened his heart may be limited to the lower, "lesser" levels of understanding.

found spotless, and our thoughts will also condemn us, and in this awful state we shall not dare look up to our Elohim. And we would be glad if we could command the rocks and the mountains to fall upon us, to hide us from his presence. But this cannot be. We must come forth and stand before him in his glory, and in his power, and in his might, majesty, and dominion, and acknowledge to our everlasting shame that all his judgments are just, that he is just in all his works, and that he is merciful unto the children of men, and that he has all power to save every man that believes on his name and brings forth fruit showing repentance.[71]

5 And now behold, I say unto you, then comes a death, even a second death, which is a spiritual death. Then is a time that whosoever dies in his sins as to the temporal death shall also die a spiritual death; yes, he shall die as to things pertaining unto righteousness. Then is the time when their torment shall be as a lake of fire and brimstone whose flames ascend up for ever and ever. And then is the time that they shall be chained down to an everlasting destruction according to the power and captivity of HaSatan, he having subjected them according to his will. Then, I say unto you, they shall be as though there had been no redemption made, for they cannot be redeemed according to Elohim's justice; and they cannot die, seeing there is no more corruption.

6 Now it came to pass that when Alma had made an end of speaking these words, the people began to be more astonished. But there was one Antionah, who was a chief ruler among them, that came forth and said unto him, What is this that you have said, that man should rise from the dead and be changed from this mortal to an immortal state, that the soul can never die? What does the scripture mean which says that Elohim **placed keruvim and a flaming sword on the east of the Garden of Eden,**[72] **for fear that** our first parents should enter **and partake of the fruit of the tree of life and live for ever?**[73] And thus we see that there was no possible chance that they should live for ever. Now Alma said unto him, This is the thing which I was

---

[71] This verse is framed around the Sefirot of the Tree of Life: "... stand before him in his glory, and in his power, and in his might, majesty, and dominion, and acknowledge to our everlasting shame, that all his judgments are just; that he is just in all his works, and that he is merciful unto the children of men, and that he has all power to save every man that believes on his name...." [72] Gen. 3:24 [73] Gen. 3:22

about to explain. Now we see that Adam did fall by partaking of the forbidden fruit,[74] according to the word of Elohim. And thus we see that by his fall, mankind became a lost and a fallen people. And now behold, I say unto you that if it had been possible for Adam to have partaken of the fruit of the tree of life at that time, there would have been no death and the word would have been void, making Elohim a liar, for he said, **If you eat, you shall surely die.**[75] And we see that death comes upon mankind, yes, the death which has been spoken of by Amulek, which is the temporal death. Nevertheless, there was a space granted unto man in which he might repent. Therefore, this life became a probationary state, a time to **prepare to meet Elohim**,[76] a time to prepare for that endless state which has been spoken of by us, which is after the resurrection of the dead. Now if it had not been for the plan of redemption which was laid from the foundation of the world, there could have been no resurrection of the dead. But there was a plan of redemption laid which shall bring to pass the resurrection of the dead, of which has been spoken.

7 And now behold, if it were possible that our first parents could have gone forth and partaken of the tree of life, they would have been for ever miserable, having no preparatory state; and thus the plan of redemption would have been frustrated, and the **word** of Elohim would have been **void**,[77] taking no effect. But behold, it was not so. But it was appointed unto man that they must die; and after death, they must come to judgment, even that same judgment of which we have spoken, which is the end. And after Elohim had appointed that these things should come unto man, behold, then he saw that it was expedient that man should know concerning the things that he had appointed unto them. Therefore, he sent angels to converse with them, who caused men to behold of his glory. And they began from that time forth to call on his name;[78] therefore, Elohim conversed with men and made known unto them the plan of redemption, which had been prepared from the foundation of the world.[79] And this he made known unto them according to their faith, and repentance, and their holy works.

---

74 The phrase "forbidden fruit" never appears in the Tanakh but is found in the Zohar (Zohar 2:144a). **75** Gen. 2:17 **76** Amos 4:12 **77** Isa. 55:11 **78** Enosh 1:1 **79** Moshiyah 8:9; Alma 12:16

⁸Wherefore, he gave mitzvot unto men — they having first transgressed the first mitzvot as to things which were temporal and **becoming as Elohim, knowing good from evil,**⁸⁰ placing themselves in a state to act, or being placed in a state to act according to their wills and pleasures, whether to do evil or to do good — therefore, Elohim gave unto them mitzvot, after having made known unto them the plan of redemption, that they should not do evil, the penalty thereof being a second death, which was an everlasting death as to things pertaining unto righteousness. For on such, the plan of redemption could have no power, for the works of justice could not be destroyed, according to the supreme goodness of Elohim. But Elohim did call on man in the name of his Son, this being the plan of redemption which was laid, saying, If you will repent and harden not your hearts, then will I have mercy upon you, through my only begotten Son. Therefore, whosoever repents and hardens not his heart, he shall have claim on mercy, through my only begotten Son, unto a remission of his sins, and these **shall enter into my rest.** And whosoever will harden his heart and will do iniquity, behold, I swear in my wrath that he **shall not enter into my rest.**⁸¹ And now, my brothers, behold, I say unto you that if you will harden your hearts, you shall not enter into the rest of YHWH. Therefore, your iniquity provokes him, that he sends down his wrath upon you as in the first provocation — yes, according to his word in the last provocation, as well as in the first, to the everlasting destruction of your souls; therefore, according to his word unto the last death, as well as the first.

⁹And now, my brothers, seeing we know these things, and they are true, let us repent and harden not our hearts, that we provoke not YHWH our Elohim to pull down his wrath upon us, in these his second mitzvot which he has given unto us; but let us enter into the rest of Elohim, which is prepared according to his word.

¹⁰And again, my brothers, I would remind you of the time when Adonai YHWH gave these mitzvot unto his children. And I would that you should remember that Adonai YHWH ordained Kohanim after his Holy Order,⁸² which was after the Order of his Son, to teach these things unto the people. And those Kohanim were ordained

---

80 Gen. 3:5, 22   81 Ps. 95:11   82 2 Nefi 5:1; Alma 3:8; 5:6; 6:2; 10:1; 20:1; 21:42

after the Order of his Son in a manner that thereby the people might know how to look forward to his Son for redemption. And this is the manner after which they were ordained: being called and prepared from the foundation of the world, according to the foreknowledge of Elohim, on account of their exceeding faith and good works in the first place, being left to choose good or evil; therefore they, having chosen good, and exercising exceedingly great faith, are called with a holy calling—yes, with that holy calling which was prepared with, and according to, a preparatory redemption for such. And thus they have been called to this holy calling on account of their faith, while others would reject the Ruach Elohim on account of the hardness of their hearts and blindness of their minds (while, if it had not been for this, they might had privilege as great as their brothers—or in short, in the first place they were on the same standing with their brothers—thus, this holy calling being prepared from the foundation of the world for such as would not harden their hearts, being in and through the atonement of the Only Begotten Son who was prepared), and thus, being called by this holy calling and ordained unto the High Priesthood of the Holy Order of Elohim to teach his mitzvot unto the children of men, that they also might enter into his rest—this High Priesthood being after the Order of his Son, which Order was from the foundation of the world, or in other words, being without beginning of days or end of years, being prepared from eternity to all eternity according to his foreknowledge of all things. Now they were ordained after this manner, being called with a holy calling, and ordained with a holy ordinance, and taking upon them the High Priesthood of the Holy Order—which calling, and ordinance, and High Priesthood is without beginning or end; thus, they become Kohanim HaGadolim for ever after the Order of the Son, the Only Begotten of the Father who is without beginning of days or end of years, who is full of grace, equity, and truth. And thus it is. Amen.

10 Now as I said concerning the Holy Order or this High Priesthood, there were many who were ordained and became Kohanim HaGadolim of Elohim. And it was on account of their exceeding faith and repentance, and their righteousness before Elohim, they choosing to repent and work righteousness rather than to perish. Therefore, they were called after this Holy Order and were

ALMA 10:2

sanctified, and their garments were washed white through the blood of the Lamb. Now they, after being sanctified by the Ruach HaKodesh, having their garments made white, being pure and spotless before Elohim, could not look upon sin except it were with abhorrence. And there were many, an exceedingly great many, who were made pure and entered into the rest of YHWH their Elohim. And now, my brothers, I would that you should humble yourselves before Elohim and bring forth fruit showing repentance, that you may also enter into that rest. Yes, humble yourselves even as the people in the days of Malki-Tzedek, who was also a **Kohen HaGadol** after this same **Order** of which I have spoken, who also took upon him the High Priesthood **for ever.**[83] And it was this same Malki-Tzedek to whom **Avraham** paid **tithes** – yes, even our father **Avraham** paid **tithes of one-tenth part of all** he possessed.[84] Now these ordinances were given after this manner, that thereby the people might look forward on the Son of Elohim, it being a type of his Order, or it being his Order,[85] and this that they might look forward to him for a remission of their sins, that they might **enter into the rest**[86] of YHWH.

2 Now this **Malki-Tzedek was a king over** the land of **Shalem**,[87] and his people had become strong in iniquity and abominations—yes, they had all gone astray; they were full of all manner of wickedness. But Malki-Tzedek, having exercised mighty faith and received the office of the High Priesthood[88] according to the Holy Order of Elohim, did preach repentance unto his people. And behold, they did repent. And Malki-Tzedek did establish shalom in the land in his days; therefore, **he was called the Prince of Shalom**,[89] for he was the King of Shalem; and he did reign under his father.[90] Now there were many before him, and also there were many afterwards, but none were greater. Therefore, of him they have more particularly made

---

83 Gen. 14:18; Ps. 110:4   84 Gen 14:20   85 A document found among the Dead Sea Scrolls, known as "The Melchizedek Document" (11Q13), speaks of a Messianic figure called "Melchizedek" who will release the people "from the debt of all their sins." The first century Jewish writer Philo of Alexandria identifies Melchizedek with the Logos (Word) and says he will "bring forward wine instead of water and shall give your souls to drink, and shall cheer them with unmixed wine in order that they may be wholly occupied with divine intoxication, more sober than sobriety itself" (Philo, *Allegorical Interpretation iii*, 82).   86 Ps. 95:11; Alma 9:9; 11:7; M'roni 7:2; 9:1   87 Gen. 14:18   88 The first century Jewish writer Philo of Alexandria writes, "God made Melchizedek…his own high priest" (Philo, *Allegorical Interpretation iii*, 79).   89 Isa. 9:6   90 According to the Talmud, Melchizedek was a title for Shem; his father was Noach (b.Nedarim 32b).

mention. Now I need not rehearse the matter; what I have said may suffice. Behold, the scriptures are before you; if you will turn from them, it shall be to your own destruction.

3 And now it came to pass that when Alma had said these words unto them, he stretched forth his hand unto them and cried with a mighty voice, saying, Now is the time to repent, for the day of salvation draws near! Yes, and the voice of YHWH by the mouth of angels does declare it unto all nations, yes, does declare it that they may have glad tidings of great joy. Yes, and he does sound these glad tidings among all his people, yes, even to them that are scattered abroad upon the face of the earth;[91] wherefore, they have come unto us. And they are made known unto us in plain terms, that we may understand, that we cannot err, and this because of our **being wanderers in a strange land**.[92] Therefore, we are thus highly favored, for we have these glad tidings declared unto us in all parts of our vineyard. For behold, angels are declaring it unto many at this time in our land; and this is for the purpose of preparing the hearts of the children of men to receive his word at the time of his coming in his glory. And now we only wait to hear the joyful news declared unto us by the mouth of angels of his coming, for the time comes, we know not how soon. Would to Elohim that it might be in my day, but let it be sooner or later, in it I will rejoice. And it shall be made known unto just and holy men by the mouth of angels at the time of his coming, that the words of our fathers may be fulfilled according to that which they have spoken concerning him, which was according to the spirit of prophecy which was in them.

4 And now, my brothers, I wish from the inmost part of my heart — yes, with great anxiety even unto pain — that you would **hearken unto my words**,[93] and cast off your sins, and not procrastinate the day of your repentance, but that you would humble yourselves before YHWH, and call on his holy name, and watch and pray continually, that you may not be tempted above that which you can bear,[94] and thus be led by the Holy Spirit, becoming humble, meek, submissive, patient, full of love and all long-suffering, having faith on YHWH, having a hope that you shall receive Eternal life, having the love of Elohim always in your hearts, that you may be lifted up

---

91 3 Nefi 7:3 **92** Ex. 2:22 **93** Deut. 18:19 **94** 3 Nefi 8:8

at the last day and enter into his rest. And may YHWH grant unto you repentance, that you may not bring down his wrath upon you, that you may not be bound down by the chains of She'ol, that you may not suffer the second death. And Alma spoke many more words unto the people which are not written in this book.

5 And after Alma had made an end of speaking unto the people, many of them did believe on his words and began to repent and to search the scriptures. But the more part of them were desirous that they might destroy Alma and Amulek, for they were angry with Alma because of the plainness of his words unto Zeezrom. And they also said that Amulek had lied unto them, and had reviled against their law, and also against their lawyers and judges. And they were also angry with Alma and Amulek; and because they had testified so plainly against their wickedness, they sought to put them away secretly. But it came to pass that they did not, but they took them, and bound them with strong cords, and took them before the chief judge of the land. And the people went forth and witnessed against them, testifying that they had reviled against the law, and their lawyers and judges of the land, and also all the people that were in the land, and also testified that there was but one Elohim, and that he should send his Son among the people, but he should not save them; and many such things did the people testify against Alma and Amulek. And now this was done before the chief judge of the land. And it came to pass that Zeezrom was astonished at the words which had been spoken. And he also knew concerning the blindness of the minds which he had caused among the people by his lying words. And his soul began to be tormented under a consciousness of his own guilt — yes, he began to be **encircled about by the pains of She'ol**.[95]

6 And it came to pass that he began to cry unto the people, saying, Behold, I am guilty, and these men are spotless before Elohim! And he began to plead for them from that time forth. But they reviled him, saying, Are you also possessed with HaSatan? And they spit upon him and cast him out from among them, and also all those who believed in the words which had been spoken by Alma and Amulek. And they cast them out and sent men to cast stones at them. And they brought their wives and children together, and whosoever believed

---

95 Ps. 116:3

or had been taught to believe in the word of Elohim, they caused that they should be **cast into the fire**.⁹⁶ And they also brought forth their records which contained the holy scriptures and **cast them into the fire**⁹⁷ also, that they might be burned and destroyed by fire.

7 And it came to pass that they took Alma and Amulek and carried them forth to the place of martyrdom, that they might witness the destruction of those who were consumed by fire. And when Amulek saw the pains of the women and children who were being consumed in the fire, he was also pained, and he said unto Alma, How can we witness this awful scene? Therefore, let us stretch forth our hands and exercise the power of Elohim which is in us, and save them from the flames. But Alma said unto him, The spirit constrains me that I must not stretch forth my hand. For behold, YHWH receives them up unto himself in glory. And he does allow that they may do this thing, or that the people may do this thing unto them according to the hardness of their hearts, that the judgments which he shall exercise upon them in his wrath may be just. And the blood of the innocent shall stand as a witness against them, yes, and cry mightily against them at the last day. Now Amulek said unto Alma, Behold, perhaps they will burn us also. And Alma said, Be it according to the will of YHWH. But behold, our work is not finished; therefore, they burn us not.

8 Now it came to pass that when the bodies of those who had been cast into the fire were consumed, and also the records which were cast in with them, the chief judge of the land came and stood before Alma and Amulek as they were bound, and he struck them with his hand upon their cheeks, and said unto them, After what you have seen, will you preach again unto this people that they shall be cast into a lake of fire and brimstone? Behold, you see that you had not power to save those who had been cast into the fire, neither has Elohim saved them because they were of your faith. And the judge struck them again upon their cheeks and asked, What say you for yourselves? Now this judge was after the order and faith of Nehor, who slew Gideon. And it came to pass that Alma and Amulek answered him nothing. And he struck them again and delivered them to the officers to be cast into prison. And when they had been

---

96 Ps. 140:11 (10) **97** Jer. 22:7

cast into prison three days, there came many lawyers, and judges, and kohanim, and teachers, who were of the profession of Nehor; and they came in unto the prison to see them. And they questioned them about many words, but they answered them nothing. And it came to pass that the judge stood before them and said, Why do you not answer the words of this people? Do you not know that I have power to deliver you up unto the flames? And he commanded them to speak, but they answered nothing.

9 And it came to pass that they departed and went their ways, but came again the next day. And the judge also struck them again on their cheeks. And many came forth also and struck them, saying, Will you stand again and judge this people and condemn our law? If you have such great power, why do you not deliver yourselves? And many such things did they say unto them, gnashing their teeth upon them and spitting upon them, and saying, How shall we look when we are damned? And many such things, yes, all manner of such things did they say unto them. And thus they did mock them for many days. And they did withhold food from them that they might hunger, and water that they might thirst; and they also did take from them their clothes that they were naked, and thus they were bound with strong cords and confined in prison.

10 And it came to pass, after they had thus suffered for many days (and it was on the twelfth day in the tenth month in the tenth year of the reign of the judges over the people of Nefi), that the chief judge over the land of Ammonihah, and many of their teachers, and their lawyers went in unto the prison where Alma and Amulek were bound with cords. And the chief judge stood before them and struck them again, and said unto them, If you have the power of Elohim, deliver yourselves from these bands, and then we will believe that YHWH will destroy this people according to your words. And it came to pass that they all went forth and struck them saying the same words, even until the last. And when the last had spoken unto them, the power of Elohim was upon Alma and Amulek, and they arose and stood upon their feet. And Alma cried, saying, How long shall we suffer these great afflictions, O YHWH? O YHWH, give us strength according to our faith which is in Mashiach, even unto deliverance. And they broke the cords with which they were bound. And when the people saw this, they began to flee, for the fear of destruction had come upon them.

¹¹ And it came to pass that so great was their fear that they fell to the earth and did not reach the outer door of the prison. And the earth shook mightily, and the walls of the prison were torn in half so that they fell to the earth; and the chief judge, and the lawyers, and kohanim, and teachers, who beat upon Alma and Amulek, were slain by the fall thereof. And Alma and Amulek came forth out of the prison, and they were not hurt, for YHWH had granted unto them power according to their faith which was in Mashiach. And they straightway came forth out of the prison, and they were loosed from their bands. And the prison had fallen to the earth, and every soul who was within the walls thereof, except it was Alma and Amulek, were slain. And they straightway came forth into the city. Now the people, having heard a great noise, came running together by multitudes to know the cause of it. And when they saw Alma and Amulek coming forth out of the prison, and the walls thereof had fallen to the earth, they were struck with great fear and fled from the presence of Alma and Amulek, even as a goat flees with her young from two lions; and thus they did flee from the presence of Alma and Amulek.

¹² And it came to pass that Alma and Amulek were commanded to depart out of that city. And they departed and came out, even into the land of Sidom. And behold, there they found all the people who had departed out of the land of Ammonihah, who had been cast out and stoned because they believed in the words of Alma. And they related unto them all that had happened unto their wives and children, and also concerning themselves and of their power of deliverance. And also Zeezrom lay sick at Sidom with a burning fever, which was caused by the great tribulations of his mind on account of his wickedness, for he supposed that Alma and Amulek were no more. And he supposed that they had been slain because of his iniquity. And this great sin, and his many other sins, did torment his mind until it did become exceedingly sore, having no deliverance; therefore, he began to be scorched with a burning heat. Now when he heard that Alma and Amulek were in the land of Sidom, his heart began to take courage. And he sent a message immediately unto them, desiring them to come unto him.

¹³ And it came to pass that they went immediately, obeying the message which he had sent unto them, and they went in unto the house, unto Zeezrom. And they found him upon his bed, sick, being

very low with a burning fever; and his mind also was exceedingly sore because of his iniquities. And when he saw them, he stretched forth his hand and implored them that they would heal him.

14 And it came to pass that Alma said unto him, taking him by the hand, Do you believe in the power of Mashiach unto salvation? And he answered and said, Yes, I believe all the words that you have taught. And Alma said, If you believe in the redemption of Mashiach, you can be healed. And he said, Yes, I believe according to your words. And then Alma cried unto YHWH, saying, O YHWH our Elohim, have mercy on this man, and heal him according to his faith which is in Mashiach. And when Alma had said these words, Zeezrom leaped upon his feet and began to walk. And this was done to the great astonishment of all the people, and the knowledge of this went forth throughout all the land of Sidom. And Alma immersed Zeezrom unto YHWH, and he began from that time forth to preach unto the people. And Alma established an assembly in the land of Sidom, and consecrated kohanim and teachers in the land, to wash by immersion unto YHWH whosoever were desirous to be immersed.

15 And it came to pass that they were many, for they did gather in from all the region round about Sidom and were immersed. But as to the people that were in the land of Ammonihah, they yet remained a hard-hearted and a stiffnecked people. And they repented not of their sins, ascribing all the power of Alma and Amulek to HaSatan, for they were of the profession of Nehor and did not believe in the repentance of their sins.

16 And it came to pass that Alma and Amulek — Amulek having abandoned all his gold, and his silver, and his precious things, which were in the land of Ammonihah, for the word of Elohim, he being rejected by those who were once his friends, and also by his father and his kindred — therefore, after Alma having established the assembly at Sidom, seeing a great restraint, yes, seeing that the people were restrained as to the pride of their hearts, and began to humble themselves before Elohim, and began to assemble themselves together at their sanctuaries to worship Elohim before the altar, watching and praying continually, that they might be delivered from HaSatan, and from death, and from destruction — now as I said, Alma having seen all these things, therefore he took Amulek and came over to the land of Zerach'mla, and took him to his own house, and

did administer unto him in his tribulations and strengthened him in YHWH. And thus ended the tenth year[98] of the reign of the judges over the people of Nefi.

11 And it came to pass in the eleventh year of the reign of the judges over the people of Nefi, on the fifth day of the second month – there having been much shalom in the land of Zerach'mla, there having been no wars nor contentions for a certain number of years, even until the fifth day of the second month in the eleventh year – there was a cry of war heard throughout the land. For behold, the armies of the Lamanites had come in on the wilderness side into the borders of the land, even into the city of Ammonihah, and began to slay the people and to destroy the city.

2 And now it came to pass, before the Nefites could raise a sufficient army to drive them out of the land, they had destroyed the people who were in the city of Ammonihah, and also some around the borders of Noach, and taken others captive into the wilderness.

3 Now it came to pass that the Nefites were desirous to obtain those who had been carried away captive into the wilderness. Therefore, he that had been appointed chief captain over the armies of the Nefites (and his name was Tzuram, and he had two sons, Lechi and Aha), now Tzuram and his two sons, knowing that Alma was Kohen HaGadol over the assembly, and having heard that he had the spirit of prophecy, therefore they went unto him and desired of him to know where YHWH would that they should go into the wilderness, in search of their brothers who had been taken captive by the Lamanites. And it came to pass that Alma inquired of YHWH concerning the matter.

4 And Alma returned and said unto them, Behold, the Lamanites will cross the river Tzidon in the south wilderness away up beyond the borders of the land of Manti. And behold, there shall you meet them on the east of the river Tzidon, and there YHWH will deliver unto you your brothers who have been taken captive by the Lamanites.

5 And it came to pass that Tzuram and his sons crossed over the river Tzidon with their armies, and marched away beyond the borders of Manti into the south wilderness which was on the east side of the river Tzidon. And they came upon the armies of the Lamanites,

---

[98] ~82 BCE

ALMA 11:6

and the Lamanites were scattered and driven into the wilderness. And they took their brothers who had been taken captive by the Lamanites; and there was not one soul of them who had been lost that were taken captive. And they were brought by their brothers to possess their own lands. And thus ended the eleventh year of the judges, the Lamanites having been driven out of the land, and the people of Ammonihah were destroyed — yes, every living soul of the Ammonihahites was destroyed, and also their great city, which they said Elohim could not destroy because of its greatness. But behold, in one day it was left desolate, and their carcasses were mangled by dogs and by wild beasts of the wilderness. Nevertheless, after many days their dead bodies were heaped up upon the face of the earth, and they were covered with a shallow covering. And now so great was the scent thereof that the people did not go in to possess the land of Ammonihah for many years. And it was called the Desolation of Nehors, for they were of the profession of Nehor who were slain; and their lands remained desolate. And the Lamanites did not come again to war against the Nefites until the fourteenth year of the reign of the judges over the people of Nefi. And thus for three years did the people of Nefi have continual shalom in all the land.

⁶And Alma and Amulek went forth preaching repentance unto the people in their Temples, and in their sanctuaries, and also in their synagogues, which were built after the manner of the Y'hudim.[99] And as many as would hear their words, unto them they did teach the word of Elohim, without any respect of persons, continually. And thus did Alma and Amulek go forth, and also many more who had been chosen for the work to preach the word throughout all the land. And the establishment of the assembly became general throughout the land, in all the region round about, among all the people of the Nefites.

⁷And there was no inequality among them, for YHWH did pour out his spirit on all the face of the land to prepare the minds of the children of men, or to prepare their hearts to receive the word which should be taught among them at the time of his coming, that they might not be hardened against the word, that they might not be unbelieving and go on to destruction, but that they might receive

---

99 2 Nefi 4:3

the word with joy, and as a branch, be grafted into the true vine,[100] that they might enter into the rest of YHWH their Elohim.

8 Now those kohanim who did go forth among the people did preach against all lyings, and deceivings, and envyings, and strifes, and malice, and revilings, and stealing, robbing, plundering, murdering, committing adultery, and all manner of lustfulness, crying that these things ought not so to be; holding forth things which must shortly come, yes, holding forth the coming of the Son of Elohim, his sufferings and death, and the resurrection of the dead. And many of the people did inquire concerning the place where the Son of Elohim should come; and they were taught that he would appear unto them after his resurrection; and this the people did hear with great joy and gladness. And now, after the assembly having been established throughout all the land, having got the victory over HaSatan, and the word of Elohim being preached in its purity in all the land, and YHWH pouring out his blessings upon the people, thus ended the fourteenth year of the reign of the judges over the people of Nefi.

An account of the sons of Moshiyah, who rejected their rights to the kingdom for the word of Elohim and went up to the land of Nefi to preach to the Lamanites. Their sufferings and deliverance according to the record of Alma.[101]

12 And now it came to pass that as Alma was journeying from the land of Gideon, southward, away to the land of Manti, behold, to his astonishment he met the sons of Moshiyah journeying towards the land of Zerach'mla. Now these sons of Moshiyah were with Alma at the time the angel first appeared unto him. Therefore, Alma did rejoice exceedingly to see his brothers; and what added more to his joy – they were still his brothers in YHWH. Yes, and they had grown strong in the knowledge of the truth, for they were men of a sound understanding, and they had searched the scriptures diligently that they might know the word of Elohim. But this is not all. They had given themselves to much prayer and fasting, therefore they had the spirit of prophecy and the spirit of revelation; and when they taught, they taught with power and authority, even as with the

---

100 1 Nefi 4:3   101 Moshiyah 11:29

ALMA 12:2

power and authority of Elohim.¹⁰² And they had been teaching the word of Elohim for the space of fourteen years among the Lamanites, having had much success in bringing many to the knowledge of the truth. Yes, by the power of their words, many were brought before the altar of Elohim to call on his name and confess their sins before him. Now these are the circumstances which attended them in their journeyings, for they had many afflictions: they did suffer much, both in the body and in mind, such as hunger, thirst, and fatigue, and also much labor in the spirit. Now these were their journeyings: having taken leave of their father Moshiyah in the first year of the reign of the judges, having refused the kingdom which their father was desirous to confer upon them (and also this was the mind of the people); nevertheless, they departed out of the land of Zerach'mla, and took their swords, and their spears, and their bows, and their arrows, and their slings – and this they did that they might provide food for themselves while in the wilderness. And thus they departed into the wilderness with their numbers which they had selected, to go up to the land of Nefi to preach the word of Elohim unto the Lamanites.

2 And it came to pass that they journeyed many days in the wilderness, and they fasted much and prayed much that YHWH would grant unto them a portion of his spirit to go with them and abide with them, that they might be an instrument in the hands of Elohim to bring, if it were possible, their brothers the Lamanites to the knowledge of the truth, to the knowledge of the baseness of the traditions of their fathers which were not correct.¹⁰³

3 And it came to pass that YHWH did visit them with his spirit, and said unto them, Be comforted; and they were comforted. And YHWH said unto them also, Go forth among the Lamanites, your brothers, and establish my word; yet you shall be patient in long-suffering and afflictions, that you may show forth good examples unto me. And I will make an instrument of you in my hands unto the salvation of many souls. And it came to pass that the hearts of the sons of Moshiyah, and also those who were with them, took courage to go forth unto the Lamanites to declare unto them the word of Elohim.

---

102 3 Nefi 5:15; Alma 3:8   103 Moshiyah 6:12

4 And it came to pass when they had arrived in the borders of the land of the Lamanites, that they separated themselves and departed one from another, trusting in YHWH that they should meet again at the close of their harvest; for they supposed that great was the work which they had undertaken. And assuredly it was great, for they had undertaken to preach the word of Elohim to a wild, and a hardened, and a ferocious people, a people who delighted in murdering the Nefites, and robbing and plundering them. **And their hearts were set upon riches**,[104] or upon gold and silver and precious stones; yet they sought to obtain these things by murdering and plundering, that they might not labor for them with their own hands. Thus, they were a very indolent people, many of whom did worship idols. And the curse of Elohim had fallen upon them because of the traditions of their fathers, even though the promises of YHWH were extended unto them on the conditions of repentance.[105] Therefore, this was the cause for which the sons of Moshiyah had undertaken the work — that perhaps they might bring them unto repentance, that perhaps they might bring them to know of the plan of redemption. Therefore, they separated themselves one from another and went forth among them, every man alone, according to the word and power of Elohim which was given unto him.

5 Now Ammon being the chief among them, or rather, he did administer unto them, he departed from them after having blessed them according to their several stations, having made known the word of Elohim unto them, or administered unto them, before his departure. And thus they took their several journeys throughout the land. And Ammon went to the land of Yishma'el, the land being called after the sons of Yishma'el who also became Lamanites. And as Ammon entered the land of Yishma'el, the Lamanites took him and bound him, as was their custom to bind all the Nefites who fell into their hands and carry them before the king. And thus it was left to the pleasure of the king to slay them, or to retain them in captivity, or to cast them into prison, or to cast them out of his land, according to his will and pleasure. And thus Ammon was carried before the king who was over the land of Yishma'el; and his name was Lamoni, and he was a descendant of Yishma'el. And the king inquired of Ammon

---

104 Ps. 62:11 (10) **105** 2 Nefi 1:1-2; Alma 7:3

ALMA 12:6

if it were his desire to dwell in the land among the Lamanites, or among his people. And Ammon said unto him, Yes, I desire to dwell among this people for a time, yes, and perhaps until the day I die.

⁶And it came to pass that king Lamoni was much pleased with Ammon, and caused that his bands should be loosed; and he would that Ammon should take one of his daughters to wife. But Ammon said unto him, No, but I will be your servant. Therefore, Ammon became a servant to king Lamoni. And it came to pass that he was set among other servants to watch the flocks of Lamoni, according to the custom of the Lamanites. And after he had been in the service of the king three days, as he was with the Lamanitish servants going forth with their flocks to the place of water, which was called the water of Sebus —and all the Lamanites drove their flocks here that they may have water— therefore, as Ammon and the servants of the king were driving forth their flocks to this place of water, behold, a certain number of the Lamanites, who had been with their flocks to water, stood and scattered the flocks of Ammon and the servants of the king; and they scattered them insomuch that they fled many ways.

⁷Now the servants of the king began to murmur, saying, Now the king will slay us, as he has our brothers, because their flocks were scattered by the wickedness of these men. And they began to weep exceedingly, saying, Behold, our flocks are scattered already. Now they wept because of the fear of being slain. Now when Ammon saw this, his heart was swollen within him with joy; for, said he, I will show forth my power unto these my fellow servants, or the power which is in me, in restoring these flocks unto the king, that I may win the hearts of these my fellow servants, that I may lead them to believe in my words. Now these were the thoughts of Ammon when he saw the affliction of those whom he termed to be his brothers.

⁸And it came to pass that he soothed them by his words, saying, My brothers, be of good cheer, and let us go in search of the flocks, and we will gather them together and bring them back unto the place of water. And thus we will reserve the flocks unto the king and he will not slay us.

⁹And it came to pass that they went in search of the flocks, and they did follow Ammon. And they rushed forth with much swiftness, and did go in front of the flocks of the king, and did gather them together again to the place of water. And those men again stood to

scatter their flocks, but Ammon said unto his brothers, Encircle the flocks round about that they flee not, and I will go and contend with these men who do scatter our flocks. Therefore, they did as Ammon had commanded them; and he went forth and stood to contend with those who stood by the waters of Sebus. And they were in number not a few, therefore they did not fear Ammon, for they supposed that one of their men could slay him according to their pleasure. For they knew not that YHWH had promised Moshiyah that he would deliver his sons out of their hands, neither did they know anything concerning YHWH. Therefore, they delighted in the destruction of their brothers, and for this cause they stood to scatter the flocks of the king.

10 But Ammon stood forth and began to cast stones at them with his sling; yes, with mighty power he did sling stones among them. And thus he slew a certain number of them, insomuch that they began to be astonished at his power. Nevertheless, they were angry because of the slain of their brothers, and they were determined that he should fall. Therefore, seeing that they could not hit him with their stones, they came forth with clubs to slay him. But behold, every man that lifted his club to strike Ammon, he cut off their arms with his sword, for he did withstand their blows by striking their arms with the edge of his sword, insomuch that they began to be astonished and began to flee before him. Yes, and they were not a few in number; and he caused them to flee by the strength of his arm. Now six of them had fallen by the sling, but he slew none except it were their leader with his sword; and he struck off as many of their arms as were lifted against him, and they were not a few. And when he had driven them afar off, he returned, and they watered their flocks and returned them to the pasture of the king, and then went in unto the king, bearing the arms which had been cut off by the sword of Ammon, of those who sought to slay him. And they were carried in unto the king for a testimony of the things which they had done.

11 And it came to pass that king Lamoni caused that his servants should stand forth and testify to all the things which they had seen concerning the matter. And when they had all testified to the things which they had seen, and he had learned of the faithfulness of Ammon in preserving his flocks, and also of his great power in contending against those who sought to slay him, he was astonished exceedingly, and said, Surely this is more than a man. Behold, is not this

the Great Spirit who does send such great punishments upon this people because of their murders? And they answered the king and said, Whether he be the Great Spirit or a man, we know not; but this much we do know, that he cannot be slain by the enemies of the king, neither can they scatter the king's flocks when he is with us because of his expertness and great strength. Therefore, we know that he is a friend to the king. And now, O king, we do not believe that a man has such great power, for we know that he cannot be slain. And now when the king heard these words, he said unto them, Now I know that it is the Great Spirit, and he has come down at this time to preserve your lives, that I might not slay you as I did your brothers. Now this is the Great Spirit of whom our fathers have spoken. Now this was the tradition of Lamoni which he had received from his father — that there was a Great Spirit. Even though they believed in a Great Spirit, they supposed that whatsoever they did was right. Nevertheless, Lamoni began to fear exceedingly, with fear[106] that he had done wrong in slaying his servants; for he had slain many of them because their brothers had scattered their flocks at the place of water. And thus, because they had had their flocks scattered, they were slain. Now it was the practice of these Lamanites to stand by the waters of Sebus to scatter the flocks of the people, that thereby they might drive away many that were scattered unto their own land, it being a practice of plunder among them.

12 And it came to pass that king Lamoni inquired of his servants, saying, Where is this man that has such great power? And they said unto him, Behold, he is feeding your horses. Now the king had commanded his servants, previous to the time of the watering of their flocks, that they should prepare his horses and his chariots and conduct him forth to the land of Nefi, for there had been a great feast appointed at the land of Nefi by the father of Lamoni, who was king over all the land. Now when king Lamoni heard that Ammon was preparing his horses and his chariots, he was more astonished because of the faithfulness of Ammon, saying, Surely there has not been any servant among all my servants that has been so faithful as this man, for even he does remember all my commandments to execute them.

---

106 Another example of the Cognate Accusative Hebraic construction. See footnote 25.

Now I surely know that this is the Great Spirit, and I would desire him that he come in unto me, but I dare not.

13 And it came to pass that when Ammon had made ready the horses and the chariots for the king and his servants, he went in unto the king. And he saw that the countenance of the king was changed. Therefore, he was about to return out of his presence, and one of the king's servants said unto him, Rabbanah[107] — which is (being interpreted) powerful or great[108] king, considering their kings to be powerful; and thus he said unto him, Rabbanah — the king desires you to stay. Therefore, Ammon turned himself unto the king and said unto him, What will you that I should do for you, O king? And the king answered him not for the space of an hour according to their time, for he knew not what he should say unto him. And it came to pass that Ammon said unto him again, What do you desire of me? But the king answered him not.

14 And it came to pass that Ammon, being filled with the Ruach Elohim, therefore he perceived the thoughts of the king. And he said unto him, Is it because you have heard that I defended your servants and your flocks? And slew seven of their brothers with the sling and with the sword, and cut off the arms of others in order to defend your flocks and your servants? Behold, is it this that causes your marvelings? I say unto you, why is it that your marvelings are so great? Behold, I am a man, and am your servant. Therefore, whatsoever you desire which is right, that will I do. Now when the king had heard these words, he marveled again, for he beheld that Ammon could discern his thoughts. But despite this, king Lamoni did open his mouth and said unto him, Who are you? Are you that Great Spirit who knows all things? Ammon answered and said unto him, I am not. And the king said, How do you know the thoughts of my heart? You may speak boldly and tell me concerning these things, and also tell me by what power you slew and cut off the arms of my brothers that scattered my flocks. And now, if you will tell me concerning these things, whatsoever you desire I will give unto you.

---

107 Compare with the Aramaic title רבנא. Defined in the Soncino Talmud (Pesachim 115b n. 6) as follows: "'Rabbana' is a Babylonian title, probably the equivalent of the Palestinian 'Rabban' lit., 'our teacher,' which is a peculiar title of honour, higher than 'Rabbi.'"   108 The Hebrew word for "great" here was likely *rav* רב, from the same root as "Rabbanah."

And if it were needed, I would guard you with my armies, but I know that you are more powerful than all they. Nevertheless, whatsoever you desire of me, I will grant it unto you. Now Ammon being wise yet harmless, he said unto Lamoni, Will you hearken unto my words if I tell you by what power I do these things? And this is the thing that I desire of you. And the king answered him and said, Yes, I will believe all your words. And thus he was caught by the craftiness of Ammon.

15 And Ammon began to speak unto him with boldness, and said unto him, Do you believe that there is an Elohim? And he answered unto him, I do not know what that means. And then Ammon said, Do you believe that there is a Great Spirit? And he said, Yes. And Ammon said, This is Elohim. And Ammon said unto him again, Do you believe that this Great Spirit, who is Elohim, created all things which are in Heaven and in the earth? And he said, Yes, I believe that he created all things which are in the earth, but I do not know the Heavens. And Ammon said unto him, The Heavens are a place where Elohim dwells, and all his holy angels. And king Lamoni said, Is it above the earth? And Ammon said, Yes, and he looks down upon all the children of men; and he knows all the thoughts and intents of the heart, for by his hand were they all created from the beginning. And king Lamoni said, I believe all these things which you have spoken. Are you sent from Elohim? Ammon said unto him, I am a man, and man in the beginning was created after the image of Elohim. And I am called by his Holy Spirit to teach these things unto this people, that they may be brought to a knowledge of that which is just and true; and a portion of that spirit dwells in me, which gives me knowledge and also power, according to my faith and desires which are in Elohim.

16 Now when Ammon had said these words, he began at the creation of the world, and also at the creation of Adam, and told him all the things concerning the fall of man, and rehearsed and laid before him the records and the holy scriptures of the people which had been spoken by the prophets, even down to the time that their father Lechi left Yerushalayim. And he also rehearsed unto them (for he spoke unto the king and to his servants) all the journeyings of their fathers in the wilderness, and all their sufferings with hunger and thirst, and their travel, and so forth. And he also rehearsed unto them concerning the rebellions of Laman, and L'mu'el, and the sons of Yishma'el — yes, all their rebellions did he relate unto them. And

he expounded unto them all the records and scriptures from the time that Lechi left Yerushalayim down to the present time. But this is not all, for he explained unto them the plan of redemption which was prepared from the foundation of the world;[109] and he also made known unto them concerning the coming of Mashiach, and all the works of YHWH did he make known unto them.[110]

17 And it came to pass that after he had said all these things and expounded them to the king, that the king believed all his words. And he began to cry unto YHWH, saying, O YHWH, have mercy, according to your abundant mercy which you have had upon the people of Nefi, have also upon me and my people. And now when he had said this, he fell unto the earth as if he were dead. And it came to pass that his servants took him, and carried him in unto his wife, and laid him upon a bed. And he lay as if he were dead for the space of two days and two nights; and his wife, and his sons, and his daughters mourned over him after the manner of the Lamanites, greatly lamenting his loss.

18 And it came to pass that after two days and two nights, they were about to take his body and lay it into a sepulcher which they had made for the purpose of burying their dead. Now the queen having heard of the fame of Ammon, therefore she sent and desired that he should come in unto her. And it came to pass that Ammon did as he was commanded and went in unto the queen, and desired to know what she would that he should do. And she said unto him, The servants of my husband have made it known unto me that you are a prophet of a holy Elohim, and that you have power to do many mighty works in his name; therefore, if this is the case, I would that you should go in and see my husband, for he has been laid upon his bed for the space of two days and two nights. And some say that he is not dead, but others say that he is dead, and that he stinks, and that he ought to be placed in the sepulcher; but as for myself, to me he does not stink.

19 Now this was what Ammon desired, for he knew that king Lamoni was under the power of Elohim; he knew that the dark veil of unbelief was being cast away from his mind, and the light which did light up his mind — which was the light of the glory of Elohim, which was a marvelous light of his goodness — yes, this light had

---

109 Alma 9:6-8 110 1 Nefi 3:8-14; Moshiyah 1:13-18

infused much joy into his soul, the cloud of darkness having been dispelled, and that the light of everlasting life was lit[111] up in his soul. Yes, he knew that this had overcome his natural frame, and he was carried away in Elohim.[112] Therefore, what the queen desired of him was his only desire. Therefore, he went in to see the king according as the queen had desired him; and he saw the king and he knew that he was not dead. And he said unto the queen, He is not dead, but he sleeps in Elohim, and tomorrow he shall rise again; therefore, bury him not. And Ammon said unto her, Do you believe this? And she said unto him, I have had no witness except your word and the word of our servants; nevertheless, I believe that it shall be according as you have said. And Ammon said unto her, Blessed are you because of your exceeding faith. I say unto you, woman, there has not been such great faith among all the people of the Nefites.

20 And it came to pass that she watched over the bed of her husband from that time, even until that time the next day which Ammon had appointed that he should rise. And it came to pass that he arose according to the words of Ammon; and as he arose, he stretched forth his hand unto the woman, and said, Blessed be the name of Elohim, and blessed are you; for as sure as you live, behold, I have seen my Redeemer;[113] and he shall come forth and be born of a woman, and he shall redeem all mankind who believe on his name. Now when he had said these words, his heart was swollen within him and he sunk again with joy; and the queen also sunk down, being overpowered by the spirit. Now Ammon, seeing the spirit of YHWH poured out according to his prayers upon the Lamanites—his brothers—who had been the cause of so much mourning among the Nefites, or among all the people of Elohim, because of their iniquities and their traditions—he fell upon his knees and began to pour out his soul in prayer and thanksgiving to Elohim for what he had done for his brothers; and he was also overpowered with joy, and thus they all three had sunk to the earth. Now when the servants of the king had seen that they had fallen, they also began to cry unto Elohim, for the fear of YHWH had come upon them also, for it was they who had stood before the king and testified unto him concerning the great power of Ammon.

---

111 Isa. 60:19-20   112 Moshiyah 11:25-28   113 2 Nefi 8:2

21 And it came to pass that they did call on the name of YHWH in their might, even until they had all fallen to the earth, except it were one of the Lamanitish women whose name was Abish. She, having been converted unto YHWH for many years on account of a remarkable vision of her father (thus having been converted to YHWH), yet she never had made it known. Therefore, when she saw that all the servants of Lamoni had fallen to the earth, and also her mistress the queen, and the king, and Ammon lay prostrate upon the earth, she knew that it was the power of Elohim; and supposing that this was an opportunity, by making known unto the people what had happened among them, that by beholding this scene it would cause them to believe in the power of Elohim, therefore she ran forth from house to house making it known unto the people. And they began to assemble themselves together unto the house of the king.

22 And there came a multitude, and to their astonishment they beheld the king, and the queen, and their servants, prostrate upon the earth; and they all lay there as though they were dead. And they also saw Ammon, and behold, he was a Nefite. And now the people began to murmur among themselves, some saying that it was a great evil that had come upon them, or upon the king and his house, because he had allowed that the Nefite should remain in the land. But others rebuked them, saying, The king has brought this evil upon his house because he slew his servants who had had their flocks scattered at the waters of Sebus. And they were also rebuked by those men who had stood at the waters of Sebus and scattered the flocks which belonged to the king, for they were angry with Ammon because of the number which he had slain of their brothers at the waters of Sebus while defending the flocks of the king. Now one of them, whose brother had been slain with the sword of Ammon, being exceedingly angry with Ammon, drew his sword and went forth, that he might let it fall upon Ammon to slay him. And as he lifted the sword to strike him, behold, he fell dead. Now we see that Ammon could not be slain, for YHWH had said unto Moshiyah, his father, I will spare him, and it shall be unto him according to your faith. Therefore, Moshiyah entrusted him unto YHWH.

23 And it came to pass that when the multitude beheld that the man had fallen dead who lifted the sword to slay Ammon, fear came upon them all, and they dared not put forth their hands to touch him, or

any of those who had fallen; and they began to marvel again among themselves about what could be the cause of this great power, or what all these things could mean.

24 And it came to pass that there were many among them who said that Ammon was the Great Spirit, and others said he was sent by the Great Spirit; but others rebuked them all, saying that he was a monster who had been sent from the Nefites to torment us. And there were some who said that Ammon was sent by the Great Spirit to afflict them because of their iniquities, and that it was the Great Spirit who had always attended the Nefites, who had continually delivered them out of their hands. And they said that it was this Great Spirit who had destroyed so many of their brothers, the Lamanites. And thus the contention began to be exceedingly sharp among them. And while they were thus contending, the woman servant who had caused the multitude to be gathered together came; and when she saw the contention which was among the multitude, she was exceedingly sorrowful, even unto tears.

25 And it came to pass that she went and took the queen by the hand, that perhaps she might raise her from the ground. And as soon as she touched her hand, she arose and stood upon her feet, and cried with a loud voice, saying, O blessed Yeshua who has saved me from an awful She'ol! O blessed Elohim, have mercy on this people! And when she had said this, she clapped her hands, being filled with joy, speaking many words which were not understood. And when she had done this, she took the king, Lamoni, by the hand; and behold, he arose and stood upon his feet. And he, immediately seeing the contention among his people, went forth and began to rebuke them and to teach them the words which he had heard from the mouth of Ammon. And as many as heard his words believed, and were converted unto YHWH. But there were many among them who would not hear his words; therefore, they went their way.

26 And it came to pass that when Ammon arose, he also administered unto them, as also did all the servants of Lamoni. And they did all declare unto the people the very same thing: that their hearts had been changed, that they had no more desire to do evil. And behold, many did declare unto the people that they had seen angels and

had conversed with them,[114] and thus they had told them things of Elohim and of his righteousness. And it came to pass that there were many that did believe in their words; and as many as did believe were washed by immersion, and they became a righteous people, and they did establish an assembly among them. And thus the work of YHWH did commence among the Lamanites; thus, YHWH did begin to pour out his spirit upon them; and we see that his arm is extended to all people who will repent and believe on his name.

27 And it came to pass that when they had established an assembly in that land, that king Lamoni desired that Ammon should go with him to the land of Nefi, that he might show him unto his father. And the voice of YHWH came to Ammon, saying, You shall not go up to the land of Nefi; for behold, the king will seek your life. But you shall go to the land of Middoni, for behold, your brother Aharon, and also Muloki and Ammah, are in prison.

28 Now it came to pass that when Ammon had heard this, he said unto Lamoni, Behold, my brother and brothers are in prison at Middoni, and I go that I may deliver them. Now Lamoni said unto Ammon, I know in the strength of YHWH you can do all things. But behold, I will go with you to the land of Middoni, for the king of the land of Middoni, whose name is Antiomno, is a friend unto me; therefore, I go to the land of Middoni that I may appease the king of the land, and he will cast your brothers out of prison. Now Lamoni said unto him, Who told you that your brothers were in prison? And Ammon said unto him, No one has told me, except it be Elohim; and he said unto me, Go and deliver your brothers, for they are in prison in the land of Middoni. Now when Lamoni had heard this, he caused that his servants should make ready his horses and his chariots. And he said unto Ammon, Come, I will go with you down to the land of Middoni, and there I will plead with the king that he will cast your brothers out of prison.

29 And it came to pass that as Ammon and Lamoni were journeying there, that they met the father of Lamoni, who was king over all the land. And behold, the father of Lamoni said unto him, Why did you not come to the feast on that great day when I made a feast unto my sons and unto my people?[115] And he also said, Where are you going

---

114 M'roni 7:6 115 This parallels David's absence from Saul's feast in honor of the New

with this Nefite who is one of the children of a liar? And it came to pass that Lamoni rehearsed unto him where he was going, for he feared to offend him. And he also told him all the cause of his remaining in his own kingdom, that he did not go unto his father to the feast which he had prepared. And now when Lamoni had rehearsed unto him all these things, behold, to his astonishment, his father was angry with him, and said, Lamoni, you are going to deliver these Nefites who are sons of a liar. Behold, he robbed our fathers, and now his children have also come among us, that they may, by their cunning and their lies, deceive us, that they again may rob us of our property. Now the father of Lamoni commanded him that he should slay Ammon with the sword. And he also commanded him that he should not go to the land of Middoni, but that he should return with him to the land of Yishma'el. But Lamoni said unto him, I will not slay Ammon, neither will I return to the land of Yishma'el, but I go to the land of Middoni that I may release the brothers of Ammon; for I know that they are just men, and holy prophets of the true Elohim.

30 Now when his father heard these words, he was angry with him, and he drew his sword that he might strike him to the earth. But Ammon stood forth and said unto him, Behold, you shall not slay your son. Nevertheless, it were better that he should fall than you, for behold, he has repented of his sins. But if you should fall at this time in your anger, your soul could not be saved. And again, it is expedient that you should stop, for if you should slay your son, he being an innocent man, his blood would cry from the ground to YHWH his Elohim for vengeance to come upon you, and perhaps you would lose your soul. Now when Ammon had said these words unto him, he answered him, saying, I know that if I should slay my son, that I should shed innocent blood; for it is you that has sought to destroy him. And he stretched forth his hand to slay Ammon, but Ammon withstood his blows, and also struck his arm, that he could not use it. Now when the king saw that Ammon could slay him, he began to plead with Ammon that he would spare his life. But Ammon raised his sword and said unto him, Behold, I will slay you, except you will grant unto me that my brothers may be cast out of prison.

Moon (1 Sam. 20:5, 18, 27) suggesting that this may also have been a New Moon feast.

Now the king, fearing that he should lose his life, said, If you will spare me, I will grant unto you whatsoever you will ask, even to the half of the kingdom.

31 Now when Ammon saw that he had worked upon the old king according to his desire, he said unto him, If you will grant that my brothers may be cast out of prison, and also that Lamoni may retain his kingdom, and that you be not displeased with him, but grant that he may do according to his own desires in whatsoever thing he thinks, then will I spare you; otherwise, I will strike you to the earth. Now when Ammon had said these words, the king began to rejoice because of his life. And when he saw that Ammon had no desire to destroy him, and when he also saw the great love he had for his son Lamoni, he was astonished exceedingly, and said, Because this is all that you have desired, that I would release your brothers and allow that my son Lamoni should retain his kingdom, behold, I will grant unto you that my son may retain his kingdom from this time and for ever, and I will govern him no more. And I will also grant unto you that your brothers may be cast out of prison, and you and your brothers may come unto me in my kingdom, for I shall greatly desire to see you. For the king was greatly astonished at the words which he had spoken, and also at the words which had been spoken by his son Lamoni; therefore, he was desirous to learn them.

32 And it came to pass that Ammon and Lamoni proceeded on their journey towards the land of Middoni. And Lamoni found favor in the eyes of the king of the land; therefore, the brothers of Ammon were brought forth out of prison. And when Ammon did meet them, he was exceedingly sorrowful; for behold, they were naked, and their skins were worn exceedingly because of being bound with strong cords. And they also had suffered hunger, thirst, and all kinds of afflictions; nevertheless, they were patient in all their sufferings. And as it happened, it was their lot to have fallen into the hands of a more hardened and a more stiffnecked people; therefore, they would not hearken unto their words, and they had cast them out, and had beaten them, and had driven them from house to house and from place to place, even until they had arrived at the land of Middoni. And there they were taken and cast into prison, and bound with strong cords, and kept in prison for many days, and were delivered by Lamoni and Ammon.

An account of the preaching of Aharon, and Muloki, and their brothers, to the Lamanites.

13 Now when Ammon and his brothers separated themselves in the borders of the land of the Lamanites, behold, Aharon took his journey towards the land which was called by the Lamanites, Yerushalayim, calling it after the land of their fathers' nativity; and it was away joining the borders of M'raman. Now the Lamanites, and the Amlicites, and the people of Amulon had built a great city which was called Yerushalayim. Now the Lamanites, of themselves, were sufficiently hardened; but the Amlicites and the Amulonites were still harder. Therefore, they did cause the Lamanites that they should harden their hearts, that they should grow stronger in wickedness and their abominations.

2 And it came to pass that Aharon came to the city of Yerushalayim, and first began to preach to the Amlicites. And he began to preach to them in their synagogues, for they had built synagogues after the order of the Nehors, for many of the Amlicites and the Amulonites were after the order of the Nehors. Therefore, as Aharon entered into one of their synagogues to preach unto the people, and as he was speaking unto them, behold, there arose an Amlicite and began to contend with him, saying, What is that that you have testified? Have you seen an angel? Why do not angels appear unto us? Behold, are not this people as good as your people? You also say, except we repent we shall perish. How do you know the thought and intent of our heart? How do you know that we have cause to repent? How do you know that we are not a righteous people? Behold, we have built sanctuaries, and we do assemble ourselves together to worship Elohim. We do believe that Elohim will save all men.

3 Now Aharon said unto him, Do you believe that the Son of Elohim shall come to redeem mankind from their sins? And the man said unto him, We do not believe that you know any such thing. We do not believe in these foolish traditions. We do not believe that you know of things to come, neither do we believe that your fathers, and also that our fathers, did know concerning the things which they spoke of — that which is to come.

4 Now Aharon began to open the scriptures unto them concerning the coming of Mashiach, and also concerning the resurrection of the

dead, and that there could be no redemption for mankind except it were through the death and sufferings of Mashiach, and the atonement of his blood. And it came to pass that as he began to explain these things unto them, they were angry with him, and began to mock him, and they would not hear the words which he spoke. Therefore, when he saw that they would not hear his words, he departed out of the synagogue and came over to a village which was called Ani-anti, and there he found Muloki preaching the word unto them, and also Ammah and his brothers. And they contended with many about the word. And it came to pass that they saw that the people would harden their hearts, therefore they departed and came over into the land of Middoni. And they did preach the word unto many, and few believed on the words which they taught. Nevertheless, Aharon and a certain number of his brothers were taken and cast into prison, and the remainder of them fled out of the land of Middoni unto the regions round about. And those who were cast into prison suffered many things, and they were delivered by the hand of Lamoni and Ammon, and they were fed and clothed. And they went forth again to declare the word; and thus they were delivered for the first time out of prison, and thus they had suffered. And they went forth wherever they were led by the spirit of YHWH, preaching the word of Elohim in every synagogue of the Amlicites, or in every assembly of the Lamanites where they could be admitted.

⁵And it came to pass that YHWH began to bless them, insomuch that they brought many to the knowledge of the truth; yes, they did convince many of their sins, and of the tradition of their fathers which were not correct.

⁶And it came to pass that Ammon and Lamoni returned from the land of Middoni to the land of Yishma'el, which was the land of their inheritance. And king Lamoni would not allow that Ammon should serve him or be his servant, but he caused that there should be synagogues built in the land of Yishma'el; and he caused that his people, or the people who were under his reign, should assemble themselves together. And he did rejoice over them, and he did teach them many things. And he did also declare unto them that they were a people who were under him, and that they were a free people, that they were free from the oppression of the king, his father, for his father had granted unto him that he might reign over the people

who were in the land of Yishma'el and in all the land round about. And he also declared unto them that they might have the liberty of worshipping YHWH their Elohim according to their desires, in whatsoever place they were in, if it were in the land which was under the reign of king Lamoni. And Ammon did preach unto the people of king Lamoni. And it came to pass that he did teach them all things concerning things pertaining to righteousness. And he did exhort them daily with all diligence; and they gave heed unto his word, and they were zealous for keeping the mitzvot of Elohim. Now, as Ammon was thus teaching the people of Lamoni continually, we will return to the account of Aharon and his other brothers; for after he departed from the land of Middoni, he was led by the spirit to the land of Nefi, even to the house of the king which was over all the land, except it were the land of Yishma'el; and he was the father of Lamoni.

7 And it came to pass that he went in unto him, into the king's palace, with his brothers, and bowed himself before the king, and said unto him, Behold, O king, we are the brothers of Ammon whom you have delivered out of prison. And now, O king, if you will spare our lives, we will be your servants. And the king said unto them, Arise, for I will grant unto you your lives, and I will not allow that you shall be my servants, but I will insist that you shall minister unto me, for I have been somewhat troubled in mind because of the generosity and the greatness of the words of your brother Ammon, and I desire to know the cause why he has not come up out of Middoni with you. And Aharon said unto the king, Behold, the spirit of YHWH has called him another way; he has gone to the land of Yishma'el to teach the people of Lamoni. Now the king said unto them, What is this that you have said concerning the spirit of YHWH? Behold, this is the thing which does trouble me. And also, what is this that Ammon said? — If you will repent, you shall be saved, and if you will not repent, you shall be cast off at the last day? And Aharon answered him, and said unto him, Do you believe that there is an Elohim? And the king said, I know that the Amlicites say that there is an Elohim, and I have granted unto them that they should build sanctuaries, that they may assemble themselves together to worship him. And if now you say there is an Elohim, behold, I will believe.[116]

---

116 3 Nefi 5:11

8 And now when Aharon heard this, his heart began to rejoice, and he said, Behold, assuredly as you live, O king, there is an Elohim. And the king said, Is Elohim that Great Spirit that brought our fathers out of the land of Yerushalayim? And Aharon said unto him, Yes, he is that Great Spirit, and **he created all things, both in Heaven and in earth.**[117] Do you believe this? And he said, Yes, I believe that the Great Spirit created all things, and I desire that you should tell me concerning all these things, and I will believe your words.[118]

9 And it came to pass that when Aharon saw that the king would believe his words, he began, from the creation of Adam, reading the scriptures unto the king: how Elohim created man after his own image, and that Elohim gave him mitzvot, and that because of transgression, man had fallen. And Aharon did expound unto him the scriptures from the creation of Adam, laying the fall of man before him, and their carnal state, and also the plan of redemption which was prepared from the foundation of the world, through Mashiach, for all whosoever would believe on his name. And since man had fallen, he could not merit anything of himself. But the suffering and death of Mashiach atones for their sins, through faith and repentance, and so forth, and that he breaks the bands of death that the grave shall have no victory, and that the sting of death should be swallowed up in the hopes of glory. And Aharon did explain all these things unto the king. And it came to pass that after Aharon had explained these things unto him, the king said, What shall I do that I may have this Eternal life of which you have spoken? Yes, what shall I do that I may be born of Elohim, having this wicked spirit rooted out of my breast, and receive his spirit that I may be filled with joy? That I may not be cast off at the last day? Behold, said he, I will give up all that I possess, yes, I will abandon my kingdom that I may receive this great joy. But Aharon said unto him, If you desire this thing, if you will bow down before Elohim — yes, if you repent of all your sins, and will bow down before Elohim, and call on his name in faith, believing that you shall receive, then shall you receive the hope which you desire.[119]

10 And it came to pass that when Aharon had said these words, the king did bow down before YHWH upon his knees, yes, even he did prostrate himself upon the earth, and cried mightily, saying, O

---

117 Gen. 1:1; Ps. 113:6   118 1 Nefi 3:6   119 3 Nefi 8:8; M'roni 7:5

Elohim, Aharon has told me that there is an Elohim, and if there is an Elohim, and if you are Elohim, will you make yourself known unto me? And I will give away all my sins to know you, and that I may be raised from the dead and be saved at the last day. And now when the king had said these words, he was struck as if he were dead.

11 And it came to pass that his servants ran and told the queen all that had happened unto the king, and she came in unto the king; and when she saw him lay as if he were dead, and also Aharon and his brothers standing as though they had been the cause of his fall, she was angry with them, and commanded that her servants, or the servants of the king, should take them and slay them. Now the servants had seen the cause of the king's fall, therefore they dared not lay their hands on Aharon and his brothers. And they pled with the queen, saying, Why do you command that we should slay these men when, behold, one of them is mightier than us all? Therefore, we shall fall before them. Now when the queen saw the fear of the servants, she also began to fear exceedingly that there should some evil come upon her. And she commanded her servants that they should go and call the people, that they might slay Aharon and his brothers.

12 Now when Aharon saw the determination of the queen, and he also knowing the hardness of the hearts of the people, feared that a multitude should assemble themselves together and there should be a great contention and a disturbance among them, therefore he put forth his hand and raised the king from the earth, and said unto him, Stand. And he stood upon his feet, receiving his strength. Now this was done in the presence of the queen and many of his servants. And when they saw it, they greatly marveled and began to fear. And the king stood forth and began to minister unto them. And he did minister unto them insomuch that his whole household was converted unto YHWH. Now there was a multitude gathered together because of the commandment of the queen, and there began to be great murmurings among them because of Aharon and his brothers. But the king stood forth among them and ministered unto them, and they were pacified towards Aharon and those who were with him.

13 And it came to pass that when the king saw that the people were pacified, he caused that Aharon and his brothers should stand forth in the midst of the multitude, and that they should preach the word unto them. And it came to pass that the king sent a proclamation

throughout all the land, among all his people who were in all his land, who were in all the regions round about, which was bordering even to the sea on the east and on the west, and which was divided from the land of Zerach'mla by a narrow strip of wilderness which ran from the sea east even to the sea west, and round about on the borders of the seashore and the borders of the wilderness which was on the north by the land of Zerach'mla, through the borders of Manti by the head of the river Tzidon running from the east towards the west; and thus were the Lamanites and the Nefites divided. Now the more idle part of the Lamanites lived in the wilderness and lived in tents. And they were spread through the wilderness on the west in the land of Nefi, yes, and also on the west of the land of Zerach'mla, in the borders by the seashore, and on the west in the land of Nefi, in the place of their fathers' first inheritance, and thus bordering along by the seashore. And also, there were many Lamanites on the east by the seashore, where the Nefites had driven them. And thus the Nefites were nearly surrounded by the Lamanites. Nevertheless, the Nefites had taken possession of all the northern parts of the land bordering on the wilderness at the head of the river Tzidon, from the east to the west, round about on the wilderness side on the north, even until they came to the land which they called Bountiful. And it bordered upon the land which they called Desolation, it being so far northward that it came into the land which had been peopled and had been destroyed, of whose bones we have spoken, which was discovered by the people of Zerach'mla, it being the place of their first landing. And they came from there up into the south wilderness. Thus, the land on the northward was called Desolation, and the land on the southward was called Bountiful, it being the wilderness which was filled with all manner of wild animals of every kind, a part of which had come from the land northward for food. And now it was only the distance of a day and a half's journey for a Nefite, on the line Bountiful and the land Desolation, from the east to the west sea; and thus the land of Nefi and the land of Zerach'mla were nearly surrounded by water, there being a small neck of land between the land northward and the land southward.

14 And it came to pass that the Nefites had inhabited the land Bountiful, even from the east unto the west sea, and thus the Nefites, in their wisdom, with their guards and their armies, had hemmed

in the Lamanites on the south, that thereby they should have no more possession on the north, that they might not overrun the land northward. Therefore, the Lamanites could have no more possessions, only in the land of Nefi and in the wilderness round about. Now this was wisdom in the Nefites, as the Lamanites were an enemy to them; they would not suffer their afflictions on every side, and also that they might have a country to where they might flee, according to their desires. And now I, after having said this, return again to the account of Ammon, and Aharon, Omner, and Himni, and their brothers.

14 Behold, now it came to pass that the king of the Lamanites sent a proclamation among all his people, that they should not lay their hands on Ammon, or Aharon, or Omner, or Himni, neither their brothers, who should go forth preaching the word of Elohim, in whatsoever place they should be, in any part of their land. Yes, he sent a decree among them that they should not lay their hands on them to bind them, or to cast them into prison, neither should they spit upon them, nor strike them, nor cast them out of their synagogues, nor scourge them, neither should they cast stones at them, but that they should have free access to their houses, and also their Temples, and their sanctuaries; and thus they might go forth and preach the word according to their desires. For the king had been converted unto YHWH, and all his household; therefore, he sent this proclamation throughout the land unto his people, that the word of Elohim might have no obstruction, but that it might go forth throughout all the land, that his people might be convinced concerning the wicked traditions of their fathers, and that they might be convinced that they were all brothers, and that they ought not to murder, nor to plunder, nor to steal, nor to commit adultery, nor to commit any manner of wickedness.

2 And now it came to pass that when the king had sent forth this proclamation, that Aharon and his brothers went forth from city to city and from one house of worship to another, establishing assemblies and consecrating kohanim and teachers throughout the land among the Lamanites, to preach and to teach the word of Elohim among them; and thus they began to have great success. And thousands were brought to the knowledge of YHWH, yes, thousands were brought to believe in the traditions of the Nefites. And they were

taught the records and the prophecies, handed down even to the present time. And as sure as YHWH lives, so sure as many as believed, or as many as were brought to the knowledge of the truth through the preaching of Ammon and his brothers, according to the spirit of revelation, and of prophecy, and the power of Elohim working miracles[120] in them — yes, I say unto you, as YHWH lives, as many of the Lamanites as believed in their preaching and were converted unto YHWH, never did fall away. For they became a righteous people; they did lay down the weapons of their rebellion, that they did not fight against Elohim anymore, neither against any of their brothers.

3 Now these are they who were converted unto YHWH: the people of the Lamanites who were in the land of Yishma'el, and also of the people of the Lamanites who were in the land of Middoni, and also of the people of the Lamanites who were in the city of Nefi, and also of the people of the Lamanites who were in the land of Shilom, and who were in the land of Shemlon, and in the city of L'mu'el, and in the city of Shimnilom; and these are the names of the cities of the Lamanites who were converted unto YHWH. And these are they that laid down the weapons of their rebellion, yes, all their weapons of war, and they were all Lamanites. And the Amlicites were not converted, except only one, neither were any of the Amulonites; but they did harden their hearts, and also the hearts of the Lamanites in that part of the land wherever they dwelt, yes, and all their villages and all their cities. Therefore, we have named all the cities of the Lamanites in which they did repent, and come to the knowledge of the truth, and were converted.

4 And now it came to pass that the king, and those people which were converted, were desirous that they might have a name, that thereby they might be distinguished from their brothers; therefore, the king consulted with Aharon and many of their kohanim concerning the name that they should take upon themselves, that they might be distinguished. And it came to pass that they called their name Anti-Nefi-Lechies; and they were called by this name and were no more called Lamanites. And they began to be a very industrious people, yes, and they were friendly with the Nefites. Therefore, they

---

120 M'raman 4:8

did open a correspondence with them, and the curse of Elohim did no more follow them.

5 And it came to pass that the Amlicites, and the Amulonites, and the Lamanites, who were in the land of Amulon, and also in the land of Helam, and who were in the land of Yerushalayim, and, in short, in all the land round about, who had not been converted and had not taken upon them the name of Anti-Nefi-Lechi, were stirred up by the Amlicites and by the Amulonites to anger against their brothers. And their hatred became exceedingly sore against them, even insomuch that they began to rebel against their king, insomuch that they would not that he should be their king. Therefore, they took up arms against the people of Anti-Nefi-Lechi.

6 Now the king conferred the kingdom upon his son, and he called his name Anti-Nefi-Lechi. And the king died in the very same year that the Lamanites began to make preparations for war against the people of Elohim. Now when Ammon, and his brothers, and all those who had come up with him saw the preparations of the Lamanites to destroy their brothers, they came forth to the land of Midian, and there Ammon met all his brothers; and from there they came to the land of Yishma'el, that they might hold a council with Lamoni, and also with his brother Anti-Nefi-Lechi, regarding what they should do to defend themselves against the Lamanites. Now there was not one soul among all the people who had been converted unto YHWH that would take up arms against their brothers; no, they would not even make any preparations for war; yes, and also their king commanded them that they should not.

7 Now these are the words which he said unto the people concerning the matter: I thank my Elohim, my beloved people, that our great Elohim has in goodness sent these, our brothers the Nefites, unto us, to preach unto us and to convince us of the traditions of our wicked fathers. And behold, I thank my great Elohim that he has given us a portion of his spirit to **soften** our **hearts**,[121] that we have opened a correspondence with these brothers, the Nefites. And behold, I also thank my Elohim that by opening this correspondence, we have been convinced of our sins and of the many murders which we have committed. And I also thank my Elohim, yes, my great Elohim, that

---

121 Job 23:16

he has granted unto us that we might repent of these things, and also that he has forgiven us of these our many sins and murders which we have committed, and took away the guilt from our hearts, through the merits of his Son. And now behold, my brothers, since it has been all that we could do — as we were the most lost of all mankind — to repent of all our sins and the many murders which we have committed, and to get Elohim to take them away from our hearts, for it was all we could do to repent sufficiently before Elohim that he would take away our stains — now, my best-beloved brothers, since Elohim has taken away our stains, and our swords have become bright, then let us stain our swords no more with the blood of our brothers.

8 Behold, I say unto you, no, let us retain our swords, that they be not stained with the blood of our brothers; for perhaps, if we should stain our swords again, they can no more be washed bright through the blood of the Son of our great Elohim, which shall be shed for the atonement of our sins. And the great Elohim has had mercy on us, and made these things known unto us that we might not perish; yes, and he has made these things known unto us beforehand because he loves our souls as well as he loves our children. Therefore, in his mercy he does visit us by his angels, that the plan of salvation might be made known unto us as well as unto future generations. O how merciful is our Elohim. And now behold, since it has been as much as we could do to get our stains taken away from us and our swords are made bright, let us hide them away, that they may be kept bright as a testimony to our Elohim at the last day, or at the day that we shall be brought to stand before him to be judged, that we have not stained our swords in the blood of our brothers since he made known his word unto us and has made us clean thereby. And now, my brothers, if our brothers seek to destroy us, behold, we will hide away our swords, yes, even we will bury them deep in the earth, that they may be kept bright as a testimony that we have never used them at the last day, and if our brothers destroy us, behold, we shall go to our Elohim and shall be saved.

9 And now it came to pass that when the king had made an end of these sayings, and all the people were assembled together, they took their swords and all the weapons which were used for the shedding of man's blood, and they did bury them up deep in the earth. And this they did, it being in their view a testimony to Elohim, and also

to men, that they never would use weapons again for the shedding of man's blood. And this they did witnessing and covenanting with Elohim, that rather than shed the blood of their brothers, they would give up their own lives; and rather than take away from a brother, they would give unto him; and rather than spend their days in idleness, they would labor abundantly with their hands. And thus we see that when these Lamanites were brought to believe and to know the truth, they were firm and would suffer, even unto death, rather than commit sin; and thus we see that they buried the weapons of shalom, or they buried the weapons of war for shalom.

10 And it came to pass that their brothers the Lamanites made preparations for war and came up to the land of Nefi for the purpose of dethroning the king, and to place another in his place, and also of destroying the people of Anti-Nefi-Lechi out of the land. Now when the people saw that they were coming against them, they went out to meet them and prostrated themselves before them to the earth, and began to call on the name of YHWH; and thus they were in this attitude when the Lamanites began to fall upon them and began to slay them with the sword. And thus without meeting any resistance, they did slay a thousand and five of them; and we know that they are blessed, for they have gone to dwell with their Elohim. Now when the Lamanites saw that their brothers would not flee from the sword, neither would they turn aside to the right hand or to the left, but that they would lie down and perish, and praised Elohim even in the very act of perishing under the sword — now when the Lamanites saw this, they did cease from slaying them; and there were many whose hearts had swollen in them for those of their brothers who had fallen under the sword, for they repented of the thing which they had done.

11 And it came to pass that they threw down their weapons of war, and they would not take them again, for they were stung for the murders which they had committed. And they came down even as their brothers, relying upon the mercies of those whose arms were lifted to slay them.

12 And it came to pass that the people of Elohim were joined that day by more than the number who had been slain; and those who had been slain were righteous people, therefore we have no reason to doubt but that they are saved. And there was not a wicked man slain among them, but there were more than a thousand brought to

the knowledge of the truth; thus we see that YHWH works in many ways to the salvation of his people.[122] Now the greatest number of those of the Lamanites who slew so many of their brothers were Amlicites and Amulonites, the greatest number of whom were after the order of the Nehors. Now among those who joined the people of YHWH, there were none who were Amlicites, or Amulonites, or who were after the order of Nehor, but they were actual descendants of Laman and L'mu'el. And thus we can plainly discern that after a people have been once enlightened by the Ruach Elohim, and have had great knowledge of things pertaining to righteousness, and then have fallen away into sin and transgression, they become more hardened; and thus their state becomes worse than if they had never known these things.

13 And behold, now it came to pass that these Lamanites were more angry because they had slain their brothers, therefore they swore vengeance upon the Nefites, and they did no more attempt to slay the people of Anti-Nefi-Lechi at that time. But they took their armies and went over into the borders of the land of Zerach'mla, and fell upon the people who were in the land of Ammonihah, and destroyed them. And after that, they had many battles with the Nefites, in the which they were driven and slain. And among the Lamanites who were slain were almost all the seed of Amulon and his brothers, who were the kohanim of Noah; and they were slain by the hands of the Nefites. And the remainder, having fled into the east wilderness and having usurped the power and authority over the Lamanites, caused that many of the Lamanites should perish by fire because of their belief; for many of them, after having suffered much loss and so many afflictions, began to be stirred up in remembrance of the words which Aharon and his brothers had preached to them in their land; therefore, they began to disbelieve the traditions of their fathers, and to believe in YHWH, and that he gave great power unto the Nefites; and thus there were many of them converted in the wilderness.

14 And it came to pass that those rulers who were the remnant of the children of Amulon caused that they should be put to death, yes, all those that believed in these things. Now this martyrdom caused that many of their brothers should be stirred up to anger; and there began

---

122 Isa. 55:8-9

to be contention in the wilderness, and the Lamanites began to hunt the seed of Amulon and his brothers and began to slay them; and they fled into the east wilderness. And behold, they are hunted at this day by the Lamanites. Thus, the words of Avinodi were brought to pass which he said concerning the seed of the kohanim who caused that he should suffer death by fire. For he said unto them, What you shall do unto me shall be a type of things to come. And now Avinodi was the first that suffered death by fire because of his belief in Elohim. Now this is what he meant: that many should suffer death by fire according as he had suffered. And he said unto the kohanim of Noah that their seed should cause many to be put to death in the like manner as he was, and that they should be scattered abroad and slain, even as a sheep having no shepherd is driven and slain by wild beasts. And now behold, these words were verified, for they were driven by the Lamanites, and they were hunted, and they were slain.[123]

15 And it came to pass that when the Lamanites saw that they could not overpower the Nefites, they returned again to their own land; and many of them came over to dwell in the land of Yishma'el and the land of Nefi, and did join themselves to the people of Elohim, who were the people of Anti-Nefi-Lechi. And they did also bury their weapons of war according as their brothers had, and they began to be a righteous people, and they did walk in the ways of YHWH and did observe to keep his mitzvot and his statutes. Yes, and they did keep the Torah of Moshe; for it was expedient that they should keep the Torah of Moshe as yet, for it was not all fulfilled.[124] But even though they kept the Torah of Moshe, they did look forward to the coming of Mashiach, considering that the Torah of Moshe was a type of his coming, and believing that they must keep those outward performances until the time[125] that he should be revealed unto them. Now they did not suppose that salvation came by the Torah of Moshe, but the Torah of Moshe did serve to strengthen their faith in Mashiach; and thus they did retain a hope, through faith, unto Eternal salvation, relying

---

[123] Moshiyah 9:5 [124] The underlying Hebrew could likely also be rendered as "for it was expedient that they should keep the Torah of Moshe, for everything was not yet fulfilled." And not one *yud* or stroke shall pass from the Torah until everything is fulfilled (Matt. 5:18; Alma 16:34; 3 Nefi 1:6; 5:22). See also "What does it mean to fulfill the Torah?" in footnote to 2 Nefi 11:8. [125] The underlying Hebrew was probably *ad* עַד (Strong's 5704), meaning "as far (or long or much) as, whether in space (even unto) or time (during, while, until [the time]) or degree (equally with)." This word could, therefore, also be translated as "to the degree that" rather than "until the time."

upon the spirit of prophecy which spoke of those things to come.[126] And now behold, Ammon, and Aharon, and Omner, and Himni, and their brothers did rejoice exceedingly for the success which they had had among the Lamanites, seeing that YHWH had granted unto them according to their prayers, and that he had also verified his word unto them in every particular.

16 And now these are the words of Ammon to his brothers, which say thus: My brothers and my friends, behold, I say unto you, how great reason have we to rejoice! For could we have supposed when we started from the land of Zerach'mla that Elohim would have granted unto us such great blessings? And now I ask, what great blessings has he bestowed upon us? Can you tell? Behold, I answer for you; our brothers, the Lamanites, were in darkness, yes, even in the darkest abyss; but behold how many of them are brought to behold the marvelous light of Elohim. And this is the blessing which has been bestowed upon us, that we have been made instruments in the hands of Elohim to bring about this great work. Behold, thousands of them do rejoice and have been brought into the fold of Elohim. Behold, the field was **ripe**, and blessed are you, for you did **thrust in the sickle**[127] and did reap with your might—yes, all the day long did you labor, and behold the number of your sheaves; and they shall be gathered into the granaries, that they are not wasted. Yes, they shall not be beaten down by the storm at the last day, yes, neither shall they be torn up by the whirlwinds; but when the storm comes, they shall be gathered together in their place, that the storm cannot penetrate to them; yes, neither shall they be driven with fierce winds wherever the enemy chooses to carry them. But behold, they are in the hands of the Adon of the Harvest and they are his, and he will raise them up at the last day. **Blessed be the name of** our **Elohim;**[128] let us sing to his praise, yes, let us give thanks to his holy name, for he does work righteousness for ever. For if we had not come up out of the land of Zerach'mla, these, our dearly beloved brothers who have so dearly loved us, would still have been racked with hatred against us; yes, and they would also have been strangers to Elohim.

---

126 2 Nefi 11:8 **127** Joel 4:13 (3:13) **128** Dan. 2:20

17 And it came to pass that when Ammon had said these words, his brother Aharon rebuked him, saying, Ammon, I fear that your joy does carry you away unto boasting. But Ammon said unto him:

I do not boast in my own strength
or in my own wisdom;
but behold, my joy is full,
yes, my heart is brimming with joy,
and **I will rejoice in my Elohim**.[129]

Yes, I know that I am nothing,
as to my strength, I am weak;
therefore, I will not boast of myself,
but I will boast of my Elohim,

for in his strength I can do all things.
Yes, behold, many mighty miracles we have worked in this land,
for which we will praise his name for ever.

Behold how many thousands of our brothers
    has he loosed from the **pains of She'ol**;[130]
And they are brought to sing redeeming love,
and this because of the power of his word which is in us;
therefore, have we not great reason to rejoice?
Yes, we have reason to praise him for ever,
for he is the El Elyon
    and has loosed these, our brothers,
        from the chains of She'ol.

Yes, they were encircled about with everlasting darkness
    and destruction;
but behold, he has brought them into his **everlasting light**,[131]
yes, into everlasting salvation;

and they are encircled about with the matchless bounty
    of his love.

---

129 Hab. 3:18; Ya'akov 3:26   **130** Ps. 116:3   **131** Isa. 60:19-20

Yes, and we have been instruments in his hands,
of doing this great and marvelous work.

Therefore, let us glory,
yes, we will glory in YHWH;
yes, we will rejoice, for our joy is full;
yes, we will praise our Elohim for ever.
¹⁸ Behold, who can glory too much in YHWH?
Yes, who can say too much of his great power,

and of his mercy, and of his long-suffering
    towards the children of men?
Behold, I say unto you, I cannot say the smallest part
which I feel.
Who could have supposed that our Elohim
would have been so merciful
as to have snatched us from our awful, sinful,
    and polluted state?
Behold, we went forth even in wrath
with mighty threatenings to destroy his assembly.

Oh then, why did he not consign us to an awful destruction?
Yes, why did he not let the sword of his justice fall upon us
and doom us to eternal despair?

Oh my soul almost, as it were, flees at the thought.

Behold, he did not exercise his justice upon us,
but in his great mercy has brought us
over that everlasting gulf of death,
and misery even to the salvation of our souls.
And now behold, my brothers, what natural man is there
    that knows these things?
I say unto you, there is none that knows these things
    except it be the penitent.
Yes, he that repents, and exercises faith,
and brings forth good works, and prays continually
    without ceasing,

unto such it is given to know the mysteries of Elohim;

yes, unto such it shall be given
to reveal things which never have been revealed.
Yes, and it shall be given unto such
to bring thousands of souls to repentance,
even as it has been given unto us
to bring these our brothers to repentance.

19 Now do you remember, my brothers,
that we said unto our brothers in the land of Zerach'mla,

We go up to the land of Nefi to preach unto our brothers
    the Lamanites,
and they laughed us to scorn?

For they said unto us, Do you suppose
    that you can bring the Lamanites
    to the knowledge of the truth?
Do you suppose that you can convince the Lamanites
    of the incorrectness of the traditions of their fathers,
as stiffnecked a people as they are,
whose hearts delight in the shedding of blood,
whose days have been spent in the most shameful iniquity,
whose ways have been the ways of a transgressor
    from the beginning?

Now, my brothers, you remember that this was their language.
And moreover, they did say,
Let us take up arms against them, that we destroy them
and their iniquity out of the land,
for fear that they overrun us and destroy us.

But behold, my beloved brothers, we came into the wilderness,
not with the intent to destroy our brothers,
but with the intent that perhaps
    we might save some few of their souls.

²⁰ Now when our hearts were depressed
>and we were about to turn back,
behold, YHWH comforted us and said,
Go among your brothers the Lamanites,
>and bear with patience your afflictions,
and I will give unto you success.

And now behold, we have come and been forth among them,
and we have been patient in our sufferings,
and we have suffered every privation;
yes, we have traveled from house to house,
relying upon the mercies of the world —
not upon the mercies of the world alone,
but upon the mercies of Elohim.

And we have entered into their houses and taught them,
and we have taught them in their streets;
yes, and we have taught them upon their hills;
and we have also entered into their Temples
>and their synagogues and taught them.
And we have been cast out, and mocked,
and spit upon, and struck upon our cheeks,
and we have been stoned,
and taken, and bound with strong cords,
and cast into prison;

and through the power and wisdom of Elohim,
>we have been delivered again.
And we have suffered all manner of afflictions,
and all this that perhaps we might be the means
>of saving some soul,
and we supposed that our joy would be full
if perhaps we could be the means of saving some.

²¹ Now behold, we can look forth and see the fruits of our labors,
>and are they few?

I say unto you, no, they are many.
Yes, and we can witness of their sincerity
because of their love towards their brothers,
    and also towards us.
For behold, they had rather sacrifice their lives
than even to take the life of their enemy;
and they have buried their weapons of war deep in the earth
because of their love towards their brothers.

And now behold, I say unto you, has there been so great love
    in all the land?
Behold, I say unto you, no, there has not,
    even among the Nefites.
For behold, they would take up arms against their brothers;
they would not allow themselves to be slain.
But behold how many of these have laid down their lives;
and we know that they have gone to their
Elohim because of their love, and of their hatred to sin.

Now, have we not reason to rejoice?
Yes, I say unto you,
there never were men that had so great reason to rejoice as we,
    since the world began.
Yes, and my joy is carried away, even unto boasting
    in my Elohim,

for he has all power, all wisdom, and all understanding;
he comprehends all things, and he is a merciful being,
even unto salvation to those who will repent
    and believe on his name.
Now if this is boasting, even so will I boast;
for this is my life and my light, my joy, and my salvation,
and my redemption from everlasting woe.

Yes, blessed is the name of my Elohim,
who **has been mindful**[132] of this people,

---

[132] Ps. 115:12

who are a branch of the tree of Isra'el,
and have been lost from its body in a strange land.
Yes, I say, blessed be the name of my Elohim,
who has been mindful of us wanderers in a strange land.

Now, my brothers, we see that Elohim is mindful
    of every people,
whatsoever land they may be in;[133]
yes, he numbers his people,
and his bowels of mercy are over all the earth.

Now this is my joy and my great thanksgiving;
yes, and I will give thanks unto my Elohim for ever.
Amen.

15 Now it came to pass that when those Lamanites who had gone to war against the Nefites had found, after their many struggles to destroy them, that it was in vain to seek their destruction, they returned again to the land of Nefi. And it came to pass that the Amlicites, because of their loss, were exceedingly angry. And when they saw that they could not seek revenge from the Nefites, they began to stir up the people in anger against their brothers, the people of Anti-Nefi-Lechi; therefore, they began again to destroy them. Now this people again refused to take up arms, and they allowed themselves to be slain according to the desires of their enemies.

2 Now when Ammon and his brothers saw this work of destruction among those whom they so dearly loved, and among those who had so dearly loved them — for they were treated as though they were angels[134] sent from Elohim to save them from everlasting destruction — therefore, when Ammon and his brothers saw this great work of destruction, they were moved with compassion. And they said unto the king, Let us gather together this people of YHWH, and let us go down to the land of Zerach'mla, to our brothers the Nefites, and flee out of the hands of our enemies, that we be not destroyed. But the king said unto them, Behold, the Nefites will

---

133 3 Nefi 7:3 **134** 2 Nefi 14:1

destroy us because of the many murders and sins we have committed against them. And Ammon said, I will go and inquire of YHWH, and if he says unto us, Go down unto our brothers, will you go? And the king said unto him, Yes, if YHWH says unto us, Go, we will go down unto our brothers, and we will be their slaves until we repair unto them the many murders and sins which we have committed against them. But Ammon said unto him, It is against the law of our brothers, which was established by my father, that there should be any slaves among them; therefore, let us go down and rely upon the mercies of our brothers. But the king said unto him, Inquire of YHWH, and if he says unto us, Go, we will go; otherwise, we will perish in the land.

3 And it came to pass that Ammon went and inquired of YHWH, and YHWH said unto him, Get this people out of this land, that they perish not, for HaSatan has great hold on the hearts of the Amlicites, who do stir up the Lamanites to anger against their brothers to slay them. Therefore, get yourselves out of this land; and blessed are this people in this generation, for I will preserve them.

4 And now it came to pass that Ammon went and told the king all the words which YHWH had said unto him. And they gathered together all their people — yes, all the people of YHWH — and did gather together all their flocks and herds, and departed out of the land, and came into the wilderness which divided the land of Nefi from the land of Zerach'mla, and came over near the borders of the land.

5 And it came to pass that Ammon said unto them, Behold, I and my brothers will go forth into the land of Zerach'mla, and you shall remain here until we return; and we will test the hearts of our brothers, whether they will that you shall come into their land.

6 And it came to pass that as Ammon was going forth into the land, that he and his brothers met Alma, over in the place of which has been spoken; and behold, this was a joyful meeting. Now the joy of Ammon was so great, even that he was full; yes, he was swallowed up in the joy of his Elohim, even to the exhausting of his strength, and he fell again to the earth. Now was not this exceeding joy? Behold, this is joy which no one receives, except it be the truly penitent and humble seeker of happiness. Now the joy of Alma in meeting his brothers was truly great, and also the joy of Aharon, of Omner, and Himni; but behold, their joy did not exceed their strength.

⁷And now it came to pass that Alma conducted his brothers back to the land of Zerach'mla, even to his own house. And they went and told the chief judge all the things that had happened unto them in the land of Nefi among their brothers the Lamanites.

⁸And it came to pass that the chief judge sent a proclamation throughout all the land, desiring the **voice of the people** concerning admitting their brothers, who were the people of Anti-Nefi-Lechi. And it came to pass that the voice of the people came, saying, Behold, we will give up the land of Yirshon, which is on the east by the sea, which joins the land Bountiful, which is on the south of the land Bountiful. And this land Yirshon is the land which we will give unto our brothers for an inheritance.[135] And behold, we will set our armies between the land Yirshon and the land Nefi, that we may protect our brothers in the land of Yirshon. And this we do for our brothers on account of their fear to take up arms against their brothers, for fear that they should commit sin. And this, their great fear, came because of their sore repentance which they had on account of the many murders and their awful wickedness. And now behold, this will we do unto our brothers, that they may inherit the land Yirshon; and we will guard them from their enemies by our armies, on condition that they will give us a portion of their substance to assist us, that we may maintain our armies.

⁹Now it came to pass that when Ammon had heard this, he returned to the people of Anti-Nefi-Lechi, and also Alma with him, into the wilderness where they had pitched their tents, and made known unto them all these things. And Alma also related unto them his conversion with Ammon, and Aharon, and his brothers. And it came to pass that it did cause great joy among them. And they went down into the land of Yirshon, and took possession of the land of Yirshon, and they were called by the Nefites, the people of Ammon; therefore, they were distinguished by that name ever after. And they were numbered among the people of Nefi, and also numbered among the people who were of the assembly of Elohim. And they were also distinguished for their zeal towards Elohim and also towards men, for they were perfectly honest and upright in all things; and

---

135 There is a wordplay here in the original Hebrew. "Yirshon" is from Hebrew ירשה (y'resha - Strong's 3424) meaning "possession, inheritance."

they were firm in the faith of Mashiach, **even unto the end**.¹³⁶ And they did look upon shedding the blood of their brothers with the greatest abhorrence, and they never could be persuaded to take up arms against their brothers; and they never did look upon death with any degree of terror, for their hope and views of Mashiach and the resurrection. Therefore, death was swallowed up to them by the victory of Mashiach over it. Therefore, they would suffer death in the most aggravating and distressing manner which could be inflicted by their brothers, before they would take the sword or the cimeter to strike them. And thus they were a zealous and beloved people, a highly favored people of YHWH.

10 And now it came to pass that after the people of Ammon were established in the land of Yirshon, and an assembly also established in the land, and the armies of the Nefites were set round about the land of Yirshon — yes, in all the borders round about the land of Zerach'mla — behold, the armies of the Lamanites had followed their brothers into the wilderness. And thus there was a tremendous battle — yes, even such a one as never had been known among all the people in the land from the time Lechi left Yerushalayim; yes, and tens of thousands of the Lamanites were slain and scattered abroad. Yes, and also there was a tremendous slaughter among the people of Nefi; nevertheless, the Lamanites were driven and scattered, and the people of Nefi returned again to their lands. And now this was a time that there was a great mourning and lamentation heard throughout all the land, among all the people of Nefi. Yes, the cry of widows mourning for their husbands, and also of fathers mourning for their sons, and the daughter for the brother; yes, and the brother for the father. And thus the cry of mourning was heard among every one of them, mourning for their kindred who had been slain. And now surely this was a sorrowful day; yes, a time of solemnity and a time of much fasting and prayer.¹³⁷ And thus ended the fifteenth year of the reign of the judges over the people of Nefi.

---

136 Ps. 119:112   137 Fasting and prayer at the turn of the year (see Alma 15:10) indicates it was Yom Kippur, just ten days after Rosh Hashanah. Verse 10 says, "...thus ended the fifteenth year" because it is summarizing and conflating Rosh Hashanah and Yom Kippur. The entire month of *Tishrei* is called "the beginning of months" (Ex. 12:1-2), and Sukkot is said to be "at the year's end" (Ex. 34:22), though it begins fifteen days after Rosh Hashanah and five days after Yom Kippur. Years were also counted from Sukkot to Sukkot (Deut. 31:10-13).

11 And this is the account of Ammon and his brothers, their journeyings into the land of Nefi, their sufferings in the land, their sorrows, and their afflictions, and their incomprehensible joy, and the reception and safety of their brothers in the land of Yirshon. And now, may YHWH, the Redeemer of all men, bless their souls for ever. And this is the account of the wars and contentions among the Nefites, and also the wars between the Nefites and the Lamanites. And the fifteenth year of the reign of the judges is ended. And from the first year to the fifteenth has brought to pass the destruction of many thousand lives; yes, it has brought to pass an awful scene of bloodshed. And the bodies of many thousands are laid low in the earth, while the bodies of many thousands are decaying in heaps upon the face of the earth. Yes, and many thousands are mourning for the loss of their kindred, because they have reason to fear, according to the promises of YHWH, that they are consigned to a state of endless woe, while many thousands of others truly mourn for the loss of their kindred, yet they rejoice and exult in the hope—yes, and even know, according to the promises of YHWH, that they are raised to dwell at the right hand of Elohim, in a state of never-ending happiness. And thus we see how great the inequality of man is because of sin, and transgression, and the power of HaSatan, which comes by the cunning plans which he has devised to ensnare the hearts of men. And thus we see the great call of the diligence of men to labor in the **vineyards of YHWH**.[138] And thus we see the great reason of sorrow, and also of rejoicing—sorrow because of death and destruction among men, and joy because of the light of Mashiach unto life.

> 12 Oh that I were an angel, and could have the wish of my heart,
> that I might go forth and speak with the shofar of Elohim,
> with a voice to shake the earth,
> and cry repentance unto every people.
> Yes, I would declare unto every soul,
> as with the voice of thunder,
> repentance and the plan of redemption—
> that they should repent and come unto our Elohim,

---

138 Isa. 5:7

> that there might be no more sorrow
>> upon all the face of the earth.
>
> But behold, I am a man, and do sin in my wish,
> for I ought to be content with the things
>> which YHWH has allotted unto me.
> I ought not to tear up in my desires the firm decree
>> of a just Elohim,
>
> for I know that he grants unto men according to their desire,
> whether it be unto death or unto life.
> Yes, I know that he grants unto men —
> yes, decrees unto them decrees which are unalterable —
>> according to their wills,
> whether they be unto salvation or unto destruction.[139]
>
> Yes, and I know that good and evil have come before all men,
> or he that knows not good from evil is blameless,
> but he that knows good and evil, to him it is given
> according to his desires,
> whether he desires good or evil, life or death,
>> joy or remorse of conscience.
>
> 13 Now, seeing that I know these things,
> why should I desire more than to perform the work
> to which I have been called?
> Why should I desire that I were an angel,
> that I could speak unto all the ends of the earth?
>
> For behold, YHWH does grant unto all nations,
>> of their own nation and tongue, to teach his word,

---

[139] A similar teaching is found in the Talmud: "In the way in which a man wishes to walk he is guided" (b.Makot 10b); "If one goes to defile himself, openings are made for him; and if he goes to purify himself, help is afforded him" (b.Shabbat 104a); "If a man defiles himself a little, he becomes much defiled: [if he defile himself] below, he becomes defiled from above; if he defile himself in this world, he becomes defiled in the world to come. Our Rabbis taught: Sanctify yourselves, therefore, and be ye holy: If a man sanctify himself a little, he becomes much sanctified. [If he sanctify himself] below, he becomes sanctified from above; if he sanctify himself in this world, he becomes sanctified in the world to come" (b.Yoma 39a).

yes, in wisdom, all that he sees fit that they should have;
therefore, we see that YHWH does counsel in his wisdom,
according to that which is just and true.

I know that which YHWH has commanded me, and I glory in it.
I do not glory of myself, but I glory in that
    which YHWH has commanded me;

yes, and this is my glory,
that perhaps I may be an instrument in the hands of Elohim
to bring some soul to repentance;
and this is my joy.
And behold, when I see many of my brothers truly penitent,
and coming to YHWH their Elohim,
then is my soul filled with joy;

then do I remember what YHWH has done for me,
yes, even that he has heard my prayer.
Yes, then do I remember his merciful arm
    which he extended towards me.

Yes, and I also remember the captivity of my fathers,
for I surely do know that YHWH did deliver them
    out of bondage,
and by this did establish his assembly.
Yes, Adonai YHWH — **the Elohim of Avraham,
and the Elohim of Yitz'chak, and the Elohim of Ya'akov**—[140]
did deliver them out of bondage.

Yes, I have always remembered the captivity of my fathers;
and that same Elohim who delivered them
    out of the hands of the Egyptians
did deliver them out of bondage.
Yes, and that same Elohim did establish his assembly
    among them.

---

140 Ex. 3:6

Yes, and that same Elohim has called me by a holy calling
to preach the word unto this people,
and has given me much success, in the which my joy is full.
But I do not joy in my own success alone,
but my joy is more full because of the success of my brothers
who have been up to the land of Nefi.

Behold, they have labored exceedingly
and have brought forth much fruit;[141]
and how great shall be their reward.

Now when I think of the success of these my brothers,
my soul is carried away,
even to the separation of it from the body,
as it were, so great is my joy.

14 And now, may Elohim grant unto these my brothers
that they may sit down in the kingdom of Elohim,
yes, and also all those who are the fruit of their labor,
that they may go no more out,
but that they may praise him for ever.
And may Elohim grant that it may be done
according to my words, even as I have spoken.
Amen.

16

Behold, now it came to pass after the people of Ammon were established in the land of Yirshon, yes, and also after the Lamanites were driven out of the land, and their dead were buried by the people of the land – now their dead were not numbered because of the greatness of their numbers, neither were the dead of the Nefites numbered – but it came to pass after they had buried their dead, and also after the days of fasting, and mourning, and prayer (and it was in the sixteenth year[142] of the reign of the judges over the people of Nefi), there began to be continual shalom throughout all the land. Yes, and the people did observe to keep the mitzvot of YHWH; and they were strict in observing the ordinances of Elohim

---

141 Ya'akov 3:28   142 ~ 77 BCE

according to the Torah of Moshe; for they were taught to keep the Torah of Moshe until[143] it should be fulfilled.[144] And thus the people did have no disturbance in all the sixteenth year of the reign of the judges over the people of Nefi.

2 And it came to pass in the commencement of the seventeenth year of the reign of the judges, there was continual shalom. But it came to pass in the latter end of the seventeenth year, there came a man into the land of Zerach'mla, and he was anti-Mashiach, for he began to preach unto the people against the prophecies which had been spoken by the prophets concerning the coming of Mashiach. Now there was no law against a man's belief, for it was strictly contrary to the mitzvot of Elohim that there should be a law which should bring men onto unequal ground. For thus says the scripture: Choose you this day whom you will serve. Now if a man desired to serve Elohim, it was his privilege, or rather if he believed in Elohim, it was his privilege to serve him; but if he did not believe in him, there was no law to punish him. But if he murdered, he was punished unto death; and if he robbed, he was also punished; and if he stole, he was also punished; and if he committed adultery, he was also punished; yes, for all this wickedness they were punished, for there was a law that men should be judged according to their crimes. Nevertheless, there was no law against a man's belief; therefore, a man was punished only for the crimes which he had done; therefore, all men were on equal grounds.

3 And this anti-Mashiach, whose name was Korihor (and the law could have no hold upon him), began to preach unto the people that there should be no Mashiach. And after this manner did he preach, saying, O you that are bound down under a foolish and a vain hope, why do you yoke yourselves with such foolish things? Why do you look for a Mashiach? For no man can know of anything which is to come. Behold, these things which you call prophecies, which you say are handed down by holy prophets, behold, they are foolish traditions of your fathers. How do you know of their surety? Behold, you cannot know of things which you do not see, therefore you cannot know

---

143 The underlying Hebrew would likely be *ad* עד (Strong's 5704), meaning "as far (or long or much) as, whether in space (even unto) or time (during, while, until) or degree (equally with)." This word could also be translated as "to the degree that" rather than "until." **144** See "What does it mean to fulfill the Torah?" footnote to 2 Nefi 11:8.

that there shall be a Mashiach. You look forward and say that you see a remission of your sins, but behold, it is the effect of a frenzied mind, and this derangement of your minds comes because of the traditions of your fathers, which lead you away into a belief of things which are not so. And many more such things did he say unto them, telling them that there could be no atonement made for the sins of men, but every man fared in this life according to the management of the creature. Therefore, every man prospered according to his genius, and that every man conquered according to his strength, and whatsoever a man did was no crime. And thus he did preach unto them, leading away the hearts of many, causing them to lift up their heads in their wickedness; yes, leading away many women, and also men, to commit whoredoms, telling them that when a man was dead, that was the end thereof.

4 Now this man went over to the land of Yirshon also, to preach these things among the people of Ammon, who were once the people of the Lamanites. But behold, they were more wise than many of the Nefites, for they took him, and bound him, and carried him before Ammon, who was a Kohen HaGadol over that people.

5 And it came to pass that he caused that he should be carried out of the land, and came over into the land of Gideon, and began to preach unto them also; and here he did not have much success, for he was taken, and bound, and carried before the Kohen HaGadol, and also the chief judge over the land.

6 And it came to pass that the Kohen HaGadol said unto him, Why do you go about perverting the ways of YHWH? Why do you teach this people that there shall be no Mashiach, to interrupt their rejoicings? Why do you speak against all the prophecies of the holy prophets? Now the Kohen HaGadol's name was Giddonah. And Korihor said unto him, Because I do not teach the foolish traditions of your fathers, and because I do not teach this people to bind themselves down under the foolish ordinances and performances which are laid down by ancient kohanim, to usurp power and authority over them, to keep them in ignorance, that they may not lift up their heads, but be brought down according to your words. You say that this people is a free people. Behold, I say, they are in bondage. You say that those ancient prophecies are true. Behold, I say that you do not know that they are true. You say that this people is a guilty and a fallen people

because of the transgression of a parent. Behold, I say that a child is not guilty because of its parents. And you also say that Mashiach shall come. But behold, I say that you do not know that there shall be a Mashiach. And you say also that he shall be slain for the sins of the world. And thus you lead away this people after the foolish traditions of your fathers, and according to your own desires. And you keep them down, even as it were in bondage, that you may gorge yourselves with the labors of their hands, that they dare not look up with boldness, and that they dare not enjoy their rights and privileges. Yes, they dare not make use of that which is their own, for fear that they should offend their kohanim, who do yoke them according to their desires, and have brought them to believe by their traditions, and their dreams, and their whims, and their visions, and their pretended mysteries, that they should, if they do not do according to their words, offend some unknown being who they say is Elohim, a being who has never been seen or known, who never was nor ever will be. Now when the Kohen HaGadol and the chief judge saw the hardness of his heart — yes, when they saw that he would revile even against Elohim — they would not make any reply to his words; but they caused that he should be bound; and they delivered him up into the hands of the officers, and sent him to the land of Zerach'mla, that he might be brought before Alma and the chief judge, who was governor over all the land.

7 And it came to pass that when he was brought before Alma and the chief judge, that he did go on in the same manner as he did in the land of Gideon; yes, he went on to blasphemy. And he did rise up in great swelling words before Alma, and did revile against the kohanim and teachers, accusing them of leading away the people after the silly traditions of their fathers, for the sake of gorging on the labors of the people. Now Alma said unto him, You know that we do not gorge ourselves upon the labors of this people; for behold, I have labored, even from the commencement of the reign of the judges until now, with my own hands for my support, despite my many travels round about the land to declare the word of Elohim unto my people. And despite the many labors which I have performed in the assembly, I have never received so much as even one senine for my labor, neither has any of my brothers, except it were in the judgment seat; and then we have received only according to law for our time. And now, if we

do not receive anything for our labors in the assembly, what does it profit us to labor in the assembly except it were to declare the truth, that we may have rejoicings in the joy of our brothers? Then why do you say that we preach unto this people to get gain, when you of yourself know that we receive no gain? And now, do you believe that we deceive this people, and that causes such joy in their hearts? And Korihor answered him, Yes.

8 Then Alma said unto him, Do you believe that there is an Elohim? And he answered, No. Now Alma said unto him, Will you deny again that there is an Elohim, and also deny the Mashiach? For behold, I say unto you, I know there is an Elohim, and also that Mashiach shall come. And now, what evidence have you that there is no Elohim? Or that Mashiach comes not? I say unto you that you have none, except it be your word only. But behold, I have all things as a testimony that these things are true, and you also have all things as a testimony unto you that they are true; and will you deny them? Do you believe that these things are true? Behold, I know that you believe, but you are possessed with a lying spirit, and you have put off the Ruach Elohim, that it may have no place in you; but HaSatan has power over you, and he does carry you about, working schemes that he may destroy the children of Elohim. And now Korihor said unto Alma, If you will, show me a sign, that I may be convinced that there is an Elohim; yes, show unto me that he has power, and then will I be convinced of the truth of your words.

9 But Alma said unto him, You have had signs enough; will you tempt your Elohim? Will you say, Show unto me a sign, when you have the testimony of all these your brothers, and also all the holy prophets? The scriptures are laid before you, yes, and all things denote there is an Elohim. Yes, even the earth, and all things that are upon the face of it, yes, and its motion, yes, and also all the planets which move in their regular order do witness that there is a supreme creator. And yet do you go about, leading away the hearts of this people, testifying unto them there is no Elohim. And yet will you deny against all these witnesses? And he said, Yes, I will deny except you shall show me a sign.

10 And now it came to pass that Alma said unto him, Behold, I am grieved because of the hardness of your heart, yes, that you will still resist the spirit of the truth, that your soul may be destroyed.

But behold, it is better that your soul should be lost, than that you should be the means of bringing many souls down to destruction by your lying and by your flattering words; therefore, if you shall deny again, behold, Elohim shall strike you, that you shall become dumb, that you shall never open your mouth anymore, that you shall not deceive this people anymore. Now Korihor said unto him, I do not deny the existence of an Elohim, but I do not believe that there is an Elohim, and I say also that you do not know that there is an Elohim; and except you show me a sign, I will not believe.

11 Now Alma said unto him, This will I give unto you for a sign, that you shall be struck dumb according to my words; and I say in the name of Elohim that you shall be struck dumb, that you shall no more have utterance. Now when Alma had said these words, Korihor was struck dumb, that he could not have utterance, according to the words of Alma. And now when the chief judge saw this, he put forth his hand and wrote unto Korihor, saying, Are you convinced of the power of Elohim? In whom you did desire that Alma should show forth his sign? Would you that he should afflict others to show unto you a sign? Now behold, he has showed unto you a sign; and now, will you dispute more?

12 And Korihor put forth his hand and wrote, saying, I know that I am dumb, for I cannot speak; and I know that nothing, except it were the power of Elohim, could bring this upon me. Yes, and I always knew that there was an Elohim; but behold, HaSatan has deceived me, for he appeared unto me in the form of an angel[145] and said unto me, Go and reclaim this people, for they have all gone astray after an unknown Elohim. And he said unto me, There is no Elohim. Yes, and he taught me that which I should say, and I have taught his words; and I taught them because they were pleasing unto the carnal mind. And I taught them even until I had much success, insomuch that I truly believed that they were true. And for this cause I withstood the truth, even until I have brought this great curse upon myself. Now when he had said this, he implored that Alma should pray unto Elohim that the curse might be taken from him. But Alma said unto him, If this curse should be taken from you, you would again lead away the hearts of this people; therefore, it shall be unto you even as YHWH will.

---

145 2 Nefi 6:3

13 And it came to pass that the curse was not taken off of Korihor, but he was cast out, and went about from house to house, begging for his food. Now the knowledge of what had happened unto Korihor was immediately published throughout all the land. Yes, the proclamation was sent forth by the chief judge to all the people in the land, declaring unto those who had believed in the words of Korihor that they must speedily repent or the same judgments would come unto them.

14 And it came to pass that they were all convinced of the wickedness of Korihor; therefore, they were all converted again unto YHWH; and this put an end to the iniquity after the manner of Korihor. And Korihor did go about from house to house, begging for his support.

15 And it came to pass that as he went forth among the people — yes, among a people who had separated themselves from the Nefites and called themselves Tzuramites, being led by a man whose name was Tzuram — and as he went forth among them, behold, he was run upon and trampled down, even until he was dead. And thus we see the end of him who perverts the ways of YHWH; and thus we see that HaSatan will not support his children at the last day, but does speedily drag them down to She'ol.

16 Now it came to pass that after the end of Korihor, Alma having received tidings that the Tzuramites were perverting the ways of YHWH, and that Tzuram, who was their leader, was leading the hearts of the people to bow down to dumb idols, and so forth, his heart again began to sicken because of the iniquity of the people. For it was the cause of great sorrow to Alma to know of iniquity among his people; therefore his heart was exceedingly sorrowful because of the separation of the Tzuramites from the Nefites. Now the Tzuramites had gathered themselves together in a land which they called Antionum, which was east of the land of Zerach'mla, which lay nearly bordering upon the seashore, which was south of the land Yirshon, which also bordered upon the wilderness south, which wilderness was full of the Lamanites. Now the Nefites greatly feared that the Tzuramites would enter into a correspondence with the Lamanites, and that it would be the means of great loss on the part of the Nefites. And now, as the preaching of the word had had a greater tendency to lead the people to do that which was just — yes, it had had a more powerful effect upon the minds of the people than the

sword or anything else which had happened unto them — therefore Alma thought it was expedient that they should act upon the virtue of the word of Elohim. Therefore, he took Ammon, and Aharon, and Omner — and Himni he did leave in the assembly in Zerach'mla, but the former three he took with him — and also Amulek and Zeezrom, who were at Melek; and he also took two of his sons. Now the eldest of his sons he took not with him, and his name was Cheleman; but the names of those whom he took with him were Shiblon and Corianton; and these are the names of those who went with him among the Tzuramites to preach unto them the word.

17 Now the Tzuramites were dissenters from the Nefites, therefore they had the word of Elohim preached unto them. But they had fallen into great errors, for they would not observe to keep the mitzvot of Elohim and his statutes according to the Torah of Moshe, neither would they observe the performances of the assembly — to continue in prayer and supplication to Elohim daily, that they might not enter into temptation. Yes, in short, they did pervert the ways of YHWH in very many instances. Therefore, for this cause, Alma and his brothers went into the land to preach the word unto them.

18 Now when they had come into the land, behold, to their astonishment they found that the Tzuramites had built synagogues, and that they did gather themselves together on one day of the week, which day they did call the day of YHWH, and they did worship after a manner which Alma and his brothers had never beheld. For they had a place built up in the center of their synagogue, a place of standing which was high above the head, and the top thereof would only admit one person. Therefore, whosoever desired to worship must go forth and stand upon the top thereof, and stretch forth his hands towards the heavens, and cry with a loud voice, saying, Holy, holy Elohim! We believe that you are Elohim, and we believe that you are holy, and that you were a spirit, and that you are a spirit, and that you will be a spirit for ever. Holy Elohim, we believe that you have separated us from our brothers; and we do not believe in the tradition of our brothers which was handed down to them by the childishness of their fathers,[146] but we believe that you have elected

---

146 "...the Pharisees have delivered to the people a great many observances by succession from their fathers, which are not written in the law of Moses; for that reason it is that the Sadducees reject them, and say that we are to esteem those observances to be obligatory

us to be your holy children; and also, you have made it known unto us that there shall be no Mashiach. But you are the same yesterday, today, and for ever; and you have elected us that we shall be saved, while all those around us are elected to be cast, by your wrath, down to Gehinnom, for which holiness, O Elohim, we thank you. And we also thank you that you have elected us, that we may not be led away after the foolish traditions of our brothers, which do bind them down to a belief of Mashiach, which does lead their hearts to wander far from you, our Elohim. And again we thank you, O Elohim, that we are a chosen and a holy people. Amen.[147]

19 Now it came to pass that after Alma, and his brothers, and his sons, had heard these prayers, they were astonished beyond all measure. For behold, every man did go forth and offer up these same prayers. Now the place was called by them Rameumptom,[148] which (being interpreted) is the holy stand. Now from this stand they did offer up, every man, the very same prayer unto Elohim, thanking their Elohim that they were chosen of him, and that he had not led them away after the tradition of their brothers, and that their hearts were not stolen away to believe in things to come, which they knew nothing about.

20 Now when the people had all offered up thanks after their manner, they returned to their homes, never speaking of their Elohim again, until they had assembled themselves together again to the holy stand to offer up thanks after their manner. Now when Alma saw this, his heart was grieved, for he saw that they were a wicked and a perverse people. Yes, he saw that their hearts were set upon gold, and upon silver, and upon all manner of fine goods. Yes, and he also saw that their hearts were lifted up unto great boasting in their pride.[149] And he lifted up his voice to Heaven and cried, saying, Oh how long, O YHWH, will you allow that your servants shall dwell here below in the flesh to behold such shameful wickedness among the children of men? Behold, O Elohim, they cry unto you, and yet their hearts are swallowed up in their pride. Behold, O Elohim, they cry unto you with their mouths while they are puffed up, even to greatness, with the

---

which are in the written word, but are not to observe what are delivered from the tradition of our forefathers..." (Josephus; Ant. 13:11:6). See also Ps. 78:1-4; Enosh 1:3. **147** 2 Nefi 11:15 **148** From the Hebrew root *rum* רום and *ram* רם (Strong's 7311), "to be high." **149** 2 Nefi 8:5

vain things of the world. Behold, O my Elohim, their costly apparel, and their ringlets, and their bracelets, and their ornaments of gold, and all their precious things which they are ornamented with. And behold, their hearts are set upon them, and yet they cry unto you and say, We thank you, O Elohim, for we are a chosen people unto you, while others shall perish.[150] Yes, and they say that you have made it known unto them that there shall be no Mashiach. O Adonai YHWH, how long will you allow that such wickedness and infidelity shall be among this people? O YHWH, will you give me strength that I may bear my infirmities? For I am infirm, and such wickedness among this people does pain my soul. O YHWH, my heart is exceedingly sorrowful; will you comfort my soul in Mashiach? O YHWH, will you grant unto me that I may have strength, that I may bear with patience these afflictions which shall come upon me because of the iniquity of this people? O YHWH, will you comfort my soul and give unto me success? And also my fellow laborers who are with me—yes, Ammon, and Aharon, and Omner, and also Amulek, and Zeezrom, and also my two sons—yes, even all these will you comfort, O YHWH? Yes, will you comfort their souls in Mashiach? Will you grant unto them that they may have strength, that they may bear their afflictions which shall come upon them because of the iniquities of this people? O YHWH, will you grant unto us that we may have success in bringing them again unto you in Mashiach? Behold, O YHWH, their souls are precious, and many of them are our near brothers. Therefore, give unto us, O YHWH, power and wisdom, that we may bring these our brothers again unto you.

21 Now it came to pass that when Alma had said these words, that he struck his hands upon all them who were with him. And behold, as he struck his hands upon them, they were filled with the Holy Spirit.[151] And after that, they did separate themselves one from another, taking no thought for themselves, what they should eat, or what they should drink, or what they should put on.[152] And YHWH provided for them, that they should hunger not, neither should they thirst; yes, and he also gave them strength, that they should suffer no manner of afflictions, except it were swallowed up in the joy of

---

150 Isa. 3:16-24; 2 Nefi 8:8   151 3 Nefi 8:10   152 3 Nefi 6:1-4

Mashiach. Now this was according to the prayer of Alma, and this because he prayed in faith.

22 And it came to pass that they did go forth, and began to preach the word of Elohim unto the people, entering into their synagogues and into their houses; yes, and even they did preach the word in their streets. And it came to pass that after much labor among them, they began to have success among the poorer class of the people. For behold, they were cast out of the synagogues because of the coarseness of their apparel, therefore they were not permitted to enter into their synagogues to worship Elohim, being esteemed as tamé.[153] Therefore, they were poor; yes, they were esteemed by their brothers as worthless; therefore, they were poor as to things of the world; and also they were poor in heart.[154]

23 Now as Alma was teaching and speaking unto the people upon the hill Onidah, there came a great multitude unto him, who were those of whom we have been speaking, who were poor in heart because of their poverty as to the things of the world. And they came unto Alma, and the one who was the most foremost among them said unto him, Behold, what shall these my brothers do? For they are despised of all men because of their poverty, yes, and more especially by our kohanim. For they have cast us out of our synagogues, which we have labored abundantly to build with our own hands; and they have cast us out because of this, our exceeding poverty, that we have no place to worship our Elohim. And now behold, what shall we do?

24 And now when Alma heard this, he turned around, his face immediately towards him. And he beheld with great joy, for he beheld that their afflictions had truly humbled them and that they were prepared to hear the word. Therefore, he did say no more to the other multitude, but he stretched forth his hand and cried unto those whom he beheld, who were truly penitent, and said unto them, I behold that you are humble in heart, and if so, blessed are you. Behold, your brother has said, What shall we do? For we are cast out of our synagogues, that we cannot worship our Elohim. Behold, I say unto you, do you suppose that you cannot worship Elohim, except it be in your synagogues only? And moreover, I would ask, do you suppose that you must not worship Elohim only once in a week?

---

153 טמא (ritually impure) 154 3 Nefi 5:12

I say unto you, it is well that you are cast out of your synagogues, that you may be humble and that you may learn wisdom; for it is necessary that you should learn wisdom. For it is because that you are cast out — that you are despised of your brothers because of your exceeding poverty — that you are brought to a humility of heart; for you are necessarily brought to be humble. And now, because you are compelled to be humble, blessed are you; for a man sometimes, if he is compelled to be humble, seeks repentance. And now surely, whosoever repents shall find mercy, and he that finds mercy and endures to the end, the same shall be saved.

25 And now, as I said unto you that because you were compelled to be humble, you were blessed, do you not suppose that they are more blessed who truly humble themselves because of the word? Yes, he that truly humbles himself, and repents of his sins, and endures to the end, the same shall be blessed,[155] yes, much more blessed than they who are compelled to be humble because of their exceeding poverty. Therefore, blessed are they who humble themselves without being compelled to be humble; or rather, in other words, blessed is he that believes in the word of Elohim and is immersed without stubbornness of heart, yes, without being brought to know the word, or even compelled to know, before they will believe.[156] Yes, there are many who do say, If you will show unto us a sign from Heaven, then we shall know of a surety; then we shall believe. Now I ask, is this faith? Behold, I say unto you, no, for if a man knows a thing, he has no cause to believe, for he knows it. And now, how much more cursed is he that knows the will of Elohim and does it not, than he that only believes, or only has cause to believe, and falls into transgression?[157] Now of this thing you must judge. Behold, I say unto you that it is on the one hand even as it is on the other; **and it shall be unto every man according to his work.**[158]

26 And now, as I said concerning faith, faith is not to have a perfect knowledge of things; therefore, if you have faith, you hope for things which are not seen which are true. And now behold, I say unto you — and I would that you should remember — that Elohim

---

[155] Alma 5:6; 10:4; 'Eter 5:5   [156] 3 Nefi 5:11   [157] This is an example of the Kal va-homer thought form, which serves as the first of the Seven Rules of Hillel. This classic Jewish thought form expresses that that which applies in a less important case will certainly apply in a more important case.   [158] Ps. 62:13 (12)

is merciful unto all who believe on his name; therefore, he desires, in the first place, that you should believe, yes, even on his word. And now, he makes known his word by angels unto men, yes, not only men, but women also. Now this is not all. Little children do have words given unto them many times which do confound the wise and the learned.[159]

27 And now, my beloved brothers, as you have desired to know of me what you shall do, because you are afflicted and cast out — now I do not desire that you should suppose that I mean to judge you, only according to that which is true — for I do not mean that you, all of you, have been compelled to humble yourselves; for I truly believe there are some among you who would humble themselves, let them be in whatsoever circumstances they might. Now as I said concerning faith, that it was not a perfect knowledge, even so it is with my words. You cannot know of their surety at first, unto perfection, any more than faith is a perfect knowledge. But behold, if you will awake and arouse your faculties, even to an experiment upon my words, and exercise a particle of faith, yes, even if you can no more than desire to believe, let this desire work in you, even until you believe in a manner that you can give place for a portion of my words.

28 Now we will compare the word unto a seed. Now, if you give place that a seed may be planted in your heart, behold, if it be a true seed, or a good seed — if you do not cast it out by your unbelief, that you will resist the spirit of YHWH — behold, it will begin to swell within your breast. And when you feel these swelling motions, you will begin to say within yourselves, It must necessarily be that this is a good seed, or that the word is good, for it begins to enlarge my soul; yes, it begins to enlighten my understanding; yes, and it begins to be delicious to me. Now behold, would not this increase your faith? I say unto you, yes. Nevertheless, it has not grown up to a perfect knowledge. But behold, as the seed swells, and sprouts, and begins to grow, then you must necessarily say that the seed is good, for behold, it swells, and sprouts, and begins to grow. And now behold, will not this strengthen your faith? Yes, it will strengthen your faith, for you will say, I know that this is a good seed, for behold, it sprouts and begins to grow. And now behold, are you sure that this is a good seed?

---

159 3 Nefi 12:2

I say unto you, yes; for every seed brings forth unto its own likeness. Therefore, if a seed grow, it is good; but if it grows not, behold, it is not good, therefore it is cast away. And now behold, because you have tried the experiment and planted the seed, and it swells, and sprouts, and begins to grow, you must necessarily know that the seed is good.

29 And now behold, is your knowledge perfect? Yes, your knowledge is perfect in that thing, and your faith is dormant, and this because you know. For you know that the word has swelled your souls, and you also know that it has sprouted up, that your understanding does begin to be enlightened and your mind does begin to expand. Oh then, is not this real? I say unto you, yes, because it is light; and whatsoever is light is good, because it is discernible; therefore, you must know that it is good.

30 And now behold, after you have tasted this light, is your knowledge perfect? Behold, I say unto you, no; neither must you lay aside your faith, for you have only exercised your faith to plant the seed, that you might try the experiment to know if the seed was good. And behold, as the tree begins to grow, you will say, Let us nourish it with great care, that it may get root, that it may grow up and bring forth fruit unto us. And now behold, if you nourish it with much care, it will get root, and grow up, and bring forth fruit. But if you neglect the tree and take no thought for its nourishment, behold, it will not get any root; and when the heat of the sun comes and scorches it, because it has no root, it withers away, and you pluck it up and cast it out. Now this is not because the seed was not good, neither is it because the fruit thereof would not be desirable, but it is because your ground is barren and you will not nourish the tree; therefore, you cannot have the fruit thereof. And thus it is: if you will not nourish the word, looking forward with an eye of faith to the fruit thereof, you can never pluck of the fruit of the tree of life. But if you will nourish the word, yes, nourish the tree as it begins to grow, by your faith, with great diligence, and with patience, looking forward to the fruit thereof, it shall take root; and behold, it shall be a tree springing up unto everlasting life. And because of your diligence, and your faith, and your patience[160] with the word, in nourishing it that it may take root in you, behold, by and by, you shall pluck the fruit

---

160 The repetition of the possessive pronoun here is normative in Hebrew, where a pronominal suffix is normally attached to each object of possession.

thereof, which is most precious, which is sweet above all that is sweet, and which is white above all that is white, yes, and pure above all that is pure. And you shall feast upon this fruit, even until you are filled, that you hunger not, neither shall you thirst. Then, my brothers, you shall reap the rewards of your faith, and your diligence, and patience, and long-suffering, waiting for the tree to bring forth fruit unto you.

31 Now after Alma had spoken these words, they sent forth unto him, desiring to know whether they should believe in one Elohim, that they might obtain this fruit of which he had spoken, or how they should plant the seed, or the word, of which he had spoken, which he said must be planted in their hearts, or in what manner they should begin to exercise their faith. And Alma said unto them, Behold, you have said that you could not worship your Elohim because you are cast out of your synagogues. But behold, I say unto you, if you suppose that you cannot worship your Elohim, you do greatly err, and you ought to search the scriptures; for if you suppose that they have taught you this, you do not understand them. Do you remember to have read what Zenos, the prophet of old, has said concerning prayer or worship? For he said, You are merciful, O Elohim, for you have heard my prayer, even when I was in the wilderness. Yes, you were merciful when I prayed concerning those who were my enemies, and you did turn them to me. Yes, O Elohim, and you were merciful unto me when I did cry unto you in my field, when I did cry unto you in my prayer, and you did hear me. And again, O Elohim, when I did turn to my house, you did hear me in my prayer. And when I did turn unto my closet, O YHWH, and prayed unto you, you did hear me. Yes, you are merciful unto your children when they cry unto you to be heard of you and not of men, and you will hear them. Yes, O Elohim, you have been merciful unto me and heard my cries in the midst of your congregations. Yes, and you have also heard me when I have been cast out and have been despised by my enemies; yes, you did hear my cries and were angry with my enemies, and you did visit them in your anger, with speedy destruction. And you did hear me because of my afflictions and my sincerity; and it is because of your Son that you have been thus merciful unto me. Therefore, I will cry unto you in all my afflictions, for in you is my joy; for you have turned your judgments away from me because of your Son.

32 And now Alma said unto them, Do you believe those scriptures which have been written by them of old? Behold, if you do, you must believe what Zenos said; for behold, he said, You have turned away your judgments because of your Son. Now behold, my brothers, I would ask if you have read these scriptures. If you have, how can you disbelieve on the Son of Elohim? For it is not written that Zenos alone spoke of these things, but Zenoch also spoke of these things, for behold, he said, You are angry, O YHWH, with this people because they will not understand of your mercies which you have bestowed upon them because of your Son. And now, my brothers, you see that a second prophet of old has testified of the Son of Elohim. And because the people would not understand his words, they stoned him to death. But behold, this is not all; these are not the only ones who have spoken concerning the Son of Elohim. Behold, he was spoken of by Moshe; yes, and behold, a type was raised up in the wilderness, that whosoever would look upon it might live. And many did look and live.[161] But few understood the meaning of those things, and this because of the hardness of their hearts. But there were many who were so hardened that they would not look; therefore, they perished. Now the reason that they would not look was because they did not believe that it would heal them. O my brothers, if you could be healed by merely casting about your eyes that you might behold, would you not behold quickly? Or would you rather harden your hearts in unbelief and be slothful, that you would not cast about your eyes, that you might perish? If so, woe shall come upon you. But if not so, then cast about your eyes and begin to believe in the Son of Elohim, that he will come to redeem his people, and that he shall suffer and die to atone for their sins, and that he shall rise again from the dead, which shall bring to pass the resurrection, that all men shall stand before him to be judged at the last and judgment day according to their works.[162] And now, my brothers, I desire that you should plant this word in your hearts. And as it begins to swell, even so nourish it by your faith. And behold, it will become a tree, springing up in you unto everlasting life. And then may Elohim grant unto you that

---

[161] Num. 21:6-9. The Hebrew word for "serpent" is *nachash* נחש, which has a gematria of 358, the same gematria as *Mashiach* משיח. See also John 3:14; 8:28; 12:32.
[162] Cheleman 3:9

your burdens may be light through the joy of his Son. And even all this can you do, if you will. Amen.

33 And now it came to pass that after Alma had spoken these words unto them, he sat down upon the ground, and Amulek arose and began to teach them, saying, My brothers, I think that it is impossible that you should be ignorant of the things which have been spoken concerning the coming of Mashiach, who is taught by us to be the Son of Elohim. Yes, I know that these things were taught unto you bountifully before your dissension from among us. And as you have desired of my beloved brother that he should make known unto you what you should do because of your afflictions — and he has spoken somewhat unto you to prepare your minds; yes, and he has exhorted you unto faith and to patience, yes, even that you would have so much faith as even to plant the word in your heart, that you may try the experiment of its goodness. And we have beheld that the great question which is in your minds is whether the word be in the Son of Elohim, or whether there shall be no Mashiach. And you also behold that my brother has proven unto you in many instances that the word is in Mashiach unto salvation. My brother has called upon the words of Zenos, that redemption comes through the Son of Elohim, and also upon the words of Zenoch, and also he has appealed unto Moshe, to prove that these things are true.

34 And now behold, I will testify unto you of myself that these things are true. Behold, I say unto you that I do know that Mashiach shall come among the children of men, to take upon him the transgressions of his people, and that he shall atone for the sins of the world, for Adonai YHWH has spoken it. For it is expedient that an atonement should be made. For according to the great plans of the Elohe Kedem, there must be an atonement made, or else all mankind must unavoidably perish. Yes, all are hardened, yes, all are fallen, and are lost, and must perish, except it be through the atonement which it is expedient should be made. For it is expedient that there should be a great and last sacrifice, yes, not a sacrifice of man, neither of beasts, neither of any manner of fowl; for it shall not be a human sacrifice, but it must be an infinite and an eternal sacrifice. Now there is not any man that can sacrifice his own blood which will atone for the sins of another. Now if a man murder, behold, will our law, which is just, take the life of his brother? I say unto you, no, but the law requires

the life of him who has murdered. Therefore, there can be nothing which is short of an infinite atonement which will suffice for the sins of the world. Therefore, it is expedient that there should be a great and last[163] sacrifice. And then shall there be, or it is expedient there should be, a stop to the shedding of blood.[164] Then shall the Torah of Moshe be fulfilled;[165] yes, it shall all be fulfilled, every yud and stroke, and none shall have passed away.[166] And behold, this is the whole meaning of the Torah, every whit pointing to that great and last sacrifice. And that great and last sacrifice will be the Son of Elohim, yes, infinite and eternal. And thus he shall bring salvation to all those who shall believe on his name, this being the intent of this last sacrifice: to bring about the bowels of mercy, which overpowers justice and brings about means unto men that they may have faith unto repentance. And thus mercy can satisfy the demands of justice, and encircle them in the arms of safety, while he that exercises no faith unto repentance is exposed to the whole Torah of the demands of justice. Therefore, only unto him that has faith unto repentance is brought about the great and eternal plan of redemption.

35 Therefore, may Elohim grant unto you, my brothers, that you may begin to exercise your faith unto repentance, that you begin to call upon his holy name, that he would have mercy upon you. Yes, cry unto him for mercy, for he is mighty to save.[167] Yes, humble yourselves and continue in prayer unto him. Cry unto him when you are in your fields, yes, over all your flocks. Cry unto him in your houses, yes, over all your household, both morning, midday, and evening.[168] Yes, cry unto him against the power of your enemies. Yes, cry unto him against HaSatan, who is an enemy to all righteousness. Cry unto him over the crops of your fields, that you may prosper in them; cry over

---

163 The underlying Hebrew may have been *acharon* אחרון (Strong's 314), which can mean "last" but can also mean "latter, following, or to come." **164** The underlying Hebrew for "stop" may have been שלא תהיה יותר, which literally means "should be no more" but could also be translated as "shall be no greater." The Hebrew word *yoter* יותר can mean "more" or "greater." Yosef ben Yosef said: "These sacrifices, as well as every ordinance belonging to the priesthood, will, when the Temple of the Lord shall be built, and the sons of Levi be purified, be fully restored and attended to in all their powers, ramifications, and blessings…" Cook, L.W. & Ehat, A.F. (Eds.) (1980) *The Words of Joseph Smith*. Salt Lake City, UT: Bookcraft, p. 43 [quote edited for grammar and punctuation]; See 3 Nefi 4:7. **165** See "What does it mean to fulfill the Torah?" footnote to 2 Nefi 11:8. **166** 3 Nefi 7:2 **167** 2 Nefi 13:4 **168** Referring to the Jewish custom of three times of daily prayer: *Shaharit* (morning prayer), *Minhah* (midday afternoon prayer), and *Maarive* (evening prayer).

the flocks of your fields, that they may increase. But this is not all. You must pour out your souls in your closets, and your secret places, and in your wilderness. Yes, and when you do not cry unto YHWH, let your hearts be full, drawn out in prayer unto him continually for your welfare, and also for the welfare of those who are around you.[169]

36 And now behold, my brothers, I say unto you, do not suppose that this is all. For after you have done all these things, if you turn away the needy and the naked, and visit not the sick and the afflicted, and impart of your substance, if you have, to those who stand in need, I say unto you, if you do not any of these things, behold, your prayer is vain and avails you nothing, and you are as hypocrites who do deny the faith. Therefore, if you do not remember to be charitable, you are as dross, which the refiners do cast out (it being of no worth) and is trampled underfoot of men.

37 And now, my brothers, I would that after you have received so many witnesses, seeing that the holy scriptures testify of these things, come forth and bring fruit unto repentance. Yes, I would that you would come forth and harden not your hearts any longer. For behold, now is the time and the day of your salvation. And therefore, if you will repent and harden not your hearts, immediately shall the great plan of redemption be brought about unto you. For behold, this life is the time for men to prepare to meet Elohim. Yes, behold, the day of this life is the day for men to perform their labors. And now, as I said unto you before, as you have had so many witnesses, therefore I implore you that you do not procrastinate the day of your repentance until the end. For after this day of life, which is given us to prepare for eternity, behold, if we do not improve our time while in this life, then comes the night of darkness in which there can be no labor performed. You cannot say when you are brought to that awful crisis that I will repent, that I will return to my Elohim. No, you cannot say this, for the same spirit you hearken to obey while living in the flesh shall, upon your death, have the same power to influence you to hearken unto that spirit in the next life. For behold, if you have procrastinated the day of your repentance, even until death, behold, you have become subjected to the spirit of HaSatan and he does seal you his. Therefore, the spirit of YHWH has withdrawn from you and

---

169 2 Nefi 15:1

has no place in you, and HaSatan has all power over you; and this is the final state of the wicked. And this I know because YHWH has said he dwells not in unholy temples, but in the hearts of the righteous does he dwell. Yes, and he has also said that the righteous should sit down in his kingdom to go no more out, but their garments should be made white through the blood of the Lamb.

38 And now, my beloved brothers, I desire that you should remember these things, and that you should work out your salvation with fear before Elohim, and that you should no more deny the coming of Mashiach; that you contend no more against the Ruach HaKodesh, but that you receive it and take upon you the name of Mashiach; that you humble yourselves even to the dust, and worship Elohim in whatsoever place you may be in, in spirit and in truth; and that you live in thanksgiving daily for the many mercies and blessings which he does bestow upon you. Yes, and I also exhort you, my brothers, that you be watchful unto prayer continually, that you may not be led away by the temptations of HaSatan, that he may not overpower you,[170] that you may not become his subjects at the last day; for behold, he rewards you no good thing. And now, my beloved brothers, I would exhort you to have patience, and that you bear with all manner of afflictions; that you do not revile against those who do cast you out because of your exceeding poverty, for fear that you become sinners like unto them, but that you have patience and bear with those afflictions with a firm hope that you shall one day rest from all your afflictions.

39 Now it came to pass that after Amulek had made an end of these words, they withdrew themselves from the multitude and came over into the land of Yirshon. Yes, and the rest of the brothers, after they had preached the word unto the Tzuramites, also came over into the land of Yirshon.

40 And it came to pass that after the more popular part of the Tzuramites had consulted together concerning the words which had been preached unto them, they were angry because of the word, for it did destroy their craft; therefore, they would not hearken unto the words. And they sent and gathered together, throughout all the land, all the people, and consulted with them concerning the words

---

170 Alma 10:4; 3 Nefi 8:8

ALMA 16:41

which had been spoken. Now their rulers, and their kohanim, and their teachers did not let the people know concerning their desires; therefore, they found out secretly the minds of all the people.

⁴¹ And it came to pass that after they had found out the minds of all the people, those who were in favor of the words which had been spoken by Alma and his brothers were cast out of the land, and they were many; and they came over also into the land of Yirshon. And it came to pass that Alma and his brothers did minister unto them.

⁴² Now the people of the Tzuramites were angry with the people of Ammon who were in Yirshon. And the chief ruler of the Tzuramites, being a very wicked man, sent over unto the people of Ammon, desiring them that they should cast out of their land all those who came over from them into their land. And he breathed out many threatenings against them. And now the people of Ammon did not fear their words, therefore they did not cast them out, but they did receive all the poor of the Tzuramites that came over unto them. And they did nourish them, and did clothe them, and did give unto them lands for their inheritance; and they did administer unto them according to their wants. Now this did stir up the Tzuramites to anger against the people of Ammon, and they began to mix with the Lamanites and to stir them up also to anger against them. And thus the Tzuramites and the Lamanites began to make preparations for war against the people of Ammon, and also against the Nefites. And thus ended the seventeenth year of the reign of the judges over the people of Nefi.

⁴³ And the people of Ammon departed out of the land of Yirshon, and came over into the land of Melek, and gave place in the land of Yirshon for the armies of the Nefites, that they might contend with the armies of the Lamanites and the armies of the Tzuramites. And thus commenced a war between the Lamanites and the Nefites in the eighteenth year of the reign of the judges; and an account shall be given of their wars hereafter.

⁴⁴ And Alma, and Ammon, and their brothers, and also the two sons of Alma returned to the land of Zerach'mla, after having been instruments in the hands of Elohim of bringing many of the Tzuramites to repentance. And as many as were brought to repentance were driven out of their land; but they have lands for their inheritance in the land of Yirshon, and they have taken up

arms to defend themselves, and their wives, and their children, and their lands.

45 Now Alma, being grieved for the iniquity of his people, yes, for the wars, and the bloodsheds, and the contentions which were among them, and having been to declare the word, or sent to declare the word, among all the people in every city, and seeing that the hearts of the people began to grow hard, and that they began to be offended because of the strictness of the word, his heart was exceedingly sorrowful. Therefore, he caused that his sons should be gathered together, that he might give unto them, every one, his charge separately, concerning the things pertaining unto righteousness. And we have an account of his commandments which he gave unto them, according to his own record.[171]

The commandments of Alma to his son Cheleman.

17 My son, give ear to my words, for I swear unto you that inasmuch as you shall keep the mitzvot of Elohim, you shall prosper in the land. I would that you should do as I have done in remembering the captivity of our fathers; for they were in bondage and none could deliver them, except it were the Elohim of Avraham, and the Elohim of Yitz'chak, and the Elohim of Ya'akov. And he surely did deliver them in their afflictions. And now, O my son

---

[171] This parallels with Ex. 13:8-16, as well as with the traditional Passover questions about the "four sons," indicating that this was a Passover Seder. (The Passover Haggadah speaks of four sons: one who is wise; one who is wicked; one who is simple; and one who does not know to ask.) Each son asks his question about the Seder in a different way, and the Haggadah recommends answering each son, according to his question, using one of the three verses in the Torah that refer to this exchange. The wise son asks, "What are the statutes, the testimonies, and the laws that God has commanded you to do?" (Deut. 6:20). One explanation for why this very detail-oriented question is categorized as "wise" is that the wise son is trying to learn how to carry out the Seder, rather than asking for someone else's understanding of its meaning. He is answered fully: "You should reply to him with [all] the laws of pesach: one may not eat any dessert after the paschal sacrifice." The wicked son asks, "What is this service to you?" (Ex. 12:26); he is characterized by the Haggadah as isolating himself from the Jewish people, standing by objectively and watching their behavior rather than participating. Therefore, he is rebuked by the explanation: "It is because God acted for my sake when I left Egypt" (Ex. 13:8)—this implies that the Seder is not for the wicked son, because the wicked son would not have deserved to be freed from Egyptian slavery; when the four sons are illustrated in the Haggadah, this son is frequently depicted as carrying weapons or wearing stylish contemporary fashions. The simple son asks, "What is this?" (Ex. 13:14) and is answered with: "With a strong hand the Almighty led us out from Egypt, from the house of bondage" (Ex. 13:14). And the one who does not know to ask is told, "It is because of what the Almighty did for me when I left Egypt" (Ex. 13:8).

Cheleman, behold, you are in your youth, and therefore I implore you that you will hear my words and learn of me. For I do know that whosoever shall put their trust in Elohim shall be supported in their trials, and their troubles, and their afflictions, and shall be lifted up at the last day. And I would not that you think that I know of myself – not of the temporal, but of the spiritual, not of the carnal mind, but of Elohim.

2 Now behold, I say unto you, if I had not been born of Elohim, I should not have known these things. But Elohim has, by the mouth of his holy angel, made these things known unto me – not of any worthiness of myself, for I went about with the sons of Moshiyah seeking to destroy the assembly of Elohim; but behold, Elohim sent his holy angel to stop us by the way. And behold, he spoke unto us as it were the voice of thunder, and the whole earth did tremble beneath our feet, and we all fell to the earth, for the fear of YHWH came upon us. But behold, the voice said unto me, Arise. And I arose, and stood up and beheld the angel. And he said unto me, If you will of yourself, be destroyed; seek no more to destroy the assembly of Elohim.

3 And it came to pass that I fell to the earth. And it was for the space of three days and three nights that I could not open my mouth, neither had I the use of my limbs. And the angel spoke more things unto me which were heard by my brothers, but I did not hear them, for when I heard the words – If you will, be destroyed of yourself; seek no more to destroy the assembly of Elohim – I was struck with such great fear and amazement, that perhaps I should be destroyed, that I fell to the earth and I did hear no more. But I was racked with Eternal torment, for my soul was torn up to the greatest degree and racked with all my sins. Yes, I did remember all my sins and iniquities, for which I was tormented with the pains of She'ol. Yes, I saw that I had rebelled against my Elohim and that I had not kept his holy mitzvot. Yes, and I had murdered many of his children, or rather led them away unto destruction. Yes, and in short, so great had been my iniquities that the very thought of coming into the presence of my Elohim did rack my soul with inexpressible horror. Oh, thought I, that I could be banished and become extinct, both soul and body, that I might not be brought to stand in the presence of my Elohim to be judged of my deeds. And now, for three days and for three nights was I racked, even with the pains of a damned soul.

4 And it came to pass that as I was thus racked with torment, while I was tormented by the memory of my many sins, behold, I remembered also to have heard my father prophesy unto the people concerning the coming of one Yeshua HaMashiach, a Son of Elohim, to atone for the sins of the world. Now as my mind caught hold upon this thought, I cried within my heart, O Yeshua, you Son of Elohim, have mercy on me, who is in the gall of bitterness and is encircled about by the everlasting chains of death. And now behold, when I thought this, I could remember my pains no more; yes, I was tormented by the memory of my sins no more.[172] And oh, what joy and what marvelous light I did behold! Yes, my soul was filled with joy as exceeding as were my pains. Yes, I say unto you, my son, that there can be nothing so exquisite and so bitter as were my pains.

5 Yes, and again I say unto you, my son, that on the other hand, there can be nothing so exquisite and sweet as was my joy. Yes, and it seemed to me that I saw, even as our father Lechi saw, Elohim sitting upon his throne, surrounded with numberless concourses of angels in the attitude of singing and praising their Elohim; yes, and my soul did long to be there.[173] But behold, my limbs did receive their strength again, and I stood upon my feet, and did manifest unto the people that I had been born of Elohim. Yes, and from that time even until now, I have labored without ceasing, that I might bring souls unto repentance, that I might bring them to taste of the exceeding joy of which I did taste, that they might also be born of Elohim and be filled with the Ruach HaKodesh.

6 Yes, and now behold, O my son, YHWH does give me exceedingly great joy in the fruits of my labors. For because of the word which he has made known unto me, behold, many have been born of Elohim, and have tasted as I have tasted, and have seen eye to eye as I have seen.[174] Therefore, they do know of these things of which I have spoken as I do know; and the knowledge which I have is of Elohim. And I have been supported under trials and troubles of every kind, yes, and in all manner of afflictions. Yes, Elohim has delivered me from prisons, and from bonds, and from death. Yes, and I do put my trust in him, and he will still deliver me. And I know that he will raise me up at the last day to dwell with him in glory. Yes, and I will

---

172 Isa. 1:18   173 1 Nefi 1:3   174 2 Nefi 8:2; 'Eter 5:3, 8

praise him for ever, for he has brought our fathers out of Egypt, and he has swallowed up the Egyptians in the Red Sea, and he led them by his power into the promised land. Yes, and he has delivered them out of bondage and captivity from time to time. Yes, and he has also brought our fathers out of the land of Yerushalayim. And he has also, by his everlasting power, delivered them out of bondage and captivity from time to time, even down to the present day. And I have always retained in remembrance their captivity; yes, and you also ought to retain in remembrance, as I have done, their captivity. But behold, my son, this is not all, for you ought to know as I do know that inasmuch as you shall keep the mitzvot of Elohim, you shall prosper in the land. And you ought to know also that inasmuch as you will not keep the mitzvot of Elohim, **you shall be cut off from his presence.**[175] Now this is according to his word.

7 And now, my son Cheleman, I command you that you take the records which have been entrusted with me. And I also command you that you keep a record of this people according as I have done, upon the plates of Nefi, and keep all these things sacred which I have kept, even as I have kept them — for it is for a wise purpose that they are kept — and these plates of brass which contain these engravings, which have the records of the holy scriptures upon them, which have the genealogy of our forefathers, even from the beginning. And behold, it has been prophesied by our fathers that they should be kept and handed down from one generation to another, and be kept and preserved by the hand of YHWH until they should go forth unto every nation, kindred, tongue, and people, that they shall know of the mysteries contained thereon. And now behold, if they are kept, they must retain their brightness, yes, and they will retain their brightness, yes, and also shall all the plates which do contain that which is holy writ.

8 Now you may suppose that this is foolishness in me, but behold, I say unto you that by small and simple things are great things brought to pass, and small means in many instances do confound the wise. And Adonai YHWH does work by means to bring about his great and eternal purposes, and by very small means YHWH does confound the wise and brings about the salvation of many souls. And now, it

---

[175] Lev. 22:3

has previously been wisdom in Elohim that these things should be preserved. For behold, they have enlarged the memory of this people, yes, and convinced many of the error of their ways and brought them to the knowledge of their Elohim, unto the salvation of their souls. Yes, I say unto you, were it not for these things that these records do contain, which are on these plates, Ammon and his brothers could not have convinced so many thousands of the Lamanites of the incorrect tradition of their fathers. Yes, these records and their words brought them unto repentance; that is, they brought them to the knowledge of YHWH their Elohim, and to rejoice in Yeshua HaMashiach their Redeemer. And who knows but that they will be the means of bringing many thousands of them, yes, and also many thousands of our stiffnecked brothers the Nefites, who are now hardening their hearts in sins and iniquities, to the knowledge of their Redeemer. Now these mysteries are not yet fully made known unto me, therefore I shall refrain. And it may suffice if I say only they are preserved for a wise purpose, which purpose is known unto Elohim; for he does counsel in wisdom over all his works, and his paths are straight, and his course is one eternal round.

9 Oh remember, remember, my son Cheleman, how strict are the mitzvot of Elohim. And he said, If you will keep my mitzvot, you shall prosper in the land, but if you keep not his mitzvot, **you shall be cut off from his presence.**[176] And now remember, my son, that Elohim has entrusted you with these things which are sacred, which he has kept sacred, and also which he will keep and preserve for a wise purpose in him, that he may show forth his power unto future generations.

10 And now behold, I tell you by the spirit of prophecy that if you transgress the mitzvot of Elohim, behold, these things which are sacred shall be taken away from you by the power of Elohim, and you shall be delivered up unto HaSatan, that he may sift you as chaff before the wind. But if you keep the mitzvot of Elohim, and do with these things which are sacred according to that which YHWH does command you — for you must appeal unto YHWH for all things whatsoever you must do with them — behold, no power of earth or She'ol can take them from you, for Elohim is powerful to the fulfilling

---

[176] Lev. 22:3

of all his words. For he will fulfill all his promises which he shall make unto you, for he has fulfilled his promise which he has made unto our fathers. For he promised unto them that he would preserve these things for a wise purpose in him, that he might show forth his power unto future generations.[177]

11 And now behold, one purpose has he fulfilled, even to the restoration of many thousands of the Lamanites to the knowledge of the truth. And he has shown forth his power in them, and he will also still show forth his power in them unto future generations; therefore, they shall be preserved. Therefore, I command you, my son Cheleman, that you be diligent in fulfilling all my words, and that you be diligent in keeping the mitzvot of Elohim as they are written.

12 And now I will speak unto you concerning those twenty-four plates,[178] that you keep them — that the mysteries, and the works of darkness, and their secret works, or the secret works of those people who have been destroyed, may be made manifest unto this people; yes, all their murders and robbings, and their plunderings, and all their wickedness and abominations may be made manifest unto this people — yes, and that you preserve these directors. For behold, YHWH saw that his people began to work in darkness, yes, work secret murders and abominations. Therefore, YHWH said if they did not repent, they should be destroyed from off the face of the earth. And YHWH said, I will prepare unto my servant Gazelem[179] a stone which shall shine forth in darkness unto light,[180] that I may uncover unto my people who serve me, that I may uncover unto them the works of their brothers — yes, their secret works, their works of darkness, and their wickedness and abominations. And now, my son, these directors were prepared that the word of Elohim might be fulfilled which he spoke, saying, I will bring forth out of darkness unto light all their secret works and their abominations, and except they repent, I will destroy them from off the face of the earth. And I will bring to light

---

[177] 2 Nefi 12:8 [178] Moshiyah 12:3-4; 'Eter 1:1 [179] The original Hebrew may have been *gazerim* גזרים from the Aramaic root גזר (Strong's 1505) "to determine." As a noun, it can refer to a diviner or astrologer or one who interprets signs to foretell the future (as in Dan. 2:27; 4:7; 5:7 and 5:11, where the KJV uses the word "soothsayers"). The Stick of Joseph was written in Hebrew using Egyptian characters (1 Nefi 1:1; Moshiyah 1:1; M'raman 4:11). Since the sound "L" is not written in Egyptian, when Hebrew words are transliterated into Egyptian characters, the Egyptian "R" does double duty for both "R" (ר) and "L" (ל). Depending on how the text is punctuated (the original manuscript had no punctuation), the word may refer either to the servant or the stone. [180] Moshiyah 12:3

all their secrets and abominations unto every nation which shall hereafter possess the land. And now, my son, we see that they did not repent. Therefore, they have been destroyed, and thus far the word of Elohim has been fulfilled. Yes, their secret abominations have been brought out of darkness and made known unto us.

¹³ And now, my son, I command you that you retain all their oaths, and their covenants, and their agreements in their secret abominations, yes, and all their signs and their wonders you shall retain from this people, that they know them not, lest perhaps they should fall into darkness also and be destroyed. For behold, there is a curse upon all this land, that destruction shall come upon all those workers of darkness, according to the power of Elohim, when they are fully ripe; therefore, I desire that this people might not be destroyed. Therefore, you shall keep these secret plans of their oaths and their covenants from this people, and only their wickedness, and their murders, and their abominations shall you make known unto them. And you shall teach them to abhor such wickedness, and abominations, and murders, and you shall also teach them that those people were destroyed on account of their wickedness and abominations, and their murders. For behold, they murdered all the prophets of YHWH who came among them to declare unto them concerning their iniquities; and the blood of those whom they murdered did cry unto YHWH their Elohim for vengeance upon those who were their murderers; and thus the judgments of Elohim did come upon those workers of darkness and secret conspiracies. Yes, and cursed be the land for ever and ever unto those workers of darkness and secret conspiracies, even unto destruction, except they repent before they are fully ripe.

¹⁴ And now, my son, remember the words which I have spoken unto you. Trust not those secret plans unto this people, but teach them an everlasting hatred against sin and iniquity. Preach unto them repentance and faith on Adonai Yeshua HaMashiach. Teach them to humble themselves and to be meek and humble in heart. Teach them to withstand every temptation of HaSatan with their faith on Adonai Yeshua HaMashiach. Teach them to never be weary of good works, but to be meek and humble in heart, for such shall find rest to their souls. Oh remember, my son, and learn wisdom in your youth; yes, learn in your youth to keep the mitzvot of Elohim. Yes, and cry unto

Elohim for all your support. Yes, let all your doings be unto YHWH, and wherever you go, let it be in YHWH. Yes, let all your thoughts be directed unto YHWH. Yes, let the affections of your heart be placed upon YHWH for ever. Counsel with YHWH in all your doings and he will direct you for good. Yes, when you lie down at night, lie down unto YHWH, that he may watch over you in your sleep; and when you rise in the morning, let your heart be full of thanks unto Elohim. And if you always do these things, you shall be lifted up at the last day.

15 And now, my son, I have somewhat to say concerning the thing which our fathers call a ball or director, or our fathers called it Liahona,[181] which is (being interpreted) a compass;[182] and YHWH prepared it.[183] And behold, there cannot any man work after the manner of such elegant workmanship. And behold, it was prepared to show unto our fathers the course which they should travel in the wilderness; and it did work for them according to their faith in Elohim. Therefore, if they had faith to believe that Elohim could cause that those spindles should point the way they should go, behold, it was done. Therefore, they had this miracle, and also many other miracles, worked by the power of Elohim, day by day. Nevertheless, because those miracles were worked by small means, it did show unto them marvelous works. They were slothful and forgot to exercise their faith and diligence, and then those marvelous works ceased and they did not progress in their journey. Therefore, they remained in the wilderness, or did not travel a direct course, and were afflicted with hunger and thirst **because of their transgression.**[184]

16 And now, my son, I would that you should understand that these things are not without a shadow. For as our fathers were slothful to give heed to this compass (now these things were temporal), they did not prosper; even so it is with things which are spiritual. For behold, it is as easy to give heed to the word of Mashiach, which will point to you a straight course to eternal bliss, as it was for our fathers to give

---

181 This is a unique but clearly Hebrew word: *liahona* ליהונא may come from the root *lawah* לוה (Strong's 3867), "to join, to bind around, to wreathe," from which come the related Hebrew words *liah* ליה (Strong's 3914), "a wreath," and *lon* לין (Strong's 3885), "to abide, to dwell, to remain or continue." The word "Liahona" combines these words to describe a device that joins the traveling party to God, a ball with two spindles that would wreathe around and direct Lechi and his party where and when to abide, dwell, remain, or continue.   182 This should not be confused with a magnetic compass, which had not yet come into use. The word compass, in common 1830 usage, may refer to a circular course, a boundary, or a device for navigation.   183 1 Nefi 5:3   184 Ps. 107:17

heed to this compass which would point unto them a straight course to the promised land. And now I say, is there not a type in this thing? For just as surely as this director did bring our fathers, by following its course, to the promised land, so shall the words of Mashiach, if we follow their course, carry us beyond this vale of sorrow into a far better land of promise.

17 O my son, do not let us be slothful because of the easiness of the way, for so was it with our fathers. For so was it prepared for them, that if they would look, they might live; even so it is with us. The way is prepared, and if we will look, we may live for ever. And now, my son, see that you take care of these sacred things, yes, see that you look to Elohim and live. Go unto this people and declare the word, and be sober. My son, shalom.

The commandments of Alma to his son Shiblon.

18 My son, give ear to my words, for I say unto you even as I said unto Cheleman, that inasmuch as you shall keep the mitzvot of Elohim, you shall prosper in the land; and inasmuch as you will not keep the mitzvot of Elohim, you shall be cast off from his presence. And now, my son, I trust that I shall have great joy in you because of your steadiness and your faithfulness unto Elohim. For as you have commenced in your youth to look to YHWH your Elohim, even so I hope that you will continue in keeping his mitzvot, for blessed is he that endures to the end.[185] I say unto you, my son, that I have had great joy in you already because of your faithfulness, and your diligence, and your patience, and your long-suffering,[186] among the people of the Tzuramites. For I knew that you were in bonds; yes, and I also knew that you were stoned for the word's sake, and you did bear all these things with patience because YHWH was with you; and now you know that YHWH did deliver you.

2 And now, my son Shiblon, I would that you should remember that as much as you shall put your trust in Elohim, even so much you shall be delivered out of your trials, and your troubles, and your afflictions, and you shall be lifted up at the last day. Now, my son, I would not that you should think that I know these things of myself, but it is the

---

[185] 2 Nefi 13:4; 3 Nefi 7:2 [186] The repetition of the possessive pronoun here is normative in Hebrew, where a pronominal suffix is normally attached to each object of possession.

Ruach Elohim which is in me which makes these things known unto me; for if I had not been born of Elohim, I should not have known these things. But behold, YHWH, in his great mercy, sent his angel to declare unto me that I must stop the work of destruction among his people; yes, and I have seen an angel face to face, and he spoke with me, and his voice was as thunder, and it shook the whole earth.[187]

3 And it came to pass that I was three days and three nights in the most bitter pain and anguish of soul, and never, until I did cry out unto Adonai Yeshua HaMashiach for mercy, did I receive a remission of my sins. But behold, I did cry unto him, and I did find shalom to my soul. And now, my son, I have told you this that you may learn wisdom, that you may learn of me that there is no other way nor means by which man can be saved, only in and through Mashiach. Behold, he is the life and the light of the world. Behold, he is the word of truth and righteousness.

4 And now, as you have begun to teach the word, even so I would that you should continue to teach; and I would that you would be diligent and temperate in all things. See that you are not lifted up unto pride. Yes, see that you do not boast in your own wisdom nor of your great strength. Use boldness, but not overbearance; and also see that you bridle all your passions, that you may be filled with love. See that you refrain from idleness. Do not pray as the Tzuramites do, for you have seen that they pray to be heard of men and to be praised for their wisdom. Do not say, O Elohim, I thank you that we are better than our brothers, but rather say, O YHWH, forgive my unworthiness and remember my brothers in mercy; yes, acknowledge your unworthiness before Elohim at all times. And may YHWH bless your soul and receive you at the last day into his kingdom to sit down in shalom. Now go, my son, and teach the word unto this people. Be sober. My son, shalom.

The commandments of Alma to his son Corianton.

19 And now, my son, I have somewhat more to say unto you than what I said unto your brother. For behold, have you not observed the steadiness of your brother? His faithfulness and his diligence in keeping the mitzvot of Elohim? Behold, has he not set

---

[187] The Hebrew word here was likely *eretz* (ארץ), which can mean "land" or "earth."

a good example for you? For you did not give so much heed unto my words as did your brother among the people of the Tzuramites. Now this is what I have against you: you did go on unto boasting in your strength and your wisdom. And this is not all, my son. You did do that which was grievous unto me, for you did abandon the ministry, and did go over into the land of Siron among the borders of the Lamanites after the harlot Isabel. Yes, she did steal away the hearts of many, but this was no excuse for you, my son. You should have tended to the ministry with which you were entrusted. Do you not know, my son, that these things are an abomination in the sight of YHWH, yes, most abominable above all sins, except it be the shedding of innocent blood or denying the Ruach HaKodesh? For behold, if you deny the Ruach HaKodesh when it once has had place in you, and you know that you deny it, behold, this is a sin which is unpardonable. Yes, and whosoever murders against the light and knowledge of Elohim, it is not easy for him to obtain forgiveness; yes, I say unto you, my son, that it is not easy for him to obtain forgiveness.

2 And now, my son, I would to Elohim that you had not been guilty of so great a crime. I would not dwell upon your crimes to torment your soul if it were not for your good. But behold, you cannot hide your crimes from Elohim, and except you repent, they will stand as a testimony against you at the last day. Now, my son, I would that you should repent, and abandon your sins, and go no more after the lusts of your eyes, but contain yourself in all these things; for except you do this, you can in no way inherit the kingdom of Elohim. Oh remember, and take it upon you, and contain yourself in these things. And I command you to take it upon you to counsel with your elder brothers in your undertakings. For behold, you are in your youth, and you stand in need to be nourished by your brothers and give heed to their counsel. Do not allow yourself to be led away by any vain or foolish thing; Do not allow HaSatan to lead away your heart again after those wicked harlots. Behold, O my son, how great iniquity you brought upon the Tzuramites; for when they saw your conduct, they would not believe in my words. And now the spirit of YHWH does say unto me, Command your children to do good, lest they lead away the hearts of many people to destruction. Therefore, I command you, my son, in the fear of Elohim, that you refrain from your iniquities, that

you turn to YHWH with all your mind, might, and strength, that you lead away the hearts of no more to do wickedly, but rather return unto them, and acknowledge your faults, and repair that wrong which you have done. Seek not after riches nor the vain things of this world, for behold, you cannot carry them with you.

3 And now, my son, I would say somewhat unto you concerning the coming of Mashiach. Behold, I say unto you that it is he that surely shall come to take away the sins of the world; yes, he comes to declare glad tidings of salvation unto his people. And now, my son, this was the ministry unto which you were called: to declare these glad tidings unto this people to prepare their minds — or rather, that salvation might come unto them, that they may prepare the minds of their children to hear the word at the time of his coming. And now I will ease your mind somewhat on this subject. Behold, you marvel why these things should be known so long beforehand. Behold, I say unto you, is not a soul at this time as precious unto Elohim as a soul will be at the time of his coming? Is it not as necessary that the plan of redemption should be made known unto this people as well as unto their children? Is it not as easy at this time for YHWH to send his angel to declare those glad tidings unto us as unto our children, or as after the time of his coming?

4 Now, my son, here is somewhat more I would say unto you, for I perceive that your mind is worried concerning the resurrection of the dead. Behold, I say unto you that there is no resurrection — or I would say in other words that this mortal does not put on immortality, this corruption does not put on incorruption — until after the coming of Mashiach. Behold, he brings to pass the resurrection of the dead. But behold, my son, the resurrection is not yet. Now I unfold unto you a mystery; nevertheless, there are many mysteries which are kept, that no one knows them except Elohim himself. But I show unto you one thing which I have inquired diligently of Elohim that I might know, that is concerning the resurrection. Behold, there is a time appointed that all shall come forth from the dead. Now when this time comes, no one knows, but Elohim knows the time which is appointed. Now whether there shall be one time, or a second time, or a third time that men shall come forth from the dead, it matters not, for Elohim knows all these things. And it suffices me to know

that this is the case — that there is a time appointed when all shall rise from the dead.

5 And now there must necessarily be a space between the time of death and the time of the resurrection. And now I would inquire, what becomes of the souls of men from this time of death to the time appointed for the resurrection? Now whether there is more than one time appointed for men to rise, it matters not, for all do not die at once, and this matters not — all is as one day with Elohim, and time only is measured unto man. Therefore, there is a time appointed unto men that they shall rise from the dead, and there is a space between the time of death and the resurrection.

6 And now, concerning this space of time, what becomes of the souls of men is the thing which I have inquired diligently of YHWH to know; and this is the thing of which I do know. And when the time comes when all shall rise, then shall they know that Elohim knows all the times which are appointed unto man. Now concerning the state of the soul between death and the resurrection, behold, it has been made known unto me by an angel that the spirits of all men, as soon as they are departed from this mortal body, yes, the spirits of all men, whether they be good or evil, are taken home to that Elohim who gave them life. And then shall it come to pass that the spirits of those who are righteous are received into a state of happiness, which is called pardes — a state of rest, a state of shalom where they shall rest from all their troubles, and from all care and sorrow, and so forth. And then shall it come to pass that the spirits of the wicked, yes, who are evil — for behold, they have no part nor portion of the spirit of YHWH; for behold, they chose evil works rather than good, therefore the spirit of HaSatan did enter into them and take possession of their house — and these shall be cast out into outer darkness. There shall be weeping, and wailing, and gnashing of teeth, and this because of their own iniquity, being led captive by the will of HaSatan. Now this is the state of the souls of the wicked, yes, in darkness and a state of awful, fearful anticipation of the fiery indignation of the wrath of Elohim upon them. Thus they remain in this state, as well as the righteous in pardes, until the time of their resurrection.

7 Now there are some that have understood that this state of happiness and this state of misery of the soul, before the resurrection, was a first resurrection. Yes, I admit it may be termed a resurrection,

ALMA 19:8

the raising of the spirit or the soul and their consignment to happiness or misery according to the words which have been spoken. And behold, again it has been spoken that there is a first resurrection, a resurrection of all those who have been, or who are, or who shall be, down to the resurrection of Mashiach from the dead. Now we do not suppose that this first resurrection, which is spoken of in this manner, can be the resurrection of the souls and their consignment to happiness or misery. You cannot suppose that this is what it means. Behold, I say unto you, no, but it means the reuniting of the soul with the body, of those from the days of Adam down to the resurrection of Mashiach. Now whether the souls and the bodies of those of whom have been spoken shall all be reunited at once, the wicked as well as the righteous, I do not say. Let it suffice that I say that they all come forth, or in other words, that their resurrection comes to pass before the resurrection of those who die after the resurrection of Mashiach. Now, my son, I do not say that their resurrection comes at the resurrection of Mashiach, but behold, I give it as my opinion that the souls and the bodies are reunited of the righteous, at the resurrection of Mashiach and his ascension into Heaven. But whether it be at his resurrection or after, I do not say.

8 But this much I say, that there is a space between death and the resurrection of the body, and a state of the soul, in happiness or in misery, until the time which is appointed of Elohim that the dead shall come forth and be reunited, both soul and body, and be brought to stand before Elohim and be judged according to their works. Yes, this brings about the restoration of those things of which have been spoken by the mouths of the prophets — the soul shall be restored to the body and the body to the soul; yes, and every limb and joint shall be restored to its body, yes, even a hair of their heads shall not be lost, but all things shall be restored to their proper and perfect frame. And now, my son, this is the restoration of which has been spoken by the mouths of the prophets. And then shall the righteous shine forth in the kingdom of Elohim. But behold, an awful death comes upon the wicked, for they die as to things pertaining to things of righteousness, for they are unclean, and no unclean thing can inherit the kingdom of Elohim.[188] But they are cast out, and consigned to partake of the

---
[188] 1 Nefi 3:5; 3 Nefi 12:5

fruits of their labors, or their works, which have been evil; and they drink the dregs of a bitter cup.

9 And now, my son, I have somewhat to say concerning the restoration of which has been spoken. For behold, some have twisted the scriptures and have gone far astray because of this thing, and I perceive that your mind has been worried also concerning this thing. But behold, I will explain it unto you. I say unto you, my son, that the plan of restoration is requisite with the justice of Elohim, for it is requisite that all things should be restored to their proper order. Behold, it is requisite and just, according to the power and resurrection of Mashiach, that the soul of man should be restored to its body, and that every part of the body should be restored to itself. And it is also requisite with the justice of Elohim that men should be judged according to their works. And if their works were good in this life and the desires of their hearts were good, that they should also, at the last day, be restored unto that which is good; and if his works are evil, they shall be restored unto him for evil. Therefore, all things shall be restored to their proper order, everything to its natural frame: mortality raised to immortality, corruption to incorruption, raised to Endless happiness to inherit the kingdom of Elohim, or to Endless misery to inherit the kingdom of HaSatan, the one on one hand, the other on the other, the one restored to happiness according to his desires of happiness, or to good according to his desires of good, and the other to evil according to his desires of evil.[189] For as he has desired to do evil all the day long, even so shall he have his reward of evil when the night comes. And so it is on the other hand: if he has repented of his sins and desired righteousness until the end of his days, even so shall he be rewarded unto righteousness. These are they that are redeemed of YHWH, yes, these are they that are taken out, that are delivered from that endless night of darkness. And thus they stand or fall. For behold, they are their own judges, whether to do good or do evil. Now the decrees of Elohim are unalterable. Therefore, the way is prepared that whosoever will may walk therein and be saved.[190]

10 And now behold, my son, do not risk one more offense against your Elohim upon those points of doctrine which you have previously

---

[189] 1 Nefi 3:27; 3 Nefi 5:38   [190] 1 Nefi 3:3; 2 Nefi 13:5; 3 Nefi 13:2; M'roni 7:6

risked to commit sin. Do not suppose because it has been spoken concerning restoration that you shall be restored from sin to happiness. Behold, I say unto you, wickedness never was happiness. And now, my son, all men that are in a state of nature — or I would say, in a carnal state — are in great bitterness of mind and in the bonds of iniquity. They are without Elohim in the world and they have gone contrary to the nature of Elohim, therefore they are in a state contrary to the nature of happiness.

11 And now behold, is the meaning of the word restoration to take a thing of a natural state and place it in an unnatural state? Or to place it in a state opposite to its nature? Oh, my son, this is not the case, but the meaning of the word restoration is to bring back again evil for evil, or carnal for carnal, or demonic for demonic; good for that which is good, righteous for that which is righteous, just for that which is just, merciful for that which is merciful. Therefore, my son, see that you are merciful unto your brothers. Deal justly, judge righteously, and do good continually; and if you do all these things, then shall you receive your reward. Yes, you shall have mercy restored unto you again, you shall have justice restored unto you again, you shall have a righteous judgment restored unto you again, and you shall have good rewarded unto you again. For that which you do send out shall return unto you again and be restored. Therefore, the word restoration more fully condemns the sinner and justifies him not at all.

12 And now, my son, I perceive there is somewhat more which does worry your mind, which you cannot understand, which is concerning the justice of Elohim in the punishment of the sinner; for you do try to suppose that it is injustice that the sinner should be consigned to a state of misery. Now behold, my son, I will explain this thing unto you. For behold, after Adonai YHWH **sent our first parents forth from the Garden of Eden to till the ground from which they were taken,**[191] **yes, he drove out the man, and he placed at the east end of the Garden of Eden keruvim and a flaming sword, which turned every way to guard the tree of life.**[192] Now we see that the **man had become as Elohim, knowing good and evil, and lest he should put forth his hand and take also of the tree of life, and eat, and live for ever,**[193] Adonai YHWH placed keruvim

---

191 Gen. 3:23   192 Gen. 3:24   193 Gen. 3:5, 22

and the flaming sword, that he should not partake of the fruit. And thus we see that there was a time granted unto man to repent, yes, a probationary time, a time to repent and serve Elohim. For behold, if Adam had put forth his hand immediately and partaken of the tree of life, he would have lived for ever, according to the word of Elohim, having no space for repentance. Yes, and also the word of Elohim **would have been void**[194] and the great plan of salvation would have been frustrated. But behold, it was appointed unto man to die. Therefore, as they were cut off from the tree of life, they should be cut off from the face of the earth, and man became lost for ever; yes, they became fallen man.

13 And now we see by this that our first parents were cut off, both temporally and spiritually, from the presence of YHWH; and thus we see they became subjects to follow after their own will. Now behold, it was not expedient that man should be reclaimed from this temporal death, for that would destroy the great plan of happiness. Therefore, as the soul could never die and the Fall had brought upon all mankind a spiritual death as well as a temporal (that is, they were cut off from the presence of YHWH), therefore it was expedient that mankind should be reclaimed from this spiritual death. Therefore, as they had become carnal, sensual, and demonic by nature, this probationary state became a state for them to prepare; it became a preparatory state.

14 And now remember, my son, if it were not for the plan of redemption (laying it aside), as soon as they were dead, their souls were miserable, being cut off from the presence of YHWH. And now there was no means to reclaim men from this fallen state, which man had brought upon himself because of his own disobedience. Therefore, according to justice, the plan of redemption could not be brought about — only on conditions of repentance of men in this probationary state, yes, this preparatory state. For except it were for these conditions, mercy could not take effect except it should destroy the work of justice. Now the work of justice could not be destroyed; if so, Elohim would cease to be Elohim.[195] And thus we see that all

---

[194] Isa. 55:11   [195] As the Zohar says: "R. Hiya discoursed on the text: Therefore hearken unto me, ye men of understanding: Far be it from God that he should do wickedness; and from the Almighty that he should commit iniquity. For the work of man will he requite unto him, and cause every man to find according to his ways (Job 34:10-11). 'God,' he

mankind were fallen, and they were in the grasp of justice, yes, the justice of Elohim, which consigned them for ever to be cut off from his presence. And now the plan of mercy could not be brought about except an atonement should be made. Therefore, Elohim himself atones for the sins of the world, to bring about the plan of mercy, to appease the demands of justice, that Elohim might be a perfect, just Elohim, and a merciful Elohim also.

15 Now repentance could not come unto men except a punishment, which was as eternal as the life of the soul, should be affixed opposite to the plan of happiness, which was as eternal also as the life of the soul. Now, how could a man repent except he should sin? How could he sin if there was no Torah? How could there be a Torah except there was a punishment? Now there was a punishment affixed and a just Torah given, which brought remorse of conscience unto man. Now if there was no Torah given (if, for example, a man murdered, he should die), would he be afraid he should die if he should murder? And also, if there was no Torah given against sin, men would not be afraid to sin. And if there was no Torah given if men sinned, what could justice do? Or mercy either? For they would have no claim upon the creature. But there is a Torah given, and a punishment affixed, and repentance granted, which repentance mercy claims. Otherwise, justice claims the creature and executes the Torah, and the Torah inflicts the punishment. If not so, the works of justice would be destroyed and Elohim would cease to be Elohim. But Elohim ceases not to be Elohim, and mercy claims the penitent, and mercy comes because of the atonement, and the atonement brings to pass the resurrection of the dead, and the resurrection of the dead brings back men into the presence of Elohim. And thus they are restored into his presence, to be judged according to their works, according to the Torah and justice. For behold, justice exercises all his demands, and also mercy claims all which is her own; and thus none but the truly penitent are saved.

16 What? Do you suppose that mercy can rob justice? I say unto you, no, not one bit. If so, Elohim would cease to be Elohim. And thus

---

said, 'in creating the world, meant it to be based on justice, and all that is done in the world would be weighed in the scales of justice, were it not that, to save the world from perishing, God screened it with mercy, which tempers pure justice and prevents it from destroying the world. The world is thus governed in mercy and thereby is able to endure'" (Zohar 1:180b).

Elohim brings about his great and eternal purposes, which were prepared from the foundation of the world. And thus comes about the salvation and the redemption of men, and also their destruction and misery. Therefore, O my son, whosoever will come may come and partake of the waters of life freely. And whosoever will not come, the same is not compelled to come, but in the last day it shall be restored unto him according to his deeds. If he has desired to do evil and has not repented in his days, behold, evil shall be done unto him according to the restoration of Elohim.

17 And now, my son, I desire that you should let these things trouble you no more, and only let your sins trouble you with that trouble which shall bring you down unto repentance. O my son, I desire that you should deny the justice of Elohim no more. Do not endeavor to excuse yourself in the least point because of your sins by denying the justice of Elohim, but do let the justice of Elohim and his mercy, and his long-suffering, have full sway in your heart, and let it bring you down to the dust in humility. And now, my son, you are called of Elohim to preach the word unto this people. And now, my son, go your way; declare the word with truth and soberness, that you may bring souls unto repentance, that the great plan of mercy may have claim upon them. And may Elohim grant unto you, yes, even according to my words. Amen.

20 And now it came to pass that the sons of Alma did go forth among the people to declare the word unto them. And Alma also, himself, could not rest, and he also went forth. Now we shall say no more concerning their preaching, except that they preached the word and the truth according to the spirit of prophecy and revelation, and they preached after the Holy Order of Elohim by which they were called.

2 And now I return to an account of the wars between the Nefites and the Lamanites in the eighteenth year of the reign of the judges. For behold, it came to pass that the Tzuramites became Lamanites. Therefore, in the commencement of the eighteenth year, the people of the Nefites saw that the Lamanites were coming upon them. Therefore, they made preparations for war, yes, they gathered together their armies in the land of Yirshon. And it came to pass that the Lamanites came with their thousands; and they came into the land of Antionum,

which was the land of the Tzuramites; and a man by the name of Zerahemnah was their leader. And now, as the Amlicites were of a more wicked and a murderous disposition than the Lamanites were, in and of themselves, therefore Zerahemnah appointed chief captains over the Lamanites and they were all Amlicites and Tzuramites. Now this he did that he might preserve their hatred towards the Nefites, that he might bring them into subjection to the accomplishment of his designs. For behold, his designs were to stir up the Lamanites to anger against the Nefites, and this he did that he might usurp great power over them, and also that he might gain power over the Nefites by bringing them into bondage, and so forth.

3 And now the design of the Nefites was to support their lands, and their houses, and their wives, and their children, that they might preserve them from the hands of their enemies, and also that they might preserve their rights and their privileges, and also their liberty, that they might worship Elohim according to their desires. For they knew that if they should fall into the hands of the Lamanites, that whosoever should worship Elohim in spirit and in truth, the true and the living Elohim, the Lamanites would destroy. Yes, and they also knew the extreme hatred of the Lamanites towards their brothers, who were the people of Anti-Nefi-Lechi, who were called the people of Ammon. And they would not take up arms, yes, they had entered into a covenant and they would not break it; therefore, if they should fall into the hands of the Lamanites, they would be destroyed. And the Nefites would not allow that they should be destroyed, therefore they gave them lands for their inheritance, and the people of Ammon did give unto the Nefites a large portion of their substance to support their armies. And thus the Nefites were compelled, alone, to stand against the Lamanites, who were a compound of Laman, and L'mu'el, and the sons of Yishma'el, and all those who had dissented from the Nefites, who were Amlicites, and Tzuramites, and the descendants of the kohanim of Noah. Now those dissenters were as numerous nearly as were the Nefites; and thus the Nefites were obliged to contend with their brothers, even unto bloodshed.

4 And it came to pass, as the armies of the Lamanites had gathered together in the land of Antionum, behold, the armies of the Nefites were prepared to meet them in the land of Yirshon. Now the leader of the Nefites, or the man who had been appointed to be the chief

captain over the Nefites — now the chief captain took the command of all the armies of the Nefites — and his name was M'roni. And M'roni took all the command and the government of their wars; and he was only twenty and five years old when he was appointed chief commander over the armies of the Nefites.

5 And it came to pass that he met the Lamanites in the borders of Yirshon, and his people were armed with swords, and with cimeters, and all manner of weapons of war. And when the armies of the Lamanites saw that the people of Nefi, or that M'roni, had prepared his people with breastplates and with armshields, yes, and also shields to defend their heads, and also they were dressed with thick clothing — now the army of Zerahemnah was not prepared with any such thing; they had only their swords and their cimeters, their bows and their arrows, their stones and their slings, but they were naked except it were a skin which was girded about their loins, yes, all were naked, except it were the Tzuramites and the Amlicites, but they were not armed with breastplates nor shields — therefore, they were exceedingly afraid of the armies of the Nefites because of their armor, despite their number being so much greater than the Nefites.

6 Behold, now it came to pass that they dared not come against the Nefites in the borders of Yirshon. Therefore, they departed out of the land of Antionum into the wilderness, and took their journey round about in the wilderness, away by the head of the river Tzidon, that they might come into the land of Manti and take possession of the land, for they did not suppose that the armies of M'roni would know where they had gone. But it came to pass, as soon as they had departed into the wilderness, M'roni sent spies into the wilderness to watch their camp. And M'roni, also knowing of the prophecies of Alma, sent certain men unto him, desiring him that he should inquire of YHWH where the armies of the Nefites should go to defend themselves against the Lamanites. And it came to pass that the word of YHWH came unto Alma, and Alma informed the messengers of M'roni that the armies of the Lamanites were marching round about in the wilderness that they might come over into the land of Manti, that they might commence an attack upon the more weak part of the people. And those messengers went and delivered the message unto M'roni.

7 Now M'roni, leaving a part of his army in the land of Yirshon, for fear that by any means a part of the Lamanites should come into that land and take possession of the city, took the remaining part of his army and marched over into the land of Manti. And he caused that all the people in that quarter of the land should gather themselves together to battle against the Lamanites, to defend their lands and their country, their rights and their liberties. Therefore, they were prepared against the time of the coming of the Lamanites. And it came to pass that M'roni caused that his army should be concealed in the valley which was near the bank of the river Tzidon, which was on the west of the river Tzidon in the wilderness. And M'roni placed spies round about, that he might know when the camp of the Lamanites should come.

8 And now, as M'roni knew the intention of the Lamanites, that it was their intention to destroy their brothers or to subject them and bring them into bondage, that they might establish a kingdom unto themselves over all the land, and he also knowing that it was the only desire of the Nefites to preserve their lands, and their liberty, and their assembly, therefore he thought it no sin that he should defend them by stratagem; therefore, he found by his spies, which course the Lamanites were to take. Therefore, he divided his army and brought a part over into the valley, and concealed them on the east and on the south of the hill Riplah; and the remainder he concealed in the west valley on the west of the river Tzidon, and so down into the borders of the land Manti. And thus having placed his army according to his desire, he was prepared to meet them.

9 And it came to pass that the Lamanites came up on the north of the hill where a part of the army of M'roni was concealed. And as the Lamanites had passed the hill Riplah and had come into the valley, and began to cross the river Tzidon, the army which was concealed on the south of the hill, which was led by a man whose name was Lechi, and he led his army forth and encircled the Lamanites about on the east, in their rear.

10 And it came to pass that the Lamanites, when they saw the Nefites coming upon them in their rear, they turned around and began to contend with the army of Lechi. And the work of death commenced on both sides, but it was more dreadful on the part of the Lamanites, for their nakedness was exposed to the heavy blows of the Nefites,

with their swords and their cimeters, which brought death almost at every stroke, while on the other hand, there was now and then a man who fell among the Nefites by their wounds and the loss of blood, they being shielded from the more vital parts of the body, or the more vital parts of the body being shielded from the strokes of the Lamanites by their breastplates, and their armshields, and their headplates. And thus the Nefites did carry on the work of death among the Lamanites. And it came to pass that the Lamanites became frightened because of the great destruction among them, even until they began to flee towards the river Tzidon. And they were pursued by Lechi and his men, and they were driven by Lechi into the waters of Tzidon, and they crossed the waters of Tzidon. And Lechi retained his armies upon the bank of the river Tzidon, that they should not cross.

11 And it came to pass that M'roni and his army met the army of the Lamanites in the valley on the other side of the river Tzidon, and began to fall upon them and to slay them. And the Lamanites did flee again before them, towards the land of Manti, and they were met again by the armies of M'roni. Now in this case, the Lamanites did fight exceedingly, yes, never had the Lamanites been known to fight with such exceedingly great strength and courage, no, not even from the beginning. And they were inspired by the Tzuramites and the Amlicites, who were their chief captains and leaders, and by Zerahemnah, who was their chief captain, or their chief leader and commander. Yes, they did fight like dragons, and many of the Nefites were slain by their hand. Yes, for they did strike in two many of their headplates, and they did pierce many of their breastplates, and they did cut off many of their arms; and thus the Lamanites did smite in their fierce anger. Nevertheless, the Nefites were inspired by a better cause; for they were not fighting for monarchy nor power, but they were fighting for their homes and their liberties, their wives and their children, and their all, yes, for their rites of worship and their assembly. And they were doing that which they felt was the duty which they owed to their Elohim, for YHWH had said unto them, and also unto their fathers, that inasmuch as you are not guilty of the first offense, neither the second, you shall not allow yourselves to be slain by the hands of your enemies. And again, YHWH has said that you shall defend your families even unto bloodshed. Therefore, for this cause were the Nefites contending with the Lamanites, to

ALMA 20:12

defend themselves, and their families, and their lands, their country, and their rights, and their religion.

12 And it came to pass that when the men of M'roni saw the fierceness and the anger of the Lamanites, they were about to shrink and flee from them. And M'roni, perceiving their intent, sent forth and inspired their hearts with these thoughts—yes, the thoughts of their lands, their liberty, yes, their freedom from bondage. And it came to pass that they turned upon the Lamanites, **and they cried with one voice unto YHWH their Elohim**[196] for their liberty and their freedom from bondage. And they began to stand against the Lamanites with power, and in that very same hour that they cried unto YHWH for their freedom, the Lamanites began to flee before them; and they fled even to the waters of Tzidon. Now the Lamanites were more numerous, yes, by more than double the number of the Nefites. Nevertheless, they were driven insomuch that they were gathered together in one body in the valley upon the bank by the river Tzidon. Therefore, the armies of M'roni encircled them about, yes, even on both sides of the river; for behold, on the east were the men of Lechi. Therefore, when Zerahemnah saw the men of Lechi on the east of the river Tzidon and the armies of M'roni on the west of the river Tzidon, that they were encircled about by the Nefites, they were struck with terror. Now M'roni, when he saw their terror, commanded his men that they should stop shedding their blood.

13 And it came to pass that they did stop and withdrew a pace from them. And M'roni said unto Zerahemnah, Behold, Zerahemnah, we do not desire to be men of blood. You know that you are in our hands, yet we do not desire to slay you. Behold, we have not come out to battle against you that we might shed your blood for power, neither do we desire to bring anyone to the yoke of bondage. But this is the very cause for which you have come against us. Yes, and you are angry with us because of our religion. But now you behold that YHWH is with us, and you behold that he has delivered you into our hands. And now I would that you should understand that this is done unto us because of our religion and our faith in Mashiach. And now you see that you cannot destroy this our faith. Now you see that this is the true faith of Elohim, yes, you see that Elohim will support,

---

[196] Neh. 9:4

and keep, and preserve us, so long as we are faithful unto him, and unto our faith, and our religion. And never will YHWH allow that we shall be destroyed, except we should fall into transgression and deny our faith. And now, Zerahemnah, I command you in the name of that all-powerful Elohim, who has strengthened our arms that we have gained power over you by our faith, by our religion, and by our rites of worship, and by our assembly, and by the sacred support which we owe to our wives and our children, and by that liberty which binds us to our lands and our country,[197] yes, and also by the maintenance of the sacred word of Elohim, to which we owe all our happiness, and by all that is most dear unto us — yes, and this is not all — I command you, by all the desires which you have for life, that you deliver up your weapons of war unto us, and we will seek not your blood, but we will spare your lives if you will go your way and come not again to war against us. And now, if you do not this, behold, you are in our hands, and I will command my men that they shall fall upon you and inflict the wounds of death in your bodies, that you may become extinct. And then we will see who shall have power over this people; yes, we will see who shall be brought into bondage.

14 And now it came to pass that when Zerahemnah had heard these sayings, he came forth and delivered up his sword, and his cimeter, and his bow, into the hands of M'roni, and said unto him, Behold, here are our weapons of war; we will deliver them up unto you. And we will not allow ourselves to take an oath unto you which we know that we shall break, and also our children. But take our weapons of war and allow that we may depart into the wilderness; otherwise, we will retain our swords and we will perish or conquer. Behold, we are not of your faith. We do not believe that it is Elohim that has delivered us into your hands, but we believe that it is your skillful craft that has preserved you from our swords. Behold, it is your breastplates and your shields that have preserved you.

15 And now when Zerahemnah had made an end of speaking these words, M'roni returned the sword and the weapons of war which he had received unto Zerahemnah, saying, Behold, we will end the conflict. Now I cannot recall the words which I have spoken; therefore,

---

197 The repetition of the possessive pronoun here is normative in Hebrew, where a pronominal suffix is normally attached to each object of possession.

ALMA 20:16

as YHWH lives, you shall not depart except you depart with an oath that you will not return again against us to war. Now as you are in our hands, we will spill your blood upon the ground, or you shall submit to the conditions to which I have proposed. And now when M'roni had said these words, Zerahemnah retained his sword; and he was angry with M'roni, and he rushed forward that he might slay M'roni. But as he raised his sword, behold, one of M'roni's soldiers smote it even to the earth and it broke by the hilt; and he also struck Zerahemnah, that he took off his scalp, and it fell to the earth. And Zerahemnah withdrew from before them into the midst of his soldiers.

16 And it came to pass that the soldier who stood by, who struck off the scalp of Zerahemnah, took up the scalp from off the ground by the hair, and laid it upon the point of his sword, and stretched it forth unto them, saying unto them with a loud voice, Even as this scalp has fallen to the earth, which is the scalp of your chief, so shall you fall to the earth except you will deliver up your weapons of war and depart with a covenant of shalom.

17 Now there were many, when they heard these words and saw the scalp which was upon the sword, that were struck with fear; and many came forth, and threw down their weapons of war at the feet of M'roni, and entered into a covenant of shalom. And as many as entered into a covenant they allowed to depart into the wilderness.

18 Now it came to pass that Zerahemnah was exceedingly angry, and he did stir up the remainder of his soldiers to anger, to contend more powerfully against the Nefites. And now M'roni was angry because of the stubbornness of the Lamanites; therefore, he commanded his people that they should fall upon them and slay them. And it came to pass that they began to slay them; yes, and the Lamanites did contend with their swords and their might. But behold, their naked skins and their bare heads were exposed to the sharp swords of the Nefites; yes, behold, they were pierced and struck, yes, and did fall exceedingly fast before the swords of the Nefites; and they began to be swept down even as the soldier of M'roni had prophesied. Now Zerahemnah, when he saw that they were all about to be destroyed, cried mightily unto M'roni, promising that he would covenant, and also his people with them, if they would spare the remainder of their lives, that they never would come to war again against them. And it

came to pass that M'roni caused that the work of death should cease again among the people. And he took the weapons of war from the Lamanites; and after they had entered into a covenant with him of shalom, they were allowed to depart into the wilderness.

19 Now the number of their dead were not numbered because of the greatness of the number; yes, the number of their dead was exceedingly great, both of the Nefites and of the Lamanites. And it came to pass that they did cast their dead into the waters of Tzidon, and they have gone forth and are buried in the depths of the sea. And the armies of the Nefites, or of M'roni, returned and came to their houses and their lands. And thus ended the eighteenth year[198] of the reign of the judges over the people of Nefi. And thus ended the record of Alma, which was written upon the plates of Nefi.

The account of the people of Nefi, and their wars and dissensions in the days of Cheleman, according to the record of Cheleman which he kept in his days.

21 Behold, now it came to pass that the people of Nefi were exceedingly joyful because YHWH had again delivered them out of the hands of their enemies. Therefore, they gave thanks unto YHWH their Elohim; yes, and they did fast much and pray much,[199] and they did worship Elohim with exceedingly great joy.[200]

2 And it came to pass in the nineteenth year of the reign of the judges over the people of Nefi, that Alma came unto his son Cheleman and said unto him, Do you believe the words which I spoke unto you concerning those records which have been kept? And Cheleman said unto him, Yes, I believe. And Alma said again, Do you believe in Yeshua HaMashiach, who shall come? And he said, Yes, I believe all the words which you have spoken. And Alma said unto him again, Will you keep my commandments? And he said, Yes, I will keep your commandments with all my heart. Then Alma said unto him, Blessed are you, and YHWH shall prosper you in this land. But behold, I have something to prophesy unto you, but what I prophesy unto you you shall not make known, yes, what I prophesy unto you shall not be made known even until the prophecy is fulfilled; therefore,

---

198 Rosh Hashanah, the 1st of Tishrei, the "head of the year," is followed by "prayer and fasting" at Yom Kippur and "great joy" at Sukkot (see footnote to Alma 21:1). **199** Prayer and fasting for Yom Kippur, the 10th of Tishrei (see footnote to Alma 20:19). **200** Rejoicing at Sukkot (Lev. 23:40) on the 15th through the 21st of Tishrei.

write the words which I shall say. And these are the words: Behold, I perceive that this very people, the Nefites, according to the spirit of revelation which is in me, in four hundred years from the time that Yeshua HaMashiach shall manifest himself unto them, shall dwindle in unbelief. Yes, and then shall they see wars and pestilences, yes, famine and bloodshed, even until the people of Nefi shall become extinct. Yes, and this because they shall dwindle in unbelief and fall into the works of darkness, and lustfulness, and all manner of iniquities. Yes, I say unto you that because they shall sin against so great light and knowledge, yes, I say unto you that from that day, even the fourth generation shall not all pass away before this great iniquity shall come. And when that great day comes, behold, the time very soon comes that those who are now, or the seed of those who are now numbered among the people of Nefi, shall no more be numbered among the people of Nefi. But whosoever remains and is not **destroyed in that great and dreadful day**[201] shall be numbered among the Lamanites, and shall become like unto them, all except it be a few who shall be called the talmidim of YHWH; and them shall the Lamanites pursue, even until they shall become extinct. And now, because of iniquity, this prophecy shall be fulfilled.[202]

3 And now it came to pass that after Alma had said these things to Cheleman, he blessed him, and also his other sons, and he also blessed the earth for the righteous' sake. And he said, Thus says Adonai YHWH: Cursed shall be the land, yes, this land, unto every nation, kindred, tongue, and people, unto destruction, which do wickedly, when they are fully ripe; and as I have said, so shall it be. For this is the cursing and the blessing of Elohim upon the land, for YHWH cannot look upon sin with the least degree of allowance. And now, when Alma had said these words, he blessed the assembly, yes, all those who should stand fast in the faith from that time henceforth. And when Alma had done this, he departed out of the land of Zerach'mla as if to go into the land of Melek. And it came to pass that he was never heard of again; and as to his death or his burial, we know not. Behold, this we know, that he was a righteous man; and the saying went abroad in the assembly that he was taken up by the spirit, or buried by the hand of YHWH, even as Moshe. But behold, the scripture says YHWH

---

201 Mal. 4:5 202 M'raman 4:1-2

took Moshe unto himself; and we suppose that he has also received Alma in the spirit unto himself. Therefore, for this cause we know nothing concerning his death and burial.[203]

4 And now it came to pass, in the commencement of the nineteenth year of the reign of the judges over the people of Nefi, that Cheleman went forth among the people to declare the word unto them. For behold, because of their wars with the Lamanites, and the many little dissensions and disturbances which had been among the people, it became expedient that the word of Elohim should be declared among them, yes, and that an ordering should be made throughout the assembly. Therefore, Cheleman and his brothers went forth to strengthen the assembly again in all the land, yes, in every city throughout all the land which was possessed by the people of Nefi. And it came to pass that they did appoint kohanim and teachers throughout all the land, over all the assemblies.

5 And now it came to pass that after Cheleman and his brothers had appointed kohanim and teachers over the assemblies, that there arose a dissension among them, and they would not give heed to the words of Cheleman and his brothers; but they grew proud, being lifted up in their hearts because of their exceedingly great riches. Therefore, they grew rich in their own eyes, and would not give heed to their words to walk uprightly before Elohim.

6 And it came to pass that as many as would not hearken to the words of Cheleman and his brothers were gathered together against their brothers. And now behold, they were exceedingly angry, insomuch that they were determined to slay them. Now the leader of those who were angry against their brothers was a large and a strong man, and his name was Amalickiah. And Amalickiah[204] was desirous to be a king; and those people who were angry were also desirous

---

[203] According to Jewish tradition, as recorded in both the Talmud and the Zohar, Moshe did not actually die, but was taken up by YHWH: "...Others declare that Moses never died; it is written here, 'So Moses died there', and elsewhere it is written: 'And he was there with the Lord.' As in the latter passage it means standing and ministering, so also in the former it means standing and ministering" (b.Sotah 13b). "Moses did not die, but he was gathered in from the world..." (Zohar 1:37b-38a). "For Moses did not die. But is it not written, 'And Moses died there'? The truth is, however, that although the departure of the righteous is always designated 'death,' this is only in reference to us. For over him who has attained completeness, and is a model of holy faith, death has no power, and so he does not, in fact, die" (Zohar 2:174a). [204] Probably from a form of the Hebrew root M-L-K (מלך) "to rule" from which we get the word *Melek* "king."

that he should be their king; and they were the greater part of those who were the lower judges of the land, and they were seeking for power. And they had been led by the flatteries of Amalickiah, that if they would support him and establish him to be their king, that he would make them rulers over the people. Thus, they were led away by Amalickiah to dissensions, despite the preaching of Cheleman and his brothers, yes, despite their exceedingly great care over the assembly, for they were Kohanim HaGadolim over the assembly. And there were many in the assembly who believed in the flattering words of Amalickiah, therefore they dissented even from the assembly; and thus were the affairs of the people of Nefi exceedingly precarious and dangerous, despite their great victory which they had had over the Lamanites, and their great rejoicings which they had had because of their deliverance by the hands of YHWH. Thus we see how quickly the children of men do forget YHWH their Elohim, yes, how quick to do iniquity and to be led away by the Evil One. Yes, and we also see the great wickedness one very wicked man can cause to take place among the children of men. Yes, we see that Amalickiah, because he was a man of cunning schemes and a man of many flattering words, that he led away the hearts of many people to do wickedly, yes, and to seek to destroy the assembly of Elohim, and to destroy the foundation of liberty which Elohim had granted unto them, or which blessing Elohim had sent upon the face of the land for the righteous' sake.

⁷And now it came to pass that when M'roni, who was the chief commander of the armies of the Nefites, had heard of these dissensions, he was angry with Amalickiah. And it came to pass that he tore his coat, and he took a piece thereof and wrote upon it: In memory of our Elohim, our religion and freedom, and our shalom, our wives, and our children. And he fastened it upon the end of a pole. And he fastened on his headplate, and his breastplate, and his shields, and girded on his armor about his loins; and he took the pole which had on the end thereof his torn coat, and he called it the Title of Liberty. And he bowed himself to the earth, and he prayed mightily unto his Elohim for the blessings of liberty to rest upon his brothers, so long as there should be a band of Messianics remain to possess the land. For thus were all the true believers of Mashiach who belonged to the assembly of Elohim called, by those who did not belong to the assembly; and those who did belong to the assembly

were faithful. Yes, all those who were true believers in Mashiach took upon them gladly the name of Mashiach — or Messianics, as they were called — because of their belief in Mashiach who should come. And therefore at this time, M'roni prayed that the cause of the Messianics and the freedom of the land might be favored.

⁸And it came to pass that when he had poured out his soul to Elohim, he named all the land which was south of the land Desolation — yes, and in short, all the land, both on the north and on the south — a chosen land, and the land of liberty. And he said, Surely Elohim shall not allow that we who are despised because we take upon us the name of Mashiach shall be trampled down and destroyed, until we bring it upon us by our own transgressions. And when M'roni had said these words, he went forth among the people, waving the torn piece of his garment in the air, that all might see the writing which he had written upon the torn piece, and crying with a loud voice, saying, Behold, whosoever will maintain this title upon the land, let them come forth in the strength of YHWH and enter into a covenant that they will maintain their rights and their religion, that Adonai YHWH may bless them!

⁹And it came to pass that when M'roni had proclaimed these words, behold, the people came running together, with their armors girded about their loins, tearing their garments in token, or as a covenant, that they would not abandon YHWH their Elohim; or in other words, if they should transgress the mitzvot of Elohim, or fall into transgression and be ashamed to take upon them the name of Mashiach, YHWH should tear them even as they had torn their garments. Now this was the covenant which they made, and they cast their garments at the feet of M'roni, saying, We covenant with our Elohim that we shall be destroyed, even as our brothers in the land northward, if we shall fall into transgression; yes, he may cast us at the feet of our enemies even as we have cast our garments at your feet, to be trampled underfoot, if we should fall into transgression.[205] M'roni said unto them, Behold, we are a remnant of the seed of Ya'akov; yes,

---

205 This is an example of a vow made by way of a euphemism or analogy. As we read in the Talmud, "All euphemisms [used to express vows] are equivalent to vows…[and] for oaths are equivalent to oaths…" (m.Nedarim 1:9; b.Nedarim 2a). For example, "[if he said, '…may it be to me] like the lamb [of the daily whole-offering]…'" (m.Nedarim 1:3; b.Nedarim 10b). In Talmudic language, the essential thought is, "if we shall fall into transgression may we be even as these garments."

ALMA 21:10

we are a remnant of the seed of Yosef, whose coat was torn by his brothers into many pieces.[206] Yes, and now behold, let us remember to keep the mitzvot of Elohim, or our garments shall be torn by our brothers and we be cast into prisons, or be sold, or be slain. Yes, let us preserve our liberty as a remnant of Yosef. Yes, let us remember the words of Ya'akov before his death; for behold, he saw that a part of the remnant of the coat of Yosef was preserved and had not decayed. And he said, Even as this remnant of garment of my son's has been preserved, so shall a remnant of the seed of my son be preserved by the hand of Elohim, and be taken unto himself, while the remainder of the seed of Yosef shall perish even as the remnant of his garment. Now behold, this gives my soul sorrow; nevertheless, my soul has joy in my son because of that part of his seed which shall be taken unto Elohim. Now behold, this was the language of Ya'akov. And now, who knows but what the remnant of the seed of Yosef, which shall perish as his garment, are those who have dissented from us? Yes, and even shall it be us if we do not stand fast in the faith of Mashiach.[207]

10 And now it came to pass that when M'roni had said these words, he went forth, and also sent forth to all the parts of the land where there were dissensions, and gathered together all the people who were desirous to maintain their liberty, to stand against Amalickiah and those who had dissented, who were called Amalickiahites.

11 And it came to pass that when Amalickiah saw that the people of M'roni were more numerous than the Amalickiahites, and he also saw that his people were doubtful concerning the justice of the cause which they had undertaken, therefore fearing that he should not gain the point, he took those of his people who would and departed into the land of Nefi.

12 Now M'roni thought it was not expedient that the Lamanites should have any more strength; therefore, he thought to cut off the people of Amalickiah, or to take them and bring them back, and put Amalickiah to death. Yes, for he knew that they would stir up the Lamanites to anger against them and cause them to come down

---

206 Compare with the *Sefer HaYashar* (The Book of Jasher): "And they [his brothers] hastened and took Joseph's coat and tore it, and they killed a kid of the goats and dipped the coat in the blood of the kid, and then trampled it in the dust, and they sent the coat to their father Jacob by the hand of Naphtali, and they commanded him to say these words" (Jasher 43:13). 207 'Eter 6:2-3

to battle against them; and this he knew that Amalickiah would do that he might obtain his purposes. Therefore, M'roni thought it was expedient that he should take his armies, which had gathered themselves together, and armed themselves, and entered into a covenant to keep the shalom. And it came to pass that he took his army and marched out with his tents into the wilderness to cut off the course of Amalickiah in the wilderness.

13 And it came to pass that he did according to his desires, and marched forth into the wilderness, and got in front of the armies of Amalickiah. And it came to pass that Amalickiah fled with a small number of his men, and the remainder were delivered up into the hands of M'roni and were taken back into the land of Zerach'mla. Now M'roni being a man who was appointed by the chief judges and the **voice of the people,** therefore he had power to do according to his will with the armies of the Nefites, to establish and to exercise authority over them.

14 And it came to pass that whomsoever of the Amalickiahites that would not enter into a covenant to support the cause of freedom, that they might maintain a free government, he caused to be put to death; and there were only a few who denied the covenant of freedom.

15 And it came to pass also that he caused the Title of Liberty to be hoisted upon every tower which was in all the land which was possessed by the Nefites; and thus M'roni planted the standard of liberty among the Nefites. And they began to have shalom again in the land; and thus they did maintain shalom in the land until nearly the end of the nineteenth year of the reign of the judges. And Cheleman and the Kohanim HaGadolim did also maintain order in the assembly; yes, even for the space of four years did they have much shalom and rejoicing in the assembly.

16 And it came to pass that there were many who died firmly believing that their souls were redeemed by Adonai Yeshua HaMashiach; thus, they went out of the world rejoicing. And there were some who died with fevers, which at some seasons of the year were very frequent in the land — but not so much so with fevers, because of the excellent qualities of the many plants and roots which Elohim had prepared to remove the cause of diseases to which men were subject by the nature of the climate — but there were many who

died with old age. And those who died in the faith of Mashiach are happy in him, as we must necessarily suppose.

17 Now we will return in our record to Amalickiah and those who fled with him into the wilderness. For behold, he had taken those who were with him, and went up into the land of Nefi, among the Lamanites, and did stir up the Lamanites to anger against the people of Nefi, insomuch that the king of the Lamanites sent a proclamation throughout all his land, among all his people, that they should gather themselves together again to go to battle against the Nefites.

18 And it came to pass that when the proclamation had gone forth among them, they were exceedingly afraid; yes, they feared to displease the king, and they also feared to go to battle against the Nefites, lest they should lose their lives. And it came to pass that they would not, or the more part of them would not, obey the commandment of the king.

19 And now it came to pass that the king was angry because of their disobedience; therefore, he gave Amalickiah the command of that part of his army which was obedient unto his commands, and commanded him that he should go forth and compel them to arms. Now behold, this was the desire of Amalickiah; for he being a very subtle man to do evil, therefore he laid the plan in his heart to dethrone the king of the Lamanites. And now he had gotten the command of those parts of the Lamanites who were in favor of the king; and he sought to gain favor of those who were not obedient. Therefore, he went forward to the place which was called Oneidah, for there had all the Lamanites fled; for they discovered the army coming, and supposing that they were coming to destroy them, therefore they fled to Oneidah, to the place of arms. And they had appointed a man to be a king and a leader over them, being fixed in their minds with a determined resolution that they would not be subjected to go against the Nefites.

20 And it came to pass that they had gathered themselves together upon the top of the mount which was called Antipas, in preparation to battle. Now it was not Amalickiah's intention to give them battle according to the commandments of the king; but behold, it was his intention to gain favor with the armies of the Lamanites, that he might place himself at their head, and dethrone the king, and take possession of the kingdom. And behold, it came to pass that he caused his army to pitch their tents in the valley which was near the mount

Antipas. And it came to pass that when it was night, he sent a secret embassy into the mount Antipas, desiring that the leader of those who were upon the mount, whose name was Lehonti, that he should come down to the foot of the mount, for he desired to speak with him.

21 And it came to pass that when Lehonti received the message, he dared not go down to the foot of the mount. And it came to pass that Amalickiah sent again the second time, desiring him to come down. And it came to pass that Lehonti would not. And he sent again the third time. And it came to pass that when Amalickiah found that he could not get Lehonti to come down from off the mount, he went up into the mount nearly to Lehonti's camp. And he sent again the fourth time his message unto Lehonti, desiring that he would come down and that he would bring his guards with him.

22 And it came to pass that when Lehonti had come down with his guards to Amalickiah, that Amalickiah desired him to come down with his army in the nighttime, and surround those men in their camps over whom the king had given him command, and that he would deliver them up into Lehonti's hands, if he would make him, Amalickiah, the second leader over the whole army.

23 And it came to pass that Lehonti came down with his men and surrounded the men of Amalickiah, so that, before they awoke at the dawn of the day, they were surrounded by the armies of Lehonti. And it came to pass that when they saw they were surrounded, they pled with Amalickiah that he would allow them to fall in with their brothers, that they might not be destroyed. Now this was the very thing which Amalickiah desired.

24 And it came to pass that he delivered his men, contrary to the commands of the king. Now this was the thing that Amalickiah desired, that he might accomplish his designs in dethroning the king. Now it was the custom among the Lamanites, if their chief leader was killed, to appoint the second leader to be their chief leader.

25 And it came to pass that Amalickiah caused that one of his servants should administer poison by degrees to Lehonti, that he died. Now when Lehonti was dead, the Lamanites appointed Amalickiah to be their leader and their chief commander. And it came to pass that Amalickiah marched with his armies (for he had gained his desires) to the land of Nefi, to the city of Nefi, which was the chief city. And the king came out to meet him with his guards, for he supposed that

Amalickiah had fulfilled his commands and that Amalickiah had gathered together so great an army to go against the Nefites to battle. But behold, as the king came out to meet him, Amalickiah caused that his servants should go forth to meet the king. And they went forth and bowed themselves before the king as if to reverence him because of his greatness. And it came to pass that the king put forth his hand to raise them, as was the custom with the Lamanites — and a token of shalom — which custom they had taken from the Nefites. And it came to pass that when he had raised the first from the ground, behold, he stabbed the king to the heart, and he fell to the earth. Now the servants of the king fled, and the servants of Amalickiah raised a cry, saying, Behold, the servants of the king have stabbed him to the heart and he has fallen, and they have fled! Behold, come and see!

26 And it came to pass that Amalickiah commanded that his armies should march forth and see what had happened to the king. And when they had come to the spot and found the king lying in his gore, Amalickiah pretended to be angry and said, Whosoever loved the king, let him go forth and pursue his servants, that they may be slain.

27 And it came to pass that all they who loved the king, when they heard these words, came forth and pursued after the servants of the king. Now when the servants of the king saw an army pursuing after them, they were frightened again and fled into the wilderness, and came over into the land of Zerach'mla, and joined the people of Ammon. And the army which pursued after them returned, having pursued after them in vain. And thus Amalickiah, by his fraud, gained the hearts of the people.

28 And it came to pass on the next day, he entered the city of Nefi with his armies and took possession of the city. And now it came to pass that the queen, when she had heard that the king was slain — for Amalickiah had sent an embassy to the queen, informing her that the king had been slain by his servants, that he had pursued them with his army, but it was in vain and they had made their escape — therefore, when the queen had received this message, she sent unto Amalickiah, desiring of him that he would spare the people of the city. And she also desired of him that he should come in unto her; and she also desired of him that he should bring witnesses with him to testify concerning the death of the king.

²⁹ And it came to pass that Amalickiah took that same servant that slew the king, and also they who were with him, and went in unto the queen, unto the place where she sat. And they all testified unto her that the king was slain by his own servants; and they said also, They have fled; does not this testify against them? And thus they satisfied the queen concerning the death of the king.

³⁰ And it came to pass that Amalickiah sought the favor of the queen and took her unto him to wife. And thus by his fraud and by the assistance of his cunning servants, he obtained the kingdom; yes, he was acknowledged king throughout all the land, among all the people of the Lamanites, who were composed of the Lamanites, and the L'mu'elites, and the Yishma'elites, and all the dissenters of the Nefites, from the reign of Nefi down to the present time. Now these dissenters, having the same instruction and the same information as the Nefites, yes, having been instructed in the same knowledge of YHWH; nevertheless, it is strange to relate, not long after their dissensions they became more hardened and impenitent, and more wild, wicked, and ferocious than the Lamanites, drinking in the traditions of the Lamanites, giving way to indolence and all manner of lustfulness—yes, entirely forgetting YHWH their Elohim.

³¹ And now it came to pass that as soon as Amalickiah had obtained the kingdom, he began to inspire the hearts of the Lamanites against the people of Nefi. Yes, he did appoint men to speak unto the Lamanites from their towers against the Nefites; and thus he did inspire their hearts against the Nefites, insomuch that in the latter end of the nineteenth year of the reign of the judges, he having accomplished his designs thus far, yes, having been made king over the Lamanites, he sought also to reign over all the land, yes, and all the people who were in the land, the Nefites as well as the Lamanites. Therefore, he had accomplished his design, for he had hardened the hearts of the Lamanites, and blinded their minds, and stirred them up to anger, insomuch that he had gathered together a numerous host to go to battle against the Nefites. For he was determined, because of the greatness of the number of his people, to overpower the Nefites and to bring them into bondage. And thus he did appoint chief captains of the Tzuramites, they being the most acquainted with the strength of the Nefites, and their places of refuge, and the weakest parts of their cities; therefore, he appointed them to be chief captains over

his armies. And it came to pass that they took their camp and moved forth towards the land of Zerach'mla in the wilderness.

32 Now it came to pass that while Amalickiah had thus been obtaining power by fraud and deceit, M'roni, on the other hand, had been preparing the minds of the people to be faithful unto YHWH their Elohim. Yes, he had been strengthening the armies of the Nefites and erecting small forts, or places of refuge, throwing up banks of earth round about to encircle his armies, and also building walls of stone to encircle them about, round about their cities and the borders of their lands, yes, all round about the land. And in their weakest fortifications he did place the greater number of men, and thus he did fortify and strengthen the land which was possessed by the Nefites. And thus he was preparing to support their liberty, their lands, their wives, and their children, and their shalom, and that they might live unto YHWH their Elohim, and that they might maintain that which was called by their enemies the cause of Messianics.

33 And M'roni was a strong and a mighty man; he was a man of a perfect understanding, yes, a man that did not delight in bloodshed; a man whose soul did joy in the liberty and the freedom of his country and his brothers from bondage and slavery; yes, a man whose heart did swell with thanksgiving to his Elohim for the many privileges and blessings which he bestowed upon his people; a man who did labor exceedingly for the welfare and safety of his people. Yes, and he was a man who was firm in the faith of Mashiach; and he had sworn with an oath to defend his people, his rights, and his country, and his religion, even to the loss of his blood.

34 Now the Nefites were taught to defend themselves against their enemies, even to the shedding of blood if it were necessary. Yes, and they were also taught never to give an offense, yes, and never to raise the sword except it were against an enemy, except it were to preserve their lives.[208] And this was their faith — that by so doing, Elohim would prosper them in the land; or in other words, if they were faithful in keeping the mitzvot of Elohim, that he would prosper them in the land, yes, warn them to flee or to prepare for war according to their danger, and also that Elohim would make it known unto them where they should go to defend themselves against their

---

[208] Alma 20:11; 3 Nefi 2:5

enemies, and by so doing, YHWH would deliver them. And this was the faith of M'roni, and his heart did glory in it — not in the shedding of blood, but in doing good, in preserving his people, yes, in keeping the mitzvot of Elohim, yes, and resisting iniquity. Yes, truly, truly I say unto you, if all men had been, and were, and ever would be like unto M'roni, behold, the very powers of She'ol would have been shaken for ever; yes, HaSatan would never have power over the hearts of the children of men. Behold, he was a man like unto Ammon, the son of Moshiyah, yes, and even the other sons of Moshiyah, yes, and also Alma and his sons, for they were all men of Elohim. Now behold, Cheleman and his brothers were not less serviceable unto the people than was M'roni, for they did preach the word of Elohim and they did immerse unto repentance all men whosoever would hearken unto their words; and thus they went forth. And the people did humble themselves because of their words, insomuch that they were highly favored of YHWH, and thus they were free from wars and contentions among themselves, yes, even for the space of four years.

35 But as I have said, in the latter end of the nineteenth year, despite their shalom among themselves, they were compelled reluctantly to contend with their brothers the Lamanites. Yes, and in short, their wars never did cease for the space of many years with the Lamanites, despite their much reluctance. Now they were sorry to take up arms against the Lamanites because they did not delight in the shedding of blood, yes, and this was not all — they were sorry to be the means of sending so many of their brothers out of this world, into an eternal world, unprepared to meet their Elohim.[209] Nevertheless, they could not consent to lay down their lives, that their wives and their children should be massacred by the barbarous cruelty of those who were once their brothers, yes, and had dissented from their assembly, and had left them, and had gone to destroy them by joining the Lamanites. Yes, they could not bear that their brothers should rejoice over the blood of the Nefites, so long as there were any who should keep the mitzvot of Elohim; for the promises of YHWH were, if they should keep his mitzvot, they should prosper in the land.

36 And now it came to pass in the eleventh month of the nineteenth year,[210] on the tenth day of the month, the armies of the Lamanites

---

209 Alma 9:4; 3 Nefi 5:31   **210** ~ 74 BCE

were seen approaching towards the land of Ammonihah. And behold, the city had been rebuilt, and M'roni had stationed an army by the borders of the city; and they had cast up dirt round about to shield them from the arrows and the stones of the Lamanites; for behold, they fought with stones and with arrows. Behold, I said that the city of Ammonihah had been rebuilt. I say unto you, yes, that it was in part rebuilt; and because the Lamanites had destroyed it once, because of the iniquity of the people, they supposed that it would again become an easy prey for them. But behold, how great was their disappointment; for behold, the Nefites had dug up a ridge of earth round about them, which was so high that the Lamanites could not cast their stones and arrows at them that they might take effect, neither could they come upon them except it was by their place of entrance.

37 Now at this time the chief captains of the Lamanites were astonished exceedingly because of the wisdom of the Nefites in repairing their places of security. Now the leaders of the Lamanites had supposed because of the greatness of their numbers, yes, they supposed that they should be privileged to come upon them as they had previously done. Yes, and they had also prepared themselves with shields, and with breastplates, and they had also prepared themselves with garments of skins, yes, very thick garments to cover their nakedness. And being thus prepared, they supposed that they should easily overpower and subject their brothers to the yoke of bondage, or slay and massacre them according to their pleasure. But behold, to their uttermost astonishment, they were prepared for them in a manner which never had been known among all the children of Lechi. Now they were prepared for the Lamanites, to battle after the manner of the instructions of M'roni.

38 And it came to pass that the Lamanites, or the Amalickiahites, were exceedingly astonished at their manner of preparation for war. Now if king Amalickiah had come down out of the land of Nefi at the head of his army, perhaps he would have caused the Lamanites to have attacked the Nefites at the city of Ammonihah; for behold, he did care not for the blood of his people. But behold, Amalickiah did not come down himself to battle. And behold, his chief captains dared not attack the Nefites at the city of Ammonihah, for M'roni had altered the management of affairs among the Nefites, insomuch

that the Lamanites were disappointed in their places of retreat and they could not come upon them. Therefore, they retreated into the wilderness, and took their camp and marched towards the land of Noach, supposing that to be the next best place for them to come against the Nefites; for they knew not that M'roni had fortified or had built forts of security for every city in all the land round about. Therefore, they marched forward to the land of Noach with a firm determination, yes, their chief captains came forward and took an oath that they would destroy the people of that city. But behold, to their astonishment, the city of Noach, which had previously been a weak place, had now, by the means of M'roni, become strong, yes, even to exceed the strength of the city Ammonihah. And now behold, this was wisdom in M'roni, for he had supposed that they would be frightened at the city Ammonihah, and as the city of Noach had previously been the weakest part of the land, therefore they would march there to battle; and thus it was according to his desires. And behold, M'roni had appointed Lechi to be chief captain over the men of that city, and it was that same Lechi who fought with the Lamanites in the valley on the east of the river Tzidon.

39 And now behold, it came to pass that when the Lamanites had found that Lechi commanded the city, they were again disappointed, for they feared Lechi exceedingly; nevertheless, their chief captains had sworn with an oath to attack the city; therefore, they brought up their armies. Now behold, the Lamanites could not get into their forts of security by any other way except by the entrance because of the highness of the bank which had been thrown up, and the depth of the ditch which had been dug round about, except it were by the entrance. And thus were the Nefites prepared to destroy all such as should attempt to climb up to enter the fort by any other way, by casting over stones and arrows at them. Thus, they were prepared, yes, a body of their strongest men, with their swords and their slings, to strike down all who should attempt to come into their place of security by the place of entrance; and thus were they prepared to defend themselves against the Lamanites.

40 And it came to pass that the captains of the Lamanites brought up their armies before the place of entrance and began to contend with the Nefites, to get into their place of security; but behold, they were driven back from time to time, insomuch that they were slain

with an immense slaughter. Now when they found that they could not obtain power over the Nefites by the pass, they began to dig down their banks of earth that they might obtain a pass to their armies, that they might have an equal chance to fight; but behold, in these attempts they were swept off by the stones and the arrows which were thrown at them; and instead of filling up their ditches by pulling down the banks of earth, they were filled up in a measure with their dead and wounded bodies. Thus, the Nefites had all power over their enemies. And thus the Lamanites did attempt to destroy the Nefites, until their chief captains were all slain — yes, and more than a thousand of the Lamanites were slain — while on the other hand, there was not a single soul of the Nefites which was slain. There were about fifty who were wounded, who had been exposed to the arrows of the Lamanites through the pass, but they were shielded by their shields, and their breastplates, and their headplates, insomuch that their wounds were upon their legs, many of which were very severe.

41 And it came to pass that when the Lamanites saw that their chief captains were all slain, they fled into the wilderness. And it came to pass that they returned to the land of Nefi to inform their king, Amalickiah, who was a Nefite by birth, concerning their great loss. And it came to pass that he was exceedingly angry with his people because he had not obtained his desires over the Nefites; he had not subjected them to the yoke of bondage. Yes, he was exceedingly angry, and he did curse Elohim, and also M'roni, and swore with an oath that he would drink his blood, and this because M'roni had kept the mitzvot of Elohim in preparing for the safety of his people. And it came to pass that on the other hand, the people of Nefi did thank YHWH their Elohim because of his miraculous power in delivering them from the hands of their enemies.

42 And thus ended the nineteenth year of the reign of the judges over the people of Nefi. Yes, and there was continual shalom among them and exceedingly great prosperity in the assembly because of their heed and diligence which they gave unto the word of Elohim, which was declared unto them by Cheleman, and Shiblon, and Corianton, and Ammon, and his brothers, and so forth, yes, and by all those which had been ordained by the Holy Order of Elohim, being immersed unto repentance and sent forth to preach among the people, and so forth.

22 And now it came to pass that M'roni did not stop making preparations for war or to defend his people against the Lamanites; for he caused that his armies should commence, in the commencement of the twentieth year[211] of the reign of the judges, that they should commence in digging up heaps of earth round about all the cities throughout all the land which was possessed by the Nefites. And upon the top of those ridges of earth, he caused that there should be timbers, yes, works of timbers, built up to the height of a man, round about the cities. And he caused that, upon those works of timbers, there should be a frame of pickets built upon the timbers round about; and they were strong and high. And he caused towers to be erected that overlooked those works of pickets; and he caused places of security to be built upon those towers, that the stones and the arrows of the Lamanites could not hurt them. And they were prepared that they could cast stones from the top thereof, according to their pleasure and their strength, and slay him who should attempt to approach near the walls of the city. Thus M'roni did prepare strongholds against the coming of their enemies, round about every city in all the land.

2 And it came to pass that M'roni caused that his armies should go forth into the east wilderness; yes, and they went forth and drove all the Lamanites who were in the east wilderness into their own lands, which were south of the land of Zerach'mla. And the land of Nefi did run in a straight course from the east sea to the west. And it came to pass that when M'roni had driven all the Lamanites out of the east wilderness, which was north of the lands of their own possessions, he caused that the inhabitants who were in the land of Zerach'mla and in the land round about should go forth into the east wilderness, even to the borders by the seashore, and possess the land. And he also placed armies on the south, in the borders of their possessions, and caused them to erect fortifications, that they might secure their armies and their people from the hands of their enemies. And thus he cut off all the strongholds of the Lamanites in the east wilderness, yes, and also on the west, fortifying the line between the Nefites and the Lamanites, between the land of Zerach'mla and the land of Nefi, from the west sea running by the head of the river Tzidon, the Nefites

---

211 ~ 73 BCE

possessing all the land northward, yes, even all the land which was northward of the land Bountiful, according to their pleasure. Thus, M'roni with his armies, which did increase daily because of the assurance of protection which his works did bring forth unto them, therefore they did seek to cut off the strength and the power of the Lamanites from off the lands of their possessions, that they should have no power upon the lands of their possessions.

3 And it came to pass that the Nefites began the foundation of a city, and they called the name of the city M'roni. And it was by the east sea, and it was on the south by the line of the possessions of the Lamanites. And they also began a foundation for a city between the city of M'roni and the city of Aharon, joining the borders of Aharon and M'roni; and they called the name of the city, or the land, Nefihah. And they also began in that same year to build many cities on the north — one in a particular manner, which they called Lechi, which was in the north by the borders of the seashore. And thus ended the twentieth year. And in these prosperous circumstances were the people of Nefi in the commencement of the twenty and first year of the reign of the judges over the people of Nefi. And they did prosper exceedingly, and they became exceedingly rich, yes, and they did multiply and grow strong in the land.

4 And thus we see how merciful and just are all the dealings of YHWH, to the fulfilling of all his words unto the children of men; yes, we can behold that his words are verified, even at this time, which he spoke unto Lechi, saying, Blessed are you and your children, and they shall be blessed; and inasmuch as they shall keep my mitzvot, they shall prosper in the land. But remember, inasmuch as they will not keep my mitzvot, they shall be cut off from the presence of YHWH. And we see that these promises have been verified to the people of Nefi, for it has been their quarrelings and their contentions, yes, their murderings, and their plunderings, their idolatry, and their whoredoms, and their abominations, which were among themselves, which brought upon them their wars and their destructions. And those who were faithful in keeping the mitzvot of YHWH were delivered at all times, while thousands of their wicked brothers have been consigned to bondage, or to perish by the sword, or to dwindle in unbelief and mingle with the Lamanites. But behold, there never was a happier time among the people of Nefi, since the

days of Nefi, than in the days of M'roni, yes, even at this time in the twenty and first year of the reign of the judges. And it came to pass that the twenty and second year of the reign of the judges also ended in shalom, yes, and also the twenty and third year.

5 And it came to pass that in the commencement of the twenty and fourth year of the reign of the judges there would also have been shalom among the people of Nefi, had it not been for a contention which took place among them concerning the land of Lechi and the land of Morionton, which joined upon the borders of Lechi, both of which were on the borders by the seashore. For behold, the people who possessed the land of Morionton did claim a part of the land of Lechi. Therefore, there began to be a heated contention between them, insomuch that the people of Morionton took up arms against their brothers, and they were determined by the sword to slay them. But behold, the people who possessed the land of Lechi fled to the camp of M'roni and appealed unto him for assistance; for behold, they were not in the wrong.

6 And it came to pass that the people of Morionton, who were led by a man whose name was Morionton, found that the people of Lechi had fled to the camp of M'roni. They were exceedingly fearful that the army of M'roni should come upon them and destroy them, therefore Morionton put it into their hearts that they should flee to the land which was northward, which was covered with large bodies of water, and take possession of the land which was northward. And behold, they would have carried this plan into effect, which would have been a cause to have been lamented, but behold, Morionton, being a man of much passion, therefore he was angry with one of his maidservants, and he fell upon her and beat her badly. And it came to pass that she fled and came over to the camp of M'roni and told M'roni all things concerning the matter, and also concerning their intentions to flee into the land northward. Now behold, the people who were in the land of Bountiful, or rather M'roni, feared that they would hearken to the words of Morionton and unite with his people, and thus he would obtain possession of those parts of the land, which would lay a foundation for serious consequences among the people of Nefi, yes, which consequences would lead to the overthrow of their liberty. Therefore, M'roni sent an army with their camp to get in front of the people of Morionton, to stop their

flight into the land northward. And it came to pass that they did not get in front of them until they had come to the borders of the land Desolation, and there they did get in front of them by the narrow pass which led by the sea into the land northward, yes, by the sea on the west and on the east.

⁷And it came to pass that the army which was sent by M'roni, which was led by a man whose name was Teancum, did meet the people of Morionton. And so stubborn were the people of Morionton, being inspired by his wickedness and his flattering words, that a battle commenced between them, in the which Teancum did slay Morionton, and defeat his army, and took them prisoners, and returned to the camp of M'roni. And thus ended the twenty and fourth year of the reign of the judges over the people of Nefi. And thus were the people of Morionton brought back. And upon their covenanting to keep the shalom, they were restored to the land of Morionton, and a union took place between them and the people of Lechi, and they were also restored to their lands.

⁸And it came to pass that in that same year that the people of Nefi had shalom restored unto them, that Nefihah, the second chief judge, died, having filled the judgment seat with perfect uprightness before Elohim. Nevertheless, he had refused Alma to take possession of those records and those things which were esteemed by Alma and his fathers to be most sacred; therefore, Alma had conferred them upon his son Cheleman.

⁹Behold, it came to pass that the son of Nefihah was appointed to fill the judgment seat in the place of his father. Yes, he was appointed chief judge and governor over the people, with an oath and sacred ordinance to judge righteously, and to keep the shalom and the freedom of the people, and to grant unto them their sacred privileges to worship YHWH their Elohim, yes, to support and maintain the cause of Elohim all his days, and to bring the wicked to justice according to their crime. Now behold, his name was Parhoron. And Parhoron did fill the seat of his father, and did commence his reign in the end of the twenty and fourth year over the people of Nefi.

23

And now it came to pass in the commencement of the twenty and fifth year[212] of the reign of the judges over the people of

---
212 ~ 68 BCE

Nefi, they having established shalom between the people of Lechi and the people of Morionton concerning their lands, and having commenced the twenty and fifth year in shalom, nevertheless, they did not long maintain an entire shalom in the land, for there began to be a contention among the people concerning the chief judge, Parhoron. For behold, there was a part of the people who desired that a few particular points of the law should be altered. But behold, Parhoron would not alter, nor allow the law to be altered; therefore, he did not hearken to those who had sent in their voices with their petitions concerning the altering of the law. Therefore, those who were desirous that the law should be altered were angry with him and desired that he should no longer be chief judge over the land. Therefore, there arose a heated dispute concerning the matter, but not unto bloodshed.

2 And it came to pass that those who were desirous that Parhoron should be dethroned from the judgment seat were called Kingmen, for they were desirous that the law should be altered in a manner to overthrow the free government and to establish a king over the land. And those who were desirous that Parhoron should remain chief judge over the land took upon them the name of Freemen; and thus was the division among them, for the Freemen had sworn or covenanted to maintain their rights and the privileges of their religion by a free government.

3 And it came to pass that this matter of their contention was settled by the **voice of the people**. And it came to pass that the **voice of the people** came in favor of the Freemen; and Parhoron retained the judgment seat, which caused much rejoicing among the brothers of Parhoron and also among the people of liberty, who also put the Kingmen to silence, that they dared not oppose, but were obliged to maintain the cause of freedom. Now those who were in favor of kings were those of high birth, and they sought to be kings; and they were supported by those who sought power and authority over the people. But behold, this was a critical time for such contentions to be among the people of Nefi; for behold, Amalickiah had again stirred up the hearts of the people of the Lamanites against the people of the Nefites, and he was gathering together soldiers from all parts of his land, and arming them, and preparing for war with all diligence, for he had sworn to drink the blood of M'roni. But behold, we shall

see that this promise which he made was rash; nevertheless, he did prepare himself and his armies to come to battle against the Nefites. Now his armies were not so great as they had previously been, because of the many thousands who had been slain by the hand of the Nefites, but despite their great loss, Amalickiah had gathered together an astonishingly great army, insomuch that he feared not to come down to the land of Zerach'mla Yes, even Amalickiah did himself come down at the head of the Lamanites. And it was in the twenty and fifth year of the reign of the judges; and it was at the same time that they had begun to settle the affairs of their contentions concerning the chief judge Parhoron.

4 And it came to pass that when the men who were called Kingmen had heard that the Lamanites were coming down to battle against them, they were glad in their hearts and they refused to take up arms; for they were so angry with the chief judge, and also with the people of liberty, that they would not take up arms to defend their country. And it came to pass that when M'roni saw this, and also saw that the Lamanites were coming into the borders of the land, he was exceedingly angry because of the stubbornness of those people whom he had labored with so much diligence to preserve; yes, he was exceedingly angry; his soul was filled with anger against them. And it came to pass that he sent a petition, with the **voice of the people,** unto the governor of the land, desiring that he should heed it and give him, M'roni, power to compel those dissenters to defend their country or to put them to death. For it was his first care to put an end to such contentions and dissensions among the people; for behold, this had been previously a cause of all their destructions. And it came to pass that it was granted according to the **voice of the people.**

5 And it came to pass that M'roni commanded that his army should go against those Kingmen to pull down their pride and their nobility, and level them with the earth, or they should take up arms and support the cause of liberty. And it came to pass that the armies did march forth against them, and they did pull down their pride and their nobility, insomuch that as they did lift their weapons of war to fight against the men of M'roni, they were cut down and leveled to the earth. And it came to pass that there were four thousand of those dissenters who were cut down by the sword; and those of their leaders who were not slain in battle were taken and cast into prison,

for there was no time for their trials at this period. And the remainder of those dissenters, rather than be struck down to the earth by the sword, yielded to the standard of liberty, and were compelled to hoist the Title of Liberty upon their towers and in their cities, and to take up arms in defense of their country. And thus M'roni put an end to those Kingmen, that there were not any known by the name of Kingmen; and thus he put an end to the stubbornness and the pride of those people who professed the blood of nobility, but they were brought down to humble themselves like unto their brothers and to fight valiantly for their freedom from bondage.

6 Behold, it came to pass that while M'roni was thus breaking down the wars and contentions among his own people, and subjecting them to shalom and civilization, and making regulations to prepare for war against the Lamanites, behold, the Lamanites had come into the land of M'roni which was in the borders by the seashore.

7 And it came to pass that the Nefites were not sufficiently strong in the city of M'roni, therefore Amalickiah did drive them, slaying many. And it came to pass that Amalickiah took possession of the city, yes, possession of all their fortifications. And those who fled out of the city of M'roni came to the city of Nefihah; and also the people of the city of Lechi gathered themselves together and made preparations, and were ready to receive the Lamanites to battle.

8 But it came to pass that Amalickiah would not allow the Lamanites to go against the city of Nefihah to battle, but he kept them down by the seashore, leaving men in every city to maintain and defend it. And thus he went on, taking possession of many cities: the city of Nefihah, and the city of Lechi, and the city of Morionton, and the city of Omner, and the city of Gid, and the city of Mulek, all of which were on the east borders by the seashore. And thus had the Lamanites obtained, by the cunning of Amalickiah, so many cities by their numberless hosts, all of which were strongly fortified after the manner of the fortifications of M'roni, all of which afforded strongholds for the Lamanites.

9 And it came to pass that they marched to the borders of the land Bountiful, driving the Nefites before them and slaying many. But it came to pass that they were met by Teancum, who had slain Morionton and had gotten in front of the people in his flight. And it came to pass that he got in front of Amalickiah also, as he

was marching forth with his numerous army that he might take possession of the land Bountiful, and also the land northward. But behold, he met with a disappointment by being repulsed by Teancum and his men, for they were great warriors; for every man of Teancum did exceed the Lamanites in their strength and in their skill of war, insomuch that they did gain advantage over the Lamanites.

10 And it came to pass that they did harass them, insomuch that they did slay them even until it was dark. And it came to pass that Teancum and his men did pitch their tents in the borders of the land Bountiful, and Amalickiah did pitch his tents in the borders on the beach by the seashore; and after this manner were they driven.

11 And it came to pass that when the night had come, Teancum and his servant stole forth and went out by night, and went into the camp of Amalickiah; and behold, sleep had overpowered them because of their much fatigue, which was caused by the labors and heat of the day.

12 And it came to pass that Teancum crept secretly into the tent of the king and put a javelin to his heart. And he did cause the death of the king immediately, that he did not awake his servants. And he returned again secretly to his own camp, and behold, his men were asleep; and he awoke them and told them all the things that he had done. And he caused that his armies should stand in readiness, for fear that the Lamanites had awoken and should come upon them. And thus ended the twenty and fifth year of the reign of the judges over the people of Nefi; and thus ended the days of Amalickiah.

24

And now it came to pass in the twenty and sixth year[213] of the reign of the judges over the people of Nefi, behold, when the Lamanites awoke on the first morning of the first month, behold, they found Amalickiah was dead in his own tent, and they also saw that Teancum was ready to give them battle on that day. And now, when the Lamanites saw this, they were frightened, and they abandoned their design of marching into the land northward, and retreated with all their army into the city of Mulek, and sought protection in their fortifications. And it came to pass that the brother of Amalickiah was appointed king over the people, and his name was

---

[213] ~ 67 BCE

Ammoron. Thus, king Ammoron, the brother of king Amalickiah, was appointed to reign in his place.

2 And it came to pass that he did command that his people should maintain those cities which they had taken by the shedding of blood, for they had not taken any cities except they had lost much blood. And now Teancum saw that the Lamanites were determined to maintain those cities which they had taken and those parts of the land which they had obtained possession of. And also seeing the enormity of their number, Teancum thought it was not expedient that he should attempt to attack them in their forts, but he kept his men round about as if making preparations for war; yes, and truly he was preparing to defend himself against them by casting up walls round about and preparing places of refuge.

3 And it came to pass that he kept thus preparing for war until M'roni had sent a large number of men to strengthen his army. And M'roni also sent orders unto him that he should retain all the prisoners who fell into his hands, for as the Lamanites had taken many prisoners, that he should retain all the prisoners of the Lamanites as a ransom for those whom the Lamanites had taken. And he also sent orders unto him that he should fortify the land Bountiful and secure the narrow pass which led into the land northward, for fear that the Lamanites should obtain that point and should have power to harass them on every side. And M'roni also sent word unto him, desiring him that he would be faithful in maintaining that quarter of the land, and that he would seek every opportunity to harass the Lamanites in that quarter, as much as was in his power, that perhaps he might take again, by stratagem or some other way, those cities which had been taken out of their hands, and that he also would fortify and strengthen the cities round about which had not fallen into the hands of the Lamanites. And he also said unto him, I would come unto you, but behold, the Lamanites are upon us in the borders of the land by the west sea, and behold, I go against them, therefore I cannot come unto you.

4 Now the king, Ammoron, had departed out of the land of Zerach'mla, and had made known unto the queen concerning the death of his brother, and had gathered together a large number of men, and had marched forth against the Nefites on the borders by the west sea. And thus he was endeavoring to harass the Nefites and

to draw away a part of their forces to that part of the land, while he had commanded those whom he had left to possess the cities which he had taken that they should also harass the Nefites on the borders by the east sea, and should take possession of their lands as much as it were in their power, according to the power of their armies. And thus were the Nefites in those dangerous circumstances in the ending of the twenty and sixth year of the reign of the judges over the people of Nefi.

5 But behold, it came to pass, in the twentieth and seventh year of the reign of the judges, that Teancum, by the command of M'roni — who had established armies to protect the south and the west borders of the land, had begun his march towards the land of Bountiful, that he might assist Teancum with his men in retaking the cities which they had lost — and it came to pass that Teancum had received orders to make an attack upon the city of Mulek and retake it if it were possible.

6 And it came to pass that Teancum made preparations to make an attack upon the city of Mulek and march forth with his army against the Lamanites, but he saw that it was impossible that he could overpower them while they were in their fortifications. Therefore, he abandoned his designs and returned again to the city Bountiful to wait for the coming of M'roni, that he might receive strength to his army.

7 And it came to pass that M'roni did arrive with his army to the land of Bountiful in the latter end of the twenty and seventh year of the reign of the judges over the people of Nefi. And in the commencement of the twenty and eighth year, M'roni and Teancum and many of the chief captains held a council of war: regarding what they should do to cause the Lamanites to come out against them to battle, or that they might by some means seduce them out of their strongholds, that they might gain advantage over them and take again the city of Mulek.

8 And it came to pass that they sent embassies to the army of the Lamanites which protected the city of Mulek, to their leader, whose name was Ya'akov, desiring him that he would come out with his armies to meet them upon the plains between the two cities. But behold, Ya'akov, who was a Tzuramite, would not come out with his army to meet them upon the plains.

9 And it came to pass that M'roni, having no hopes of meeting them upon even grounds, therefore he resolved upon a plan that he might decoy the Lamanites out of their strongholds. Therefore, he caused that Teancum should take a small number of men and march down near the seashore, and M'roni and his army, by night, marched into the wilderness on the west of the city Mulek. And thus the next day, when the guards of the Lamanites had discovered Teancum, they ran and told it unto Ya'akov, their leader.

10 And it came to pass that the armies of the Lamanites did march forth against Teancum, supposing by their numbers to overpower Teancum because of the smallness of his numbers. And as Teancum saw the armies of the Lamanites coming out against him, he began a retreat down by the seashore northward.

11 And it came to pass that when the Lamanites saw that he began to flee, they took courage and pursued them with vigor. And while Teancum was thus leading away the Lamanites who were pursuing them in vain, behold, M'roni commanded that a part of his army who were with him should march forth into the city and take possession of it. And thus they did, and slew all those who had been left to protect the city — yes, all those who would not yield up their weapons of war. And thus M'roni had obtained possession of the city Mulek with a part of his army, while he marched with the remainder to meet the Lamanites when they should return from the pursuit of Teancum.

12 And it came to pass that the Lamanites did pursue Teancum until they came near the city Bountiful, and then they were met by Lechi and a small army which had been left to protect the city Bountiful. And now behold, when the chief captains of the Lamanites had beheld Lechi with his army coming against them, they fled in much confusion, for fear that perhaps they should not obtain the city Mulek before Lechi should overtake them; for they were wearied because of their march and the men of Lechi were fresh. Now the Lamanites did not know that M'roni had been in their rear with his army, and all they feared was Lechi and his men. Now Lechi was not desirous to overtake them till they should meet M'roni and his army. And it came to pass that before the Lamanites had retreated far, they were surrounded by the Nefites, by the men of M'roni on one hand and the men of Lechi on the other, all of whom were fresh and full of strength; but the Lamanites were wearied because of their long march. And

M'roni commanded his men that they should fall upon them until they had given up their weapons of war.

13 And it came to pass that Ya'akov, being their leader, being also a Tzuramite and having an unconquerable spirit, he led the Lamanites forth to battle with exceeding fury against M'roni, M'roni being in their course of march, therefore Ya'akov was determined to slay them and cut his way through to the city of Mulek. But behold, M'roni and his men were more powerful, therefore they did not give way before the Lamanites.

14 And it came to pass that they fought on both sides with exceeding fury, and there were many slain on both sides; yes, and M'roni was wounded and Ya'akov was killed. And Lechi pressed upon their rear with such fury with his strong men that the Lamanites in the rear delivered up their weapons of war; and the remainder of them, being greatly confused, knew not where to go or to strike. M'roni, seeing their confusion, said unto them, If you will bring forth your weapons of war and deliver them up, behold, we will cease shedding your blood. And it came to pass that when the Lamanites had heard these words, their chief captains, all those who were not slain, came forth and threw down their weapons of war at the feet of M'roni, and also commanded their men that they should do the same; but behold, there were many that would not. And those who would not deliver up their swords were taken and bound, and their weapons of war were taken from them, and they were compelled to march with their brothers forth into the land Bountiful. And now the number of prisoners who were taken exceeded more than the number of those who had been slain, yes, more than those who had been slain on both sides.

15 And it came to pass that they did set guards over the prisoners of the Lamanites and did compel them to go forth and bury their dead, yes, and also the dead of the Nefites who were slain; and M'roni placed men over them to guard them while they should perform their labors. And M'roni went to the city of Mulek with Lechi and took command of the city and gave it unto Lechi. Now behold, this Lechi was a man who had been with M'roni in the more part of all his battles, and he was a man like unto M'roni; and they rejoiced in each other's safety, yes, they were beloved by each other, and also beloved by all the people of Nefi.

16 And it came to pass that after the Lamanites had finished burying their dead, and also the dead of the Nefites, they were marched back into the land Bountiful; and Teancum, by the orders of M'roni, caused that they should commence laboring in digging a ditch round about the land, or the city Bountiful. And he caused that they should build a breastwork of timbers upon the inner bank of the ditch, and they cast up dirt out of the ditch against the breastwork of timbers; and thus they did cause the Lamanites to labor until they had encircled the city of Bountiful round about with a strong wall of timbers and earth to an exceeding height. And this city became an exceeding stronghold ever after. And in this city they did guard the prisoners of the Lamanites, yes, even within a wall which they had caused them to build with their own hands. Now M'roni was compelled to cause the Lamanites to labor because it was easy to guard them while at their labor; and he desired all his forces when he should make an attack upon the Lamanites.

17 And it came to pass that M'roni had thus gained a victory over one of the greatest of the armies of the Lamanites, and had obtained possession of the city Mulek, which was one of the strongest holds of the Lamanites in the land of Nefi; and thus he had also built a stronghold to retain his prisoners. And it came to pass that he did no more attempt a battle with the Lamanites in that year, but he did employ his men in preparing for war, yes, and in making fortifications to guard against the Lamanites, yes, and also delivering their women and their children from famine and affliction, and providing food for their armies.

18 And now it came to pass that the armies of the Lamanites on the west sea south, while in the absence of M'roni — on account of some intrigue among the Nefites which caused dissensions among them — had gained some ground over the Nefites, yes, insomuch that they had obtained possession of a number of their cities in that part of the land. And thus, because of iniquity among themselves,[214] yes, because of dissensions and intrigue among themselves, they were placed in the most dangerous circumstances.

19 And now behold, I have somewhat to say concerning the people of Ammon, who in the beginning were Lamanites, but by Ammon

---

[214] Cheleman 4:9

and his brothers (or rather by the power and word of Elohim) they had been converted unto YHWH, and they had been brought down into the land of Zerach'mla, and had ever since been protected by the Nefites. And because of their oath, they had been kept from taking up arms against their brothers, for they had taken an oath that they never would shed blood more; and according to their oath, they would have perished. Yes, they would have allowed themselves to have fallen into the hands of their brothers, had it not been for the pity and the exceeding love which Ammon and his brothers had had for them. And for this cause they were brought down into the land of Zerach'mla, and they ever had been protected by the Nefites.

20 But it came to pass that when they saw the danger, and the many afflictions and tribulations which the Nefites bore for them, they were moved with compassion and were desirous to take up arms in the defense of their country. But behold, as they were about to take their weapons of war, they were overpowered by the persuasions of Cheleman and his brothers, for they were about to break the oath which they had made; and Cheleman feared that by so doing they should lose their souls. Therefore, all those who had entered into this covenant were compelled to watch their brothers wade through their afflictions in their dangerous circumstances at this time. But behold, it came to pass they had many sons who had not entered into a covenant that they would not take their weapons of war to defend themselves against their enemies. Therefore, they did assemble themselves together at this time, as many as were able to take up arms, and they called themselves Nefites. And they entered into a covenant to fight for the liberty of the Nefites, yes, to protect the land unto the laying down of their lives; yes, even they covenanted that they never would give up their liberty, but they would fight in all cases to protect the Nefites and themselves from bondage.

21 Now behold, there were two thousand of those young men who entered into this covenant and took their weapons of war to defend their country. And now behold, as they never had previously been a disadvantage to the Nefites, they became now at this period of time also a great support; for they took their weapons of war and they would that Cheleman should be their leader. And they were all young men, and they were exceedingly valiant for courage, and also for strength and activity. But behold, this was not all. They were men

who were true at all times in whatsoever thing they were entrusted. Yes, they were men of truth and soberness, for they had been taught to keep the mitzvot of Elohim and to walk uprightly before him.[215]

22 And now it came to pass that Cheleman did march at the head of his two thousand stripling soldiers to the support of the people in the borders of the land on the south by the west sea. And thus ended the twenty and eighth year of the reign of the judges over the people of Nefi, and so forth.

25

And now it came to pass in the commencement of the twenty and ninth year[216] of the judges that Ammoron sent word unto M'roni desiring that he would exchange prisoners. And it came to pass that M'roni felt to rejoice exceedingly at this request, for he desired the provisions which were imparted for the support of the Lamanite prisoners for the support of his own people; and he also desired his own people for the strengthening of his army. Now the Lamanites had taken many women and children, and there was not a woman nor a child among all the prisoners of M'roni, or the prisoners whom M'roni had taken. Therefore, M'roni resolved upon a stratagem to obtain as many prisoners of the Nefites from the Lamanites as it were possible; therefore he wrote a letter and sent it by the servant of Ammoron, the same who had brought a letter to M'roni.

2 Now these are the words which he wrote unto Ammoron, saying, Behold, Ammoron, I have written unto you somewhat concerning this war which you have waged against my people, or rather which your brother has waged against them and which you are still determined to carry on after his death. Behold, I would tell you something concerning the justice of Elohim, and the sword of his almighty wrath which does hang over you except you repent and withdraw your armies into your own lands, or the lands of your possessions, which is the land of Nefi. Yes, I would tell you these things if you were capable of hearkening unto them. Yes, I would tell you concerning that awful Gehinnom that awaits to receive such murderers as you and your brother have been except you repent and withdraw your murderous purposes, and return with your armies to your own lands;

---

215 Prov. 2:1-12; Moshiyah 2:3 **216** ~64 BCE

but as you have once rejected these things and have fought against the people of YHWH, even so I may expect you will do it again.

3 And now behold, we are prepared to receive you; yes, and except you withdraw your purposes, behold, you will pull down the wrath of that Elohim whom you have rejected upon you, yes, even to your utter destruction. **But as YHWH lives,**[217] our armies shall come upon you except you withdraw, and you shall soon be visited with death; for we will retain our cities and our lands, yes, and we will maintain our religion and the cause of our Elohim. But behold, I suppose that I talk to you concerning these things in vain, or I suppose that you are a child of She'ol. Therefore, I will close my letter by telling you that I will not exchange prisoners except it be on conditions that you will deliver up a man, and his wife, and his children for one prisoner. If this be the case that you will do it, I will exchange. And behold, if you do not this, I will come against you with my armies. Yes, even I will arm my women and my children, and I will come against you, and I will follow you even into your own land, which is the land of our first inheritance. Yes, and it shall be blood for blood, yes, life for life; and I will give you battle even until you are destroyed from off the face of the earth. Behold, I am in my anger, and also my people; you have sought to murder us, and we have only sought to defend our lives. But behold, if you seek to destroy us more, we will seek to destroy you; yes, and we will seek our lands, the lands of our first inheritance. Now I close my letter. I am M'roni; I am a leader of the people of the Nefites.

4 Now it came to pass that Ammoron, when he had received this letter, he was angry, and he wrote another letter unto M'roni. And these are the words which he wrote, saying, I am Ammoron, the king of the Lamanites; I am the brother of Amalickiah whom you have murdered. Behold, I will avenge his blood upon you, yes, and I will come upon you with my armies, for I fear not your threatenings. For behold, your fathers did wrong their brothers, insomuch that they did rob them of their right to the government when it rightfully belonged unto them. And now behold, if you will lay down your arms and subject yourselves to be governed by those to whom the government does rightly belong, then will I cause that my people

---

217 2 Kings 5:20; 1 Nefi 1:20

shall lay down their weapons and shall be at war no more. Behold, you have breathed out many threatenings against me and my people, but behold, we fear not your threatenings. Nevertheless, I will grant to exchange prisoners according to your request gladly, that I may preserve my food for my men of war. And we will wage a war which shall be eternal, either to the subjecting the Nefites to our authority, or to their eternal extinction. And as concerning that Elohim whom you say we have rejected, behold, we know not such a being, neither do you. But if it so be that there is such a being, we know not but that he has made us as well as you. And if it so be that there is an adversary and a Gehinnom, behold, will he not send you there to dwell with my brother whom you have murdered? Whom you have hinted that he has gone to such a place? But behold, these things matter not. I am Ammoron, and a descendant of Tzuram, whom your fathers forced and brought out of Yerushalayim. And behold, I am now a bold Lamanite. Behold, this war has been waged to avenge their wrongs, and to maintain and to obtain their rights to the government. And I close my letter to M'roni.

5 Now it came to pass that when M'roni had received this letter, he was more angry, because he knew that Ammoron had a perfect knowledge of his fraud; yes, he knew that Ammoron knew that it was not a just cause that had caused him to wage a war against the people of Nefi. And he said, Behold, I will not exchange prisoners with Ammoron except he will withdraw his purpose as I have stated in my letter, for I will not grant unto him that he shall have any more power than what he has gotten. Behold, I know the place where the Lamanites do guard my people whom they have taken prisoners. And as Ammoron would not grant unto my letter, behold, I will give unto him according to my words; yes, I will seek death among them until they shall petition for shalom. And now it came to pass that when M'roni had said these words, he caused that a search should be made among his men, that perhaps he might find a man who was a descendant of Laman's among them.

6 And it came to pass that they found one whose name was Laman, and he was one of the servants of the king who was murdered by Amalickiah. Now M'roni caused that Laman and a small number of his men should go forth unto the guards who were over the Nefites. Now the Nefites were guarded in the city of Gid; therefore, M'roni

caused that Laman, and a small number of men who were appointed, go with him.

7 And when it was evening, Laman went to the guards who were over the Nefites, and behold, they saw him coming and they hailed him. But he said unto them, Fear not. Behold, I am a Lamanite. Behold, we have escaped from the Nefites and they sleep; and behold, we have taken of their wine and brought with us. Now when the Lamanites heard these words, they received him with joy. And they said unto him, Give us of your wine, that we may drink. We are glad that you have thus taken wine with you, for we are weary. But Laman said unto them, Let us keep of our wine till we go against the Nefites to battle. But this saying only made them more desirous to drink of the wine. For, said they, we are weary, therefore let us take of the wine, and by and by we shall receive wine for our rations, which will strengthen us to go against the Nefites. And Laman said unto them, You may do according to your desires. And it came to pass that they did take of the wine freely, and it was pleasant to their taste, therefore they took of it more freely; and it was strong, having been prepared in its strength.

8 And it came to pass they did drink and were merry, and by and by they were all drunken. And now when Laman and his men saw that they were all drunken and were in a deep sleep, they returned to M'roni and told him all the things that had happened. And now this was according to the design of M'roni. And M'roni had prepared his men with weapons of war; and he went to the city Gid while the Lamanites were in a deep sleep and drunken, and cast in weapons of war, in unto the prisoners, insomuch that they were all armed, yes, even to their women and all their children, as many as were able to use a weapon of war. When M'roni had armed all those prisoners (and all those things were done in a profound silence, but had they awoken the Lamanites, behold, they were drunken and the Nefites could have slain them; but behold, this was not the desire of M'roni. He did not delight in murder or bloodshed, but he delighted in saving his people from destruction. And for this cause, that he might not bring upon him injustice, he would not fall upon the Lamanites and destroy them in their drunkenness. But he had obtained his desire, for he had armed those prisoners of the Nefites who were within the walls of the city, and had given them power to gain possession of those parts which were within the walls) and then he caused his men

who were with him to withdraw a pace from them and surround the armies of the Lamanites. Now behold, this was done in the nighttime so that when the Lamanites awoke in the morning, they beheld that they were surrounded by the Nefites without and that their prisoners were armed within. And thus they saw that the Nefites had power over them; and in these circumstances they found that it were not expedient that they should fight with the Nefites. Therefore, their chief captains demanded their weapons of war, and they brought them forth and cast them at the feet of the Nefites, pleading for mercy. Now behold, this was the desire of M'roni. He took them prisoners of war, and took possession of the city, and caused that all the prisoners should be liberated who were Nefites. And they did join the army of M'roni and were a great strength to his army.

9 And it came to pass that he did cause the Lamanites whom he had taken prisoners that they should commence a labor in strengthening the fortifications round about the city Gid. And it came to pass that when he had fortified the city Gid according to his desires, he caused that his prisoners should be taken to the city Bountiful. And he also guarded that city with an exceedingly strong force. And it came to pass that they did, despite all the intrigues of the Lamanites, keep and protect all the prisoners whom they had taken, and also maintain all the ground and the advantage which they had retaken. And it came to pass that the Nefites began again to be victorious and to reclaim their rights and their privileges. Many times did the Lamanites attempt to encircle them about by night, but in these attempts they did lose many prisoners. And many times did they attempt to administer of their wine to the Nefites, that they might destroy them with poison or with drunkenness. But behold, the Nefites were not slow to remember YHWH their Elohim in these their times of affliction. They could not be taken in their snares, yes, they would not partake of their wine, yes, they would not take of wine except they had first given to some of the Lamanite prisoners. And they were thus cautious that no poison should be administered among them; for if their wine would poison a Lamanite, it would also poison a Nefite; and thus they did try all their liquors. And now it came to pass that it was expedient for M'roni to make preparations to attack the city Morionton. For behold, the Lamanites had, by their labors, fortified the city Morionton until it had become an exceeding stronghold. And they were continually

bringing new forces into that city, and also new supplies of provisions. And thus ended the twenty and ninth year of the reign of the judges over the people of Nefi.

26 And now it came to pass in the commencement of the thirtieth year[218] of the reign of the judges, in the second day on the first month, M'roni received a letter from Cheleman stating the affairs of the people in that quarter of the land. And these are the words which he wrote, saying, My dearly beloved brother M'roni, as well in YHWH as in the tribulations of our warfare, behold, my beloved brother, I have somewhat to tell you concerning our warfare in this part of the land. Behold, two thousand of the sons of those men whom Ammon brought down out of the land of Nefi – now you have known that these were descendants of Laman, who was the eldest son of our father Lechi – now I need not rehearse unto you concerning their traditions or their unbelief, for you know concerning all these things, therefore it suffices me that I tell you that two thousand of these young men have taken their weapons of war and would that I should be their leader; and we have come forth to defend our country.

2 And now you also know concerning the covenant which their fathers made, that they would not take up their weapons of war against their brothers to shed blood. But in the twenty and sixth year, when they saw our afflictions and our tribulations for them, they were about to break the covenant which they had made and take up their weapons of war in our defense. But I would not allow them that they should break this covenant which they had made, supposing that Elohim would strengthen us, insomuch that we should not suffer more because of the fulfilling the oath which they had taken. But behold, here is one thing in which we may have great joy. For behold, in the twenty and sixth year, I, Cheleman, did march at the head of these two thousand young men to the city of Judea, to assist Antipus, whom you had appointed a leader over the people of that part of the land. And I did join my two thousand sons – for they are worthy to be called sons – to the army of Antipus, in the which strength Antipus did rejoice exceedingly. For behold, his army had

---

218 ~63 BCE

been reduced by the Lamanites because of the enormity of their forces, having slain a vast number of our men, for which cause we have to mourn. Nevertheless, we may console ourselves in this point: that they have died in the cause of their country and of their Elohim, yes, and they are happy. And the Lamanites had also retained many prisoners, all of whom are chief captains, for none other have they spared alive. And we suppose that they are now at this time in the land of Nefi; it is so if they are not slain.

3 And now these are the cities which the Lamanites have obtained possession of by shedding the blood of so many of our valiant men: the land of Manti, or the city of Manti, and the city of Zeezrom, and the city of Cumeni, and the city of Antiparah. And these are the cities which they possessed when I arrived at the city of Judea and I found Antipus and his men laboring with their might to fortify the city. Yes, and they were depressed in body as well as in spirit, for they had fought valiantly by day and labored by night to maintain their cities; and thus they had suffered great afflictions of every kind. And now they were determined to conquer in this place or die. Therefore, you may well suppose that the little force which I brought with me — yes, those sons of mine — gave them great hopes and much joy.

4 And now it came to pass that when the Lamanites saw that Antipus had received a greater strength to his army, they were compelled by the orders of Ammoron to not come against the city of Judea or against us to battle; and thus were we favored of YHWH. For had they come upon us in this our weakness, they might have perhaps destroyed our little army; but thus were we favored: they were commanded by Ammoron to maintain those cities which they had taken. And thus ended the twenty and sixth year. And in the commencement of the twenty and seventh year,[219] we had prepared our city and ourselves for defense. Now we were desirous that the Lamanites should come upon us, for we were not desirous to make an attack upon them in their strongholds. And it came to pass that we kept spies out round about to watch the movements of the Lamanites, that they might not pass us by night or by day to make an attack upon our other cities which were on the northward, for we knew in those cities they were not sufficiently strong to meet them. Therefore, we

---

[219] ~66 BCE

were desirous, if they should pass by us, to fall upon them in their rear, and thus bring them up in the rear at the same time they were met in the front. We supposed that we could overpower them, but behold, we were disappointed in this our desire. They dared not pass by us with their whole army, neither dared they with a part, for fear that they should not be sufficiently strong and they should fall. Neither dared they march down against the city of Zerach'mla, neither dared they cross the head of Tzidon over to the city of Nefihah. And thus, with their forces, they were determined to maintain those cities which they had taken.

⁵And now it came to pass, in the second month of this year, there were brought unto us many provisions from the fathers of my two thousand sons. And also, there were sent two thousand men unto us from the land of Zerach'mla. And thus we were prepared with ten thousand men, and provisions for them, and also for their wives and their children. And the Lamanites, thus seeing our forces increase daily and provisions arrive for our support, they began to be fearful and began to rush forth, if it were possible, to put an end to our receiving provisions and strength. Now when we saw that the Lamanites began to grow uneasy in this way, we were desirous to bring a stratagem into effect upon them. Therefore, Antipus ordered that I should march forth with my little sons to a neighboring city, as if we were carrying provisions to a neighboring city. And we were to march near the city Antiparah as if we were going to the city beyond, on the borders by the seashore. And it came to pass that we did march forth, as if with our provisions, to go to that city. And it came to pass that Antipus did march forth with a part of his army, leaving the remainder to maintain the city. But he did not march forth until I had gone forth with my little army and come near the city Antiparah. And now, in the city Antiparah was stationed the strongest army of the Lamanites, yes, the most numerous. And it came to pass that when they had been informed by their spies, they came forth with their army and marched against us.

⁶And it came to pass that we did flee before them northward. And thus we did lead away the most powerful army of the Lamanites, yes, even to a considerable distance, insomuch that when they saw the army of Antipus pursuing them with their might, they did not turn to the right nor to the left, but pursued their march in a straight

course after us. And we supposed that it was their intent to slay us before Antipus should overtake them — and this that they might not be surrounded by our people. And now Antipus, beholding our danger, did speed the march of his army. But behold, it was night, therefore they did not overtake us, neither did Antipus overtake them; therefore we did camp for the night.

7 And it came to pass that before the dawn of the morning, behold, the Lamanites were pursuing us. Now we were not sufficiently strong to contend with them; yes, I would not allow that my little sons should fall into their hands. Therefore we did continue our march, and we took our march into the wilderness. Now they dared not turn to the right nor to the left, for fear that they should be surrounded. Neither would I turn to the right or to the left, for fear that they should overtake me and we could not stand against them, but be slain, and they would make their escape; and thus we did flee all that day into the wilderness, even until it was dark.

8 And it came to pass that again, when the light of the morning came, we saw the Lamanites upon us and we did flee before them. But it came to pass that they did not pursue us far before they halted; and it was in the morning of the third day on the seventh month. And now, whether they were overtaken by Antipus, we knew not, but I said unto my men, Behold, we know not but they have halted for the purpose that we should come against them, that they may catch us in their snare. Therefore, what say you, my sons? Will you go against them to battle? And now I say unto you, my beloved brother M'roni, that never had I seen so great courage, no, not among all the Nefites. For as I had always called them my sons (for they were all of them very young), even so they said unto me, Father, behold, our Elohim is with us, and he will not allow that we shall fall;[220] then let us go forth. We would not slay our brothers if they would leave us alone; therefore let us go, lest they should overpower the army of Antipus. Now they never had fought, yet they did not fear death, and they did think more upon the liberty of their fathers than they did upon their lives. Yes, they had been taught by their mothers that if they did not doubt, that Elohim would deliver them. And they rehearsed

---

[220] 1 Sam. 17:32-37, 45-47

unto me the words of their mothers, saying, We do not doubt our mothers knew.[221]

9 And it came to pass that I did return with my two thousand against these Lamanites who had pursued us. And now behold, the armies of Antipus had overtaken them and a terrible battle had commenced. The army of Antipus, being weary because of their long march in so short a space of time, were about to fall into the hands of the Lamanites, and had I not returned with my two thousand, they would have obtained their purpose; for Antipus had fallen by the sword, and many of his leaders, because of their weariness, which was occasioned by the speed of their march. Therefore, the men of Antipus, being confused because of the fall of their leaders, began to give way before the Lamanites.

10 And it came to pass that the Lamanites took courage and began to pursue them. And thus were the Lamanites pursuing them with great vigor when Cheleman came upon their rear with his two thousand and began to slay them exceedingly, insomuch that the whole army of the Lamanites halted and turned upon Cheleman. Now when the people of Antipus saw that the Lamanites had turned around, they gathered together their men and came again upon the rear of the Lamanites.

11 And now it came to pass that we, the people of Nefi — the people of Antipus, and I with my two thousand — did surround the Lamanites and did slay them, yes, insomuch that they were compelled to deliver up their weapons of war, and also themselves as prisoners of war.

12 And now it came to pass that when they had surrendered themselves up unto us, behold, I numbered those young men who had fought with me, fearing that there were many of them slain. But behold, to my great joy, there had not one soul of them fallen to the earth. Yes, and they had fought as if with the strength of Elohim, yes, never were men known to have fought with such miraculous strength; and with such mighty power did they fall upon the Lamanites that they did frighten them.[222] And for this cause did the Lamanites deliver themselves up as prisoners of war. And as we had no place for our prisoners that we could guard them to keep them from the armies of

---

221 Prov. 15:33; M'raman 4:9   222 Isa. 41:8–14

the Lamanites, therefore we sent them to the land of Zerach'mla, and a part of those men who were not slain of Antipus with them; and the remainder I took and joined them to my stripling Ammonites, and took our march back to the city of Judea.

13 And now it came to pass that I received a letter from Ammoron, the king, stating that if I would deliver up those prisoners of war whom we had taken, that he would deliver up the city of Antiparah unto us. But I sent a letter unto the king that we were sure that our forces were sufficient to take the city of Antiparah by our force, and by delivering up the prisoners for that city we should suppose ourselves unwise, and that we would only deliver up our prisoners on exchange. And Ammoron refused my letter, for he would not exchange prisoners, therefore we began to make preparations to go against the city of Antiparah. But the people of Antiparah did leave the city and fled to their other cities which they had possession of, to fortify them; and thus the city of Antiparah fell into our hands. And thus ended the twenty and eighth year of the reign of the judges.

14 And it came to pass that in the commencement of the twenty and ninth year we received a supply of provisions, and also an addition to our army, from the land of Zerach'mla and from the land round about, to the number of six thousand men, besides sixty of the sons of the Ammonites who had come to join their brothers, my little band of two thousand. And now behold, we were strong, yes, and we had also plenty of provisions brought unto us.

15 And it came to pass that it was our desire to wage a battle with the army which was placed to protect the city Cumeni. And now behold, I will show unto you that we soon accomplished our desire; yes, with our strong force, or with a part of our strong force, we did surround by night the city Cumeni a little before they were to receive a supply of provisions. And it came to pass that we did camp round about the city for many nights, but we did sleep upon our swords and keep guards, that the Lamanites could not come upon us by night and slay us, which they attempted many times. But as many times as they attempted this, their blood was spilt. At length their provisions did arrive, and they were about to enter the city by night. And we, instead of being Lamanites, were Nefites; therefore we did take them and their provisions. And even though the Lamanites were cut off from their support after this manner, they were still determined to

maintain the city. Therefore, it became expedient that we should take those provisions and send them to Judea, and our prisoners to the land of Zerach'mla.

16 And it came to pass that not many days had passed away before the Lamanites began to lose all hopes of relief, therefore they yielded up the city into our hands; and thus we had accomplished our designs in obtaining the city Cumeni. But it came to pass that our prisoners were so numerous, that, despite the enormity of our number, we were obliged to employ all our force to keep them, or put them to death. For behold, they would break out in great numbers, and would fight with stones and with clubs, or whatsoever thing they could get into their hands, insomuch that we did slay upwards of two thousand of them after they had surrendered themselves prisoners of war. Therefore, it became expedient for us that we should put an end to their lives, or guard them, sword in hand, down to the land of Zerach'mla. And also our provisions were not any more than sufficient for our own people, despite that which we had taken from the Lamanites. And now, in those critical circumstances it became a very serious matter to determine concerning those prisoners of war; nevertheless, we did resolve to send them down to the land of Zerach'mla. Therefore, we selected a part of our men and gave them charge over our prisoners to go down to the land of Zerach'mla.

17 But it came to pass that the next day they did return. And now behold, we did not inquire of them concerning the prisoners, for behold, the Lamanites were upon us and they returned in time to save us from falling into their hands. For behold, Ammoron had sent to their support a new supply of provision, and also a numerous army of men.

18 And it came to pass that those men whom we sent with the prisoners did arrive in time to thwart them as they were about to overpower us. But behold, my little band of two thousand and sixty fought most desperately, yes, they were firm before the Lamanites and did administer death unto all those who opposed them. And as the remainder of our army were about to give way before the Lamanites, behold, these two thousand and sixty were firm and undaunted. Yes, and they did obey and observe to perform every word of command with exactness, yes, and even according to their faith it was done

unto them;[223] and I did remember the words which they said unto me that their mothers had taught them. And now behold, it was these, my sons, and those men who had been selected to accompany the prisoners, to whom we owe this great victory, for it was they who did beat the Lamanites. Therefore, they were driven back to the city of Manti. And we retained our city Cumeni and were not all destroyed by the sword; nevertheless, we had suffered great loss.

19 And it came to pass that after the Lamanites had fled, I immediately gave orders that my men who had been wounded should be taken from among the dead, and caused that their wounds should be dressed. And it came to pass that there were two hundred, out of my two thousand and sixty, who had fainted because of the loss of blood; nevertheless, according to the goodness of Elohim and to our great astonishment, and also the joy of our whole army, there was not one soul of them who did perish; yes, and neither was there one soul among them who had not received many wounds. And now, their preservation was astonishing to our whole army, yes, that they should be spared while there was a thousand of our brothers who were slain. And we do justly ascribe it to the miraculous power of Elohim, because of their exceeding faith in that which they had been taught to believe: that there was a just Elohim,[224] and whosoever did not doubt, that they should be preserved by his marvelous power. Now this was the faith of these of whom I have spoken. They are young and their minds are firm, and they do put their trust in Elohim continually.[225]

20 And now it came to pass that after we had thus taken care of our wounded men and had buried our dead, and also the dead of the Lamanites, who were many, behold, we did inquire of Gid concerning the prisoners whom they had started to go down to the land of Zerach'mla with. Now Gid was the chief captain over the band which was appointed to guard them down to that land. And now, these are the words which Gid said unto me: Behold, we did start to go down to the land of Zerach'mla with our prisoners. And it came to pass that we did meet the spies of our armies who had been sent out to watch the camp of the Lamanites. And they cried unto us, saying, Behold, the armies of the Lamanites are marching towards the city of Cumeni! And behold, they will fall upon them, yes, and will destroy our people!

---

223 'Eter 5:3   224 Moshiyah 1:16   225 2 Nefi 3:8

21 And it came to pass that our prisoners did hear their cries, which caused them to take courage, and they did raise up in rebellion against us. And it came to pass because of their rebellion, we did cause that our swords should come upon them. And it came to pass that they did, in a body, run upon our swords, in the which the greater number of them were slain; and the remainder of them broke through and fled from us. And behold, when they had fled and we could not overtake them, we took our march with speed towards the city Cumeni; and behold, we did arrive in time that we might assist our brothers in preserving the city. And behold, we were again delivered out of the hands of our enemies. And blessed is the name of our Elohim, for behold, it is he that has delivered us, yes, that has done this great thing for us.

22 Now it came to pass that when I, Cheleman, had heard these words of Gid, I was filled with exceeding joy because of the goodness of Elohim in preserving us, that we might not all perish; yes, and I trust that the souls of those who have been slain have entered into the rest of their Elohim.

23 And behold, now it came to pass that our next object was to obtain the city of Manti, but behold, there was no way that we could lead them out of the city by our small bands. For behold, they remembered that which we had previously done, therefore we could not decoy them away from their strongholds. And they were so exceedingly more numerous than was our army that we dared not go forth and attack them in their strongholds. Yes, and it became expedient that we should employ our men to the maintaining those parts of the land of which we had retained of our possessions. Therefore, it became expedient that we should wait, that we might receive more strength from the land of Zerach'mla, and also a new supply of provisions.

24 And it came to pass that I thus did send an embassy to the great governor of our land to acquaint him concerning the affairs of our people. And it came to pass that we did wait to receive provisions and strength from the land of Zerach'mla. But behold, this did profit us but little, for the Lamanites were also receiving great strength from day to day, and also many provisions; and thus were our circumstances at this period of time. And the Lamanites were rushing forth against us from time to time, resolving by stratagem

to destroy us; nevertheless, we could not come to battle with them because of their retreats and their strongholds.

25 And it came to pass that we did wait in these difficult circumstances for the space of many months, even until we were about to perish for the want of food. But it came to pass that we did receive food which was guarded to us with an army of two thousand men to our assistance; and this is all the assistance which we did receive to defend ourselves and our country from falling into the hands of our enemies, yes, to contend with an enemy which was innumerable. And now the cause of these our deprivations, or the cause why they did not send more strength unto us, we knew not. Therefore, we were grieved and also filled with fear that by any means the judgments of Elohim should come upon our land, to our overthrow and utter destruction. Therefore, we did pour out our souls in prayer to Elohim that he would strengthen us and deliver us out of the hands of our enemies, yes, and also give us strength that we might retain our cities, and our lands, and our possessions, for the support of our people. Yes, and it came to pass that YHWH our Elohim did visit us with assurances that he would deliver us, yes, insomuch that he did speak shalom to our souls, and did grant unto us great faith, and did cause us that we should hope for our deliverance in him. And we did take courage with our small force which we had received, and were fixed with a determination to conquer our enemies, and to maintain our lands, and our possessions, and our wives, and our children, and the cause of our liberty. And thus we did go forth with all our might against the Lamanites who were in the city of Manti. And we did pitch our tents by the wilderness side, which was near to the city. And it came to pass on the next day, that when the Lamanites saw that we were in the borders by the wilderness which was near the city, that they sent out their spies round about us, that they might discover the number and the strength of our army.

26 And it came to pass that when they saw that we were not strong according to our numbers, and fearing that we should cut them off from their support except they should come out to battle against us and kill us, and also supposing that they could easily destroy us with their numerous hosts, therefore they began to make preparations to come out against us to battle. And when we saw that they were making preparations to come out against us, behold, I caused that

Gid, with a small number of men, should conceal himself in the wilderness, and also that Teomner should, with a small number of men, conceal himself also in the wilderness. Now Gid and his men were on the right and the other on the left; and when they had thus concealed themselves, behold, I remained with the remainder of my army in that same place where we had first pitched our tents against the time that the Lamanites should come out to battle.

27 And it came to pass that the Lamanites did come out with their numerous army against us. And when they had come, and were about to fall upon us with the sword, I caused that my men, those who were with me, should retreat into the wilderness.

28 And it came to pass that the Lamanites did follow after us with great speed, for they were exceedingly desirous to overtake us that they might slay us; therefore they did follow us into the wilderness. And we did pass by in the midst of Gid and Teomner, insomuch that they were not discovered by the Lamanites.

29 And it came to pass that when the Lamanites had passed by, or when the army had passed by, Gid and Teomner did rise up from their secret places and did cut off the spies of the Lamanites, that they should not return to the city. And it came to pass that when they had cut them off, they ran to the city and fell upon the guards who were left to guard the city, insomuch that they did destroy them and did take possession of the city. Now this was done because the Lamanites did allow their whole army, except a few guards only, to be led away into the wilderness.

30 And it came to pass that Gid and Teomner, by this means, had obtained possession of their stronghold. And it came to pass that we took our course, after having traveled much in the wilderness, towards the land of Zerach'mla. And when the Lamanites saw that they were marching towards the land of Zerach'mla, they were exceedingly afraid, that there was a plan laid to lead them on to destruction; therefore they began to retreat into the wilderness again, yes, even back by the same way which they had come. And behold, it was night and they did pitch their tents, for the chief captains of the Lamanites had supposed that the Nefites were weary because of their march. And supposing that they had driven their whole army, therefore they took no thought concerning the city of Manti.

31 Now it came to pass that when it was night, that I caused that my men should not sleep, but that they should march forward by another way towards the land of Manti. And because of this our march in the nighttime, behold, the next day we were beyond the Lamanites, insomuch that we did arrive before them to the city of Manti. And thus it came to pass that by this stratagem we did take possession of the city of Manti without the shedding of blood.

32 And it came to pass that when the armies of the Lamanites did arrive near the city and saw that we were prepared to meet them, they were astonished exceedingly and struck with great fear, insomuch that they did flee into the wilderness. Yes, and it came to pass that the armies of the Lamanites did flee out of all this quarter of the land. But behold, they have carried with them many women and children out of the land. And those cities which had been taken by the Lamanites, all of them are at this period of time in our possession; and our fathers, and our women, and our children are returning to their homes, all except it be those who have been taken prisoners and carried off by the Lamanites. But behold, our armies are small to maintain so great a number of cities and so great possessions. But behold, we trust that our Elohim, who has given us victory over those lands, insomuch that we have obtained those cities and those lands which were our own.

33 Now we do not know the cause that the government does not grant us more strength, neither do those men who came up unto us know why we have not received greater strength. Behold, we do not know but what you are unsuccessful and you have drawn away the forces into that quarter of the land; if so, we do not desire to murmur. And if it is not so, behold, we fear that there is some dissension in the government, that they do not send more men to our assistance, for we know that they are more numerous than that which they have sent. But behold, it matters not; we trust Elohim will deliver us, despite the weakness of our armies, yes, and deliver us out of the hands of our enemies. Behold, this is the twenty and ninth year, in the latter end, and we are in the possession of our lands, and the Lamanites have fled to the land of Nefi.

34 And those sons of the people of Ammon, of whom I have so highly spoken, are with me in the city of Manti, and YHWH has supported them, yes, and kept them from falling by the sword, insomuch that not even one soul has been slain. But behold, they have received

many wounds. Nevertheless, they stand fast in that liberty with which Elohim has made them free. And they are strict to remember YHWH their Elohim from day to day, yes, they do observe to **keep his statutes, and his judgments, and his mitzvot continually,**[226] and their faith is strong in the prophecies concerning that which is to come. And now, my beloved brother M'roni, that YHWH our Elohim, who has redeemed us and made us free, may keep you continually in his presence, yes, and that he may favor this people, even that you may have success in obtaining the possession of all that which the Lamanites have taken from us which was for our support. And now behold, I close my letter. I am Cheleman, the son of Alma.

27

Now it came to pass in the thirtieth year of the reign of the judges over the people of Nefi, after M'roni had received and had read Cheleman's letter, he rejoiced exceedingly because of the welfare, yes, the exceeding success which Cheleman had had in obtaining those lands which were lost. Yes, and he did make it known unto all his people in all the land round about in that part where he was, that they might rejoice also.

2 And it came to pass that he immediately sent a letter to Parhoron, desiring that he should cause men to be gathered together to strengthen Cheleman, or the armies of Cheleman, insomuch that he might with ease maintain that part of the land which he had been so miraculously prospered in retaining. And it came to pass when M'roni had sent this letter to the land of Zerach'mla, he began again to lay a plan that he might obtain the remainder of those possessions and cities which the Lamanites had taken from them.

3 And it came to pass that while M'roni was thus making preparations to go against the Lamanites to battle, behold, the people of Nefihah who were gathered together from the city of M'roni, and the city of Lechi, and the city of Morionton, were attacked by the Lamanites. Yes, even those who had been compelled to flee from the land of Manti and from the land round about had come over and joined the Lamanites in this part of the land. And thus being exceedingly numerous, yes, and receiving strength from day to day by the command of Ammoron, they came forth against the people of

---

[226] Deut. 11:1

Nefihah and they did begin to slay them with an exceedingly great slaughter. And their armies were so numerous that the remainder of the people of Nefihah were obliged to flee before them; and they came even and joined the army of M'roni. And now, as M'roni had supposed that there should be men sent to the city of Nefihah, to the assistance of the people to maintain that city, and knowing that it was easier to keep the city from falling into the hands of the Lamanites than to retake it from them, he supposed that they would easily maintain that city; therefore he retained all his force to maintain those places which he had recovered.

⁴And now when M'roni saw that the city of Nefihah was lost, he was exceedingly sorrowful and began to doubt, because of the wickedness of the people, whether they should not fall into the hands of their brothers. Now this was the case with all his chief captains. They doubted and marveled also because of the wickedness of the people, and this because of the success of the Lamanites over them. And it came to pass that M'roni was angry with the government because of their indifference concerning the freedom of their country.

⁵And it came to pass that he wrote again to the governor of the land, who was Parhoron, and these are the words which he wrote, saying, Behold, I direct my letter to Parhoron in the city of Zerach'mla, who is the chief judge and the governor over the land, and also to all those who have been chosen by this people to govern and manage the affairs of this war; for behold, I have somewhat to say unto them by the way of condemnation. For behold, you yourselves know that you have been appointed to gather together men and arm them with swords, and with cimeters, and all manner of weapons of war of every kind, and send forth against the Lamanites in whatsoever parts they should come into our land. And now behold, I say unto you that myself, and also my men, and also Cheleman and his men, have suffered exceedingly great sufferings—yes, even hunger, thirst, and fatigue, and all manner of afflictions of every kind. But behold, were this all we had suffered, we would not murmur nor complain; but behold, great has been the slaughter among our people, yes, thousands have fallen by the sword, while it might have been otherwise if you had rendered unto our armies sufficient strength and relief for them. Yes, great has been your neglect towards us.

⁶And now behold, we desire to know the cause of this exceedingly great neglect; yes, we desire to know the cause of your thoughtless state. Can you think to sit upon your thrones in a state of thoughtless stupor while your enemies are spreading the work of death around you? Yes, while they are murdering thousands of your brothers? Yes, even they who have looked up to you for protection, yes, have placed you in a situation that you might have relieved them. Yes, you might have sent armies unto them to have strengthened them and have saved thousands of them from falling by the sword. But behold, this is not all. You have withheld your provisions from them, insomuch that many have fought and bled out their lives because of their great desires which they had for the welfare of this people; yes, and this they have done when they were about to perish with hunger because of your exceedingly great neglect towards them. And now, my beloved brothers—for you ought to be beloved, yes, and you ought to have stirred yourselves more diligently for the welfare and the freedom of this people. But behold, you have neglected them, insomuch that the blood of thousands shall come upon your heads for vengeance; yes, for known unto Elohim were all their cries and all their sufferings. Behold, could you suppose that you could sit upon your thrones and because of the exceeding goodness of Elohim you could do nothing and he would deliver you? Behold, if you have supposed this, you have supposed in vain. Do you suppose that because so many of your brothers have been killed, it is because of their wickedness? I say unto you, if you have supposed this, you have supposed in vain. For I say unto you, there are many who have fallen by the sword, and behold, it is to your condemnation. For YHWH allows the righteous to be slain that his justice and judgment may come upon the wicked; therefore you need not suppose that the righteous are lost because they are slain, but behold, they do enter into the rest of YHWH their Elohim.

⁷And now behold, I say unto you, I fear exceedingly that the judgments of Elohim will come upon this people because of their exceeding slothfulness, yes, even the slothfulness of our government and their exceedingly great neglect towards their brothers, yes, towards those who have been slain. For were it not for the wickedness which first commenced at our head, we could have withstood our enemies, that they could have gained no power over us. Yes, had it not been for the war which broke out among ourselves, yes, were it not

for those Kingmen who caused so much bloodshed among ourselves, yes, at the time we were contending among ourselves — if we had united our strength as we previously had done, yes, had it not been for the desire of power and authority which those Kingmen had over us, had they been true to the cause of our freedom and united with us, and gone forth against our enemies instead of taking up their swords against us, which was the cause of so much bloodshed among ourselves — yes, if we had gone forth against them in the strength of YHWH, we should have dispersed our enemies, for it would have been done according to the fulfilling of his word. But behold, now the Lamanites are coming upon us and they are murdering our people with the sword, yes, our women and our children, taking possession of our lands, and also carrying them away captive, causing them that they should suffer all manner of afflictions, and this because of the great wickedness of those who are seeking for power and authority, yes, even those Kingmen.

8 But why should I say much concerning this matter? For we know not but what you yourselves are seeking for authority; we know not but what you are also traitors to your country. Or is it that you have neglected us because you are in the heart of our country and you are surrounded by security, that you do not cause food to be sent unto us and also men to strengthen our armies? Have you forgotten the mitzvot of YHWH your Elohim? Yes, have you forgotten the captivity of our fathers? Have you forgotten the many times we have been delivered out of the hands of our enemies? Or do you suppose that YHWH will still deliver us while we sit upon our thrones and do not make use of the means which YHWH has provided for us? Yes, will you sit in idleness while you are surrounded with thousands of those, yes, and tens of thousands, who do also sit in idleness, while there are thousands round about in the borders of the land who are falling by the sword? Yes, wounded and bleeding? Do you suppose that Elohim will look upon you as guiltless while you sit still and behold these things? Behold, I say unto you, no.

9 Now I would that you should remember that Elohim has said that the inward vessel shall be cleansed first, and then shall the outer vessel be cleansed also. And now except you do repent of that which you have done, and begin to be up and doing, and send forth food and men unto us, and also unto Cheleman, that he may support

those parts of our country which he has retained, and that we may also recover the remainder of our possessions in these parts, behold, it will be expedient that we contend no more with the Lamanites until we have first cleansed our inward vessel, yes, even the great head of our government. And except you grant my letter, and come out and show unto me a true spirit of freedom, and strive to strengthen and fortify our armies, and grant unto them food for their support, behold, I will leave a part of my Freemen to maintain this part of our land, and I will leave the strength and the blessings of Elohim upon them, that none other power can operate against them — and this because of their exceeding faith and their patience in their tribulations — and I will come unto you; and if there be any among you that has a desire for freedom, yes, if there be even a spark of freedom remaining, behold, I will stir up insurrections among you, even until those who have desires to usurp power and authority shall become extinct. Yes, behold, I do not fear your power nor your authority, but it is my Elohim whom I fear; and it is according to his mitzvot that I do take my sword to defend the cause of my country, and it is because of your iniquity that we have suffered so much loss.

10 Behold, it is time, yes, the time is now at hand that except you do act quickly in the defense of your country and your little ones, the sword of justice does hang over you, yes, and it shall fall upon you and visit you, even to your utter destruction. Behold, I wait for assistance from you; and except you do administer unto our relief, behold, I come unto you, even into the land of Zerach'mla, and strike you with the sword, insomuch that you can have no more power to impede the progress of this people in the cause of our freedom. For behold, YHWH will not allow that you shall live and grow strong in your iniquities to destroy his righteous people. Behold, can you suppose that YHWH will spare you and come out in judgment against the Lamanites when it is the tradition of their fathers that has caused their hatred — yes, and it has been redoubled by those who have dissented from us — while your iniquity is for the cause of your love of glory and the vain things of the world? You know that you do transgress the laws of Elohim, and you do know that you do trample them under your feet. Behold, YHWH says unto me, If those whom you have appointed your governors do not repent of their sins and iniquities, you shall go up to battle against them.

11 And now behold, I, M'roni, am constrained according to the covenant which I have made to keep the mitzvot of my Elohim, therefore I would that you should adhere to the word of Elohim and send speedily unto me of your provisions and of your men, and also to Cheleman. And behold, if you will not do this, I come unto you speedily. For behold, Elohim will not allow that we should perish with hunger, therefore he will give unto us of your food, even if it must be by the sword. Now see that you fulfill the word of Elohim. Behold, I am M'roni, your chief captain. I seek not for power, but to pull it down. I seek not for honor of the world, but for the glory of my Elohim and the freedom and welfare of my country. And thus I close my letter.

28

Behold, now it came to pass that soon after M'roni had sent his letter unto the chief governor, he received a letter from Parhoron, the chief governor. And these are the words which he received: I, Parhoron, who am the chief governor of this land, do send these words unto M'roni, the chief captain over the army. Behold, I say unto you, M'roni, that I do not joy in your great afflictions, yes, it grieves my soul. But behold, there are those who do joy in your afflictions, yes, insomuch that they have risen up in rebellion against me, and also those of my people who are Freemen, yes, and those who have risen up are exceedingly numerous. And it is they who have sought to take away the judgment seat from me that have been the cause of this great iniquity; for they have used great flattery and they have led away the hearts of many people, which will be the cause of sore affliction among us. They have withheld our provisions and have intimidated our Freemen, that they have not come unto you. And behold, they have driven me out before them, and I have fled to the land of Gideon with as many men as it were possible that I could get. And behold, I have sent a proclamation throughout this part of the land; and behold, they are flocking to us daily, to their arms, in the defense of their country and their freedom, and to avenge our wrongs. And they have come unto us insomuch that those who have risen up in rebellion against us are set at defiance, yes, insomuch that they do fear us and dare not come out against us to battle. They have gotten possession of the land or the city of Zerach'mla. They have appointed a king over them and he has written unto the king of the Lamanites, in the which he has joined an alliance with him, in the which alliance he has agreed to maintain the city of Zerach'mla, which maintenance he supposes will enable the Lamanites to conquer the remainder of the land. And he shall be placed king over this people when they shall be conquered under the Lamanites.

2 And now, in your letter you have censured me, but it matters not. I am not angry, but do rejoice in the greatness of your heart. I, Parhoron, do not seek for power, except only to retain my judgment seat, that I may preserve the rights and the liberty of my people. My soul stands fast in that liberty in the which Elohim has made us free.

3 And now behold, we will resist wickedness, even unto bloodshed. We would not shed the blood of the Lamanites if they would stay in their own land. We would not shed the blood of our brothers if they would not rise up in rebellion and take the sword against us. We would subject ourselves to the yoke of bondage if it were requisite with the justice of Elohim or if he should command us so to do. But behold, he does not command us that we shall subject ourselves to our enemies, but that we should put our trust in him, and he will deliver us. Therefore, my beloved brother M'roni, let us resist evil. And whatsoever evil we cannot resist with our words, yes, such as rebellions and dissensions, let us resist them with our swords, that we may retain our freedom, that we may rejoice in the great privilege of our assembly and in the cause of our Redeemer and our Elohim. Therefore, come unto me speedily with a few of your men and leave the remainder in the charge of Lechi and Teancum. Give unto them power to conduct the war in that part of the land according to the Ruach Elohim — which is also the spirit of freedom — which is in them. Behold, I have sent a few provisions unto them, that they may not perish until you can come unto me. Gather together whatsoever force you can upon your march here and we will go speedily against those dissenters in the strength of our Elohim, according to the faith which is in us. And we will take possession of the city of Zerach'mla, that we may obtain more food to send forth unto Lechi and Teancum, yes, we will go forth against them in the strength of YHWH and we will put an end to this great iniquity.

⁴And now, M'roni, I do joy in receiving your letter, for I was somewhat worried concerning what we should do, whether it should be just for us to go against our brothers. But you have said except they repent, YHWH has commanded you that you should go against them. See that you strengthen Lechi and Teancum in YHWH. Tell them to fear not, for Elohim will deliver them, yes, and also all those who stand fast in that liberty with which Elohim has made them free. And now I close my letter to my beloved brother M'roni.

29

And now it came to pass that when M'roni had received this letter, his heart did take courage and was filled with exceedingly great joy because of the faithfulness of Parhoron, that he was not also a traitor to the freedom and cause of his country. But he did also mourn exceedingly because of the iniquity of those who had driven Parhoron from the judgment seat, yes, in short, because of those who had rebelled against their country and also their Elohim.

²And it came to pass that M'roni took a small number of men according to the desire of Parhoron, and gave Lechi and Teancum command over the remainder of his army, and took his march towards the land of Gideon. And he did raise the standard of liberty in whatsoever place he did enter, and gained whatsoever force he could in all his march towards the land of Gideon.

³And it came to pass that thousands did flock unto his standard and did take up their swords in the defense of their freedom, that they might not come into bondage. And thus when M'roni had gathered together whatsoever men he could in all his march, he came to the land of Gideon; and uniting his forces with that of Parhoron's, they became exceedingly strong, even stronger than the men of Pachus, who was the king of those dissenters who had driven out the Freemen, out of the land of Zerach'mla, and had taken possession of the land.

⁴And it came to pass that M'roni and Parhoron went down with their armies into the land of Zerach'mla, and went forth against the city and did meet the men of Pachus, insomuch that they did come to battle. And behold, Pachus was slain and his men were taken prisoners, and Parhoron was restored to his judgment seat. And the men of Pachus received their trial according to the law, and also those Kingmen who had been taken and cast into prison, and they

were executed according to the law; yes, those men of Pachus and those Kingmen — whosoever would not take up arms in the defense of their country, but would fight against it — were put to death. And thus it became expedient that this law should be strictly observed for the safety of their country, yes, and whosoever was found denying their freedom was speedily executed according to the law. And thus ended the thirtieth year of the reign of the judges over the people of Nefi, M'roni and Parhoron having restored shalom to the land of Zerach'mla among their own people, having inflicted death upon all those who were not true to the cause of freedom.

5 And it came to pass in the commencement of the thirty and first year of the reign of the judges over the people of Nefi, M'roni immediately caused that provisions should be sent, and also an army of six thousand men should be sent unto Cheleman, to assist him in preserving that part of the land. And he also caused that an army of six thousand men, with a sufficient quantity of food, should be sent to the armies of Lechi and Teancum. And it came to pass that this was done to fortify the land against the Lamanites.

6 And it came to pass that M'roni and Parhoron, leaving a large body of men in the land of Zerach'mla, took their march with a large body of men towards the land of Nefihah, being determined to overthrow the Lamanites in that city.

7 And it came to pass that as they were marching towards the land, they took a large body of men of the Lamanites, and slew many of them, and took their provisions and their weapons of war. And it came to pass, after they had taken them, they caused them to enter into a covenant that they would no more take up their weapons of war against the Nefites. And when they had entered into this covenant, they sent them to dwell with the people of Ammon; and they were in number about four thousand who had not been slain.

8 And it came to pass that when they had sent them away, they pursued their march towards the land of Nefihah. And it came to pass that when they had come to the city Nefihah, they did pitch their tents in the plains of Nefihah, which is near the city Nefihah. Now M'roni was desirous that the Lamanites should come out to battle against them upon the plains. But the Lamanites, knowing of their exceedingly great courage and beholding the greatness of their numbers, therefore they dared not come out against them; therefore

they did not come to battle in that day. And when the night came, M'roni went forth in the darkness of the night and came up on the top of the wall to spy out in what part of the city the Lamanites did camp with their army.

9 And it came to pass that they were on the east, by the entrance, and they were all asleep. And now M'roni returned to his army and caused that they should prepare in haste strong cords and ladders to be let down from the top of the wall into the inner part of the wall.

10 And it came to pass that M'roni caused that his men should march forth and come up upon the top of the wall, and let themselves down into that part of the city, yes, even on the west, where the Lamanites did not camp with their armies.

11 And it came to pass that they were all let down into the city by night, by the means of their strong cords and their ladders. Thus when the morning came, they were all within the walls of the city. And now when the Lamanites awoke and saw that the armies of M'roni were within the walls, they were exceedingly frightened, insomuch that they did flee out by the pass. And now when M'roni saw that they were fleeing before him, he did cause that his men should march forth against them, and slew many, and surrounded many others and took them prisoners; and the remainder of them fled into the land of M'roni which was in the borders by the seashore. Thus had M'roni and Parhoron obtained the possession of the city of Nefihah without the loss of one soul; and there were many of the Lamanites who were slain.

12 Now it came to pass that as many of the Lamanites that were prisoners were desirous to join the people of Ammon and become a free people, and it came to pass that as many as were desirous, unto them it was granted according to their desires. Therefore, all the prisoners of the Lamanites did join the people of Ammon and did begin to labor exceedingly, tilling the ground, raising all manner of grain, and flocks, and herds of every kind. And thus were the Nefites relieved from a great burden, yes, insomuch that they were relieved from all the prisoners of the Lamanites.

13 Now it came to pass that M'roni, after he had obtained possession of the city of Nefihah, having taken many prisoners, which did reduce the armies of the Lamanites exceedingly, and having retained many of the Nefites who had been taken prisoners, which did strengthen

the army of M'roni exceedingly, therefore M'roni went forth from the land of Nefihah to the land of Lechi.

14 And it came to pass that when the Lamanites saw that M'roni was coming against them, they were again frightened, and fled before the army of M'roni. And it came to pass that M'roni and his army did pursue them from city to city until they were met by Lechi and Teancum; and the Lamanites fled from Lechi and Teancum, even down upon the borders by the seashore until they came to the land of M'roni. And the armies of the Lamanites were all gathered together, insomuch that they were all in one body in the land of M'roni. Now Ammoron, the king of the Lamanites, was also with them.

15 And it came to pass that M'roni, and Lechi, and Teancum did encamp with their armies round about in the borders of the land of M'roni, insomuch that the Lamanites were encircled about in the borders by the wilderness on the south and in the borders by the wilderness on the east; and thus they did encamp for the night. For behold, the Nefites, and the Lamanites also, were weary because of the greatness of the march, therefore they did not resolve upon any stratagem in the nighttime, except it were Teancum. For he was exceedingly angry with Ammoron, insomuch that he considered that Ammoron, and Amalickiah his brother, had been the cause of this great and lasting war between them and the Lamanites, which had been the cause of so much war and bloodshed, yes, and so much famine.

16 And it came to pass that Teancum, in his anger, did go forth into the camp of the Lamanites and did let himself down over the walls of the city. And he went forth with a cord from place to place, insomuch that he did find the king; and he did cast a javelin at him, which did pierce him near the heart. But behold, the king did awake his servant before he died, insomuch that he did pursue Teancum and slew him.

17 Now it came to pass that when Lechi and M'roni knew that Teancum was dead, they were exceedingly sorrowful; for behold, he had been a man who had fought valiantly for his country, yes, a true friend to liberty, and he had suffered very many exceedingly sore afflictions. But behold, he was dead and had gone the way of all the earth.

18 Now it came to pass that M'roni marched forth the next day and came upon the Lamanites, insomuch that they did slay them

with a great slaughter and they did drive them out of the land. And they did flee, even that they did not return at that time against the Nefites. And thus ended the thirty and first year of the reign of the judges over the people of Nefi. And thus they had had wars, and bloodsheds, and famine, and affliction, for the space of many years. And there had been murders, and contentions, and dissensions, and all manner of iniquity among the people of Nefi. Nevertheless for the righteous' sake, yes, because of the prayers of the righteous,[227] they were spared. But behold, because of the exceedingly great length of the war between the Nefites and the Lamanites, many had become hardened because of the exceedingly great length of the war; and many were softened because of their afflictions, insomuch that they did humble themselves before Elohim, even in the depths of humility.

19 And it came to pass that after M'roni had fortified those parts of the land which were most exposed to the Lamanites until they were sufficiently strong, he returned to the city of Zerach'mla. And also Cheleman returned to the place of his inheritance; and there was once more shalom established among the people of Nefi. And M'roni yielded up the command of his armies into the hands of his son whose name was M'ronihah; and he retired to his own house, that he might spend the remainder of his days in shalom. And Parhoron did return to his judgment seat, and Cheleman did take upon him again to preach unto the people the word of Elohim; for because of so many wars and contentions, it had become expedient that a regulation should be made again in the assembly. Therefore, Cheleman and his brothers went forth and did declare the word of Elohim with much power, unto the convincing of many people of their wickedness, which did cause them to repent of their sins and to be washed by immersion unto YHWH their Elohim.

20 And it came to pass that they did strengthen again the assembly of Elohim throughout all the land. Yes, and regulations were made concerning the law; and their judges and their chief judges were chosen. And the people of Nefi began to prosper again in the land, and began to multiply and to grow exceedingly strong again in the land. And they began to grow exceedingly rich, but despite their riches, or their strength, or their prosperity, they were not lifted

---

227 Alma 8:5

up in the pride of their eyes, neither were they slow to remember YHWH their Elohim, but they did humble themselves exceedingly before him. Yes, they did remember how great things YHWH had done for them, that he had delivered them from death, and from bonds, and from prisons, and from all manner of afflictions, and he had delivered them out of the hands of their enemies. And they did pray unto YHWH their Elohim continually, insomuch that YHWH did bless them according to his word so that they did grow strong and prosper in the land. And it came to pass that all these things were done. And Cheleman died in the thirty and fifth year[228] of the reign of the judges over the people of Nefi.

30 And it came to pass, in the commencement of the thirty and sixth year[229] of the reign of the judges over the people of Nefi, that Shiblon took possession of those sacred things which had been delivered unto Cheleman by Alma. And he was a just man, and he did walk uprightly before Elohim, and he did observe to do good continually, **to keep the mitzvot of YHWH**[230] his Elohim, and also did his brother.

2 And it came to pass that M'roni died also. And thus ended the thirty and sixth year of the reign of the judges. And it came to pass that in the thirty and seventh year of the reign of the judges, there was a large company of men, even to the amount of five thousand and four hundred men, with their wives and their children, departed out of the land of Zerach'mla into the land which was northward.

3 And it came to pass that Hagoth, he being an exceedingly curious man, therefore he went forth and built him an exceedingly large ship on the borders of the land Bountiful, by the land Desolation, and launched it forth into the west sea, by the narrow neck which led into the land northward. And behold, there were many of the Nefites who did enter therein and did sail forth with many provisions, and also many women and children; and they took their course northward. And thus ended the thirty and seventh year. And in the thirty and eighth year, this man built other ships. And the first ship did also return, and many more people did enter into it, and they also took many provisions and set out again to the land northward.

---

228 ~58 BCE   229 ~57 BCE   230 Deut. 10:13

⁴And it came to pass that they never were heard of more. And we suppose that they are drowned in the depths of the sea. And it came to pass that one other ship also did sail forth, and where she did go, we know not. And it came to pass that in this year there were many people who went forth into the land northward. And thus ended the thirty and eighth year.

⁵And it came to pass, in the thirty and ninth year of the reign of the judges, Shiblon died also. And Corianton had gone forth to the land northward in a ship to carry forth provisions unto those people who had gone forth into that land; therefore it became expedient for Shiblon to confer those sacred things, before his death, upon the son of Cheleman, who was called Cheleman, being called after the name of his father. Now behold, all those engravings which were in the possession of Cheleman were written and sent forth among the children of men throughout all the land, except it were those parts which had been commanded by Alma should not go forth. Nevertheless, these things were to be kept sacred and handed down from one generation to another, therefore in this year they had been conferred upon Cheleman before the death of Shiblon.

⁶And it came to pass also in this year that there were some dissenters who had gone forth unto the Lamanites, and they were stirred up again to anger against the Nefites. And also in this same year, they came down with a numerous army to war against the people of M'ronihah, or against the army of M'ronihah, in the which they were beaten and driven back again to their own lands, suffering great loss. And thus ended the thirty and ninth year of the reign of the judges over the people of Nefi. And thus ended the account of Alma, and Cheleman his son, and also Shiblon, who was his son.

ספר חלמן
CHELEMAN
THE BOOK OF CHELEMAN

An account of the Nefites, their wars and contentions, and their dissensions, and also the prophecies of many holy prophets before the coming of Mashiach, according to the record of Cheleman, who was the son of Cheleman, and also according to the records of his sons, even down to the coming of Mashiach. And also many of the Lamanites are converted — an account of their conversion. An account of the righteousness of the Lamanites, and the wickedness and abominations of the Nefites, according to the record of Cheleman and his sons, even down to the coming of Mashiach, which is called The Book of Cheleman, and so forth.

And now behold, it came to pass in the commencement of the fortieth year[1] of the reign of the judges over the people of Nefi, there began to be a serious difficulty among the people of the Nefites. For behold, Parhoron had died and gone the way of all the earth; therefore, there began to be a serious contention concerning who should have the judgment seat[2] among the brothers who were the sons of Parhoron. Now these are the names who did contend for the judgment seat, who did also cause the people to contend: Parhoron, Paanchi, and Pacumeni. Now these are not all the sons of Parhoron, for he had many, but these are they who did contend for the judgment seat; therefore, they did cause three divisions among the people. Nevertheless, it came to pass that Parhoron was appointed by the **voice of the people** to be a chief judge[3] and a governor over the people of Nefi.

2 And it came to pass that Pacumeni, when he saw that he could not obtain the judgment seat, he did unite with the **voice of the people**. But behold, Paanchi, and that part of the people that were desirous that he should be their governor, was exceedingly angry; therefore, he was about to flatter away those people to rise up in rebellion against their brothers.

---

1 ~53 BCE   **2** Moshiyah 13:9-10   **3** Deut. 16:18

³And it came to pass as he was about to do this, behold, he was taken, and was tried according to the **voice of the people,** and condemned unto death;⁴ for he had risen up in rebellion and sought to destroy the liberty of the people. Now when those people who were desirous that he should be their governor saw that he was condemned unto death, therefore they were angry; and behold, they sent forth one Kishcumen, even to the judgment seat of Parhoron, and murdered Parhoron as he sat upon the judgment seat. And he was pursued by the servants of Parhoron; but behold, so speedy was the flight of Kishcumen that no man could overtake him. And he went unto those that sent him, and they all entered into a covenant, yes, swearing by their everlasting Maker that they would tell no man that Kishcumen had murdered Parhoron. Therefore, Kishcumen was not known among the people of Nefi, for he was in disguise at the time that he murdered Parhoron. And Kishcumen and his band who had covenanted with him did mingle themselves among the people in a manner that they all could not be found; but as many as were found were condemned unto death. And now behold, Pacumeni was appointed according to the **voice of the people** to be a chief judge and a governor over the people, to reign in the place of his brother Parhoron, and it was according to his right. And all this was done in the fortieth year of the reign of the judges, and it had an end.

⁴And it came to pass in the forty and first year of the reign of the judges that the Lamanites had gathered together an innumerable army of men and armed them with swords, and with cimeters, and with bows, and with arrows, and with headplates, and with breastplates, and with all manner of shields of every kind, and they came down again that they might commence battle against the Nefites. And they were led by a man whose name was Coriantumr, and he was a descendant of Zerach'mla,⁵ and he was a dissenter from among the Nefites, and he was a large and a mighty man. Therefore, the king of the Lamanites, whose name was Tubaloth, who was the son of Ammoron, supposing that Coriantumr, being a mighty man, could stand against the Nefites, insomuch (with his strength and also with his great wisdom) that by sending him forth, he should gain power over the Nefites, therefore he did stir them up to anger, and

---

4 Alma 21:14; 23:4   5 Moshiyah 11:13

he did gather together his armies, and he did appoint Coriantumr to be their leader, and did cause that they should march down to the land of Zerach'mla to battle against the Nefites.

⁵And it came to pass that because of so much contention and so much difficulty in the government, they had not kept sufficient guards in the land of Zerach'mla; for they had supposed that the Lamanites dared not come into the heart of their lands and attack that great city Zerach'mla. But it came to pass that Coriantumr did march forth at the head of his numerous host and came upon the inhabitants of the city, and their march was with such exceedingly great speed that there was no time for the Nefites to gather together their armies. Therefore, Coriantumr did cut down the watch by the entrance of the city and did march forth with his whole army into the city, and they did slay everyone who did oppose them, insomuch that they did take possession of the whole city. And it came to pass that Pacumeni, who was the chief judge, did flee before Coriantumr, even to the walls of the city. And it came to pass that Coriantumr did smite him against the wall, insomuch that he died. And thus ended the days of Pacumeni.

⁶And now when Coriantumr saw that he was in possession of the city of Zerach'mla, and saw that the Nefites had fled before them, and were slain, and were taken, and were cast into prison, and that he had obtained possession of the strongest hold in all the land, his heart took courage, insomuch that he was about to go forth against all the land. And now he did not remain in the land of Zerach'mla, but he did march forth with a large army, even towards the city of Bountiful; for it was his determination to go forth and cut his way through with the sword, that he might obtain the north parts of the land. And supposing that their greatest strength was in the center of the land, therefore he did march forth, giving them no time to assemble themselves together except it was in small bodies, and in this manner they did fall upon them and cut them down to the earth.

⁷But behold, this march of Coriantumr's through the center of the land gave M'ronihah great advantage over them, despite the greatness of the number of the Nefites who were slain. For behold, M'ronihah had supposed that the Lamanites dared not come into the center of the land, but that they would attack the cities round about in the borders as they had previously done; therefore, M'ronihah had

caused that their strong armies should maintain those parts round about by the borders. But behold, the Lamanites were not frightened according to his desire, but they had come into the center of the land and had taken the capital city, which was the city of Zerach'mla, and were marching through the most important parts of the land, slaying the people with a great slaughter — both men, women, and children — taking possession of many cities and of many strongholds. But when M'ronihah had discovered this, he immediately sent forth Lechi with an army, round about to get in front of them before they should come to the land Bountiful. And thus he did, and he did get in front of them before they came to the land Bountiful, and gave unto them battle insomuch that they began to retreat back towards the land of Zerach'mla. And it came to pass that M'ronihah did get in front of them in their retreat and did give unto them battle, insomuch that it became an exceedingly bloody battle, yes, many were slain, and among the number who were slain, Coriantumr was also found. And now behold, the Lamanites could not retreat either way, neither on the north, nor on the south, nor on the east, nor on the west, for they were surrounded on every side by the Nefites. And thus had Coriantumr plunged the Lamanites into the midst of the Nefites, insomuch that they were in the power of the Nefites, and he himself was slain. And the Lamanites did yield themselves up into the hands of the Nefites.

8 And it came to pass that M'ronihah took possession of the city of Zerach'mla again, and caused that the Lamanites who had been taken prisoners should depart out of the land in shalom. And thus ended the forty and first year of the reign of the judges.

9 And it came to pass in the forty and second year[6] of the reign of the judges, after M'ronihah had established again shalom between the Nefites and the Lamanites, behold, there was no one to fill the judgment seat; therefore, there began to be a contention again among the people concerning who should fill the judgment seat. And it came to pass that Cheleman, who was the son of Cheleman, was appointed to fill the judgment seat by the **voice of the people**. But behold, Kishcumen, who had murdered Parhoron, did lay wait to destroy Cheleman also. And he was upheld by his band who had entered into

---

6 ~51 BCE

a covenant that no one should know his wickedness. For there was one Gaddianton, who was exceedingly expert in many words, and also in his craft to carry on the secret work of murder and of robbery, therefore he became the leader of the band of Kishcumen. Therefore, he did flatter them, and also Kishcumen, that if they would place him in the judgment seat, he would grant unto those who belonged to his band that they should be placed in power and authority among the people. Therefore, Kishcumen sought to destroy Cheleman.

10 And it came to pass as he went forth towards the judgment seat to destroy Cheleman, behold, one of the servants of Cheleman, having been out by night and having obtained, through disguise, a knowledge of those plans which had been laid by this band to destroy Cheleman — and it came to pass that he met Kishcumen, and he gave unto him a sign. Therefore Kishcumen made known unto him the object of his desire, desiring that he would conduct him to the judgment seat, that he might murder Cheleman. And when the servant of Cheleman had known all the heart of Kishcumen, and how that it was his object to murder, and also that it was the object of all those who belonged to his band to murder, and to rob, and to gain power (and this was their secret plan and their conspiracy),[7] the servant of Cheleman said unto Kishcumen, Let us go forth unto the judgment seat. Now this did please Kishcumen exceedingly, for he did suppose that he should accomplish his design; but behold, the servant of Cheleman, as they were going forth unto the judgment seat, did stab Kishcumen, even to the heart, that he fell dead without a groan. And he ran and told Cheleman all the things which he had seen, and heard, and done.

11 And it came to pass that Cheleman did send forth to take this band of robbers and secret murderers, that they might be executed according to the law. But behold, when Gaddianton had found that Kishcumen did not return, he feared that he should be destroyed; therefore, he caused that his band should follow him, and they took their flight out of the land by a secret way into the wilderness. And thus when Cheleman sent forth to take them, they could nowhere be found. And more of this Gaddianton shall be spoken hereafter. And thus ended the forty and second year of the reign of the judges over

---

7 3 Nefi 3:6–7; 'Eter 3:17–18

the people of Nefi. And behold, in the end of this book you shall see that this Gaddianton did prove the overthrow, yes, almost the entire destruction of the people of Nefi.[8] Behold, I do not mean the end of The Book of Cheleman, but I mean the end of The Book of Nefi, from which I have taken all the account which I have written.

2 And now it came to pass in the forty and third year[9] of the reign of the judges, there was no contention among the people of Nefi, except it were a little pride[10] which was in the assembly, which did cause some little dissension among the people, which affairs were settled in the ending of the forty and third year. And there was no contention among the people in the forty and fourth year, neither was there much contention in the forty and fifth year. And it came to pass in the forty and sixth year, there were many contentions and many dissensions, in the which there were an exceedingly great many who departed out of the land of Zerach'mla and went forth unto the land northward to inherit the land. And they did travel to an exceedingly great distance, insomuch that they came to large bodies of water and many rivers, yes, and even they did spread forth into all parts of the land, in whatsoever parts had not been rendered desolate and without timber because of the many inhabitants who had before inherited the land. And now no part of the land was desolate except it was for timber, and so forth. But because of the greatness of the destruction of the people who had before inhabited the land, it was called desolate. And there being but little timber upon the face of the land, nevertheless, the people who went forth became exceedingly expert in the working of cement; therefore, they did build houses of cement in the which they did dwell.

2 And it came to pass that they did multiply and spread, and did go forth from the land southward to the land northward, and did spread insomuch that they began to cover the face of the whole earth,[11] from the sea south to the sea north, from the sea west to the sea east. And the people who were in the land northward did dwell in tents and in houses of cement, and they did allow whatsoever tree should spring up upon the face of the land that it should grow up, that in

---

8 M'raman 4:1-2 **9** ~50 BCE **10** Ya'akov 2:4-6; M'raman 4:5 **11** The Hebrew word here was likely *eretz* (ארץ), which can mean "land" or "earth."

CHELEMAN 2:3

time they might have timber to build their houses, yes, their cities, and their Temples, and their synagogues, and their sanctuaries, and all manner of their buildings.

3 And it came to pass, as timber was exceedingly scarce in the land northward, they did send forth much by the way of shipping; and thus they did enable the people in the land northward that they might build many cities both of wood and of cement. And it came to pass that there were many of the people of Ammon who were Lamanites by birth that did also go forth into this land.

4 And now there are many records kept of the proceedings of this people, by many of this people, which are detailed and very large concerning them; but behold, a hundredth part of the proceedings of this people — yes, the account of the Lamanites and of the Nefites, and their wars, and contentions, and dissensions, and their preaching, and their prophecies, and their shipping, and their building of ships,[12] and their building of Temples and of synagogues, and their sanctuaries, and their righteousness, and their wickedness, and their murders, and their robbings, and their plunderings,[13] and all manner of abominations and whoredoms — cannot be contained in this work. But behold, there are many books and many records of every kind,[14] and they have been kept chiefly by the Nefites. And they have been handed down from one generation to another by the Nefites, even until they have fallen into transgression and have been murdered, plundered, and hunted, and driven forth, and slain, and scattered upon the face of the earth, and mixed with the Lamanites until they are no more called the Nefites, becoming wicked, and wild, and ferocious, yes, even becoming Lamanites.

5 And now I return again to my account. Therefore, what I have spoken had passed; after there had been great contentions, and disturbances, and wars, and dissensions among the people of Nefi, the forty and sixth year of the reign of the judges ended. And it came to pass that there were still great contentions in the land, yes, even in the forty and seventh year, and also in the forty and eighth year. Nevertheless, Cheleman did fill the judgment seat with justice and equity, yes, he did observe to keep the statutes, and the judgments,

---

[12] Alma 30:3 [13] The repetition of the possessive pronoun here is normative in Hebrew, where a pronominal suffix is normally attached to each object of possession. [14] Words of M'raman 1:2; Moshiyah 1:1

and the mitzvot of Elohim. And he did do that which was right in the sight of Elohim continually, and he did walk after the ways of his father, insomuch that he did prosper in the land.

6 And it came to pass that he had two sons. He gave unto the eldest the name of Nefi and unto the youngest the name of Lechi. And they began to grow up unto YHWH.[15] And it came to pass that the wars and contentions began to cease in a small degree among the people of the Nefites in the latter end of the forty and eighth year of the reign of the judges over the people of Nefi. And it came to pass in the forty and ninth year of the reign of the judges, there was continual shalom established in the land, all except it were the secret conspiracies which Gaddianton[16] the robber had established in the more settled parts of the land, which at that time were not known unto those who were at the head of government; therefore they were not destroyed out of the land.

7 And it came to pass that in this same year, there was exceedingly great prosperity in the assembly, insomuch that there were thousands who did join themselves unto the assembly and were immersed[17] unto repentance. And so great was the prosperity of the assembly, and so many the blessings which were poured out upon the people, that even the Kohanim HaGadolim and the teachers were themselves astonished beyond measure. And it came to pass that the work of YHWH did prosper, unto the washing by immersion and uniting to the assembly of Elohim, many souls, yes, even tens of thousands. Thus we may see that YHWH is merciful unto all who will, in the sincerity of their hearts, call upon his holy name. Yes, thus we see that the gate of Heaven is open unto all, even to those who will believe on the name of Yeshua HaMashiach, who is the Son of Elohim; yes, we see that whosoever will lay hold upon the word of Elohim, which is alive and powerful, which shall divide asunder all the cunning, and the snares, and the wiles of HaSatan, and lead the follower of Mashiach in a strait and narrow[18] course across that everlasting gulf of misery which is prepared to engulf the wicked, and land their souls, yes, their immortal souls, at the right hand of Elohim in the kingdom of Heaven, to sit down with Avraham, and Yitz'chak, and

---

15 Cheleman 2:16, 19   **16** Cheleman 1:9, 11   **17** 2 Nefi 6:7; 13:1-2; Cheleman 5:17-18; 3 Nefi 3:12; 5:10; 12:3   **18** 2 Nefi 13:3-4

with Ya'akov, and with all our holy fathers, to go no more out. And in this year, there was continual rejoicing in the land of Zerach'mla and in all the regions round about, even in all the land which was possessed by the Nefites. And it came to pass that there was shalom and exceedingly great joy in the remainder of the forty and ninth year, yes, and also there was continual shalom and great joy in the fiftieth year of the reign of the judges.

8 And in the fifty and first year of the reign of the judges, there was shalom also, except it were the pride which began to enter into the assembly — not into the assembly of Elohim, but into the hearts of the people who professed to belong to the assembly of Elohim; and they were lifted up in pride,[19] even to the persecution of many of their brothers. Now this was a great evil, which did cause the more humble part of the people to suffer great persecutions and to wade through much affliction. Nevertheless, they did fast and pray[20] often, and did grow stronger and stronger in their humility, and firmer and firmer in the faith of Mashiach, unto the filling their souls with joy and consolation, yes, even to the purifying and the sanctification of their hearts, which sanctification comes because of their yielding their hearts unto Elohim. And it came to pass that the fifty and second year ended in shalom also, except it was the exceedingly great pride which had gotten into the hearts of the people — and it was because of their exceedingly great riches and their prosperity in the land — and it did grow upon them from day to day.

9 And it came to pass in the fifty and third year of the reign of the judges, Cheleman died and his eldest son Nefi began to reign in his place. And it came to pass that he did fill the judgment seat with justice and equity, yes, he did keep the mitzvot of Elohim and did walk in the ways of his father. And it came to pass in the fifty and fourth year,[21] there were many dissensions in the assembly, and there was also a contention among the people, insomuch that there was much bloodshed; and the rebellious part were slain and driven out of the land, and they did go unto the king of the Lamanites.

10 And it came to pass that they did endeavor to stir up the Lamanites to war against the Nefites; but behold, the Lamanites were exceedingly afraid, insomuch that they would not hearken to

---

19 Ya'akov 2:4-6; M'raman 4:5 20 Ameni 1:10; M'roni 6:2 21 ~39 BCE

the words of those dissenters. But it came to pass in the fifty and sixth year of the reign of the judges, there were dissenters who went up from the Nefites unto the Lamanites, and they succeeded with those others in stirring them up to anger against the Nefites, and they were all that year preparing for war. And in the fifty and seventh year they did come down against the Nefites to battle, and they did commence the work of death; yes, insomuch that in the fifty and eighth year of the reign of the judges, they succeeded in obtaining possession of the land of Zerach'mla, yes, and also all the lands, even unto the land which was near the land Bountiful. And the Nefites and the armies of M'ronihah were driven even into the land of Bountiful; and there they did fortify against the Lamanites, from the west sea even unto the east, it being a day's journey for a Nefite on the line which they had fortified and stationed their armies to defend their north country. And thus those dissenters of the Nefites, with the help of a numerous army of the Lamanites, had obtained all the possession of the Nefites which was in the land southward. And all this was done in the fifty and eighth and ninth years of the reign of the judges.

11 And it came to pass in the sixtieth year of the reign of the judges, M'ronihah did succeed with his armies in obtaining many parts of the land, yes, they retained many cities which had fallen into the hands of the Lamanites.

12 And it came to pass in the sixty and first year of the reign of the judges, they succeeded in retaining even the half of all their possessions. Now this great loss of the Nefites and the great slaughter which was among them would not have happened had it not been for their wickedness and their abomination which was among them. Yes, and it was among those also who professed to belong to the assembly of Elohim. And it was because of the pride of their hearts, because of their exceeding riches, yes, it was because of their oppression to the poor, withholding their food from the hungry, withholding their clothing from the naked, and striking their humble brothers upon the cheeks,[22] making a mockery of that which was sacred, denying the spirit of prophecy and of revelation, murdering, plundering, lying, stealing, committing adultery, raising up in great contentions, and dissenting away into the land of Nefi among the Lamanites. And

---

22 3 Nefi 5:30

because of this, their great wickedness and their boastings in their own strength, they were left in their own strength; therefore, they did not prosper, but were afflicted, and slain, and driven before the Lamanites, until they had lost possession of almost all their lands. But behold, M'ronihah did preach many things unto the people because of their iniquity, and also Nefi and Lechi, who were the sons of Cheleman, did preach many things unto the people, yes, and did prophesy many things unto them concerning their iniquities, and what should come unto them if they did not repent of their sins. And it came to pass that they did repent, and inasmuch as they did repent, they did begin to prosper. For when M'ronihah saw that they did repent, he did venture to lead them forth from place to place and from city to city, even until they had retained the one half of their property and the one half of all their lands. And thus ended the sixty and first year of the reign of the judges.

13 And it came to pass in the sixty and second year of the reign of the judges that M'ronihah could obtain no more possessions over the Lamanites; therefore, they did abandon their design to obtain the remainder of their lands. For so numerous were the Lamanites that it became impossible for the Nefites to obtain more power over them. Therefore, M'ronihah did employ all his armies in maintaining those parts which he had taken.

14 And it came to pass, because of the greatness of the number of the Lamanites, the Nefites were in great fear that they would be overpowered, and trampled down, and slain, and destroyed. Yes, they began to remember the prophecies of Alma, and also the words of Moshiyah. And they saw that they had been a stiffnecked people, and that they had despised the mitzvot of Elohim, and that they had altered and trampled under their feet the laws of Moshiyah, or that which YHWH commanded him to give unto the people, and thus seeing that their laws had become corrupt and that they had become a wicked people, insomuch that they were wicked even like unto the Lamanites. And because of their iniquity, the assembly had begun to dwindle. And they began to disbelieve in the spirit of prophecy and in the spirit of revelation,[23] and the judgments of Elohim did stare them in the face. And they saw they had become weak like unto their

---

23 Ya'akov 3:2; 3 Nefi 13:8

brothers the Lamanites, and that the spirit of YHWH did no more preserve them. Yes, it had withdrawn[24] from them because the spirit of YHWH does not dwell in unholy temples. Therefore, YHWH did cease to preserve them by his miraculous and matchless power, for they had fallen into a state of unbelief[25] and awful wickedness. And they saw that the Lamanites were exceedingly more numerous than they, and except they should cling unto YHWH their Elohim, they must unavoidably perish. For behold, they saw that the strength of the Lamanites was as great as their strength, even man for man. And thus had they fallen into this great transgression; yes, thus had they become weak because of their transgression in the space of not many years.[26]

15 And it came to pass that in this same year, behold, Nefi delivered up the judgment seat[27] to a man whose name was Cezoram. For as their laws and their governments were established by the **voice of the people,** and they who chose evil were more numerous than they who chose good, therefore they were ripening for destruction. For the laws had become corrupted, yes, and this was not all; they were a stiffnecked people, insomuch that they could not be governed by the law nor justice, except it were to their destruction.

16 And it came to pass that Nefi had become weary because of their iniquity, and he yielded up the judgment seat, and took it upon himself to preach the word of Elohim all the remainder of his days, and his brother Lechi also, all the remainder of his days. For they remembered the words which their father Cheleman spoke unto them. And these are the words which he spoke: Behold, my sons, I desire that you should remember to keep the mitzvot of Elohim; and I would that you should declare unto the people these words. Behold, I have given unto you the names of our first parents[28] who came out of the land of Yerushalayim, and this I have done that when you remember your names, that you may remember them; and when you remember them, you may remember their works; and when you remember their works, you may know how that it is said and also written that they were good. Therefore, my sons, I would that you should do that which is good, that it may be said of you, and also

---

24 Moshiyah 1:11; Cheleman 2:34; 5:3   25 Cheleman 2:34; M'roni 7:7; 10:4-5
26 Cheleman 2:34; 3:1; 4:5   27 Moshiyah 13:2-3, 9-10   28 1 Nefi 1:1-6

written, even as it has been said and written of them. And now, my sons, behold, I have somewhat more to desire of you, which desire is that you may not do these things that you may boast, but that you may do these things to lay up for yourselves a treasure[29] in Heaven, yes, which is eternal and which fades not away; yes, that you may have that precious gift of Eternal life,[30] which we have reason to suppose has been given to our fathers.

17 Oh remember, remember, my sons, the words which king Binyamin spoke unto his people. Yes, remember that there is no other way nor means by which man can be saved, only through the atoning blood of Yeshua HaMashiach who shall come; yes, remember that he comes to redeem the world. And remember also the words which Amulek spoke unto Zeezrom in the city of Ammonihah, for he said unto him that YHWH surely should come to redeem his people, but that he should not come to redeem them in their sins, but to redeem them from their sins. And he has power given unto him from the Father to redeem them from their sins because of repentance. Therefore, he has sent his angels to declare the tidings of the conditions of repentance, which brings unto the power of the Redeemer, unto the salvation of their souls. And now, my sons, remember, remember that it is upon the rock of our Redeemer, who is Mashiach, the Son of Elohim, that you must build your foundation, that when HaSatan shall send forth his mighty winds, yes, his shafts in the whirlwind, yes, when all his hail and his mighty storm shall beat upon you, it shall have no power over you to drag you down to the gulf of misery and endless woe because of the rock upon which you are built, which is a sure foundation, a foundation whereon if men build, they cannot fall.[31]

18 And it came to pass that these were the words which Cheleman taught to his sons; yes, he did teach them many things which are not written, and also many things which are written. And they did remember his words, and therefore they went forth keeping the mitzvot of Elohim to teach the word of Elohim among all the people of Nefi, beginning at the city Bountiful, and from that place to the city of Gid, and from the city of Gid to the city of Mulek, and even

---

29 3 Nefi 5:36   30 2 Nefi 13:3-4; 3 Nefi 4:7   31 3 Nefi 5:9; 8:7

from one city to another, until they had gone forth among all the people of Nefi who were in the land southward, and from that place into the land of Zerach'mla among the Lamanites.

19 And it came to pass that they did preach with great power, insomuch that they did confound many of those dissenters who had gone over from the Nefites, insomuch that they came forth and did confess their sins, and were immersed unto repentance,[32] and immediately returned to the Nefites to endeavor to repair unto them the wrongs which they had done. And it came to pass that Nefi and Lechi did preach unto the Lamanites with such great power and authority, for they had power and authority given unto them that they might speak; and they also had what they should speak given unto them. Therefore, they did speak unto the great astonishment of the Lamanites, to the convincing them, insomuch that there were eight thousand of the Lamanites, who were in the land of Zerach'mla and round about, immersed unto repentance, and convinced of the wickedness of the traditions of their fathers.

20 And it came to pass that Nefi and Lechi did proceed from that place to go to the land of Nefi. And it came to pass that they were taken by an army of the Lamanites and cast into prison, yes, even in that same prison in which Ammon and his brothers were cast by the servants of Limhi. And after they had been cast into prison many days without food, behold, they went forth into the prison to take them, that they might slay them. And it came to pass that Nefi and Lechi were encircled about as if by fire, even insomuch that they dared not lay their hands upon them for fear that they should be burned. Nevertheless, Nefi and Lechi were not burned; and they were as standing in the midst of fire and were not burned. And when they saw that they were encircled about with a pillar of fire[33] and that it burned them not, their hearts did take courage, for they saw that the Lamanites dared not lay their hands upon them, neither dared they come near unto them, but stood as if they were struck dumb with amazement.

21 And it came to pass that Nefi and Lechi did stand forth and began to speak unto them, saying, Fear not, for behold, it is Elohim that has

---

32 2 Nefi 6:7; 13:2; 3 Nefi 3:12; 12:5; 4 Nefi 1:1; M'roni 6:1; 7:6   **33** Ex. 13:21-22; 1 Nefi 1:3; 3 Nefi 8:5; 9:2

shown unto you this marvelous thing, in which it is shown unto you that you cannot lay your hands on us to slay us.[34] And behold, when they had said these words, the earth shook exceedingly and the walls of the prison did shake as if they were about to tumble to the earth; but behold, they did not fall. And behold, they that were in the prison were Lamanites, and Nefites who were dissenters. And it came to pass that they were overshadowed with a cloud of darkness, and an awful solemn fear came upon them. And it came to pass that there came a voice,[35] as if it were above the cloud of darkness,[36] saying, Repent, repent, and seek no more to destroy my servants whom I have sent unto you to declare good tidings.

22 And it came to pass when they heard this voice and beheld that it was not a voice of thunder, neither was it a voice of a great tumultuous noise, but behold, it was a still voice[37] of perfect mildness, as if it had been a whisper, and it did pierce even to the very soul — and despite the mildness of the voice, behold, the earth shook exceedingly. And the walls of the prison trembled again, as if it were about to tumble to the earth; and behold, the cloud of darkness which had overshadowed them did not disperse. And behold, the voice came again, saying, Repent, repent, for the kingdom of Heaven is at hand; and seek no more to destroy my servants. And it came to pass that the earth shook again, and the walls trembled; and also again the third time the voice came and did speak unto them marvelous words which cannot be uttered by man.[38] And the walls did tremble again, and the earth shook as if it were about to divide asunder.

23 And it came to pass that the Lamanites could not flee because of the cloud of darkness which did overshadow them; yes, and also, they were immovable because of the fear which did come upon them. Now there was one among them who was a Nefite by birth, who had once belonged to the assembly of Elohim but had dissented from them. And it came to pass that he turned around, and behold, he saw through the cloud of darkness the faces of Nefi and Lechi; and behold, they did shine exceedingly,[39] even as the faces of angels. And he beheld that they did lift up their eyes to Heaven, and they were in

---

[34] 1 Nefi 5:22; Moshiyah 7:19-20   [35] Ex. 3:4; 3 Nefi 4:6; 5:2   [36] Deut. 4:11-12; 5:22
[37] 1 Kings 19:12; 1 Nefi 5:21; 3 Nefi 5:2   [38] Alma 9:3; 3 Nefi 8:4; 9:5; 12:2   [39] Ex. 34:29-35; Moshiyah 7:20

the attitude as if talking or lifting their voices to some being whom they beheld.

24 And it came to pass that this man did cry unto the multitude that they might turn and look. And behold, there was power given unto them that they did turn and look; and they did behold the faces of Nefi and Lechi. And they said unto the man, Behold, what do all these things mean? And who is it with whom these men do converse? Now the man's name was Aminadab. And Aminadab said unto them, They do converse with the angels of Elohim. And it came to pass that the Lamanites said unto him, What shall we do that this cloud of darkness may be removed from overshadowing us? And Aminadab said unto them, You must repent and cry unto the voice,[40] even until you shall have faith in Mashiach, which was taught unto you by Alma and Amulek, and by Zeezrom; and when you shall do this, the cloud of darkness shall be removed from overshadowing you.

25 And it came to pass that they all did begin to cry unto the voice of him who had shaken the earth, yes, they did cry even until the cloud of darkness was dispersed. And it came to pass that when they cast their eyes about and saw that the cloud of darkness was dispersed from overshadowing them, and behold, they saw that they were encircled about (yes, every soul) by a pillar of fire.[41] And Nefi and Lechi were in the midst of them, yes, they were encircled about, yes, they were as if in the midst of a flaming fire, yet it did harm them not, neither did it take hold upon the walls of the prison; and they were filled with that joy which is unspeakable and full of glory. And behold, the holy Ruach Elohim did come down from Heaven and did enter into their hearts, and they were filled as if with fire, and they could speak forth marvelous words.

26 And it came to pass that there came a voice unto them, yes, a pleasant voice, as if it were a whisper,[42] saying, Shalom, shalom be unto you because of your faith in my Well Beloved,[43] who was from the foundation of the world.[44] And now when they heard this, they cast up their eyes as if to behold from where the voice came, and behold, they saw the Heavens open, and angels came down out of Heaven[45] and ministered unto them. And there were about three

---

40 2 Nefi 15:1; Enosh 1:1, 4; Alma 16:35; 'Eter 1:3   **41** Ex. 13:21-22; 14:24; Num. 14:14; Neh. 9:19; 1 Nefi 1:3   **42** 2 Nefi 15:1; Enosh 1:1, 4; 'Eter 1:3   **43** 3 Nefi 5:2   **44** 1 Nefi 3:5; 2 Nefi 6:7; Moshiyah 2:2   **45** 3 Nefi 8:5; 9:2

hundred souls who saw and heard[46] these things, and they were bidden to go forth and marvel not, neither should they doubt. And it came to pass that they did go forth and did minister unto the people, declaring throughout all the regions round about all the things which they had heard and seen, insomuch that the more part of the Lamanites were convinced of them because of the greatness of the evidences which they had received. And as many as were convinced did lay down their weapons of war,[47] and also their hatred and the tradition of their fathers. And it came to pass that they did yield up unto the Nefites the lands of their possession.

27 And it came to pass that when the sixty and second year[48] of the reign of the judges had ended, all these things had happened, and the Lamanites had become, the more part of them, a righteous people, insomuch that their righteousness did exceed that of the Nefites, because of their firmness and their steadiness in the faith. For behold, there were many of the Nefites who had become hardened, and impenitent, and enormously wicked, insomuch that they did reject the word of Elohim, and all the preaching and the prophesying which did come among them. Nevertheless, the people of the assembly did have great joy because of the conversion of the Lamanites, yes, because of the assembly of Elohim which had been established among them. And they did fellowship one with another, and did rejoice one with another, and did have great joy. And it came to pass that many of the Lamanites did come down into the land of Zerach'mla and did declare unto the people of the Nefites the manner of their conversion, and did exhort them to faith and repentance. Yes, and many did preach with exceedingly great power and authority, unto the bringing down many of them into the depths of humility, to be the humble followers[49] of Elohim and the Lamb.

28 And it came to pass that many of the Lamanites did go into the land northward, and also, Nefi and Lechi went into the land northward, to preach unto the people. And thus ended the sixty and third year. And behold, there was shalom in all the land, insomuch that the Nefites did go into whatsoever part of the land they would, whether among the Nefites or the Lamanites. And it came to pass

---

46 Ex. 24:9–11; 3 Nefi 8:4; 12:2–3; 13:4 **47** Cheleman 5:15; M'raman 3:5 **48** ~30 BCE
49 Isa. 5:15; 2 Chron. 34:27; Alma 3:5; 10:1, 4

that the Lamanites did also go wherever they would, whether it were among the Lamanites or among the Nefites. And thus they did have free commerce one with another, to buy, and to sell, and to get gain, according to their desire.

29 And it came to pass that they became exceedingly rich,[50] both the Lamanites and the Nefites; and they did have an exceeding plenty of gold, and of silver, and of all manner of precious metals, both in the land south and in the land north. Now the land south was called Lechi, and the land north was called Muloch, which was after the son of Tzidkiyahu;[51] for YHWH did bring Muloch into the land north and Lechi into the land south. And behold, there was all manner of gold in both these lands, and of silver, and of precious ore of every kind; and there were also meticulous workmen who did work all kinds of ore, and did refine it. And thus they did become rich. They did raise grain in abundance, both in the north and in the south, and they did flourish exceedingly, both in the north and in the south. And they did multiply and grow exceedingly strong in the land. And they did raise many flocks and herds, yes, many fatlings. Behold, their women did labor and spin, and did make all manner of cloth of fine twined linen, and cloth of every kind, to clothe their nakedness. And thus the sixty and fourth year did pass away in shalom. And in the sixty and fifth year they did also have great joy and shalom, yes, much preaching and many prophecies concerning that which was to come. And thus passed away the sixty and fifth year.

30 And it came to pass that in the sixty and sixth year of the reign of the judges, behold, Cezoram was murdered by an unknown hand as he sat upon the judgment seat. And it came to pass that in the same year, that his son, who had been appointed by the people in his place, was also murdered. And thus ended the sixty and sixth year. And in the commencement of the sixty and seventh year, the people began to grow exceedingly wicked again. For behold, YHWH had blessed them so long with the riches of the world that they had not been stirred up to anger, to wars, nor to bloodsheds; therefore, they began to set their hearts upon their riches, yes, they began to seek to get gain that they might be lifted up one above another. Therefore, they

---

50 Yahram 1:4; Alma 22:3; 29:20; 'Eter 4:4　**51** 2 Kings 25:7; Ameni 1:6–7; Moshiyah 11:13; Cheleman 3:9

began to commit secret murders, and to rob, and to plunder, that they might get gain.⁵² And now behold, those murderers and plunderers were a band who had been formed by Kishcumen and Gaddianton. And now it had come to pass that there were many, even among the Nefites, of Gaddianton's band. But behold, they were more numerous among the more wicked part of the Lamanites. And they were called Gaddianton's robbers and murderers; and it was they who did murder the chief judge Cezoram and his son while in the judgment seat; and behold, they were not found.

31 And now it came to pass that when the Lamanites found that there were robbers among them, they were exceedingly sorrowful; and they did use every means, whatsoever was in their power, to destroy them off the face of the earth. But behold, HaSatan did stir up the hearts⁵³ of the more part of the Nefites, insomuch that they did unite with those bands of robbers, and did enter into their covenants and their oaths, that they would protect and preserve one another in whatsoever difficult circumstances they should be placed in, that they should not suffer for their murders, and their plunderings, and their stealings.

32 And it came to pass that they did have their signs, yes, their secret signs and their secret words, and this that they might distinguish a brother who had entered into the covenant, that whatsoever wickedness his brother should do, he should not be injured by his brother, nor by those who did belong to his band who had taken this covenant. And thus they might murder, and plunder, and steal, and commit whoredoms and all manner of wickedness, contrary to the laws of their country, and also the laws of their Elohim. And whosoever of those who belonged to their band should reveal unto the world their wickedness and their abominations should be tried, not according to the laws of their country, but according to the laws of their wickedness, which had been given by Gaddianton and Kishcumen. Now behold, it is these secret oaths and covenants which Alma commanded his son should not go forth unto the world for fear that they should be a means of bringing down the people unto destruction.

---

52 'Eter 3:17-18   53 3 Nefi 5:8; M'raman 2:1

33 Now behold, those secret oaths and covenants did not come forth unto Gaddianton from the records which were delivered unto Cheleman, but behold, they were put into the heart of Gaddianton by that same being who did entice our first parents to partake of the forbidden fruit,[54] yes, that same being who did plot with Kayin that if he would murder his brother Hevel, it should not be known unto the world. And he did plot with Kayin and his followers from that time forth. And also, it is that same being who put it into the hearts of the people to build a tower sufficiently high that they might get to Heaven. And it was that same being who led the people who came from that tower into this land who spread the works of darkness and abominations over all the face of the land, until he dragged the people down to an entire destruction and to an everlasting Gehinnom. Yes, it is that same being who put it into the heart of Gaddianton to still carry on the work of darkness and of secret murder; and he has brought it forth from the beginning of man, even down to this time. And behold, it is he who is the author of all sin. And behold, he does carry on his works of darkness and secret murder, and does hand down their plots, and their oaths, and their covenants, and their plans of awful wickedness, from generation to generation, according as he can get hold upon the hearts[55] of the children of men. And now behold, he had gotten great hold upon the hearts of the Nefites, yes, insomuch that they had become exceedingly wicked. Yes, the more part of them had turned out of the way of righteousness, and did trample under their feet the mitzvot of Elohim, and did turn unto their own ways, and did build up unto themselves idols of their gold and their silver.

34 And it came to pass that all these iniquities did come unto them in the space of not many years,[56] insomuch that a more part of it had come unto them in the sixty and seventh year of the reign of the judges over the people of Nefi. And they did grow in their iniquities in the sixty and eighth year also, to the great sorrow and lamentation of the righteous. And thus we see that the Nefites did begin to dwindle in unbelief, and grow in wickedness and abominations, while the Lamanites began to grow exceedingly in the knowledge of their

---

54 The phrase "forbidden fruit" never appears in the Tanakh, but is found in the Zohar (Zohar 2:144a). 55 Alma 6:4; 8:6; Cheleman 3:3; 5:21; 4 Nefi 1:6 56 Cheleman 2:14; 3:1; 4:5

Elohim;[57] yes, they did begin to keep his statutes and mitzvot, and to walk in truth and uprightness before him. And thus we see that the spirit of YHWH began to withdraw[58] from the Nefites because of the wickedness and the hardness of their hearts. And thus we see that YHWH began to pour out his spirit[59] upon the Lamanites because of their easiness and willingness to believe in his word.

35 And it came to pass that the Lamanites did hunt the band of robbers of Gaddianton, and they did preach the word of Elohim among the more wicked part of them, insomuch that this band of robbers was utterly destroyed from among the Lamanites. And it came to pass that on the other hand, that the Nefites did build them up and support them, beginning at the more wicked part of them, until they had overspread all the land of the Nefites, and had seduced the more part of the righteous until they had come down to believe in their works, and partake of their spoils, and to join with them in their secret murders and conspiracies. And thus they did obtain the sole management of the government, insomuch that they did trample under their feet, and smite, and tear, and turn their backs upon the poor and the meek and humble followers[60] of Elohim. And thus we see that they were in an awful state and ripening for an everlasting destruction. And it came to pass that thus ended the sixty and eighth year of the reign of the judges over the people of Nefi.

THE PROPHECY OF NEFI, THE SON OF CHELEMAN

Elohim threatens the people of Nefi that he will visit them in his anger, to their utter destruction, except they repent of their wickedness. Elohim smites the people of Nefi with pestilence; they repent and turn unto him. Sh'mu'el, a Lamanite, prophesies unto the Nefites.

3 Behold, now it came to pass in the sixty and ninth year[61] of the reign of the judges over the people of the Nefites, that Nefi, the son of Cheleman, returned to the land of Zerach'mla from the land northward. For he had been forth among the people who were in the land northward, and did preach the word of Elohim unto them,

---

57 Hos. 6:6; Words of M'raman 1:3; Moshiyah 9:10; Alma 17:8; 'Eter 1:14   58 Hos. 5:6; Moshiyah 1:11; Alma 16:37; Cheleman 2:14; 5:3   59 Ezek. 39:29; Joel 2:28; Prov. 1:23; Moshiyah 2:4; 9:7-8; 11:17; Alma 6:4; 11:7; 12:26   60 2 Chron. 34:27; Isa. 5:15; 2 Nefi 12:2; Alma 2:5   61 ~24 BCE

and did prophesy many things unto them; and they did reject all his words, insomuch that he could not stay among them, but returned again unto the land of his nativity. And seeing the people in a state of such awful wickedness, and those Gaddianton robbers filling the judgment seats, having usurped the power and authority of the land, laying aside the mitzvot of Elohim and not in the least blameless before him, doing no justice unto the children of men, condemning the righteous because of their righteousness, letting the guilty and the wicked go unpunished because of their money; and moreover, to be held in office at the head of government, to rule and do according to their wills, that they might get gain and glory of the world; and moreover, that they might more easily commit adultery, and steal, and kill, and do according to their own wills — now this great iniquity had come upon the Nefites in the space of not many years[62] — and when Nefi saw it, his heart was swollen with sorrow within his breast. And he did exclaim in the agony of his soul, Oh that I could have had my days in the days when my father Nefi first came out of the land of Yerushalayim, that I could have joyed with him in the promised land! Then were his people easy to be entreated, firm to keep the mitzvot of Elohim, and slow to be led to do iniquity, and they were quick to hearken unto the words of YHWH. Yes, if my days could have been in those days, then would my soul have had joy in the righteousness of my brothers. But behold, I am consigned that these are my days and that my soul shall be filled with sorrow because of this the wickedness of my brothers.

2 And behold, now it came to pass that it was upon a tower which was in the garden of Nefi, which was by the highway which led to the chief market, which was in the city of Zerach'mla. Therefore, as Nefi had bowed himself upon the tower which was in his garden — which tower was also near unto the garden gate which led by the highway — and it came to pass that there were certain men passing by, and saw Nefi as he was pouring out his soul[63] unto Elohim upon the tower; and they ran and told the people what they had seen. And the people came together in multitudes that they might know the cause of so great mourning for the wickedness of the people.

---

62 Cheleman 2:14; 2:34; 4:5   63 1 Sam. 1:15; Enosh 1:2; Moshiyah 11:20; M'raman 1:11

3 And now when Nefi arose, he beheld the multitudes of people who had gathered together. And it came to pass that he opened his mouth and said unto them, Behold, why have you gathered yourselves together? That I may tell you of your iniquities? Yes, because I have got upon my tower that I might pour out my soul unto my Elohim because of the exceeding sorrow of my heart, which is because of your iniquities? And because of my mourning and lamentation, you have gathered yourselves together and do marvel, yes, and you have great need to marvel; yes, you ought to marvel because you are given away that HaSatan has got so great hold upon your hearts.[64] Yes, how could you have given away to the enticing of him who is seeking to hurl away your souls down to everlasting misery and endless woe?

4 Oh repent, repent. Why will you die? Turn, turn unto YHWH your Elohim. **Why has he abandoned**[65] you? It is because you have hardened your hearts, yes, you will not hearken unto the voice of the good shepherd;[66] yes, you have provoked him to anger against you. And behold, instead of gathering you, except you will repent, behold, he shall scatter you forth[67] that you shall become meat for dogs and wild beasts. Oh how could you have forgotten your Elohim in the very day that he has delivered you? But behold, it is to get gain, to be praised of men, yes, and that you might get gold and silver. And you have set your hearts upon the riches and the vain things of this world, for the which you do murder, and plunder, and steal, and bear false witness against your neighbor, and do all manner of iniquity; and for this cause, woe[68] shall come unto you except you shall repent. For if you will not repent, behold, this great city, and also all those great cities which are round about, which are in the land of our possession, shall be taken away, that you shall have no place in them. For behold, YHWH will not grant unto you strength, as he has previously done, to withstand against your enemies. For behold, thus says YHWH: I will not show unto the wicked of my strength, to one more than the other, except it be unto those who repent of their sins and hearken unto my words.

---

64 Alma 6:4; 8:6; Cheleman 2:33; 5:21; 4 Nefi 1:6   65 Ps. 22:2 (1)   66 Isa. 40:11; Ezek. 34:12; Ps. 23:1; 1 Nefi 7:5; Alma 3:7–8, 11; Cheleman 5:16; 3 Nefi 7:3   67 Lev. 26:33; Deut. 4:27; Jer. 9:16; Ezek. 20:23; 22:15; Ps. 44:11; Neh. 1:8; M'raman 2:5   68 2 Nefi 6:10; 12:3

⁵ Now therefore I would that you should behold, my brothers, that it shall be better for the Lamanites than for you, except you shall repent. For behold, they are more righteous than you, for they have not sinned against that great knowledge which you have received; therefore, YHWH will be merciful unto them. Yes, he will lengthen out[69] their days and increase their seed, even when you shall be utterly destroyed, except you shall repent. Yes, woe be unto you because of that great abomination which has come among you, and you have united yourselves unto it, yes, to that secret band which was established by Gaddianton. Yes, woe shall come unto you because of that pride[70] which you have allowed to enter your hearts, which has lifted you up beyond that which is good because of your exceedingly great riches. Yes, woe be unto you because of your wickedness and abominations, and except you repent, you shall perish. Yes, even your lands shall be taken from you and you shall be destroyed from off the face of the earth. Behold, now I do not say that these things shall be, of myself, because it is not of myself that I know these things. But behold, I know that these things are true because Adonai YHWH has made them known unto me;[71] therefore, I testify that they shall be.

⁶ And now it came to pass that when Nefi had said these words, behold, there were men who were judges who also belonged to the secret band of Gaddianton, and they were angry,[72] and they cried out against him, saying unto the people, Why do you not seize upon this man and bring him forth, that he may be condemned according to the crime which he has done? Why do you see this man and hear him revile against this people and against our law? For behold, Nefi had spoken unto them concerning the corruptness of their law. Yes, many things did Nefi speak which cannot be written; and nothing did he speak which was contrary to the mitzvot of Elohim. And those judges were angry with him because he spoke plainly unto them concerning their secret works of darkness; nevertheless, they dared not lay their own hands upon him, for they feared the people, that they should cry out against them. Therefore, they did cry unto the people, saying, Why do you allow this man to revile against us? For behold, he does condemn all this people, even unto destruction, yes,

---

69 2 Nefi 1:9   70 Ya'akov 2:4–6; Alma 3:5, 10; M'raman 4:5   71 Moshiyah 1:13; Alma 8:14; 17:2, 6   72 1 Nefi 1:5; 2:4; 5:22; 2 Nefi 3:6; Moshiyah 7:14; Alma 13:4; 3 Nefi 3:4, 10

and also that these our great cities shall be taken from us, that we shall have no place in them. And now we know that this is impossible, for behold, we are powerful and our cities great, therefore our enemies can have no power over us.

7 And it came to pass that thus they did stir up the people to anger against Nefi and raised contentions among them; for there were some who did cry out, Let this man alone, for he is a good man, and those things which he says will surely come to pass except we repent. Yes, behold, all the judgments will come upon us which he has testified unto us, for we know that he has testified rightly unto us concerning our iniquities; and behold, they are many. And he knows as well all things which shall befall us as he knows our iniquities; yes, and behold, if he had not been a prophet, he could not have testified concerning those things.

8 And it came to pass that those people who sought to destroy Nefi were compelled, because of their fear, that they did not lay their hands on him. Therefore, he began again to speak unto them, seeing that he had gained favor in the eyes of some, insomuch that the remainder of them did fear. Therefore, he was constrained to speak more unto them, saying, Behold, my brothers, have you not read that Elohim gave power unto one man, even Moshe, to strike the waters of the Red Sea,[73] and they departed hither and thither, insomuch that the Isra'elites, who were our fathers, came through upon dry ground, and the waters closed upon the armies of the Egyptians and swallowed them up?

9 And now behold, if Elohim gave unto this man such power, then why should you dispute among yourselves and say that he has given unto me no power by which I may know concerning the judgments that shall come upon you except you repent? But behold, you not only deny my words, but you also deny all the words which have been spoken by our fathers, and also the words which were spoken by this man, Moshe, who had such great power given unto him — yes, the words which he has spoken concerning the coming of the Mashiach. Yes, did he not bear record that the Son of Elohim should come? And as he lifted up the brazen serpent[74] in the wilderness, even so shall

---

73 Ex. 14:16; Josh. 2:10; 1 Nefi 1:15; 5:18; Moshiyah 5:7; Alma 17:6 **74** Num. 21:9; 2 Kings 18:4; John 3:14; Alma 16:32

he be lifted up who should come. And as many as should look upon that serpent should live, even so as many as should look upon the Son of Elohim with faith, having a contrite spirit,[75] might live, even unto that life which is eternal.[76] And now behold, Moshe did not only testify of these things, but also all the holy prophets from his day, even to the days of Avraham. Yes, and behold, Avraham saw of his coming, and was filled with gladness and did rejoice.[77] Yes, and behold, I say unto you that Avraham not only knew of these things, but there were many before the days of Avraham who were called by the Order of Elohim, yes, even after the Order of his Son — and this that it should be shown unto the people a great many thousand years before his coming that even redemption should come unto them. And now I would that you should know that even since the days of Avraham there have been many prophets that have testified these things; yes, behold, the prophet Zenos did testify boldly, for the which he was slain, and behold, also Zenoch, and also Ezaias, and also Yesha'yahu,[78] and Yirmeyahu,[79] Yirmeyahu being that same prophet who testified of the destruction of Yerushalayim[80] — and now, we know that Yerushalayim was destroyed according to the words of Yirmeyahu — oh then why not the Son of Elohim come according to his prophecy? And now will you dispute that Yerushalayim was not destroyed? Will you say that the sons of Tzidkiyahu were not slain, all except it were Muloch? Yes, and do you not behold that the seed of Tzidkiyahu are with us and they were driven out of the land of Yerushalayim?[81] But behold, this is not all. Our father Lechi was driven out of Yerushalayim because he testified of these things. Nefi also testified of these things, and also almost all of our fathers, even down to this time; yes, they have testified of the coming of Mashiach, and have looked forward and have rejoiced in his day which is to come. And behold, he is Elohim, and he is with them, and he did manifest himself unto them, that they were redeemed by him; and they gave unto him glory because of that which is to come.

---

[75] Isa. 57:15; 66:2; Ps. 34:19 (18); 51:19 (17); 2 Nefi 1:6; Cheleman 3:9; 3 Nefi 4:7; 5:23; 'Eter 1:19; M'roni 6:1   [76] Num. 21:6-9. The Hebrew word for "serpent" is *nachash* נחש (Strong's 5175), which has a gematria of 358, the same gematria as *Mashiach* משיח (Strong's 4899). See also John 3:14; 8:28; 12:32; Alma 16:32.   [77] As we read in Targum Onkelos: "And he believed in the Word (Memra) of YHWH. And He counted it to him for righteousness" (Targum Onkelos Gen. 15:6).   [78] Isa. 53:1-12. See also footnotes to Moshiyah 8:3-5, 8   [79] Jer. 23:5-6   [80] Jer. 26:17-18   [81] Thus fulfilling Ezek. 17:1-24

10 And now, seeing you know these things and cannot deny them, except you shall lie, therefore in this you have sinned, for you have rejected all these things, despite so many evidences which you have received. Yes, even you have received all things, both things in heaven and all things which are in earth, as a witness that they are true. But behold, you have rejected the truth and rebelled against your holy Elohim. And even at this time, instead of laying up for yourselves treasures in Heaven,[82] where nothing does corrupt and where nothing can come which is unclean, you are heaping up for yourselves wrath against the day of judgment. Yes, even at this time you are ripening because of your murders, and your fornication, and wickedness, for everlasting destruction. Yes, and except you repent, it will come unto you soon; yes, behold, it is now even at your doors. Yes, go in unto the judgment seat and search; and behold, your judge is murdered, and he lies in his blood, and he has been murdered by his brother who seeks to sit in the judgment seat. And behold, they both belong to your secret band whose author is Gaddianton and the Evil One[83] who seeks to destroy the souls[84] of men.

11 Behold, now it came to pass that when Nefi had spoken these words, certain men who were among them ran to the judgment seat, yes, even there were five who went. And they said among themselves as they went, Behold, now we will know of a surety whether this man be a prophet, and Elohim has commanded him to prophesy such marvelous things unto us. Behold, we do not believe that he has, yes, we do not believe that he is a prophet; nevertheless, if this thing which he has said concerning the chief judge be true, that he be dead, then will we believe that the other words which he has spoken are true. And it came to pass that they ran in their might and came in unto the judgment seat; and behold, the chief judge had fallen to the earth and did lie in his blood. And now behold, when they saw this, they were astonished exceedingly, insomuch that they fell to the earth, for they had not believed the words which Nefi had spoken concerning the chief judge. But now when they saw, they believed,

---

82 3 Nefi 5:36   83 2 Nefi 3:8; 6:9; Alma 21:6; Cheleman 5:20; M'raman 1:4   84 Gen. 2:7; Yosef ben Yosef said, "God made a tabernacle & put a spirit in it and it became a human soul..." (Ehat, A.F. & Cook, L.W. (Eds.) (1980) *The Words of Joseph Smith*. Salt Lake City, UT: Bookcraft, p. 346; see also pgs. 352, 359). See also Ya'akov 2:5; Moshiyah 13:2; Alma 16:10; 19:7-8; 3 Nefi 9:6.

and fear came upon them that all the judgments which Nefi had spoken should come upon the people. Therefore, they did quake and had fallen to the earth.

12 Now immediately when the judge had been murdered, he being stabbed by his brother, by a garb[85] of secrecy, and he fled, and the servants ran and told the people, raising the cry of murder among them. And behold, the people did gather themselves together unto the place of the judgment seat, and behold, to their astonishment they saw those five men who had fallen to the earth. And now behold, the people knew nothing concerning the multitude which had gathered together at the garden of Nefi, therefore they said among themselves, These men are they who have murdered the judge, and Elohim has struck them down that they could not flee from us.

13 And it came to pass that they laid hold on them, and bound them, and cast them into prison. And there was a proclamation sent abroad that the judge was slain, and that the murderers had been taken and were cast into prison. And it came to pass that on the next day,[86] the people did assemble themselves together to mourn and to fast at the burial of the great and chief judge who had been slain. And thus those judges, who were at the garden of Nefi and heard his words, were also gathered together at the burial.

14 And it came to pass that they inquired among the people, saying, Where are the five who were sent to inquire concerning the chief judge, whether he was dead? And they answered and said, Concerning the five whom you say you have sent, we know not, but there are five who are the murderers whom we have cast into prison. And it came to pass that the judges desired that they should be brought, and they were brought; and behold, they were the five who were sent. And behold, the judges inquired of them to know concerning the matter. And they told them all that they had done, saying, We ran and came to the place of the judgment seat; and when we saw all things even as Nefi had testified, we were astonished, insomuch that we fell to the earth. And when we were recovered from our astonishment, behold, they cast us into prison. Now as for the murder of this man, we know not who has done it; and only this much we know, we ran and came

---

85 The Hebrew word *beged* בגד (Strong's 899) means both "garment" or "garb" and "treachery." This is an obvious Hebrew word play. 86 The ancient Jewish practice was to bury the body within 24 hours.

according as you desired, and behold, he was dead according to the words of Nefi.

15 And now it came to pass that the judges did explain the matter unto the people, and did cry out against Nefi, saying, Behold, we know that this Nefi must have agreed with someone to slay the judge, and then he might declare it unto us, that he might convert us unto his faith, that he might raise himself to be a great man, chosen of Elohim and a prophet. And now behold, we will detect this man, and he shall confess his fault and make known unto us the true murderer of this judge. And it came to pass that the five were liberated[87] on the day of the burial. Nevertheless, they did rebuke the judges in the words which they had spoken against Nefi, and did contend with them one by one, insomuch that they did confound them.

16 Nevertheless, they caused that Nefi should be taken, and bound, and brought before the multitude; and they began to question him in diverse ways, that they might cross him, that they might accuse him to death, saying unto him, You are in league. Who is this man that has done this murder? Now tell us and acknowledge your fault; saying, Behold, here is money;[88] and also, we will grant unto you your life if you will tell us and acknowledge the agreement which you have made with him. But Nefi said unto them, O you fools, you **uncircumcised of heart**,[89] you blind and you stiffnecked people, do you know how long YHWH your Elohim will allow you that you shall go on in this your ways of sin? Oh you ought to begin to howl and mourn because of the great destruction at this time which does await you except you shall repent. Behold, you say that I have agreed with a man that he should murder Seezoram, our chief judge. But behold, I say unto you that this is because I have testified unto you, that you might know concerning this thing, yes, even for a witness unto you that I did know of the wickedness and abominations which are among you. And because I have done this, you say that I have agreed with a man that he should do this thing. Yes, because I showed unto you this sign,[90] you are angry with me and seek to destroy my life.

---

87 Without at least two witnesses, there were no grounds for a conviction of the five men (Deut. 17:6; 19:15). 88 Ex. 23:7-8; 1 Sam. 8:3; Isa. 1:23; Amos 5:12; Ps. 26:10; Moshiyah 13:9; Alma 8:12-13; 'Eter 4:3 89 Lev. 26:40-42; Deut. 10:16; Jer. 4:4; 9:24-25 (25-26); Ezek. 44:9 90 Ya'akov 5:3-4; Alma 16:8-11, 25

¹⁷ And now behold, I will show unto you another sign, and see if you will in this thing seek to destroy me. Behold, I say unto you, go to the house of Seantum, who is the brother of Seezoram, and say unto him, Has Nefi, the pretended prophet who does prophesy so much evil concerning this people, agreed with you, in the which you have murdered Seezoram, who is your brother? And behold, he shall say unto you, No. And you shall say unto him, Have you murdered your brother? And he shall stand with fear and suppose not what to say. And behold, he shall deny unto you, and he shall make as if he were astonished; nevertheless, he shall declare unto you that he is innocent. But behold, you shall examine him, and you shall find blood upon the skirts of his cloak. And when you have seen this, you shall say, From where comes this blood? Do we not know that it is the blood of your brother? And then shall he tremble and shall look pale, even as if death had come upon him. And then shall you say, Because of this fear and this paleness which has come upon your face, behold, we know that you are guilty. And then shall greater fear come upon him; and then shall he confess unto you, and deny no more that he has done this murder. And then shall he say unto you that I, Nefi, knew nothing concerning the matter, except it were given unto me by the power of Elohim. And then shall you know that I am an honest man and that I am sent unto you from Elohim.

¹⁸ And it came to pass that they went and did even according as Nefi had said unto them. And behold, the words which he had said were true; for according to the words, he did deny, and also according to the words, he did confess. And he was brought to prove that he himself was the very murderer, insomuch that the five were set at liberty, and also was Nefi.[91] And there were some of the Nefites who believed on

---

[91] Without at least two witnesses, there were no grounds for a conviction of the five men or of Nefi (Deut. 17:6; 19:15). The confession of Seantum alone would not have been sufficient for his conviction, in the absence of witnesses. As the Talmud says, "No man may call himself a wrongdoer" (b.Sanhedrin 9b), just as no man can testify in his own favor (b.Ketubot 27a). If a man testified to his own guilt, that in itself made him disreputable and an invalid witness (b.Sanhedrin 25a; b.Baba Kamma 72b). There are biblical instances of convictions associated with confessions (Josh. 7:19-20; 2 Sam. 1:10-16; compare Judg. 17:1-4; 1 Sam. 14:43; 2 Sam. 4:8-12). The Talmud points out that these were all confessions made after trial and conviction, made for the sole purpose of expiating the sin before YHWH (b.Sanhedrin 43b) or as special case exceptions to the rule (for example, trials before kings rather than judges). One type of exception was when a confession was "corroborated by an ordeal as well as by the production of the corpus delecti" (Falk, Z. (1964) *Hebrew Law in Biblical Times*. Jerusalem, Israel: Wahrmann, p.

the words of Nefi; and there were some also who believed because of the testimony of the five, for they had been converted while they were in prison. And now there were some among the people who said that Nefi was a prophet; and there were others who said, Behold, he is a god, for except he was a god, he could not know of all things. For behold, he has told us the thoughts of our hearts, and also has told us things, and even he has brought unto our knowledge the true murderer of our chief judge.

19 And it came to pass that there arose a division among the people, insomuch that they divided hither and thither and went their ways, leaving Nefi alone as he was standing in the midst of them. And it came to pass that Nefi went his way towards his own house, pondering upon the things which YHWH had shown unto him. And it came to pass as he was thus pondering, being much cast down because of the wickedness of the people of the Nefites, their secret works of darkness, and their murderings, and their plunderings, and all manner of iniquities — and it came to pass as he was thus pondering in his heart, behold, a voice came unto him, saying, Blessed are you,[92] Nefi, for those things which you have done. For I have beheld how you have with unwearyingness declared the word which I have given unto you, unto this people. And you have not feared them, and have not sought your own life, but have sought my will and to keep my mitzvot. And now because you have done this with such unwearyingness, behold, I will bless you for ever. And I will make you mighty in word and in deed, in faith and in works, yes, even that all things shall be done unto you according to your word, for you will not ask that which is contrary to my will. Behold, you are Nefi, and I am Elohim. Behold, I declare it unto you in the presence of my angels that you shall have power over this people and shall smite the earth[93] with famine, and with pestilence, and destruction, according to the wickedness of this people. Behold, I give unto you power that whatsoever you shall seal on earth shall be sealed in Heaven,[94] and whatsoever you shall loose on earth shall be loosed in Heaven. And thus shall you have power

---

71). Such was the case of Achan (Josh. 7:19-20), who was exposed by casting of lots and whose confession was corroborated by the discovery of the goods under the floor of his tent. Similarly, Seantum was exposed by Nefi's revelations and by the discovery of blood on his garment.   **92** 1 Nefi 1:6, 9; 3:6; 2 Nefi 2:7; Moshiyah 11:20; Alma 6:5   **93** The Hebrew word here was likely *eretz* (ארץ), which can mean "land" or "earth."   **94** 1 Kings 17:1; 2 Nefi 15:3

among this people. And thus, if you shall say unto this Temple, It shall be split in two — and it shall be done. And if you shall say unto this mountain, Be you cast down and become smooth — and it shall be done. And behold, if you shall say that Elohim shall smite this people, it shall come to pass. And now behold, I command you that you shall go and declare unto this people that thus says Adonai YHWH, who is the Almighty: Except you repent, you shall be smitten, even unto destruction.

20 And behold, now it came to pass that when YHWH had spoken these words unto Nefi, he did stop and did not go unto his own house, but did return unto the multitudes who were scattered about upon the face of the land, and began to declare unto them the word of YHWH which had been spoken unto him concerning their destruction if they did not repent. Now behold, in spite of that great miracle which Nefi had done in telling them concerning the death of the chief judge, they did harden their hearts and did not hearken unto the words of YHWH; therefore, Nefi did declare unto them the word of YHWH, saying, Except you repent, thus says YHWH, you shall be smitten, even unto destruction.[95] And it came to pass that when Nefi had declared unto them the word, behold, they did still harden their hearts, and would not hearken unto his words. Therefore they did revile against him and did seek to lay their hands upon him, that they might cast him into prison. But behold, the power of Elohim was with him and they could not take him to cast him into prison, for he was taken by the spirit and carried away out of the midst of them.[96]

21 And it came to pass that thus he did go forth in the spirit[97] from multitude to multitude, declaring the word of Elohim, even until he had declared it unto them all, or sent it forth among all the people. And it came to pass that they would not hearken unto his words. And there began to be contentions, insomuch that they were divided against themselves, and began to slay one another with the sword. And thus ended the seventy and first year of the reign of the judges over the people of Nefi.

4 And now it came to pass in the seventy and second year[98] of the reign of the judges that the contentions did increase, insomuch

---

95 2 Nefi 4:4; Ya'akov 2:8, 11   96 Isa. 52:11; Ezek. 37:1   97 Ya'akov 3:6; Alma 6:4; 12:1
98 ~21 BCE

that there were wars throughout all the land, among all the people of Nefi. And it was this secret band of robbers who did carry on this work of destruction and wickedness. And this war did last all that year. And in the seventy and third year it did also last.

2 And it came to pass that in this year Nefi did cry unto YHWH, saying, O YHWH, do not allow that this people shall be destroyed by the sword, but O YHWH, rather let there be a famine in the land to stir them up in remembrance of YHWH their Elohim, and perhaps they will repent and turn unto you. And so it was done according to the words of Nefi, and there was a great famine upon the land, among all the people of Nefi.[99] And thus in the seventy and fourth year the famine did continue, and the work of destruction did cease by the sword, but became sore by famine. And this work of destruction did also continue in the seventy and fifth year. For the earth was smitten, that it was dry and did not yield forth grain in the season of grain; and the whole earth was smitten, even among the Lamanites as well as among the Nefites, so that they were afflicted that they did perish by thousands in the more wicked parts of the land.

3 And it came to pass that the people saw that they were about to perish by famine, and they began to remember the words of Nefi. And the people began to plead with their chief judges and their leaders, that they would say unto Nefi, Behold, we know that you are a man of Elohim, and therefore cry unto YHWH our Elohim that he turn away from us this famine, for fear that all the words which you have spoken concerning our destruction be fulfilled. And it came to pass that the judges did say unto Nefi according to the words which had been desired. And it came to pass that when Nefi saw that the people had repented and did humble themselves in sackcloth, he cried again unto YHWH, saying, O YHWH, behold, this people repent, and they have swept away the band of Gaddianton from among them, insomuch that they have become extinct and they have concealed their secret plans in the earth. Now, O YHWH, because of this their humility, will you turn away your anger and let your anger be appeased in the destruction of those wicked men whom you have already destroyed? O YHWH, will you turn away your anger, yes, your fierce anger, and cause that this famine may cease in

---

99 1 Kings 17:1; Cheleman 3:19

this land? O YHWH, will you hearken unto me and cause that it may be done according to my words, and send forth rain upon the face of the earth that she may bring forth her fruit and her grain in the season of grain? O YHWH, you did hearken unto my words when I said, Let there be a famine, that the pestilence of the sword might cease. And I know that you will even at this time hearken unto my words, for you said that if this people repent, I will spare them. Yes, O YHWH, and you see that they have repented because of the famine, and the pestilence, and destruction which has come unto them. And now, O YHWH, will you turn away your anger and try again if they will serve you? And if so, O YHWH, you can bless them according to your word which you have said.

4 And it came to pass that in the seventy and sixth year, YHWH did turn away his anger from the people, and caused that rain should fall upon the earth, insomuch that it did bring forth her fruit in the season of her fruit. And it came to pass that it did bring forth her grain in the season of her grain.[100] And behold, the people did rejoice and glorify Elohim, and the whole face of the land was filled with rejoicing. And they did no more seek to destroy Nefi, but they did esteem him as a great prophet and a man of Elohim, having great power and s'mikhah given unto him from Elohim. And behold, Lechi, his brother, was not a bit behind him as to things pertaining to righteousness. And thus it did come to pass that the people of Nefi began to prosper again in the land, and began to build up their waste places, and began to multiply and spread, even until they did cover the whole face of the land, both on the northward and on the southward, from the sea west to the sea east. And it came to pass that the seventy and sixth year did end in shalom. And the seventy and seventh year began in shalom, and the assembly did spread throughout the face of all the land, and the more part of the people, both the Nefites and the Lamanites, did belong to the assembly; and they did have exceedingly great shalom in the land. And thus ended the seventy and seventh year. And also, they had shalom in the seventy and eighth year, except it were a few contentions concerning the points of doctrine which had been laid down by the prophets; and in the seventy and ninth year there began to be much strife. But it came

---

100 See footnote to Cheleman 4:2.

to pass that Nefi, and Lechi, and many of their brothers, who knew concerning the true points of doctrine, having many revelations[101] daily, therefore they did preach unto the people, insomuch that they did put an end to their strife in that same year.

5 And it came to pass that in the eightieth year of the reign of the judges over the people of Nefi, there were a certain number of the dissenters[102] from the people of Nefi, who had some years before gone over unto the Lamanites and took upon themselves the name of Lamanites, and also a certain number who were real descendants of the Lamanites being stirred up to anger by them, or by those dissenters, therefore they commenced a war with their brothers. And they did commit murder and plunder, and then they would retreat back into the mountains, and into the wilderness and secret places, hiding themselves that they could not be discovered, receiving daily an addition to their numbers, inasmuch as there were dissenters that went forth unto them. And thus in time, yes, even in the space of not many years,[103] they became an exceedingly great band of robbers; and they did search out all the secret plans of Gaddianton, and thus they became robbers of Gaddianton.

6 Now behold, these robbers did make great havoc, yes, even great destruction among the people of Nefi, and also among the people of the Lamanites. And it came to pass that it was expedient that there should be a stop put to this work of destruction, therefore they sent an army of strong men into the wilderness and upon the mountains to search out this band of robbers and to destroy them. But behold, it came to pass that in that same year they were driven back, even into their own lands. And thus ended the eightieth year of the reign of the judges over the people of Nefi.

7 And it came to pass in the commencement of the eighty and first year, they did go forth again against this band of robbers and did destroy many; and they were also visited with much destruction. And they were again obliged to return out of the wilderness and out of the mountains unto their own lands, because of the exceeding greatness of the numbers of those robbers who infested the mountains and the wilderness. And it came to pass that thus ended this year.

---

101 Ya'akov 1:1; 3:2; 5:1; Yahram 1:2   102 Alma 21:30; 29:3; 30:6; 3 Nefi 1:7; 3:7
103 Cheleman 2:34; 3:1

⁸And the robbers did still increase and grow strong, insomuch that they did defy the whole armies of the Nefites, and also of the Lamanites; and they did cause great fear to come unto the people upon all the face of the land. Yes, for they did visit many parts of the land and did do great destruction unto them, yes, did kill many and did carry away others captive into the wilderness,[104] yes, and more especially their women and their children. Now this great evil, which came unto the people because of their iniquity, did stir them up again in remembrance of YHWH their Elohim. And thus ended the eighty and first year of the reign of the judges. And in the eighty and second year they began again to forget YHWH their Elohim. And in the eighty and third year they began to grow strong in iniquity. And in the eighty and fourth year they did not mend their ways. And it came to pass in the eighty and fifth year they did grow stronger and stronger in their pride and in their wickedness; and thus they were ripening again for destruction. And thus ended the eighty and fifth year.

⁹And thus we can behold how false, and also the unsteadiness of the hearts of the children of men. Yes, we can see that YHWH in his great infinite goodness does bless and prosper those who put their trust in him. Yes, and we may see at the very time when he does prosper his people — yes, in the increase[105] of their fields, their flocks, and their herds, and in gold, and in silver, and in all manner of precious things of every kind and art; sparing their lives and delivering them out of the hands of their enemies, softening the hearts of their enemies, that they should not declare wars against them, yes, and in short, doing all things for the welfare and happiness of his people — yes, then is the time that they do harden their hearts, and do forget YHWH their Elohim, and do trample[106] under their feet HaKodesh, yes, and this because of their ease and their exceedingly great prosperity. And thus we see that except YHWH does chasten his people with many afflictions, yes, except he does visit them with death, and with terror, and with famine, and with all manner of pestilences, they will not remember him. Oh how foolish, and how vain, and how evil, and demonic, and how quick to do iniquity,[107] and how slow to do good, are the children of men; yes, how quick

---

104 Alma 11:2-5   105 Alma 16:35   106 1 Nefi 5:36; Alma 3:10; 27:10; Cheleman 2:33; 3 Nefi 13:5   107 Ex. 32:8; Judg. 2:17; Isa. 59:7; Jer. 4:22; Moshiyah 8:1; Alma 21:6

to hearken unto the words of the Evil One and to set their hearts[108] upon the vain things of the world, yes, how quick to be lifted up in pride,[109] yes, how quick to boast and do all manner of that which is iniquity; and how slow are they to remember YHWH their Elohim and to give ear unto his counsels, yes, how slow to walk in wisdom's paths! Behold, they do not desire that YHWH their Elohim who has created them should rule and reign over them; despite his great goodness and his mercy towards them, they despise his counsels, and they do not want him to be their guide.

10 Oh how great is the nothingness[110] of the children of men, yes, even they are less than the dust of the earth! For behold, the dust of the earth moves hither and thither, to the dividing asunder, at the command of our great and El Olam. Yes, behold, at his voice do the hills and the mountains tremble and quake, and by the power of his voice they are broken up and become smooth, yes, even like unto a valley. Yes, by the power of his voice does the whole earth shake,[111] yes, by the power of his voice do the foundations rock, even to the very center. Yes, and if he says unto the earth, Move — it is moved. Yes, if he says unto the earth, You shall go back, that it lengthens out the day for many hours — and[112] it is done. And thus according to his word the earth goes back,[113] and it appears unto man that the sun stands still. Yes, and behold, this is so, for surely it is the earth that moves and not the sun. And behold also, if he says unto the waters of the great deep, Be you dried up — and it is done. Behold, if he says unto this mountain,[114] Be you raised up, and come over and fall upon that city, that it be buried up — and behold, it is done. And behold, if a man hide up a treasure in the earth, and YHWH shall say, Let it be cursed because of the iniquity of he who has hid it up — and behold, it shall be cursed. And if YHWH shall say, Be you cursed that no man shall find you from this time henceforth and for ever — and behold, no man gets it henceforth and for ever.[115] And behold, if YHWH shall say unto a man, Because of your iniquities, you shall be cursed for

---

108 Gen. 6:5 109 Ya'akov 2:4-6; Alma 3:5, 10; M'raman 4:5 110 Isa. 40:17; Dan. 4:35; Moshiyah 2:3 111 1 Nefi 5:21; M'raman 2:7; 'Eter 1:18 112 The "if...and" conditional structure seems stilted in English, which prefers "if...then." However, in Hebrew, this construction is correct. The numerous examples appearing in this paragraph, as well as elsewhere in the text, indicate the Hebraic nature of the underlying original. 113 Isa. 38:8 114 Ps. 46:3 (2); Zech. 14:4; 1 Nefi 5:37; Ya'akov 3:2; Cheleman 3:19; 3 Nefi 4:2, 6 115 Cheleman 5:5; 'Eter 6:7

ever — and it shall be done. And if YHWH shall say, Because of your iniquities, you shall be cut off from my presence — and he will cause that it shall be so. And woe unto him to whom he shall say this, for it shall be unto him that will do iniquity, and he cannot be saved; therefore, for this cause, that men might be saved, has repentance been declared.

11 Therefore, blessed are they who will repent and hearken unto the voice of YHWH their Elohim, for these are they that shall be saved. And may Elohim grant, in his great fulness, that men might be brought unto repentance and good works, that they might be restored unto grace for grace according to their works. And I would that all men might be saved. But we read that in that great and last day,[116] there are some who shall be cast out,[117] yes, who shall be cast off from the presence of YHWH, yes, who shall be consigned to a state of Endless misery, fulfilling the words which say: They that have done good shall have Everlasting life, and they that have done evil shall have Everlasting damnation. And thus it is. Amen.

The prophecy of Sh'mu'el, the Lamanite, to the Nefites.

5 And now it came to pass in the eighty and sixth year,[118] the Nefites did still remain in wickedness, yes, in great wickedness, while the Lamanites did observe strictly to keep the mitzvot of Elohim according to the Torah of Moshe. And it came to pass that in this year there was one Sh'mu'el, a Lamanite, who came into the land of Zerach'mla and began to preach unto the people. And it came to pass that he did preach repentance many days unto the people, and they did cast him out. And he was about to return to his own land, but behold, the voice of YHWH came unto him that he should return again and prophesy unto the people whatsoever things should come into his heart.

2 And it came to pass that they would not allow that he should enter into the city, therefore he went and got upon the wall thereof, and stretched forth his hand, and cried with a loud voice, and prophesied unto the people whatsoever things YHWH put into his heart. And he said unto them, Behold, I, Sh'mu'el, a Lamanite, do speak the words

---

116 Mal. 3:23 (4:5)   **117** Ya'akov 4:1; Moshiyah 8:13; Alma 3:4; 16:36; 19:6; 3 Nefi 5:20
118 ~ 7 BCE

of YHWH which he does put into my heart. And behold, he has put it into my heart to say unto this people that the sword of justice hangs over this people. And four hundred years passes not away except the sword of justice falls upon this people, yes, heavy destruction awaits this people, and it surely comes unto this people. And nothing can save this people, except it be repentance and faith on Adonai Yeshua HaMashiach, who surely shall come into the world, and shall suffer many things, and shall be slain for his people. And behold, an angel of YHWH has declared it unto me, and he did bring glad tidings to my soul. And behold, I was sent unto you to declare it unto you also, that you might have glad tidings; but behold, you would not receive me.

3 Therefore, thus says YHWH: Because of the hardness of the hearts of the people of the Nefites, except they repent, I will take away my word from them, and I will withdraw my spirit from them, and I will sustain them no longer, and I will turn the hearts of their brothers against them, and four hundred years shall not pass away before I will cause that they shall be smitten. Yes, I will visit them **with the sword, and with famine, and with pestilence;**[119] yes, I will visit them in my fierce anger. And there shall be those of the fourth generation[120] who shall live, of your enemies, to behold your utter destruction. And this shall surely come except you repent, says YHWH, and those of the fourth generation shall visit your destruction. But if you will repent and return unto YHWH your Elohim, I will turn away my anger, says YHWH. Yes, thus says YHWH: Blessed are they who will repent and turn unto me, but woe unto him that repents not. Yes, woe unto this great city of Zerach'mla, for behold, it is because of those who are righteous that it is saved.[121] Yes, woe unto this great city, for I perceive, says YHWH, that there are many, yes, even the more part of this great city, that will harden their hearts against me, says YHWH. But blessed are they who will repent, for them will I spare. But behold, if it were not for the righteous who are in this great city, behold, I would cause that fire should come down out of heaven[122] and destroy it. But behold, it is for the righteous' sake that it is spared. But behold, the time comes, says YHWH, that when you shall cast out the righteous from among you, then shall you be ripe for destruction.

---

119 Jer. 27:8 120 Gen. 15:16; Ex. 20:5; 34:7; Num. 14:18; Deut. 5:9; 2 Kings 10:30 121 Gen. 18:23-33 122 Gen. 19:24; Ex. 9:23; 3 Nefi 4:6

⁴Yes, woe be unto this great city because of the wickedness and abominations which are in her; yes, and woe be unto the city of Gideon for the wickedness and abominations which are in her; yes, and woe be unto all the cities which are in the land round about, which are possessed by the Nefites, because of the wickedness and the abominations which are in them. And behold, a curse[123] shall come upon the land, says YHWH Tzva'ot, because of the people's sake who are upon the land, yes, because of their wickedness and their abominations.

⁵And it shall come to pass, says YHWH Tzva'ot, yes, our great and true Elohim, that whoever shall hide up treasures in the earth shall find them again no more, because of the great curse of the land, except he be a righteous man and shall hide it up unto YHWH; for I will, says YHWH, that they shall hide up their treasures unto me. And cursed be they who hide not up their treasures unto me, for none hides up their treasures unto me except it be the righteous. And he that hides not up his treasure unto me, cursed is he, and also the treasure; and none shall redeem it because of the curse of the land. And the day shall come that they shall hide up their treasures because they have set their hearts upon riches. And because they have set their hearts upon their riches and will hide up their treasures when they shall flee before their enemies, because they will not hide them up unto me, cursed be they and also their treasures; and in that day shall they be smitten, says YHWH.

⁶Behold, you people of this great city, and hearken unto my words, yes, hearken unto the words which YHWH says. For behold, he says that you are cursed because of your riches, and also are your riches cursed, because you have set your hearts upon them and have not hearkened unto the words of him who gave them unto you. You do not remember YHWH your Elohim in the things which he has blessed you, but you do always remember your riches — not to thank YHWH your Elohim for them. Yes, your hearts are not drawn out unto YHWH, but they do swell with great pride unto boasting, and unto great swelling, envyings, strifes, malice, persecutions, and murders, and all manner of iniquities. For this cause has Adonai YHWH caused that a curse should come upon the land, and also upon your riches, and

---

123 1 Nefi 5:19; Alma 21:3

CHELEMAN 5:7

this because of your iniquities. Yes, woe unto this people because of this time which has arrived that you do cast out the prophets,[124] and do mock them, and cast stones at them, and do slay them, and do do all manner of iniquity unto them, even as they did of old time.

7 And now when you talk, you say, If our days had been in the days of our fathers of old, we would not have slain the prophets,[125] we would not have stoned them and cast them out. Behold, you are worse than they; for, as YHWH lives, if a prophet come among you and declares unto you the word of YHWH, which testifies of your sins and iniquities, you are angry with him, and cast him out, and seek all manner of ways to destroy him. Yes, you will say that he is a false prophet, and that he is a sinner and of HaSatan, because he testifies that your deeds are evil. But behold, if a man shall come among you and shall say, Do this and there is no iniquity, do that and you shall not suffer — yes, he will say, Walk after the pride of your own hearts, yes, walk after the pride of your eyes and do whatsoever your heart desires — and if a man shall come among you and say this, you will receive him and you will say that he is a prophet. Yes, you will lift him up and you will give unto him of your substance, you will give unto him of your gold and of your silver, and you will clothe him with costly apparel.[126] And because he speaks soothing words unto you and he says that all is well, then you will not find fault with him.

8 O you wicked and you perverse generation, you hardened and you stiffnecked[127] people, how long will you suppose that YHWH will sustain you? Yes, how long will you allow yourselves to be led by foolish and blind guides? Yes, how long will you choose darkness rather than light? Yes, behold, the anger of YHWH is already kindled against you. Behold, he has cursed the land because of your iniquity; and behold, the time comes that he curses your riches, that they become slippery, that you cannot hold them. And in the days of your poverty you cannot retain them, and in the days of your poverty you shall cry unto YHWH; and in vain shall you cry, for your desolation is already come upon you and your destruction is made sure. And then shall you weep and howl in that day, says YHWH Tzva'ot. And then shall you lament and say, Oh that I had repented and had not

---

124 1 Kings 19:10; 2 Chron. 24:21; 2 Nefi 11:10 **125** Matt. 23:30 **126** Alma 1:1 **127** Ex. 32:9; Deut. 9:6-7; 2 Nefi 11:9; Ya'akov 3:5; 4:1; Enosh 1:6; Moshiyah 1:16

killed the prophets, and stoned them, and cast them out. Yes, in that day shall you say, Oh that we had remembered YHWH our Elohim in the day that he gave us our riches, and then they would not have become slippery, that we should lose them; for behold, our riches are gone from us. Behold, we lay a tool here and on the next day it is gone. And behold, our swords are taken from us in the day we have sought them for battle. Yes, we have hid up our treasures and they have slipped away from us because of the curse of the land. Oh that we had repented in the day that the word of YHWH came unto us, for behold, the land is cursed, and all things have become slippery and we cannot hold them. Behold, we are surrounded by demons, yes, we are encircled about by the angels of him who has sought to destroy our souls. Behold, our iniquities are great. O YHWH, can you not turn away your anger from us? And this shall be your language in these days.

9 But behold, your days of probation are past. You have procrastinated[128] the day of your salvation until it is everlastingly too late and your destruction is made sure; yes, for you have sought all the days of your lives for that which you could not obtain, and you have sought for happiness in doing iniquity,[129] which thing is contrary to the nature of that righteousness which is in our great and Eternal Head. O you people of the land, that you would hear my words. And I pray that the anger of YHWH be turned away from you and that you would repent and be saved.

10 And now it came to pass that Sh'mu'el, the Lamanite, did prophesy a great many more things which cannot be written. And behold, he said unto them, Behold, I give unto you a sign; for five more years come, and behold, then comes[130] the Son of Elohim to redeem all those who shall believe on his name. And behold, this will I give unto you for a sign at the time of his coming: for behold, there shall be great lights in heaven, insomuch that in the night before he comes there shall be no darkness,[131] insomuch that it shall appear unto man as if it was day. Therefore, there shall be one day and a night and a day, as if it were one day and there were no night; and this shall be unto you for a sign. For you shall know of the rising of the sun, and also of its setting, therefore you shall know of a surety that there shall

---

128 Alma 10:4; 16:37   **129** 2 Nefi 1:7; Alma 19:10   **130** 3 Nefi 1:4–5   **131** 3 Nefi 1:4–5

be two days and a night. Nevertheless, the night shall not be darkened, and it shall be the night before he is born. And behold, there shall be a new **star** arise,[132] such an one as you never have beheld, and this also shall be a sign unto you. And behold, this is not all; there shall be many signs and wonders in heaven. And it shall come to pass that you shall all be amazed and wonder, insomuch that you shall fall to the earth.[133] And it shall come to pass that whosoever shall believe on the Son of Elohim, the same shall have everlasting life.

11 And behold, thus has YHWH commanded me by his angel[134] that I should come and tell this thing unto you, yes, he has commanded that I should prophesy these things unto you. Yes, he has said unto me, Cry unto this people, Repent and prepare the way of YHWH. And now because I am a Lamanite, and have spoken unto you the words which YHWH has commanded me, and because it was hard against you, you are angry with me, and do seek to destroy me and have cast me out from among you. And you shall hear my words, for, for this intent have I come up upon the walls of this city, that you might hear and know of the judgments of Elohim which do await you because of your iniquities, and also that you might know the conditions of repentance, and also that you might know of the coming of Yeshua HaMashiach, the Son of Elohim the Father of Heaven and of earth, the Creator of all things from the beginning, and that you might know of the signs of his coming, to the intent that you might believe on his name. And if you believe on his name, you will repent of all your sins, that thereby you may have a remission of them through his merits.[135]

12 And behold again, another sign I give unto you, yes, a sign of his death; for behold, he surely must die, that salvation may come. Yes, it is necessary and becomes expedient that he die to bring to pass the resurrection of the dead, that thereby men may be brought into the presence of YHWH. Yes, behold, this death brings to pass the resurrection and redeems[136] all mankind from the first death (that spiritual death); for all mankind, by the Fall of Adam,[137] being cut off from the presence of YHWH, are considered as dead, both as to things temporal and to things spiritual.[138] But behold, the

---

132 Num. 24:17; 3 Nefi 1:5 **133** 3 Nefi 1:4; 5:4 **134** 1 Nefi 3:8-15; Moshiyah 1:13; 2:1; 11:26 **135** 2 Nefi 1:6; 13:4; M'roni 6:1 **136** Isa. 29:22; 52:7-9; 2 Nefi 1:3; 3 Nefi 7:6; 9:7-9; 'Eter 1:13; M'raman 4:7 **137** 2 Nefi 1:9-10; Moshiyah 1:15-18; Alma 9:6; 13:9; M'raman 4:7 **138** 1 Nefi 4:6; 2 Nefi 1:6; Alma 9:5; 17:1, 16; 19:13

resurrection of Mashiach redeems mankind, yes, even all mankind, and brings them back into the presence of YHWH. Yes, and it brings to pass the conditions of repentance — that whosoever repents, the same is not cut down and cast into the fire,[139] but whosoever repents not is cut down and cast into the fire, and there comes upon them again a spiritual death, yes, a second death, for they are cut off again as to things pertaining to righteousness. Therefore, repent, repent, lest by knowing these things and not doing them you shall allow yourselves to come under condemnation, and you are brought down unto this second death.

13 But behold, as I said unto you concerning another sign, a sign of his death, behold, in that day that he shall suffer death, **the sun shall be darkened** and **refuse to give** his **light** unto you, and also **the moon and the stars**.[140] And there shall be no light upon the face of this land, even from the time that he shall suffer death, for the space of three days, to the time that he shall rise again from the dead. Yes, at the time that he shall yield up the ghost, there shall be thunderings and lightnings for the space of many hours, and the earth shall shake and tremble, and the rocks[141] which are upon the face of this earth,[142] which are both above the earth and beneath, which you know at this time are solid (or the more part of it is one solid mass) shall be broken up, yes, they shall be split in two, and shall ever after be found in seams, and in cracks, and in broken fragments, upon the face of the whole earth, yes, both above the earth and beneath. And behold, there shall be great tempests,[143] and there shall be many mountains laid low like unto a valley, and there shall be many places which are now called valleys which shall become mountains, whose height thereof is great. And many highways shall be broken up, and many cities shall become desolate, and many graves shall be opened and shall yield up many of their dead, and many k'doshim shall appear unto many. And behold, thus has the angel spoken unto me, for he said unto me that there should be thunderings and lightnings for the space of many hours; and he said unto me that while the thunder and the lightning lasted, and the tempest, that these things should be, and that darkness should cover the face of the whole earth for the

---

139 Ya'akov 3:7, 28; Alma 3:6, 9-10; 3 Nefi 12:4-5   **140** Isa. 13:10; Joel 2:10; 4:15 (3:15)
141 3 Nefi 4:2   **142** The Hebrew word here was likely *eretz* (ארץ), which can mean "land" or "earth."   **143** 3 Nefi 4:2-3

space of three days. And the angel said unto me that many shall see greater things than these, to the intent that they might believe; that these signs and these wonders should come to pass upon all the face of this land, to the intent that there should be no cause for unbelief among the children of men — and this to the intent that whosoever will believe might be saved, and that whosoever will not believe, a righteous judgment might come upon them. And also, if they are condemned, they bring upon themselves their own condemnation.

14 And now remember, remember, my brothers, that whosoever perishes, perishes unto himself, and whosoever does iniquity, does it unto himself. For behold, you are free; you are permitted to act for yourselves. For behold, Elohim has given unto you a knowledge, and he has made you free. He has given unto you that you might know good from evil, and he has given unto you that you might choose life or death. And you can do good and be restored unto that which is good, or have that which is good restored unto you; or you can do evil and have that which is evil restored unto you. And now my beloved brothers, behold, I declare unto you that except you shall repent, your houses shall be left unto you desolate.[144] Yes, except you repent, your women shall have great cause to mourn in the day that they shall nurse; for you shall attempt to flee and there shall be no place for refuge. Yes, and woe unto them which are with child, for they shall be heavy and cannot flee; therefore, they shall be trampled down and shall be left to perish. Yes, woe unto this people who are called the people of Nefi, except they shall repent when they shall see all those signs and wonders which shall be showed unto them; for behold, they have been a chosen people of YHWH. Yes, the people of Nefi has he loved, and also has he chastened them, yes, in the days of their iniquities has he chastened them because he loves them.

15 But behold, my brothers, the Lamanites has he hated because their deeds have been evil continually, and this because of the iniquity of the tradition of their fathers. But behold, salvation has come unto them through the preaching of the Nefites, and for this intent has YHWH prolonged their days. And I would that you should behold that the more part of them are in the path of their duty, and **they do walk** circumspectly before Elohim, and they do observe to **keep his**

---

144 2 Nefi 8:12; 3 Nefi 4:2, 9

mitzvot, and his statutes,[145] and his judgments, according to the Torah of Moshe. Yes, I say unto you that the more part of them are doing this, and they are striving, with unwearied diligence, that they may bring the remainder of their brothers to the knowledge of the truth; therefore, there are many who do add to their numbers daily. And behold, you do know of yourselves, for you have witnessed it, that as many of them as are brought to the knowledge of the truth, and to know of the wicked and abominable traditions of their fathers, and are led to believe the holy scriptures — yes, the prophecies of the holy prophets which are written, which lead them to faith on YHWH and unto repentance, which faith and repentance bring a change of heart[146] unto them — therefore, as many as have come to this, you know of yourselves, are firm and steadfast in the faith, and in the thing with which they have been made free. And you know also that they have buried their weapons[147] of war, and they fear to take them up lest by any means they shall sin. Yes, you can see that they fear to sin, for behold, they will allow themselves that they be trampled down and slain by their enemies, and will not lift their swords against them, and this because of their faith in Mashiach.

16 And now because of their steadfastness when they do believe in that thing which they do believe, for because of their firmness when they are once enlightened, behold, YHWH shall bless them and prolong their days, despite their iniquity. Yes, even if they should dwindle in unbelief,[148] YHWH shall prolong their days until the time shall come which has been spoken of by our fathers, and also by the prophet Zenos,[149] and many other prophets, concerning the restoration of our brothers the Lamanites again to the knowledge of the truth. Yes, I say unto you that in the latter times, the promises of YHWH have been extended to our brothers, the Lamanites; and despite the many afflictions which they shall have, and even though they shall be driven to and fro upon the face of the earth, and be hunted, and shall be slain and scattered abroad, having no place for refuge, YHWH shall be merciful unto them, and this is according to the prophecy that they shall again be brought to the true knowledge, which is the knowledge of their Redeemer, and their great and their

---

[145] Deut. 30:16 [146] Alma 3:5 [147] Alma 14:19, 21 [148] 1 Nefi 1:17; 3:18, 23; 4:3; Cheleman 2:14, 34; M'roni 7:7; 10:4-5 [149] 1 Nefi 5:36-37; Ya'akov 3:7; 4:1; Alma 16:31-33; Cheleman 3:9; 3 Nefi 4:11

true Shepherd,[150] and be numbered among his sheep. Therefore, I say unto you, it shall be better for them than for you, except you repent. For behold, had the mighty works been shown unto them which have been shown unto you, yes, unto them who have dwindled in unbelief because of the traditions of their fathers, you can see of yourselves that they never would again have dwindled in unbelief. Therefore, says YHWH, I will not utterly destroy them, but I will cause that in the day of my wisdom they shall return again unto me, says YHWH. And now behold, says YHWH, concerning the people of the Nefites, if they will not repent and observe to do my will, I will utterly destroy them, says YHWH, because of their unbelief, despite the many mighty works which I have done among them. And as surely as YHWH lives shall these things be, says YHWH.

17 And now it came to pass that there were many who heard the words of Sh'mu'el, the Lamanite, which he spoke upon the walls of the city. And as many as believed on his words went forth and sought for Nefi; and when they had come forth and found him, they confessed unto him their sins and denied not, desiring that they might be washed by immersion unto YHWH. But as many as there were who did not believe in the words of Sh'mu'el were angry with him, and they cast stones at him upon the wall, and also many shot arrows at him as he stood upon the wall. But the spirit of YHWH was with him, insomuch that they could not hit him with their stones, neither with their arrows.

18 Now when they saw this, that they could not hit him, there were many more who did believe on his words, insomuch that they went away unto Nefi to be immersed. For behold, Nefi was immersing, and prophesying, and preaching, crying repentance unto the people, showing signs and wonders, working miracles among the people, that they might know that the Mashiach must shortly come, telling them of things which must shortly come, that they might know and remember at the time of their coming that they had been made known unto them beforehand, to the intent that they might believe. Therefore, as many as believed on the words of Sh'mu'el went forth unto him to be washed by immersion,[151] for they came repenting and confessing their sins.

---

150 Isa. 40:11; Ezek. 34:12; Ps. 23:1; 1 Nefi 7:5; Alma 3:7–8, 11; 3 Nefi 7:3   151 3 Nefi 5:7-11

19 But the more part of them did not believe in the words of Sh'mu'el; therefore, when they saw that they could not hit him with their stones and their arrows, they cried out unto their captains, saying, Take this fellow and bind him, for behold, he has a demon![152] And because of the power of the demon which is in him, we cannot hit him with our stones and our arrows; therefore take him, and bind him, and away with him! And as they went forth to lay their hands on him, behold, he did cast himself down from the wall and did flee out of their lands, yes, even unto his own country, and began to preach and to prophesy among his own people. And behold, he was never heard of again among the Nefites; and thus were the affairs of the people. And thus ended the eighty and sixth year of the reign of the judges over the people of Nefi. And thus ended also the eighty and seventh year of the reign of the judges, and the more part of the people remaining in their pride and wickedness, and the lesser part walking more circumspectly before Elohim. And thus were the conditions also in the eighty and eighth year of the reign of the judges. And there was but little alteration in the affairs of the people, except it were the people began to be more hardened in iniquity, and do more and more of that which was contrary to the mitzvot of Elohim in the eighty and ninth year of the reign of the judges.

20 But behold, it came to pass in the ninetieth year[153] of the reign of the judges, there were great signs given unto the people, and wonders; and the words of the prophets began to be fulfilled, and angels[154] did appear unto men — wise men — and did declare unto them glad tidings of great joy; and thus in this year, the scriptures began to be fulfilled. Nevertheless, the people began to harden their hearts — all except it were the most believing part of them, both of the Nefites and also of the Lamanites — and began to depend upon their own strength and upon their own wisdom, saying, Some things they may have guessed right among so many, but behold, we know that all these great and marvelous works cannot come to pass of which have been spoken. And they began to reason and to contend among themselves, saying that it is not reasonable that such a being as a Mashiach shall come. If so, and he be the Son of Elohim the Father of Heaven and of earth, as it has been spoken, why will he not show

---

152 Alma 8:7   153 ~3 BCE   154 1 Nefi 3:8; Moshiyah 1:13; 2:1

himself unto us as well as unto them who shall be at Yerushalayim? Yes, why will he not show himself in this land as well as in the land of Yerushalayim? But behold, we know that this is a wicked tradition which has been handed down unto us by our fathers, to cause us that we should believe in some great and marvelous thing which should come to pass, but not among us, but in a land which is far distant, a land which we know not; therefore, they can keep us in ignorance, for we cannot witness with our own eyes that they are true. And they will, by the cunning and the mysterious arts of the Evil One, work some great mystery which we cannot understand, which will keep us down to be servants to their words, and also servants unto them (for we depend upon them to teach us the word), and thus will they keep us in ignorance if we will yield ourselves unto them all the days of our lives.

21 And many more things did the people imagine[155] up in their hearts which were foolish and vain; and they were much disturbed, for HaSatan did stir them up[156] to do iniquity continually. Yes, he did go about spreading rumors and contentions upon all the face of the land, that he might harden the hearts of the people against that which was good and against that which should come. And despite the signs and the wonders which were worked among the people of YHWH, and the many miracles which they did, HaSatan did get great hold upon the hearts[157] of the people upon all the face of the land. And thus ended the ninetieth year of the reign of the judges over the people of Nefi. And thus ended The Book of Cheleman, according to the record of Cheleman and his sons.

ספר נפי בן נפי אשר היה בן חלמן
3 NEFI
THE BOOK OF NEFI
THE SON OF NEFI, WHO WAS THE SON OF CHELEMAN

And Cheleman was the son of Cheleman, who was the son of Alma, who was the son of Alma, being a descendant of Nefi, who was the son of Lechi, who came out of Yerushalayim in the first year of the reign of Tzidkiyahu, the king of Y'hudah.

---

155 Zech. 7:10; 8:17; Ps. 140:3 (2); 3 Nefi 1:8   156 3 Nefi 3:3   157 Alma 6:4; 8:6; Cheleman 2:33; 3:3; 4 Nefi 1:6

Now it came to pass that the ninety and first year[1] had passed away, and it was six hundred years from the time that Lechi left Yerushalayim; and it was in the year that Lachoneus[2] was the chief judge and the governor over the land. And Nefi, the son of Cheleman, had departed out of the land of Zerach'mla, giving charge unto his son Nefi, who was his eldest son, concerning the plates of brass,[3] and all the records which had been kept, and all those things which had been kept sacred from the departure of Lechi out of Yerushalayim. Then he departed out of the land, and where he went, no man knows.[4] And his son Nefi did keep the record in his place, yes, the record of this people.

2 And it came to pass that in the commencement of the ninety and second year, behold, the prophecies of the prophets began to be fulfilled more fully, for there began to be greater signs and greater miracles worked among the people. But there were some who began to say that the time was past for the words to be fulfilled which were spoken by Sh'mu'el, the Lamanite. And they began to rejoice over their brothers, saying, Behold, the time is past and the words of Sh'mu'el are not fulfilled; therefore, your joy and your faith concerning this thing have been vain. And it came to pass that they did make a great uproar throughout the land; and the people who believed began to be very sorrowful, for fear that by any means those things which had been spoken might not come to pass. But behold, they did watch steadfastly for that day and that night and that day which should be as one day[5] as if there were no night, that they might know that their faith had not been vain.

3 Now it came to pass that there was a day set apart by the unbelievers that all those who believed in those traditions should be put to death, except the sign should come to pass which had been given by Sh'mu'el, the prophet. Now it came to pass that when Nefi, the son of Nefi, saw this wickedness of his people, his heart was exceedingly sorrowful. And it came to pass that he went out and bowed himself down upon the earth, and cried mightily to his Elohim in behalf of his people, yes, those who were about to be destroyed because of their faith in the tradition of their fathers. And it came to pass that

---

1 ~2 BCE 2 Regarding the appearance of Greek names in ancient America, see citation for *Timothy* in 3 Nefi 9:2 3 1 Nefi 1:10, 22-23; 2 Nefi 3:1; Moshiyah 1:3; 3 Nefi 4:11 4 Gen. 5:24; Deut. 34:5-6; 2 Kings 2:16; Alma 21:3 5 Cheleman 5:10

he cried mightily unto YHWH all that day. And behold, the voice of YHWH came unto him, saying, Lift up your head and be of good cheer. For behold, the time is at hand, and on this night shall the sign be given, and tomorrow I come into the world, to show unto the world that I will fulfill all that which I have caused to be spoken by the mouth of my holy prophets.[6] Behold, I come unto my own to fulfill all things which I have made known unto the children of men from the foundation of the world, and to do the will both of the Father and of the Son — of the Father because of me, and of the Son because of my flesh. And behold, the time is at hand and this night shall the sign be given.

4 And it came to pass that the words which came unto Nefi were fulfilled according as they had been spoken; for behold, at the going down of the sun there was no darkness, and the people began to be astonished because there was no darkness when the night came. And there were many, who had not believed the words of the prophets, who fell to the earth and became as if they were dead, for they knew that the great plan of destruction which they had laid for those who believed in the words of the prophets had been frustrated. For the sign which had been given was already at hand, and they began to know that the Son of Elohim must shortly appear. Yes, and in short, all the people upon the face of the whole earth, from the west to the east, both in the land north and in the land south, were so exceedingly astonished that they fell to the earth, for they knew that the prophets had testified of these things for many years, and that the sign which had been given was already at hand. And they began to fear because of their iniquity and their unbelief.

5 And it came to pass that there was no darkness in all that night, but it was as light as though it was midday. And it came to pass that the sun did rise in the morning again according to its proper order; and they knew that it was the day that YHWH should be born, because of the sign which had been given. And it had come to pass, yes, all things, every point, according to the words of the prophets. And it came to pass also that a new star[7] did appear according to the word. And it came to pass that from this time forth there began to be lyings

---

[6] Num. 24:17; Deut. 18:15; Isa. 7:14; 9:6; 25:9; 50:6; 53:5; Hos. 11:1; Zech. 11:13; 13:6; Mal. 3:1; Ps. 22:17 (16); 118:22; 1 Nefi 1:5; 2 Nefi 11:6; Moshiyah 8:2; Cheleman 3:9; 5:10, 13; 3 Nefi 4:11 [7] Cheleman 5:10

sent forth among the people by HaSatan to harden their hearts, to the intent that they might not believe in those signs and wonders which they had seen. But despite these lyings and deceivings, the more part of the people did believe and were converted unto YHWH.

6 And it came to pass that Nefi went forth among the people, and also many others, immersing unto repentance, in the which there was a great remission of sins. And thus the people began again to have shalom in the land. And there were no contentions, except it were a few that began to preach, endeavoring to prove by the scriptures that it was no longer necessary to observe the Torah of Moshe. Now in this thing they did err, having not understood the scriptures. But it came to pass that they soon became converted and were convinced of the error which they were in, for it was made known unto them that the Torah was not yet fulfilled[8] and that it must be fulfilled in every point. Yes, the word came unto them that it must be fulfilled, yes, that not one yud nor stroke should pass away till it should all be fulfilled.[9] Therefore, in this same year were they brought to a knowledge of their error and did confess their faults. And thus the ninety and second year did pass away, bringing glad tidings unto the people because of the signs which did come to pass according to the words of the prophecy of all the holy prophets.

7 And it came to pass that the ninety and third year did also pass away in shalom, except it were for the Gaddianton robbers who did dwell upon the mountains, who did infest the land; for so strong were their holds and their secret places that the people could not overpower them; therefore, they did commit many murders and did do much slaughter among the people. And it came to pass that in the ninety and fourth year they began to increase in a great degree because there were many dissenters[10] of the Nefites who did flee unto them, which did cause much sorrow unto those Nefites who did remain in the land. And there was also a cause of much sorrow among the Lamanites, for behold, they had many children who came of age that they became responsible for themselves,[11] and were led away by some who were Tzuramites, by their lyings and their flattering words, to join those Gaddianton robbers. And thus were the Lamanites afflicted also, and

---

8 See "What does it mean to fulfill the Torah?" footnote to 2 Nefi 11:8.   **9** 2 Nefi 11:8-9; Alma 14:15; 16:1, 34; 3 Nefi 5:22-23, 31; 7:2; 'Eter 5:2   **10** Alma 21:30; 29:3; 30:6; 3 Nefi 1:7; 3:7   **11** M'roni 8:2-5

began to decrease as to their faith and righteousness because of the wickedness of the rising generation.

8 And it came to pass that thus passed away the ninety and fifth[12] year also; and the people began to forget those signs and wonders which they had heard, and began to be less and less astonished at a sign or a wonder from Heaven, insomuch that they began to be hard in their hearts and blind in their minds, and began to disbelieve all which they had heard and seen, imagining up some vain thing in their hearts: that it was worked by men and by the power of HaSatan to lead away and deceive the hearts of the people. And thus did HaSatan get possession of the hearts of the people again, insomuch that he did blind their eyes and lead them away to believe that the doctrine[13] of Mashiach was a foolish and a vain thing.

9 And it came to pass that the people began to grow strong in wickedness and abominations, and they did not believe that there should be any more signs or wonders given. And HaSatan did go about leading away the hearts of the people, tempting them and causing them that they should do great wickedness in the land. And thus did pass away the ninety and sixth year, and also the ninety and seventh year, and also the ninety and eighth year, and also the ninety and ninth year, and also a hundred years had passed away since the days of Moshiyah, who was king over the people of the Nefites. And six hundred and nine years had passed away since Lechi left Yerushalayim;[14] and nine years had passed away from the time when the sign was given which was spoken of by the prophets that Mashiach should come into the world. Now the Nefites began to reckon their time[15] from this period when the sign was given, or from the coming of Mashiach. Therefore, nine years had passed away, and Nefi, who was the father of Nefi, who had the charge of the records, did not return to the land of Zerach'mla and could nowhere be found in all the land.

10 And it came to pass that the people did still remain in wickedness, despite the much preaching and prophesying which was sent among them. And thus passed away the tenth year also, and the eleventh year also passed away in iniquity. And it came to pass in the thirteenth year, there began to be wars and contentions throughout all the

---

12 ~3 CE 13 2 Nefi 13:1, 5; 14:1; Ya'akov 5:1–2; 3 Nefi 5:8–9 14 1 Nefi 1:7 15 3 Nefi 4:1

land, for the Gaddianton robbers had become so numerous, and did slay so many of the people, and did lay waste so many cities, and did spread so much death and carnage throughout the land, that it became expedient that all the people, both the Nefites and the Lamanites, should take up arms against them. Therefore, all the Lamanites who had become converted unto YHWH did unite with their brothers, the Nefites, and were compelled, for the safety of their lives, and their women, and their children, to take up arms against those Gaddianton robbers, yes, and also to maintain their rights and their privileges of their assembly, and of their worship, and their freedom, and their liberty.[16]

11 And it came to pass that before this thirteenth year had passed away, the Nefites were threatened with utter destruction because of this war which had become exceedingly sore. And it came to pass that those Lamanites who had united with the Nefites were numbered among the Nefites, and their curse was taken from them,[17] and their skin became white like unto the Nefites, and their young men and their daughters became exceedingly fair, and they were numbered among the Nefites and were called Nefites. And thus ended the thirteenth year.

12 And it came to pass in the commencement of the fourteenth year, the war between the robbers and the people of Nefi did continue and did become exceedingly sore. Nevertheless, the people of Nefi did gain some advantage over the robbers, insomuch that they did drive them back out of their lands, into the mountains and into their secret places. And thus ended the fourteenth year. And in the fifteenth year they did come forth again against the people of Nefi. And because of the wickedness of the people of Nefi, and their many contentions and dissensions, the Gaddianton robbers did gain many advantages over them. And thus ended the fifteenth year. And thus were the people in a state of many afflictions; and the sword of destruction did hang over them, insomuch that they were about to be struck down by it, and this because of their iniquity.

2 And now it came to pass that in the sixteenth year[18] from the coming of Mashiach, Lachoneus, the governor of the land,

---

16 Alma 21:6-15   17 2 Nefi 4:4   18 ~15 CE. The Nefites began to reckon their time from the sign of Mashiach's birth (3 Nefi 1:9). Because there was no "year 0," the sign was given

received a letter from the leader and the governor of this band of robbers. And these are the words which were written, saying, Lachoneus, most noble and chief governor of the land, behold, I write this letter unto you and do give unto you exceedingly great praise because of your firmness, and also the firmness of your people, in maintaining that which you suppose to be your right and liberty. Yes, you do stand well, as if you were supported by the hand of a god in the defense of your liberty, and your property, and your country, or that which you do call so. And it seems a pity unto me, most noble Lachoneus, that you should be so foolish and vain as to suppose that you can stand against so many brave men who are at my command, who do now at this time stand in their arms and do await with great anxiety for the word, Go down upon the Nefites and destroy them. And I, knowing of their unconquerable spirit, having proved them in the field of battle, and knowing of their everlasting hatred towards you because of the many wrongs which you have done unto them, therefore if they should come down against you, they would visit you with utter destruction. Therefore, I have written this letter, sealing it with my own hand, feeling for your welfare because of your firmness in that which you believe to be right, and your noble spirit in the field of battle.

2 Therefore, I write unto you desiring that you would yield up unto this my people your cities, your lands, and your possessions, rather than that they should visit you with the sword and that destruction should come upon you. Or in other words, yield yourselves up unto us and unite with us, and become acquainted with our secret works[19] and become our brothers, that you may be like unto us — not our slaves, but our brothers and partners in all our substance. And behold, I swear unto you, if you will do this with an oath, you shall not be destroyed. But if you will not do this, I swear unto you with an oath that on the next month I will command that my armies shall come down against you, and they shall not stay their hand and shall spare not, but shall slay you and shall let fall the sword upon you, yes, even until you shall become extinct. And behold, I am Giddianhi, and I am the governor of this the secret society of Gaddianton, which

---

in 1 BCE. Therefore, one year after the sign, began the year 1 CE. "In the sixteenth year" means that 15 years had been completed since the sign, but 16 years had not. Hence, the proper notation is 15 CE.   **19** Cheleman 2:32–33

society and the works thereof I know to be good; and they are of an ancient[20] date, and they have been handed down unto us. And I write this letter unto you, Lachoneus, and I hope that you will deliver up your lands and your possessions without the shedding of blood, that this my people may recover their rights and government, who have dissented away from you because of your wickedness in retaining from them their rights of government. And except you do this, I will avenge their wrongs. I am Giddianhi.

3 And now it came to pass when Lachoneus received this letter, he was exceedingly astonished because of the boldness of Giddianhi in demanding the possession of the land of the Nefites, and also of threatening the people and avenging the wrongs of those that had received no wrong, except it were they had wronged themselves by dissenting away unto those wicked and abominable robbers. And now behold, this Lachoneus, the governor, was a just man, and could not be frightened by the demands and the threatenings of a robber. Therefore, he did not hearken to the letter of Giddianhi, the governor of the robbers, but he did cause that his people should cry unto YHWH for strength against the time that the robbers should come down against them. Yes, he sent a proclamation among all the people that they should gather together their women and their children, their flocks and their herds, and all their substance except it were their land, unto one place. And he caused that fortifications should be built round about them and the strength thereof should be exceedingly great. And he caused that there should be armies, both of the Nefites and of the Lamanites (or of all them who were numbered among the Nefites) that should be placed as guards round about, to watch them and to guard them from the robbers, day and night. Yes, he said unto them, As YHWH lives, except you repent of all your iniquities and cry unto YHWH, that they would in no way be delivered out of the hands of those Gaddianton robbers. And so great and marvelous were the words and prophecies of Lachoneus that they did cause fear to come upon all the people; and they did exert themselves in their might to do according to the words of Lachoneus.

4 And it came to pass that Lachoneus did appoint chief captains over all the armies of the Nefites to command them at the time that

---

20 'Eter 3:15-19

the robbers should come down out of the wilderness against them. Now the most eminent among all the chief captains and the great commander of all the armies of the Nefites was appointed, and his name was Gidgiddoni. Now it was the custom among all the Nefites to appoint for their chief captains, except it were in their times of wickedness, someone that had the spirit of revelation, and also of prophecy.[21] Therefore, this Gidgiddoni was a great prophet among them, and also was the chief judge.

5 Now the people said unto Gidgiddoni, Pray unto YHWH, and let us go up upon the mountains and into the wilderness, that we may fall upon the robbers and destroy them in their own lands. But Gidgiddoni said unto them, YHWH forbid; for if we should go up against them, YHWH would deliver us into their hands. Therefore, we will prepare ourselves in the center of our lands, and we will gather all our armies together, and we will not go against them, but we will wait till they shall come against us. Therefore, as YHWH lives, if we do this, he will deliver them into our hands.

6 And it came to pass in the seventeenth year, in the latter end of the year, the proclamation of Lachoneus had gone forth throughout all the face of the land, and they had taken their horses, and their chariots, and their cattle, and all their flocks, and their herds, and their grain, and all their substance, and did march forth by thousands and by tens of thousands, until they had all gone forth to the place which had been appointed that they should gather themselves together to defend themselves against their enemies. And the land which was appointed was the land of Zerach'mla and the land which was between the land of Zerach'mla and the land Bountiful, yes, to the line which was between the land Bountiful and the land Desolation. And there were a great many thousand people who were called Nefites, who did gather themselves together in this land. Now Lachoneus did cause that they should gather themselves together in the land southward because of the great curse which was upon the land northward; and they did fortify themselves against their enemies. And they did dwell in one land and in one body, and they did fear the words which had been spoken by Lachoneus, insomuch that they did repent of all their sins. And they did put up their prayers unto

---

21 Ya'akov 3:2; Alma 6:7; 12:1; 20:1; 3 Nefi 13:8

YHWH their Elohim that he would deliver them in the time that their enemies should come down against them to battle. And they were exceedingly sorrowful because of their enemy. And Gidgiddoni did cause that they should make weapons of war of every kind, that they should be strong with armor, and with shields, and with bucklers, after the manner of his instruction.

7 And it came to pass that in the latter end of the eighteenth year,[22] those armies of robbers had prepared for battle, and began to come down, and to rush forth from the hills, and out of the mountains, and the wilderness, and their strongholds, and their secret places, and began to take possession of the lands, both which were in the land south and which were in the land north, and began to take possession of all the lands which had been deserted by the Nefites and the cities which had been left desolate. But behold, there were no wild beasts nor game in those lands which had been deserted by the Nefites, and there was no game for the robbers except it were in the wilderness. And the robbers could not exist except it were in the wilderness, for the want of food; for the Nefites had left their lands desolate and had gathered their flocks, and their herds, and all their substance, and they were in one body. Therefore, there was no chance for the robbers to plunder and to obtain food except it were to come up in open battle against the Nefites. And the Nefites being in one body and having so great a number, and having reserved for themselves provisions, and horses, and cattle, and flocks of every kind, that they might subsist for the space of seven years,[23] in the which time they did hope to destroy the robbers from off the face of the land. And thus the eighteenth year did pass away.

8 And it came to pass that in the nineteenth year, Giddianhi found that it was expedient that he should go up to battle against the Nefites, for there was no way that they could subsist except it were to plunder, and rob, and murder. And they dared not spread themselves upon the face of the land insomuch that they could raise grain, for fear that the Nefites should come upon them and slay them. Therefore, Giddianhi gave commandment unto his armies that in this year they should go up to battle against the Nefites.

---

22 ~17 CE   23 Gen. 41:36; 3 Nefi 2:12

9 And it came to pass that they did come up to battle, and it was in the sixth month. And behold, great and terrible was the day that they did come up to battle. And they were girded about after the manner of robbers, and they had a lambskin about their loins, and they were dyed in blood, and their heads were shorn, and they had headplates upon them. And great and terrible was the appearance of the armies of Giddianhi because of their armor and because of their being dyed in blood. And it came to pass that the armies of the Nefites, when they saw the appearance of the army of Giddianhi, had all fallen to the earth and did lift their cries to YHWH their Elohim that he would spare them and deliver them out of the hands of their enemies. And it came to pass that when the armies of Giddianhi saw this, they began to shout with a loud voice because of their joy, for they had supposed that the Nefites had fallen with fear because of the terror of their armies. But in this thing they were disappointed, for the Nefites did not fear them, but they did fear their Elohim and did supplicate him for protection. Therefore, when the armies of Giddianhi did rush upon them, they were prepared to meet them, yes, in the strength of YHWH [24] they did receive them.

10 And the battle commenced in this the sixth month, and great and terrible was the battle thereof, yes, great and terrible was the slaughter thereof, insomuch that there never was known so great a slaughter among all the people of Lechi since he left Yerushalayim. And despite the threatenings and the oaths which Giddianhi had made, behold, the Nefites did beat them insomuch that they did fall back from before them.

11 And it came to pass that Gidgiddoni commanded that his armies should pursue them as far as to the borders of the wilderness and that they should not spare any that should fall into their hands by the way. And thus they did pursue them and did slay them to the borders of the wilderness, even until they had fulfilled the commandment of Gidgiddoni. And it came to pass that Giddianhi, who had stood and fought with boldness, was pursued as he fled; and being weary because of his much fighting, he was overtaken and slain. And thus was the end of Giddianhi the robber. And it came to pass that the armies of the Nefites did return again to their place of security.

---

24 Words of M'raman 1:5; Moshiyah 6:5, 11, 12; Alma 21:8; 27:7; 28:3; M'raman 1:8

¹² And it came to pass that this nineteenth year did pass away and the robbers did not come again to battle, neither did they come again in the twentieth year. But in the twenty and first year, they did not come up to battle, but they came up on all sides to lay siege[25] round about the people of Nefi; for they did suppose that if they should cut off the people of Nefi from their lands and should hem them in on every side, and if they should cut them off from all their outward privileges, that they could cause them to yield themselves up according to their wishes. Now they had appointed unto themselves another leader, whose name was Zemnarihah; therefore, it was Zemnarihah that did cause that this siege should take place. But behold, this was an advantage unto the Nefites, for it was impossible for the robbers to lay siege sufficiently long to have any effect upon the Nefites because of their many provisions which they had laid up in store, and because of the scantiness of provisions among the robbers. For behold, they had nothing except it were meat for their subsistence, which meat they did obtain in the wilderness. And it came to pass that the wild game became scarce in the wilderness, insomuch that the robbers were about to perish with hunger. And the Nefites were continually marching out by day and by night and falling upon their armies, and cutting them off by thousands and by tens of thousands. And thus it became the desire of the people of Zemnarihah to withdraw from their design because of the great destruction which came upon them by night and by day.

¹³ And it came to pass that Zemnarihah did give command unto his people that they should withdraw themselves from the siege and to march into the furthermost parts of the land northward. And now Gidgiddoni, being aware of their design, and knowing of their weakness because of the want of food and the great slaughter which had been made among them, therefore he did send out his armies in the nighttime and did cut off the way of their retreat, and did place his armies in the way of their retreat. And this did they do in the nighttime, and made their march beyond the robbers, so that the next day, when the robbers began their march, they were met by the armies of the Nefites, both in their front and in their rear. And

---

25 Isa. 29:3; Ezek. 4:2–8; 'Eter 6:7

the robbers who were on the south were also cut off in their places of retreat. And all these things were done by command of Gidgiddoni.

14 And there were many thousands who did yield themselves up prisoners unto the Nefites, and the remainder of them were slain; and their leader, Zemnarihah, was taken and **hanged upon a tree**,[26] yes, even upon the top thereof until he was dead. And when they had hanged him until he was dead, they did fell the tree[27] to the earth and did cry with a loud voice, saying, May YHWH preserve his people in righteousness and in holiness of heart, that they may cause to be felled to the earth all who shall seek to slay them because of power and secret conspiracies, even as this man has been felled to the earth! And they did rejoice and cry again with one voice,[28] saying, May the Elohim of Avraham, and the Elohim of Yitz'chak, and the Elohim of Ya'akov, protect this people in righteousness so long as they shall call on the name of their Elohim for protection! And it came to pass that they did break forth, all as one, in singing and praising their Elohim for the great thing which he had done for them in preserving them from falling into the hands of their enemies. Yes, they did cry, Hoshianna to the El Elyon! And they did cry, Blessed be the name of Adonai YHWH Tzva'ot, the El Elyon! And their hearts were swollen with joy unto the gushing out of many tears because of the great goodness of Elohim in delivering them out of the hands of their enemies. And they knew it was because of their repentance and their humility that they had been delivered from an everlasting destruction. And now behold, there was not a living soul among all the people of the Nefites who did doubt in the least the words of all the holy prophets[29] which had been spoken, for they knew that they must necessarily be fulfilled. And they knew it must be true that Mashiach had come, because of

---

26 Deut. 21:22   27 This follows the ancient Jewish custom of felling the tree after hanging. We read in the Torah, "And if a man have committed a sin worthy of death, and he be put to death, and you hang him on a tree: His body shall not remain all night upon the tree, but you shall in any wise bury him that day; (for he that is hanged is accursed of Elohim;) that your land be not defiled, which YHWH your Elohim gives you for an inheritance" (Deut. 21:22-23). The Hebrew says, literally, "burying you shall bury him/it." The repetition of the verb is taken by the Talmud to mean that the tree is felled and also buried (b.Sanhedrin 46b). Maimonides comments, "In order that it should not serve as a sad reminder, people saying: 'This is the tree in which so and so was hanged'" (Maimonides, b.Sanhedrin, XV, 9).   28 Ex. 24:3; Moshiyah 2:1; 3:1; Alma 20:12; 3 Nefi 9:6   29 Num. 24:17; Deut. 18:15; Isa. 7:14; 9:6; 25:9; 50:6; 53:5; Hos. 11:1; Zech. 11:13; 13:6; Mal. 3:1; Ps. 22:17 (16); 118:22; 1 Nefi 1:5; 2 Nefi 11:6; Moshiyah 8:2; Cheleman 3:9; 5:10, 13; 3 Nefi 4:11

the many signs[30] which had been given according to the words of the prophets. And because of the things which had come to pass already, they knew it must be that all things should come to pass according to that which had been spoken. Therefore, they did abandon all their sins, and their abominations, and their whoredoms, and did serve Elohim with all diligence, day and night.

15 And now it came to pass that when they had taken all the robbers prisoners, insomuch that none did escape who were not slain, they did cast their prisoners into prison and did cause the word of Elohim to be preached unto them. And as many as would repent of their sins and enter into a covenant that they would murder no more were set at liberty. But as many as there were who did not enter into a covenant, and who did still continue to have those secret murders[31] in their hearts, yes, as many as were found breathing out threatenings against their brothers, were condemned and punished according to the law. And thus they did put an end to all those wicked, and secret, and abominable conspiracies in the which there was so much wickedness and so many murders committed. And thus had the twenty and second year[32] passed away, and the twenty and third year also, and the twenty and fourth, and the twenty and fifth. And thus had twenty and five years passed away.

16 And there had many things transpired which, in the eyes of some, would be great and marvelous; nevertheless, they cannot all be written in this book, yes, this book cannot contain even a hundredth part of what was done among so many people in the space of twenty and five years. But behold, there are records which do contain all the proceedings of this people,[33] and a shorter but a true account was given by Nefi; therefore, I have made my record of these things according to the record of Nefi which was engraved on the plates which were called the plates of Nefi.[34]

17 And behold, I do make this record on plates which I have made with my own hands. And behold, I am called M'raman,[35] being called after the land of M'raman,[36] the land in which Alma did establish the assembly among this people, yes, the first assembly which was

---

30 Cheleman 5:10, 20   **31** Alma 17:12; Cheleman 2:30, 35; 3 Nefi 4:6   **32** ~ 22 CE   **33** Cheleman 2:4   **34** 1 Nefi 2:14; Yahram 1:6; Words of M'raman 1:2, 4; Moshiyah 1:1; 12:3; Alma 17:7; 4 Nefi 1:4; M'raman 1:1, 7; 3:2   **35** Words of M'raman 1:2-4   **36** Moshiyah 9:6; Alma 3:1

established among them after their transgression. Behold, I am a talmid of Yeshua HaMashiach, the Son of Elohim. I have been called of him³⁷ to declare his word among his people, that they might have everlasting life. And it has become expedient that I, according to the will of Elohim — that the prayers of those who have gone before, who were the holy ones, should be fulfilled according to their faith — should make a record³⁸ of these things which have been done, yes, a small record of that which has taken place from the time that Lechi left Yerushalayim, even down until the present time. Therefore, I do make my record from the accounts which have been given by those who were before me until the commencement of my day, and then do I make a record of the things which I have seen with my own eyes. And I know the record which I make to be a just and a true record; nevertheless, there are many things which, according to our language,³⁹ we are not able to write.

18 And now I make an end of my saying which is of myself, and proceed to give my account of the things which have been before me. I am M'raman and a pure descendant of Lechi.⁴⁰ I have reason to bless my Elohim and my Savior, Yeshua HaMashiach, that he brought our fathers out of the land of Yerushalayim — and no one knew it, except it were himself and those whom he brought out of that land — and that he has given me and my people so much knowledge unto the salvation of our souls. Surely he has blessed the house of Ya'akov, and has been merciful unto the seed of Yosef,⁴¹ and inasmuch as the children of Lechi have kept his mitzvot, he has blessed them and prospered them according to his word. Yes, and surely shall he again bring a remnant of the seed of Yosef to the knowledge of YHWH their Elohim. And as surely as YHWH lives will **he gather in from the four quarters of the earth**⁴² all the remnant of the seed of Ya'akov who are scattered abroad upon all the face of the earth. And as he has covenanted with all the house of Ya'akov, even so shall the covenant with which he has covenanted with the house of Ya'akov be fulfilled, in his own due time, unto the restoring all the house of Ya'akov unto the knowledge of the covenant that he has covenanted with them.⁴³

---

37 M'roni 7:2 38 Enosh 1:4; Words of M'raman 1:2-4 39 1 Nefi 1:1; Moshiyah 1:1 40 1 Nefi 1:22 41 Gen. 37-50; Deut. 33:13-17; 1 Nefi 1:22; 2:1; 4:3; 2 Nefi 2:2-7; Ya'akov 2:7; Alma 8:1; 21:9; 3 Nefi 4:11; 'Eter 6:2-4 42 Deut. 30:4; Isa. 11:12; 54:7; Zech. 2:6 43 Gen. 13:15-18; Jer. 31:30-33 (31-34); 1 Nefi 3:26-29; 4:3; 2 Nefi 2:2-7; 6:1; M'raman 4:3-4, 11; 'Eter 6:3; M'roni 10:6

And then shall they know their Redeemer, who is Yeshua HaMashiach, the Son of Elohim; and then shall they be **gathered in from the four quarters of the earth** unto their own lands, from where they have been dispersed; yes, as YHWH lives, so shall it be. Amen.

3 And now it came to pass that the people of the Nefites did all return to their own lands in the twenty and sixth year,[44] every man with his family, his flocks and his herds, his horses and his cattle, and all things whatsoever did belong unto them. And it came to pass that they had not eaten up all their provisions, therefore they did take with them all that they had not devoured of all their grain of every kind, and their gold, and their silver, and all their precious things, and they did return to their own lands and their possessions, both on the north and on the south, both on the land northward and on the land southward. And they granted unto those robbers who had entered into a covenant to keep the shalom of the land (who were desirous to remain Lamanites) lands according to their numbers, that they might have, with their labors, the means to subsist upon. And thus they did establish shalom in all the land, and they began again to prosper and to grow great. And the twenty and sixth and seventh years passed away and there was great order in the land, and they had formed their laws according to equity and justice. And now there was nothing in all the land to hinder the people from prospering continually except they should fall into transgression. And now it was Gidgiddoni, and the judge Lachoneus, and those who had been appointed leaders who had established this great shalom in the land.

2 And it came to pass that there were many cities built anew, and there were many old cities repaired, and there were many highways cast up and many roads made which led from city to city, and from land to land, and from place to place. And thus passed away the twenty and eighth year, and the people had continual shalom. But it came to pass in the twenty and ninth year, there began to be some disputes among the people; and some were lifted up unto pride[45] and boasting because of their exceedingly great riches, yes, even unto great persecution, for there were many merchants in the land, and also many lawyers and many officers. And the people began to

---

44 ~25 CE   45 Ya'akov 2:4–6; M'raman 4:5

be distinguished by ranks according to their riches and their chance for learning—yes, some were ignorant because of their poverty, and others did receive great learning because of their riches. Some were lifted up in pride, and others were exceedingly humble; some did return insults for insults, while others would receive insults, and persecution, and all manner of afflictions, and would not turn and revile again,[46] but were humble and penitent before Elohim. And thus there became a great inequality in all the land, insomuch that the assembly began to be broken up, yes, insomuch that in the thirtieth year, the assembly was broken up in all the land, except it were among a few of the Lamanites who were converted unto the true faith; and they would not depart from it, for they were firm, and steadfast, and immovable, willing with all diligence to keep the mitzvot of YHWH.

3 Now the cause of this iniquity of the people was this: HaSatan had great power to stir up[47] the people to do all manner of iniquity and to puff them up with pride, tempting them to seek for power, and authority, and riches, and the vain things of the world. And thus HaSatan did lead away the hearts of the people to do all manner of iniquity; therefore, they had only enjoyed shalom but a few years. And thus in the commencement of the thirtieth year—the people having been delivered up for the space of a long time to be carried about by the temptations of HaSatan, wherever he desired to carry them, and to do whatsoever iniquity he desired they should—and thus in the commencement of this, the thirtieth year, they were in a state of awful wickedness. Now they did not sin ignorantly, for they knew the will of Elohim concerning them, for it had been taught unto them; therefore, they did willfully rebel against Elohim.

4 And now it was in the days of Lachoneus, the son of Lachoneus—for Lachoneus did fill the seat of his father and did govern the people that year—and there began to be men, inspired from Heaven and sent forth, standing among the people in all the land, preaching and testifying boldly of the sins and iniquities of the people, and testifying unto them concerning the redemption which YHWH would make for his people, or in other words, the resurrection[48] of Mashiach; and they did testify boldly of his death and

---

46 3 Nefi 5:30; 4 Nefi 1:5–6 **47** 3 Nefi 5:8; M'raman 2:1 **48** 1 Sam. 2:6; Isa. 25:8; 26:19; Ezek. 37:12; Hos. 13:14; Job 14:14; 19:26; Dan. 12:2; 2 Nefi 1:6; 6:2, 4, 7; 11:10; Moshiyah 8:2, 9–11, 14; Alma 9:2, 6; 19:4–9; Cheleman 5:12; M'raman 4:7

sufferings. Now there were many of the people who were exceedingly angry because of those who testified of these things; and those who were angry were chiefly the chief judges and they who had been Kohanim HaGadolim and lawyers; yes, all those who were lawyers were angry with those who testified of these things. Now there was no lawyer, nor judge, nor Kohen HaGadol, that could have power to condemn anyone to death, except their condemnation was signed by the governor of the land. Now there were many of those who testified of the things pertaining to Mashiach who testified boldly, who were taken and put to death secretly by the judges, that the knowledge of their death came not unto the governor of the land until after their death.[49] Now behold, this was contrary to the laws of the land, that any man should be put to death except they had power from the governor of the land. Therefore, a complaint came up unto the land of Zerach'mla to the governor of the land against these judges who had condemned the prophets of YHWH unto death not according to the law.

5 Now it came to pass that they were taken and brought up before the judge, to be judged of their crime which they had done, according to the law which had been given by the people. Now it came to pass that those judges had many friends and kindreds, and the remainder — yes, even almost all the lawyers and the Kohanim HaGadolim — did gather themselves together and unite with the kinsfolk of those judges who were to be tried according to the law. And they did enter into a covenant one with another, yes, even into that covenant which was given by them of old,[50] which covenant was given and administered by HaSatan to combine against all righteousness. Therefore, they did combine against the people of YHWH and enter into a covenant to destroy them and to deliver those who were guilty of murder from the grasp of justice which was about to be administered according to the law. And they did set at defiance[51] the law and the rights of their country. And they did covenant one with another to destroy the governor and to establish a king over the land, that the land should no more be at liberty, but should be subject unto kings.[52]

---

49 3 Nefi 4:6 **50** 'Eter 3:17 **51** Alma 28:1 **52** 2 Nefi 7:2

⁶ Now behold, I will show unto you that they did not establish a king over the land, but in this same year, yes, the thirtieth year,⁵³ they did destroy upon the judgment seat, yes, did murder the chief judge of the land. And the people were divided one against another and they did separate one from another into tribes, every man according to his family, and his kinsfolk, and friends; and thus they did destroy the government of the land. And every tribe did appoint a chief or a leader over them; and thus they became tribes and leaders of tribes. Now behold, there was no man among them except he had much family and many kinsfolk and friends, therefore their tribes became exceedingly great. Now all this was done, and there were no wars as yet among them. And all this iniquity had come upon the people because they did yield themselves unto the power of HaSatan. And the regulations of the government were destroyed because of the secret conspiracy⁵⁴ of the friends and the kinsfolk of those who murdered the prophets. And they did cause a great contention in the land, insomuch that the more righteous part of the people — although they had nearly all become wicked, yes, there were but few⁵⁵ righteous men among them — and thus six years had not passed away since the more part of the people had turned from their righteousness, like the dog to his vomit⁵⁶ or like the sow to her wallowing in the mire.

⁷ Now this secret conspiracy, which had brought such great iniquity upon the people, did gather themselves together and did place at their head a man whom they did call Ya'akov, and they did call him their king; therefore, he became a king over this wicked band. And he was one of the most eminent who had given his voice against the prophets who testified of Yeshua. And it came to pass that they were not so strong in numbers as the tribes of the people, who were united together — except it were their leaders who did establish their laws, every one according to his tribe — nevertheless, they were enemies; though they were not a righteous people, yet they were united in the hatred of those who had entered into a covenant to destroy the government. Therefore Ya'akov, seeing that their enemies were more numerous than they, he being the king of the band, therefore he commanded his people that they should take their flight into the northernmost part of the land, and there build up unto themselves a

---

53 ~29 CE   54 2 Nefi 6:3   55 2 Nefi 12:2   56 Prov. 26:11

kingdom[57] until they were joined by dissenters — for he flattered them that there would be many dissenters — and they become sufficiently strong to contend with the tribes of the people; and they did so. And so speedy was their march that it could not be impeded until they had gone forth out of the reach of the people. And thus ended the thirtieth year; and thus were the affairs of the people of Nefi.

8 And it came to pass in the thirty and first year that they were divided into tribes, every man according to his family, kinsfolk, and friends. Nevertheless, they had come to an agreement that they would not go to war one with another. But they were not united as to their laws and their manner of government, for they were established according to the minds of those who were their chiefs and their leaders. But they did establish very strict laws that one tribe should not trespass against another, insomuch that in some degree they had shalom in the land. Nevertheless, their hearts were turned from YHWH their Elohim, and they did stone the prophets and did cast them out[58] from among them.

9 And it came to pass that Nefi, having been visited by angels, and also by the voice of YHWH, therefore having seen angels,[59] and being an eyewitness, and having had power given unto him, that he might know concerning the ministry of Mashiach, and also being an eyewitness to the quick return of the people from righteousness unto their wickedness and abominations, therefore being grieved for the hardness of their hearts and the blindness of their minds, he went forth among them in that same year and began to testify boldly repentance and remission of sins through faith[60] on Adonai Yeshua HaMashiach. And he did minister many things unto them, and all of them cannot be written, and a part of them would not suffice; therefore, they are not written in this book. And Nefi did teach with power and with great authority.[61]

10 And it came to pass that they were angry with him, even because he had greater power than they, for it was not possible that they could disbelieve his words. For so great was his faith on Adonai Yeshua HaMashiach that angels did minister unto him daily, and in the name of Yeshua did he cast out demons and unclean spirits;[62] and even his

---

57 3 Nefi 3:5 58 1 Nefi 1:5; Cheleman 5:6-8; 3 Nefi 4:5-6; 'Eter 4:7 59 1 Nefi 3:8; Moshiyah 1:13; 2:1 60 Matt. 17:20; Rom. 4:16; Heb. 11-12; 2 Nefi 13:5; Alma 16:26-30; 'Eter 5:2-3 61 Moshiyah 7:20; 9:10; 11:3; Alma 12:1 62 Zech. 13:2; 1 Nefi 3:13

brother did he raise from the dead,[63] after he had been stoned and suffered death by the people. And the people saw it and did witness it and were angry with him because of his power; and he did also do many more miracles in the sight of the people in the name of Yeshua.

11 And it came to pass that the thirty and first year did pass away and there were but few who were converted unto YHWH. But as many as were converted did truly signify unto the people that they had been visited by the power and Ruach Elohim which was in Yeshua HaMashiach, in whom they believed. And as many as had demons cast out from them and were healed of their sicknesses and their infirmities did truly manifest unto the people that they had been worked upon by the Ruach Elohim and had been healed,[64] and they did show forth signs also, and did do some miracles[65] among the people.

12 And thus passed away the thirty and second year also. And Nefi did cry unto the people in the commencement of the thirty and third year, and he did preach unto them repentance and remission of sins. Now I would have you remember also that there were none who were brought unto repentance who were not washed by immersion with water. Therefore, there were ordained of Nefi men unto this ministry, that all such as should come unto them should be immersed with water,[66] and this as a witness and a testimony before Elohim and unto the people that they had repented and received a remission of their sins. And there were many in the commencement of this year that were immersed unto repentance; and thus the more part of the year did pass away.

4 And now it came to pass that according to our record – and we know our record to be true, for behold, it was a just man who did keep the record, for he truly did many miracles in the name of Yeshua, and there was not any man who could do a miracle in the name of Yeshua except he were cleansed every whit from his iniquity – and now it came to pass, if there was no mistake made by this man in the reckoning of our time,[67] the thirty and third year[68] had passed

---

[63] 3 Nefi 9:2; 4 Nefi 1:2   [64] 1 Nefi 3:13; 2 Nefi 11:5; Alma 10:14; 3 Nefi 8:2-3; 4 Nefi 1:2
[65] Cheleman 5:18, 21; 3 Nefi 4:1; 9:5; 13:8; 4 Nefi 1:2, 6; 'Eter 5:2-3   [66] 2 Nefi 6:7; 13:1-2; Cheleman 2:7, 19; 5:17-18; 3 Nefi 5:10; 12:3   [67] 3 Nefi 1:9   [68] ~33 CE

away. And the people began to look with great earnestness for the sign which had been given by the prophet Sh'mu'el, the Lamanite, yes, for the time that there should be darkness for the space of three days over the face of the land.[69] And there began to be great doubtings and disputations among the people, even though so many signs had been given.

2 And it came to pass in the thirty and fourth year, in the first month, on the fourteenth day of the month, there arose a great storm, such an one as never had been known in all the land; and there was also a great and terrible tempest; and there was terrible thunder; insomuch that it did shake the whole earth as if it was about to divide asunder. And there were exceedingly sharp lightnings, such as never had been known in all the land.[70] And the city of Zerach'mla did take fire; and the city of M'roni did sink into the depths of the sea and the inhabitants thereof were drowned. And the earth was carried up upon the city of M'ronihah, that in the place of the city thereof, there became a great mountain. And there was a great and terrible destruction in the land southward. But behold, there was greater and more terrible destruction in the land northward; for behold, the whole face of the land was changed because of the tempests, and the whirlwinds, and the thunderings, and the lightnings, and the exceedingly great quaking of the whole earth. And the highways were broken up, and the level roads were spoiled, and many smooth places became rough. And many great and notable cities were sunk, and many were burned, and many were shaken till the buildings thereof had fallen to the earth and the inhabitants thereof were slain, and the places were left desolate. And there were some cities which remained, but the damage thereof was exceedingly great, and there were many in them who were slain. And there were some who were carried away in the whirlwind, and where they went, no man knows, except they know that they were carried away. And thus the face of the whole earth became deformed because of the tempests, and the thunderings, and the lightnings, and the quaking of the earth. And behold, the rocks were split in two, yes, they were broken up upon

---

[69] Cheleman 5:13 [70] The Hebrew word here was likely *eretz* (ארץ), which can mean "land" or "earth." It is used in parallel later in the paragraph, in the phrase, "And thus the face of the whole earth."

the face of the whole earth, insomuch that they were found in broken fragments, and in seams, and in cracks, upon all the face of the land.

3 And it came to pass that when the thunderings, and the lightnings, and the storm, and the tempest, and the quakings of the earth did cease — for behold, they did last for about the space of three hours; and it was said by some that the time was greater, nevertheless, all these great and terrible things were done in about the space of three hours — and then, behold, there was darkness upon the face of the land.

4 And it came to pass that there was thick darkness upon the face of all the land, insomuch that the inhabitants thereof who had not fallen could feel the vapor of darkness.[71] And there could be no light because of the darkness, neither candles, neither torches, neither could there be fire kindled with their fine and exceedingly dry wood, so that there could not be any light at all. And there was not any light seen, neither fire, nor glimmer, neither the sun, nor the moon, nor the stars, for so great were the mists of darkness which were upon the face of the land.

5 And it came to pass that it did last for the space of three days[72] that there was no light seen; and there was great mourning, and howling, and weeping among all the people continually, yes, great were the groanings of the people because of the darkness and the great destruction which had come upon them. And in one place they were heard to cry, saying, Oh that we had repented before this great and terrible day, and then would our brothers have been spared, and they would not have been burned in that great city Zerach'mla. And in another place they were heard to cry and mourn, saying, Oh that we had repented before this great and terrible day and had not killed and stoned the prophets and cast them out, then would our mothers, and our fair daughters, and our children have been spared and not have been buried up in that great city M'ronihah. And thus were the howlings of the people great and terrible.

6 And it came to pass that there was a voice heard among all the inhabitants of the earth[73] upon all the face of this land, crying, Woe, woe, woe unto this people. Woe unto the inhabitants of the whole

---

71 1 Nefi 5:37   72 Cheleman 5:13; 3 Nefi 4:1   73 The Hebrew word here was likely *eretz* (ארץ), which can mean "land" or "earth."

earth except they shall repent, for HaSatan laughs and his angels rejoice because of the slain of the fair sons and daughters of my people; and it is because of their iniquity and abominations that they are fallen. Behold, that great city Zerach'mla have I burned with fire, and the inhabitants thereof. And behold, that great city M'roni have I caused to be sunk in the depths of the sea, and the inhabitants thereof to be drowned. And behold, that great city M'ronihah have I covered with earth, and the inhabitants thereof, to hide their iniquities and their abominations from before my face, that the blood of the prophets and the k'doshim shall not come up anymore unto me against them. And behold, the city of Gilgal have I caused to be sunk, and the inhabitants thereof, to be buried up in the depths of the earth; yes, and the city Onihah and the inhabitants thereof, and the city of Mocum and the inhabitants thereof, and the city of Yerushalayim and the inhabitants thereof. And waters have I caused to come up in the place thereof, to hide their wickedness and abominations from before my face, that the blood of the prophets and the k'doshim shall not come up anymore unto me against them. And behold, the city of Gadiandi, and the city of Gadiomnah, and the city of Ya'akov, and the city Gimgimno — all these have I caused to be sunk, and made hills and valleys in the places thereof; and the inhabitants thereof have I buried up in the depths of the earth, to hide their wickedness and abominations from before my face, that the blood of the prophets and the k'doshim should not come up anymore unto me against them. And behold, that great city Ya'akov-ugath, which was inhabited by the people of king Ya'akov,[74] have I caused to be burned with fire because of their sins and their wickedness, which was above all the wickedness of the whole earth because of their secret murders and conspiracies, for it was they that did destroy the shalom of my people and the government of the land. Therefore, I did cause them to be burned to destroy them from before my face, that the blood of the prophets and the k'doshim should not come up unto me anymore against them. And behold, the city of Laman, and the city of Yosh, and the city of Gad, and the city of Kishcumen have I caused to be burned with fire, and the inhabitants thereof, because of their wickedness in casting out the prophets and stoning them

---

[74] 3 Nefi 3:7

whom I did send to declare unto them concerning their wickedness and their abominations. And because they did cast them all out, that there were none righteous among them, I did send down fire and destroy them, that their wickedness and abominations might be hid from before my face, that the blood of the prophets and the k'doshim whom I sent among them might not cry unto me from the ground against them. And many great destructions have I caused to come upon this land and upon this people because of their wickedness and their abominations.

7 O all you that are spared because you were more righteous than they, will you not now return unto me, and repent of your sins, and be converted, that I may heal you? Yes, truly I say unto you, if you will come unto me, you shall have Eternal life. Behold, my arm of mercy is extended towards you, and whosoever will come, him will I receive; and blessed are those who come unto me. Behold, I am Yeshua HaMashiach, the Son of Elohim. **I created the heavens and the earth**,[75] and all things that in them are. I was with the Father from the beginning. I am in the Father and the Father in me, and in me has the Father glorified his name. I came unto my own and my own received me not. And the scriptures concerning my coming are fulfilled. And as many as have received me, to them have I given to become the sons of Elohim; and even so will I to as many as shall believe on my name. For behold, by me redemption comes, and in me is the Torah of Moshe fulfilled.[76] I am the light and the life of the world. I am Alef and Tav,[77] the beginning and the end. And you shall offer up unto me no more the shedding of blood,[78] yes, your sacrifices and your burnt offerings shall be done away,[79] for I will accept none of your sacrifices and your burnt offerings;[80] and you shall offer for

---

[75] Gen. 1:1   [76] See "What does it mean to fulfill the Torah?" footnote to 2 Nefi 11:8.   [77] א and ת, the first and last letters in the Hebrew alphabet, expressing the idea of the beginning and the end.   [78] The Hebrew may have been לא יותר שפיכות דמים. The Hebrew word *yoter* יותר (Strong's 3148) can mean "more" or "greater"; thus, the passage would be understood as "no greater shedding of blood." See footnotes to Alma 16:34.   [79] As in 2 Nefi 11:8, the underlying Hebrew may have been *chalaf* חלף (Strong's 2498), which can also be understood as "renewed." Yosef ben Yosef said: "These sacrifices, as well as every ordinance belonging to the priesthood, will, when the Temple of the Lord shall be built, and the sons of Levi be purified, be fully restored and attended to in all their powers, ramifications, and blessings..." Cook, L.W. & Ehat, A.F. (Eds.) (1980) *The Words of Joseph Smith*. Salt Lake City, UT: Bookcraft, p. 43 [quote edited for grammar and punctuation].   [80] The 1830 version has "for I will accept none of your sacrifices and your burnt offerings"; however, in Hebrew this could read as a rhetorical question: "for will I not accept your sacrifices and your burnt offerings?" (See footnote to Moshiyah 8:1.)

a sacrifice unto me a broken heart and a contrite spirit. And whoever comes unto me with a broken heart and a contrite spirit,[81] him will I cleanse with fire and with the Ruach HaKodesh, even as the Lamanites, because of their faith in me at the time of their conversion, were cleansed with fire[82] and with the Ruach HaKodesh and they knew it not. Behold, I have come unto the world to bring redemption unto the world, to save the world from sin. Therefore, whoever repents and comes unto me as a little child, him will I receive, for of such is the kingdom of Elohim.[83] Behold, for such I have laid down my life and have taken it up again; therefore, repent and come unto me you ends of the earth and be saved.

8 And now behold, it came to pass that all the people of the land did hear these sayings and did witness of it. And after these sayings, there was silence in the land for the space of many hours, for so great was the astonishment of the people that they did cease lamenting and howling for the loss of their kinsfolk which had been slain; therefore there was silence in all the land for the space of many hours.

9 And it came to pass that there came a voice[84] again unto the people, and all the people did hear and did witness of it, saying, O you people of these great cities which have fallen, who are descendants of Ya'akov, yes, who are of the house of Isra'el, O you people of the house of Isra'el, how often have I gathered you as a hen gathers her chickens under her wings, and have nourished you! And again, how often would I have gathered you as a hen gathers her chickens under her wings, yes, O you people of the house of Isra'el who have fallen! Yes, O you people of the house of Isra'el, you that dwell at Yerushalayim as you that have fallen, yes, how often would I have gathered you as a hen gathers her chickens, and you would not! O you house of Isra'el whom I have spared, how often will I gather you as a hen gathers her chickens under her wings if you will repent and return unto me with full purpose of heart! But if not, O house of Isra'el, the places of your dwellings shall become desolate until the time of the fulfilling of the covenant[85] to your fathers.

---

81 Isa. 57:15; 66:2; Ps. 34:19 (18); 51:18-19 (16-17); 2 Nefi 1:6; 3:8; Cheleman 3:9; 3 Nefi 5:23; M'raman 1:6; 'Eter 1:19; M'roni 6:1   82 3 Nefi 5:9; 9:2; M'raman 3:5; 'Eter 5:3   83 1 Nefi 4:6; 2 Nefi 13:5; Ya'akov 4:1; Alma 5:5; 4 Nefi 1:3; M'roni 10:4-5   84 3 Nefi 5:2   85 Gen. 13:15-18; Jer. 31:30-33 (31-34); 1 Nefi 3:26-29; 4:3; 2 Nefi 2:2-7; 6:1; M'raman 4:3-4, 11; 'Eter 6:3; M'roni 10:6

¹⁰ And now it came to pass that after the people had heard these words, behold, they began to weep and howl again because of the loss of their kindred and friends. And it came to pass that thus did the three days pass away. And it was in the morning and the darkness dispersed from off the face of the land, and the earth did cease to tremble, and the rocks did cease to split, and the dreadful groanings did cease, and all the tumultuous noises did pass away, and the earth did hold together again that it stood, and the mourning and the weeping and the wailing of the people who were spared alive did cease. And their mourning was turned into joy, and their lamentations into the praise and thanksgiving unto Adonai Yeshua HaMashiach, their Redeemer. And thus far were the scriptures fulfilled which had been spoken by the prophets. And it was the more righteous part of the people who were saved, and it was they who received the prophets and stoned them not, and it was they who had not shed the blood of the k'doshim, who were spared. And they were spared, and were not sunk and buried up in the earth, and they were not drowned in the depths of the sea, and they were not burned by fire, neither were they fallen upon and crushed to death; and they were not carried away in the whirlwind, neither were they overpowered by the vapor of smoke and of darkness.

¹¹ And now whoever reads, let him understand; he that has the scriptures, let him search them, and see, and behold if all these deaths, and destructions by fire, and by smoke, and by tempests and by whirlwinds, and by the opening of the earth to receive them, and all these things are not unto the fulfilling of the prophecies of many of the holy prophets. Behold, I say unto you, yes, many have testified of these things at the coming of Mashiach[86] and were slain because they testified of these things — yes, the prophet Zenos did testify of these things, and also Zenoch spoke concerning these things, because they testified in particular concerning us,[87] who are the remnant[88] of their seed. Behold, our father Ya'akov also testified concerning a remnant of the seed of Yosef. And behold, are not we a remnant of the seed of Yosef?[89] And these things which testify of

---

86 Num. 24:17; Deut. 18:15; Isa. 7:14; 9:6; 25:9; 50:6; 53:5; Hos. 11:1; Zech. 11:13; 13:6; Mal. 3:1; Ps. 22:17 (16); 118:22; 1 Nefi 1:5; 2 Nefi 11:6; Moshiyah 8:2; Cheleman 5:10, 13
87 Cheleman 3:9   88 3 Nefi 2:18; M'raman 3:5; 'Eter 6:3   89 Gen. 37-50; Deut. 33:13-17; 1 Nefi 1:22; 2:1; 4:3; 2 Nefi 2:2-7; Ya'akov 2:7; Alma 21:9; 3 Nefi 4:11; 'Eter 6:2-4

us, are they not written upon the plates of brass[90] which our father Lechi brought out of Yerushalayim? And it came to pass that in the ending of the thirty and fourth year,[91] behold, I will show unto you that the people of Nefi who were spared, and also those who had been called Lamanites who had been spared, did have great favors shown unto them and great blessings poured out upon their heads, insomuch that soon after the ascension of Mashiach into Heaven, he did truly manifest himself unto them, showing his body unto them and ministering unto them; and an account of his ministry shall be given hereafter. Therefore, for this time, I make an end of my sayings.

Yeshua HaMashiach showed himself unto the people of Nefi, as the multitude were gathered together in the land Bountiful, and did minister unto them; and in this manner did he show himself unto them.

5 And now it came to pass that there was a great multitude[92] gathered together of the people of Nefi, round about the Temple which was in the land Bountiful; and they were marveling and wondering one with another, and were showing one to another the great and marvelous change which had taken place. And they were also conversing about this Yeshua HaMashiach, of whom the sign had been given concerning his death.

2 And it came to pass that while they were thus conversing one with another, they heard a voice[93] as if it came out of Heaven. And they cast their eyes round about, for they understood not the voice which they heard; and it was not a harsh voice, neither was it a loud voice. Nevertheless, and despite it being a small voice, it did pierce them that did hear to the center, insomuch that there was no part of their frame that it did not cause to quake, yes, it did pierce them to the very soul and did cause their hearts to burn. And it came to pass that again they heard the voice and they understood it not. And again the third time they did hear the voice and did open their ears to hear it, and their eyes were towards the sound thereof, and they did look steadfastly towards Heaven, from where the sound came.

---

90 1 Nefi 1:10, 22-23; 2 Nefi 3:1; Moshiyah 1:3; 3 Nefi 4:11   91 The destruction at the death of Mashiach occurred "in the thirty and fourth year, in the first month, on the fourteenth day of the month" (3 Nefi 4:2). The record is then silent for approximately 11 months, resuming at this point, "in the ending of the thirty and fourth year."   92 3 Nefi 8:5 "And they were in number about two thousand and five hundred souls, and they did consist of men, women, and children."   93 3 Nefi 4:6, 9

And behold, the third time they did understand the voice which they heard, and it said unto them, Behold my Beloved Son[94] in whom I am well pleased, in whom I have glorified my name; hear you him.

3 And it came to pass, as they understood, they cast their eyes up again towards Heaven. And behold, they saw a man descending out of Heaven, and he was clothed in a white robe, and he came down and stood in the midst of them. And the eyes of the whole multitude were turned upon him and they dared not open their mouths, even one to another, and could not imagine what it meant, for they thought it was an angel that had appeared unto them.

4 And it came to pass that he stretched forth his hand[95] and spoke unto the people, saying, Behold, I am Yeshua HaMashiach, of whom the prophets testified should come into the world. And behold, I am the light and the life of the world; and I have drunk out of that bitter cup which the Father has given me, and have glorified the Father in taking upon me the sins of the world, in the which I have suffered the will of the Father in all things from the beginning. And it came to pass that when Yeshua had spoken these words, the whole multitude fell to the earth, for they remembered that it had been prophesied among them that Mashiach should show himself[96] unto them after his ascension into Heaven.

5 And it came to pass that YHWH spoke unto them, saying, Arise and come forth unto me,[97] that you may thrust your hands into my side, and also that you may feel the prints of the nails in my hands and in my feet, that you may know that I am the Elohim of Isra'el, and the Elohim of the whole earth, and have been slain for the sins of the world.[98]

6 And it came to pass that the multitude went forth, and thrust their hands into his side, and did feel the prints of the nails in his hands and in his feet. And this they did do, going forth one by one, until they had all gone forth and did see with their eyes, and did feel with their hands, and did know of a surety, and did bear record that it was he — of whom it was written by the prophets[99] — that should come, and when they had all gone forth and had witnessed for themselves,

---

[94] Ps. 2:7; Matt. 3:17; 17:5 [95] 1 Nefi 5:23; Moshiyah 7:10; 8:13; Alma 8:6 [96] Alma 11:8 [97] 3 Nefi 8:8 [98] 1 Nefi 3:14; Alma 16:6; 3 Nefi 10:2 [99] Num. 24:17; Deut. 18:15; Isa. 7:14; 9:6; 25:9; 50:6; 53:5; Hos. 11:1; Zech. 11:13; 13:6; Mal. 3:1; Ps. 22:17 (16); 118:22; 1 Nefi 1:5; 2 Nefi 11:6; Moshiyah 8:2; Cheleman 5:10, 13

they did cry out with one accord, saying, Hoshianna! Blessed be the name of the El Elyon! And they did fall down at the feet of Yeshua and did worship him.

7 And it came to pass that he spoke unto Nefi[100] (for Nefi was among the multitude) and commanded him that he should come forth. And Nefi arose and went forth, and bowed himself before YHWH, and he did kiss his feet. And YHWH commanded him that he should arise. And he arose and stood before him. And YHWH said unto him, I give unto you power that you shall wash this people by immersion[101] when I am again ascended into Heaven.

8 And again, YHWH called others and said unto them likewise, and he gave unto them power to wash by immersion. And he said unto them, In this way shall you immerse to wash, and there shall be no disputations among you. Truly I say unto you that whosoever repents of his sins through your words and desires to be washed by immersion in my name, in this way shall you immerse them: behold, you shall go down and stand in the water, and in my name shall you immerse them. And now behold, these are the words which you shall say, calling them by name, saying, Having authority given me of Yeshua HaMashiach, I immerse you in the name of the Father, and of the Son, and of the Ruach HaKodesh. Amen. And then shall you immerse them in the water and come forth again out of the water. And after this manner shall you wash by immersion in my name, for behold, truly I say unto you that the Father and the Son and the Ruach HaKodesh are echad; and I am in the Father, and the Father in me, and the Father and I are echad. And according as I have commanded you, thus shall you immerse to wash. And there shall be no disputations among you, as there have previously been, neither shall there be disputations among you concerning the points of my doctrine, as there have previously been. For truly, truly I say unto you, he that has the spirit of contention is not of me, but is of HaSatan, who is the father of contention; and he stirs up the hearts of men to contend with anger, one with another. Behold, this is not my doctrine, to stir up the hearts of men with anger, one against another, but this is my doctrine, that such things should be done away.

---

100 3 Nefi 1:1-6; 3:9-12; 9:2; 10:5 **101** Cheleman 5:17-18; 3 Nefi 3:12; 5:10; 12:3

9 Behold, truly, truly I say unto you, I will declare unto you my doctrine.[102] And this is my doctrine, and it is the doctrine which the Father has given unto me — and I bear record of the Father, and the Father bears record of me, and the Ruach HaKodesh bears record of the Father and me — and I bear record that the Father commands all men everywhere to **repent**[103] and **believe**[104] in me. And whoever believes in me, and is **washed by immersion**,[105] the same shall be saved, and they are they who shall inherit the kingdom of Elohim. And whoever believes not in me, and is not immersed, shall be damned. Truly, truly I say unto you that this is my doctrine, and I bear record of it from the Father. And whoever believes in me believes in the Father also, and unto him will the Father bear record of me, for he will visit him with fire and with the Ruach HaKodesh.[106] And thus will the Father bear record of me, and the **Ruach HaKodesh** will bear record unto him of the Father and me, for the Father and I and the Ruach HaKodesh are echad. And again I say unto you, you must repent, and **become as a little child**,[107] and be immersed in my name, or you can in no way receive these things. And again I say unto you, you must repent, and be washed by immersion in my name, and become as a little child, or you can in no way inherit the kingdom of Elohim. Truly, truly I say unto you that this is my doctrine. And whosoever builds upon this builds upon my **rock**,[108] and the gates of She'ol shall not prevail against them. And whoever shall declare more or less[109] than this, and establish it for my doctrine, the same comes of evil and is not built upon my rock, but he builds upon a sandy foundation, and the gates of She'ol stand open to receive such when the floods come and the winds beat upon them. Therefore, go forth unto this people and declare the words which I have spoken unto the ends of the earth.

10 And it came to pass that when Yeshua had spoken these words unto Nefi and to those who had been called — now the number of them who had been called, and received power and s'mikhah to wash by immersion, was twelve — and behold, he stretched forth his hand[110] unto the multitude and cried unto them, saying, Blessed are

---

102 2 Nefi 13:1-5; 14:1; 3 Nefi 9:11   103 Alma 5:4; 3 Nefi 4:7; 9:11-12; 10:1   104 M'raman 4:6; 'Eter 1:18   105 2 Nefi 6:7; Alma 5:4; 3 Nefi 10:4; M'raman 3:5   106 1 Nefi 3:4-5; 2 Nefi 13:2; 15:1; 3 Nefi 8:10   107 Moshiyah 1:16; 3 Nefi 4:7   108 Cheleman 2:17; 3 Nefi 6:12; 8:7   109 3 Nefi 8:7   110 Moshiyah 7:10; 8:13; Alma 8:6; 3 Nefi 5:4

you if you shall give heed unto the words of these twelve whom I have chosen from among you to minister unto you and to be your servants. And unto them I have given power[111] that they may immerse you with water; and after that you are washed by immersion with water, behold, I will immerse you with fire and with the Ruach HaKodesh. Therefore, blessed are you if you shall believe in me and be immersed after you have seen me and know that I am.

11 And again, more blessed are they who shall believe in your words because that you shall testify that you have seen me and that you know that I am. Yes, blessed are they who shall believe in your words, and come down into the depths of humility,[112] and be washed by immersion, for they shall be visited with fire and with the Ruach HaKodesh and shall receive a remission of their sins.

12 Yes, blessed are the **poor in spirit**[113] who come unto me, for theirs is the kingdom of Heaven.

13 And again, blessed are all **they that mourn**, for they **shall be comforted**.[114]

14 And blessed are **the meek**, for they **shall inherit the earth**.[115]

15 And blessed are all they who do hunger and thirst after righteousness, for they shall be filled with the Ruach HaKodesh.

16 And blessed are the merciful, for they shall obtain mercy.[116]

17 And blessed are all the **pure in heart**,[117] for they shall see Elohim.

18 And blessed are all the peacemakers, for they shall be called the children of Elohim.

19 And blessed are all they who are persecuted for my name's sake, for theirs is the kingdom of Heaven. And blessed are you when men shall revile you, and persecute, and shall say all manner of evil against you falsely, for my sake, for you shall have great joy and be exceedingly glad, for great shall be your reward in Heaven; for so persecuted they the prophets who were before you.

20 Truly, truly I say unto you, I give unto you to be the salt of the earth,[118] but if the salt shall lose its savor, with what shall the earth

---

111 Moshiyah 9:8; 3 Nefi 5:7–8   112 Isa. 57:15; 66:2; Ps. 34:19 (18); 51:3–19 (1–17); 2 Nefi 1:6; 'Eter 1:19; M'roni 6:1   113 Isa. 57:15; 66:2   114 Isa. 61:2; 66:10, 13   115 Ps. 37:11; The Hebrew word for "earth" is *eretz* ארץ, which can mean "earth" or "land." In Psalm 37:11, the verse refers to "the land of Israel."   116 As the Talmud says, "…he who is merciful to others, mercy is shown to him by Heaven" (b.Shabbat 151b).   117 Ps. 24:4; 51:12 (10); 73:1   118 The word for "earth" here in the original Hebrew was *eretz* (ארץ), which can mean "earth" or "land." In the parallel in Matthew 5:13, the phrase "salt of

be salted? The salt shall be thereafter good for nothing but to be cast out and to be trampled under foot of men.

21 Truly, truly I say unto you, I give unto you to be the **light** of this people.[119] A city that is set on a hill cannot be hid. Behold, do men light a candle and put it under a bushel? No, but on a candlestick, and it gives light to all that are in the house. Therefore, let your light so shine before this people, that they may see your good works and glorify your Father who is in Heaven.

22 Think not that I am come to destroy the Torah or the prophets. I am not come to destroy, but to fulfill;[120] for truly I say unto you, not one yud nor one stroke has passed away from the Torah, but in me it has all been fulfilled.

23 And behold, I have given unto you the Torah and the mitzvot of my Father, that you shall believe in me, and that you shall repent of your sins, and come unto me with a **broken heart and a contrite spirit**.[121] Behold, you have the mitzvot before you and the Torah is fulfilled. Therefore, come unto me and be saved. For truly I say unto you that except you shall keep my mitzvot which I have commanded you at this time, you shall in no case enter into the kingdom of Heaven.

24 You have heard that it has been said by them of old time, and it is also written before you, that you **shall not kill**,[122] and whosoever shall kill shall be in danger of the judgment of Elohim. But I say unto you that whosoever is angry with his brother[123] shall be in danger of

---

the earth" runs parallel to "light of the world," where "earth" is parallel to "world." However, in 3 Nefi "*eretz*" is parallel to "this people." HaEretz ("the Land") is a common euphemism for "the Land of Israel." So "*eretz*" in this case, might be better understood as "land" in parallel to "this people."   **119** This verse runs parallel with Mat. 5:14-16, but has "light of this people" where Matt. 5:14 has "light of the world." This points to a scribal error between the Hebrew words עולם "world" and עם "people," which is a common scribal error in Hebrew and Aramaic. For example, in Matt. 1:21, the Old Syriac Siniatic and Aramaic Peshitta versions have "he shall save his people (לעמה)," while the Old Syriac Curetonian version has "he shall save the world (לעלם)." It has also been suggested that a similar scribal error in a Hebrew or Aramaic original language source text, may have caused the variance in Acts 2:47 between the readings "finding favor before all the people" (in the Alexandrian and Byzantine text types), and "finding favor with all the world" (in the Western text type). The phrase "light of this people" seems to allude to Isa. 49:6 "a light to the Gentiles," which reads in the Aramaic Peshitta version of Isaiah "a light to the people/nation (לעממא)." This reading of "light of this people" in 3 Nefi 5:21, points to a Hebrew origin for both 3 Nefi and Matthew, and suggests that the reading in 3 Nefi may be the correct reading, offering a possible correction to a scribal error in our received text of Matt. 5:14. See "What does it mean to fulfill the Torah?" footnote to 2 Nefi 11:8.   **121** Isa. 57:15; 66:2; Ps. 34:19 (18); 51:3-19 (1-17); 2 Nefi 1:6; 'Eter 1:19; M'roni 6:1   **122** Ex. 20:13; Deut. 5:17   **123** The KJV of this sermon renders the phrase, "whosoever is angry with his brother without a cause". *The Stick of Joseph* version

his judgment. And whosoever shall say to his brother, Raca,[124] shall be in danger of the council, and whosoever shall say, You fool, shall be in danger of Gehinnom.

25 Therefore, if you shall come unto me, or shall desire to come unto me, and remember that your brother has anything against you, go your way unto your brother and first be reconciled to your brother, and then come unto me with full purpose of heart and I will receive you.

26 Agree with your adversary quickly while you are in the way with him, lest at any time he shall seize you and you shall be cast into prison. Truly I say unto you, you shall by no means come out from that place until you have paid the uttermost senine. And while you are in prison, can you pay even one senine? Truly, truly I say unto you, no.

27 Behold, it is written by them of old time that **you shall not commit adultery;**[125] but I say unto you that whosoever looks on a woman to lust after her has committed adultery already in his heart. Behold, I give unto you a mitzvah that you allow none of these things to enter into your heart, for it is better that you should deny yourselves of these things, in which you will take up your Tz'lav,[126] than that you should be cast into Gehinnom.

28 It has been written **that whosoever shall put away his wife, let him give her a get.**[127] Truly, truly I say unto you that whosoever shall put away his wife, saving for the cause of fornication, causes her to commit adultery; and whoever shall marry her who is divorced commits adultery.

29 And again it is written, **You shall not forswear yourself, but shall perform unto YHWH your oaths;**[128] but truly, truly I say unto you, swear not at all, neither by **Heaven**, for **it is Elohim's throne**, nor by **the earth,** for it is **his footstool**,[129] neither shall you swear

---

eliminates the phrase "without a cause," agreeing with the Hebrew manuscripts of Matthew (Shem Tob, DuTillet, and Munster), which also lack the phrase. Some Greek manuscripts of Matthew have subscriptions referencing alternate readings from a standard version "on Zion the Holy Mount" called "The Judaikon" (Jewish version). One of these subscriptions is to Matthew 5:22 and says "The phrase 'without cause' is not written in some copies, nor in the Judaikon (Jewish version)."   **124** The Aramaic word *raka* רקא is here transliterated into English. This Aramaic word means "worthless, empty, a fool."   **125** Ex. 20:13 (14); Deut. 5:18   **126** A wooden instrument of execution by hanging or crucifixion, translated "cross" or "gallows." In this case it implies carrying a burden, as Yeshua carried the burden of our sin in his suffering and death.   **127** A get (גט) is a divorce document that a husband must give to a wife to make a divorce valid. See Deut. 24:1   **128** Lev. 19:12; Num. 30:3 (2); Deut. 23:22 (21)   **129** Isa. 66:1

by your head, because you cannot make one hair black or white, but let your communication be, Yes, yes, no, no; for whatsoever comes of more than these is evil.

30 And behold, it is written, **An eye for an eye and a tooth for a tooth;**[130] but I say unto you that you shall not resist evil, but whosoever shall strike you on your right cheek, turn to him the other also. And if any man will sue you at the law and take away your coat, let him have your cloak also. And whosoever shall compel you to go a mile, go with him two. Give to him that asks you, and to him that would borrow from you, turn not away.

31 And behold, it is written also **that you shall love your neighbor**[131] and hate your enemy; but behold, I say unto you, love your enemies, bless them that curse you, do good to them that hate you, and pray for them who despitefully use you and persecute you, that you may be the children of your Father who is in Heaven, for he makes his sun to rise on the evil and on the good. Therefore, those things which were of old time, which were under the Torah, in me are all fulfilled. Old things are done away[132] and all things have become new. Therefore, I would that you should be perfect, even as I or your Father who is in Heaven is perfect.

32 Truly, truly I say that I would that you should do tzedakah[133] unto the poor, but take heed that you do not your tzedakah before men to be seen of them; otherwise, you have no reward of your Father who is in Heaven. Therefore, when you shall do your tzedakah, do not sound a shofar before you, as will hypocrites do in the synagogues and in the streets, that they may have glory of men. Truly I say unto you, they have their reward. But when you do tzedakah, let not your left hand know what your right hand does, that your tzedakah may be in secret; and your Father who sees in secret himself shall reward you openly.

33 And when you pray, you shall not do as the hypocrites, for they love to pray standing in the synagogues and in the corners of the streets, that they may be seen of men. Truly I say unto you, they have their reward. But you, when you pray, enter into your closet, and when you have shut your door, pray[134] to your Father who is in

---

130 Ex. 21:24; Lev. 24:20; Deut. 19:21 131 Lev. 19:18 132 See footnote to "done away" in 3 Nefi 4:7. 133 This Hebrew term (צדקה) means "justice" or "righteousness" and signifies the obligation to help those in need. 134 Alma 16:31; 18:4

secret; and your Father who sees in secret shall reward you openly. But when you pray, use not vain repetitions as the heathen, for they think that they shall be heard for their much speaking. Be not, therefore, like unto them, for your Father knows what things you have need of before you ask him.

34 After this manner, therefore, you should pray: Our Father who is in Heaven, hallowed be your name. Your will be done on earth as it is in Heaven.[135] And forgive us our debts as we forgive our debtors.[136] And lead us not into temptation,[137] but deliver us from evil. For **yours is the kingdom, and the power, and the glory**,[138] for ever. Amen. For if you forgive men their trespasses, your Heavenly Father will also forgive you, but if you forgive not men their trespasses, neither will your Father forgive your trespasses.

35 Moreover, when you fast,[139] be not as the hypocrites, of a sad countenance, for they disfigure their faces that they may appear unto men to fast. Truly, I say unto you, they have their reward. But you, when you fast, anoint your head and wash your face, that you appear not unto men to fast, but unto your Father who is in secret; and your Father who sees in secret shall reward you openly.

36 Lay not up for yourselves treasures upon earth, where moth and rust do corrupt and thieves break through and steal, but lay up for yourselves treasures[140] in Heaven, where neither moth nor rust does corrupt and where thieves do not break through nor steal; for where your treasure is, there will your heart be also.

37 The light of the body is the eye; if, therefore, your eye be single,[141] your whole body shall be full of light. But if your eye be evil, your

---

135 Similarly, the Tosefta says, "May your will be done in Heaven and also on earth" (t.Berakhot 3:7). **136** As we read in the Talmud, "Also all who have trespassed against us...even as we also forgive all" (b.Megillah 28a). **137** "And lead us not into temptation" is a KJV-ism from Matt. 6:13. This is actually a Hebrew idiom by which an active verb is used to indicate not that Elohim does a thing but that, in his sovereignty, he allows it to happen. The Yosef ben Yosef translation of Matthew gets the idiom correct with, "And suffer us not to be led into temptation" (JST Matt. 6:14). **138** 1 Chron. 29:11-13 **139** Isa. 58:1-12 **140** Cheleman 2:16 **141** The underlying Hebrew may have been "good eye," a Hebrew idiom meaning to be generous. In Matt. 6:22, the *Jewish New Testament* says "good," where the KJV says "single." David Stern writes in his "Introduction" to the *Jewish New Testament*: "...much of what is written in the New Testament is incomprehensible apart from its Jewish context. Here (Matt. 6:22-23) is an example, only one of many...in Hebrew, having an *'ayin ra'ah*, an 'evil eye,' means being stingy; while having an *'ayin tovah*, a 'good eye,' means being generous" (Stern, D. (1989) *Jewish New Testament: A Translation of the New Testament that Expresses its Jewishness*. Jerusalem, Israel: Jerusalem New Testament Publications, p. x). See also M'raman 4:3, where the Hebrew

whole body shall be full of darkness. If, therefore, the light that is in you be darkness, how great is that darkness.

38 No man can serve two masters, for either he will hate the one and love the other, or else he will hold to the one and despise the other. You cannot serve Elohim and mammon.[142]

6 And now it came to pass that when Yeshua had spoken these words, he looked upon the twelve whom he had chosen, and said unto them, Remember the words which I have spoken. For behold, you are they whom I have chosen to minister unto this people.

2 Therefore, I say unto you, take no thought for your life, what you shall eat or what you shall drink, nor yet for your body, what you shall put on. Is not the life more than meat? And the body than raiment? Behold the fowls of the air, for they sow not, neither do they reap nor gather into barns; yet your Heavenly Father feeds them. Are you not much better than they?[143]

3 Which of you, by taking thought, can add one cubit unto his stature? And why take you thought for raiment? Consider the lilies of the field, how they grow. They labor not, neither do they spin; and yet I say unto you that even Solomon in all his glory was not arrayed like one of these. Wherefore, if Elohim so clothes the grass of the field, which today is, and tomorrow is cast into the oven, even so will he clothe you if you are not of little faith. Therefore, take no thought, saying, What shall we eat? Or, What shall we drink? Or, With what shall we be clothed? For your Heavenly Father knows that you have need of all these things. But seek you first the kingdom of Elohim and his righteousness, and all these things shall be added unto you.

4 Take, therefore, no thought for tomorrow, for tomorrow shall take thought for the things of itself. Sufficient is the day unto the evil thereof.

5 And now it came to pass that when Yeshua had spoken these words, he turned again to the multitude and did open his mouth

---

idiom is used correctly, according to the "Jewish context" of this idiomatic phrase (compare Prov. 23:6; 28:22). See footnote to M'raman 4:3. **142** The Aramaic word *mammon* ממון is here transliterated into English. This Aramaic word means "money, accumulation of wealth." **143** This is an example of the Kal va-homer thought form, which serves as the first of the Seven Rules of Hillel. This classic Jewish thought form expresses that that which applies in a less important case will certainly apply in a more important case.

unto them again, saying, Truly, truly I say unto you, judge not, that you be not judged;[144] for with what judgment you judge, you shall be judged, and what standard you apply, it shall be applied to you again.[145]

6 And why do you behold the sliver that is in your brother's eye, but consider not the beam that is in your own eye? Or how will you say to your brother, Let me pull the sliver out of your eye, and behold, a beam is in your own eye? You hypocrite, first cast out the beam out of your own eye, and then shall you see clearly to cast out the sliver out of your brother's eye. Give not that which is holy unto the dogs, neither cast your pearls before swine, for fear that they trample them under their feet, and turn again, and tear you.

7 Ask[146] and it shall be given unto you, seek and you shall find, knock[147] and it shall be opened unto you; for everyone that asks, receives, and he that seeks, finds, and to him that knocks, it shall be opened.

8 Or what man is there of you, whom if his son ask bread, will he give him a stone? Or if he ask a fish, will he give him a serpent? If you then, being evil, know how to give good gifts unto your children, how much more shall your Father who is in Heaven give good things to them that ask him?[148] Therefore, all things whatsoever you would that men should do to you, do you even so to them,[149] for this is the Torah and the prophets.

9 Enter in at the strait gate,[150] for wide is the gate and broad is the way that leads to destruction, and many there be who go in at that gate; because strait is the gate and narrow is the way which leads unto life, and few there be that find it.

10 Beware of false prophets who come to you in sheep's clothing,[151] but inwardly they are ravening wolves. You shall know them by their fruits. Do men gather grapes of thorns? Or figs of thistles? Even so, every good tree brings forth good fruit, but a corrupt tree brings forth evil fruit. A good tree cannot bring forth evil fruit, neither a corrupt tree bring forth good fruit. Every tree that brings not forth

---

144 Lev. 19:15; Zech. 7:9; M'raman 4:3   145 As we read in the Mishnah, "By the same measure by which a man metes out, they mete out to him…" (m.Sotah 1:7).   146 1 Nefi 4:2; 2 Nefi 14:1; M'roni 7:5; 10:2   147 3 Nefi 13:1   148 Another example of the Kal vahomer thought form. See footnote 143.   149 The Talmud records a similar saying of Hillel: "What is hateful to you, do not to your neighbor, this is the whole Torah" (b.Shabbat 31a).   150 2 Nefi 6:11; 13:3; Ya'akov 4:2; 3 Nefi 13:2   151 Ezek. 34:2-11

good fruit is cut down and cast into the fire. Wherefore, by their fruits you shall know them.

11 Not everyone that says unto me, Adon, Adon, shall enter into the kingdom of Heaven, but he that does the will of my Father who is in Heaven. Many will say to me in that day, Adon, Adon, have we not prophesied in your name? And in your name have cast out demons? And in your name done many wonderful works? And then will I profess unto them, I never knew you. **Depart from me, you that work iniquity.**[152]

12 Therefore, whoever hears these sayings of mine and does them, I will compare him to a wise man who built his house upon a rock;[153] and the rain descended, and the floods came, and the winds blew and beat upon that house, and it fell not, for it was founded upon a rock. And everyone that hears these sayings of mine and does them not shall be compared to a foolish man who built his house upon the sand; and the rain descended, and the floods came, and the winds blew and beat upon that house, and it fell, and great was the fall of it.

7 And now it came to pass that when Yeshua had ended these sayings, he cast his eyes round about on the multitude and said unto them, Behold, you have heard the things which I taught before I ascended to my Father. Therefore, whoever remembers these sayings of mine and does them, him will I raise up at the last day.

2 And it came to pass that when Yeshua had said these words, he perceived that there were some among them who marveled, and wondered what he desired concerning the Torah of Moshe, for they understood not the saying that old things had passed away[154] and that all things had become new. And he said unto them, Marvel not that I said unto you that old things had passed away and that all things had become new. Behold, I say unto you that the Torah is fulfilled that was given unto Moshe.[155] Behold, I am he that gave the Torah, and I am he who covenanted with my people Isra'el. Therefore, the Torah in me is fulfilled, for I have come to fulfill the Torah;[156] therefore, it has an end.[157] Behold, I do not destroy the prophets, for as many as

---

152 Ps. 6:9 (8); 119:115   153 See footnote to "rock" in 3 Nefi 5:9.   154 See footnote to "done away" in 3 Nefi 4:7.   155 See "What does it mean to fulfill the Torah?" in footnote to 2 Nefi 11:8.   156 See previous footnote.   157 In the "Introduction" to his *Jewish New Testament*, Jewish writer David Stern writes concerning a parallel verse in Rom. 10:4:

have not been fulfilled in me, truly I say unto you, shall all be fulfilled. And because I said unto you that old things have passed away,[158] I do not destroy that which has been spoken concerning things which are to come. For behold, the covenant which I have made with my people is not all fulfilled, but the Torah which was given unto Moshe[159] has an end in me. Behold, I am the Torah and the light. Look unto me and endure to the end and you shall live; for unto him that endures to the end will I give Eternal life. Behold, I have given unto you the mitzvot; therefore, keep my mitzvot. And this is the Torah and the prophets, for they truly testified of me.

3 And now it came to pass that when Yeshua had spoken these words, he said unto those twelve whom he had chosen, You are my talmidim, and you are a light unto this people, who are a remnant of the house of Yosef.[160] And behold, this is the land of your inheritance,[161] and the Father has given it unto you. And not at any time has the Father given me mitzvah that I should tell it unto your brothers at Yerushalayim; neither at any time has the Father given me mitzvah that I should tell unto them concerning the other tribes of the house of Isra'el whom the Father has led away out of the land. This much did the Father command me that I should tell unto them, that other sheep[162] I have which are not of this fold; them also I must bring, and they shall hear my voice, and there shall be one fold and one shepherd. And now because of stiffneckedness and unbelief, they understood not my words; therefore, I was commanded of the Father to say no

---

"But Greek telos, which gives the English word 'teleology,' usually means 'goal, purpose, consummation,' not 'termination.' The Messiah did not bring the Torah to an end. Rather, as the Jewish New Testament renders it, 'the goal at which the Torah aims is the Messiah, who offers righteousness to everyone who trusts'" (Stern, D. (1989) *Jewish New Testament: A Translation of the New Testament that Expresses its Jewishness*. Jerusalem, Israel: Jerusalem New Testament Publications, p. xxiii). James Murdock S.T.D. (who translated the Aramaic Peshitta New Testament into English for the first time in 1893) translated the Aramaic word (used in the Aramaic Peshitta in Rom. 10:4) as "aim." A note in the margin shows that the Aramaic word is *saka* and can also be understood as "end, scope, summary." The word "end" was likely *tak'lit* תכלית (Strong's 8503), which can mean "end" but can also mean "purpose, aim, intention, or goal." There are several other passages in *The Stick of Joseph* that confirm that Yeshua HaMashiach is the "end of the Torah," not because He is the termination of the Torah, but because He is the goal of the Torah: "...for this end ['goal,' not termination] has the Torah of Moshe been given." (2 Nefi 8:2); "Behold, he offers himself a sacrifice for sin, to answer the ends of the Torah unto all those who have a broken heart and a contrite spirit, and unto none else can the ends of the Torah be answered." (2 Nefi 1:6). **158** See footnote to 3 Nefi 4:7. **159** Ya'akov 3:2 **160** Gen. 37-50; Deut. 33:13-17; 1 Nefi 1:22; 2:1; 4:3; 2 Nefi 2:2-7; Ya'akov 2:7; 21:9; 3 Nefi 1:1; 'Eter 6:2-4 **161** 2 Nefi 1:1-2; 2:1; 7:4 **162** 1 Kings 22:17; John 10:16; 1 Nefi 7:5

more concerning this thing unto them. But truly I say unto you that the Father has commanded me, and I tell it unto you, that you were separated from them because of their iniquity; therefore, it is because of their iniquity that they know not of you. And truly I say unto you again that the other tribes has the Father separated from them, and it is because of their iniquity that they know not of them. And truly I say unto you that you are they of whom I said, Other sheep I have, which are not of this fold; them also I must bring, and they shall hear my voice, and there shall be one fold and one shepherd. And they understood me not, for they supposed it had been the Goyim;[163] for they understood not that the Goyim should be converted through their preaching. And they understood me not, that I said, They shall hear my voice, and they understood me not that the Goyim should not at that time hear my voice, that I should not manifest myself unto them except it were by the Ruach HaKodesh. But behold, you have both heard my voice and seen me, and you are my sheep, and you are numbered among those whom the Father has given me. And truly, truly I say unto you that I have other sheep which are not of this land, neither of the land of Yerushalayim, neither in any parts of that land round about where I have been to minister. For they of whom I speak are they who have not as yet heard my voice, neither have I at any time manifested myself unto them. But I have received a mitzvah of the Father that I shall go unto them, and that they shall hear my voice and shall be numbered among my sheep, that there may be one fold and one shepherd; therefore, I go to show myself unto them.

4 And I command you that you shall write these sayings after I am gone, that if it so be that my people at Yerushalayim — they who have seen me and been with me in my ministry — do not ask the Father in my name that they may receive a knowledge of you by the Ruach HaKodesh, and also of the other tribes[164] whom they know not of, that these sayings which you shall write shall be kept and shall be manifested unto the Goyim; that through the Milo HaGoyim,[165] the

---

163 Isa. 11:10; 42:6; 54:3; 60:3; 66:19; Jer.16:19; Mal. 1:11; 1 Nefi 3:4,19-26; 2 Nefi 5:5; 9:22; 3 Nefi 9:7-8, 11-12; M'raman 2:5-7; 'Eter 5:4-8   164 2 Nefi 12:10; 3 Nefi 8:1; 13:5; M'raman 1:12   165 "Fulness of the Gentiles." See Gen. 48:19; Rom. 11:25; 1 Nefi 4:3. This phrase (מלא הגוים) appears in Rom. 11:25 where the KJV has "fulness of the Gentiles" as part of the explanation of the Olive Tree parable. It also appears in Gen. 48:19, where the KJV translates it as "a multitude of nations" as part of Jacob's blessing on Ephraim. Jacob plainly states that Ephraim's descendants will become the Milo HaGoyim. Hence

remnant of their seed, who shall be scattered[166] forth upon the face of the earth because of their unbelief, may be brought in, or may be brought to a knowledge of me, their Redeemer. And then will I **gather them in from the four quarters of the earth,**[167] and then will I fulfill the covenant[168] which the Father has made unto all the people of the house of Isra'el. And blessed are the Goyim because of their belief in me, in and of the Ruach HaKodesh, which witness unto them of me and of the Father. Behold, because of their belief in me, says the Father, and because of the unbelief of you, O house of Isra'el, in the latter day shall the truth come unto the Goyim, that the fulness of these things shall be made known unto them.

5 But woe, says the Father, unto the unbelieving of the Goyim, for — even though they have come forth upon the face of this land, and have scattered my people who are of the house of Isra'el, and my people who are of the house of Isra'el have been cast out from among them and have been trampled under feet by them; and because of the mercies of the Father unto the Goyim, and also the judgments of the Father upon my people who are of the house of Isra'el — truly, truly I say unto you that after all this — and I have caused my people who are of the house of Isra'el to be smitten, and to be afflicted, and to be slain, and to be cast out from among them, and to become hated by them, and to become a hiss and a byword among them — and, thus commands the Father that I should say unto you: At that day when the Goyim shall sin against my besorah, and shall reject the fulness of my besorah, and shall be lifted up in the pride of their hearts above all nations and above all the people of the whole earth, and shall be filled with all manner of lies, and of deceits, and of mischiefs, and all manner of hypocrisy, and murders, and priestcrafts, and whoredoms, and of secret abominations, and if they shall do all these things, and shall reject the fulness of my besorah, Behold, says the Father, I will bring the fulness of my besorah from among them. And then will I remember my covenant which I have made unto my people, O house of Isra'el, and I will bring my besorah unto them. And I will show

---

this work began among the Gentiles and goes to all of scattered Isra'el in the hand of Ephraim. See also Ezek. 37:19.   **166** Lev. 26:33; Deut. 28:64; 1 Kings 22:17; 2 Kings 17:6; 25:7; Jer. 29:18; Ezek. 5:10; 6:8; Hos. 9:17   **167** Deut. 30:4; Isa. 11:12; Jer. 23:3–8; Zech. 2:6; 3 Nefi 4:9. See also Ezek. 37 (and Appendix E), where the restoration and gathering of Israel is prophesied in conjunction with this record.   **168** Gen. 13:15-18; Jer. 31:30-33 (31–34); 1 Nefi 3:26-29; 4:3; 2 Nefi 2:2-7; 6:1; M'raman 4:3-4, 11; 'Eter 6:3; M'roni 10:6

unto you, O house of Isra'el, that the Goyim shall not have power over you, but I will remember my covenant unto you, O house of Isra'el, and you shall come unto the knowledge of the fulness of my besorah. But if the Goyim will repent and return unto me, says the Father, behold, they shall be numbered among my people, O house of Isra'el. And I will not allow my people who are of the house of Isra'el to go through among them and tread them down, says the Father. But if they will not turn unto me and hearken unto my voice, I will allow them—yes, I will allow my people, O house of Isra'el—that they shall go through among them and shall tread them down[169] and they shall be as salt that has lost its savor, which is thereafter good for nothing but to be cast out and to be trampled under foot of my people, O house of Isra'el.

6 Truly, truly I say unto you, thus has the Father commanded me, that I should give unto this people this land for their inheritance, and when the words of the prophet Yesha'yahu shall be fulfilled, which say: **Your watchmen shall lift up the voice, with the voice together shall they sing, for they shall see eye to eye when YHWH shall bring again Tziyon. Break forth into joy, sing together you waste places of Yerushalayim, for YHWH has comforted his people, he has redeemed Yerushalayim. YHWH has made bare his holy arm in the eyes of all the nations and all the ends of the earth shall see the salvation of Elohim.**[170]

8 Behold, now it came to pass that when Yeshua had spoken these words, he looked round about again on the multitude and he said unto them, Behold, my time is at hand. I perceive that you are weak, that you cannot understand all my words which I am commanded of the Father to speak unto you at this time; therefore, go unto your homes, and ponder[171] upon the things which I have said, and ask of the Father, in my name, that you may understand and prepare your minds for tomorrow, and I will come unto you again. But now I go unto the Father, and also to show myself unto the lost tribes[172] of Isra'el, for they are not lost unto the Father, for he knows where he has taken them.

---

169 Mic. 5:7 (8); M'raman 2:7   170 Isa. 52:8-10   171 Prov. 4:20-27; 1 Nefi 3:6; Cheleman 3:19; M'roni 10:2   172 1 Kings 22:17; John 10:16; 1 Nefi 7:5

2 And it came to pass that when Yeshua had thus spoken, he cast his eyes round about again on the multitude, and beheld they were in tears and did look steadfastly upon him, as if they would ask him to remain a little longer with them. And he said unto them, Behold, my bowels are filled with compassion towards you. Have you any that are sick among you? Bring them here. Have you any that are lame, or blind, or crippled, or maimed, or leprous, or that are withered, or that are deaf, or that are afflicted in any manner? Bring them here and I will heal them, for I have compassion upon you, my bowels are filled with mercy; for I perceive that you desire that I should show unto you what I have done unto your brothers at Yerushalayim, for I see that your faith is sufficient that I should heal you.

3 And it came to pass that when he had thus spoken, all the multitude with one accord did go forth with their sick, and their afflicted, and their lame, and with their blind, and with their dumb, and with all they that were afflicted in any manner; and he did heal[173] them, every one, as they were brought forth unto him. And they did all — both they who had been healed and they who were whole — bow down at his feet and did worship him; and as many as could come for the multitude did kiss his feet, insomuch that they did bathe his feet with their tears.

4 And it came to pass that he commanded that their little children should be brought; so they brought their little children and sat them down upon the ground round about him, and Yeshua stood in the midst. And the multitude gave way until they had all been brought unto him. And it came to pass that when they had all been brought and Yeshua stood in the midst, he commanded the multitude that they should kneel down upon the ground. And it came to pass that when they had knelt upon the ground, Yeshua groaned within himself, and said, Father, I am troubled because of the wickedness of the people of the house of Isra'el. And when he had said these words, he himself also knelt upon the earth, and behold, he prayed unto the Father, and the things which he prayed cannot be written; and the multitude did bear record, who heard him. And after this manner do they bear record: **The eye has never seen, neither has the ear heard**[174] before, so great and marvelous things as we saw and heard

---

173 1 Nefi 3:13; 4 Nefi 1:2   174 Isa. 64:3 (4). There is a direct connection here with a

Yeshua speak unto the Father. And no tongue can speak,[175] neither can there be written[176] by any man, neither can the hearts of men conceive so great and marvelous things as we both saw and heard Yeshua speak. And no one can conceive of the joy which filled our souls at the time we heard him pray for us unto the Father.

5 And it came to pass that when Yeshua had made an end of praying unto the Father, he arose, but so great was the joy of the multitude that they were overcome. And it came to pass that Yeshua spoke unto them and told them to arise. And they arose from the earth, and he said unto them, Blessed are you because of your faith.[177] And now behold, my joy is full. And when he had said these words, he wept, and the multitude bore record of it. And he took their little children, one by one, and blessed them and prayed unto the Father for them. And when he had done this, he wept again. And he spoke unto the multitude, and said unto them, Behold your little ones. And as they looked to behold, they cast their eyes towards Heaven, and they saw the Heavens open, and they saw angels descending out of Heaven, as it were in the midst of fire.[178] And they came down and encircled those little ones about — and they were encircled about with fire — and the angels did minister unto them. And the multitude did see, and hear, and bear record; and they know that their record is true, for they, all of them, did see and hear, every man for himself. And they were in number about two thousand and five hundred souls,[179] and they did consist of men, women, and children.

6 And it came to pass that Yeshua commanded his talmidim that they should bring forth some matzah[180] and wine[181] unto him. And

---

Baraita (pre-Talmudic tradition), which is quoted twice in the Talmud (and in the Midrash Rabbah and Zohar): "What is the meaning of 'Eye has not seen' (Isa. 64:3)? Rabbi Joshua ben Levi said: This is the wine that has been kept in its grapes from the six days in the beginning" (b.Berakhot 34b; b.Sanhedrin 99a). [The *Yayin HaMeshumar*—the wine that has been kept] And the Midrash Rabbah says: "Because he bared his soul unto death (Isa. 53:12) and bruised themselves with the Torah which is sweeter than honey, the Holy One, blessed be He, will hereafter give them to drink of the wine kept in its grapes since the six days in the beginning" (Midrash Rabbah to Numbers 13:2 [500]). And we read in the Zohar: "The Tzadik (The Righteous) is the Yesod (foundation) in Yah, the mystery (*sod*) which is the wine which has been kept in its grapes from the six days in the beginning" (Zohar; Roeh M'haimna on Pinchas). This Baraita directly connects with the partaking of the wine of the Seder in 3 Nefi 8:6-7 and with Mashiach as the suffering servant of Isa. 53 (See notes to Moshiyah 8). **175** 3 Nefi 9:5 **176** Alma 9:3; Cheleman 3:6; 3 Nefi 3:9; 8:4; 9:5 **177** Matt. 17:20; Rom. 4:16; Heb. 11-12; Alma 16:26-30; **178** Cheleman 2:20-26 **179** 3 Nefi 5:1 **180** Ex. 12:15; Lev. 23:4-5; Num. 2:10; 3 Nefi 9:6; M'roni 4 **181** M'roni 5; 6:2

while they were gone for matzah and wine, he commanded the multitude that they should sit themselves down upon the earth. And when the talmidim had come with matzah and wine, he took of the matzah, and broke and blessed it, and he gave unto the talmidim and commanded that they should eat. And when they had eaten and were filled, he commanded that they should give unto the multitude. And when the multitude had eaten and were filled, he said unto the talmidim, Behold, there shall one be ordained among you, and to him will I give power that he shall break matzah and bless it, and give it unto the people of my assembly, unto all those who shall believe and be immersed in my name. And this shall you always observe to do, even as I have done,[182] even as I have broken matzah and blessed it, and given it unto you. And this shall you do in remembrance of my body which I have shown unto you. And it shall be a testimony unto the Father that you do always remember me. And if you do always remember me, you shall have my spirit to be with you.

7 And it came to pass that when he had said these words, he commanded his talmidim that they should take of the wine of the cup and drink of it,[183] and that they should also give unto the multitude that they might drink of it. And it came to pass that they did so, and did drink of it and were filled. And they gave unto the multitude, and they did drink and they were filled. And when the talmidim had done this, Yeshua said unto them, Blessed are you for this thing which you have done, for this is fulfilling my mitzvot, and this does witness unto the Father that you are willing to do that which I have commanded you. And this shall you always do unto those who repent and are washed by immersion in my name; and you shall do it in remembrance of my blood which I have shed[184] for you, that you may witness unto the Father that you do always remember me. And if you do always remember me, you shall have my spirit to be with you. And I give unto you a mitzvah that you shall do these things, and if you shall always do these things, blessed are you, for you are built upon my rock. But whoever among you shall do more or less than these are not built upon my rock,[185] but are built upon a sandy foundation. And when the rain descends, and the floods come, and

---

[182] John 6:54; 1 Cor. 11:26; Rev. 3:20; M'roni 6:2   [183] Compare with the *Yayin HaMeshumar* (wine of the keeping, see note to 3 Nefi 8:4 re: eye has not seen).   [184] Ex. 12:21; 24:8; Moshiyah 1:14-16   [185] Cheleman 2:17; 3 Nefi 6:12; 8:7

the winds blow and beat upon them, they shall fall, and the gates of She'ol are already open to receive them. Therefore, blessed are you if you shall keep my mitzvot which the Father has commanded me that I should give unto you. Truly, truly I say unto you, you must watch and pray always,[186] for fear that you be tempted by HaSatan and you are led away captive by him. And as I have prayed among you, even so shall you pray in my assembly, among my people who do repent and are immersed in my name. Behold, I am the light; I have set an example for you.

8 And it came to pass that when Yeshua had spoken these words unto his talmidim, he turned again unto the multitude and said unto them, Behold, truly, truly I say unto you, you must watch and pray always so that you do not enter into temptation, for HaSatan desires to have you, that he may sift you as wheat; therefore, you must always pray unto the Father in my name. And whatsoever you shall ask the Father in my name, which is right, believing that you shall receive, behold, it shall be given unto you. Pray in your families unto the Father always in my name, that your wives and your children may be blessed. And behold, you shall meet together often,[187] and you shall not forbid any man from coming unto you when you shall meet together, but allow them that they may come unto you, and forbid them not. But you shall pray for them, and shall not cast them out, and if it so be that they come unto you often, you shall pray for them unto the Father in my name. Therefore, hold up your light, that it may shine unto the world. Behold, I am the light which you shall hold up, that which you have seen me do. Behold, you see that I have prayed unto the Father, and you all have witnessed. And you see that I have commanded that none of you should go away, but rather have commanded that you should come unto me, that you might feel and see; even so shall you do unto the world. And whosoever breaks this mitzvah allows himself to be led into temptation.

9 And now it came to pass that when Yeshua had spoken these words, he turned his eyes again upon the talmidim whom he had chosen, and said unto them, Behold, truly, truly I say unto you, I give unto you another mitzvah, and then I must go unto my Father, that I may fulfill other mitzvot which he has given me. And now behold,

---

[186] Alma 10:4; 3 Nefi 8:7   [187] 4 Nefi 1:2; M'roni 6:2

this is the mitzvah which I give unto you, that you shall not allow anyone knowingly to partake of my flesh and blood unworthily[188] when you shall administer it. For whoever eats and drinks my flesh and blood unworthily eats and drinks damnation to his soul;[189] therefore, if you know that a man is unworthy to eat and drink of my flesh and blood, you shall forbid him. Nevertheless, you shall not cast him out from among you, but you shall minister unto him and shall pray for him unto the Father in my name; and if it so be that he repents and is washed by immersed in my name, then shall you receive him and shall administer unto him of my flesh and blood. But if he repent not, he shall not be numbered among my people, that he may not destroy my people. For behold, I know my sheep[190] and they are numbered. Nevertheless, you shall not cast him out of your synagogues or your places of worship, for unto such shall you continue to minister; for you know not but that they will return and repent and come unto me with full purpose of heart,[191] and I shall heal them, and you shall be the means of bringing salvation unto them. Therefore, keep these sayings which I have commanded you, that you come not under condemnation, for woe unto him whom the Father condemns. And I give you these mitzvot because of the disputations[192] which have been among you. And blessed are you if you have no disputations among you. And now I go unto the Father because it is expedient that I should go unto the Father for your sakes.

10 And it came to pass that when Yeshua had made an end of these sayings, he touched with his hand the talmidim whom he had chosen, one by one, even until he had touched them all, and spoke unto them as he touched them. And the multitude heard not the words which he spoke, therefore they did not bear record, but the talmidim bore record that he gave them power to give the Ruach HaKodesh. And I will show unto you hereafter that this record is true.[193] And it came to pass that when Yeshua had touched them all, there came a cloud[194] and overshadowed the multitude, that they could not see Yeshua. And while they were overshadowed, he departed from them and

---

188 The Torah prohibits uncircumcised males from partaking of the Passover (Ex. 12:42-45). 189 This is almost identical to 1 Cor. 11:29, "drinks damnation to himself," pointing to an underlying Hebrew word *nefesh* נפש, which can mean "soul, life, or self" (see Moshiyah 1:10, 16, 18). 190 John 10:14-16; 1 Nefi 7:5 191 2 Nefi 13:2; Ya'akov 4:2 192 3 Nefi 4:1; 5:8; M'roni 8:2 193 M'roni 2:1 194 Deut. 31:15; Mark 9:7; Moshiyah 11:26; 'Eter 1:6-8

ascended into Heaven. And the talmidim saw and did bear record that he ascended again into Heaven.

9 And now it came to pass that when Yeshua had ascended into Heaven, the multitude did disperse, and every man did take his wife and his children and did return to his own home. And it was noised abroad among the people immediately, before it was yet dark, that the multitude had seen Yeshua, and that he had ministered unto them, and that he would also show himself the next day unto the multitude; yes, and even all the night it was noised abroad concerning Yeshua. And insomuch did they send forth unto the people that there were many, yes, an exceedingly great number did labor exceedingly all that night that they might be, the next day, in the place where Yeshua should show himself unto the multitude.

2 And it came to pass that the next day, when the multitude was gathered together, behold, Nefi and his brother whom he had raised from the dead,[195] whose name was Timothy,[196] and also his son whose name was Yonah, and also Mattani, and Mattanihah his brother, and Kumen, and Kumenonhi, and Yirmeyahu, and Shemnon, and Yonah, and Tzidkiyahu, and Yesha'yahu — now these were the names of the talmidim whom Yeshua had chosen — and it came to pass that they went forth and stood in the midst of the multitude. And behold, the multitude was so great that they did cause that they should be separated into twelve bodies, and the twelve did teach the multitude. And behold, they did cause that the multitude should kneel down upon the face of the earth and should pray unto the Father in the name[197] of Yeshua. And the talmidim did pray unto the Father also in the name of Yeshua. And it came to pass that they arose and ministered unto the people. And when they had taught them the same words which Yeshua had spoken, nothing varying from the words which Yeshua had spoken, behold, they knelt again

---

[195] 3 Nefi 3:10; 4 Nefi 1:2 [196] The appearance of the Greek name "Timothy" (*Timo-Theos*) "honoring God" should come as no surprise. No less a scholar than Dr. Cyrus Gordon suggests the Greek word "Theos" migrated to Ancient America. He writes of the Uto-Aztecan (Nahuatl) word *teo-tl*: "For example *teo-tl* 'god' could have been introduced from Greek *theo-s*... Greek influence in Ancient America does not come as a complete surprise. Since Mycenaean times, the Greeks have been a nautical people" (Gordon, C.H. (1971) *Before Columbus*. New York, NY: Crown. p. 136). [197] 2 Nefi 14:3; 3 Nefi 9:9; M'raman 4:10; M'roni 10:2

and prayed to the Father in the name of Yeshua; and they did pray for that which they most desired. And they desired that the Ruach HaKodesh should be given unto them. And when they had thus prayed, they went down unto the water's edge, and the multitude followed them. And it came to pass that Nefi went down into the water and was washed by immersion.[198] And he came up out of the water and began to immerse, and he immersed all those whom Yeshua had chosen. And it came to pass when they were all washed by immersion and had come up out of the water, the Ruach HaKodesh[199] did fall upon them, and they were filled with the Ruach HaKodesh and with fire. And behold, they were encircled about as if it were fire, and it came down from Heaven, and the multitude did witness it and do bear record. And angels[200] did come down out of Heaven and did minister unto them. And it came to pass that while the angels were ministering unto the talmidim, behold, Yeshua came and stood in the midst, and ministered unto them. And it came to pass that he spoke unto the multitude and commanded them that they should kneel down again upon the earth, and also that his talmidim should kneel down upon the earth. And it came to pass that when they had all knelt down upon the earth, he commanded his talmidim that they should pray. And behold, they began to pray, and they did pray unto Yeshua, calling him their Adonai and their Elohim.

³And it came to pass that Yeshua departed out of the midst of them, and went a little way off from them, and bowed himself to the earth, and he said, Father, I thank you that you have given the Ruach HaKodesh unto these whom I have chosen, and it is because of their belief in me that I have chosen them out of the world. Father, I pray that you will give the Ruach HaKodesh unto all them that shall believe[201] in their words. Father, you have given them the Ruach HaKodesh because they believe in me; and you see that they believe in me because you hear them and they pray unto me; and they pray unto me because I am with them. And now Father, I pray unto you for them, and also for all those who shall believe on their words, that they may believe in me, that I may be in them as you, Father, are in me, that we may be one.

---

198 2 Nefi 13:1-2; Moshiyah 9:8; 3 Nefi 5:8 **199** 2 Nefi 13:2; 3 Nefi 5:11 **200** 1 Nefi 3:12; 3 Nefi 3:10; 8:5; M'roni 7:7 **201** 2 Nefi 11:12; 3 Nefi 5:9-11; 13:4

4 And it came to pass that when Yeshua had thus prayed unto the Father, he came unto his talmidim, and behold, they did still continue without ceasing to pray unto him. And they did not multiply many words, for it was given unto them what they should pray, and they were filled with desire. And it came to pass that Yeshua blessed them as they did pray unto him, and his countenance did smile upon them, and the light of his countenance did shine upon them. And behold, they were as white as the countenance and also the garments of Yeshua. And behold, the whiteness thereof did exceed all whiteness, yes, even there could be nothing upon earth so white as the whiteness thereof. And Yeshua said unto them, Pray on. Nevertheless, they did not cease to pray. And he turned from them again and went a little way off, and bowed himself to the earth, and he prayed again unto the Father, saying, Father, I thank you that you have purified these whom I have chosen because of their faith;[202] and I pray for them, and also for them who shall believe on their words, that they may be purified in me through faith on their words, even as they are purified in me. Father, I pray not for the world, but for them which you have given unto me out of the world because of their faith, that they may be purified in me, that I may be in them as you, Father, are in me, that we may be echad,[203] that I may be glorified in them. And when Yeshua had spoken these words, he came again unto his talmidim, and behold, they did pray steadfastly without ceasing unto him; and he did smile upon them again, and behold, they were white, even as Yeshua.

5 And it came to pass that he went again a little way off and prayed unto the Father, and tongue cannot speak[204] the words which he prayed, neither can be written by man the words which he prayed. And the multitude did hear, and do bear record, and their hearts were open, and they did understand in their hearts the words which he prayed. Nevertheless, so great and marvelous were the words which he prayed that they cannot be written,[205] neither can they be uttered by man. And it came to pass that when Yeshua had made an end of praying, he came again to the talmidim and said unto them, So great faith as yours have I never seen among all the Y'hudim; wherefore, I

---

202 Matt. 17:20; Rom. 4:16; Alma 16:26–30   203 John 17:9–11; 3 Nefi 5:8; 9:9; 13:3. See *echad* in Glossary.   204 3 Nefi 8:4   205 Alma 9:3

could not show unto them so great miracles because of their unbelief. Truly I say unto you, there are none of them that have seen so great things as you have seen, neither have they heard so great things as you have heard.

6 And it came to pass that he commanded the multitude that they should cease to pray, and also his talmidim. And he commanded them that they should not cease to pray in their hearts. And he commanded them that they should arise and stand up upon their feet, and they arose and stood upon their feet. And it came to pass that he broke matzah[206] again, and blessed it, and gave to the talmidim to eat. And when they had eaten, he commanded them that they should break matzah and give unto the multitude. And when they had given unto the multitude, he also gave them wine to drink, and commanded them that they should give unto the multitude. Now there had been no matzah, neither wine, brought by the talmidim, neither by the multitude; but he truly gave unto them matzah to eat, and also wine to drink. And he said unto them, He that eats this matzah, eats of my body to their soul, and he that drinks of this wine,[207] drinks of my blood to their soul; and their soul shall never hunger nor thirst, but shall be filled.[208] Now when the multitude had all eaten and drunk, behold, they were filled with the spirit, and they did cry out with one voice and gave glory to Yeshua, whom they both saw and heard.

7 And it came to pass that when they had all given glory unto Yeshua, he said unto them, Behold, now I finish the mitzvah which the Father has commanded me concerning this people who are a remnant of the house of Isra'el. You remember that I spoke unto you and said that when the words of Yesha'yahu should be fulfilled — behold, they are written, you have them before you, therefore search them — and truly, truly I say unto you that when they shall be fulfilled, then is the fulfilling of the covenant[209] which the Father has made unto his people, O house of Isra'el. Then shall the remnants which shall be scattered[210] abroad upon the face of the earth be gathered in from the east, and from the west, and from the south, and from the north;

---

[206] 3 Nefi 8:6   [207] Compare with the *Yayin HaMeshumar* (wine of the keeping, see note to 3 Nefi 8:4 re: eye has not seen).   [208] John 6:54; 3 Nefi 8:6-7   [209] Gen. 13:15-18; Jer. 31:30-33 (31-34); 1 Nefi 3:26-29; 4:3; 2 Nefi 2:2-7; 6:1; M'raman 4:3-4, 11; 'Eter 6:3; M'roni 10:6   [210] Lev. 26:33; Deut. 28:64; 1 Kings 22:17; 2 Kings 17:6; 25:7; Jer. 29:18; Ezek. 5:10; 6:8; Hos. 9:17

and they shall be brought to the knowledge of YHWH their Elohim who has redeemed them. And the Father has commanded me that I should give unto you this land for your inheritance. And I say unto you that if the Goyim do not repent after the blessing which they shall receive after they have scattered my people, then shall you who are **a remnant of the house of Ya'akov go forth among them. And you shall be in the midst of them who shall be many, and you shall be among them as a lion among the beasts of the forest, and as a young lion among the flocks of sheep, who, if he goes through, both treads down and tears in pieces, and none can deliver. Your hand shall be lifted up upon your adversaries, and all your enemies shall be cut off.**[211] And I will gather[212] my people together as a man gathers his **sheaves into the floor,** for I will make my people with whom the Father has covenanted, yes, **I will make your horn iron and I will make your hoofs brass, and you shall beat in pieces many people. And I will consecrate their gain unto YHWH and their substance unto the Adon of the whole earth.**[213] And behold, I am he who does it. And it shall come to pass, says the Father, that the sword of my justice shall hang over them at that day; and except they repent, it shall fall upon them, says the Father, yes, even upon all the nations of the Goyim.[214]

8 And it shall come to pass that I will establish[215] my people, O house of Isra'el. And behold, this people will I establish in this land unto the fulfilling of the covenant which I made with your father Ya'akov, and it shall be a New Yerushalayim.[216] And the Powers of Heaven[217] shall be in the midst of this people, yes, even I will be in the midst of you. Behold, I am he of whom Moshe spoke, saying, **A prophet shall YHWH your Elohim raise up unto you of your brothers, like unto me; him shall you hear in all things whatsoever he shall say unto you. And it shall come to pass that every soul who will not hear that prophet shall be cut off from among the people.**[218] Truly I say unto you, yes, and all the prophets from Sh'mu'el and those that follow after, as many as have spoken, have testified of me. And

---

211 Mic. 5:8-9   212 Deut. 30:4; Isa. 11:12; Jer. 23:3-8; Zech. 2:6; 3 Nefi 4:9. See also Ezek. 37, where the restoration and gathering of Israel is prophesied in conjunction with this record.   213 Mic. 4:12-13   214 1 Nefi 3:26; 2 Nefi 5:5; 3 Nefi 7:3-5; M'raman 2:7; 'Eter 3:18   215 Deut. 28:9; Isa. 2:2; Ps. 89:5 (4); 3 Nefi 9:11; 10:1   216 3 Nefi 10:1; 'Eter 6:1-3   217 3 Nefi 10:1; 13:3   218 Deut. 18:15, 18-19

behold, you are the children of the prophets, and you are of the house of Isra'el, and you are of the covenant[219] which the Father made with your fathers, saying unto Avraham, And **in your seed shall all the kindreds of the earth be blessed**,[220] the Father having raised me up unto you first, and sent me to bless you in turning away every one of you from his iniquities — and this because you are the children of the covenant. And after that you were blessed, then fulfills the Father the covenant which he made with Avraham, saying, **In your seed shall all the kindreds of the earth be blessed**, unto the pouring out of the Ruach HaKodesh through me upon the Goyim, which blessing upon the Goyim shall make them mighty above all, unto the scattering of my people, O house of Isra'el. And they shall be a scourge unto the people of this land. Nevertheless, when they shall have received the fulness of my besorah, then, if they shall harden their hearts against me, I will return their iniquities upon their own heads, says the Father. And I will remember the covenant which I have made with my people, and I have covenanted with them that I would gather them together in my own due time, that I would give unto them again the land of their fathers for their inheritance, which is the land of Yerushalayim, which is the promised land unto them for ever, says the Father.

9 And it shall come to pass that the time comes when the fulness of my besorah shall be preached unto them, and they shall believe in me, that I am Yeshua HaMashiach, the Son of Elohim, and shall pray unto the Father in my name. **Then shall their watchmen lift up their voice, and with the voice together shall they sing, for they shall see eye to eye. Then will the Father gather them together again and give unto them Yerushalayim for the land of their inheritance. Then shall they break forth into joy. Sing together, you waste places of Yerushalayim, for the Father has comforted his people, he has redeemed Yerushalayim. The Father has made bare his holy arm in the eyes of all the nations, and all the ends of the earth shall see the salvation of**[221] the Father. And the Father and I are echad. And then shall be brought to pass that which is written: **Awake, awake again and put on your strength,**

---

[219] Gen. 13:15-18; Jer. 31:30-33 (31-34); 1 Nefi 3:26-29; 4:3; 2 Nefi 2:2-7; 6:1; M'raman 4:3-4, 11; 'Eter 6:3; M'roni 10:6   [220] Gen. 12:3; 22:17; 1 Nefi 7:3; 2 Nefi 7:2; 12:10   [221] Isa. 52:8-10; Moshiyah 8:12; 3 Nefi 7:6

O Tziyon. Put on your beautiful garments, O Yerushalayim, the holy city, for henceforth there shall no more come into you the uncircumcised and the unclean. Shake yourself from the dust, arise; sit down, O Yerushalayim. Loose yourself from the bands of your neck, O captive daughter of Tziyon. For thus says YHWH: You have sold yourselves for no value and you shall be redeemed without money.[222]

10 Truly, truly I say unto you that my people shall know my name, yes, in that day they shall know that I am he that does speak. And then shall they say, How beautiful upon the mountains are the feet of him that brings good tidings unto them, that publishes shalom,[223] that brings good tidings unto them of good, that publishes salvation, that says unto Tziyon, Your Elohim reigns! And then shall a cry go forth, Depart, depart, go out from there, touch not that which is unclean, go out of the midst of her, be you clean that bear the vessels of YHWH. For you shall not go out with haste, nor go by flight, for YHWH will go before you and the Elohim of Isra'el shall be your rearguard. Behold, my servant shall deal prudently, he shall be exalted and extolled, and be very high.[224] As many were astonished at you — his visage was so marred, more than any man, and his form more than the sons of men — so shall he sprinkle many nations. The kings shall shut their mouths at him, for that which had not been told them shall they see, and that which they had not heard shall they consider.[225] Truly, truly I say unto you, all these things shall surely come even as the Father has commanded me. And then shall this covenant which the Father has covenanted with his people be fulfilled; and then shall Yerushalayim be inhabited again with my people, and it shall be the land of their inheritance.

---

222 Isa. 52:1-3   223 Isa. 52:6-7; Moshiyah 8:8-9. We read in the Talmud and Midrash Rabbah: "Rabbi Jose the Galilean says: Great is peace — or at the hour the King Messiah reveals himself unto Israel, he will begin in no other way than with 'peace' as it is written: 'How beautiful upon the mountains are the feet of the messenger of good news, that announces peace' (Isa. 52:7)" (Perek HaShalom in some Talmud editions and Numbers Rabbah XI, 16-20).   224 Isa 52:7-13. Targum Jonathan translates Isa. 52:13 as, "Behold, My Servant the Messiah shall prosper; he shall be exalted and great and very powerful" (Targum Jonathan on Isa. 52:13).   225 Isa. 52:14-15; Rambam says: "Regarding the mission by which Messiah will present himself, Isaiah states, 'He grew like a tender plant and as a root out of dry land at him will kings shut their mouths, for what had not been told unto them shall they see, and what they never heard shall they understand'" (Rambam on Isa. 52:15-53:2).

11 And truly I say unto you, I give unto you a sign, that you may know the time when these things shall be about to take place, that I shall gather[226] in from their long dispersion my people, O house of Isra'el, and shall establish again among them my Tziyon. And behold, this is the thing which I will give unto you for a sign: for truly I say unto you that when these things which I declare unto you — and which I shall declare unto you hereafter of myself and by the power of the Ruach HaKodesh, which shall be given unto you of the Father — shall be made known unto the Goyim, that they may know concerning this people who are a remnant of the house of Ya'akov, and concerning this my people who shall be scattered by them, truly, truly I say unto you, when these things shall be made known unto them of the Father and shall come forth of the Father from them unto you — for it is wisdom in the Father that they should be established in this land and be set up as a free people by the power of the Father, that these things might come forth from them unto a remnant of your seed, that the covenant of the Father may be fulfilled which he has covenanted with his people, O house of Isra'el — therefore, when these works and the works which shall be worked among you hereafter shall come forth from the Goyim unto your seed which shall dwindle in unbelief because of iniquity — for it is required by the Father that it should come forth from the Goyim, that he may show forth his power unto the Goyim for this cause, that the Goyim, if they will not harden their hearts, that they may repent, and come unto me, and be washed by immersion in my name, and know of the true points of my doctrine, that they may be numbered among my people, O house of Isra'el — and when these things come to pass, that your seed shall begin to know these things, it shall be a sign unto them that they may know that the work of the Father has already commenced unto the fulfilling of the covenant which he has made unto the people who are of the house of Isra'el. And when that day shall come, it shall come to pass that **kings shall shut their mouths, for that which had not been told them shall they see, and that which they had not heard shall they consider.**[227]

---

226 Deut. 30:3-4; Isa. 11:12; Jer. 23:3-8; Zech. 2:6; 3 Nefi 4:9. See also Ezek. 37, where the restoration and gathering of Israel is prophesied in conjunction with this record.
227 Isa. 52:15

12 For in that day, for my sake, shall the Father work a work which shall be a great and **a marvelous work**[228] among them, and there shall be among them those who will not believe it, although a man shall declare it unto them. But behold, the life of my servant shall be in my hand; therefore, they shall not hurt him, although **he shall be marred**[229] because of them. Yet I will heal him, for I will show unto them that my wisdom is greater than the cunning of HaSatan. Therefore, it shall come to pass that whosoever will not believe in my words, who am Yeshua HaMashiach, which the Father shall cause him to bring forth unto the Goyim, and shall give unto him power that he shall bring them forth unto the Goyim, it shall be done even as Moshe said — They shall be cut off from among my people who are of the covenant. **And my people who are a remnant of Ya'akov shall be among the Goyim, yes, in the midst of them as a lion among the beasts of the forest, as a young lion among the flocks of sheep, who, if he go through, both treads down and tears in pieces, and none can deliver. Their hand shall be lifted up upon their adversaries, and all their enemies shall be cut off. Yes, woe be unto the Goyim except they repent, for it shall come to pass in that day, says the Father, that I will cut off your horses out of the midst of you, and I will destroy your chariots, and I will cut off the cities of your land and throw down all your strongholds. And I will cut off witchcrafts out of your land, and you shall have no more soothsayers. Your graven images I will also cut off and your standing images out of your midst, and you shall no more worship the works of your hands. And I will pluck up your groves out of your midst; so will I destroy your cities.**[230] And it shall come to pass that all lyings, and deceivings, and envyings, and strifes, and priestcrafts, and whoredoms shall be done away. For it shall come to pass, says the Father, that at that day, whosoever will not repent and come unto my Beloved Son, them will I cut off from among my people, O house of Isra'el, **and I will execute vengeance and fury upon them, even as upon the heathen, such as they have not heard.**[231]

---

228 Isa. 29:14; 1 Nefi 3:26; 3 Nefi 13:5   **229** Isa. 52:14   **230** Mic. 5:8-14   **231** Mic. 5:15

10 But if they will repent, and hearken unto my words, and harden not their hearts, I will establish my assembly among them, and they shall come in unto the covenant[232] and be numbered among this the remnant of Ya'akov, unto whom I have given this land for their inheritance. And they shall assist my people, the remnant of Ya'akov, and also as many of the house of Isra'el as shall come, that they may build a city which shall be called the New Yerushalayim.[233] And then shall they assist my people, that they may be gathered in, who are scattered upon all the face of the land, in unto the New Yerushalayim. And then shall the Powers of Heaven[234] come down among them, and I also will be in the midst. And then shall the work of the Father commence at that day, even when this besorah shall be preached among the remnant of this people. Truly I say unto you, at that day shall the work of the Father commence among all the dispersed of my people, yes, even the tribes which have been lost, which the Father has led away out of Yerushalayim. Yes, the work shall commence among all the dispersed of my people, with the Father to prepare the way by which they may come unto me, that they may call on the Father in my name. Yes, and then shall the work commence with the Father among all nations, in preparing the way by which his people may be gathered[235] home to the land of their inheritance. **And they shall go out from all nations, and they shall not go out in haste nor go by flight, for I will go before them,** says the Father, **and I will be their rearguard.**[236]

2 And then shall that which is written come to pass: **Sing, O barren, you that did not bear; break forth into singing and cry aloud, you that did not travail with child; for more are the children of the desolate than the children of the married wife, says YHWH. Enlarge the place of your tent and let them stretch forth the curtains of your habitations; spare not, lengthen your cords and strengthen your stakes, for you shall break forth on the right hand and on the left, and your seed shall inherit the Goyim and make the desolate cities to be inhabited. Fear not, for you shall not be ashamed, neither be you confounded, for you shall not be put to shame; for you shall forget the shame of your**

---

232 2 Nefi 5:5; 12:11; 3 Nefi 7:5; 9:8, 11   **233** 'Eter 6:1-3   **234** 3 Nefi 9:8   **235** Deut. 30:4; Isa. 11:12; Jer. 23:3-8; Zech. 2:6; 3 Nefi 4:9. See also Ezek. 37, where the restoration and gathering of Israel is prophesied in conjunction with this record.   **236** Isa. 52:12

youth and shall not remember the reproach of your widowhood anymore. For your Maker, your husband, YHWH Tzva'ot is his name; and your Redeemer, HaKodesh of Isra'el, the Elohim of the whole earth shall he be called. For YHWH has called you as a woman abandoned and grieved in spirit, and a wife of youth when you were refused, says your Elohim. For a small moment have I abandoned you, but with great mercies will I gather you. In a little wrath I hid my face from you for a moment, but with everlasting kindness will I have mercy on you, says YHWH your Redeemer. For this, the waters of Noach unto me, for as I have sworn that the waters of Noach should no more go over the earth, so have I sworn that I would not be angry with you. For the mountains shall depart and the hills be removed, but my kindness shall not depart from you, neither shall the covenant of my shalom be removed, says YHWH that has mercy on you.

3 O you afflicted, tossed with tempest and not comforted, behold, I will lay your stones with fair colors and lay your foundations with sapphires. And I will make your windows of agates, and your gates of carbuncles, and all your borders of pleasant stones. And all your children shall be taught of YHWH, and great shall be the shalom of your children. In righteousness shall you be strengthened; you shall be far from oppression, for you shall not fear, and from terror, for it shall not come near you. Behold, they shall surely gather together against you, not by me; whosoever shall gather together against you shall fall for your sake. Behold, I have created the smith that blows the coals in the fire and that brings forth an instrument for his work, and I have created the waster to destroy. No weapon that is formed against you shall prosper, and every tongue that shall rise against you in judgment you shall condemn. This is the heritage of the servants of YHWH, and their righteousness is of me, says YHWH.[237]

4 And now behold, I say unto you that you ought to search these things. Yes, a mitzvah I give unto you that you search these things diligently, for great are the words of Yesha'yahu. For surely he spoke as touching all things concerning my people which are of the house

---

237 Isa. 54:1-17

of Isra'el. Therefore, it must necessarily be that he speak also to the Goyim. And all things that he spoke have been and shall be, even according to the words which he spoke. Therefore, give heed to my words. Write the things which I have told you, and, according to the time and the will of the Father, they shall go forth unto the Goyim. And whosoever will hearken unto my words, and repents and is washed by immersion, the same shall be saved. Search the prophets, for many there be that testify of these things.

5 And now it came to pass that when Yeshua had said these words, he said unto them again, after he had expounded[238] all the scriptures unto them which they had received, he said unto them, Behold, other scriptures I would that you should write, that you have not. And it came to pass that he said unto Nefi, Bring forth the record which you have kept. And when Nefi had brought forth the records and laid them before him, and he cast his eyes upon them and said, Truly I say unto you, I commanded my servant Sh'mu'el, the Lamanite, that he should testify unto this people that at the day that the Father should glorify his name in me, that there were many k'doshim who should arise from the dead, and should appear unto many, and should minister unto them. And he said unto them, Was it not so? And his talmidim answered him and said, Yes, Adon, Sh'mu'el did prophesy according to your words, and they were all fulfilled. And Yeshua said unto them, How is it that you have not written this thing, that many k'doshim[239] did arise and appear unto many and did minister unto them? And it came to pass that Nefi remembered that this thing had not been written. And it came to pass that Yeshua commanded that it should be written, therefore it was written according as he commanded.

11 And now it came to pass that when Yeshua had expounded all the scriptures in one which they had written, he commanded them that they should teach the things which he had expounded unto them. And it came to pass that he commanded them that they should write the words which the Father had given unto Mal'akhi, which he should tell unto them. And it came to pass that after they were written, he expounded them. And these are the words

---

238 3 Nefi 11:1, 6   **239** "Holy ones" or "saints"

which he did tell them, saying, Thus said the Father unto Mal'akhi: Behold, I will send my messenger and he shall prepare the way before me, and YHWH whom you seek shall suddenly come to his Temple, even the messenger of the covenant whom you delight in. Behold, he shall come, says YHWH Tzva'ot, but who may abide the day of his coming? And who shall stand when he appears? For he is like a refiner's fire and like fullers' soap. And he shall sit as a refiner and purifier of silver, and he shall purify the sons of Levi and purge them as gold and silver, that they may offer unto YHWH an offering in righteousness. Then shall the offering of Y'hudah and Yerushalayim be pleasant unto YHWH, as in the days of old and as in former years. And I will come near to you in judgment, and I will be a swift witness against the sorcerers, and against the adulterers, and against false swearers, and against those that oppress the laborer in his wages, the widow, and the fatherless, and that turn aside the stranger, and fear not me, says YHWH Tzva'ot. For I am YHWH, I change not; therefore, you sons of Ya'akov are not consumed.

2 Even from the days of your fathers, you are gone away from my ordinances and have not kept them. Return unto me and I will return unto you, says YHWH Tzva'ot. But you said, In what way shall we return? Will a man rob Elohim? Yet you have robbed me. But you say, In what way have we robbed you? In tithes and offerings. You are cursed with a curse, for you have robbed me, even this whole nation. Bring you all the tithes into the storehouse, that there may be meat in my house, and prove me now by this, says YHWH Tzva'ot, if I will not open you the windows of Heaven and pour you out a blessing that there shall not be room enough to receive it. And I will rebuke the devourer for your sakes, and he shall not destroy the fruits of your ground, neither shall your vine cast her fruit before the time in the field, says YHWH Tzva'ot. And all nations shall call you blessed, for you shall be a delightful land, says YHWH Tzva'ot.

3 Your words have been stout against me, says YHWH. Yet you say, What have we spoken against you? You have said, It is vain to serve Elohim. And what does it profit that we have kept his ordinance and that we have walked mournfully before YHWH Tzva'ot? And now we call the proud happy; yes, they that work

wickedness are set up, yes, them that tempt Elohim are even delivered.

⁴Then they that feared YHWH spoke often one to another, and YHWH hearkened and heard. And a book of remembrance was written before him for them that feared YHWH and that thought upon his name. And they shall be mine, says YHWH Tzva'ot, in that day when I make up my jewels. And I will spare them as a man spares his own son that serves him. Then shall you return and discern between the righteous and the wicked, between him that serves Elohim and him that serves him not.[240] For behold, the day comes that shall burn as an oven, and all the proud, yes, and all that do wickedly, shall be stubble; and the day that comes shall burn them up, says YHWH Tzva'ot, that it shall leave them neither root nor branch.

⁵But unto you that fear my name shall the Son of Righteousness[241] arise with healing in his wings.[242] And you shall go forth and grow up as calves in the stall; and you shall tread down the wicked, for they shall be ashes under the soles of your feet in the day that I shall do this, says YHWH Tzva'ot. Remember you the Torah of Moshe, my servant whom I commanded, unto him in Horev for all Isra'el, with the statutes and judgments. Behold, I will send you Eliyahu the prophet

---

240 Mal. 3:1-18   241 The phrase in Malachi (Mal. 3:20 [4:2]) is correctly translated as "sun of righteousness," however *The Stick of Joseph* has instead rendered the phrase "Son of Righteousness." This is not an error of diction in English, but a deliberate and important interpretive term. The sixth of the ten Sefirot is known as *tiferet*, which is "often symbolized by the sun, also by the tree of life" (The Zohar; Soncino Press; Volume III Glossary, p. 420). We read in the Zohar concerning *tiferet*: "The Holy One, blessed be He, has a Son, whose glory (*tifret*) shines from one end of the world to another. He is a great and mighty tree, whose head reaches heaven, and whose roots are set in the holy ground, and his name is 'Mispar' and his place is in the uppermost heaven, as it is written, 'The heavens declare (me-SaPRim) the glory (*tifret*) of God' (Ps. 19:1). Were it not for this 'Mispar' there would be neither hosts nor offspring in any of the worlds" (Zohar 2:105a).
242 Mal. 3:20 (4:1). This verse is never cited as a Messianic prophecy in the New Testament. However, it is used as a Messianic prophecy in the Midrash Rabbah: "Moses asked: 'Shall they remain in pledge for ever?' God replied: 'No, only until the sun appears' that is, till the coming of the Messiah; for it says, But unto you that fear My name shall the sun of righteousness arise with healing in its wings (Mal. 3:20)" (Midrash Rabbah on Ex. 31:10). The Hebrew word for "wing" in this verse of Malachi is *kanaf*, a word which means "wing" or "corner." The Hebrew word for "corner" is found in Num. 15:37-41, where we are told to put the *tzitzit* on the "corners" of our garments. In Matt. 9:20-22; 14:36; Mark 3:10; and Luke 6:19, persons were healed after touching Yeshua's *tzitzit* because there was healing in his "wings." It appears the same thing happened with the resurrected Mashiach among the Nefites. See 2 Nefi 11:5, 10-11.

before the coming of the great and dreadful day of YHWH, and he shall turn the heart of the fathers to the children and the heart of the children to their fathers, lest I come and smite the earth with a curse.[243]

6 And now it came to pass that when Yeshua had said these things, he expounded them unto the multitude. And he did expound[244] all things unto them, both great and small. And he said, These scriptures which you had not with you, the Father commanded that I should give unto you, for it was wisdom in him that they should be given unto future generations.[245] And he did expound all things, even from the beginning until the time that he should come in his glory — yes, even all things which should come upon the face of the earth, even until the elements should **melt** with fervent heat, and the earth **should be wrapped together as a scroll**,[246] and the heavens and the earth should pass away, and even unto the great and last day when all people, and all kindreds, and all nations and tongues shall stand before Elohim to be judged of their works, whether they be good or whether they be evil; if they be good, to the resurrection[247] of everlasting life, and if they be evil, to the resurrection of damnation — being on a parallel, the one on the one hand and the other on the other hand, according to the mercy, and the justice,[248] and the holiness which is in Mashiach, who was before the world began.

12 And now there cannot be written in this book even a hundredth part of the things which Yeshua did truly teach unto the people. But behold, the plates of Nefi do contain the more part of the things which he taught the people. And these things have I written, which are a lesser part of the things which he taught the people, and I have written them to the intent that they may be brought again unto this people from the Goyim, according to the words which Yeshua has spoken. And when they shall have received this, which is expedient that they should have first to try their faith,[249]

---

243 Mal. 3:19-24 (4:1-6) **244** Alma 12:16-17; 13:9; 3 Nefi 11:6 **245** 2 Nefi 3:1; Alma 14:8; 17:9-11; 3 Nefi 11:1 **246** Isa. 34:3-4; Nah. 1:5-6; Mic. 1:4; Ps. 97:5 **247** 1 Sam. 2:6; Isa. 25:8; 26:19; Ezek. 37:12; Hos. 13:14; Job 19:26; Dan. 12:2; 2 Nefi 1:6; 6:2, 4, 7; 7:5; Moshiyah 8:2, 9-11, 14; Alma 9:2, 6; 19:4-9; Cheleman 5:12; 3 Nefi 3:4; M'raman 3:5; 4:7; M'roni 7:8 **248** Gen. 18:19; Isa. 9:7; Jer. 23:5; Ps. 89:15 (14); 1 Nefi 3:17; 2 Nefi 6:7; Ya'akov 4:2; Moshiyah 8:7; Alma 16:34; M'raman 3:4 **249** 'Eter 1:17

and if it should so be that they shall believe these things, then shall the greater things be made manifest unto them. And if it so be that they will not believe these things, then shall the greater things[250] be withheld from them unto their condemnation. Behold, I was about to write them all, which were engraved upon the plates of Nefi, but YHWH forbade it, saying, I will try the faith of my people. Therefore I, M'raman, do write the things which have been commanded me of YHWH. And now I, M'raman, make an end of my sayings and proceed to write the things which have been commanded me. Therefore, I would that you should behold that YHWH truly did teach the people for the space of three days, and after that, he did show himself unto them often, and did break bread[251] often, and blessed it, and gave it unto them.

2 And it came to pass that he did teach and minister unto the children of the multitude of whom has been spoken. And he did loose their tongues, and they did speak unto their fathers great and marvelous things, even greater than he had revealed unto the people, and loosed their tongues that they could utter. And it came to pass that after he had ascended into Heaven, the second time that he showed himself unto them, and had gone unto the Father, after having healed[252] all their sick and their lame, and opened the eyes of the blind, and unstopped the ears of the deaf, and even had done all manner of cures among them, and raised a man from the dead, and had shown forth his power unto them, and had ascended unto the Father, behold, it came to pass on the next day that the multitude gathered themselves together, and they both saw and heard these children; yes, even babes did open their mouths and utter marvelous things. And the things which they did utter were forbidden, that there should not any man write them.[253]

3 And it came to pass that the talmidim whom Yeshua had chosen began from that time forth to immerse and to teach as many as did come unto them. And as many as were washed by immersion in the name of Yeshua were filled with the Ruach HaKodesh. And many of them saw and heard unspeakable things which are not lawful to be written. And they taught and did minister one to another, and they

---

250 Alma 9:3; Cheleman 5:13; 'Eter 1:17-19   251 3 Nefi 8:6-7; 9:6; M'roni 4:1; 6:2   252 1 Nefi 3:13; Moshiyah 1:14; 3 Nefi 8:2-3   253 2 Nefi 14:2; 3 Nefi 8:4; 9:5

had all things common among them, every man dealing justly one with another. And it came to pass that they did do all things even as Yeshua had commanded them. And they who were immersed in the name of Yeshua were called the assembly of Mashiach.

4 And it came to pass that as the talmidim of Yeshua were journeying, and were preaching the things which they had both heard and seen, and were immersing in the name of Yeshua, it came to pass that the talmidim were gathered together and were united in mighty prayer and fasting. And Yeshua again showed himself unto them, for they were praying unto the Father in his name; and Yeshua came and stood in the midst of them, and said unto them, What will you that I shall give unto you? And they said unto him, Adon, we will that you would tell us the name by which we shall call this assembly, for there are disputes among the people concerning this matter. And YHWH said unto them, Truly, truly I say unto you, why is it that the people should murmur and dispute because of this thing? Have they not read the scriptures which say you must take upon you the name of Mashiach, which is my name? For by this name shall you be called at the last day. And whoever takes upon him my name and endures to the end, the same shall be saved at the last day. Therefore, whatsoever you shall do, you shall do it in my name. Therefore, you shall call the assembly in my name, and you shall call upon the Father in my name, that he will bless the assembly for my sake. And how is it my assembly unless it is called in my name? For if an assembly is called in Moshe's name, then it is Moshe's assembly; or if it is called in the name of a man, then it is the assembly of a man; but if it is called in my name, then it is my assembly, if it so be that they are built upon my besorah. Truly I say unto you that you are built upon my besorah; therefore, you shall call whatsoever things you do call in my name. Therefore, if you call upon the Father for the assembly, if it be in my name, the Father will hear you. And if it so be that the assembly is built upon my besorah, then will the Father show forth his own works in it. But if it be not built upon my besorah, and is built upon the works of men or upon the works of HaSatan, truly I say unto you, they have joy in their works for a season, and by and by the end comes, and they are cut down and cast into the fire[254] from where there is no return, for

---

[254] Ya'akov 3:7, 18-25; Cheleman 5:12; 3 Nefi 12:4-5; M'raman 4:3

their works do follow them. For it is because of their works that they are cut down. Therefore, remember the things that I have told you.

5 Behold, I have given unto you my besorah,[255] and this is the besorah which I have given unto you: that I came into the world to do the will of my Father because my Father sent me. And my Father sent me that I might be lifted up upon the Tz'lav. And after that I had been lifted up upon the Tz'lav, I might draw all men unto me, that as I have been lifted up by men, even so should men be lifted up by the Father to stand before me, to be judged of their works, whether they be good or whether they be evil. And for this cause have I been lifted up.[256] Therefore, according to the power of the Father, I will draw all men unto me, that they may be judged according to their works. And it shall come to pass that whoever repents and is washed by immersion in my name shall be filled, and if he endures to the end,[257] behold, him will I hold guiltless before my Father at that day when I shall stand to judge the world. And he that endures not unto the end, the same is he that is also cut down and cast into the fire from where they can no more return, because of the justice of the Father. And this is the word which he has given unto the children of men, and for this cause he fulfills the words which he has given; and he lies not, but fulfills all his words. And no unclean thing can enter into his kingdom, therefore nothing enters into his rest except it be those who have washed their garments[258] in my blood because of their faith, and the repentance of all their sins, and their faithfulness unto the end. Now this is the mitzvah: Repent all you ends of the earth, and come unto me, and be washed by immersion in my name, that you may be sanctified by the reception of the Ruach HaKodesh, that you may stand spotless before me at the last day. Truly, truly I say unto you, this is my besorah, and you know the things that you must do in my assembly, for the works which you have seen me do, that shall you also do. For that which you have seen me do, even that shall you do. Therefore, if you do these things, blessed are you, for you shall be lifted up at the last day.

---

255 1 Nefi 3:21-23; 4:3; 7:3; 3 Nefi 7:5   256 Numbers 21:6-9; 1 Nefi 3:14; 5:36; Cheleman 3:9   257 1 Nefi 7:6; 2 Nefi 13:3-4; 6:7; Ameni 1:10; 3 Nefi 7:2; M'raman 4:10   258 Alma 3:3; 10:1; 'Eter 6:3

13 Write the things which you have seen and heard, except it be those which are forbidden.²⁵⁹ Write the works of this people which shall be, even as has been written of that which has been. For behold, out of the books which have been written and which shall be written shall this people be judged, for by them shall their works be known unto men. And behold, all things are written by the Father. Therefore, out of the books²⁶⁰ which shall be written shall the world be judged. And know you that you shall be judges of this people according to the judgment which I shall give unto you, which shall be just. Therefore, what manner of men ought you to be? Truly I say unto you, even as I am. And now I go unto the Father. And truly I say unto you, whatsoever things you shall ask the Father in my name, it shall be given unto you. Therefore, ask²⁶¹ and you shall receive, knock and it shall be opened unto you; for he that asks, receives, and unto him that knocks, it shall be opened. And now behold, my joy is great, even unto fulness, because of you, and also this generation; yes, and even the Father rejoices, and also all the holy angels, because of you and this generation, for none of them are lost. Behold, I would that you should understand, for I mean those which are now alive of this generation, and none of them are lost, and in them I have fulness of joy. But behold, it sorrows me because of the fourth generation from this generation, for they are led away captive by him, even as was the son of perdition,²⁶² for they will sell me for silver, and for gold, and for that which moth does corrupt, and which thieves can break through and steal. And in that day will I visit them, even in turning their works upon their own heads.

2 And it came to pass that when Yeshua had ended these sayings, he said unto his talmidim, Enter you in at the strait gate,²⁶³ for strait is the gate and narrow is the way that leads to life, and few there be that find it; but wide is the gate and broad the way which leads to death, and many there be who travel therein until the night comes, in which no man can work.

3 And it came to pass when Yeshua had said these words, he spoke unto his talmidim one by one, saying unto them, What is it that you desire of me after that I am gone to the Father? And they all spoke,

---

259 Alma 9:3; Cheleman 3:6; 3 Nefi 8:4; 9:5; 13:4   260 Ezek. 37:15-19; 1 Nefi 1:3-5, 22; 2 Nefi 11:19-21; 12:1, 12   261 1 Nefi 4:2; 2 Nefi 14:1; M'roni 7:5; 10:2   262 3 Nefi 13:8   263 2 Nefi 6:11; 13:3; Ya'akov 4:2; 3 Nefi 6:9

except it were three, saying, We desire that after we have lived unto the age of man, that our ministry in which you have called us may have an end, that we may speedily come unto you in your kingdom. And he said unto them, Blessed are you because you desire this thing of me; therefore, after that you are seventy and two years old, you shall come unto me in my kingdom, and with me you shall find rest. And when he had spoken unto them, he turned himself unto the three and said unto them, What will you that I should do unto you[264] when I am gone unto the Father? And they sorrowed in their hearts, for they dared not speak unto him the thing which they desired. And he said unto them, Behold, I know your thoughts, and you have desired the thing which Yochanan, my beloved,[265] who was with me in my ministry before that I was lifted up by the Judeans, desired of me. Therefore, more blessed are you, for you shall never taste of death, but you shall live to behold all the doings of the Father unto the children of men, even until all things shall be fulfilled according to the will of the Father, when I shall come in my glory with the Powers of Heaven.[266] And you shall never endure the pains of death, but when I shall come in my glory, you shall be changed in the twinkling of an eye from mortality to immortality;[267] and then shall you be blessed in the kingdom of my Father. And again, you shall not have pain while you shall dwell in the flesh, neither sorrow, except it be for the sins of the world. And all this will I do because of the thing which you have desired of me, for you have desired that you might bring the souls of men unto me while the world shall stand. And for this cause you shall have fulness of joy, and you shall sit down in the kingdom of my Father. Yes, your joy shall be full, even as the Father has given me fulness of joy, and you shall be even as I am, and I am even as the Father, and the Father and I are echad. And the Ruach HaKodesh bears record of the Father and me, and the Father gives the Ruach HaKodesh unto the children of men because of me.

4 And it came to pass that when Yeshua had spoken these words, he touched every one of them with his finger, except it were the three who were to remain, and then he departed. And behold, the Heavens were opened, and they were caught up into Heaven and saw and heard unspeakable things. And it was forbidden them that

---

264 3 Nefi 13:6; 4 Nefi 1:3, 7   **265** John 21:21-24   **266** 3 Nefi 9:8; 10:1   **267** 3 Nefi 13:6

they should utter,²⁶⁸ neither was it given unto them power that they could utter, the things which they saw and heard. And whether they were in the body or out of the body, they could not tell; for it did seem unto them like a transfiguration of them, that they were changed from this body of flesh into an immortal state, that they could behold the things of Elohim. But it came to pass that they did again minister upon the face of the earth. Nevertheless, they did not teach the things which they had heard and seen because of the mitzvah which was given them in Heaven. And now whether they were mortal or immortal from the day of their transfiguration, I know not; but this much I know according to the record which has been given — they did go forth upon the face of the land and did minister unto all the people, uniting as many to the assembly as would believe in their preaching, immersing them; and as many as were washed by immersion did receive the Ruach HaKodesh. And they were cast into prison by them who did not belong to the assembly, and the prisons could not hold them, for they were broken in two. And they were cast down into the earth, but they did smite the earth with the word of Elohim, insomuch that by his power²⁶⁹ they were delivered out of the depths of the earth, and therefore they could not dig pits sufficiently to hold them. And thrice they were cast into a furnace²⁷⁰ and received no harm. And twice were they cast into a den of wild beasts, and behold, they did play with the beasts as a child with a suckling lamb and received no harm.²⁷¹ And it came to pass that thus they did go forth among all the people of Nefi, and did preach the besorah of Mashiach unto all people upon the face of the land, and they were converted unto YHWH and were united unto the assembly of Mashiach. And thus the people of that generation were blessed, according to the word of Yeshua.

⁵And now I, M'raman, make an end of speaking concerning these things for a time. Behold, I was about to write the names of those who were never to taste of death, but YHWH forbade. Therefore, I write them not, for they are hidden from the world. But behold, I have seen them and they have ministered unto me,²⁷² and behold, they will be among the Goyim and the Goyim know them not. They will

---

268 Alma 9:3; Cheleman 3:6; 3 Nefi 8:4; 9:5; 13:1   269 Ya'akov 3:2   270 Dan. 3:19–29; Cheleman 2:20, 25   271 Dan. 6:17-24 (16–23)   272 M'raman 4:2

also be among the Y'hudim and the Y'hudim shall know them not. And it shall come to pass, when YHWH sees fit in his wisdom, that they shall minister unto all the scattered tribes of Isra'el, and unto all nations, kindreds, tongues, and people, and shall bring out of them unto Yeshua many souls, that their desire may be fulfilled, and also because of the convincing power of Elohim which is in them. And they are as the angels[273] of Elohim, and if they shall pray unto the Father in the name of Yeshua, they can show themselves unto whatsoever man it seems good to them. Therefore, great and marvelous works shall be worked by them before the great and coming day when all people must surely stand before the judgment seat of Mashiach. Yes, even among the Goyim shall there be a great and marvelous work performed by them before that judgment day. And if you had all the scriptures which give an account of all the marvelous works of Mashiach, you would, according to the words of Mashiach, know that these things must surely come. And woe be unto him that will not hearken unto the words of Yeshua and also to them whom he has chosen[274] and sent among them; for whoever receives not the words of Yeshua and the words of those whom he has sent, receives not him, and therefore he will not receive them at the last day. And it would be better for them if they had not been born. For do you suppose that you can get rid of the justice of an offended Elohim who has been trampled under feet[275] of men, that thereby salvation might come?

⁶And now behold, as I spoke concerning those whom YHWH had chosen, yes, even three[276] who were caught up into the Heavens, that I knew not whether they were cleansed from mortality to immortality, but behold, since I wrote, I have inquired of YHWH; and he has made it manifest unto me that there must necessarily be a change[277] worked upon their bodies, or else they must taste of death. Therefore, that they might not taste of death, there was a change worked upon their bodies, that they might not suffer pain nor sorrow except it were for the sins of the world. Now this change was not equal to that which should take place at the last day, but there was a change worked upon them insomuch that HaSatan could have no power over them, that he could not tempt them. And they were sanctified in the flesh,

---

273 Moshiyah 2:1; 11:26   274 3 Nefi 5:10   275 1 Nefi 5:36; Alma 3:10; Cheleman 4:9
276 3 Nefi 13:3-4   277 Gen. 5:24; Alma 21:3; 3 Nefi 13:3

that they were holy and that the powers of the earth could not hold them, and in this state they were to remain until the judgment day of Mashiach. And at that day, they were to receive a greater change and to be received into the kingdom of the Father, to go no more out, but to dwell with Elohim eternally in the Heavens.

7 And now behold, I say unto you that when YHWH shall see fit in his wisdom that these sayings shall come[278] unto the Goyim according to his word, then you may know that the covenant[279] which the Father has made with the children of Isra'el concerning their restoration to the lands of their inheritance is already beginning to be fulfilled. And you may know that the words of YHWH which have been spoken by the holy prophets shall all be fulfilled. And you need not say that YHWH delays his coming unto the children of Isra'el. And you need not imagine in your hearts that the words which have been spoken are vain, for behold, YHWH will remember his covenant which he has made unto his people of the house of Isra'el. And when you shall see these sayings coming forth among you, then you need not any longer oppose the doings of YHWH, for the sword of his justice is in his right hand. And behold, at that day, if you shall oppose his doings, he will cause it that it shall soon overtake you.

8 Woe unto him that opposes the doings of YHWH. Yes, woe unto him that shall deny[280] the Mashiach and his works. Yes, woe unto him that shall deny the revelations of YHWH, and that shall say YHWH no longer works by revelation, or by prophecy,[281] or by gifts, or by tongues, or by healings, or by the power of the Ruach HaKodesh. Yes, and woe unto him that shall say at that day that there can be no miracle worked by Yeshua HaMashiach, in order to get gain; for he that does this shall become like unto the son of perdition, for whom there was no mercy according to the words of Mashiach. Yes, and you need not any longer hiss, nor reject, nor make game of the Y'hudim, nor of any of the remnant of the house of Isra'el, for behold, YHWH remembers his covenant unto them, and he will do unto them according to that which he has sworn. Therefore, you need not suppose that you can turn the right hand of YHWH unto

---

278 2 Nefi 12:12 279 Gen. 13:15-18; Jer. 31:30-33 (31-34); 1 Nefi 3:26-29; 4:3; 2 Nefi 2:2-7; 6:1; M'raman 4:3-4, 11; 'Eter 6:3; M'roni 10:6 280 2 Nefi 11:9; 4 Nefi 1:5-6; M'raman 4:6-7; M'roni 1:1 281 Ya'akov 1:1; Alma 6:7; 12:1; 20:1; 3 Nefi 2:4

the left, that he may not execute judgment unto the fulfilling of the covenant which he has made unto the house of Isra'el.

14 Hearken, O you Goyim, and hear the words of Yeshua HaMashiach, the Son of the living Elohim, which he has commanded me that I should speak concerning you; for behold, he commands me that I should write, saying, Turn, all you Goyim, from your wicked ways, and repent of your evil doings — of your lies and deceivings, and of your whoredoms, and of your secret abominations, and your idolatries, and of your murders, and your priestcrafts, and your envyings, and your strifes,[282] and from all your wickedness and abominations — and come unto me[283] and be washed by immersion in my name, that you may receive a remission of your sins and be filled with the Ruach HaKodesh, that you may be numbered with my people who are of the house of Isra'el.

ספר נפי אשר היה בן נפי
אשר אחד מתלמדים ישוע המשיח

4 NEFI

THE BOOK OF NEFI
WHO IS THE SON OF NEFI,
ONE OF THE TALMIDIM OF YESHUA HAMASHIACH

An account of the people of Nefi, according to his record.

AND it came to pass that the thirty and fourth year[1] passed away, and also the thirty and fifth, and behold, the talmidim of Yeshua had formed an assembly of Mashiach in all the lands round about. And as many as did come unto them and did truly repent of their sins were immersed[2] in the name of Yeshua, and they did also receive the Ruach HaKodesh. And it came to pass in the thirty and sixth year, the people were all converted unto YHWH, upon all the face of the land, both Nefites and Lamanites; and there were no contentions and disputations among them, and every man did deal justly one with another. And they had all things common among them; therefore,

---

282 The repetition of the possessive pronoun here is normative in Hebrew, where a pronominal suffix is normally attached to each object of possession. 283 2 Nefi 11:16; Alma 3:6; 3 Nefi 5:23; 'Eter 1:19; M'roni 7:6   1 ~ 34 CE   2 2 Nefi 6:7; 13:2; 3 Nefi 5:8–10

4 NEFI 1:2

there were not rich and poor,³ bond and free, but they were all made free and partakers of the Heavenly gift.⁴

2 And it came to pass that the thirty and seventh year passed away also, and there still continued to be shalom in the land. And there were great and marvelous works performed by the talmidim of Yeshua, insomuch that they did heal the sick, and raise the dead, and cause the lame to walk, and the blind to receive their sight, and the deaf to hear. And all manner of miracles⁵ did they work among the children of men, and in nothing did they work miracles except it were in the name of Yeshua. And thus did the thirty and eighth year pass away, and also the thirty and ninth, and the forty and first, and the forty and second, yes, even until forty and nine years had passed away, and also the fifty and first, and the fifty and second, yes, and even until fifty and nine years had passed away. And YHWH did prosper⁶ them exceedingly in the land, yes, insomuch that they did build cities again where there had been cities burned, yes, even that great city Zerach'mla⁷ did they cause to be built again. But there were many cities which had been sunk, and waters came up in the place thereof; therefore, these cities could not be renewed. And now behold, it came to pass that the people of Nefi did grow strong, and did multiply exceedingly fast, and became an exceedingly fair and delightful people. And they were married and given in marriage, and were blessed according to the multitude of the promises which YHWH had made unto them. And they did not walk anymore after the performances and ordinances of the Torah of Moshe,⁸ but they did walk after the mitzvot which they had received from their Adonai and their Elohim, continuing in fasting and prayer, and in meeting together often,⁹ both to pray and to hear the word of YHWH. And it came to pass that there was no contention¹⁰ among all the people in all the land, but there were mighty miracles worked among the talmidim of Yeshua.

3 And it came to pass that the seventy and first year¹¹ passed away, and also the seventy and second year, yes, and in short, until the

---

3 2 Nefi 6:10 4 'Eter 5:2 5 M'raman 4:8 6 Alma 17: 9; 29:20 7 3 Nefi 4:6 8 3 Nefi 4:7; 7:2. The original Hebrew might also be understood as a rhetorical question: "And did they not walk more after the performances and ordinances of the Torah of Moshe?" See note to Moshiyah 8:1 on the issue of rhetorical questions and statements in Hebrew.
9 M'roni 6:2 10 Moshiyah 9:9 11 ~71 CE

seventy and ninth year had passed away. Yes, even a hundred years had passed away, and the talmidim[12] of Yeshua whom he had chosen had all gone to the pardes of Elohim — except it were the three[13] who should remain. And there were other talmidim ordained in their place, and also many of that generation had passed away. And it came to pass that there was no contention[14] in the land because of the love of Elohim which did dwell in the hearts of the people; and there were no envyings, nor strifes, nor tumults, nor whoredoms, nor lyings, nor murders, nor any manner of lustfulness. And surely there could not be a happier people among all the people who had been created by the hand of Elohim. There were no robbers, nor murderers, neither were there Lamanites nor any manner of -ites, but they were one,[15] the children of Mashiach and heirs to the kingdom of Elohim. And how blessed were they, for YHWH did bless them in all their doings, yes, even they were blessed and prospered until a hundred and ten years had passed away. And the first generation from Mashiach had passed away, and there was no contention in all the land.

4 And it came to pass that Nefi,[16] he that kept this last record (and he kept it upon the plates of Nefi) died, and his son Amos kept it in his place. And he kept it upon the plates of Nefi also, and he kept it eighty and four years. And there was still shalom in the land, except it were a small part of the people who had revolted from the assembly and took upon them the name of Lamanites; therefore, there began to be Lamanites again in the land. And it came to pass that Amos died also, and it was a hundred and ninety and four years from the coming of Mashiach; and his son Amos kept the record in his place. And he also kept it upon the plates of Nefi, and it was also written in The Book of Nefi, which is this book. And it came to pass that two hundred years[17] had passed away and the second generation had all passed away except it were a few.

5 And now I, M'raman, would that you should know that the people had multiplied insomuch that they were spread upon all the face of the land, and that they had become exceedingly rich because of their prosperity in Mashiach. And now in this two hundred and first year, there began to be among them those who were lifted up in pride,

---

12 3 Nefi 5:8, 10   **13** 3 Nefi 13:3   **14** 3 Nefi 5:8   **15** Moshiyah 9:9   **16** 3 Nefi 1:1   **17** ~200 CE

such as the wearing of costly apparel, and all manner of fine pearls, and of the fine things of the world. And from that time forth, they did have their goods and their substance no more common among them, and they began to be divided into classes.[18] And they began to build up assemblies unto themselves to get gain, and began to deny the true assembly[19] of Mashiach.

6 And it came to pass that when two hundred and ten years had passed away, there were many assemblies in the land. Yes, there were assemblies which professed to know the Mashiach, and yet they did deny[20] the greater parts of his besorah, insomuch that they did receive all manner of wickedness, and did administer that which was sacred unto him to whom it had been forbidden because of unworthiness. And this assembly did multiply exceedingly because of iniquity and because of the power of HaSatan, who did get hold upon their hearts. And again, there was another assembly which denied[21] the Mashiach, and they did persecute[22] the true assembly of Mashiach because of their humility and their belief in Mashiach. And they did despise them because of the many miracles which were worked among them. Therefore, they did exercise power and authority over the talmidim of Yeshua who did remain with them, and they did cast them into prison; but by the power of the word of Elohim which was in them, the prisons were broken in two,[23] and they went forth doing mighty miracles among them. Nevertheless, and despite all these miracles, the people did harden their hearts and did seek to kill them, even as the Judeans at Yerushalayim sought to kill[24] Yeshua, according to his word. And they did cast them into furnaces of fire, and they came forth receiving no harm.[25] And they also cast them into dens of wild beasts, and they did play with the wild beasts, even as a child with a lamb; and they did come forth from among them, receiving no harm. Nevertheless, the people did harden their hearts, for they were led by many kohanim[26] and false prophets to build up many assemblies and to do all manner of iniquity.[27] And they did smite[28] upon the people of Yeshua, but the people of Yeshua did not smite again. And thus they did dwindle in unbelief[29] and wickedness from year to year, even until two hundred and thirty years had passed away.

---

18 Alma 16:22 19 M'roni 6:1 20 M'raman 4:7 21 Cheleman 3:9 22 Alma 1:5 23 Alma 10:11; 3 Nefi 13:4 24 2 Nefi 7:1 25 M'raman 4:4 26 Moshiyah 7:1 27 3 Nefi 3:3 28 Alma 1:5 29 Alma 21:2

⁷And now it came to pass in this year, yes, in the two hundred and thirty and first year,³⁰ there was a great division among the people. And it came to pass that in this year, there arose a people who were called the Nefites,³¹ and they were true believers in Mashiach. And among them there were those who were called by the Lamanites: Ya'akovites, and Yosefites, and Tzuramites. Therefore, the true believers in Mashiach and the true worshipers of Mashiach, among whom were the three talmidim of Yeshua who should remain, were called Nefites, and Ya'akovites, and Yosefites, and Tzuramites. And it came to pass that they who rejected the besorah were called Lamanites,³² and L'mu'elites, and Yishma'elites. And they did not dwindle in unbelief, but they did willfully rebel against the besorah of Mashiach, and they did teach their children that they should not believe, even as their fathers from the beginning did dwindle. And it was because of the wickedness and abominations of their fathers, even as it was in the beginning. And they were taught to hate the children of Elohim, even as the Lamanites were taught to hate the children of Nefi from the beginning. And it came to pass that two hundred and forty and four years had passed away, and thus were the affairs of the people. And the more wicked part³³ of the people did grow strong, and became exceedingly more numerous than were the people of Elohim. And they did still continue to build up³⁴ assemblies unto themselves and adorn them with all manner of precious things. And thus did two hundred and fifty years pass away, and also two hundred and sixty years.

⁸And it came to pass that the wicked part of the people began again to build up the secret oaths and conspiracies of Gaddianton.³⁵ And also, the people who were called the people of Nefi began to be proud in their hearts because of their exceeding riches,³⁶ and became³⁷ vain like unto their brothers the Lamanites. And from this time the talmidim began to sorrow for the sins of the world. And it came to pass that when three hundred years had passed away, both the people of Nefi and the Lamanites had become exceedingly wicked, one like unto another. And it came to pass that the robbers of Gaddianton did spread³⁸ over all the face of the land, and there were none that

---

30 ~ 230 CE 31 Alma 1:19; 14:2; Cheleman 5:15 32 Alma 17:8; Cheleman 5:15 33 3 Nefi 3:6 34 M'raman 4:5 35 Cheleman 2:33 36 Cheleman 2:12 37 Cheleman 2:14 38 3 Nefi 1:10

were righteous except it were the talmidim of Yeshua. And gold and silver did they lay up in store in abundance, and did traffic in all manner of traffic.

⁹And it came to pass that after three hundred and five years had passed away — and the people did still remain in wickedness — and Amos died, and his brother Ammaron did keep the record in his place. And it came to pass that when three hundred and twenty years had passed away, Ammaron, being constrained by the Ruach HaKodesh, did hide[39] up the records which were sacred — yes, even all the sacred records[40] which had been handed down from generation to generation, which were sacred, even until the three hundred and twentieth year[41] from the coming of Mashiach. And he did hide them up unto YHWH, that they might come again unto the remnant of the house of Ya'akov[42] according to the prophecies and the promises of YHWH. And thus is the end of the record of Ammaron.

ספר מרמן
M'RAMAN
THE BOOK OF M'RAMAN

AND now I, M'raman, make a record of the things which I have both seen and heard, and call it The Book of M'raman. And about the time that Ammaron[1] hid up the records unto YHWH, he came unto me, I being about ten years of age — and I began to be learned somewhat after the manner of the learning of my people — and Ammaron said unto me, I perceive that you are a sober child, and are quick to observe. Therefore, when you are about twenty and four years old, I would that you should remember the things that you have observed concerning this people. And when you are of that age, go to the land of Antum, unto a hill which shall be called Shim,[2] and there have I deposited unto YHWH all the sacred engravings concerning this people. And behold, you shall take the plates of Nefi[3] unto yourself, and the remainder shall you leave in the place where they are. And you shall engrave upon the plates of Nefi all the things that you have observed

---

39 M'raman 1:1 **40** 1 Nefi 5:34; 3 Nefi 1:1; M'raman 3:2 **41** ~319 CE **42** M'raman 3:5
1 4 Nefi 1:9 **2** M'raman 2:3. Likely from the Hebrew root *sim* שים (Strong's 7760), "to put or place something, to deposit." **3** 1 Nefi 2:14

concerning this people. And I, M'raman, being a descendant of Nefi (and my father's name was M'raman) and I remembered the things which Ammaron commanded me.

2 And it came to pass that I, being eleven years old, was carried by my father into the land southward, even to the land of Zerach'mla, the whole face of the land having become covered with buildings, and the people were as numerous almost as it were the sand of the sea.

3 And it came to pass in this year, there began to be a war between the Nefites — who consisted of the Nefites, and the Ya'akovites, and the Yosefites, and the Tzuramites — and this war was between the Nefites and the Lamanites, and the L'mu'elites, and the Yishma'elites. Now the Lamanites, and the L'mu'elites, and the Yishma'elites were called Lamanites, and the two parties were Nefites and Lamanites. And it came to pass that the war began to be among them in the borders of Zerach'mla by the waters of Tzidon. And it came to pass that the Nefites had gathered together a great number of men, even to exceed the number of thirty thousand. And it came to pass that they did have in this same year a number of battles, in the which the Nefites did beat the Lamanites and did slay many of them.

4 And it came to pass that the Lamanites withdrew their design, and there was shalom settled in the land; and shalom did remain for the space of about four years, that there was no bloodshed. But wickedness did prevail upon the face of the whole land, insomuch that YHWH did take away his beloved talmidim; and the work of miracles and of healing did cease because of the iniquity of the people. And there were no gifts from YHWH, and the Ruach HaKodesh did not come upon any, because of their wickedness and unbelief. And I, being fifteen years of age, and being somewhat of a sober mind, therefore I was visited of YHWH, and tasted and knew of the goodness of Yeshua. And I did endeavor to preach unto this people, but my mouth was shut. And I was forbidden that I should preach unto them, for behold, they had willfully rebelled against their Elohim; and the beloved talmidim[4] were taken away out of the land because of their iniquity. But I did remain among them, but I was forbidden to preach unto them because of the hardness of their hearts. And because of the hardness of their hearts, the land was cursed for their sake. And these

---

4 4 Nefi 1:3; M'raman 4:2;

Gaddianton robbers[5] who were among the Lamanites did infest the land, insomuch that the inhabitants thereof began to hide up their treasures in the earth; and they became slippery,[6] because YHWH had cursed the land, that they could not hold them nor retain them again. And it came to pass that there were sorceries, and witchcrafts, and magics, and the power of the Evil One was worked upon all the face of the land, even unto the fulfilling of all the words of Avinodi, and also Sh'mu'el, the Lamanite.[7]

5 And it came to pass in that same year, there began to be a war again between the Nefites and the Lamanites. And despite being young, I was large in stature; therefore, the people of Nefi appointed me, that I should be their leader, or the leader of their armies. Therefore, it came to pass that in my sixteenth year I did go forth at the head of an army of the Nefites against the Lamanites; therefore, three hundred and twenty and six years[8] had passed away. And it came to pass that in the three hundred and twenty and seventh year, the Lamanites did come upon us with exceedingly great power, insomuch that they did frighten my armies. Therefore, they would not fight, and they began to retreat towards the north countries. And it came to pass that we did come to the city of Angolah, and we did take possession of the city and make preparations to defend ourselves against the Lamanites. And it came to pass that we did fortify the city with our might; but despite all our fortifications, the Lamanites did come upon us and did drive us out of the city. And they did also drive us forth out of the land of David. And we marched forth and came to the land of Y'hoshua, which was in the borders west by the seashore. And it came to pass that we did gather in our people as fast as it were possible, that we might get them together in one body. But behold, the land was filled with robbers and with Lamanites; and despite the great destruction which hung over my people, they did not repent of their evil doings. Therefore, there was blood and carnage spread throughout all the face of the land, both on the part of the Nefites and also on the part of the Lamanites. And it was one complete revolution throughout all the face of the land. And now the Lamanites had a king, and his name was Aharon, and he came against us with an army of forty and

---

5 Cheleman 1:11; 2:35   6 Cheleman 5:5   7 For Avinodi's words, see Moshiyah 7–9. For Sh'mu'el's words, see Cheleman 5.   8 ~326 CE

four thousand. And behold, I withstood him with forty and two thousand. And it came to pass that I beat him with my army, that he fled before me. And behold, all this was done, and three hundred and thirty years[9] had passed away.

6 And it came to pass that the Nefites began to repent of their iniquity and began to cry even as had been prophesied by Sh'mu'el, the prophet. For behold, no man could keep that which was his own, because of the thieves, and the robbers, and the murderers, and the magic art, and the witchcraft which was in the land. Thus, there began to be a mourning and a lamentation in all the land because of these things, and more especially among the people of Nefi. And it came to pass that when I, M'raman, saw their lamentation, and their mourning, and their sorrowing before YHWH, my heart did begin to rejoice within me, knowing the mercies and the long-suffering of YHWH, therefore supposing that he would be merciful unto them, that they would again become a righteous people. But behold, this my joy was vain, for their sorrowing was not unto repentance because of the goodness of Elohim, but it was rather the sorrowing of the damned because YHWH would not always allow them to take happiness in sin. And they did not come unto Yeshua with broken hearts and contrite spirits,[10] but they did curse Elohim and wish to die. Nevertheless, they would struggle with the sword for their lives. And it came to pass that my sorrow did return unto me again, and I saw that the day of grace was past with them, both temporally and spiritually, for I saw thousands of them cut down in open rebellion against their Elohim and heaped up as dung upon the face of the land. And thus three hundred and forty and four years had passed away.

7 And it came to pass that in the three hundred and forty and fifth year, the Nefites did begin to flee before the Lamanites, and they were pursued until they came even to the land of Yashon before it was possible to stop them in their retreat. And now the city of Yashon was near the land where Ammaron had deposited the records unto YHWH, that they might not be destroyed. And behold, I had gone according to the word of Ammaron and taken the plates of Nefi, and did make a record according to the words of Ammaron. And upon the plates of Nefi I did make a full account of all the wickedness

---

9 ~330 CE **10** 3 Nefi 5:23

and abominations. But upon these plates I did decline to make a full account of their wickedness and abominations, for behold, a continual scene of wickedness and abominations has been before my eyes ever since I have been sufficient to behold the ways of man. And woe is me because of their wickedness, for my heart has been filled with sorrow because of their wickedness all my days. Nevertheless, I know that I shall be lifted up[11] at the last day.

8 And it came to pass that in this year the people of Nefi again were hunted and driven. And it came to pass that we were driven forth until we had come northward to the land which was called Shem. And it came to pass that we did fortify the city of Shem and we did gather in our people as much as it were possible, that perhaps we might save them from destruction. And it came to pass in the three hundred and forty and sixth year, they began to come upon us again. And it came to pass that I did speak unto my people, and did urge them with great energy that they would stand boldly before the Lamanites and fight for their wives, and their children, and their houses, and their homes. And my words did arouse them somewhat to vigor, insomuch that they did not flee from before the Lamanites, but did stand with boldness against them. And it came to pass that we did contend with an army of thirty thousand against an army of fifty thousand. And it came to pass that we did stand before them with such firmness that they did flee from before us. And it came to pass that when they had fled, we did pursue them with our armies, and did meet them again, and did beat them. Nevertheless, the strength of YHWH was not with us, yes, we were left to ourselves, that the spirit of YHWH did not abide in us. Therefore, we had become weak like unto our brothers. And my heart did sorrow because of this the great calamity of my people, because of their wickedness and their abominations. But behold, we did go forth against the Lamanites and the robbers of Gaddianton until we had again taken possession of the lands of our inheritance. And the three hundred and forty and ninth year had passed away. And in the three hundred and fiftieth year, we made a treaty with the Lamanites and the robbers of Gaddianton, in the which we did get the lands of our inheritance divided. And the Lamanites did give unto us the land northward, yes, even to the narrow passage which

---
11 1 Ne 3:23; Alma 10:4; 17:1

led into the land southward. And we did give unto the Lamanites all the land southward.

⁹And it came to pass that the Lamanites did not come to battle again until ten years more had passed away. And behold, I had employed my people, the Nefites, in preparing their lands and their arms against the time of battle. And it came to pass that YHWH did say unto me, Cry unto this people: Repent, and come unto me, and be washed by immersion, and build up again my assembly, and you shall be spared. And I did cry unto this people, but it was in vain, and they did not realize that it was YHWH that had spared them and granted unto them a chance for repentance. And behold, they did harden their hearts against YHWH their Elohim. And it came to pass that after this tenth year had passed away, making in the whole three hundred and sixty years from the coming of Mashiach, and the king of the Lamanites sent a letter unto me which gave unto me to know that they were preparing to come again to battle against us. And it came to pass that I did cause my people that they should gather themselves together at the land Desolation, to a city which was in the borders by the narrow pass which led into the land southward, and there we did place our armies, that we might stop the armies of the Lamanites, that they might not get possession of any of our lands. Therefore, we did fortify against them with all our force.

¹⁰And it came to pass that in the three hundred and sixty and first year, the Lamanites did come down to the city of Desolation to battle against us. And it came to pass that in that year, we did beat them, insomuch that they did return to their own lands again. And in the three hundred and sixty and second year,[12] they did come down again to battle. And we did beat them again and did slay a great number of them, and their dead were cast into the sea. And now because of this great thing which my people, the Nefites, had done, they began to boast in their own strength and began to swear before the Heavens that they would avenge themselves of the blood of their brothers who had been slain by their enemies. And they did swear by the Heavens, and also by the throne of Elohim, that they would go up to battle against their enemies and would cut them off from the face of the land.

---

[12] ~361 CE

11 And it came to pass that I, M'raman, did utterly refuse from this time forth to be a commander and a leader of this people because of their wickedness and abomination. Behold, I had led them, despite their wickedness, I had led them many times to battle — and I had loved them according to the love of Elohim which was in me, with all my heart. And my soul had been poured out in prayer unto my Elohim all the day long for them. Nevertheless, it was without faith because of the hardness of their hearts. And thrice have I delivered them out of the hands of their enemies, and they have repented not of their sins. And when they had sworn by all that had been forbidden them by our Adonai and Savior Yeshua HaMashiach, that they would go up unto their enemies to battle and avenge themselves of the blood of their brothers, behold, the voice of YHWH came unto me, saying, Vengeance[13] is mine, and I will repay. And because this people repented not after I had delivered them, behold, they shall be cut off from the face of the earth.

12 And it came to pass that I utterly refused to go up against my enemies. And I did even as YHWH had commanded me, and I did stand as an idle witness to manifest unto the world the things which I saw and heard, according to the manifestations of the spirit, which had testified of things to come. Therefore, I write unto you Goyim, and also unto you, house of Isra'el, when the work shall commence, that you shall be about to prepare to return to the land of your inheritance. Yes, behold, I write unto all the ends of the earth, yes, unto you, twelve tribes of Isra'el, which shall be judged according to your works by the twelve[14] whom Yeshua chose to be his talmidim in the land of Yerushalayim. And I write also unto the remnant of this people, who shall also be judged by the twelve whom Yeshua chose in this land. And they shall be judged by the other twelve whom Yeshua chose in the land of Yerushalayim. And these things does the spirit manifest unto me; therefore, I write unto you all. And for this cause I write unto you, that you may know that you must all stand before[15] the judgment seat of Mashiach, yes, every soul who belongs to the whole human family of Adam, and you must stand to be judged of your works, whether they be good or evil; and also that you may believe the besorah of Yeshua HaMashiach, which you shall have among you;

---

13 Deut. 32:35; Rom. 12:19 14 Mark 3:13–14; Luke 6:12–16; 1 Nefi 3:16 15 Alma 8:16

and also that the Y'hudim, the covenant people of YHWH, shall have other witnesses, besides him whom they saw and heard, that Yeshua whom they slew was the very Mashiach and the very Elohim. And I would that I could persuade all you ends of the earth to repent and prepare to stand before the judgment seat of Mashiach.

2 And now it came to pass that in the three hundred and sixty and third year,[16] the Nefites did go up with their armies to battle against the Lamanites, out of the land of Desolation. And it came to pass that the armies of the Nefites were driven back again to the land of Desolation. And while they were yet weary, a fresh army of the Lamanites did come upon them. And they had a sore battle, insomuch that the Lamanites did take possession of the city Desolation, and did slay many of the Nefites, and did take many prisoners; and the remainder did flee and join the inhabitants of the city Teancum. Now the city Teancum lay in the borders by the seashore, and it was also near the city Desolation. And it was because the armies of the Nefites went up unto the Lamanites that they began to be slain – for were it not for that, the Lamanites could have had no power over them. But behold, the judgments of Elohim will overtake the wicked; and it is by the wicked that the wicked are punished, for it is the wicked that stir up the hearts of the children of men unto bloodshed. And it came to pass that the Lamanites did make preparations to come against the city Teancum.

2 And it came to pass in the three hundred and sixty and fourth year, the Lamanites did come against the city Teancum, that they might take possession of the city Teancum also. And it came to pass that they were repulsed and driven back by the Nefites. And when the Nefites saw that they had driven the Lamanites, they did again boast of their own strength; and they went forth in their own might and took possession again of the city Desolation. And now all these things had been done, and there had been thousands slain on both sides, both the Nefites and the Lamanites. And it came to pass that the three hundred and sixty and sixth year had passed away. And the Lamanites came again upon the Nefites to battle, and yet the Nefites repented not of the evil they had done, but persisted in their

---

[16] ~ 362 CE

wickedness continually. And it is impossible for the tongue to describe or for man to write a perfect description of the horrible scene of the blood and carnage which was among the people, both of the Nefites and of the Lamanites. And every heart was hardened so that they delighted in the shedding of blood continually. And there never had been so great wickedness among all the children of Lechi, nor even among all the house of Isra'el (according to the words of YHWH), as were among this people.

3 And it came to pass that the Lamanites did take possession of the city Desolation, and this because their number did exceed the number of the Nefites. And they did also march forward against the city Teancum, and did drive the inhabitants forth out of her, and did take many prisoners of women and of children, and did offer them up as sacrifices unto their idol gods. And it came to pass that in the three hundred and sixty and seventh year, the Nefites being angry because the Lamanites had sacrificed their women and their children, that they did go against the Lamanites with exceedingly great anger, insomuch that they did beat again the Lamanites and drive them out of their lands. And the Lamanites did not come again against the Nefites until the three hundred and seventy and fifth year.[17] And in this year they did come down against the Nefites with all their powers, and they were not numbered because of the greatness of their number. And from this time forth did the Nefites gain no power over the Lamanites, but began to be swept off by them, even as dew before the sun. And it came to pass that the Lamanites did come down against the city Desolation, and there was an exceedingly sore battle fought in the land Desolation, in the which they did beat the Nefites. And they fled again from before them, and they came to the city Boaz; and there they did stand against the Lamanites with exceeding boldness, insomuch that the Lamanites did not beat them until they had come again the second time. And when they had come the second time, the Nefites were driven and slaughtered with an exceedingly great slaughter; their women and their children were again sacrificed unto idols. And it came to pass that the Nefites did again flee from before them, taking all the inhabitants with them, both in towns and villages. And now I, M'raman, seeing that the

---

17 ~ 374 CE

Lamanites were about to overthrow the land, therefore I did go to the hill Shim and did take up all the records which Ammaron[18] had hidden up unto YHWH.

4 And it came to pass that I did go forth among the Nefites and did turn from the oath which I had made that I would no more assist them. And they gave me command again of their armies, for they looked upon me as though I could deliver them from their afflictions. But behold, I was without hope, for I knew the judgments of YHWH which should come upon them; for they turned not from their iniquities, but did struggle for their lives without calling upon that Being who had created them. And it came to pass that the Lamanites did come against us as we had fled to the city of Yarden, but behold, they were driven back that they did not take the city at that time. And it came to pass that they came against us again, and we did maintain the city. And there were also other cities which were maintained by the Nefites, which strongholds did cut them off, that they could not get into the country which lay before us to destroy the inhabitants of our land. But it came to pass that whatsoever lands we had passed by and the inhabitants thereof were not gathered in were destroyed by the Lamanites; and their towns, and villages, and cities were burned with fire. And thus three hundred and seventy and nine years passed away. And it came to pass that in the three hundred and eightieth year,[19] the Lamanites did come again against us to battle, and we did stand against them boldly; but it was all in vain, for so great were their numbers that they did tread the people of the Nefites under their feet. And it came to pass that we did again take flight, and those whose flight was swifter than the Lamanites did escape, and those whose flight did not exceed the Lamanites were swept down and destroyed.

5 And now behold, I, M'raman, do not desire to torment the souls of men in casting before them such an awful scene of blood and carnage as was laid before my eyes. But I, knowing that these things must surely be made known, and that all things which are hid must be revealed upon the housetops,[20] and also that a knowledge of these things must come unto the remnant of this people, and also unto the Goyim which YHWH has said should scatter this people — and this people should be counted as nothing among them — therefore

---

[18] 4 Nefi 1:9 [19] ~379 CE [20] Luke 12:2-3

I write a small abridgement, daring not to give a full account of the things which I have seen, because of the commandment which I have received, and also that you might not have too great sorrow because of the wickedness of this people.

6 And now behold, this I speak unto their seed, and also to the Goyim who have care for the house of Isra'el, that realize and know from where their blessings come. For I know that such will sorrow for the calamity of the house of Isra'el, yes, they will sorrow for the destruction of this people. They will sorrow that this people had not repented, that they might have been clasped in the arms of Yeshua. Now these things are written unto the remnant of the house of Ya'akov, and they are written after this manner because it is known of Elohim that wickedness will not bring them forth unto them. And they are to be hid up unto YHWH, that they may come forth in his own due time. And this is the commandment which I have received. And behold, they shall come forth according to the mitzvah of YHWH, when he shall see fit in his wisdom. And behold, they shall go unto the unbelieving of the Y'hudim. And for this intent shall they go, that they may be persuaded that Yeshua is the Mashiach, the Son of the living Elohim; that the Father may bring about, through his Most Beloved, his great and eternal purpose in restoring the Y'hudim, or all the house of Isra'el, to the land of their inheritance which YHWH their Elohim has given them, unto the fulfilling of his covenant; and also that the seed of this people may more fully believe his besorah which shall go forth unto them from the Goyim. For this people shall be scattered, and shall become a dark, an unclean, and a loathsome people, beyond the description of that which ever has been among us, yes, even that which has been among the Lamanites, and this because of their unbelief and idolatry. For behold, the spirit of YHWH has already ceased to strive with their fathers, and they are without Mashiach and Elohim in the world, and they are driven about as chaff before the wind. They were once a delightful people, and they had Mashiach for their shepherd. Yes, they were led even by Elohim the Father. But now behold, they are led about by HaSatan, even as chaff is driven before the wind, or as a vessel is tossed about upon the waves without sail or anchor, or without anything with which to steer her; and even as she is, so are they. And behold, YHWH has reserved their blessing, which they might have received in the land,

for the Goyim who shall possess the land. But behold, it shall come to pass that they shall be driven and scattered by the Goyim. And after they have been driven and scattered by the Goyim, behold, then will YHWH remember the covenant which he made unto Avraham and unto all the house of Isra'el. And also YHWH will remember the prayers of the righteous which have been put up unto him for them.

7 And then, O you Goyim, how can you stand before the power of Elohim except you shall repent and turn from your evil ways? Do you not know that you are in the hands of Elohim? Do you not know that he has all power, and at his great command the earth **shall be rolled together as a scroll?**[21] Therefore, repent, and humble yourselves before him, or he shall come out in justice against you, and **a remnant** of the seed of Ya'akov shall go forth among you **as a lion and tear you in pieces, and there is none to deliver.**[22]

3 And now I finish my record concerning the destruction of my people, the Nefites. And it came to pass that we did march forth before the Lamanites. And I, M'raman, wrote a letter unto the king of the Lamanites, and desired of him that he would grant unto us that we might gather together our people unto the land of Kumorah, by a hill which was called Kumorah,[23] and there we would give them battle. And it came to pass that the king of the Lamanites did grant unto me the thing which I desired. And it came to pass that we did march forth to the land of Kumorah, and we did pitch our tents round about the hill Kumorah. And it was in a land of many waters, rivers, and fountains, and here we had hope to gain advantage over the Lamanites. And when three hundred and eighty and four years[24] had passed away, we had gathered in all the remainder of our people unto the land Kumorah.

2 And it came to pass that when we had gathered in all our people in one to the land of Kumorah, behold, I, M'raman, began to be old. And knowing it to be the last struggle of my people, and having been commanded of YHWH that I should not allow that the records which had been handed down by our fathers, which were sacred, to fall

---

21 Isa. 34:3-4   22 Mic. 5:8   23 Likely from the Hebrew root *kum* קום (Strong's 6965), "to rise up." This was the same hill which the Yeredites called "Ramah" ('Eter 6:14), from the Hebrew root *ram* רם (Strong's 7410), "to be high." Kumorah might be a contraction for *Kum-Rammah*, "to rise up high."   24 ~384 CE

into the hands of the Lamanites — for the Lamanites would destroy them[25] — therefore I made this record out of the plates of Nefi and hid up in the hill Kumorah all the records which had been entrusted to me by the hand of YHWH, except it were these few plates which I gave unto my son M'roni.[26]

3 And it came to pass that my people, with their wives and their children, did now behold the armies of the Lamanites marching towards them; and with that awful fear of death which fills the breasts of all the wicked did they await to receive them. And it came to pass that they came to battle against us, and every soul was filled with terror because of the greatness of their numbers. And it came to pass that they did fall upon my people with the sword, and with the bow, and with the arrow, and with the ax, and with all manner of weapons of war. And it came to pass that my men were cut down, yes, or even my ten thousand who were with me, and I fell wounded in the midst, and they passed by me, that they did not put an end to my life. And when they had gone through and cut down all my people except it were twenty and four of us, among whom was my son M'roni, and we, having survived the destruction of our people, did behold the next day, when the Lamanites had returned unto their camps, from the top of the hill Kumorah, the ten thousand[27] of my people who were cut down, being led in the front by me. And we also beheld the ten thousand of my people who were led by my son M'roni. And behold, the ten thousand of Gidgiddonah had fallen, and he also in the midst. And Lamah had fallen with his ten thousand, and Gilgal had fallen with his ten thousand, and Limhah had fallen with his ten thousand, and Joneum had fallen with his ten thousand, and Cumenihah, and M'ronihah, and Antionum, and Shiblom, and Shem, and Yosh had fallen with their ten thousand

---

25 2 Nefi 11:14 **26** M'raman 4:1 **27** The underlying Hebrew may have been *eleph* אלף (Strong's 505). In its strictest sense, this word means "thousand," but is also used poetically for large numbers. This root (אלף) can also mean "chieftain," indicating one with command of a large group of soldiers, but not necessarily numbering one thousand. The same word is used for the rank of Colonel and above in the modern Israeli Defense Forces. The Nefite practice of appointing "captains, and higher captains, and chief captains, according to their numbers" (Alma 1:10) indicates that a captain over "ten thousand" was likely the "chief captain" commander of a large unit, consisting of smaller divisions and units, but not necessarily numbering anything close to ten thousand. See Wenham, J.W. (1967) Large Numbers in the Old Testament. *Tyndale Bulletin*, Volume 18, pgs. 19-53. See also 1 Chron. 12:18-20; 13:1.

each. And it came to pass that there were ten more who did fall by the sword with their ten thousand each. Yes, even all my people — except it were those twenty and four who were with me, and also a few who had escaped into the south countries, and a few who had dissented over unto the Lamanites — had fallen. And their flesh, and bones, and blood lay upon the face of the earth, being left by the hands of those who slew them, to decay upon the land, and to crumble, and to return to their mother earth.

4 And my soul was torn with anguish because of the slain of my people, and I cried, Oh[28] you fair ones, how could you have departed from the ways of YHWH? O you fair ones, how could you have rejected that Yeshua, who stood with open arms to receive you? Behold, if you had not done this, you would not have fallen. But behold, you are fallen, and I mourn your loss. O you fair sons and daughters, you fathers and mothers, you husbands and wives, you fair ones, how is it that you could have fallen? But behold, you are gone, and my sorrows cannot bring your return. And the day soon comes that your mortal must put on immortality, and these bodies which are now decaying in corruption must soon become incorruptible[29] bodies. And then you must stand before the judgment seat of Mashiach to be judged according to your works. And if it so be that you are righteous, then are you blessed with your fathers who have gone before you. Oh that you had repented before this great destruction had come upon you. But behold, you are gone, and the Father, yes, the Eternal Father of Heaven, knows your state, and he does with you according to his justice and mercy.

5 And now behold, I would speak somewhat unto the remnant of this people who are spared, if it so be that Elohim may give unto them my words, that they may know of the things of their fathers. Yes, I speak unto you, you remnant of the house of Isra'el, and these are the words which I speak: Know you that you are of the house of Isra'el. Know you that you must come unto repentance, or you cannot be saved.[30] Know you that you must lay down your weapons of war, and delight no more in the shedding of blood, and take them not again, except it be that Elohim shall command you. Know you that you must come to the knowledge of your fathers, and repent of all

---

28 2 Nefi 11:11   **29** 1 Cor. 15:53   **30** 2 Nefi 13:3; Alma 8:15

your sins and iniquities, and believe in Yeshua HaMashiach — that he is the Son of Elohim, and that he was slain by the Y'hudim, and by the power of the Father he has risen again, by which he has gained the victory[31] over the grave; and also in him is the sting of death swallowed up. And he brings to pass the resurrection of the dead, by which man must be raised to stand before his judgment seat. And he has brought to pass the redemption of the world, by which he that is found guiltless before him at the judgment day has it given unto them to dwell in the presence of Elohim in his kingdom, to sing ceaseless praises with the choirs above unto the Father, and unto the Son, and unto the Ruach HaKodesh, which are echad,[32] in a state of happiness which has no end. Therefore, repent and be immersed in the name of Yeshua, and lay hold upon the besorah of Mashiach which shall be set before you, not only in this record, but also in the record which shall come unto the Goyim from the Y'hudim, which record shall come from the Goyim unto you. For behold, this is written for the intent that you may believe that. And if you believe that, you will believe this also. And if you believe this, you will know concerning your fathers, and also the marvelous works which were worked by the power of Elohim among them. And you will also know that you are a remnant of the seed of Ya'akov. Therefore, you are numbered among the people of the first covenant. And if it so be that you believe in Mashiach and are immersed, first with water, then with fire and with the Ruach HaKodesh, following the example of our Savior according to that which he has commanded us, it shall be well with you in the day of judgment. Amen.

4 Behold, I, M'roni, do finish the record of my father M'raman. Behold, I have but few things to write, which things I have been commanded of my father. And now it came to pass that after the great and tremendous battle at Kumorah, behold, the Nefites who had escaped into the country southward were hunted by the Lamanites until they were all destroyed, and my father also was killed by them. And I, even I, remain alone to write the sad tale of the destruction of my people. But behold, they are gone, and I fulfill the commandment of my father. And whether they will slay me, I know not; therefore,

---

31 Isa. 25:8; Moshiyah 8:14   32 Deut. 6:4; 2 Nefi 13:5

I will write and hide up the records in the earth, and where I go, it matters not. Behold, my father has made this record and he has written the intent thereof. And behold, I would write it also, if I had room upon the plates, but I have not. And ore I have none, for I am alone; my father has been slain in battle, and all my kinsfolk, and I have not friends nor anywhere to go. And how long YHWH will allow that I may live, I know not. Behold, four hundred years[33] have passed away since the coming of our Adonai and Savior. And behold, the Lamanites have hunted my people, the Nefites, down, from city to city and from place to place, even until they are no more; and great has been their fall. Yes, great and marvelous is the destruction of my people, the Nefites. And behold, it is the hand of YHWH which has done it. And behold also, the Lamanites are at war one with another, and the whole face of this land is one continual round of murder and bloodshed, and no one knows the end of the war.

2 And now behold, I say no more concerning them, for there are none, except it be Lamanites and robbers that do exist upon the face of the land. And there are none that do know the true Elohim, except it be the talmidim[34] of Yeshua who did remain in the land until the wickedness of the people was so great that YHWH would not allow them to remain with the people. And where they be upon the face of the land, no man knows. But behold, my father and I have seen them, and they have ministered unto us. And whoever receives this record, and shall not condemn it because of the imperfections which are in it, the same shall know of greater things[35] than these. Behold, I am M'roni, and were it possible, I would make all things known unto you.

3 Behold, I make an end of speaking concerning this people. I am the son of M'raman, and my father was a descendant of Nefi, and I am the same who hides up this record unto YHWH. The plates thereof are of no worth because of the mitzvah of YHWH, for he truly said that no one shall have them to get gain. But the record thereof is of great worth,[36] and whoever shall bring it to light, him will YHWH bless. For none can have power to bring it to light except it be given him of Elohim. For Elohim will that it shall be done with an eye single[37] to

---

33 ~ 400 CE   34 4 Nefi 1:3   35 3 Nefi 12:1   36 2 Nefi 2:3   37 The underlying Hebrew may have been "good eye," a Hebrew idiom meaning to be generous. In Matt. 6:22, the *Jewish New Testament* says "good," where the KJV says "single." David Stern writes in his "Introduction" to the *Jewish New Testament*: "…much of what is written in the New

his glory, or the welfare of the ancient and long dispersed covenant people of YHWH; and blessed be him that shall bring this thing to light, for it shall be brought out of darkness unto light according to the word of Elohim. Yes, it **shall be brought out of the earth,**[38] and it shall shine forth out of darkness and come unto the knowledge of the people, and it shall be done by the power of Elohim. And if there be faults, they be the faults of a man. But behold, we know no fault; nevertheless, Elohim knows all things. Therefore, he that condemns, let him be aware that he shall be in danger of Gehinnom. And he that says, Show unto me or you shall be smitten — let him be aware that he commands that which is forbidden of YHWH. For behold, the same that judges[39] rashly shall be judged rashly again, for according to his works shall his wages be. Therefore, he that smites shall be smitten again of YHWH. Behold what the scripture says: Man shall not smite, neither shall he judge, for judgment is mine, says YHWH, and vengeance[40] is mine also, and I will repay. And he that shall breathe out anger and strifes against the work of YHWH and against the covenant people of YHWH, who are the house of Isra'el, and shall say, We will destroy the work of YHWH and YHWH will not remember his covenant which he has made unto the house of Isra'el, the same is in danger to be cut down and cast into the fire. For the eternal purposes of YHWH shall roll on until all his promises shall be fulfilled.

4 Search the prophecies of Yesha'yahu.[41] Behold, I cannot write them. Yes, behold, I say unto you that those k'doshim who have gone before me, who have possessed this land, shall cry, yes, even **from the dust**[42] will they cry unto YHWH. And as YHWH lives, he will remember the covenant which he has made with them. And he knows their prayers, that they were in behalf of their brothers. And he knows their faith, for in his name could they remove mountains,[43] and in his name could they cause the earth to shake, and by the power of his word did they cause prisons[44] to tumble to the earth. Yes, even the fiery furnace

---

Testament is incomprehensible apart from its Jewish context. Here (Matt. 6:22-23) is an example, only one of many... in Hebrew, having an 'ayin ra'ah, an 'evil eye,' means being stingy; while having an 'ayin tovah, a 'good eye,' means being generous" (Stern, D. (1989) *Jewish New Testament: A Translation of the New Testament that Expresses its Jewishness.* Jerusalem, Israel: Jerusalem New Testament Publications, p. x). Here in M'raman 4:3, the Hebrew idiom is used correctly, according to the "Jewish context" of this idiomatic phrase (compare Prov. 23:6; 28:22; see also 3 Nefi 5:37).   **38** Ps. 85:12 (11)   **39** Matt. 7:1; 3 Nefi 6:5   **40** Deut. 32:35; Rom. 12:19   **41** Isa. 6:8; 3 Nefi 10:4   **42** Isa. 29:4; 2 Nefi 2:6; 'Eter 3:18   **43** Cheleman 3:19; 4:10   **44** 3 Nefi 13:5

could not harm them, neither wild beasts nor poisonous serpents, because of the power of his word. And behold, their prayers were also in behalf of him that YHWH should allow to bring these things forth. And no one need say, They shall not come, for they surely shall, for YHWH has spoken it. **For out of the earth**[45] shall they come by the hand of YHWH, and none can stay it. And it shall come in a day when it shall be said that miracles are done away. And it shall come even as if one should speak from the dead.[46] And it shall come in a day when the blood of k'doshim shall cry unto YHWH because of secret conspiracies and the works of darkness. Yes, it shall come in a day when the power of Elohim shall be denied,[47] and assemblies become defiled and shall be lifted up in the pride of their hearts, yes, even in a day when leaders of assemblies and teachers, shall be lifted up in the pride of their hearts, even to the envying of them who belong to their assemblies. Yes, it shall come in a day when there shall be heard of fires, and tempests, and vapors of smoke in foreign lands; and there shall also be heard of wars, and rumors of wars, and earthquakes in diverse places. Yes, it shall come in a day when there shall be great pollutions upon the face of the earth — there shall be murders, and robbing, and lying, and deceivings, and whoredoms, and all manner of abominations — when there shall be many who will say, Do this or do that and it matters not, for YHWH will uphold[48] such at the last day. But woe unto such, for they are in the gall of bitterness and in the bonds of iniquity. Yes, it shall come in a day when there shall be churches built up that shall say, Come unto me, and for your money[49] you shall be forgiven of your sins.

5 O you wicked, and perverse, and stiffnecked people, why have you built up churches unto yourselves to get gain? Why have you transfigured the holy word of Elohim that you might bring damnation upon your souls? Behold, look you unto the revelations of Elohim, for behold, the time comes at that day when all these things must be fulfilled. Behold, YHWH has shown unto me great and marvelous things concerning that which must shortly come at that day when these things shall come forth among you. Behold, I speak unto you as if you were present, and yet you are not. But behold, Yeshua HaMashiach has shown you unto me, and I know your doing,

---

45 Ps. 85:12 (11) **46** Isa. 29:4 **47** 2 Nefi 12:5 **48** 2 Nefi 12:1 **49** Isa. 55:1; 2 Nefi 6:13

and I know that you do walk in the pride of your hearts. And there are none, except a few only, who do not lift themselves up in the pride of their hearts, unto the wearing of very fine apparel, unto envying, and strifes, and malice, and persecutions, and all manner of iniquity. And your assemblies, yes, even every one, have become polluted because of the pride of your hearts. For behold, you do love money, and your substance, and your fine apparel, and the adorning of your assemblies, more than you love the poor and the needy, the sick and the afflicted. O you pollutions, you hypocrites, you teachers who sell yourselves for that which will canker, why have you polluted the holy assembly of Elohim? Why are you ashamed to take upon you the name of Mashiach? Why do you not think that greater is the value of an Endless happiness than that misery which never dies? Because of the praise of the world? Why do you adorn yourselves with that which has no life, and yet allow the hungry, and the needy, and the naked, and the sick, and the afflicted to pass by you and notice them not? Yes, why do you build up your secret abominations to get gain? And cause that widows should mourn before YHWH, and also orphans to mourn before YHWH, and also the blood of their fathers and their husbands to cry unto YHWH from the ground for vengeance upon your heads? Behold, the sword of vengeance hangs over you, and the time soon comes that he avenges the blood of the k'doshim upon you, for he will not allow their cries any longer.

6 And now, I speak also concerning those who do not believe in Mashiach. Behold, will you believe in the day of your visitation, behold, when YHWH shall come? Yes, even that great day when the earth **shall be rolled together as a scroll**[50] and the elements **shall melt**[51] with fervent heat? Yes, in that great day when you shall be brought to stand before the Lamb of Elohim, then will you say that there is no Elohim? Then will you longer deny the Mashiach? Or can you behold the Lamb of Elohim? Do you suppose that you shall dwell with him under a consciousness of your guilt? Do you suppose that you could be happy to dwell with that holy Being when your souls are racked with a consciousness of guilt that you have continually abused his laws? Behold, I say unto you that you would be more miserable to dwell with a holy and a just Elohim under a consciousness of

---

50 Isa. 34:4   51 Isa. 34:3-4; Nah. 1:5-6; Mic. 1:4; Ps. 97:5

your uncleanness before him than you would to dwell with the damned souls in Gehinnom. For behold, when you shall be brought to see your nakedness before Elohim, and also the glory of Elohim, and the holiness of Yeshua HaMashiach, it will kindle a flame of unquenchable fire upon you. Oh then, you unbelieving, turn unto YHWH. Cry mightily unto the Father in the name of Yeshua that perhaps you may be found spotless, pure, fair, and white, having been cleansed by the blood of the Lamb, at that great and last day.

7 And again I speak unto you who deny the revelations of Elohim and say that they are done away, that there are no revelations, nor prophecies, nor gifts, nor healing, nor speaking with tongues, and the interpretation of tongues. Behold, I say unto you, he that denies these things knows not the besorah of Mashiach. Yes, he has not read the scriptures; if so, he does not understand them. For do we not read that Elohim is the same [52] yesterday, today, and for ever? And in him there is no variableness neither shadow of changing? And now, if you have imagined up unto yourselves a god who does vary, and in him there is shadow of changing, then have you imagined up unto yourselves a god who is not an Elohim of miracles. But behold, I will show unto you an Elohim of miracles, even **the Elohim of Avraham, and the Elohim of Yitz'chak, and the Elohim of Ya'akov.**[53] And it is that same **Elohim** who **created the heavens and the earth,**[54] and all things that in them are. Behold, he created Adam, and by Adam came the Fall of man. And because of the Fall of man came Yeshua HaMashiach, even the Father and the Son; and because of Yeshua HaMashiach came the redemption of man. And because of the redemption[55] of man which came by Yeshua HaMashiach, they are brought back into the presence of YHWH — yes, this is the way in which all men are redeemed, because the death of Mashiach brings to pass the resurrection, which brings to pass a redemption from an endless sleep, from which sleep all men shall be awakened by the power of Elohim when the shofar shall sound; and they shall come forth, both small and great, and all shall stand before his bar, being redeemed and loosed from this eternal band of death, which death is a temporal death. And then comes the judgment of HaKodesh upon them. And then comes the time that he that is unclean shall

---

52 Ps. 102:28 (27); Mal. 3:6; Heb. 13:8 **53** Ex. 3:6 **54** Gen. 1:1 **55** 'Eter 1:13

be unclean[56] still, and he that is righteous shall be righteous still; he that is happy shall be happy still, and he that is unhappy shall be unhappy still.

8 And now, O all you that have imagined up unto yourselves a god who can do no miracles, I would ask of you, Have all these things passed of which I have spoken? Has the end come yet? Behold, I say unto you, no, and Elohim has not ceased to be an Elohim of miracles. Behold, are not the things that Elohim has worked marvelous in our eyes? Yes, and who can comprehend the marvelous works of Elohim? Who shall say that it was not a miracle that by his word the heaven and the earth should be? And by the power of his word, man was created of the dust of the earth? And by the power of his word have miracles been worked? And who shall say that Yeshua HaMashiach did not do many mighty miracles? And there were many mighty miracles worked by the hands of the emissaries. And if there were miracles worked, then why has Elohim ceased to be an Elohim of miracles and yet be an unchangeable being? And behold, I say unto you, he changes not; if so, he would cease[57] to be Elohim. And he ceases not to be Elohim, and is an Elohim of miracles. And the reason why he ceases to do miracles among the children of men is because they dwindle in unbelief, and depart from the right way, and know not the Elohim in whom they should trust.

9 Behold, I say unto you that whosoever believes in Mashiach, doubting nothing, whatsoever he shall ask[58] the Father, in the name of Mashiach, it shall be granted him. And this promise is unto all, even unto the ends of the earth. For behold, thus said Yeshua HaMashiach, the Son of Elohim, unto his talmidim who should remain, yes, and also to all his talmidim, in the hearing of the multitude: Go[59] into all the world and preach the besorah to every creature. And he that believes and is washed by immersion shall be saved, but he that believes not shall be damned. And these signs shall follow them that believe: In my name shall they cast out demons, they shall speak with new tongues, they shall take up serpents, and if they drink any deadly thing, it shall not hurt them; they shall lay hands on the sick, and they shall recover. And whosoever shall believe in my name, doubting nothing, unto him will I confirm all my words, even unto

---

56 2 Nefi 6:6　57 Alma 19:16　58 John 14:13　59 Mark 16:15-18

the ends of the earth. And now behold, who can stand against the works of YHWH? Who can deny his sayings? Who will rise up against the almighty power of YHWH? Who will despise the works of YHWH? Who will despise the children of Mashiach? Behold, all you who are despisers of the works of YHWH, for you shall wonder and perish.

10 Oh then despise not and wonder not, but hearken unto the words of YHWH and ask the Father in the name of Yeshua for whatsoever things of which you shall stand in need. Doubt not, but be believing, and begin as in times of old, and come unto YHWH with all your heart, and work out your own salvation with fear and trembling before him. Be wise in the days of your probation; strip yourselves of all uncleanness. Ask, not that you may consume it on your lusts, but ask with a firmness unshaken that you will yield to no temptation, but that you will serve the true and living Elohim. See that you are not immersed unworthily. See that you partake not of the sacred meal of Mashiach unworthily, but see that you do all things in worthiness, and do it in the name of Yeshua HaMashiach, the Son of the living Elohim. And if you do this and endure to the end, you will in no way be cast out. Behold, I speak unto you as though I speak from the dead, for I know that you shall hear my words.

11 Condemn me not because of my imperfection, neither my father because of his imperfection, neither they who have written before him. But rather, give thanks unto Elohim that he has made manifest unto you our imperfections, that you may learn to be more wise than we have been. And now behold, we have written this record according to our knowledge, in the characters which are called among us reformed Egyptian, being handed down and altered by us according to our manner of speech. And if our plates had been sufficiently large, we should have written in Hebrew; but the Hebrew has been altered by us also. And if we could have written in Hebrew, behold, you would have had no imperfection in our record. But YHWH knows the things which we have written, and also that no other people knows our language; and because no other people knows our language, therefore he has prepared means for the interpretation thereof. And these things are written that we may rid our garments[60] of the blood of our brothers who have dwindled in unbelief. And behold, these things which we

---

60 2 Nefi 6:12; Moshiyah 1:9

have desired concerning our brothers, yes, even their restoration to the knowledge of Mashiach, is according to the prayers of all the k'doshim who have dwelt in the land. And may Adonai Yeshua HaMashiach grant that their prayers may be answered according to their faith, and may Elohim the Father remember the covenant which he has made with the house of Isra'el, and may he bless them for ever through faith on the name of Yeshua HaMashiach. Amen.

ספר אתר
'ETER
THE BOOK OF 'ETER

AND now I, M'roni, proceed to give an account of those ancient inhabitants who were destroyed by the hand of YHWH upon the face of this north country. And I take my account from the twenty and four plates which were found by the people of Limhi, which is called The Book of 'Eter.[1] And as I suppose that the first part of this record – which speaks concerning the creation of the world, and also of Adam, and an account from that time even to the great tower, and whatsoever things transpired among the children of men until that time – is had among the Y'hudim,[2] therefore I do not write those things which transpired from the days of Adam until that time; but they are had upon the plates, and whoever finds them, the same will have power that he may get the full account. But behold, I give not the full account, but a part of the account I give, from the tower down until they were destroyed.

2 And in this way do I give the account: He that wrote this record was 'Eter, and he was a descendant of Coriantor. And Coriantor was the son of Moron, and Moron was the son of Ethem, and Ethem was the son of Ahah, and Ahah was the son of Shet, and Shet was the son of Shiblon, and Shiblon was the son of Com, and Com was the son of Coriantum, and Coriantum was the son of Amnigaddah, and Amnigaddah was the son of Aharon. And Aharon was a descendant of Heth, who was the son of Hearthom. And Hearthom was the son of Lib, and Lib was the son of Kish, and Kish was the son of Corom,

---

[1] Moshiyah 12:3-4 [2] Gen. 1-11

and Corom was the son of Levi, and Levi was the son of Kim, and Kim was the son of Morionton. And Morionton was a descendant of Riplakish, and Riplakish was the son of Shez, and Shez was the son of Heth, and Heth was the son of Com, and Com was the son of Coriantum, and Coriantum was the son of Emer, and Emer was the son of Omer, and Omer was the son of Shule, and Shule was the son of Kib, and Kib was the son of Orihah,[3] who was the son of Yered, which Yered came forth with his brother and their families, with some others and their families, from the great **tower**,[4] at the time YHWH **confounded the language**[5] of the people and swore in his wrath that they should be **scattered upon all the face of the earth**. And according to the word[6] of YHWH, the people were **scattered**.[7]

3 And the brother of Yered being a large and a mighty man, and being a man highly favored[8] of YHWH, for Yered his brother said unto him, Cry unto YHWH that he will not confound us that we may not understand our words.[9] And it came to pass that the brother of Yered did cry unto YHWH, and YHWH had compassion upon Yered. Therefore, he did not confound the language of Yered, and Yered and his brother were not confounded. Then Yered said unto his brother, Cry again unto YHWH, and it may be that he will turn away his anger from those who are our friends,[10] that he confound not their language. And it came to pass that the brother of Yered did cry unto YHWH, and YHWH had compassion upon their friends and their families also, that they were not confounded. And it came to pass that Yered spoke again unto his brother, saying, Go and inquire of YHWH whether he will drive us out of the land. And if he will drive us out of the land, cry unto him, Where shall we go? And who knows but YHWH will carry us forth into a land which is choice above all the earth. And if it so be, let us be faithful unto YHWH, that we may receive it for our inheritance. And it came to pass that the brother of Yered did cry unto YHWH according to that which had been spoken

---

3 Probably meaning "my light" (אורי) is *Yah* (the suffix "ihah" appears in many Yeredite names).   4 Gen. 11:8   5 Gen. 11:7   6 This agrees with Targum Jonathan on Gen. 11, which reads, "And the Word of YHWH was revealed against the city, and with Him seventy angels, having reference to seventy nations, each having its own language, and thence the writing of its own hand: and He dispersed them from thence upon the face of all the earth into seventy languages. And one knew not what his neighbor would say: but one slew the other; and they ceased from building the city" (Targum Jonathan on Gen. 11:8).
7 Gen. 11:1-9   8 1 Nefi 1:1; Alma 7:4   9 Ameni 1:8; Moshiyah 12:4   10 Enosh 1:2; M'roni 7:9

by the mouth of Yered. And it came to pass that YHWH did hear the brother of Yered and had compassion upon him, and said unto him, Go to and gather together your flocks, both male and female of every kind, and also of the seed of the earth of every kind, and your family, and also Yered your brother and his family, and also your friends and their families, and the friends of Yered and their families.

4 And when you have done this, you shall go at the head of them down into the valley which is northward, and there will I meet you, and I will go before you into a land which is choice above all the land of the earth.[11] And there will I bless you and your seed, and raise up unto me — of your seed, and the seed of your brother, and they who shall go with you — a great nation. And there shall be none greater than the nation which I will raise up unto me of your seed upon all the face of the earth. And this I will do unto you because this long time which you have cried unto me.

5 And it came to pass that Yered, and his brother, and their families, and also the friends of Yered and his brother and their families, went down into the valley which was northward (and the name of the valley was Nimrod, being called after the mighty hunter[12]) with their flocks which they had gathered together, male and female of every kind. And they did also lay snares and catch fowls of the air. And they did also prepare a vessel in which they did carry with them the fish of the waters. And they did also carry with them deseret, which (by interpretation) is a honey bee. And thus they did carry with them swarms of bees, and all manner of that which was upon the face of the land, seeds of every kind.[13]

6 And it came to pass that when they had come down into the valley of Nimrod, YHWH came down and talked with the brother of Yered. And he was in a cloud, and the brother of Yered saw him not. And it came to pass that YHWH commanded them that they should go forth into the wilderness, yes, into that quarter where there never had man been. And it came to pass that YHWH did go before them, and did talk with them as he stood in a cloud,[14] and gave directions where they should travel. And it came to pass that they did travel in the wilderness and did build barges in which they did cross many

---

[11] Deut. 31:7-8; 2 Nefi 1:1-2 [12] Gen. 10:8-9 [13] Gen. 1:12, 20, 24, 28; Gen. 6:18-21; 1 Nefi 2:6; 5:4 [14] Ex. 13:21; Num. 14:14; 2 Nefi 8:10

waters, being directed continually by the hand of YHWH.¹⁵ And YHWH would not allow that they should stop beyond the sea in the wilderness, but he would that they should come forth even unto the land of promise, which was choice above all other lands, which Adonai YHWH had preserved for a righteous people. And he had sworn in his anger unto the brother of Yered that whoever should possess this land of promise, from that time henceforth and for ever should serve him, the true and only Elohim, or they should be swept off when the fulness of his anger should come upon them.

7 And now we can behold the decrees of Elohim concerning this land, that it is a land of promise, and whatsoever nation shall possess it shall serve Elohim or they shall be swept off when the fulness of his anger shall come upon them. And the fulness of his anger comes upon them when they are ripened in iniquity. For behold, this is a land which is choice above all other lands. Wherefore, he that does possess it shall serve Elohim or shall be swept off, for it is the everlasting decree of Elohim. And it is not until the fulness of iniquity among the children of the land that they are swept off. And this comes unto you, O you Goyim, that you may know the decrees of Elohim, that you may repent and not continue in your iniquities until the fulness comes, that you may not bring down the fulness of the anger of Elohim upon you as the inhabitants of the land have previously done. Behold, this is a choice land; and whatsoever nation shall possess it shall be free from bondage, and from captivity, and from all other nations under Heaven if they will but serve the Elohim of the land, who is Yeshua HaMashiach, who has been manifested by the things which we have written.¹⁶

8 And now I proceed with my record. For behold, it came to pass that YHWH did bring Yered and his brothers forth, even to that great sea which divides the lands. And as they came to the sea, they pitched their tents, and they called the name of the place Moriancumer. And they dwelt in tents upon the seashore for the space of four years. And it came to pass at the end of the four years that YHWH came again unto the brother of Yered, and stood in a cloud and talked with him. And for the space of three hours did YHWH talk with the brother of Yered, and chastened him because he remembered not to call upon the

---

15 1 Nefi 5:16   16 2 Nefi 1:1-2

name of YHWH. And the brother of Yered repented of the evil which he had done and did call upon the name of YHWH for his brothers who were with him. And YHWH said unto him, I will forgive you and your brothers of their sins, but you shall not sin anymore. For you shall remember that my spirit will not always strive with man. Wherefore, if you will sin until you are fully ripe, you shall be cut off from the presence of YHWH. And these are my thoughts upon the land which I shall give you for your inheritance, for it shall be a land of choice above all other lands.

9 And YHWH said, Go to work and build after the manner of barges which you have previously built. And it came to pass that the brother of Yered did go to work, and also his brothers, and built barges after the manner which they had built, according to the instructions of YHWH.[17] And they were small and they were light upon the water, even like unto the lightness of a fowl upon the water. And they were built after a manner that they were exceedingly tight, even that they would hold water like unto a dish; and the bottom thereof was tight like unto a dish, and the sides thereof were tight like unto a dish, and the ends thereof were peaked, and the top thereof was tight like unto a dish, and the length thereof was the length of a tree, and the door thereof, when it was shut, was tight like unto a dish. And it came to pass that the brother of Yered cried unto YHWH, saying, O YHWH, I have performed the work which you have commanded me and I have made the barges according as you have directed me. And behold, O YHWH, in them there is no light. Where shall we steer? And also we shall perish, for in them we cannot breathe except it is the air which is in them; therefore we shall perish. And YHWH said unto the brother of Yered, Behold, you shall make a hole in the top thereof, and also in the bottom thereof, and when you shall suffer for air, you shall unstop the hole thereof and receive air. And if it so be that the water come in upon you, behold, you shall stop the hole thereof, that you may not perish in the flood.

10 And it came to pass that the brother of Yered did so, according as YHWH had commanded. And he cried again unto YHWH, saying, O YHWH, behold, I have done even as you have commanded me and I have prepared the vessels for my people. And behold, there is no

---

17 1 Nefi 5:15

light in them. Behold, O YHWH, will you allow that we shall cross this great water in darkness? And YHWH said unto the brother of Yered, What will you that I should do that you may have light in your vessels? For behold, you cannot have windows, for they will be dashed in pieces. Neither shall you take fire with you, for you shall not go by the light of fire. For behold, you shall be as a whale in the midst of the sea, for the mountain waves shall dash upon you. Nevertheless, I will bring you up again out of the depths of the sea, for the winds have gone forth out of my mouth, and also the rains and the floods have I sent forth. And behold, I prepare you against these things, for how be it, you cannot cross this great deep except I prepare you against the waves of the sea, and the winds which have gone forth, and the floods which shall come. Therefore, what do you desire that I should prepare for you, that you may have light when you are swallowed up in the depths of the sea?

11 And it came to pass that the brother of Yered — now the number of the vessels which had been prepared was eight — therefore the brother of Yered went forth unto the mount which they called mount Shelem because of its great height, and did molten out of a rock sixteen small stones; and they were white and clear, even as transparent glass. And he did carry them in his hands up on the top of the mount, and cried again unto YHWH, saying, O YHWH, you have said that we must be encompassed about by the floods. Now behold, O YHWH, and do not be angry with your servant because of his weakness before you, for we know that you are holy and dwell in the Heavens, and that we are unworthy before you — because of the fall, our natures have become evil continually; nevertheless, O YHWH, you have given us a mitzvah that we must call upon you, that from you we may receive according to our desires. Behold, O YHWH, you have afflicted us because of our iniquity and have driven us forth, and for these many years we have been in the wilderness;[18] nevertheless, you have been merciful unto us. O YHWH, look upon me in pity, and turn away your anger from this your people, and allow not that they shall go forth across this raging deep in darkness, but behold these things which I have molten out of the rock. And I know, O YHWH, that you have all power and can do whatsoever you will for the benefit of

---

[18] 1 Nefi 5:11–12

man. Therefore, touch these stones, O YHWH, with your finger, and prepare them that they may shine forth in darkness, and they shall shine forth unto us in the vessels which we have prepared, that we may have light while we shall cross the sea.[19] Behold, O YHWH, you can do this. We know that you are able to show forth great power which looks small unto the understanding of men.

12 And it came to pass that when the brother of Yered had said these words, behold, YHWH stretched forth his hand and touched the stones one by one with his finger. And the veil was taken from off the eyes of the brother of Yered, and he saw the finger of YHWH; and it was as the finger of a man, like unto flesh and blood. And the brother of Yered fell down before YHWH, for he was struck with fear. And YHWH saw that the brother of Yered had fallen to the earth, and YHWH said unto him, Arise. Why have you fallen? And he said unto YHWH, I saw the finger of YHWH, and I feared that he should smite me, for I knew not that YHWH had flesh and blood. And YHWH said unto him, Because of your faith, you have seen that I shall take upon me flesh and blood.[20] And none of those now living have come before me with such great faith as you have, for were it not so, you could not have seen my finger. Did you see more than this? And he answered, No, YHWH. Show yourself unto me. And YHWH said unto him, Will you believe the words which I shall speak? And he answered, Yes, YHWH. I know that you speak the truth, for you are an Elohim of truth and cannot lie.

13 And when he had said these words, behold, YHWH showed himself unto him and said, Because you know these things, you are redeemed from the Fall. Therefore, you are brought back into my presence; therefore I show myself unto you.[21] Behold, I am he who was prepared from the foundation of the world to redeem my people. Behold, I am Yeshua HaMashiach. I am the Father and the Son. In me shall all mankind have life; and that eternally, even they who shall believe on my name. And they shall become my sons and my daughters.[22] And to none of those now living whom I created have I appeared, for none have believed in me as you have. Do you see that you are created after my own image? Yes, even all men were created

---

[19] According to the Midrash Rabbah on Gen. 6:16 (as well as Rashi on Gen. 6:16), Noach's Ark was lit by a precious stone called the *tzohar* which "glowed brightly." [20] Moshiyah 1:14 [21] 2 Nefi 14:1; Alma 26:34; Cheleman 3:9 [22] Moshiyah 3:2

in the beginning after my own image. Behold, this body which you now behold is the body of my spirit. And man have I created after the body of my spirit. And even as I appear unto you to be in the spirit will I appear unto my people in the flesh.²³

14 And now as I, M'roni, said I could not make a full account of these things which are written, therefore it suffices me to say that Yeshua showed himself unto this man in the spirit, even after the manner and in the likeness of the same body even as he showed himself unto the Nefites. And he ministered unto him even as he ministered unto the Nefites,²⁴ and all this that this man might know that he was Elohim, because of the many great works which YHWH had shown unto him. And because of the knowledge of this man, he could not be kept from beholding within the veil. And he saw the finger of Yeshua, which when he saw, he fell with fear, for he knew that it was the finger of YHWH. And he had faith no longer, for he knew, nothing doubting. Wherefore, having this perfect knowledge of Elohim, he could not be kept from within the veil.²⁵ Therefore, he saw Yeshua, and he did minister unto him.

15 And it came to pass that YHWH said unto the brother of Yered, Behold, you shall not allow these things which you have seen and heard to go forth unto the world until the time comes that I shall glorify my name in the flesh. Wherefore, you shall treasure up the things which you have seen and heard, and show it to no man. And behold, when you shall come unto me, you shall write them and shall seal them up that no one can interpret them, for you shall write them in a language that they cannot be read. And behold, these two stones will I give unto you, and you shall seal them up also with the things which you shall write. For behold, the language which you shall write I have confounded. Wherefore, I will cause, in my own due time, that these stones shall magnify to the eyes of men these things which you shall write.²⁶ And when YHWH had said these words, he showed unto the brother of Yered all the inhabitants of the earth which had been, and also all that would be. And YHWH withheld them not from his sight, even unto the ends of the earth. For YHWH had said unto him in times before that if he would believe in him, that he could show unto him all things, it should be shown unto him. Therefore, YHWH

---

23 2 Nefi 5:4   24 3 Nefi 5:4-6   25 Ya'akov 3:4   26 Moshiyah 12:3

could not withhold anything from him, for he knew that YHWH could show him all things.²⁷

16 And YHWH said unto him, Write these things and seal them up, and I will show them in my own due time unto the children of men. And it came to pass that YHWH commanded him that he should seal up the two stones which he had received and show them not until YHWH should show them unto the children of men. And YHWH commanded the brother of Yered to go down out of the mount from the presence of YHWH and write the things which he had seen. And they were forbidden to come unto the children of men until after that he should be lifted up upon the Tz'lav. And for this cause did king Binyamin keep them, that they should not come unto the world until after Mashiach should show himself unto his people. And after that Mashiach truly had showed himself unto his people, he commanded that they should be made manifest.

17 And now, after that they have all dwindled in unbelief and there is none except it be the Lamanites — and they have rejected the besorah of Mashiach — therefore I am commanded that I should hide them up again in the earth. Behold, I have written upon these plates the very things which the brother of Yered saw. And there never was greater things made manifest than that which was made manifest unto the brother of Yered. Wherefore, YHWH has commanded me to write them, and I have written them. And he commanded me that I should seal them up. And he also has commanded that I should seal up the interpretation thereof; wherefore, I have sealed up the interpreters according to the mitzvah of YHWH. For YHWH said unto me, They shall not go forth unto the Goyim until the day that they shall repent of their iniquity and become clean before YHWH. And in that day that they shall exercise faith in me, said YHWH, even as the brother of Yered did, that they may become sanctified in me, then will I manifest unto them the things which the brother of Yered saw, even to the unfolding unto them all my revelations, said Yeshua HaMashiach, the Son of Elohim the Father of the heavens, and of the earth, and all things that in them are.²⁸

18 And he that will contend against the word of YHWH, let him be cursed. And he that shall deny these things, let him be cursed. For

---

27 1 Nefi 3:30-31 28 1 Nefi 3:5; 3 Nefi 11:6

unto them will I show no greater things, said Yeshua HaMashiach; for I am he who speaks, and at my command the heavens are opened and are shut, and at my word the earth shall shake, and at my command the inhabitants thereof shall pass away, even so as by fire. And he that believes not my words believes not my talmidim. And if it so be that I do not speak, judge you, for you shall know that it is I that speaks at the last day.[29] But he that believes these things which I have spoken, him will I visit with the manifestations of my spirit. And he shall know and bear record, for because of my spirit, he shall know that these things are true, for it persuades men to do good. And whatsoever thing persuades men to do good is of me, for good comes of none except it be of me. I am the same that leads men to all good.[30]

19 He that will not believe my words will not believe me, that I am. And he that will not believe me will not believe the Father who sent me. For behold, I am the Father. I am the light, and the life, and the truth of the world. Come unto me, O you Goyim, and I will show unto you the greater things, the knowledge which is hid up because of unbelief. Come unto me, O you house of Isra'el, and it shall be made manifest unto you how great things the Father has laid up for you from the foundation of the world; and it has not come unto you because of unbelief.[31] Behold, when you shall tear that veil of unbelief which does cause you to remain in your awful state of wickedness, and hardness of heart, and blindness of mind, then shall the great and marvelous things which have been hid up from the foundation of the world from you — yes, when you shall call upon the Father in my name with a broken heart and a contrite spirit — then shall you know that the Father has remembered the covenant which he made unto your fathers, O house of Isra'el.[32] And then shall my revelations which I have caused to be written by my servant Yochanan be unfolded in the eyes of all the people. Remember, when you see these things, you shall know that the time is at hand that they shall be made manifest in very deed. Therefore, when you shall receive this record, you may know that the work of the Father has commenced upon all the face of the land.[33] Therefore, repent, all you ends of the earth, and come unto me, and believe in my besorah, and be washed by immersion

---

29 2 Nefi 15:2; 3 Nefi 9:10   **30** M'roni 7:3   **31** M'roni 7:6–7   **32** 2 Nefi 6:1; 3 Nefi 9:8   **33** 3 Nefi 10:1

in my name. For he that believes and is immersed shall be saved, but he that believes not shall be damned. And signs shall follow them that believe in my name.³⁴ And blessed is he that is found faithful unto my name at the last day, for he shall be lifted up to dwell in the kingdom prepared for him from the foundation of the world. And behold, it is I that has spoken it. Amen.

2 And now I, M'roni, have written the words which were commanded me, according to my memory, and I have told you the things which I have sealed up. Therefore, touch them not in order that you may translate, for that thing is forbidden you, except by and by it shall be wisdom in Elohim. And behold, you may be privileged that you may show the plates unto those who shall assist to bring forth this work. And unto three shall they be shown by the power of Elohim; wherefore, they shall know of a surety that these things are true. And in the mouth of three witnesses shall these things be permanently decreed, and the testimony of three, and this work – in the which shall be shown forth the power of Elohim, and also his word, of which the Father and the Son and the Ruach HaKodesh bears record – and all this shall stand as a testimony against the world at the last day. And if it so be that they repent and come unto the Father in the name of Yeshua, they shall be received into the kingdom of Elohim. And now, if I have no s'mikhah for these things, judge you, for you shall know that I have s'mikhah when you shall see me and we shall stand before Elohim at the last day. Amen.

3 And now I, M'roni, proceed to give the record of Yered and his brother. For it came to pass after YHWH had prepared the stones which the brother of Yered had carried up into the mount, the brother of Yered came down out of the mount, and he did put forth the stones into the vessels which were prepared, one in each end thereof. And behold, they did give light unto the vessels thereof. And thus YHWH caused stones to shine in darkness, to give light unto men, women, and children, that they might not cross the great waters in darkness.³⁵

²And it came to pass that when they had prepared all manner of food, that thereby they might subsist upon the water, and also food for

---

34 2 Nefi 13:2-3; M'raman 4:9   35 'Eter 1:11

their flocks, and herds, and whatsoever beast, or animal, or fowl that they should carry with them — and it came to pass that when they had done all these things, they got aboard their vessels, or barges, and set forth into the sea, commending themselves unto YHWH their Elohim. And it came to pass that Adonai YHWH caused that there should a furious wind blow upon the face of the waters towards the promised land; and thus they were tossed upon the waves of the sea before the wind. And it came to pass that they were many times buried in the depths of the sea because of the mountain waves which broke upon them, and also the great and terrible tempests which were caused by the fierceness of the wind.

³And it came to pass that when they were buried in the deep, there was no water that could hurt them, their vessels being tight like unto a dish; and also they were tight like unto the ark of Noach. Therefore, when they were encompassed about by many waters, they did cry unto YHWH and he did bring them forth again upon the top of the waters.

⁴And it came to pass that the wind did never cease to blow towards the promised land while they were upon the waters, and thus they were driven forth before the wind. And they did sing praises unto YHWH, yes, the brother of Yered did sing praises unto YHWH and he did thank and praise YHWH all the day long. And when the night came, they did not cease to praise YHWH. And thus they were driven forth, and no monster of the sea could break them, neither whale that could mar them. And they did have light continually, whether it was above the water or under the water. And thus they were driven forth three hundred and forty and four days upon the water, and they did land upon the shore of the promised land. And when they had set their feet upon the shores of the promised land, they bowed themselves down upon the face of the land and did humble themselves before YHWH, and did shed tears of joy before YHWH because of the multitude of his tender mercies over them. And it came to pass that they went forth upon the face of the land and began to till the earth.

⁵And Yered had four sons, and they were called Jacom, and Gilgah, and Mahah, and Orihah. And the brother of Yered also fathered sons and daughters. And the friends of Yered and his brother were in number about twenty and two souls. And they also fathered sons and daughters before they came to the promised land, and therefore they began to be many. And they were taught to walk humbly before

YHWH, and they were also taught from on high. And it came to pass that they began to spread upon the face of the land, and to multiply, and to till the earth; and they did become strong in the land.

⁶And the brother of Yered began to be old, and saw that he must soon go down to the grave; wherefore, he said unto Yered, Let us gather together our people, that we may number them, that we may know of them what they will desire of us before we go down to our graves. And accordingly, the people were gathered together. Now the number of the sons and the daughters of the brother of Yered were twenty and two souls, and the number of the sons and daughters of Yered were twelve, he having four sons. And it came to pass that they did number their people. And after that they had numbered them, they did desire of them the things which they would that they should do before they went down to their graves. And it came to pass that the people desired of them that they should anoint one of their sons to be a king over them. And now behold, this was grievous unto them. But the brother of Yered said unto them, Surely this thing leads into captivity. But Yered said unto his brother, Allow them that they may have a king. And therefore he said unto them, Choose you out from among our sons a king, even whom you will.

⁷And it came to pass that they chose the first born of the brother of Yered, and his name was Pagag. And it came to pass that he refused and would not be their king. And the people desired that his father should constrain him, but his father would not. And he commanded them that they should constrain no man to be their king. And it came to pass that they chose all the brothers of Pagag, and they refused. And it came to pass that neither would the sons of Yered, even all, except it were one — and Orihah was anointed to be king over the people. And he began to reign, and the people began to prosper, and they became exceedingly rich.

⁸And it came to pass that Yered died, and his brother also. And it came to pass that Orihah did walk humbly before YHWH, and did remember how great things YHWH had done for his father, and also taught his people how great things YHWH had done for their fathers. And it came to pass that Orihah did execute judgment upon the land in righteousness all his days, whose days were exceedingly many. And he fathered sons and daughters, yes, he fathered thirty and one, among whom were twenty and three sons.

9 And it came to pass that he also fathered Kib in his old age. And it came to pass that Kib reigned in his place. And Kib fathered Corihor. And when Corihor was thirty and two years old, he rebelled against his father, and went over and dwelt in the land of Nehor. And he fathered sons and daughters, and they became exceedingly fair; wherefore, Corihor drew away many people after him. And when he had gathered together an army, he came up unto the land of Moron where the king dwelt and took him captive, which brought to pass the saying of the brother of Yered that they would be brought into captivity. Now the land of Moron where the king dwelt was near the land which is called Desolation by the Nefites. And it came to pass that Kib dwelt in captivity, and his people, under Corihor his son, until he became exceedingly old. Nevertheless, Kib fathered Shule in his old age while he was yet in captivity.

10 And it came to pass that Shule was angry with his brother. And Shule grew strong and became mighty as to the strength of a man, and he was also mighty in judgment. Wherefore, he came to the hill Efrayim, and he did molten out of the hill and made swords out of steel for those whom he had drawn away with him. And after he had armed them with swords, he returned to the city Nehor and gave battle unto his brother Corihor, by which means he obtained the kingdom and restored it unto his father Kib. And now because of the thing which Shule had done, his father bestowed upon him the kingdom; therefore, he began to reign in the place of his father. And it came to pass that he did execute judgment in righteousness. And he did spread his kingdom upon all the face of the land, for the people had become exceedingly numerous. And it came to pass that Shule also fathered many sons and daughters. And Corihor repented of the many evils which he had done, wherefore Shule gave him power in his kingdom. And it came to pass that Corihor had many sons and daughters. And among the sons of Corihor, there was one whose name was Noah.

11 And it came to pass that Noah rebelled against Shule the king, and also his father Corihor, and drew away Corihor his brother, and also all his brothers, and many of the people. And he gave battle unto Shule the king, in which he did obtain the land of their first inheritance; and he became a king over that part of the land. And it came to pass that he gave battle again unto Shule the king; and he

took Shule the king, and carried him away captive into Moron. And it came to pass as he was about to put him to death, the sons of Shule crept into the house of Noah by night and slew him, and broke down the door of the prison, and brought out their father, and placed him upon his throne in his own kingdom. Wherefore, the son of Noah did build up his kingdom in his place. Nevertheless, they did not gain power any more over Shule the king. And the people who were under the reign of Shule the king did prosper exceedingly and became great. And the country was divided, and there were two kingdoms: the kingdom of Shule and the kingdom of Cohor, the son of Noah. And Cohor, the son of Noah, caused that his people should give battle unto Shule, in which Shule did beat them and did slay Cohor. And now Cohor had a son who was called Nimrod, and Nimrod gave up the kingdom of Cohor unto Shule, and he did gain favor in the eyes of Shule; wherefore, Shule did bestow great favors upon him, and he did do in the kingdom of Shule according to his desires. And also in the reign of Shule there came prophets among the people, who were sent from YHWH, prophesying that the wickedness and idolatry of the people was bringing a curse upon the land, and they should be destroyed if they did not repent.[36]

12 And it came to pass that the people did revile against the prophets and did mock them. And it came to pass that king Shule did execute judgment against all those who did revile against the prophets. And he did execute a law throughout all the land which gave power unto the prophets that they should go wherever they would. And by this cause the people were brought unto repentance. And because the people did repent of their iniquities and idolatries, YHWH did spare them, and they began to prosper again in the land.

13 And it came to pass that Shule fathered sons and daughters in his old age. And there were no more wars in the days of Shule. And he remembered the great things that YHWH had done for his fathers in bringing them across the great deep into the promised land; wherefore, he did execute judgment in righteousness all his days. And it came to pass that he fathered Omer, and Omer reigned in his place. And Omer fathered Yered; and Yered fathered sons and daughters.

---

36 1 Nefi 1:2; Moshiyah 1:15; 7:8

14 And Yered rebelled against his father, and came and dwelt in the land of Heth. And it came to pass that he did flatter many people because of his cunning words until he had gained the half of the kingdom. And when he had gained the half of the kingdom, he gave battle unto his father; and he did carry away his father into captivity and did make him serve in captivity. And now in the days of the reign of Omer, he was in captivity the half of his days. And it came to pass that he fathered sons and daughters, among whom were Esrom and Coriantumr. And they were exceedingly angry because of the doings of Yered, their brother, insomuch that they did raise an army and gave battle unto Yered. And it came to pass that they did give battle unto him by night. And it came to pass that when they had slain the army of Yered, they were about to slay him also; and he pled with them that they would not slay him, and he would give up the kingdom unto his father. And it came to pass that they did grant unto him his life.

15 And now Yered became exceedingly sorrowful because of the loss of the kingdom, for he had set his heart upon the kingdom and upon the glory of the world. Now the daughter of Yered being exceedingly expert, and seeing the sorrow of her father, thought to devise a plan by which she could redeem the kingdom unto her father. Now the daughter of Yered was exceedingly fair. And it came to pass that she did talk with her father and said unto him, Why has my father so much sorrow? Has he not read the record which our fathers brought across the great deep? Behold, is there not an account concerning them of old, that they by their secret plans did obtain kingdoms and great glory? And now therefore, let my father send for Akish, the son of Kimnor. And behold, I am fair; and I will dance before him and I will please him, that he will desire me to wife. Wherefore, if he shall desire of you that you shall give me unto him to wife, then shall you say, I will give her if you will bring unto me the head of my father, the king.

16 And now Omer was a friend to Akish. Wherefore, when Yered had sent for Akish, the daughter of Yered danced before him that she pleased him, insomuch that he desired her to wife. And it came to pass that he said unto Yered, Give her unto me to wife. And Yered said unto him, I will give her unto you if you will bring unto me the head of my father, the king. And it came to pass that Akish gathered in unto the house of Yered all his kinsfolk and said unto them, Will

you swear unto me that you will be faithful unto me in the thing which I shall desire of you? And it came to pass that they all swore unto him — by the Elohim of Heaven, and also by the Heavens, and also by the earth, and by their heads — that whoever should vary from the assistance which Akish desired should lose his head, and whoever should divulge whatsoever thing Akish made known unto them, the same should lose his life.

17 And it came to pass that thus they did agree with Akish. And Akish did administer unto them the oaths which were given by them of old who also sought power, which had been handed down even from Kayin, who was a murderer from the beginning. And they were kept up by the power of HaSatan to administer these oaths unto the people, to keep them in darkness, to help such as sought power to gain power, and to murder, and to plunder, and to lie, and to commit all manner of wickedness and whoredoms. And it was the daughter of Yered who put it into his heart to search up these things of old, and Yered put it into the heart of Akish. Wherefore, Akish administered it unto his kindred and friends, leading them away by fair promises to do whatsoever thing he desired. And it came to pass that they formed a secret conspiracy, even as they of old, which conspiracy is most abominable and wicked above all in the sight of Elohim. For YHWH works not in secret conspiracies, neither does he will that man should shed blood, but in all things has forbidden it from the beginning of man.

18 And now I, M'roni, do not write the manner of their oaths and conspiracies, for it has been made known unto me that they are had among all people; and they are had among the Lamanites. And they have caused the destruction of this people of whom I am now speaking, and also the destruction of the people of Nefi. And whatsoever nation shall uphold such secret conspiracies, to get power and gain, until they shall spread over the nation, behold, they shall be destroyed; for YHWH will not allow that the blood of his k'doshim which shall be shed by them shall always cry unto him from the ground for vengeance upon them and yet he avenges them not. Wherefore, O you Goyim, it is wisdom in Elohim that these things should be shown unto you, that thereby you may repent of your sins and allow not that these murderous conspiracies shall get above you — which are built up to get power and gain — and the work, yes,

even the work of destruction come upon you, yes, even the sword of the justice of the Elohe Kedem shall fall upon you to your overthrow and destruction if you shall allow these things to be. Wherefore, YHWH commands you, when you shall see these things come among you, that you shall awake to a sense of your awful situation because of this secret conspiracy which shall be among you; or woe be unto it because of the blood of them who have been slain, for they cry from the dust for vengeance upon it, and also upon those who build it up.

19 For it comes to pass that whoever builds it up seeks to overthrow the freedom of all lands, nations, and countries. And it brings to pass the destruction of all people, for it is built up by HaSatan, who is the father of all lies, even that same liar who beguiled our first parents, yes, even that same liar who has caused man to commit murder from the beginning, who has hardened the hearts of men that they have murdered the prophets, and stoned them, and cast them out from the beginning. Wherefore I, M'roni, am commanded to write these things, that evil may be done away and that the time may come that HaSatan may have no power upon the hearts of the children of men, but that they may be persuaded to do good continually, that they may come unto the fountain of all righteousness and be saved.

4 And now I, M'roni, proceed with my record. Therefore behold, it came to pass that because of the secret conspiracies of Akish and his friends, behold, they did overthrow the kingdom of Omer. Nevertheless, YHWH was merciful unto Omer, and also to his sons and to his daughters who did not seek his destruction. And YHWH warned Omer in a dream that he should depart out of the land. Wherefore, Omer departed out of the land with his family, and traveled many days, and came over and passed by the hill of Shim, and came over by the place where the Nefites were destroyed, and from that place eastward, and came to a place which was called Ablom, by the seashore. And there he pitched his tent, and also his sons, and his daughters, and all his household, except it were Yered and his family.

2 And it came to pass that Yered was anointed king over the people by the hand of wickedness, and he gave unto Akish his daughter to wife. And it came to pass that Akish sought the life of his father-in-law, and he applied unto those whom he had sworn by the oath of the

ancients. And they obtained the head of his father-in-law as he sat upon his throne giving audience to his people. For so great had been the spreading of this wicked and secret society that it had corrupted the hearts of all the people. Therefore, Yered was murdered upon his throne, and Akish reigned in his place.

³And it came to pass that Akish began to be jealous of his son. Therefore, he shut him up in prison and kept him upon a little or no food until he had suffered death. And now the brother of him that suffered death (and his name was Nimrah) and he was angry with his father because of that which his father had done unto his brother. And it came to pass that Nimrah gathered together a small number of men and fled out of the land, and came over and dwelt with Omer. And it came to pass that Akish fathered other sons; and they won the hearts of the people, even though they had sworn unto him to do all manner of iniquity according to that which he desired. Now the people of Akish were desirous for gain, even as Akish was desirous for power. Wherefore, the sons of Akish did offer them money, by which means they drew away the more part of the people after them. And there began to be a war between the sons of Akish and Akish, which lasted for the space of many years, yes, unto the destruction of nearly all the people of the kingdom, yes, even all except it were thirty souls, and they who fled with the house of Omer. Wherefore, Omer was restored again to the land of his inheritance.

⁴And it came to pass that Omer began to be old. Nevertheless, in his old age he fathered Emer; and he anointed Emer to be king, to reign in his place. And after that he had anointed Emer to be king, he saw shalom in the land for the space of two years, and he died, having seen exceedingly many days which were full of sorrow. And it came to pass that Emer did reign in his place and did fill the steps of his father. And YHWH began again to take the curse from off the land. And the house of Emer did prosper exceedingly under the reign of Emer. And in the space of sixty and two years they had become exceedingly strong, insomuch that they became exceedingly rich, having all manner of fruit, and of grain, and of silks, and of fine linen, and of gold, and of silver, and of precious things, and also all manner of cattle, of oxen and cows, and of sheep, and of swine,[37] and

---

37 The mitzvah in the Mosaic Law against eating swine had not yet been given.

of goats, and also many other kinds of animals which were useful for the food of man. And they also had horses and asses, and there were elephants, and cureloms, and cumoms, all of which were useful unto man, and more especially the elephants, and cureloms, and cumoms. And thus YHWH did pour out his blessings upon this land which was choice above all other lands. And he commanded that whoever should possess the land should possess it unto YHWH, or they should be destroyed when they were ripened in iniquity. For upon such, said YHWH, I will pour out the fulness of my wrath.

5 And Emer did execute judgment in righteousness all his days, and he fathered many sons and daughters; and he fathered Coriantum, and he anointed Coriantum to reign in his place. And after that he had anointed Coriantum to reign in his place, he lived four years and he saw shalom in the land. Yes, and he even saw the Son of Righteousness and did rejoice and glory in his day, and he died in shalom.

6 And it came to pass that Coriantum did walk in the steps of his father, and did build many mighty cities, and did administer that which was good unto his people in all his days. And it came to pass that he had no children, even until he was exceedingly old. And it came to pass that his wife died, being a hundred and two years old. And it came to pass that Coriantum took to wife in his old age a young maid, and fathered sons and daughters; wherefore, he lived until he was a hundred and forty and two years old. And it came to pass that he fathered Com, and Com reigned in his place. And he reigned forty and nine years, and he fathered Heth, and he also fathered other sons and daughters. And the people had spread again over all the face of the land. And there began again to be an exceedingly great wickedness upon the face of the land; and Heth began to embrace the secret plans again of old, to destroy his father. And it came to pass that he did dethrone his father, for he slew him with his own sword; and he did reign in his place.

7 And there came prophets in the land again, crying repentance unto them, that they must prepare the way of YHWH or there should come a curse upon the face of the land; yes, even there should be a great famine, in the which they should be destroyed if they did not repent. But the people believed not the words of the prophets, but they cast them out. And some of them they cast into pits and left them to perish. And it came to pass that they did all these things

according to the commandment of king Heth. And it came to pass that there began to be a great scarcity upon the land. And the inhabitants began to be destroyed exceedingly fast because of the famine, for there was no rain upon the face of the earth. And there came forth poisonous serpents also upon the face of the land, and did poison many people. And it came to pass that their flocks began to flee before the poisonous serpents towards the land southward, which was called by the Nefites, Zerach'mla. And it came to pass that there were many of them which did perish by the way; nevertheless, there were some which fled into the land southward. And it came to pass that YHWH did cause the serpents that they should pursue them no more, but that they should hedge up the way, that the people could not pass, that whoever should attempt to pass might fall by the poisonous serpents. And it came to pass that the people did follow the course of the beasts, and did devour the carcasses of those which fell by the way until they had devoured them all.

8 Now when the people saw that they must perish, they began to repent of their iniquities and cry unto YHWH. And it came to pass that when they had humbled themselves sufficiently before YHWH, YHWH did send rain upon the face of the earth. And the people began to revive again, and there began to be fruit in the north countries and in all the countries round about. And YHWH did show forth his power unto them in preserving them from famine.[38]

9 And it came to pass that Shez, who was a descendant of Heth (for Heth had perished by the famine, and all his household except it were Shez), wherefore Shez began to build up again a broken people. And it came to pass that Shez did remember the destruction of his fathers, and he did build up a righteous kingdom; for he remembered what YHWH had done in bringing Yered and his brother across the deep. And he did walk in the ways of YHWH, and he fathered sons and daughters. And his eldest son, whose name was also Shez, did rebel against him. Nevertheless, Shez was killed by the hand of a robber because of his great riches, which brought shalom again unto his father. And it came to pass that his father did build up many cities upon the face of the land. And the people began again to spread over

---

38 Cheleman 4:3–4

all the face of the land. And Shez did live to a great old age, and he fathered Riplakish, and he died. And Riplakish reigned in his place.

10 And it came to pass that Riplakish did not do that which was right in the sight of YHWH, for he did have many wives and concubines, and did lay that upon men's shoulders which was grievous to be borne. Yes, he did tax them with heavy taxes, and with the taxes he did build many spacious buildings. And he did erect for himself an exceedingly beautiful throne. And he did build many prisons. And whoever would not be subject unto taxes he did cast into prison. And whoever was not able to pay taxes he did cast into prison. And he did cause that they should labor continually for their support. And whoever refused to labor he did cause to be put to death. Wherefore, he did obtain all his fine work; yes, even his fine gold he did cause to be refined in prison, and all manner of fine workmanship he did cause to be worked in prison.

11 And it came to pass that he did afflict the people with his whoredoms and abominations. And when he had reigned for the space of forty and two years, the people did rise up in rebellion against him. And there began to be war again in the land, insomuch that Riplakish was killed and his descendants were driven out of the land. And it came to pass, after the space of many years, Morionton (he being a descendant of Riplakish) gathered together an army of outcasts, and went forth and gave battle unto the people. And he gained power over many cities, and the war became exceedingly sore and did last for the space of many years; and he did gain power over all the land and did establish himself king over all the land. And after that he had established himself king, he did ease the burden of the people, by which he did gain favor in the eyes of the people; and they did anoint him to be their king. And he did do justice unto the people, but not unto himself because of his many whoredoms; wherefore, he was cut off from the presence of YHWH.

12 And it came to pass that Morionton built up many cities. And the people became exceedingly rich under his reign, both in buildings, and in gold, and in silver, and in raising grain, and in flocks, and herds, and such things which had been restored unto them. And Morionton did live to an exceedingly great age, and then he fathered Kim. And Kim did reign in the place of his father; and he did reign eight years, and his father died. And it came to pass that Kim did not

reign in righteousness; wherefore, he was not favored of YHWH. And his brother did rise up in rebellion against him, in the which he did bring him into captivity. And he did remain in captivity all his days, and he fathered sons and daughters in captivity. And in his old age he fathered Levi, and he died.

13 And it came to pass that Levi did serve in captivity, after the death of his father, for the space of forty and two years. And he did make war against the king of the land, by which he did obtain unto himself the kingdom. And after he had obtained unto himself the kingdom, **he did that which was right in the sight of YHWH.**[39] And the people did prosper in the land. And he did live to a good old age and fathered sons and daughters; and he also fathered Corom, whom he anointed king in his place.

14 And it came to pass that Corom did that which was good in the sight of YHWH all his days, and he fathered many sons and daughters. And after that he had seen many days, he did pass away, even like unto the rest of the earth; and Kish reigned in his place. And it came to pass that Kish passed away also, and Lib reigned in his place. And it came to pass that Lib also did that which was good in the sight of YHWH. And in the days of Lib the poisonous serpents were destroyed. Wherefore, they did go into the land southward to hunt food for the people of the land, for the land was covered with animals of the forest; and Lib also himself became a great hunter. And they built a great city by the narrow neck of land, by the place where the sea divides the land. And they did preserve the land southward for a wilderness to get game. And the whole face of the land northward was covered with inhabitants. And they were exceedingly industrious, and they did buy, and sell, and traffic one with another, that they might get gain. And they did work in all manner of ore, and they did make gold, and silver, and iron, and brass, and all manner of metals; and they did dig it out of the earth. Wherefore, they did cast up mighty heaps of earth to get ore, of gold, and of silver, and of iron, and of copper. And they did work all manner of fine work.[40] And they did have silks and fine-twined linen, and they did work all manner of cloth, that they might clothe themselves from their nakedness. And

---

39 2 Kings 12:2; Words of M'raman 1:5–6 **40** This is an example of the Hebraism known as the Cognate Accusative, where a noun pairs with the verb which is the noun's root.

they did make all manner of tools to till the earth, both to plow and to sow, to reap and to hoe, and also to thresh. And they did make all manner of tools, with which they did work their beasts. And they did make all manner of weapons of war. And they did work all manner of work of exceedingly elegant workmanship. And never could be a people more blessed than were they, and more prospered by the hand of YHWH. And they were in a land that was choice above all lands, for YHWH had spoken it.

15 And it came to pass that Lib did live many years and fathered sons and daughters, and he also fathered Hearthom. And it came to pass that Hearthom reigned in the place of his father. And when Hearthom had reigned twenty and four years, behold, the kingdom was taken away from him. And he served many years in captivity, yes, even all the remainder of his days. And he fathered Heth. And Heth lived in captivity all his days, and Heth fathered Aharon. And Aharon dwelt in captivity all his days, and he fathered Amnigaddah. And Amnigaddah also dwelt in captivity all his days, and he fathered Coriantum. And Coriantum dwelt in captivity all his days, and he fathered Com.

16 And it came to pass that Com drew away the half of the kingdom, and he reigned over the half of the kingdom forty and two years. And he went to battle against the king Amgid, and they fought for the space of many years, during which time Com gained power over Amgid and obtained power over the remainder of the kingdom. And in the days of Com there began to be robbers in the land, and they adopted the old plans and administered oaths after the manner of the ancients, and sought again to destroy the kingdom. Now Com did fight against them much; nevertheless, he did not prevail against them.

17 And there came also in the days of Com many prophets and prophesied of the destruction of that great people, except they should repent and turn unto YHWH, and abandon their murders and wickedness. And it came to pass that the prophets were rejected by the people and they fled unto Com for protection, for the people sought to destroy them. And they prophesied unto Com many things, and he was blessed in all the remainder of his days. And he lived to a good old age and fathered Shiblon. And Shiblon reigned in his place.

18 And the brother of Shiblon rebelled against him, and there began to be an exceedingly great war in all the land. And it came to pass that the brother of Shiblon caused that all the prophets who prophesied of the destruction of the people should be put to death. And there was great calamity in all the land — for they had testified that a great curse should come upon the land, and also upon the people, and that there should be a great destruction among them, such a one as never had been upon the face of the earth, and their bones should become as heaps of earth upon the face of the land, except they should repent of their wickedness.[41] And they hearkened not unto the voice of YHWH because of their wicked conspiracies; wherefore, there began to be wars and contentions in all the land, and also many famines and pestilences, insomuch that there was a great destruction, such a one as never had been known upon the face of the earth. And all this came to pass in the days of Shiblon. And the people began to repent of their iniquity; and inasmuch as they did, YHWH did have mercy on them.

19 And it came to pass that Shiblon was slain, and Shet was brought into captivity and he did dwell in captivity all his days. And it came to pass that Ahah, his son, did obtain the kingdom, and he did reign over the people all his days. And he did do all manner of iniquity in his days, by which he caused the shedding of much blood; and few were his days. And Ethem, being a descendant of Ahah, did obtain the kingdom, and he also did do that which was wicked in his days. And it came to pass in the days of Ethem, there came many prophets and prophesied again unto the people; yes, they did prophesy that YHWH would utterly destroy them from off the face of the earth except they repented of their iniquities. And it came to pass that the people hardened their hearts and would not hearken unto their words. And the prophets mourned and withdrew from among the people.

20 And it came to pass that Ethem did execute judgment in wickedness all his days, and he fathered Moron. And it came to pass that Moron did reign in his place, and Moron did that which was wicked before YHWH. And it came to pass that there arose a rebellion among the people because of that secret conspiracy which was built up to get power and gain. And there arose a mighty man among them

---

41 Moshiyah 5:12

in iniquity and gave battle unto Moron, by which he did overthrow the half of the kingdom; and he did maintain the half of the kingdom for many years. And it came to pass that Moron did overthrow him and did obtain the kingdom again. And it came to pass that there arose another mighty man, and he was a descendant of the brother of Yered. And it came to pass that he did overthrow Moron and obtain the kingdom; wherefore, Moron dwelt in captivity all the remainder of his days, and he fathered Coriantor.

21 And it came to pass that Coriantor dwelt in captivity all his days. And in the days of Coriantor there also came many prophets and prophesied of great and marvelous things, and cried repentance unto the people, and except they should repent, Adonai YHWH would execute judgment against them to their utter destruction, and that Adonai YHWH would send or bring forth another people to possess the land by his power, after the manner which he brought their fathers. And they did reject all the words of the prophets because of their secret society and wicked abominations. And it came to pass that Coriantor fathered 'Eter, and he died having dwelt in captivity all his days.

5 And it came to pass that the days of 'Eter were in the days of Coriantumr, and Coriantumr was king over all the land. And 'Eter was a prophet of YHWH; wherefore, 'Eter came forth in the days of Coriantumr and began to prophesy unto the people, for he could not be constrained because of the spirit of YHWH which was in him. For he did cry from the morning even until the going down of the sun, exhorting the people to believe in Elohim unto repentance for fear that they should be destroyed, saying unto them that by faith all things are fulfilled. Wherefore, whoever believes in Elohim might with surety hope for a better world, yes, even a place at the right hand of Elohim,[42] which hope comes of faith, makes an anchor to the souls of men, which would make them sure and steadfast, always abounding in good works, being led to glorify Elohim. And it came to pass that 'Eter did prophesy great and marvelous things unto the people, which they did not believe because they saw them not.

---

[42] Moshiyah 3:2; 11:21; M'roni 7:5

2 And now I, M'roni, would speak somewhat concerning these things. I would show unto the world that faith is things which are hoped for and not seen. Wherefore, dispute not because you see not, for you receive no witness — not until after the trial of your faith. For it was by faith that Mashiach showed himself unto our fathers after he had risen from the dead, and he showed not himself unto them until after they had faith in him; wherefore, it must necessarily be that some had faith in him, for he showed himself not unto the world but because of the faith of men. He has shown himself unto the world, and glorified the name of the Father, and prepared a way that thereby others might be partakers of the Heavenly gift, that they might hope for those things which they have not seen; wherefore, you may also have hope and be partakers of the gift if you will but have faith.[43] Behold, it was by faith that they of old were called after the Holy Order of Elohim.[44] Wherefore, by faith was the Torah of Moshe given. But in the gift of the Son has Elohim prepared a more excellent way, and it is by faith that it has been fulfilled.[45] For if there be no faith among the children of men, Elohim can do no miracle among them; wherefore, he showed not himself until after their faith.[46]

3 Behold, it was the faith of Alma and Amulek that caused the prison to tumble to the earth. Behold, it was the faith of Nefi and Lechi that worked the change upon the Lamanites, that they were cleansed with fire and with the Ruach HaKodesh. Behold, it was the faith of Ammon and his brothers which worked so great a miracle among the Lamanites. Yes, and even all they which worked miracles worked them by faith, even those who were before Mashiach, and also them which were after. And it was by faith that the three talmidim obtained a promise that they should not taste of death, and they obtained not the promise until after their faith.[47] And neither at any time have any worked miracles until after their faith; wherefore, they first believed in the Son of Elohim. And there were many whose faith was so exceedingly strong, even before Mashiach came, who could not be kept from within the veil, but truly saw with their eyes the things which they had beheld with an eye of faith;[48] and they were glad. And behold, we have seen in this record that one of these was

---

[43] 4 Nefi 1:1 [44] Alma 9:10; 10:2 [45] 2 Nefi 8:2; 3 Nefi 7:2 [46] 'Eter 1:12-13; M'roni 7:4-9
[47] 3 Nefi 13:4-6 [48] Alma 16:26, 30; 'Eter 1:12

the brother of Yered, for so great was his faith in Elohim that when Elohim put forth his finger, he could not hide it from the sight of the brother of Yered because of his word which he had spoken unto him, which word he had obtained by faith. And after the brother of Yered had beheld the finger of YHWH because of the promise which the brother of Yered had obtained by faith, YHWH could not withhold anything from his sight; wherefore, he showed him all things, for he could no longer be kept without the veil. And it is by faith that my fathers have obtained the promise that these things should come unto their brothers through the Goyim. Therefore, YHWH has commanded me, yes, even Yeshua HaMashiach.[49]

4 And I said unto him, YHWH, the Goyim will mock at these things because of our weakness in writing; for YHWH, you have made us mighty in word by faith, but you have not made us mighty in writing. For you have made all this people that they could speak much because of the Ruach HaKodesh, which you have given them. And you have made us that we could write but little because of the awkwardness of our hands. Behold, you have not made us mighty in writing like unto the brother of Yered, for you made him that the things which he wrote were mighty, even as you are, unto the overpowering of man to read them. You have also made our words powerful and great, even that we cannot write them. Wherefore, when we write, we behold our weakness and stumble because of the placing of our words. And I fear that the Goyim shall mock at our words.

5 And when I had said this, YHWH spoke unto me, saying, Fools mock, but they shall mourn. And my grace is sufficient for the meek, that they shall take no advantage of your weakness. And if men come unto me, I will show unto them their weakness. I give unto men weakness, that they may be humble. And my grace is sufficient for all men that humble themselves before me; for if they humble themselves before me and have faith in me, then will I make weak things become strong unto them. Behold, I will show unto the Goyim their weakness. And I will show unto them that faith, hope, and charity brings unto me, the fountain of all righteousness.

6 And I, M'roni, having heard these words, was comforted, and said, O YHWH, your righteous will be done, for I know that you work unto

---

49 2 Nefi 12:12; Enosh 1:3-4

the children of men according to their faith. For the brother of Yered said unto the mountain Zerin, Remove — and it was removed. And if he had not had faith, it would not have moved. Wherefore, you work after men have faith. For thus did you manifest yourself unto your talmidim; for after they had faith and did speak in your name, you did show yourself unto them in great power. And I also remember that you have said that you have prepared a house for man, yes, even among the mansions of your Father, in the which man might have a more excellent hope. Wherefore, man must hope, or he cannot receive an inheritance in the place which you have prepared. And again I remember that you have said that you have loved the world, even unto the laying down of your life for the world, that you might take it again, to prepare a place for the children of men. And now I know that this love which you have had for the children of men is charity.[50] Wherefore, except men shall have charity, they cannot inherit that place which you have prepared in the mansions of your Father. Wherefore, I know by this thing which you have said that if the Goyim have not charity because of our weakness, that you will prove them and take away their talent, yes, even that which they have received, and give unto them who shall have more abundantly.

7 And it came to pass that I prayed unto YHWH that he would give unto the Goyim grace, that they might have charity. And it came to pass that YHWH said unto me, If they have not charity, it matters not unto you. You have been faithful; wherefore, your garments shall be made clean. And because you have seen your weakness, you shall be made strong, even unto the sitting down in the place which I have prepared in the mansions of my Father.

8 And now I, M'roni, bid shalom unto the Goyim, yes, and also unto my brothers, whom I love, until we shall meet before the judgment seat of Mashiach, where all men shall know that my garments are not spotted with your blood. And then shall you know that I have seen Yeshua, and that he has talked with me face to face, and that he told me in plain humility, even as a man tells another, in my own language, concerning these things. And only a few have I written because of my weakness in writing. And now I would commend you to seek this Yeshua of whom the prophets and emissaries have

---

50 M'roni 7:9

written, that the grace of Elohim the Father, and also Adonai Yeshua HaMashiach, and the Ruach HaKodesh, which bears record of them, may be and abide in you for ever. Amen.

6 And now I, M'roni, proceed to finish my record concerning the destruction of the people of whom I have been writing. For behold, they rejected all the words of 'Eter, for he truly told them of all things from the beginning of man; and that after the waters had receded from off the face of this land, it became a choice land above all other lands, a chosen land of YHWH — wherefore, YHWH would have that all men should serve him who dwelt upon the face thereof — and that it was the place of the New Yerushalayim, which should come down out of Heaven, and the holy sanctuary of YHWH.

2 Behold, 'Eter saw the days of Mashiach, and he spoke concerning a New Yerushalayim upon this land. And he spoke also concerning the house of Isra'el, and the Yerushalayim from where Lechi should come — after it should be destroyed, it should be built up again, a holy city unto YHWH (wherefore, it could not be a New Yerushalayim, for it had been in a time of old, but it should be built up again and become a holy city of YHWH, and it should be built up unto the house of Isra'el) and that a New Yerushalayim should be built up upon this land unto the remnant of the seed of Yosef, for which things there has been a type. For as Yosef brought his father down into the land of Egypt, even so he died there. Wherefore, YHWH brought a remnant of the seed of Yosef out of the land of Yerushalayim, that he might be merciful unto the seed of Yosef, that they should perish not, even as he was merciful unto the father of Yosef, that he should perish not.

3 Wherefore, the remnant of the house of Yosef shall be built up upon this land, and it shall be a land of their inheritance. And they shall build up a holy city unto YHWH like unto the Yerushalayim of old. And they shall no more be confounded until the end come, when the earth shall pass away. And there shall be a new heaven and a new earth. And they shall be like unto the old, except the old have passed away and all things have become new. And then comes the New Yerushalayim; and blessed are they who dwell therein, for it is they whose garments are white through the blood of the Lamb; and they are they who are numbered among the remnant of the seed of Yosef, who were of the house of Isra'el. And then also comes the

Yerushalayim of old and the inhabitants thereof; blessed are they, for they have been washed in the blood of the Lamb. And they are they who were scattered, and **gathered in from the four quarters of the earth**[51] and from the north countries, and are partakers of the fulfilling of the covenant which Elohim made with their father, Avraham. And when these things come, brings to pass the scripture which says, There are they who were first who shall be last, and there are they who were last who shall be first.[52]

4 And I was about to write more, but I am forbidden; but great and marvelous were the prophecies of 'Eter. But they esteemed him as nothing and cast him out. And he hid himself in the cavity of a rock by day, and by night he went forth, viewing the things which should come upon the people. And as he dwelt in the cavity of a rock, he made the remainder of this record, viewing the destructions which came upon the people by night.

5 And it came to pass that in that same year which he was cast out from among the people, there began to be a great war among the people, for there were many who rose up who were mighty men and sought to destroy Coriantumr by their secret plans of wickedness, of which have been spoken. And now Coriantumr, having studied himself in all the arts of war and all the cunning of the world, wherefore he gave battle unto them who sought to destroy him. But he repented not, neither his fair sons nor daughters, neither the fair sons and daughters of Cohor, neither the fair sons and daughters of Corihor. And in short, there were none of the fair sons and daughters upon the face of the whole earth[53] who repented of their sins. Wherefore, it came to pass that in the first year that 'Eter dwelt in the cavity of a rock, there were many people who were slain by the sword, by those secret conspiracies fighting against Coriantumr that they might obtain the kingdom. And it came to pass that the sons of Coriantumr fought much and bled much. And in the second year, the word of YHWH came to 'Eter that he should go and prophesy unto Coriantumr that if he would repent, and all his household, YHWH would give unto him his kingdom and spare the people.[54] Otherwise, they should be destroyed, and all his household,

---

51 Deut. 30:3–4; Isa. 11:12; Zech. 2:6   52 1 Nefi 3:24; Ya'akov 3:25   53 The Hebrew word for "earth" is *eretz* ארץ, which can mean "earth" or "land." This verse refers only to Yeredites; thus, "land" fits the context better than "earth."   54 3 Nefi 4:9

except it were himself. And he should only live to see the fulfilling of the prophecies which had been spoken concerning another people receiving the land for their inheritance, and Coriantumr should receive a burial by them, and every soul should be destroyed except it were Coriantumr. And it came to pass that Coriantumr repented not, neither his household, neither the people; and the wars ceased not. And they sought to kill 'Eter, but he fled from before them and hid again in the cavity of the rock.

6 And it came to pass that there arose up Shared, and he also gave battle unto Coriantumr; and he did beat him, insomuch that in the third year he did bring him into captivity. And the sons of Coriantumr in the fourth year did beat Shared and did obtain the kingdom again unto their father. Now there began to be a war upon all the face of the land, every man with his band fighting for that which he desired. And there were robbers, and in short, all manner of wickedness upon all the face of the land. And it came to pass that Coriantumr was exceedingly angry with Shared, and he went against him with his armies to battle. And they did meet in great anger, and they did meet in the valley of Gilgal, and the battle became exceedingly sore. And it came to pass that Shared fought against him for the space of three days. And it came to pass that Coriantumr beat him, and did pursue him until he came to the plains of Heshlon. And it came to pass that Shared gave him battle again upon the plains. And behold, he did beat Coriantumr and drove him back again to the valley of Gilgal. And Coriantumr gave Shared battle again in the valley of Gilgal, in which he beat Shared and slew him. And Shared wounded Coriantumr in his thigh, that he did not go to battle again for the space of two years, in which time all the people upon all the face of the land were shedding blood; and there was none to constrain them.

7 And now there began to be a great curse upon the land because of the iniquity of the people, in which if a man should lay his tool or his sword upon the shelf, or upon the place where he would keep it, and behold, the next day he could not find it, so great was the curse upon the land. Wherefore, every man did cling unto that which was his own with his hands, and would not borrow, neither would he lend. And every man kept the hilt of his sword in his right hand, in the defense of his property, and his own life, and of his wives and children. And now after the space of two years, and after the death

of Shared, behold, there arose the brother of Shared, and he gave battle unto Coriantumr, in which Coriantumr did beat him and did pursue him to the wilderness of Akish. And it came to pass that the brother of Shared did give battle unto him in the wilderness of Akish, and the battle became exceedingly sore, and many thousands fell by the sword. And it came to pass that Coriantumr did lay siege to the wilderness. And the brother of Shared did march forth out of the wilderness by night and slew a part of the army of Coriantumr as they were drunken; and he came forth to the land of Moron and placed himself upon the throne of Coriantumr. And it came to pass that Coriantumr dwelt with his army in the wilderness for the space of two years, in which he did receive great strength to his army.

⁸ Now the brother of Shared, whose name was Gilead, also received great strength to his army because of secret conspiracies. And it came to pass that his Kohen HaGadol murdered him as he sat upon his throne. And it came to pass that one of the secret conspirators murdered him in a secret pass and obtained unto himself the kingdom, and his name was Lib. And Lib was a man of great stature, more than any other man among all the people. And it came to pass that in the first year of Lib, Coriantumr came up unto the land of Moron and gave battle unto Lib. And it came to pass that he fought with Lib, in which Lib did strike upon his arm, that he was wounded. Nevertheless, the army of Coriantumr did press forward upon Lib, that he fled to the borders upon the seashore. And it came to pass that Coriantumr pursued him, and Lib gave battle unto him upon the seashore. And it came to pass that Lib did smite the army of Coriantumr, that they fled again to the wilderness of Akish. And it came to pass that Lib did pursue him until he came to the plains of Agosh. And Coriantumr had taken all the people with him as he fled before Lib, in that quarter of the land where he fled. And when he had come to the plains of Agosh, he gave battle unto Lib, and he smote upon him until he died. Nevertheless, the brother of Lib did come against Coriantumr in the place thereof; and the battle became exceedingly severe, in the which Coriantumr fled again before the army of the brother of Lib.

⁹ Now the name of the brother of Lib was called Shiz. And it came to pass that Shiz pursued after Coriantumr, and he did overthrow many cities, and he did slay both women and children, and he did

burn the cities thereof. And there went a fear of Shiz throughout all the land; yes, a cry went forth throughout the land, Who can stand before the army of Shiz? Behold, he sweeps the earth before him!

10 And it came to pass that the people began to flock together in armies throughout all the face of the land, and they were divided; and a part of them fled to the army of Shiz, and a part of them fled to the army of Coriantumr. And so great and lasting had been the war, and so long had been the scene of bloodshed and carnage, that the whole face of the land was covered with the bodies of the dead. And so swift and speedy was the war that there was none left to bury the dead, but they did march forth from the shedding of blood to the shedding of blood, leaving the bodies of men, women, and children, strewn upon the face of the land, to become a prey to the worms of the flesh. And the scent thereof went forth upon the face of the land, even upon all the face of the land. Wherefore, the people became troubled by day and by night because of the scent thereof. Nevertheless, Shiz did not cease to pursue Coriantumr, for he had sworn to avenge himself upon Coriantumr of the blood of his brother, who had been slain; and the word of YHWH came to 'Eter that Coriantumr should not fall by the sword. And thus we see that YHWH did visit them in the fulness of his anger. And their wickedness and abominations had prepared a way for their everlasting destruction.

11 And it came to pass that Shiz did pursue Coriantumr eastward, even to the borders by the seashore. And there he gave battle unto Shiz for the space of three days. And so terrible was the destruction among the armies of Shiz that the people began to be frightened and began to flee before the armies of Coriantumr. And they fled to the land of Corihor and swept off the inhabitants before them, all they that would not join them. And they pitched their tents in the valley of Corihor, and Coriantumr pitched his tents in the valley of Shurr. Now the valley of Shurr was near the hill Comron; wherefore, Coriantumr did gather his armies together upon the hill Comron, and did sound a shofar unto the armies of Shiz to invite them forth to battle. And it came to pass that they came forth, but were driven again. And they came the second time, and they were driven again the second time. And it came to pass that they came again the third time, and the battle became exceedingly sore. And it came to pass that Shiz smote upon Coriantumr, that he gave him many deep wounds.

And Coriantumr, having lost his blood, fainted and was carried away as though he were dead. Now the loss of men, women, and children on both sides was so great that Shiz commanded his people that they should not pursue the armies of Coriantumr; wherefore, they returned to their camp.

12 And it came to pass, when Coriantumr had recovered of his wounds, he began to remember the words which 'Eter had spoken unto him. He saw that there had been slain by the sword already nearly two millions of his people, and he began to sorrow in his heart; yes, there had been slain two millions of mighty men, and also their wives and their children. He began to repent of the evil which he had done. He began to remember the words which had been spoken by the mouth of all the prophets, and he saw them, that they were fulfilled thus far every bit. And his soul mourned and refused to be comforted.

13 And it came to pass that he wrote a letter unto Shiz, desiring him that he would spare the people, and he would give up the kingdom for the sake of the lives of the people. And it came to pass that when Shiz had received his letter, he wrote a letter unto Coriantumr that if he would give himself up that he might slay him with his own sword, that he would spare the lives of the people. And it came to pass that the people repented not of their iniquity. And the people of Coriantumr were stirred up to anger against the people of Shiz, and the people of Shiz were stirred up to anger against the people of Coriantumr; wherefore, the people of Shiz did give battle unto the people of Coriantumr.

14 And when Coriantumr saw that he was about to fall, he fled again before the people of Shiz. And it came to pass that he came to the waters of Ripliancum, which (by interpretation) is large, or to exceed all; wherefore, when they came to these waters, they pitched their tents. And Shiz also pitched his tents near unto them, and therefore the next day they did come to battle. And it came to pass that they fought an exceedingly serious battle, in the which Coriantumr was wounded again, and he fainted with the loss of blood. And it came to pass that the armies of Coriantumr did press upon the armies of Shiz, that they beat them, that they caused them to flee before them. And they did flee southward and did pitch their tents in a place which was called Ogath. And it came to pass that the army of Coriantumr

did pitch their tents by the hill Ramah,[55] and it was that same hill where my father M'raman did hide up the records unto YHWH which were sacred. And it came to pass that they did gather together all the people upon all the face of the land who had not been slain, except it were 'Eter.

15 And it came to pass that 'Eter did behold all the doings of the people. And he beheld that the people who were for Coriantumr were gathered together to the army of Coriantumr, and the people who were for Shiz were gathered together to the army of Shiz. Wherefore, they were for the space of four years gathering together the people, that they might get all who were upon the face of the land, and that they might receive all the strength which it were possible that they could receive. And it came to pass that when they were all gathered together, every one to the army which he would, with their wives and their children—men, women, and children being armed with weapons of war, having shields, and breastplates, and headplates, and being clothed after the manner of war—and they did march forth one against another to battle; and they fought all that day and conquered not.

16 And it came to pass that when it was night, they were weary, and retired to their camps. And after they had retired to their camps, they took up a howling and a lamentation for the loss of the slain of their people. And so great were their cries, their howlings and lamentations, that it did split the air exceedingly. And it came to pass that the next day they did go again to battle. And great and terrible was that day; nevertheless, they conquered not. And when the night came, again they did split the air with their cries, and their howlings, and their mournings for the loss of the slain of their people.

17 And it came to pass that Coriantumr wrote again a letter unto Shiz, desiring that he would not come again to battle, but that he would take the kingdom and spare the lives of the people. But behold, the spirit of YHWH had ceased striving with them and HaSatan had full power over the hearts of the people, for they were given up unto the hardness of their hearts and the blindness of their minds, that they might be destroyed; wherefore, they went again to battle. And it came to pass that they fought all that day. And when the night came,

---

55 From the Hebrew root *ram* רם (Strong's 7410), "to be high." (See footnote to M'raman 3:1.)

they slept upon their swords. And the next day, they fought even until the night came. And when the night came, they were drunken with anger, even as a man who is drunken with wine. And they slept again upon their swords.

18 And the next day, they fought again. And when the night came, they had all fallen by the sword except it were fifty and two of the people of Coriantumr and sixty and nine of the people of Shiz. And it came to pass that they slept upon their swords that night. And the next day they fought again, and they contended in their might, with their swords and with their shields, all that day. And when the night came, there were thirty and two of the people of Shiz and twenty and seven of the people of Coriantumr. And it came to pass that they ate, and slept, and prepared for death the next day. And they were large and mighty men as to the strength of men. And it came to pass that they fought for the space of three hours, and they fainted with the loss of blood. And it came to pass that when the men of Coriantumr had received sufficient strength that they could walk, they were about to flee for their lives. But behold, Shiz arose, and also his men, and he swore in his anger that he would slay Coriantumr or he would perish by the sword; wherefore, he did pursue them.

19 And the next day, he did overtake them, and they fought again with the sword. And it came to pass that when they had all fallen by the sword, except it were Coriantumr and Shiz, behold, Shiz had fainted with loss of blood. And it came to pass that when Coriantumr had leaned upon his sword, that he rested a little, and he cut off the head of Shiz. And it came to pass that after he had cut off the head of Shiz, that Shiz raised upon his hands and fell. And after that he had struggled for breath, he died. And it came to pass that Coriantumr fell to the earth and became as if he had no life.

20 And YHWH spoke unto 'Eter and said unto him, Go forth. And he went forth and beheld that the words of YHWH had all been fulfilled. And he finished his record (and the hundredth part I have not written) and he hid them in a manner that the people of Limhi did find them.[56] Now the last words which are written by 'Eter are these: Whether YHWH desires that I be translated or that I suffer the

---

56 Moshiyah 5:12

will of YHWH in the flesh, it matters not, if it so be that I am saved in the kingdom of Elohim. Amen.

ספר מרני
M'RONI
THE BOOK OF M'RONI

Now I, M'roni, after having made an end of abridging the account of the people of Yered, I had supposed not to have written more, but I have not as yet perished. And I make not myself known to the Lamanites for fear that they should destroy me. For behold, their wars are exceedingly fierce among themselves; and because of their hatred, they put to death every Nefite that will not deny[1] the Mashiach. And I, M'roni, will not deny the Mashiach. Wherefore, I wander wherever I can for the safety of my own life. Wherefore, I write a few more things, contrary to that which I had supposed, for I had supposed not to have written any more. But I write a few more things, that perhaps they may be of worth[2] unto my brothers the Lamanites in some future day, according to the will of YHWH.[3]

2 The words of Mashiach which he spoke unto his talmidim, the twelve whom he had chosen, as he laid his hands upon them. And he called them by name, saying, You shall call on the Father in my name in mighty prayer, and after that you have done this, you shall have power that on him whom you shall lay your hands, you shall give the Ruach HaKodesh.[4] And in my name shall you give it, for thus do my emissaries. Now Mashiach spoke these words unto them at the time of his first appearing, and the multitude heard it not, but the talmidim heard it. And on as many as they laid their hands fell the Ruach HaKodesh.

3 The manner which the talmidim, which were called the elders of the assembly, ordained kohanim and teachers. After they had prayed unto the Father in the name of Mashiach, they laid their hands upon them and said, In the name of Yeshua HaMashiach, I ordain

---

1 2 Nefi 11:9; M'raman 4:6 **2** 1 Nefi 7:3 **3** Enosh 1:3 **4** 3 Nefi 8:10

you to be a kohen (or if he be a teacher, I ordain you to be a teacher) to preach repentance and remission of sins through Yeshua HaMashiach by the endurance of faith on his name to the end. Amen. And after this manner did they ordain kohanim and teachers, according to the gifts and callings of Elohim unto men. And they ordained them by the power[5] of the Ruach HaKodesh which was in them.

4 The manner of their elders and kohanim administering the flesh and blood[6] of Mashiach unto the assembly. And they administered it according to the mitzvot of Mashiach; wherefore, we know that the manner to be true. And the elder or kohen did minister it; and they did kneel down with the assembly and pray to the Father in the name of Mashiach, saying, O Elohim the Eternal Father, we ask you in the name of your Son Yeshua HaMashiach to bless and sanctify this bread to the souls of all those who partake of it, that they may eat in remembrance of the body of your Son, and witness unto you, O Elohim the Eternal Father, that they are willing to take upon them the name of your Son, and always remember him, and keep his mitzvot which he has given them, that they may always have his ruach to be with them. Amen.

5 The manner of administering the wine.[7] Behold, they took the cup and said, O Elohim the Eternal Father, we ask you in the name of your Son Yeshua HaMashiach to bless and sanctify this wine to the souls of all those who drink of it, that they may do it in remembrance of the blood of your Son, which was shed for them, that they may witness unto you, O Elohim the Eternal Father, that they do always remember him, that they may have his ruach to be with them. Amen.

6 And now I speak concerning immersion. Behold, elders, kohanim, and teachers were washed by immersion; and they were not immersed except they brought forth fruit showing that they were worthy of it. Neither did they receive any unto immersion save they came forth **with a broken heart and a contrite spirit**,[8] and witnessed unto the assembly that they truly repented of all their sins. And none were received unto immersion except they took

---

5 3 Nefi 9:2 **6** 3 Nefi 9:6 **7** 3 Nefi 9:6 **8** Ps. 34:19 (18)

upon them the name of Mashiach, having a determination to serve him unto the end. And after they had been received unto washing by immersion, and were worked upon[9] and cleansed by the power of the Ruach HaKodesh, they were numbered among the people of the assembly of Mashiach. And their names were taken, that they might be remembered and nourished by the good word of Elohim, to keep them in the right way, to keep them continually watchful unto prayer, relying alone upon the merits of Mashiach, who was the author and the finisher of their faith.

2 And the assembly did meet together often[10] to fast, and to pray, and to speak one with another concerning the welfare of their souls. And they did meet together often to partake of bread and wine in remembrance[11] of Adonai Yeshua.[12] And they were strict to observe that there should be no iniquity[13] among them. And whoever was found to commit iniquity, and three witnesses of the assembly did condemn them before the elders, and if they repented not and confessed not, their names were blotted out and they were not numbered among the people of Mashiach. But as often as they repented and sought forgiveness with real intent, they were forgiven. And their meetings were conducted by the assembly after the manner of the workings of the spirit, and by the power[14] of the Ruach HaKodesh, for as the power of the Ruach HaKodesh led them, whether to preach, or exhort, or to pray, or to supplicate, or to sing, even so it was done.

7 And now I, M'roni, write a few of the words of my father, M'raman, which he spoke concerning faith, hope, and charity, for after this manner did he speak unto the people as he taught them in the synagogue which they had built for the place of worship:

2 And now I, M'raman, speak unto you, my beloved brothers. And it is by the grace of Elohim the Father and our Adonai Yeshua HaMashiach and his holy will, because of the gift of his calling unto me, that I am permitted to speak[15] unto you at this time. Wherefore, I would speak unto you that are of the assembly,[16] that are the peaceable followers of Mashiach, and that have obtained a sufficient hope by

---

9 Enosh 1:7 **10** 3 Nefi 8:8 **11** Moshiyah 2:3 **12** See note to 3 Nefi 8:4 concerning the *Yayin HaMeshumar*. **13** 2 Nefi 1:5 **14** 2 Nefi 14:1 **15** Alma 16:16 **16** 1 Nefi 3:27

which you can enter into the rest of YHWH, from this time henceforth, until you shall rest with him in Heaven. And now, my brothers, I judge these things of you because of your peaceable walk with the children of men. For I remember the word of Elohim which says, By their works, you shall know them. For if their works be good, then they are good also.[17] For behold, Elohim has said, A man being evil cannot do that which is good; for if he offers a gift or prays unto Elohim, except he shall do it with real intent, it profits him nothing.[18] For behold, it is not counted unto him for righteousness. For behold, if a man being evil gives a gift, he does it grudgingly; wherefore, it is counted unto him the same as if he had retained the gift. Wherefore, he is counted evil before Elohim.[19] And likewise, also is it counted evil unto a man if he shall pray and not with real intent of heart. Yes, and it profits him nothing, for Elohim receives none such. Wherefore, a man being evil cannot do that which is good, neither will he give a good gift. For behold, a bitter fountain cannot bring forth good water, neither can a good fountain bring forth bitter water. Wherefore, a man being the servant of HaSatan cannot follow Mashiach; and if he follow Mashiach, he cannot be a servant of HaSatan. Wherefore, all things which are good come of Elohim, and that which is evil comes of HaSatan. For HaSatan is an enemy unto Elohim, and fights against him continually, and invites and entices to sin, and to do that which is evil continually. But behold, that which is of Elohim invites and entices to do good continually.

3 Wherefore, everything which invites and entices to do good, and to love Elohim, and to serve him, is inspired of Elohim. Wherefore, take heed, my beloved brothers, that you do not judge that which is evil to be of Elohim, or that which is good and of Elohim to be of HaSatan. For behold, my brothers, it is given unto you to judge, that you may know good from evil.[20] And the way to judge is as plain, that you may know with a perfect knowledge as the daylight is from the dark night. For behold, the spirit of Mashiach is given to every man, that they may know good from evil. Wherefore, I show unto you

---

17 Alma 19:11 **18** As we read in the Mishnah: "...all are the same, the one who offers much and the one who offers little, on condition that a man will direct his intention to Heaven" (m.Menachot 13:11). **19** As we read in the Talmud: "...all the charity and kindness done by the heathen is counted to them as sin, because they only do it to magnify themselves" (b.Baba Batra 10b). **20** 2 Nefi 1:6, 10

the way to judge. For everything which invites to do good and to persuade to believe[21] in Mashiach is sent forth by the power and gift of Mashiach. Wherefore, you may know with a perfect knowledge it is of Elohim. But whatsoever thing persuades men to do evil, and believe not in Mashiach, and deny him, and serve not Elohim, then you may know with a perfect knowledge it is of HaSatan, for after this manner does HaSatan work; for he persuades no man to do good,[22] no not one, neither do his angels, neither do they who subject themselves unto him. And now, my brothers, seeing that you know the light by which you may judge, which light is the light of Mashiach, see that you do not judge wrongfully; for with that same judgment which you judge, you shall also be judged. Wherefore, I implore you, brothers, that you should search diligently in the light of Mashiach that you may know good from evil. And if you will lay hold upon every good thing and condemn it not, you certainly will be a child of Mashiach.

⁴And now my brothers, how is it possible that you can lay hold upon every good thing? And now I come to that faith of which I said I would speak, and I will tell you the way by which you may lay hold on every good thing. For behold, Elohim knowing all things, being from everlasting to everlasting, behold, he sent angels to minister unto the children of men, to make manifest concerning the coming of Mashiach, and in Mashiach there should come every good thing. And Elohim also declared[23] unto prophets by his own mouth that Mashiach should come. And behold, there were diverse ways that he did manifest things unto the children of men which were good, and all things which are good come of Mashiach; otherwise, men were fallen and there could no good thing come unto them. Wherefore, by the ministering of angels[24] and by every word which proceeded forth out of the mouth of Elohim, men began to exercise faith[25] in Mashiach; and thus by faith they did lay hold upon every good thing, and thus it was until the coming of Mashiach; and after that he came, men also were saved by faith in his name. And by faith they become the sons of Elohim.

⁵And as sure as Mashiach lives, he spoke these words unto our fathers, saying, Whatsoever thing you shall ask the Father in my

---

21 2 Nefi 11:6, 9   **22** M'roni 7:2   **23** Moshiyah 1:15; Cheleman 5:10   **24** Ameni 1:10
25 Alma 14:15

name, which is good, in faith, believing that you shall receive, behold, it shall be done unto you. Wherefore, my beloved brothers, have miracles[26] ceased because Mashiach has ascended into Heaven? And has sat down on the right hand of Elohim to claim of the Father his rights of mercy which he has upon the children of men? For he has answered the ends of the Torah, and he claims all those who have faith[27] in him; and they who have faith in him will cling to every good thing. Wherefore, he advocates the cause of the children of men. And he dwells eternally in the Heavens.

6 And because he has done this, my beloved brothers, have miracles ceased? Behold, I say unto you, no; neither have angels ceased to minister unto the children of men. For behold, they are subject[28] unto him, to minister according to the word of his command, showing themselves unto them of strong faith and a firm mind in every form of godliness. And the office of their ministry is to call men unto repentance, and to fulfill and to do the work of the covenants of the Father which he has made unto the children of men, to prepare the way among the children of men by declaring the word of Mashiach unto the chosen vessels of YHWH, that they may bear testimony of him; and by so doing, Adonai YHWH prepares the way that the residue of men may have faith in Mashiach, that the Ruach HaKodesh may have place in their hearts, according to the power thereof; and after this manner brings to pass the Father the covenants which he has made unto the children of men. And Mashiach has said, If you will have faith in me, you shall have power[29] to do whatsoever thing is expedient in me. And he has said, Repent, all you ends of the earth, and come unto me, and be washed by immersion[30] in my name, and have faith in me, that you may be saved.

7 And now, my beloved brothers, if this be the case, that these things are true which I have spoken unto you—and Elohim will show unto you with power and great glory at the last day that they are true—and if they are true, has the day of miracles ceased? Or have angels ceased to appear unto the children of men? Or has he withheld the power of the Ruach HaKodesh from them? Or will he so long as time shall last, or the earth shall stand, or there shall be one man upon the

---

26 M'raman 4:8-10   27 2 Nefi 11:8   28 2 Nefi 6:2; M'roni 9:5   29 3 Nefi 3:9   30 3 Nefi 9:11

face thereof to be saved? Behold, I say unto you, no. For it is by faith that miracles are worked,[31] and it is by faith that angels appear and minister unto men. Wherefore, if these things have ceased, woe be unto the children of men, for it is because of unbelief, and all is vain. For no man can be saved, according to the words of Mashiach, except they shall have faith in his name. Wherefore, if these things have ceased, then has faith ceased also, and awful is the state of man, for they are as though there had been no redemption[32] made.

8 But behold, my beloved brothers, I judge better things of you, for I judge that you have faith in Mashiach, because of your meekness; for if you have not faith in him, then you are not fit to be numbered among the people of his assembly. And again, my beloved brothers, I would speak unto you concerning hope. How is it that you can attain unto faith except you shall have hope?[33] And what is it that you shall hope for? Behold, I say unto you that you shall have hope[34] through the atonement of Mashiach and the power of his resurrection to be raised unto life Eternal, and this because of your faith in him, according to the promise. Wherefore, if a man have faith, he must necessarily have hope; for without faith, there cannot be any hope. And again, behold, I say unto you that he cannot have faith and hope except he shall be meek and humble of heart. If so, his faith and hope is vain, for none is acceptable before Elohim except the meek and humble of heart.

9 And if a man be meek and humble in heart, and confesses by the power of the Ruach HaKodesh that Yeshua is the Mashiach, he must necessarily have charity.[35] For if he have not charity, he is nothing; wherefore, he must necessarily have charity. And charity suffers long and is kind, and envies not, and is not puffed up, seeks not her own, is not easily provoked, thinks no evil and rejoices not in iniquity, but rejoices in the truth, bears all things, believes all things, hopes all things, endures all things. Wherefore, my beloved brothers, if you have not charity, you are nothing, for charity never fails. Wherefore, cling[36] unto charity, which is the greatest of all. For all things must fail, but charity is the pure love of Mashiach, and it endures for ever. And whoever is found possessed of it at the last day, **it shall be**

---

[31] 2 Nefi 11:12; 3 Nefi 9:5 [32] Alma 8:15 [33] 2 Nefi 13:4; Ya'akov 3:2 [34] Alma 10:4 [35] 2 Nefi 15:1; Alma 5:6 [36] Ya'akov 4:2

well with them.³⁷ Wherefore, my beloved brothers, pray unto the Father with all the energy of heart that you may be filled with this love, which he has bestowed upon all who are true followers of his Son Yeshua HaMashiach; that you may become the sons³⁸ of Elohim; that when he shall appear, we shall be like him, for we shall see him as he is; that we may have this hope; that we may be purified, even as he is pure. Amen.

8 A letter of my father, M'raman, written to me, M'roni; and it was written unto me soon after my calling to the ministry. And in this manner did he write unto me, saying, My beloved son M'roni, I rejoice exceedingly that your Adonai Yeshua HaMashiach has been mindful of you and has called you to his ministry and to his holy work. I am mindful of you always in my prayers, continually praying unto Elohim the Father in the name of his holy child Yeshua, that he, through his infinite goodness and grace, will keep you through the endurance of faith on his name to the end.

2 And now, my son, I speak unto you concerning that which grieves me exceedingly, for it grieves me that there should disputations rise among you. For if I have learned the truth, there have been disputations among you concerning the immersion of your little children. And now, my son, I desire that you should labor diligently that this shameful error should be removed from among you, for, for this intent I have written this letter. For immediately after I had learned these things of you, I inquired of YHWH concerning the matter; and the word of YHWH came to me by the power of the Ruach HaKodesh, saying, Listen to the words of Mashiach, your Redeemer, your Adonai, and your Elohim. Behold, I came into the world not to call the righteous, but sinners to repentance. The whole need no physician, but they that are sick. Wherefore, little children are whole, for they are not capable of committing sin. Wherefore, the curse of Adam is taken from them in me, that it has no power over them. And the law of circumcision is done away³⁹ in me. And after this manner did the Ruach HaKodesh manifest the word of Elohim unto me.

---

37 Deut. 5:29   38 3 Nefi 4:7   39 The seventh rule of Hillel tells us that a passage must be understood in context, and the fifth rule of Hillel tells us that general statements and specific statements must be understood in context of one another. The general subject of this section of text deals with the principle that children below the age of accountability

³Wherefore, my beloved son, I know that it is solemn mockery before Elohim that you should immerse little children. Behold, I say unto you that this thing shall you teach: repentance and immersion unto those who are accountable and capable of committing sin. Yes, teach parents that they must repent, and be washed by immersion, and humble themselves as their little children, and they shall all be saved with their little children. And their little children[40] need no repentance, neither immersion. Behold, immersion is unto repentance, to the fulfilling the mitzvot unto the remission of sins; but little children are alive[41] in Mashiach, even from the foundation of the world. If not so, Elohim is a partial Elohim, and also a changeable Elohim, and a respecter of persons. For how many little children have died without immersion? Wherefore, if little children could not be saved without washing by immersion, these must have gone to an endless Gehinnom. Behold, I say unto you that he that supposes that little children need immersion is in the gall of bitterness and in the bonds of iniquity, for he has neither faith, hope, nor charity. Wherefore, should he be cut off while in the thought, he must go down to She'ol. For awful is the wickedness to suppose that Elohim saves one child because of immersion, and the other must perish because he has no washing by immersion. Woe be unto him that shall pervert the ways of YHWH after this manner, for they shall perish except they repent.

⁴Behold, I speak with boldness, having authority from Elohim. And I fear not what man can do, for perfect love casts out all fear. And I am filled with charity, which is everlasting love. Wherefore, all children are alike unto me; wherefore, I love little children with a perfect love, and they are all alike and partakers of salvation. For I know that Elohim is not a partial Elohim, neither a changeable[42] being, but he is unchangeable from all eternity to all eternity. Little children cannot repent. Wherefore, it is awful wickedness to deny the pure mercies of Elohim unto them, for they are all alive in him because

---

are not culpable to Elohim in regards to Torah observance. Moreover the "law of circumcision" is incumbent, not upon an infant, but upon a parent. "Wherefore, little children…are not capable of committing sin. Wherefore, the curse of Adam is taken away from them in me, that it has no power over them." The "law of circumcision" is given as a specific example of this principle. In other words, a child below the age of accountability is not culpable to Elohim in regards to the law of circumcision.   **40** Moshiyah 1:16   **41** Moshiyah 8:9-10   **42** M'raman 4:8

of his mercy. And he that says that little children need immersion denies the mercies of Mashiach, and does not value the atonement of him and the power of his redemption. Woe unto such, for they are in danger of death, She'ol, and an Endless torment. I speak it boldly; Elohim has commanded me. Listen unto them and give heed, or they stand against you at the judgment seat of Mashiach. For behold that all little children are alive in Mashiach, and also all they that are without the Torah, for the power of redemption comes on all they that have no Torah. Wherefore, he that is not condemned, or he that is under no condemnation, cannot repent, and unto such, immersion avails nothing, but it is mockery before Elohim, denying the mercies of Mashiach and the power of his Holy Spirit, and putting trust in dead works.

5 Behold, my son, this thing ought not to be, for repentance is unto them that are under condemnation and under the curse of a broken law. And the firstfruits of repentance is washing by immersion. And immersion comes by faith unto the fulfilling the mitzvot, and the fulfilling the mitzvot brings remission of sins, and the remission of sins brings meekness and humility of heart. And because of meekness and humility of heart comes the visitation of the Ruach HaKodesh, which Comforter fills with hope and perfect love, which love endures by diligence unto prayer until the end shall come, when all the k'doshim shall dwell with Elohim. Behold, my son, I will write unto you again if I go not out soon against the Lamanites. Behold, the pride[43] of this nation, or the people of the Nefites, has proved their destruction, except they should repent. Pray for them, my son, that repentance may come unto them. But behold, I fear that the spirit has ceased striving[44] with them. And in this part of the land, they are also seeking to put down all power and s'mikhah which comes from Elohim, and they are denying[45] the Ruach HaKodesh. And after rejecting so great a knowledge, my son, they must perish soon, unto the fulfilling of the prophecies which were spoken by the prophets, as well as the words of our Savior himself. Shalom, my son, until I shall write unto you or shall meet you again. Amen.

---

43 2 Nefi 11:11 **44** 'Eter 6:17 **45** 2 Nefi 11:9

The second letter of M'raman to his son M'roni

9 My beloved son, I write unto you again, that you may know that I am yet alive; but I write somewhat that which is grievous. For behold, I have had a sore battle with the Lamanites in the which we did not conquer. And Archeantus has fallen by the sword, and also Luram, and Emron; yes, and we have lost a great number of our choice men. And now behold, my son, I fear that the Lamanites shall destroy this people, for they do not repent. And HaSatan stirs them up continually to anger[46] one with another. Behold, I am laboring with them continually. And when I speak the word of Elohim with sharpness, they tremble and anger against me. And when I use no sharpness, they harden their hearts against it. Wherefore, I fear that the spirit of YHWH has ceased striving with them. For so exceedingly do they anger, that it seems to me that they have no fear of death. And they have lost their love one towards another, and they thirst after blood and revenge continually. And now, my beloved son, despite their hardness, let us labor diligently; for if we should cease to labor, we should be brought under condemnation. For we have a labor[47] to perform while in this tabernacle of clay, that we may conquer[48] the enemy of all righteousness and rest our souls in the kingdom of Elohim.

2 And now I write somewhat concerning the sufferings of this people. For according to the knowledge which I have received from Amoron, behold, the Lamanites have many prisoners which they took from the tower of Sherrizah, and there were men, women, and children. And the husbands and fathers of those women and children they have slain; and they feed the women upon the flesh of their husbands, and the children upon the flesh of their fathers. And no water, except a little, do they give unto them. And despite this great abomination of the Lamanites, it does not exceed that of our people in Moriantum. For behold, many of the daughters of the Lamanites have they taken prisoners; and after depriving them of that which was most dear and precious above all things, which is chastity and virtue, and after they had done this thing, they did murder them in a most cruel manner, torturing their bodies even unto death. And

---

46 2 Nefi 12:4; M'raman 2:2 **47** Alma 16:37 **48** Moshiyah 1:16

after they have done this, they devour their flesh like wild beasts because of the hardness of their hearts; and they do it for a token of bravery. O my beloved son, how can a people like this, that are without civilization — and only a few years have passed away, and they were a civil and a delightful people — but O my son, how can a people like this, whose delight is in so much abomination, how can we expect that Elohim will stay his hand in judgment against us? Behold, my heart cries, Woe unto this people. Come out in judgment, O Elohim, and hide their sins, and wickedness, and abominations from before your face.

3 And again, my son, there are many widows and their daughters who remain in Sherrizah. And that part of the provisions which the Lamanites did not carry away, behold, the army of Zenefi has carried away, and left them to wander wherever they can for food. And many old women do faint by the way and die. And the army which is with me is weak. And the armies of the Lamanites are between Sherrizah and me. And as many as have fled to the army of Aharon have fallen victims to their awful brutality. Oh the depravity of my people; they are without order and without mercy. Behold, I am but a man, and I have but the strength of a man, and I cannot any longer enforce my commands. And they have become strong in their perversion, and they are alike brutal, sparing none, neither old nor young. And they delight in everything except that which is good. And the sufferings of our women and our children upon all the face of this land do exceed everything. Yes, tongue cannot tell, neither can it be written.

4 And now, my son, I dwell no longer upon this horrible scene. Behold, you know the wickedness of this people. You know that they are without principle and past feeling, and their wickedness does exceed that of the Lamanites. Behold, my son, I cannot recommend them unto Elohim for fear that he should smite me. But behold, my son, I recommend you unto Elohim. And I trust in Mashiach that you will be saved. And I pray unto Elohim that he would spare your life, to witness the return of his people unto him or their utter destruction; for I know that they must perish except they repent and return unto him. And if they perish, it will be like unto the Yeredites, because of the willfulness[49] of their hearts seeking for blood and revenge. And

---

49 Moshiyah 8:11

if it so be that they perish, we know that many of our brothers have dissented over unto the Lamanites, and many more will also dissent over unto them. Wherefore, write somewhat a few things if you are spared and I should perish and not see you. But I trust that I may see you soon, for I have sacred records that I would deliver up unto you.

⁵ My son, be faithful[50] in Mashiach. And may not the things which I have written grieve you, to weigh you down unto death; but may Mashiach lift you up. And may his sufferings and death, and the showing his body unto our fathers, and his mercy and long-suffering, and the hope of his glory and of Eternal life rest in your mind for ever. And may the grace of Elohim the Father, whose throne is high in the Heavens, and our Adonai Yeshua HaMashiach, who **sits on the right hand**[51] of his power until all things shall become subject unto him, be and abide with you for ever. Amen.

10 Now I, M'roni, write somewhat as seems me good, and I write unto my brothers the Lamanites. And I would that they should know that more than four hundred and twenty years[52] have passed away since the sign was given of the coming of Mashiach. And I seal up these records after I have spoken a few words by way of exhortation unto you.

2 Behold, I would exhort you that when you shall read these things, if it be wisdom in Elohim that you should read them, that you would remember how merciful[53] YHWH has been unto the children of men, from the creation of Adam even down until the time that you shall receive these things, and ponder it in your hearts.[54] And when you

---

50 2 Nefi 1:11 51 Ps. 110:1; Moshiyah 3:2 52 ~ 420 CE 53 Ya'akov 4:1; Alma 22:4
54 M'roni's admonition to "ponder" the "wisdom" of *The Stick of Joseph* parallels the process described by the Rebbe Zalman in the Tanya, whereby the wisdom of the Word of Elohim gestates in our understanding to produce a testimony through an awe and a love for Elohim "like burning coals, with a passion" for His Word. We read in the Tanya: "The intellect of the rational soul, which is the faculty that conceives any thing, is given the appellation of chochmah [wisdom]... when [a person] cogitates with his intellect in order to understand a thing truly and profoundly as it evolves from the concept which he has conceived in his intellect, this is called binah [understanding]. These [chochmah and binah] are the very 'father' and 'mother' which give birth to love of G-d, and awe and dread of Him. For when the intellect in the rational soul deeply contemplates and immerses itself exceedingly in the greatness of G-d, how He fills all worlds and encompasses all worlds, and in the presence of Whom everything is considered as nothing — there will be born and aroused in his mind and thought the emotion of awe for the Divine Majesty, to fear and be humble before His blessed greatness, which is without end or limit, and to have the dread of G-d in his heart. Next, his heart will glow

shall receive these things, I would exhort you that you would ask[55] Elohim the Eternal Father, in the name of Mashiach, if these things are not true. And if[56] you shall ask with a sincere heart, with real intent,[57] having faith in Mashiach, and he will manifest the truth of it unto you by the power of the Ruach HaKodesh. And by the power of the Ruach HaKodesh, you may know the truth of all things. And whatsoever thing is good is just and true. Wherefore, nothing that is good denies the Mashiach, but acknowledges that he is; and you may know that he is by the power of the Ruach HaKodesh. Wherefore, I would exhort you that you deny not the power of Elohim, for he works by power according to the faith of the children of men, the same today, and tomorrow, and for ever.

3 And again I exhort you, my brothers, that you deny[58] not the gifts of Elohim, for they are many, and they come from the same Elohim. And there are different ways that these gifts are administered, but it is the same Elohim who works all in all. And they are given by the manifestations of the Ruach Elohim unto men to profit them. For behold, to one is given by the Ruach Elohim that he may teach the word of wisdom, and to another that he may teach the word of knowledge by the same spirit, and to another exceedingly great faith, and to another the gifts of healing by the same spirit; and again, to another that he may work mighty miracles; and again, to another that he may prophesy concerning all things; and again, to another the beholding of angels and ministering spirits; and again, to another all kinds of tongues; and again, to another the interpretation of languages and of diverse kinds of tongues. And all these gifts come by the spirit of Mashiach, and they come unto every man severally, according as he will. And I would exhort you, my beloved brothers, that you remember that every good gift comes of Mashiach.

4 And I would exhort you, my beloved brothers, that you remember that he is the same[59] yesterday, today, and for ever, and that all these

---

with an intense love, like burning coals, with a passion, desire and longing, and a yearning soul, towards the greatness of the blessed Eyn Sof. This constitutes the culminating passion of the soul, of which Scripture speaks, as 'My soul longeth, yea, even fainteth...' and 'My soul thirsteth for G-d...' and 'My soul thirsteth for Thee...'" (Tanya; Likutei Amarim Chapter 3).   **55** 2 Nefi 14:1   **56** The "if...and" conditional structure seems stilted in English, which prefers "if...then." However, in Hebrew, this construction is correct. Its appearance here and elsewhere in the text indicates the Hebraic nature of the underlying original.   **57** 2 Nefi 13:2   **58** 3 Nefi 13:8   **59** 2 Nefi 1:6

gifts of which I have spoken, which are spiritual, never will be done away, even as long as the world shall stand — only according to the unbelief of the children of men. Wherefore, there must be faith; and if there must be faith, there must also be hope; and if there must be hope, there must also be charity. And except you have charity, you can in no way be saved in the kingdom of Elohim; neither can you be saved in the kingdom of Elohim if you have not faith; neither can you if you have no hope. And if you have no hope, you must necessarily be in despair; and despair comes because of iniquity. And Mashiach truly said unto our fathers, If you have faith, you can do all things which are expedient unto me.

5 And now I speak unto all the ends of the earth, that if the day comes that the power and gifts of Elohim shall be done away among you, it shall be because of unbelief. And woe be unto the children of men if this be the case, for there shall be none that does good among you, no not one; for if there be one among you that does good, he shall work by the power and gifts of Elohim. And woe unto them which shall do these things away and die, for they die in their sins and they cannot be saved in the kingdom of Elohim. And I speak it according to the words of Mashiach, and I lie not. And I exhort you to remember[60] these things, for the time speedily comes that you shall know that I lie not, for you shall see me at the bar of Elohim. And Adonai YHWH will say unto you, Did I not declare my words unto you, which were written by this man like as one crying from the dead? Yes, even **as one speaking out of the dust**?[61] I declare these things unto the fulfilling of the prophecies. And behold, they shall proceed forth out of the mouth of the El Olam, and his word shall hiss forth from generation to generation. And Elohim shall show unto you that that which I have written is true.

6 And again I would exhort you that you would come unto Mashiach and lay hold upon every good gift, and **touch not** the evil gift, **nor the unclean thing**.[62] And **awake** and **arise** from the dust, **O Yerushalayim**. Yes, **and put on your beautiful garments, O daughter of Tziyon**,[63] **and strengthen your stakes and enlarge** your borders for ever, that **you may no more be confounded**, that **the covenants**[64] of the Eternal Father which he has made unto you,

---

60 Alma 16:38   **61** Isa. 29:4   **62** Isa. 52:11   **63** Isa. 52:1-2   **64** Isa. 54:2, 4, 10; 1 Nefi

O house of Isra'el, may be fulfilled. Yes, come unto Mashiach, and be perfected in him, and deny yourselves of all ungodliness. And if you shall deny yourselves of all ungodliness, **and love Elohim with all your might, mind, and strength,**[65] then is his grace sufficient for you, that by his grace you may be perfect in Mashiach. And if, by the grace of Elohim, you are perfect in Mashiach, you can in no way deny the power of Elohim. And again if you, by the grace of Elohim, are perfect in Mashiach, and deny not his power, then are you sanctified in Mashiach by the grace of Elohim, through the shedding of the blood of Mashiach, which is in the covenant of the Father unto the remission of your sins, that you become holy, without spot.

7 And now I bid unto all shalom. I soon go to rest in the pardes of Elohim until my spirit and body shall again reunite[66] and I am brought forth triumphant through the air to meet you before the pleasing bar of the great YHWH, the Eternal Judge of both living and dead. Amen.

Glossary

A note on proper names: Many of the proper names from the 1830 translation have been changed to their Hebraic versions in this edition. Some are noted here, along with their original 1830 spellings or, in cases where the name appears in the King James Version of the Bible, with their KJV spellings. Personal names are also given in their most likely Hebrew spelling.

Achaz (אחז) *Ahaz* in the KJV
Adon Lord, Master
Adon Yeshua The Lord Yeshua
Adon Yeshua HaMashiach Lord Yeshua the Messiah
Adonai Lord (used only in referring to deity)
Adonai YHWH Lord God
Adonai YHWH Tzva'ot Lord God Almighty or Lord God of Hosts
Aharon (אהרון) *Aaron* in the KJV
Alef The first letter of the Hebrew alphabet (א); given as *alpha* in Greek translations
Alma (עלמא) The Aramaic equivalent of *Elam*
Ameni (אמני) *Omni* in the 1830 translation
Avinodam (אבינודעם) *Abinadom* in the 1830 translation
Avinodi (אבינודי) My father was a wanderer/nomad; *Abinadi* in the 1830 translation
Avraham (אברהם) *Abraham* in the KJV
Bavel Babel or Babylon
Beit Avarah *Bethabara* in the KJV
Besorah (בשורה Strong's 1309) good tidings, good news; *gospel* in the 1830 translation
Binyamin (בנימן) *Benjamin* in the 1830 translation
Brass Plates See *Plates of Brass* in Appendix B.
Chamesh (חמש) *Chemish* in the 1830 translation
Cheleman (חלמן) *Helaman* in the 1830 translation
Echad The number one. Implies alike, together, united.
Efrayim (אפרים) *Ephraim* in the KJV
El, Eloah God in the singular
El Elyon Most High God
El Olam Everlasting God

El Shaddai God Almighty, literally "God, the double breasted." Identified in the Zohar with the *Shekinah* (Zohar 1 95a), the feminine aspect of Elohim.

Eliyahu (אליהו) *Elijah* in the KJV

Elohim God (technically plural, but normally matched with singular verbs and adjectives)

Elohe Kedem Eternal God

Elyon Most High

Enosh (אנוש) *Enos* in the 1830 translation

'Eter (עתר) *Ether* in the 1830 translation

Get A divorce document that a husband must give to a wife to make a divorce valid.

Gehinnom Hell, the place of the post-resurrection afterlife for the unrighteous. Gehinnom was a valley just outside of Jerusalem (Josh. 15:8; 18:16; Neh. 11:30; Jer. 19:2, 6) in which pagans had once sacrificed their own children to Ba'al and Molech (2 Kings 23:10; 2 Chron. 28:3; 33:6; Jer. 7:31-32; 19:2, 6; 32:35). In the first century, all of the refuse of the city was cast into this valley and burned there. In the Mishnah and Talmud, it is contrasted with the Garden of Eden, the World to Come, and Heaven; it is the final afterlife of the wicked (m. Avot 5:19-20; m. Eduyot 2:10; b. Berakhot 28a). According to the Talmud, Gehinnom is huge (b. Pesahim 94a) and has seven compartments (b. Sotah 19b). There is some debate in the Rabbinic literature as to whether souls are punished eternally in Gehinnom. The Targum Jonathan to Isaiah 66:24 describes it as a place where "their souls shall not die." Rabban Johanan ben Zakkai describes it as a place where one is imprisoned "forever" with an "everlasting death" (b. Ber. 28b), while Rabbi Akiva taught punishment in Gehinnom was limited to twelve months (m. Eduyot 2:10).

Giv'at-Sh'ul *Gibeah of Saul* in the KJV

Goy, Goyim (singular/plural) Gentile(s); literally: nation(s). Used in this text to refer to those who are not of the House of Israel or who have lost or forgotten their connection to the House of Israel.

HaElyon The Most High

HaKodesh The Holy One

HaMashiach The Messiah; literally, "the anointed one."

HaSatan The Devil, the Adversary, Satan

Havah (חוה) *Eve* in the KJV; the mother of the human family
Hellel Day star; also the angelic name of HaSatan, *Lucifer* in the KJV
Hevel (הבל) *Abel* in the KJV
Horev Horeb
Isra'el Israel; literally, "prevails with God" or "a man seeing God"
Isra'elite Israelite
Kayin (קין) *Cain* in the KJV; he murdered his brother Hevel
Kadosh, K'doshim (singular/plural); One who is holy or set apart to YHWH; saint/saints in the KJV
Keruvim Cherubim; angelic beings
Kohen, Kohanim Priest, priests
Kohen HaGadol High Priest
Kumorah A hill where sacred records were hidden. The name may come from the contraction *KumRamah* (to rise to a height). The Yeredites called the same hill *Ramah* (high).
Lashon Hara Wicked speech, derogatory speech about another person; *babblings* in the 1830 translation.
Lavan (לבן) *Laban* in the 1830 translation
Lechi (לחי) *Lehi* in the 1830 translation
Liahona A ball or director that gave the Nefites divine direction in their journey. Liahona (ליהונא) may come from the root *lawah* לוה (Strong's 3867), "to join, to bind around, to wreathe," from which come the related Hebrew words *liah* ליה (Strong's 3914), "a wreath," and *lon* לון (Strong's 3885), "to abide, to dwell, to remain or continue." The word "Liahona" combines these words to describe a device that joins the traveling party to God, a ball with two spindles that would wreathe around and direct Lechi and his party where and when to abide, dwell, remain, or continue.
L'mu'el (למואל) *Lemuel* in the 1830 translation
L'mu'elite *Lemuelite* in the 1830 translation
L'vanon Lebanon
Mal'akhi (מלאכי) *Malachi* in the KJV
Malki-Tzedek (מלכיצדק) *Melchizedek* in the KJV
Mashiach Messiah; literally, "anointed one"
Mattani (מתני) "My gift"; *Mathoni* in the 1830 translation
Mattanihah (מתניהה) *Mathonihah* in the 1830 translation
Matzah Unleavened bread, commonly used at Passover

Milo HaGoyim "Fulness of the Gentiles," defined in Rom. 11:25 as the time when blindness ends for Israel, and the natural branches are grafted back into their own olive tree (Rom. 11:11-24). The same Hebrew phrase is commonly translated "multitude of nations" in Gen. 48:19, where Ephraim is blessed to become a "multitude of nations."

Miryam (מרים) *Mary* in the KJV

Mitzvah, Mitzvot (singular/plural) Commandment(s)

M'nasheh (מנשה) *Manasseh* in the KJV

Moshe (משה) *Moses* in the KJV

Moshiyah (מושעיה) *Mosiah* in the 1830 translation

M'raman (מרמן) *Mormon* in the 1830 translation

M'roni (מרני) *Moroni* in the 1830 translation

Naftali (נפתלי) *Naphtali* in the KJV

Natzrat (נצרת) *Nazareth* in the KJV

Nefi The name "Nefi" deserves some special attention. At the time Nefi lived, Egyptian culture held a great deal of influence in Israel, especially among the upper class, to which Lechi (Nefi's father) appears to have belonged. The name Nefi may come from the Egyptian word "nefi," which Budge defines as "to breathe, to blow at, to give breath to, i.e. to set free (a prisoner)...compare Heb. נפח" (*An Egyptian Hieroglyphic Dictionary*, E. A. Wallis Budge; Dover Publications, Inc.; Vol. I, p. 369). The Hebrew word *naphach* (נפח Strong's 5301) means to "to blow upon, to breathe." The Egyptian word "nefi" is clearly related to "naphach" and, given the textual origin of this work, the text is entirely accurate to name Nefi using an Egyptian word with a related Hebrew root. This same Hebrew root appears in Gen. 2:7 and Ezek. 37:9, both in reference to moving the spirit or breath of life.

Nefihah (נפיהה) *Nephihah* in the 1830 translation

Nefite *Nephite* in the 1830 translation

Ne'um (נאם) *Neum* in the 1830 translation

Noach (נח) *Noah* in the KJV, the patriarch who built the ark; not to be confused with the wicked king Noah in this text, whose name has been left with its 1830 spelling.

Ofir (אופיר) *Ophir* in the KJV

Olam World, age, forever

'Orev *Oreb* in the KJV

Pardes Paradise, often a synonym for the Garden of Eden. A compartment in She'ol where the righteous await the resurrection; additionally, a metonym for a mystical experience. PaRDeS is also an acronym in Hebrew for the four levels of understanding the Scriptures: *Pashat* (plain, literal, simple); *Remez* (hinted, implied); *Drash* (allegorical, homiletical); and *Sod* (hidden, secret, mystical).

Patros *Pathros* in the KJV

Pekach (פקח) *Pekah* in the KJV

Pesach A major holiday commemorating the liberation of Israel from Egyptian captivity. One of three holidays that anciently required a pilgramage to the temple at Jerusalem. It is observed for seven (or eight) days and begins with the Seder meal on the evening of the 15th of Nisan. Also called Passover.

Plates of Brass See *Plates of Brass* in Appendix B

P'leshet *Palestina* in the KJV

P'lishti/P'lishtim *Philistine/Philistines* in the KJV

Rahav (רחב) *Rahab* in the KJV

Remalyah (רמליהו) *Remaliah* in the KJV

Retzin (רצין) *Rezin* in the KJV

Rosh Hashanah "The Head of the Year," or the Jewish New Year. The biblical name for this holiday is *Yom Teruah*, literally "day of shouting or blasting," commonly translated "Feast of Trumpets."

Ruach This Hebrew term means spirit, wind, or breath. When applied to deity, it refers to the influence, glory, and power exerted by God on man. When applied to man, it refers to the inner essence of the being, as opposed to the physical body. The presence of the *ruach* gives life to the body. In Judaism, *Nefesh* (soul) is the animating life force, *Ruach* (spirit) is the seat of the emotions and moral capacity, and *Neshama* is the rational mind.

Ruach Elohim Spirit of God

Ruach HaKodesh Holy Spirit, Holy Ghost. Because the 1830 text makes some distinction between these terms, "Holy Ghost" has been translated *Ruach HaKodesh*, while "Holy Spirit" has been left as original.

Saryah (שריה) "My prince is Yah"; *Sariah* in the 1830 translation

Seder A ritual meal observed at Passover (Pesach), at which the story of Israel's liberation from Egyptian bondage is commemorated and retold.

Shalem *Salem* in the KJV

Shalom Peace, harmony, wholeness, completeness, prosperity, welfare, and tranquility. Also used as a greeting or goodbye.

She'ol Hell, the place of the pre-resurrection afterlife. Within She'ol is a compartment called *Pardes*, where the righteous await their resurrection, while the wicked await in She'ol proper. The *Encyclopedia Judaica* states, "Several names are given to the abode of the dead, the most common being She'ol — always feminine and without the definite article — a sign of proper nouns. The term does not occur in other Semitic languages, except as a loan word from Hebrew She'ol, and its etymology is obscure" (*Encyclopedia Judaica*; article "Netherworld" p. 996).

Shet (שת) *Seth* in the KJV

Shin'ar *Shinar* in the KJV

Shofar A ram's-horn trumpet, traditionally sounded in battle and at Rosh Hashanah and Yom Kippur.

Sh'mu'el (שמואל) *Samuel* in the KJV

S'mikhah Authority, ordination; from a word meaning "laying on of hands."

Sukkah Booth A tabernacle, a temporary dwelling hut topped with branches, constructed for use during the week-long Feast of Sukkot (sometimes called the Feast of Tabernacles).

Sukkot The Feast of Tabernacles, a biblical Feast that begins on the 15th day of the seventh month, *Tishrei*. During the time of the Jerusalem Temple, it was one of the Three Pilgrimage Festivals on which the Israelites were commanded to make a pilgrimage to the Temple.

Talmid, Talmidim (singular/plural) A student or disciple

Tamé Ritually impure

Tav (ת) The last letter of the Hebrew alphabet; "Omega" in translations from Greek.

Torah The divine Law; literally, "guidance, instruction."

Tu B'Av The 15th day of Av. An ancient minor Jewish festival marking the beginning of the grape harvest. It is similar in romantic character with Valentine's Day and is traditionally celebrated with maidens dancing. Rabbi Simeon ben Gamliel said, "There never were in Israel greater days of joy than the Fifteenth of Av and the Day of Atonement...what happened on the fifteenth of Av?...Rabbi Joseph said in the name of Rabbi Nahman: 'It is the day on which the tribe of Benjamin was permitted to re-enter the congregation [of Israel], as it is said, Now the men of Israel had sworn in Mizpah, saying: There shall not any of us give his daughter unto Benjamin to wife. (Judg. 21:1) From what was their exposition?' Rab said: 'From the phrase "any of us" which was interpreted to mean, "but not from any of our children" ' (b. Ta'anit 30b)."

Tum'ah Ritual uncleanness

Tzedakah Alms, charitable giving; one's duty to the needy

Tzidkiyahu (צדקיהו) *Zedekiah* in the KJV

Tzidon *Sidon* in the KJV

Tziyon *Zion* in the KJV

Tz'lav, Tz'livot (singular/plural) A wooden instrument of execution by hanging or crucifixion; "cross" in the 1830 translation.

Tzuram (צורעם) *Zoram* in the 1830 translation, possibly meaning "Rock of the Nation." *Tzur* was used as a metaphor for Elohim as protector of Isra'el (Deut. 32:37; Isa. 30:29; Ps. 18:3, 32, 47).

Tzuramite *Zoramite* in the 1830 translation

Tzva'ot *Hosts* in KJV; also "armies"

Uziyahu (עזיהו) *Uzziah* in the KJV

Ya, Yah Abbreviation of YHWH

Ya'akov (יעקב) *Jacob* in the KJV

Ya'akovite *Jacobite* in the 1830 translation

Yah YHWH *The Lord Jehovah* in the KJV

Yahram (יהרם) *Jarom* in the 1830 translation

Yarden *Jordan* in the KJV

Yered (ירד) *Jared* in the KJV

Yeredite *Jaredite* in the 1830 translation

Yerushalayim *Jerusalem* in the KJV

Yesha'yahu (ישעיהו) *Isaiah* in the KJV

Yeshua A Greek form of this name is often recognized as *Jesus*, but the informed understand that the current "Christian" Jesus has become nothing more than a caricature and a mockery of the Jew named Yeshua to whom this book is dedicated.

Yeshua HaMashiach (ישוע המשיח) Literally, "Yeshua the anointed." Translated in the KJV as *Jesus Christ*, though that Greek-based name has become associated with a false portrayal of the Mashiach. See "Yeshua" above.

Y'hoshua (יהושוע) *Joshua* in the KJV

Y'hudah (יהודה) *Judea, Judah* in the KJV

Y'hudi/Y'hudim *Jew/Jews* in the KJV

YHWH The personal name of the Creator, written without vowels. Also translated as "Lord" or "the Lord."

YHWH Elohim Omnipotent Lord God Omnipotent

YHWH Omnipotent The Lord Omnipotent

YHWH our Elohim The Lord our God

YHWH their Elohim The Lord their God

YHWH Tzva'ot Lord of Hosts

YHWH your Elohim The Lord your God

Yirmeyahu (ירמיהו) *Jeremiah* in the KJV

Yirshon *Jershon* in the 1830 translation

Yishai (ישי) *Jesse* in the KJV

Yishma'el (ישמעאל) *Ishmael* in the KJV

Yishma'elite *Ishmaelite* in the 1830 translation

Yitz'chak (יצחק) *Isaac* in the KJV

Yochanan (יוחנן) *John* in the KJV

Yom Kippur The Day of Atonement. A biblical holy day observed as a day of fasting and intensive prayer.

Yonah (יונה) *Jonas* in the 1830 translation

Yosef (יוסף) *Joseph* in the KJV

Yosef ben Yosef Literally, "Joseph, son of Joseph." In this text, the name refers to Joseph Smith, Jr., the original translator of the text into English. His translation is referred to herein as the 1830 translation. See Appendices B and F for more information.

Yosefite *Josephite* in the 1830 translation

Yosh (יוש) *Josh* in the 1830 translation

Yotam (יותם) *Jotham* in the KJV

Yud (י) The smallest Hebrew letter

Y'verekhyahu (יברכיהו) *Jeberechiah* in the KJV

Zerach'mla (זרעחמלא) *Zarahemla* in the 1830 translation; possibly from the Aramaic roots *Zera* (seed/dispersed) and *Ch'mla* (gathered in).

Z'kharyahu (זכריהו) *Zechariah* in the KJV

Appendices and Reference Information

Appendix A: Abbreviations and References

Appendix B: Source Documents and Groups

Appendix C: Hebraic Nature of the Underlying Text

Appendix D: Selected Tanakh Prophecies Fulfilled by *The Stick of Joseph in the Hand of Ephraim*

Appendix E: Ezekiel's Prophecy of this Work

Appendix F: Testimonies and Dedication from the 1830 Translation

Appendix A: Abbreviations and References

All Tanakh and Bible references use the standard English names and spellings in footnotes and references. Those abbreviations are as follows:

Tanakh:

Gen.	2 Kings	Nah.	Ruth
Ex.	Isa.	Hab.	Lam.
Lev.	Jer.	Zeph.	Eccles.
Num.	Ezek.	Hag.	Est.
Deut.	Hos.	Zech.	Dan.
Josh.	Joel	Mal.	Ezra
Judg.	Amos	Ps.	Neh.
1 Sam.	Obad.	Prov.	1 Chron.
2 Sam.	Jonah	Job	2 Chron.
1 Kings	Mic.	Song	

New Testament:

Matt.	2 Cor.	1 Tim.	2 Pet.
Mark	Gal.	2 Tim.	1 John
Luke	Eph.	Titus	2 John
John	Phil.	Philem.	3 John
Acts	Col.	Heb.	Jude
Rom.	1 Thess.	James	Rev.
1 Cor.	2 Thess.	1 Pet.	

The Stick of Joseph book names are given in their short form, but not abbreviated. They are listed as follows:

1 Nefi	Yahram	Moshiyah	4 Nefi
2 Nefi	Ameni	Alma	M'raman
Ya'akov	Words of M'raman	Cheleman	'Eter
Enosh		3 Nefi	M'roni

Other Abbreviations Used in References

2 Macc. 2 Maccabees
b. ——— Babylonian Talmud
b. Baba Kamma Babylonian Talmud Tractate Baba Kamma
b. Baba Batra Babylonian Talmud Tractate Baba Batra
b. Berakhot Babylonian Talmud Tractate Berakhot
b. Hullin Babylonian Talmud Tractate Hullin
b. Ketubot Babylonian Talmud Tractate Ketubot
b. Makot Babylonian Talmud Tractate Makot
b. Megillah Babylonian Talmud Tractate Megillah
b. Menachot Babylonian Talmud Tractate Menachot
b. Nedarim Babylonian Talmud Tractate Nedarim
b. Niddah Babylonian Talmud Tractate Niddah
b. Pesahim Babylonian Talmud Tractate Pesahim
b. Rosh Hashanah Babylonian Talmud Tractate Rosh Hashanah
b. Sanhedrin Babylonian Talmud Tractate Sanhedrin
b. Shabbat Babylonian Talmud Tractate Shabbat
b. Sotah Babylonian Talmud Tractate Sotah
b. Sukkah Babylonian Talmud Tractate Sukkah
b. Ta'anit Babylonian Talmud Tractate Ta'anit
b. Yevamot Babylonian Talmud Tractate Yevamot
b. Yoma Babylonian Talmud Tractate Yoma
CJB *Complete Jewish Bible* by David H. Stern
ISR Institute for Scripture Research version of the Bible
JST Joseph Smith Translation of the Bible
KJV King James Version of the Bible
m. ——— Mishnah
m. Avot Mishnah Tractate Pirkei Avot
m. Chagigah Mishnah Tractate Chagigah
m. Menachot Mishnah Tractate Menachot
m. Nedarim Mishnah Tractate Nedarim
m. Sanhedrin Mishnah Tractate Sanhedrin
m. Sotah Mishnah Tractate Sotah
NJPS New Jewish Publication Society version of the Tanakh
O.T. Old Testament (i.e. the Tanakh)
R. Rabbi

Strom *Stromateis* by Clement of Alexandria
Strong's *The Exhaustive Concordance of the Bible* by James Strong
t. Berakhot Tosefta Tractate Berakhot
y. ——— Jerusalem Talmud.
y. Betzah Jerusalem Talmud Tractate Betzah

Citation Numbering

Standard chapter and verse numbers are used for Bible and Tanakh references. In cases where Jewish versions and Christian versions differ in numbering, the Jewish numbering is used, with the Christian numbering given in parenthesis directly after. References from *The Stick of Joseph* are given in the form of Book Chapter:Paragraph(s). For example, (M'roni 10:6) means the Book of M'roni, chapter 10, paragraph 6.

Spelling and Terminology

Hebraic forms of many names and terms are used in the text of *The Stick of Joseph*. For definitions and explanations of Hebrew terms, please see the Glossary. Standard English, non-Hebraicized spellings of most names are used in footnotes, references, and appendices.

Appendix B: Source Documents and Groups

The Stick of Joseph primarily spans a period of approximately one thousand years, between 600 BCE and 400 CE. Numerous prophets wrote the record, and one of the final writers, M'raman, abridged the lengthy history into a single book, which was subsequently completed by his son, M'roni. This M'roni buried the abridged record in approximately 420 CE, in the area that is now New York State, in the United States of America.

Yosef ben Yosef (Joseph Smith, Jr.) was shown the site of the hidden record by an angel who gave him the record and the means to translate it on Rosh Hashanah, 5588 (1827 CE). Yosef completed the translation and published the book three years later, in 1830. This first-published work was named after M'raman, who compiled and abridged the ancient records. The Anglicized book title for the Gentile audience was *The Book of Mormon*.

As happened with the Bible, Gentile churches and institutions attempted to claim the book as their own, make profit from it, and use it to gain converts—all while utterly failing to appreciate its authors, purpose, message, or destiny (see 2 Nefi 12:8). This is a fundamentally Jewish text, prepared for the House of Israel, for their benefit and blessing. For more information about the first English translation, visit www.Scriptures.info.

The text given to Yosef ben Yosef was compiled by ancient authors from several sources, all of which consisted of records engraved on metal writing tablets, referred to as "plates." Though the various sets of plates overlapped (as to time period covered or the group that kept the record), still each is unique in purpose and content.

Groups

The Stick of Joseph in the Hand of Ephraim details the ancient migrations of three specific groups to the American continent, as follows:

- **The people of Lechi** left Jerusalem in 601 BCE and separated into two main groups known as the Nefites and the Lamanites, each named for one of Lechi's sons. This is the primary group that created and kept this record.

- **The people of Muloch** also left Jerusalem at the time of the Babylonian destruction. Muloch was one of the sons of King Tzidkiyahu (Zedekiah), the last king of Y'hudah (Judah) (see Jer. 39:1–2). Internal evidence in the text suggests the group that came with Muloch (commonly called Mulochites) may have spoken Aramaic. The Mulochites joined with the Nefites and became one people (see Ameni 1:8).
- **The people of Yered** (commonly called the Yeredites) left the Tower of Bavel (Babel) at the time of the confounding of languages and traveled to the American continent. Their civilization ended around the time the Mulochites arrived.

Records

The text refers to the following plates kept by these groups, all of which contributed material to *The Stick of Joseph in the Hand of Ephraim*:

- The *Plates of Brass* are a record containing "the five books of Moshe [Moses]...and also a record of the Y'hudim [Jews] from the beginning...and also the prophecies of the holy prophets" up to and including some of the prophecies of Yirmeyahu (Jeremiah) (see 1 Nefi 1:10, 22). Additionally, these plates contained records of Israelite prophets now lost to history, including Zenoch, Zenos, Ezaias, and Neum (see Cheleman 3:9). These plates were taken from Yerushalayim (Jerusalem) by Nefi, son of Lechi, and carried to the American continent with Lechi's family.
- The *Small Plates of Nefi* are a record started by Nefi, concerning the events leading up to and including his family's travels from Yerushalayim to the American continent, as well as the ministries of Nefi and his brother Ya'akov. Subsequent prophets and writers continued this record until the plates were full. Their purpose was to record ministry work and "the things of Elohim," rather than a secular history (see 1 Nefi 2:1, 14; 2 Nefi 3:6; Words of M'raman 1:2–3). Their content was included, unabridged, to replace the material contained in 116 pages of manuscript that were lost by one of Yosef ben Yosef's assistants in the early days of translation work. They

encompass the books of 1 Nefi, 2 Nefi, Ya'akov, Enosh, Yahram, and Ameni.

- The *Large Plates of Nefi* are a historical record kept by Nefi, son of Lechi, and subsequently added to by other writers. This record contains more secular information than the Small Plates of Nefi, including "the reigns of the kings, and the wars and contentions" of the Nefite people (see 1 Nefi 2:14). These records were abridged by M'raman to create his record (see Plates of M'raman, below, and Dedication, in Appendix F).
- The *Plates of 'Eter* are a record of an earlier civilization called the Yeredite people who left the Tower of Bavel at the time of the confounding of languages and traveled to the American continent. Their record was recorded by the prophet 'Eter on twenty-four gold plates (see Moshiyah 5:12; 'Eter 1:1). Their civilization ended with the destruction of their people, during the lifetime of Nefi, son of Lechi.
- The *Plates of M'raman* is the abridgment, made by M'raman, of the Large Plates of Nefi (that was subsequently added to by M'raman's son, M'roni, who also included the above Small Plates of Nefi and an abridgment of the Plates of 'Eter). M'raman's commentary and abridgment of the Large Plates of Nefi begins at Words of M'raman and ends at M'raman 3:5. M'roni's completion of the record includes M'raman 4, 'Eter, and M'roni. The Plates of M'raman were then buried in the earth by M'roni ca. 420 CE, after the destruction of the Nefite civilization. These plates were given to Yosef ben Yosef in 1827 by the resurrected Nefi, son of Lechi. While in the possession of Yosef, the Plates of M'raman were commonly called the "Gold Plates" or "Gold Bible" by those who were aware of the ongoing translation work, due to the golden appearance of the metal plates upon which the records were engraved. The unsealed portion of the plates was translated by the gift and power of Elohim, and the sealed portion of the plates was left untranslated. When the work of translation was completed, Yosef reburied the plates (see 2 Nefi 11:20).

The Stick of Joseph is primarily the work of three authors: Nefi (son of Lechi), M'raman, and M'roni. Nefi's small plates are included without abridgment, while the rest of the record consists of M'raman and M'roni's abridgments of prior records written by other authors, as well as their own writings. Though Joseph Smith, Jr. (Yosef ben Yosef) was initially listed as author for copyright purposes, he claimed only to have received the translation by divine power and did not claim original authorship of any part of the book.

In instances where lengthy quotes appear from the Tanakh (entire chapters of Isaiah, for example), the text, with exceptions, most closely matches the King James Version of the Bible, which would have been most familiar to Yosef's Gentile audience at the time and most readily available to Yosef.

Appendix C: Hebraic Nature of the Underlying Text

In the opening words of this book, Nefi declares:

> Yes, I make a record in the language of my father, which consists of the learning of the Y'hudim [Jews] and the language of the Egyptians. (1 Nefi 1:1)

This statement seems unusual because Hebrew, not Egyptian, was the primary language of the Jews living in and around Jerusalem in Nefi's day. The following explanation appears later in the text:

> And now behold, we have written this record according to our knowledge, in the characters which are called among us reformed Egyptian, being handed down and altered by us according to our manner of speech. And if our plates had been sufficiently large, we should have written in Hebrew; but the Hebrew has been altered by us also. And if we could have written in Hebrew, behold, you would have had no imperfection in our record. But YHWH knows the things which we have written, and also that no other people knows our language; and because no other people knows our language, therefore he has prepared means for the interpretation thereof. (M'raman 4:11)

Taken together, these statements convey that what Nefi designated "the language of my father" was spoken Hebrew, while "the language of the Egyptians" referred to the written language called "the characters which are called among us reformed Egyptian." The phrase "the learning of the Y'hudim [Jews] and the language of the Egyptians" means that the record was written in the Hebrew language, but written using a form of Egyptian characters to represent the underlying Hebrew.

Yosef ben Yosef confirmed that regardless of what type of "characters" were used, *The Stick of Joseph* was written in Hebrew. Referring to M'raman's dedicatory page he wrote:

> I wish also to mention here that the title page of the [book] is a literal translation, taken from the very last leaf on the left hand side of the collection or book of plates which contained the record which has been translated, the language of the whole running **the same as all Hebrew writing in general**, and that said title page is not by any means a

> *modern composition, either of mine or of any other man's who has lived or does live in this generation.* (Joseph Smith History, Part 16, paragraph 30, emphasis added; see also Dedication in Appendix F)

The Stick of Joseph may be thought of as having two parts. The first portion is taken directly from the Small Plates of Nefi. This material would have been written in a form of Biblical Hebrew, using the reformed Egyptian characters. The second portion is taken from M'raman's abridgement and was written about a thousand years after the Nefites left Jerusalem. It would have been written in an otherwise unknown dialect of late-Nefite Hebrew, which M'roni described as having been "altered by us" over that thousand year period and, likewise, recorded using the reformed Egyptian characters (see M'raman 4:11).

A great deal of internal evidence demonstrates that this record was originally written in Hebrew dialects, with some Aramaic influences. We will begin with the indications of Aramaic influence, then continue to the voluminous evidence of Hebraic origin.

Aramaic Influence

Although Hebrew is given as the primary language of the text, Aramaic may have also played an important role. When the two groups known as the Mulochites and the Nefites first encountered one another, they faced a language barrier, as we read in Ameni:

> *And they discovered a people who were called the people of Zerach'mla. Now, there was great rejoicing among the people of Zerach'mla, and also, Zerach'mla did rejoice exceedingly because* YHWH *had sent the people of Moshiyah with the plates of brass, which contained the record of the Y'hudim. Behold, it came to pass that Moshiyah discovered that the people of Zerach'mla came out from Yerushalayim at the time that Tzidkiyahu king of Y'hudah was carried away captive into Babylon. And they journeyed in the wilderness and were brought by the hand of* YHWH *across the great waters, into the land where Moshiyah discovered them; and they had dwelt there from that time forth. And at the time that Moshiyah discovered them, they had become exceedingly numerous. Nevertheless, they had had many wars and serious contentions, and had fallen by the sword from time to time. And their language had become*

> *corrupted; and they had brought no records with them; and they denied the being of their Creator. And neither Moshiyah, nor the people of Moshiyah, could understand them. But it came to pass that Moshiyah caused that they should be taught in his language. And it came to pass that after they were taught in the language of Moshiyah, Zerach'mla gave a genealogy of his fathers, according to his memory. And they are written, but not in these plates. And it came to pass that the people of Zerach'mla and of Moshiyah did unite together, and Moshiyah was appointed to be their king.* (Ameni 1:6–8)

Each of these two groups had come to the American continent from Judea about 400 years earlier. Yet after only 400 years of separation, the Mulochites (people of Zerach'mla) could not understand the Nefite language. By comparison, the average English speaker today can reasonably understand the English of the King James Version of the Bible, published in 1611. This raises the question of why these two groups would be unable to communicate after a similar period of separation.

The answer may be that, whereas the Nefites spoke Hebrew, the Mulochites may have spoken Aramaic, which may have been easily mistaken for "corrupt" Hebrew by the Nefites. Hebrew and Aramaic are similar languages in that they both use the same twenty-two letters, share many of the same roots, and share much of the same grammar. However, the two languages differ enough that a speaker of one cannot understand the other.

The Mulochites originated when an unidentified group rescued Muloch, one of king Tzidkiyahu's (Zedekiah's) sons, from execution. The Tanakh tells us that Tzidkiyahu's sons were executed by the king of Babylon (see 2 Kings 25:7; Jer. 39:6-7). A prophecy in Ezek. 17:1–24 speaks of a "tender one" or "twig" (apparently a son of Tzidkiyahu) transplanted to a "mountain" to flourish elsewhere.

An unknown group rescued Muloch from certain death at the hands of Babylon and smuggled him across the sea to the American continent (see Ameni 1:7 and Cheleman 2:29, 3:9). But this group kept no records, and their identity remains unknown. However, a group of "fifth column" Babylonians, or perhaps Jews culturally allied with Babylon, would have been most likely positioned to rescue Muloch from the king of Babylon. If this were the case, it would explain why the Mulochites spoke a language unintelligible to the Nefites. Such a group would likely have spoken Aramaic, not Hebrew.

An example of this language barrier also occurs in the Tanakh:

> *Eliakim son of Hilkiah, Shebna, and Joah replied to the Rabshakeh, "Please, speak to your servants in Aramaic, for we understand it; do not speak to us in Judean [Hebrew] in the hearing of the people on the wall." But the Rabshakeh answered them, "Was it to your master and to you that my master sent me to speak those words? It was precisely to the men who are sitting on the wall–who will have to eat their dung and drink their urine with you." And the Rabshakeh stood and called out in a loud voice in Judean: "Hear the words of the great king, the king of Assyria."* (2 Kings 18:26–28)

In this passage, the Assyrians spoke Aramaic, and the Jews spoke Hebrew. The Jewish leadership did not want their soldiers to hear the Assyrian king's message, so they requested the messenger speak Aramaic, not Hebrew. The leadership had been educated in Aramaic and could understand it, while the common Jews could not. This demonstrates the barrier presented, even between these similar languages.

In the period after the merger of the Nefites and the Mulochites, several Aramaic words appear transliterated into the text, such as *Rabbanah* (Alma 12:13), *Raca* (3 Nefi 5:24), and *mammon* (3 Nefi 5:38). The major writer Alma bears an Aramaic name (Alma is the Aramaic form of the Hebrew name Elam). Even the name of the non-Hebrew-speaking people (the people of Zerach'mla) reflects a compound of the Aramaic roots *zera* (seed/dispersed) and *ch'mla* (gathered in). Moreover, the "n" ending on many proper nouns in the text may point to Aramaic influence. While the plural masculine ending in Hebrew is -im, in Aramaic it is -in. Many pronouns that end in "m" in Hebrew, end in "n" in their Aramaic forms.

Evidence of Underlying Hebrew

This text was first published in English in 1830. Prior to that, the text had been hidden for approximately 1400 years. Although the first modern translation was rendered in English, the grammar and construction of the English was quite unconventional and even awkward in some cases. Though the text's 24-year-old translator,

Yosef ben Yosef, had no education in Hebrew or Aramaic, the record he published is overwhelmingly Hebraic in nature, which accounts for the unconventional English grammar. The only explanation given of the translation process is that it was done "by the gift and power of Elohim" (see Testimony of Three Witnesses in Appendix F).

The following examples of Hebraisms in the text are by no means isolated. In each case, some few examples are offered to illustrate the underlying Hebrew construction. Although many more examples of each instance could be offered, space constraints require brevity in this treatment. The reader is invited to discover further examples within the text itself.

"And It Came to Pass"

The frequent use of the phrase "and it came to pass" (ויהי) in *The Stick of Joseph* may seem unusual to the English reader. However, the frequent use of this phrase is very indicative of Biblical Hebrew.

"Behold"

The frequent use of the term "behold" (הנה) is another Hebraism in *The Stick of Joseph*. While considered an unnecessary interjection in English, it is used over a thousand times in the Tanakh and appears frequently in *The Stick of Joseph*.

The Prophetic Perfect

In the Hebrew language, actions are presented in verb forms as being either complete (perfect) or incomplete (imperfect). However, one special idiom in Hebrew is known as the prophetic perfect in which a future action is presented with a perfect, rather than an imperfect, verb or verbs, because the prophet has seen it as if it had already been completed. Here are some examples from the Tanakh:

> *Therefore my people **are gone** into captivity...* (Isa. 5:13), despite the fact that this captivity was future to Isaiah's time.
>
> *The people who walk in darkness **have seen** a great light...* (Isa. 9:2).
>
> *For unto us a child **is** [literally "has been"] born...* (Isa. 9:6).

And from *The Stick of Joseph*:

> *But behold, I **have obtained** a land of promise…* (1 Nefi 1:21).

> *Wherefore, after **he was** immersed with water, the Ruach HaKodesh **descended** upon him in the form of a dove* (2 Nefi 13:2).

> *For these are they whose sins **he has** borne; these are they for whom **he has** died…* (Moshiyah 8:8).

Compound Prepositions

Hebrew commonly uses compound prepositions. For example:

> *…and Abram went **down into** Egypt…* (Gen. 12:10).

> *How our fathers went **down into** Egypt…* (Num. 20:15).

> *…the Lord God of Israel hath disposed the Amorites **from before** his people Israel…* (Judg. 11:23).

> *Turn you behind me.* (literal Hebrew *turn you **to behind** me*) (2 Kings 9:19).

And here are several similar examples from *The Stick of Joseph*:

> *And they fled **from before** my presence…* (1 Nefi 1:19).

> *…and the servant went **down into** the vineyard…* (Ya'akov 3:16).

> *…and they went **down into** the Land of Nefi* (Moshiyah 5:2).

> *…they did not flee **from before** the Lamanites…* (M'raman 1:8).

The Construct State

In Biblical Hebrew, nouns are often used like adjectives, to modify other nouns. In English translation, this is expressed by joining the two words with the word "of," though in Hebrew, the definite article (ה) is used in the same way.

Examples from the Tanakh:

> *pillar of stone* (Gen. 35:14)

> *tablets of stone* (Ex. 24:12)

Examples from *The Stick of Joseph*:

river of water (1 Nefi 1:7)

land of promise (1 Nefi 1:9)

plates of brass (1 Nefi 1:11)

rod of iron (1 Nefi 2:10)

mist of darkness (1 Nefi 2:10)

words of plainness (Ya'akov 3:5)

night of darkness (Alma 16:37)

works of darkness (Alma 17:12)

Repetition of the Definite Article

In English, a series of nouns can be introduced by a single definite article (the). However, in Hebrew, the definite article (ה) is repeated for each noun. *The Stick of Joseph* follows this Hebrew grammar in passages like 2 Nefi 4:2, *We did observe to keep **the** judgments, and **the** statutes, and **the** mitzvot of* YHWH….

Repetition of Preposition

In Hebrew, when a preposition governs multiple objects, it is repeated for each one in the series.

Examples from the Tanakh:

*And Pharaoh was wroth **against** two of his officers, **against** the chief of the butlers, and **against** the chief of the bakers.* (Gen. 40:2)

And David and all the house of Israel played before YHWH *on all manner of instruments made of fir wood, even **on** harps, and **on** psalteries, and **on** timbrels, and **on** cornets, and **on** cymbals.* (2 Sam. 6:5)

*But I will have mercy upon the house of Judah, and will save them **by*** YHWH *their Elohim, and will not save them **by** bow, nor **by** sword, nor **by** battle, **by** horses, nor **by** horsemen.* (Hos. 1:7)

Examples from *The Stick of Joseph*:

> *And I did teach my people to build buildings, and to work in all manner of wood, and of iron, and of copper, and of brass, and of steel, and of gold, and of silver, and of precious ores, which were in great abundance.* (2 Nefi 4:3)

> *And we multiplied exceedingly, and spread upon the face of the land, and became exceedingly rich in gold, and **in** silver, and **in** precious things, and **in** fine workmanship of wood, **in** buildings, and **in** machinery, and also **in** iron, and copper, and brass, and steel, making all manner of tools of every kind to till the ground, and weapons of war–yes, the sharp pointed arrow, and the quiver, and the dart, and the javelin, and all preparations for war.* (Yahram 1:4)

> *And it came to pass in the forty and first year of the reign of the judges that the Lamanites had gathered together an innumerable army of men and armed them **with** swords, and **with** cimeters, and **with** bows, and **with** arrows, and **with** headplates, and **with** breastplates, and **with** all manner of shields of every kind....* (Cheleman 1:4)

The Cognate Accusative

This is a grammatical form common to Hebrew but very awkward in English, in which a noun drawn from the same root as its verb is used to strengthen the impact of the verb action.

Examples from the Tanakh:

> *cried with a great and exceedingly bitter cry* (Gen. 27:34)

> *we have dreamed a dream* (Gen. 40:8)

> *vowed a vow* (Judg. 11:30)

> *thundered with a great thunder* (1 Sam. 7:10)

Examples in *The Stick of Joseph*:

> *curse them even with a sore curse* (1 Nefi 1:9)

> *I have dreamed a dream* (1 Nefi 1:10)

> *yokes them with a yoke* (1 Nefi 3:19)

> *work a great and marvelous work* (1 Nefi 3:26)

> *desire which I desired* (Enosh 1:3)
>
> *taxed with a tax* (Moshiyah 5:5)

The Redundant "And"

Contrary to English usage, Biblical Hebrew is distinguished by its frequent use of the conjunction "and" (ו), both at the introduction of sentences and in connecting lists and series within a sentence.

Examples from the Tanakh:

> *And* YHWH *has blessed my master greatly;* **and** *he is become great:* **and** *he hath given him flocks,* **and** *herds,* **and** *silver,* **and** *gold,* **and** *menservants,* **and** *maidservants,* **and** *camels,* **and** *asses.* (Gen. 24:35)

> *And Joshua,* **and** *all Israel with him, took Achan the son of Zerah,* **and** *the silver,* **and** *the garment,* **and** *the wedge of gold,* **and** *his sons,* **and** *his daughters,* **and** *his oxen,* **and** *his asses,* **and** *his sheep,* **and** *his tent,* **and** *all that he had:* **and** *they brought them unto the valley of Achor.* (Josh. 7:24)

> *And David said unto Saul, Thy servant kept his father's sheep,* **and** *there came a lion,* **and** *a bear,* **and** *took a lamb out of the flock:* **And** *I went out after him,* **and** *smote him,* **and** *delivered it out of his mouth:* **and** *when he arose against me, I caught him by his beard,* **and** *smote him,* **and** *slew him.* (1 Sam. 17:34-35)

Example from *The Stick of Joseph*:

> *And it came to pass that the angel spoke unto me again, saying, Look.* **And** *I looked,* **and** *I beheld the Heavens open again,* **and** *I saw angels descending upon the children of men,* **and** *they did minister unto them.* **And** *he spoke unto me again, saying, Look.* **And** *I looked,* **and** *I beheld the Lamb of Elohim going forth among the children of men.* **And** *I beheld multitudes of people who were sick,* **and** *who were afflicted with all manner of diseases,* **and** *with demons and unclean spirits;* **and** *the angel spoke* **and** *showed all these things unto me.* **And** *they were healed by the power of the Lamb of Elohim;* **and** *the demons* **and** *the unclean spirits were cast out.* **And** *it came to pass that the angel spoke unto me again, saying, Look. And I looked* **and** *beheld the Lamb of Elohim, that he was taken by the people, yes, the Son of the El Olam was judged of the world;* **and** *I saw and bear record.* (1 Nefi 3:12–14)

Other examples are 1 Nefi 3:15; Enosh 1:6; Moshiyah 6:9; Alma 21:8; and Cheleman 2:4, just to cite a few.

The "if...and" Conditional Clause

In the English language, a conditional idea is most commonly expressed in the form of "if...then." The same conditional idea, expressed in Hebrew, takes the form of "if...and." Although English speakers find this wording ungrammatical or perhaps even nonsensical, Yosef ben Yosef's original 1830 translation contained thirteen instances of this unique Hebrew construction. Some were edited out in subsequent editions in an effort to improve the English grammar of the text and have been restored in this current translation. Cheleman 4:10 contains several of these instances:

> *Yes, and **if** he says unto the earth, Move — **and** it is moved. Yes, **if** he says unto the earth, You shall go back, that it lengthens out the day for many hours — **and** it is done.... And behold also, **if** he says unto the waters of the great deep, Be you dried up — **and** it is done. Behold, **if** he says unto this mountain, Be you raised up, and come over and fall upon that city, that it be buried up — **and** behold, it is done.... And behold, **if** YHWH shall say unto a man, Because of your iniquities, you shall be cursed for ever — **and** it shall be done. And **if** YHWH shall say, Because of your iniquities, you shall be cut off from my presence — **and** he will cause that it shall be so.*

Another notable occurrence is found in M'roni 10:2.

Repetition of the Possessive Pronoun

Another Hebrew grammatical form found in *The Stick of Joseph* is that of the repetition of the possessive pronoun.

Example from the Tanakh:

> *These are the sons of Ham, after **their** families, after **their** tongues, in **their** countries, and in **their** nations.* (Gen. 10:20)

Additional examples can be found in Ex. 10:9, Lev. 26:30, Deut. 26:7, and Neh. 9:32.

Examples in *The Stick of Joseph*:

> But this much I can tell you, that if you do not watch **your**selves, and **your** thoughts, and **your** words, and **your** deeds, and observe to keep the mitzvot of Elohim, and continue in the faith of what you have heard concerning the coming of our Adonai, even unto the end of **your** lives, you must perish. And now, O man, remember and perish not. (Moshiyah 2:6)

> And he laid a tax of one-fifth part of all they possessed: a fifth part of **their** gold and of **their** silver, and a fifth part of **their** ziff, and of **their** copper, and of **their** brass and **their** iron, and a fifth part of **their** fatlings, and also a fifth part of all **their** grain. (Moshiyah 7:1)

> And because of **your** diligence, and **your** faith, and **your** patience with the word, in nourishing it that it may take root in you, behold, by and by, you shall pluck the fruit thereof, which is most precious, which is sweet above all that is sweet, and which is white above all that is white, yes, and pure above all that is pure. And you shall feast upon this fruit even until you are filled, that you hunger not, neither shall you thirst. (Alma 16:30)

More examples can be found in Alma 18:1, Cheleman 2:4, and 3 Nefi 14:1.

The Redundant Pronoun

Hebrew often uses a noun as a direct object and then refers back to the noun with a pronoun in a following clause. This seems redundant in English. For example, in Genesis 1:4, *Elohim saw the **light**, that **it** was good*, rather than simply, "Elohim saw that the light was good."

Some examples among many in *The Stick of Joseph*:

> I beheld, and saw **the people** of the seed of my brothers that **they** had overcome my seed. (1 Nefi 3:18)

> I beheld the **wrath** of Elohim, that **it** was upon the seed of my brothers (1 Nefi 3:20)

The Emphatic Pronoun

Biblical Hebrew often repeats a personal pronoun for emphasis. For example, *I, even I do bring a flood of waters* (Gen. 6:17), and *Bless me, even me* (Gen. 27:38). *The Stick of Joseph* contains many similar instances. For example, *I, even I whom you call your king* (Moshiyah 1:9).

Adverbials

Hebrew has very few adverbs, and thus often uses a prepositional phrase where English would simply use an adverb. Examples in *The Stick of Joseph* are *with much harshness* (1 Nefi 5:30), *in righteousness* (1 Nefi 6:2), *with gladness* (2 Nefi 12:5), *with joy* (Ya'akov 3:1), *with patience* (Moshiyah 11:9), and *in spirit and in truth* (Alma 16:38).

Subordinate Clause

Another common Hebraism in *The Stick of Joseph* is the Hebrew use of the subordinate clause, in which a preposition is followed by the word "that" (אשר), such as in Ezekiel 40:1 "after (אחר) that (אשר) the city was smitten."

Examples in *The Stick of Joseph*:

> *after that I have abridged* (1 Nefi 1:4)*
>
> *after that he has commanded to flee* (1 Nefi 1:12)*
>
> *before that they were slain* (1 Nefi 3:20)*
>
> *because that they hardened their hearts* (1 Nefi 5:7)*
>
> *And because that they are redeemed* (2 Nefi 1:10)
>
> *because that my heart is broken* (2 Nefi 3:8)
>
> *because that you are of the house of Israel* (2 Nefi 5:2)*
>
> *because that you shall receive more of my word* (2 Nefi 12:9)*
>
> *before that he manifest himself in the flesh* (Enosh 1:1)*
>
> *and after that I had been lifted up upon the cross* (3 Nefi 12:5)

* These examples have been revised in many English versions to read more clearly in English, but this Hebraism is found in these verses in the 1830 edition.

Relative Clause

In Hebrew, the word "who" or "which" (אשר) indicates the beginning of a relative clause but does not always immediately follow the word to which it refers. The following are examples of this in *The Stick of Joseph*:

> And **Laman said unto L'mu'el** and also unto the sons of Yishma'el, Behold, let us slay our father, and also our brother Nefi, who has taken it upon him to be our ruler and our teacher, **who are his elder brothers**. (1 Nefi 5:10)

> But you know that **the Egyptians** were drowned in the Red Sea, **who were the armies of Pharaoh**. (1 Nefi 5:18)

> Yes, every knee shall bow, and every tongue confess before him. Yes, even at the last day, when **all men** shall stand to be judged of him, then shall they confess that he is Elohim; then shall they confess, **who live without Elohim** in the world, that the judgment of an everlasting punishment is just upon them. And they shall quake, and tremble, and shrink beneath the glance of his all-searching eye. (Moshiyah 11:28)

Interchangeable Prepositions

The Hebrew prepositions ב and ל (generally translated "in" and "to," respectively) each carry a much wider range of meaning than their English counterparts, with a certain amount of overlap that can, at times, make them interchangeable. In the 1830 edition, 1 Nefi 2:3 reads, *let us be faithful in him*, which is perfectly good Hebrew but very awkward English. In another example, the 1830 text had *after you have arrived to the promised land* (1 Nefi 5:16), which is bad English but perfectly good Hebrew. Because these Hebrew uses are so unacceptable to English speakers, many later editions revised these passages to use acceptable English prepositions.

Pronominal Suffixes

In Hebrew, possession is often indicated by a pronominal suffix appended to a noun. *The Stick of Joseph* shows evidence of such pronominal suffixes in the Hebrew underlying the English with terms like *power of him* (2 Nefi 6:7), *eyes of me* (2 Nefi 7:2), *mysteries of him* (Ya'akov 3:3), *words of me* (Ya'akov 3:7), and *atonement of him* (M'roni 8:4).

Speaker in Compound Subjects

In English, when the speaker is included as part of a compound subject, the speaker is always referenced last. For example, "My wife and I went to the store." But in Hebrew, exactly the opposite is true—the speaker is always listed first. For example, *I and the lad* (Gen. 22:5), *I and Jonathan my son* (1 Sam. 14:40), and *I and my son* (1 Kings 1:21). In several instances, *The Stick of Joseph* follows the Hebrew rather than the English grammatical rule for this situation. For example, *I and my brothers* (1 Nefi 1:11; Alma 15:5), *I and my father* (1 Nefi 7:6), and *I and my people* (Moshiyah 6:5).

Hebrew Idioms

The Stick of Joseph makes use of many unique Hebrew idioms. For example, *before my face* (3 Nefi 4:6), meaning "in my presence"; "*give ear*" (Cheleman 4:9), meaning "to hear"; "*in their ears*" (2 Nefi 12:4); "*lift up the voice*" (Moshiyah 7:17); "*lift up your heads*" (Moshiyah 5:7), just to state a few.

One especially significant example is the use of the "good eye/bad eye" idiom. David Stern writes of this idiom as it is used in Matthew 6:22-23:

> ...much of what is written in the New Testament is incomprehensible apart from its Jewish context. Here (Matt. 6:22-23) is an example, only one of many...in Hebrew, having an "ayin ra'ah," an "evil eye," means being stingy; while having an "ayin tovah," a "good eye," means being generous (Stern, D. (1989) *Jewish New Testament: A Translation of the New Testament that Expresses its Jewishness*. Jerusalem, Israel: Jerusalem New Testament Publications, p. x)

The King James Version uses "eye be single" for this idiom in Matthew 6:22 (as does the parallel in 3 Nefi 5:37).

In M'raman 4:3, we read:

> ...and I am the same who hides up this record unto YHWH. The plates thereof are of no worth, because of the mitzvah of YHWH, for he truly

> *said that no one shall have them to get gain. But the record thereof is of great worth, and whoever shall bring it to light, him will yhwh bless. For none can have power to bring it to light save it be given him of Elohim. For Elohim will that it shall be done with an eye single to his glory, or the welfare of the ancient and long dispersed covenant people of* YHWH...

It appears that, as in the KJV, "eye single" stands for the "good eye" idiom and is used according to its correct context here, that the one who would bring forth the plates would not do so "to get gain."

Variants with Parallel "New Testament" Phrases Due to Hebrew Original

There are a number of instances where almost identical phrases appear both in *The Stick of Joseph* and the New Testament, with only a slight variation, which points to a single underlying Hebrew word, as shown in the examples below:

2 Nefi 3:7 / 2 Timothy 1:12

> *I know in whom I have trusted* (2 Nefi 3:7).

> *I know whom I have believed* (2 Tim. 1:12).

The underlying Hebrew word behind both must have been *aman* (אמן), which can mean "to trust, to have faith, or to believe." This points to a Hebrew original behind 2 Nefi 3:7.

Moshiyah 2:33 / 1 Corinthians 11:29

> *drinks damnation to his own soul* (Moshiyah 1:10)

> *drinks damnation to his soul* (3 Nefi 8:9)

> *drinketh damnation to himself* (1 Cor. 11:29)

The variations between this phrase as it appears in *The Stick of Joseph* and as it appears in the New Testament, point to a single underlying Hebrew term *nefesho* (נפשו), which can mean either "himself" or "his soul."

Moshiyah 1:7 / 1 Peter (1 Kefa) 3:21

> *that I can answer a clear conscience before Elohim* (Moshiyah 1:7)
>
> *the answer of a good conscience toward Elohim* (1 Pet. [1 Kefa] 3:21)

The difference between these two phrases points to an underlying Hebrew word *pashat* (פשט) that is strongly affected by the meaning of its Aramaic cognate *peshitta* (פשיטא).

The word *peshitta* can be translated "clear," as in the Jerusalem Talmud:

> ...*things doubtful to the Rabbis are **clear** to you; those clear to the Rabbis are doubtful to you.* (y. Betzah I, 60b)

But the word *peshitta* can also be translated as "good," as in Matthew 6:22. In this verse we find the Hebrew idiom "good eye," meaning "to be generous."

And in Matthew 6:22 of the Aramaic Peshitta Text, the Aramaic word *peshitta* is used to mean "good,"—*If your eye therefore is **good** [peshitta]*.

Variants with Parallel Tanakh Phrases Due to Hebrew Original

When *The Stick of Joseph* quotes the phrase, *you shall not kill* (Ex. 20:13; Deut. 5:17; Matt. 5:21), it follows the KJV (in Moshiyah 7:21 and 3 Nefi 5:24). Here, the Hebrew word *ratsach* (רצח) is rendered, in a general manner as "kill," as it is in the KJV.

However, when this commandment is more loosely referenced, Yosef ben Yosef renders the same word more specifically as "murder":

> *And again, Adonai YHWH has commanded that men should not **murder*** (2 Nefi 11:17). See also Alma 16:2.

This points to an underlying Hebrew text.

Another example is found in Moshiyah 8:3, which is quoting Isaiah 53:3:

> *He is despised and rejected of men – a man of sorrows, and acquainted with grief. And we hid, as it were, our faces from him. He was despised and we esteemed him not* (Moshiyah 8:3).

Here, *The Stick of Joseph* follows the language of the KJV.

However, when this material is only loosely referenced, different words are used:

> *And he shall go forth suffering pains, and afflictions, and temptations of every kind, and this that the word might be fulfilled which says, He will take upon him the pains and the sicknesses of his people.* (Alma 5:3)

The Hebrew word translated in the KJV as "sorrows" in Isaiah 53:3 is *makov* (מכאב), which the 1955 Jewish Publication Society Tanakh translates as "pains."

The Hebrew word translated by the KJV as "grief" in Isaiah 53:3 is *holi* (חלי Strong's 2483), which the 1955 and 1985 Jewish Publication Society Tanakh translates as "disease."

Underlying Ambiguous Hebrew Words as Evidence of Hebrew Original

Another evidence for a Hebrew original is to be found in ambiguous Hebrew words that appear to lie behind the English text.

John Tvedtnes writes:

> Some passages of [*The Stick of Joseph*] can be better understood in Hebrew than in English because the Hebrew reflects word-play or a range of meaning which gives more sense to the passage. (Tvedtnes, J.A. (Oct. 1986) "Is the Writing in the Book of Mormon Characteristic of the Hebrew Language?" *The Ensign*, p.64)

Tvedtnes gives an example:

> Many...passages in [*The Stick of Joseph*] take on richer meaning if the passages are read as translations of Hebrew. For example, in [1 Nefi] we read that as [Lechi] "prayed unto the Lord, there came a pillar of fire and **dwelt** upon a rock before him."...Here, English usage would prefer the verb "sat" rather than "dwelt." But the Hebrew verb, in fact, has both meanings. *(ibid.)*

The Hebrew word in question here is *yashav* (ישב).

Another example is in 1 Nefi 1:3 where Nefi, describing the results of his father Lechi's vision of the destruction of Jerusalem, says, "his soul did rejoice." The Hebrew word behind "rejoice," here, may likely have been *gil* (גיל Strong's 1523), which can mean "rejoice" but can also mean "tremble." Certainly Lechi's soul did not "rejoice" at seeing the destruction of Jerusalem, but rather it "trembled."

Finally, let us look at the way *The Stick of Joseph* renders the Hebrew word *eretz* (ארץ), which can mean either "land" or "earth."

In 'Eter 6:5, we read:

> *But he repented not, neither his fair sons nor daughters, neither the fair sons and daughters of Cohor, neither the fair sons and daughters of Corihor. And in short, there were none of the fair sons and daughters upon the face of the whole earth who repented of their sins.*

Since the Hebrew word behind "earth" would have been *eretz*, the English "land" would actually make better sense in this passage.

In 3 Nefi, we read the following at the death of Yeshua:

> *And thus the face of the whole earth became deformed, because of the tempests, and the thunderings, and the lightnings, and the quaking of the earth.* (3 Nefi 4:2)

However, the context seems to refer only to the lands occupied by the Nefites and Lamanites, so that *eretz* here is also better understood as "land," rather than as "earth."

Finally, in its parallel to the Sermon on the Mount, 3 Nefi says, *the meek shall inherit the earth* (3 Nefi 5:14), which agrees with the KJV wording of Matthew 5:5. However, both are quoting Psalms 37:11, where the context seems to be that of the inheritance of "the land [of Israel]."

Wordplays in the Hebrew Original

There are also several examples of wordplays in the underlying Hebrew behind the English of *The Stick of Joseph*.

For example in 2 Nefi:

> *And because of the **intercession** for all, all men come unto Elohim. Wherefore, they stand in the presence of him, to be judged of him according to the truth and holiness which is in him. Wherefore, the ends of the Torah which HaKodesh has given, unto the **inflicting** of the punishment which is affixed, which punishment that is affixed is*

> *in opposition to that of the happiness which is affixed, to answer the ends of the atonement....* (2 Nefi 1:6-7)

There is a wordplay here in the original Hebrew between the words *yap'gia* (יפגיע) "intercession" and *p'ga* (פגע) "inflicting," pointing to the Hebrew nature of the underlying language.

Another example of a wordplay in the Hebrew is found in Alma:

> *And it came to pass that the voice of the people came, saying: Behold, we will give up the Land of **Yirshon**, which is on the east by the sea, which joins the land Bountiful, which is on the south of the land Bountiful. And this land **Yirshon** is the land which we will give unto our brothers for an inheritance.* (Alma 15:8)

There is a wordplay here in the original Hebrew. "Yirshon" is from Hebrew *y'resha* (ירשה Strong's 3424), meaning "possession, inheritance."

Another example of a wordplay in the Hebrew is found in Cheleman:

> *Now, immediately when the judge had been murdered, he being stabbed by his brother by a garb of secrecy, and he fled, and the servants ran and told the people, raising the cry of murder among them.* (Cheleman 3:12)

The Hebrew word for "garb," *beged* (בגד) can mean "garb" or "garment," but can also mean "treachery."

Scribal Errors Evidenced by the Hebrew Original

Demonstrable scribal errors in other texts, which are made apparent from the underlying Hebrew of *The Stick of Joseph*, offer further evidence of the book's Hebrew origin. For example, the *Plates of Brass* reading of Isaiah 13:3, recorded in 2 Nefi 10:1, points to a scribal error in the Masoretic Text.

Isaiah 13:3 / 2 Nefi 10:1

The 2 Nefi reading of *my anger is not upon them that rejoice in my highness* must have read לא אפי על עליזי גאותי. The Masoretic Text appears to reflect a scribal error with the similar-appearing text לאפי עליזי גאותי *mine anger, [even] them that rejoice in my highness*. With the two versions aligned, the potential error is readily seen:

לא אפי על עליזי גאותי
לאפי׳ עליזי גאותי

Another example can be found in 3 Nefi 5:21. This verse runs parallel with Matthew 5:14–16, but it has *light of this people* where Matthew 5:14 has *light of the world*. This points to a scribal error between the Hebrew words עולם "world" and עם "people," which is a common scribal error in Hebrew and Aramaic. For example, in Matthew 1:21, the Old Syriac Siniatic and Aramaic Peshitta versions have *he shall save **his people*** (לעמה), while the Old Syriac Curetonian version has *he shall save the world* (לעם). It has also been suggested that a similar scribal error in a Hebrew or Aramaic original language source text may have caused the variance in Acts 2:47 between the readings "finding favor before all the people" (in the Alexandrian and Byzantine text types) and "finding favor with all the world" (in the Western text type). The phrase "light of this people" seems to allude to Isaiah 49:6, "a light to the Gentiles," which reads in the Aramaic Peshitta version of Isaiah as "a light to the people/nation (לעממא)." This reading of "light of this people" in 3 Nefi 5:21 points to a Hebrew origin for both 3 Nefi and Matthew and suggests that the reading in 3 Nefi may be the correct reading, offering a possible correction to a scribal error in our received text of Matthew 5:14.

Hebrew and Aramaic Behind Proper Nouns

Several proper nouns demonstrate a Hebrew (and Aramaic) origin for *The Stick of Joseph*. For example, the very name of the city Zerach'mla comes from the Aramaic word *Z'ra* (זרע), meaning "seed, scattered, or dispersed," as in the Aramaic Peshitta version of James 1:1:

> James, a servant of Elohim and of the Adon Yeshua the Mashiach to the twelve tribes that are **scattered** among the nations: Shalom.

And in the Aramaic Peshitta text of 1 Peter (1 Kefa) 1:1:

> Peter, an emissary of Yeshua the Mashiach to the chosen and sojourners who are **scattered** in Pontus and in Galatia and in Cappadocia and in Asia and in Bithynia,

Additionally, the Aramaic word *Kh'mal* (חמל) has the meaning of "did gather in (as grain into a barn)," as we see in the Aramaic Peshitta:

> *Look at the bird in the sky, which does not **sow** (**scatter**) nor reap and does not **gather** into storehouses, yet your father who is in heaven feeds them. Are you not more important than they?* (Matt. 6:26 from the Peshitta)

Here the word "sow" is a form of *z'ra*, and the word "gather" is a form of *Kh'mal*.

And in Luke:

> *And he thought within himself and said, What shall I do because I have no place where I can **gather** in my crops.* (Luke 12:17, from the Peshitta)

So the name "Zerach'mla" is an Aramaic term with the meaning that the scattered ones are gathered in. Even the "-a" ending is a standard Aramaic noun ending.

Another example can be found in the name "Alma," which is an Aramaic form of the Biblical Hebrew name "Elam."

In Alma 17:15, we find the unique (but clearly Hebrew) word *Liahona* (ליהונא), which derives from the root *lawah* (לוה Strong's 3867), meaning "to join, to bind around, to wreathe," from which comes the related Hebrew words *liah* (ליה Strong's 3914), meaning "a wreath," and *lon* (לון Strong's 3885), meaning "to abide, to dwell, to remain or continue." The word "Liahona" combines these words to describe a device that joins the traveling party to God, a ball with two spindles that would wreathe around and direct Lechi and his party where and when to abide, dwell, remain, or continue.

Conclusion

With all of this evidence, it is very difficult to avoid the conclusion that *The Stick of Joseph in the Hand of Ephraim* was originally written in Hebrew, with some Aramaic influence, and then later translated into English. It is, therefore, equally difficult to avoid the conclusion that *The Stick of Joseph in the Hand of Ephraim* is an authentic record of ancient Hebrews.

Bibliography

Some of the information presented here came from the following sources:

Parry, D.W., Peterson, D.C., & Welch J.W. (Eds.). (2002) *Echoes and Evidences of the Book of Mormon*. Provo, Utah: Foundation for Ancient Research and Mormon Studies.

Sorenson, J.L. & Thorne, M.J. (Eds.). (1991) *Rediscovering the Book of Mormon: Insights you may have missed before*. Salt Lake City, Utah: Deseret Book.

Skousen, R. (2014) *Analysis of Textual Variants of the Book of Mormon*, (six parts). Provo, UT: FARMS

Recent Book of Mormon Developments: Articles from the Zarahemla Record. (1992) Independence, Missouri: Zarahemla Research Foundation

Appendix D: Selected Tanakh Prophecies Fulfilled by *The Stick of Joseph in the Hand of Ephraim*

The Stick of Joseph in the Tanakh:

> The word of the Lord came to me: And you, O mortal, take a stick and write on it, "Of Judah and the Israelites associated with him"; and take another stick and write on it, "Of Joseph—the stick of Ephraim—and all the House of Israel associated with him." Bring them close to each other, so that they become one stick, joined together in your hand. And when any of your people ask you, "Won't you tell us what these actions of yours mean?" answer them, "Thus said the Lord God: I am going to take the stick of Joseph—which is in the hand of Ephraim—and of the tribes of Israel associated with him, and I will place the stick of Judah upon it and make them into one stick; they shall be joined in My hand. (Ezek. 37:15–19 NJPS)

The Stick of Joseph in this text:

> Wherefore, the fruit of your loins shall write, and the fruit of the loins of Y'hudah shall write. And that which shall be written by the fruit of your loins, and also that which shall be written by the fruit of the loins of Y'hudah, shall grow together unto the confounding of false doctrines, and laying down of contentions, and establishing shalom among the fruit of your loins, and bringing them to the knowledge of their fathers in the latter days, and also to the knowledge of my covenants, says YHWH. (2 Nefi 2:4)

The Tribe of Yosef (Joseph) to be led across the sea:

> Yosef is a fruitful plant, a fruitful plant by a spring, with branches climbing over the wall. (Gen. 49:22 CJB)

> Shepherd of Isra'el, listen! You who lead Yosef like a flock, you whose throne is on the k'ruvim [cherubim], shine out!...It put out branches as far as the sea and shoots to the River. (Ps. 80:2, 12 CJB)

> I am a descendant of Yosef who was carried captive into Egypt. And great were the covenants of YHWH which he made unto Yosef. Wherefore, Yosef truly saw our day. And he obtained a promise of YHWH that, out

> of the fruit of his loins, Adonai YHWH would raise up a righteous branch unto the house of Isra'el, not the Mashiach, but a branch which was to be broken off, nevertheless to be remembered in the covenants of YHWH, that the Mashiach should be made manifest unto them in the latter days in the spirit of power unto the bringing of them out of darkness unto light, yes, out of hidden darkness and out of captivity unto freedom. (2 Nefi 2:2)

Consider also the obvious comparison between Yosef ben Yosef, who produced the first translation of this book, and Yosef ben Ya'akov, who preserved the House of Israel against famine. Both were situated at the central hubs of world powers in their respective epochs. Yosef ben Ya'akov resided in Egypt, the greatest world power at that time. It comes as no surprise, therefore, that Yosef ben Yosef was situated in New York, USA.

The destruction of Israel and the coming forth of a sealed book:

> I will encamp all around you, besiege you with towers and mount siegeworks against you. Prostrate, you will speak from the ground; your words will be stifled by the dust; your voice will sound like a ghost in the ground, your words like squeaks in the dust. (Isaiah 29:3-4 CJB)

> So that all prophecy has been to you
> Like the words of a sealed document.
> If it is handed to one who can read and he is asked to read it, he will say, "I can't, because it is sealed"; and if the document is handed to one who cannot read and he is asked to read it, he will say, "I can't read."(Isaiah 29:11-12 NJPS)

> But behold, I prophesy unto you concerning the last days, concerning the days when Adonai YHWH shall bring these things forth unto the children of men. After my seed and the seed of my brothers shall have dwindled in unbelief, and shall have been slain by the Goyim, yes, after Adonai YHWH shall have camped against them round about, and shall have laid siege against them with a mount, and raised forts against them, and after they shall have been brought down low in the dust, even that they are not, yet the words of the righteous shall be written, and the prayers of the faithful shall be heard, and all those who have dwindled in unbelief shall not be forgotten. For those who shall be destroyed shall

speak unto them out of the ground, and their speech shall be low out of the dust, and their voice shall be as one that has a familiar spirit, for Adonai YHWH *will give unto him power that he may whisper concerning them, even as it were out of the ground, and their speech shall whisper out of the dust. For thus says Adonai* YHWH: *They shall write the things which shall be done among them, and they shall be written and sealed up in a book....*(2 Nefi 11:13–14; see also 11:18–21)

Truth to come out of the Earth:

Truth springs up from the earth;
justice looks down from heaven. (Psalm 85:11 NJPS)

A prince of Tzidkiyahu (Zedekiah) transplanted:

Say: The king of Babylon came to Jerusalem, and carried away its king and its officers and brought them back with him to Babylon. He took one of the seed royal and made a covenant with him and imposed an oath on him, and he carried away the nobles of the land– so that it might be a humble kingdom and not exalt itself, but keep his covenant and so endure. (Ezekiel 17:12–14 NJPS)

Thus said the Lord God: Then I in turn will take and set [in the ground a slip] from the lofty top of the cedar; I will pluck a tender twig from the tip of its crown, and I will plant it on a tall, towering mountain. I will plant it in Israel's lofty highlands, and it shall bring forth boughs and produce branches and grow into a noble cedar. Every bird of every feather shall take shelter under it, shelter in the shade of its boughs. Then shall all the trees of the field know that it is I the Lord who have abased the lofty tree and exalted the lowly tree, who have dried up the green tree and made the withered tree bud. (Ezekiel 17:22–24 NJPS)

And now will you dispute that Yerushalayim was not destroyed? Will you say that the sons of Tzidkiyahu were not slain, all except it were Muloch? Yes, and do you not behold that the seed of Tzidkiyahu are with us and they were driven out of the Land of Yerushalayim? (Cheleman 3:9)

Appendix E: Ezekiel's Prophecy of this Work

One of the most memorable prophecies in the Book of Ezekiel is the famous "Two Sticks" Prophecy of Ezekiel 37, which reads as follows in the King James Version:

> *The word of the* LORD *came again unto me, saying, Moreover, thou son of man, take thee one stick, and write upon it, For Judah, and for the children of Israel his companions: then take another stick, and write upon it, For Joseph,* **the stick of Ephraim,** *and for all the house of Israel his companions: And join them one to another into one stick; and they shall become one in thine hand. And when the children of thy people shall speak unto thee, saying, Wilt thou not shew us what thou meanest by these? Say unto them, Thus saith the Lord* GOD; *Behold, I will* **take the stick of Joseph, which is in the hand of Ephraim,** *and the tribes of Israel his fellows, and will put them with him, even with the stick of Judah, and make them one stick, and they shall be one in mine hand. And the sticks whereon thou writest shall be in thine hand before their eyes.* (Ezek. 37:15–20, emphasis added)

We learn several things from these verses. To begin with, the obvious *Pashat* (plain, simple) meaning is that of a promised reunion of the two divisions of Israel. But there is more. On the *Remez* level (implied, hinted), we see that the stick of Joseph is "in the hand of Ephraim" but is also called the "stick of Ephraim" earlier in the passage. If the stick of Joseph simply represents Ephraim (the House of Israel), then how can Ephraim be in the hand of Ephraim? This implies that there must be a deeper meaning to the phrase "stick of Joseph" than simply a reference to the House of Israel (although that is its *Pashat*, or plain, simple meaning).

The next level of understanding, the *Drash* (allegorical, homiletical understanding), can be found in the Targum on Ezekiel 37. The Targums are Aramaic paraphrases of the books of the Tanakh that were anciently read in the Synagogues, alongside the Hebrew readings from the Torah and the Prophets. The Targums explained, in Aramaic, what the Hebrew was understood to mean. Therefore, the Targums were highly interpretive and "Midrashic."

E · EZEKIEL'S PROPHECY OF THIS WORK

The official Targum of the Prophets was composed some 2000 years ago by Jonathan ben Uzziel, who was a talmid (student) of Hillel. (Hillel taught as an old man when Yeshua was a small child, so this was one or two generations before Yeshua.) The Talmud describes this Targum as follows:

> The Targum of the Prophets was composed by Jonathan ben Uzziel under the guidance of [traditions handed down from] Haggai, Zechariah and Malachi, and the land of Israel [thereupon] quaked over an area of four hundred parasangs by four hundred parasangs, and a Bath Kol [voice from heaven] came forth and exclaimed, Who is this that has revealed My secrets to mankind? Jonathan b. Uzziel thereupon arose and said, It is I who have revealed Thy secrets to mankind. It is fully known to Thee that I have not done this for my own honour or for the honour of my father's house, but for Thy honour I have done it, that dissension may not increase in Israel. (b. Megillah 3a)

By examining how the Targum Jonathan paraphrases this prophecy in Ezekiel 37, we learn how this prophecy was understood by the ancients.

> And it came to pass a sentence came upon me from before YHWH saying: And you son of man, take you one **plate** and write upon it for the tribes of Judah, and to the sons of Israel, their brothers. And take one **plate** and write upon it for the tribe of Joseph which is the tribe of Ephraim, and all the House of Israel their brothers. And join the **plates** one to another, and they shall become one in your hand. And when the children of your people shall speak to you saying: "Will you not show us what these are?" I prophesied to them thus says YHWH Elohim, behold I shall join the tribe of Joseph which is the tribe of Ephraim, and the tribes of Israel their brothers, and I will cause them to have fellowship with the tribe of Judah and I will make them one people and they shall be one before me. And the **plates which were written upon** will be in your hand to their eyes. (Ezek. 37:15-20 Targum Jonathan, emphasis added.)

The Targum paraphrases the Hebrew word meaning "stick" with the Aramaic word "lucha," which means a plate or tablet that is inscribed or engraved. **The same word in Hebrew is** *luach* **(לוח Strong's 3871, plural** *luchot***), which is the very word used in Exodus for the inscribed stone tablets of the Torah (see Ex. 24:12). The**

Targum reveals to us a deeper layer of meaning, said to be handed down from the prophets themselves, identifying the two "sticks" as two records, or two inscribed sets of plates, which are united into one record.

The Targum is in total agreement with *The Stick of Joseph*, which alludes to Ezekiel's prophecy saying:

> *Wherefore, the fruit of your loins shall write, and the fruit of the loins of Y'hudah shall write. And that which shall be written by the fruit of your loins, and also that which shall be written by the fruit of the loins of Y'hudah,* **shall grow together** *unto the confounding of false doctrines, and laying down of contentions, and establishing shalom among the fruit of your loins, and bringing them to the knowledge of their fathers in the latter days, and* **also to the knowledge of my covenants**, *says* YHWH. *And out of weakness he shall be made strong, in that day when my work shall commence among all my people, unto the restoring you, oh house of Isra'el, says* YHWH. (2 Nefi 2:4 emphasis added)

The two sets of plates are the "stick of Judah" (represented by the *Plates of Brass*) and the stick of Joseph, which was inscribed on the *Plates of M'raman* (see *Appendix B: Source Documents and Groups*).

There is yet much more we can learn about these two "sticks" or records. Let us consider the above passage of Nefi on the Remez (hinted, implied) level. Notice that Nefi says that the two sticks will "grow together." How do two "sticks" grow together? What does this imply?

At this point, it is helpful to know that the Hebrew word for "stick" in Ezekiel 37 is *ets* (עץ Strong's 6086), which can mean "stick," but it can also mean "wood" or "tree." So here we have, to the Hebrew mind, not only a prophecy of two "sticks" but also of two "trees."

This brings us to Paul's parable of the two trees in Romans 11—a tame, cultivated olive tree and a wild olive tree. The wild olive tree represents the "House of Israel" who are counted among the Gentiles, and the cultivated, or tame, olive tree represents the house of Judah. Notice also that this parable speaks of branches from the wild olive tree, "Ephraim," being grafted into the natural olive tree, "Judah," just as Ezekiel's prophecy predicts.

The prophet Lechi also recounted this parable in *The Stick of Joseph*, as recorded by Nefi:

> *Yes, even my father spoke much concerning the Goyim, and also concerning the house of Isra'el, that they should be compared like unto an olive tree whose branches should be broken off and should be scattered upon all the face of the earth. Wherefore, he said it must necessarily be that we should be led with one accord into the land of promise, unto the fulfilling of the word of* YHWH *that we should be scattered upon all the face of the earth. And after the house of Isra'el should be scattered, they should be gathered together again, or in short, after the Goyim had received the fulness of the besorah,* **the natural branches of the olive tree – or the remnants of the house of Isra'el – should be grafted in, or come to the knowledge of the true Mashiach, their Adon and their Redeemer.** (1 Nefi 3:4 emphasis added)

The use of this parable by both Lechi and Paul points to an earlier source yet. That earlier, and much longer, version comes to us from the prophet Zenos—as recorded in the *Plates of Brass* of the stick of Judah. This more fulsome version is quoted at length in *The Stick of Joseph* in Ya'akov chapter 3 and outlines the entire history of the House of Israel, from its founding to its eventual glorious reunification.

In summary, Ezekiel's prophecy of two sticks carried the following two meanings in documented, ancient Jewish sources:

First, the two "sticks" are two *luchot*, which are inscribed tablets or plates, and are understood to refer to two records—one for Joseph and one for Judah. The prophecy predicts the record of Joseph will be added to the record of Judah in the last days, and the two records will become one in uniting scattered Israel. This will be done "before their eyes" or publicly and openly, before "all the House of Israel."

Second, the two "trees" are two olive trees, representing Judah and Joseph, the Southern kingdom and the Northern kingdom, or the Jews and those "Gentiles" among the gentiles, who are actually scattered Israel. Lengthy prophecies discuss the return and "grafting" back in of the scattered branches of Israel—representing not only a return to, and gathering within, the land of Israel, but also a return to the covenants and favor of YHWH.

Considered in its fulness, the scope of YHWH's prophecy, given through Ezekiel, is sweeping and magnificent. Chapter 37 begins with the vision of the dry bones, representing Israel in its scattered and fallen condition, separated from YHWH and bereft of life. The themes of the vision proceed as follows:

1. YHWH re-assembles the dry bones and restores them as complete bodies.
2. The spirit breathes life into them, making them alive and whole again—a vast army of Israel that is restored, remembered, and raised again by YHWH.
3. Two records are joined together: The Stick of Judah and *The Stick of Joseph*. The joining of these two records is the key to what follows.
4. Scattered Israel returns and gathers into their own lands, no longer divided into two kingdoms but united as a single people under a single king, who is called David.
5. YHWH cleanses and restores Israel to His true faith, and they no longer defile themselves with idolatry or apostasy.
6. The Temple is rebuilt, and YHWH comes to dwell in shalom with His people.

Ezekiel's prophecy is unfolding now, in our day and before our eyes, exactly as YHWH said it would. The nation of Israel has been established, and all of scattered Israel now has homelands to which they can return and dwell. The second record, preserved for over 2500 years and prepared by YHWH for this purpose, has come forth to remind Israel of God's covenants with their fathers and to teach them of Mashiach. It is here to destroy idolatry, establish truth, and gather all of Israel home to their Redeemer.

You are holding that record in your hand. It is real, it is true, and it is absolutely what it purports to be. How you respond to what you read in this book will determine whether you participate in the rest of Ezekiel's prophecy, yet to unfold in this generation. YHWH decreed the prophecy, and His word *must* be fulfilled. All that was prophesied will unavoidably happen, and this record is the sign it is happening now. Look to Mashiach, and live.

Appendix F: Testimonies and Dedication from the 1830 Translation

The Testimony Of Three Witnesses[1]

Be it known unto all nations, kindreds, tongues, and people, unto whom this work shall come, that we, through the grace of Elohim the Father and our Adon Yeshua HaMashiach, have seen the plates which contain this record, which is a record of the people of Nefi, and also of the Lamanites, his brothers, and also of the people of Yered, who came from the tower of which has been spoken. And we also know that they have been translated by the gift and power of Elohim, for his voice has declared it unto us; wherefore, we know of a surety that the work is true. And we also testify that we have seen the engravings which are upon the plates, and they have been shown unto us by the power of Elohim and not of man. And we declare with words of soberness that an angel of Elohim came down from Heaven, and he brought and laid before our eyes, that we beheld and saw the plates, and the engravings thereon; and we know that it is by the grace of Elohim the Father and our Adon Yeshua HaMashiach that we beheld and bear record that these things are true; and it is marvelous in our eyes. Nevertheless, the voice of YHWH commanded us that we should bear record of it; wherefore, to be obedient unto the mitzvot of Elohim, we bear testimony of these things. And we know that if we are faithful in Mashiach, we shall rid our garments of the blood of all men, and be found spotless before the judgment seat of Mashiach, and shall dwell with him eternally in the Heavens. And the honor be to the Father, and to the Son, and to the Ruach HaKodesh, which are echad. Amen.

OLIVER COWDERY,
DAVID WHITMER,
MARTIN HARRIS.

---

[1] See 2 Nefi 11:19. These witnesses satisfy the law of witnesses in Deut.17:6 and 19:15. Note: Certain terms from the original language of these signed statements have been translated to more culturally appropriate terms for Jewish readership. No meanings have been changed.

And also the Testimony of Eight Witnesses

Be it known unto all nations, kindreds, tongues, and people, unto whom this work shall come, that Joseph Smith, Jr., the translator of this work, has shown unto us the plates of which have been spoken, which have the appearance of gold; and as many of the leaves as the said Smith has translated, we did handle with our hands. And we also saw the engravings thereon, all of which has the appearance of ancient work and of elegant workmanship. And this we bear record with words of soberness, that the said Smith has shown unto us, for we have seen, and lifted, and know of a surety that the said Smith has got the plates of which we have spoken. And we give our names unto the world to witness unto the world that which we have seen; and we lie not, Elohim bearing witness of it.

CHRISTIAN WHITMER,
JACOB WHITMER,
PETER WHITMER JR.,
JOHN WHITMER,
HIRAM PAGE,
JOSEPH SMITH SEN.,
HYRUM SMITH,
SAMUEL H. SMITH.

Dedication

(from the 1830 edition)

THE BOOK OF M'RAMAN
AN ACCOUNT WRITTEN BY THE HAND OF M'RAMAN
UPON PLATES TAKEN FROM THE PLATES OF NEFI

Wherefore, it is an abridgment of the record of the people of Nefi, and also of the Lamanites; written to the Lamanites which are a remnant of the house of Isra'el and also to Y'hudi and Goy; written by way of mitzvah, and also by the spirit of prophecy and of revelation. Written, and sealed, and hid up unto YHWH, that they might not be destroyed; to come forth by the gift and power of Elohim unto the interpretation thereof; sealed up by the hand of M'roni and hid up unto YHWH, to come forth in due time by the way of Goy; the interpretation thereof by the gift of Elohim.

An abridgment taken from The Book of 'Eter also, which is a record of the people of Yered, which were scattered at the time YHWH confounded the language of the people when they were building a tower to get to Heaven: which is to show unto the remnant of the house of Isra'el how great things YHWH has done for their fathers, and that they may know the covenants of YHWH, that they are not cast off for ever. And also to the convincing of the Y'hudi and Goy that Yeshua is the Mashiach, the Elohe Kedem, manifesting himself unto all nations. And now if there is fault, it is the mistake of men; wherefore, condemn not the things of Elohim, that you may be found spotless at the judgment seat of Mashiach.

—M'RONI

www.ingramcontent.com/pod-product-compliance
Lightning Source LLC
Chambersburg PA
CBHW050308120526
44592CB00014B/1833